Lecture Notes in Computer Sci

Edited by G. Goos, J. Hartmanis and J. var

Springer
Berlin
Heidelberg
New York
Barcelona
Hong Kong
London
Milan
Paris
Singapore
Tokyo

Alexander Gelbukh (Ed.)

Computational Linguistics and Intelligent Text Processing

Second International Conference, CICLing 2001
Mexico City, Mexico, February 18-24, 2001
Proceedings

 Springer

Series Editors

Gerhard Goos, Karlsruhe University, Germany
Juris Hartmanis, Cornell University, NY, USA
Jan van Leeuwen, Utrecht University, The Netherlands

Volume Editor

Alexander Gelbukh Unidad Profecional "Adolfo López Mateos"
CIC (Centro de Investigación en Computatción
IPN (Instituto Politécnico Nacional)
Av. Juan Dios Bátiz s/n esq. M. Othon Mendizabal
Col. Nuevo Vallejo, CP. 07738, México, Mexico
E-mail: gelbukh@cic.ipn.mx

Cataloging-in-Publication Data applied for

Die Deutsche Bibliothek - CIP-Einheitsaufnahme

Computational linguistics and intelligent text processing : second
international conference ; proceedings / CICLing 2001, Mexico City,
Mexico, February 18 - 24, 2001. Alexander Gelbukh (ed.). - Berlin ;
Heidelberg ; New York ; Barcelona ; Hong Kong ; London ; Milan ;
Paris ; Singapore ; Tokyo : Springer, 2001
   (Lecture notes in computer science ; Vol. 2004)
   ISBN 3-540-41687-0

CR Subject Classification (1998): I.2.7, I.7, F.4.3, I.2, H.3

ISSN 0302-9743
ISBN 3-540-41687-0 Springer-Verlag Berlin Heidelberg New York

Springer-Verlag Berlin Heidelberg New York
a member of BertelsmannSpringer Science+Business Media GmbH
© Springer-Verlag Berlin Heidelberg 2001
Printed in Germany

Typesetting: Camera-ready by author, data conversion by Boller Mediendesign
Printed on acid-free paper   SPIN 10781959   06/3142   5 4 3 2 1 0

Preface

CICLing 2001 is the second annual Conference on Intelligent text processing and Computational Linguistics (hence the name CICLing), see www.CICLing.org. It is intended to provide a balanced view of the cutting edge developments in both theoretical foundations of computational linguistics and practice of natural language text processing with its numerous applications. A feature of the CICLing conferences is their wide scope that covers nearly all areas of computational linguistics and all aspects of natural language processing applications. The conference is a forum for dialogue between the specialists working in these two areas.

This year our invited speakers were Graeme Hirst (U. Toronto, Canada), Sylvain Kahane (U. Paris 7, France), and Ruslan Mitkov (U. Wolverhampton, UK). They delivered excellent extended lectures and organized vivid discussions.

A total of 72 submissions were received, all but very few of surprisingly high quality. After careful reviewing, the Program Committee selected for presentation 53 of them, 41 as full papers and 12 as short papers, by 98 authors from 19 countries: Spain (19 authors), Japan (15), USA (12), France, Mexico (9 each), Sweden (6), Canada, China, Germany, Italy, Malaysia, Russia, United Arab Emirates (3 each), Argentina (2), Bulgaria, The Netherlands, Ukraine, UK, and Uruguay (1 each).

In addition to their high scientific level, one of the success factors of CICLing conferences is their excellent cultural program. CICLing 2001 was held in Mexico, a wonderful country very rich in culture, history, and nature. The participants of the conference – in their souls active researchers of the world – had a chance to see the solemn 2000-years-old pyramids of legendary Teotihuacanas, a Monarch butterfly wintering site where the old pines are covered with millions of butterflies as if they were leaves, a great cave with 85-meter halls and a river flowing from it, Aztec warriors dancing in the street in their colorful plumages, and the largest anthropological museum in the world; see photos at www.CICLing.org.

A conference is the result of the work of many people. First of all I would like to thank the members of the Program Committee for the time and effort they devoted to the reviewing of the submitted articles and to the selection process. Especially helpful were Igor Bolshakov, Nicoletta Calzolari, Ted Pedersen, Grigori Sidorov, Karin Verspoor, Manuel Vilares-Ferro, and many others – a complete list would be too long. I also thank David Escorial for his constant help.

Obviously I thank the authors for their patience in the preparation of the papers, not to mention the very development of their scientific results that form this book. I also express my most cordial thanks to the members of the local Organizing Committee for their considerable contribution to making this conference become a reality. Last but not least, I thank our sponsoring organization – the Center for Computing Research (CIC, www.cic.ipn.mx) of the National Polytechnic Institute (IPN), Mexico, for hosting the conference for the second time.

December 2000   Alexander Gelbukh

Program Committee

Additional Reviewers

Cox, Clive (Vocalis, UK),
Graña Gil, Jorge (U. La Coruña, Spain),
Martinez Barco, Patricio (U. Alicante, Spain),
Muñoz, Rafael (U. Alicante, Spain),
Olivares Ceja, Jesus M. (CIC-IPN, Mexico),
Vert, Jean-Philippe (Ecole Normale Supérieure, France).

Organizing Committee

Gelbukh, Alexander (*Chair*),
Salcedo Camarena, Teresa,
Ulloa Castillejos, Carlos,
Vargas Garcia, Soila,
Vizcaíno Sahagún, Carlos.

Organization

The conference was organized by the Natural Language Laboratory (www.cic.ipn.mx/Investigacion/ltexto.html) of the Center for Computing Research (CIC, Centro de Investigación en Computación, www.cic.ipn.mx) of the National Polytechnic Institute (IPN, Instituto Politécnico Nacional, www.ipn.mx), Mexico City, Mexico.

Website and Contact

The website of the CICLing conferences is http://www.CICLing.org currently mirrored at http://www.cic.ipn.mx/cicling. Specifically, this conference's website is http://www.CICLing.org/2001. The contact email address is gelbukh@CICLing.org; also gelbukh@cic.ipn.mx or gelbukh@earthling.net.

Table of Contents

Computational Linguistics

Computational Linguistic Theories

Semantics

Anaphora and Reference

Disambiguation

Translation

Text Generation

Intelligent Text Processing

Text Categorization

Information Retrieval

Structure Identification. Text Mining

What Is a Natural Language
and How to Describe It?
Meaning-Text Approaches
in Contrast with Generative Approaches

Sylvain Kahane

CNRS & Lattice-Talana, Université Paris 7, UFRL, case 7003,
2, place Jussieu, 75251 Paris Cedex 05, France
sk@ccr.jussieu.fr
http://www.linguist.jussieu.fr/~skahane

Abstract. The paper expounds the general conceptions of the Meaning-Text theory about what a natural language is and how it must be described. In a second part, a formalization of these conceptions – the transductive grammars – is proposed and compared with generative approaches.[1]

1 Introduction

The Meaning-Text theory (MTT) was put forward in Moscow, thirty-five years ago, by Žolkovski and Mel'čuk ([29], [30]), in the framework of research in machine translation. Presentations of MTT can be found in [20], [21], [25].

MTT considers that a natural language is a correspondence between meanings and texts. Although this conception of language is a more or less accepted by everybody, it appears that most contemporary linguistic theories do not model natural languages in the same ways as MTT. The postulates of MTT will be explained, commented and compared with other conceptions of language in Section 2. In Section 3, I propose a formal definition of what a grammar is in the spirit of MTT, that is, a grammar which defines a correspondence between meanings and texts or, more generally, between any two sets of structures. My definition will by exemplified by a very simple grammar which ensures the correspondence between syntactic and morphological representations. Various definitions of this grammar will be proposed, which allows me to make various comparisons with other formal modelings of natural languages (Sect. 4).

2 What Is a Natural Language?

The answer of MTT to the central question-What is a natural language?-is based on the three following postulates.

---

[1] I want to thank Kim Gerdes, Alain Polguère and Pascal Amsili for many valuable comments and corrections. I want also to thank Alexander Gelbukh for his suggestions about the topic of this paper.

A. Gelbukh (Ed.): CICLing 2001, LNCS 2004, pp. 1–17, 2001.

Postulate 1

Natural language is (considered as) a many-to-many correspondence between meanings and texts.[2]

Postulate 2

The Meaning-Text correspondence is described by a formal device which simulates the linguistic activity of a native speaker.

Postulate 3

Given the complexity of the Meaning-text correspondence, intermediate levels of (utterance) representation have to be distinguished; more precisely, a syntactic and a morphological level.

1) The first postulate of MTT means that the description of a natural language $\mathcal{L}$ consists of the description of the correspondence between the set of meanings of $\mathcal{L}$ and the set of texts of $\mathcal{L}$. This point of view must be compared with the one of Chomsky 1957 ([6]), which has had an enormous influence on linguistics and formal language theory: the description of a natural language $\mathcal{L}$ consists of a formal device deriving the set of all (acceptable) sentences of $\mathcal{L}$. For a long time, his outlook has had a rather restrictive interpretation, a sentence being understood as a string of characters[3]-that is, a text in the MTT terminology-or, in the best case, a sentence being understood as a phrase structure tree. Nevertheless, Chomsky's postulate is formally equivalent to MTT's first postulate, provided a sentence is considered in its Saussurian sense, that is, a linguistic sign with a *signifié* (meaning) and a *signifiant* (text). From a mathematical point of view, it is indeed equivalent to define a correspondence between the set of meanings and the set of texts and to define the set of couples consisting of a meaning and its corresponding text, we can call a sentence.[4]

2) The second postulate stresses on the fact that a natural language must be described as a correspondence. A speaker speaks. A Meaning-Text model must model the speaker activity, that is, model how a speaker transforms what he wants to say (a meaning) into what he says (a text). It is certainly the main specificity of MTT to say that a natural language must be described as a (Meaning-Text) correspondence and moreover that the direction from meaning to text must be privileged. This point will be looked at in more details in Section 3.

3) The third postulate asks for several comments. Most of linguistic theories consider a morphological and a syntactic level of representations. What is important here is that these levels are intermediate between the semantic and

---

[2] *Text* refers to any fragment of speech, of whatever length, and *sound* could be a better term.

[3] Perhaps, the best example of the restrictive interpretation of Chomsky's works is the definition of the term *formal language*, as a set of string of characters. In this sense, a formal language can never model the essence of a natural language.

[4] We forget the fact that the description of a natural language cannot be reduced to the description of isolated sentences.

phonological levels (= meanings and texts). This means that the correspondence from meanings to texts will be completely modular: a correspondence between the semantic and the syntactic level, a correspondence between the syntactic and the morphological level and a correspondence between the morphological and the phonological level (in fact, MTT consider more than two intermediate levels of representations, but this does not change anything to our discussion).

The result is that the syntactic module, which ensures the correspondence between the syntactic representations and the morphological representations, only associates syntactic representations with morphological representations. It does not, as a generative grammar would do, give a complete characterization of the representations it handles. In the synthesis direction, a syntactic module handles syntactic representations which have been synthetized by deeper modules from well-formed semantic representations which represent real meanings. Consequently, a well-formed syntactic representation is characterized by all the modules, by the fact that it is a possible intermediary between a well-formed semantic representation and a corresponding phonological representation. It is not the aim of MTT to give an explicit characterization of well-formed syntactic representations.

I want to insist on the fact that MTT clearly separates the different levels of representation. Representations of different levels have different structural organizations: semantic representations are graphs (of predicate-argument relations), syntactic representations are (non ordered) dependency trees and morphological representations are strings. In the MTT approach, everything that can be differentiated is differentiated. And objects with different organizations must be represented by different means. Moreover, MTT carefully pays attention to the geometry of the representation: a morphological representation is one-dimensional (a string), a syntactic representation is two-dimensional (a tree) and a semantic representation is multi-dimensional (a graph).

One other point should be underlined. MTT uses dependency trees as syntactic representations contrary to most of other linguistic theories, which use phrase structure trees. In fact, ever since the X-bar theory ([13]), the constituents of a phrase structure are considered as projections of lexical heads, and dependency trees and phrase structure trees contain more or less the same information (see [14] for a formal comparison of the two means of representation). Nevertheless, there is a fundamental distinction: a phrase structure contains the linear order of the words of the sentence. In other words, a phrase structure tree does not separate the syntactic structure from the morphological structure. Contemporary theories, such as HPSG ([28]), even mix the semantic representation with the phrase structure representation and use a single formalism-feature structures-to represent all these objects. Moreover, the primacy is given to the syntactic structure, that is, the structure of the whole representation-mixing semantic, syntactic, morphological and phonological information-is a phrase structure tree and the geometry of the other structures does not appear explicitly.

I think that, now, thirty-five years after their first description (!), the MTT postulates, even if they are given different formulations, are more or less ac-

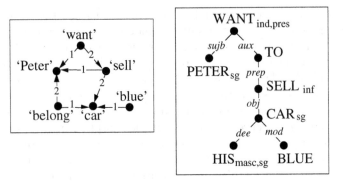

$$\text{PETER}_{sg} \ \text{WANT}_{ind,pres,3,sg} \ \text{TO} \ \text{SELL}_{inf} \ \text{HIS}_{masc,sg} \ \text{BLUE} \ \text{CAR}_{sg}$$

Fig. 1. Semantic[5], syntactic and morphological representations of *Peter wants to sell his blue car*

cepted by the whole linguistic community. For instance, I can quote the first sentences of Brody's Minimalist Program presentation ([5]): "It is a truism that grammar relates sound and meaning. Theories that account for this relationship with reasonable success postulate representational levels corresponding to sound and meaning and assume that the relationship is mediated through complex representations that are composed of smaller units." The main point that is not clearly taken into account by most of the contemporary formal description of natural language is the fact that a natural language must be described as a correspondence. This point will be emphasized now.

3   How to Describe a Language?

To introduce our discussion, let us recall what Mel'čuk says: "The MTM [= Meaning-Text model] is by no means a generative or, for that matter, transformational system; it is a purely EQUATIVE (or TRANSLATIVE) device. The rules of the MTM do not generate (i.e., enumerate, specify) the set of all and only grammatically correct or meaningful texts. They simply match any given SemR [= Semantic Representation] with all PhonRs [= Phonological representations] which, in accordance with native speakers' linguistic intuition, can convey the corresponding meaning; inversely, they match any given PhonR with all SemRs that can be expressed by the corresponding text." ([20]:45). He adds: "Un MST [= Modèle Sens-Texte] est purement ÉQUATIF ou TRADUCTIF; à la différence

---

[5] The semantic representation of Fig. 1 is far to be complete. In fact, a semantic graph, which indicates the predicate-argument relations between the meanings of the full words of the sentence, cannot be interpreted as a semantic representation without a communicative organization, such as a theme-rheme partition with communicative dominant nodes ([27]).

de beaucoup de ses contemporains, ce n'est pas un modèle génératif. [...] Il fait correspondre à chaque SemR toutes les PhonR qui peuvent l'exprimer dans une langue donnée; c'est pourquoi il est qualifié d'"équatif". [...] Un MST essaie de se comporter comme un locuteur, qui ne passe son temps ni à générer des ensembles de phrases grammaticalement correctes ou à distinguer entre phrases correctes et incorrectes, ni à transformer des structures abstraites; un locuteur parle, c'est-à-dire qu'il exprime, au moyen de textes, les sens qu'il veut communiquer. Un MST doit faire la même chose: "traduire" un sens donné en un texte qui l'exprime (voilà pourquoi ce modèle est "traductif")." ([21]:16).

Although sizeable fragments of natural languages have been described in the MTT framework (see [23], [20], [22]), an MTT formalism has never been achieved. Many rules have been written but no directions for use have been proposed explicitly. Mel'čuk justifies this, saying: "The transition mechanism, i.e., the dynamic device, or procedure, for moving from actual complex SemRs to actual complex PhonRs and vice-versa is not considered [by an MTM]. I believe that such a dynamic device, while necessary to put the above static mapping to work, lies outside the field of linguistics, at least as yet. The MTM can be compared to a bilingual dictionary, which presupposes, but does not include, rules looking up the words it contains; then the dynamic device driving the MTM correspondence compares to the psychological ability of a human to use these rules in order to actually look up any given word. It stands to reason that such an ability is not part of the dictionary and should not concern the lexicographer too much." ([20]:45). Indeed, a Meaning-Text model is a grammar of a particular language and the directions for use of such a grammar must be separated from the grammar itself, as it is done in other formalisms. But, the problem with MTT is that this information is nowhere or only implicit.

The goal of this part will be to propose a formalization of the concept of Meaning-Text grammar and to compare this concept with the framework of reference, the generative grammars, and the canonical example of such grammars, context-free grammars.

3.1 Transductive Grammars and Supercorrespondence

In this section, I will propose a very general formal definition of what a grammar is in the spirit of MTT. Such a grammar will be called a transductive grammar, by analogy with transducer (see, for instance, [1]) (although, as far as I know, the transducer theory is limited to the correspondence between strings).

Let S and S' be two sets of structures (graphs, trees, orders ...). A transductive grammar G between S and S' is a formal grammar which associates elements of S with elements of S'. As a formal grammar, G contains a finite set of rules, which are called the correspondence rules. A correspondence rule associates a piece of structure from elements of S with a piece of structure from elements of S'. Consequently, a transductive grammar G defines more than a correspondence between the sets of structures S and S'. Indeed, for each couple (S, S') that are associated by G, G also defines partitions of the structures S

and S' and a one-to-one mapping $\varphi_{(S,S')}$ between the pieces of these two partitions. This will be called a *supercorrespondence* between the sets S and S'. The supercorrespondence defined by a transductive grammar G between two sets of structures $\mathcal{S}$ and $\mathcal{S}'$ is mathematically equivalent to a family of product structures $(S, S', \varphi_{(S,S')})$, with $S \in \mathcal{S}$, $S' \in \mathcal{S}'$ and $\varphi_{(S,S')}$ a correspondence between the pieces of partitions of S and S'.[6]

We see now that the first postulate of MTT has not been well enounced. A natural language is more than a correspondence between meanings and texts, that is, a set of couples meaning-text. A natural language is a supercorrespondence between meanings and texts, that is, a set of product structures meaning-text. And similarly, a sentence is not a couple meaning-text or *signifié-signifiant*, but a product structure, each piece of the meaning being related to a piece of the text. I am just giving a new expression of the well-known notion of *compositionality*: a sequence is a sign that can be decomposed into smaller signs.

3.2   Example of Syntactic Transductive Grammar

We will now focus our discussion on a particular module of a Meaning-Text model. We have chosen the syntactic module, because it is the module which receives the biggest attention in most of the natural language models.

The MTT syntactic module ensures the correspondence between syntactic and morphological representations. A *syntactic representation* is a *non ordered* dependency tree (assorted with other pieces of information, such as the theme-rheme partition ...). The nodes of a syntactic tree are labeled by lexical units[7] and the branches are labeled by *syntactic relations* (*subj(ect)*, *obj(ect)*, *mod(ifier)* ...). A *morphological representation* is a linearly ordered string of lexical units, that is, a *linear order* on a set of lexical units (assorted with other pieces of information such as prosody ...). Each lexical unit points to a dictionary entry. In order to simplify, only the part of speech will be considered and it will be added on the node labeling.

All our notions will be exemplified with the following trivial example:

(1) Peter eats red beans.

 Peter$_{(N)sg}$ eat$_{(V)ind,pres,3,sg}$ red$_{(A)}$ bean$_{(N)pl}$

We will now define a family of syntactic transductive grammars, which we will call atomic dependency grammars. These grammars are atomic because they associate only atoms of structures, that is, nodes and edges. Two kinds of rules

---

[6] In mathematics, a *product structure* is a structure obtained by combining two structures on a same set. For instance, if S is a tree and S' is a string and if $\varphi_{(S,S')}$ is one-to-one mapping between the nodes of S and the elements of S', then $(S, S', \varphi_{(S,S')})$ is equivalent to a linearly ordered tree, that is, to the product of tree structure and a linear order structure on a same set of nodes.

[7] In fact, each lexical unit is accompanied by grammemes [= inflections], but our presentation is oversimplified in order to focus only on our topic, the comparison between transductive and generative approaches.

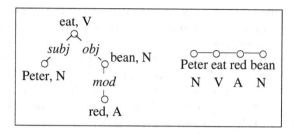

Fig. 2. (Simplified) syntactic tree and morphological string of (1)

are considered: *sagittal rules* (Lat. *sagitta* 'arrow'), which associate a dependency between two nodes with an order relation between two nodes, and *nodal rules*, which associate a node with a node. The nodal rules are trivial here and do not appear in the formal definition. (They will be introduced in the generative definition, cf. Section 4.)

An *atomic dependency grammar* is a 5-tuple $G = (\Sigma, \mathcal{C}, \mathcal{R}, \mathcal{O}, \Delta)$, where Σ is the set of lexical units, $\mathcal{C}$ is the set of (grammatical) categories, $\mathcal{R}$ is the set of syntactic relations, $\mathcal{O}$ is the set of linear positions and Δ is the set of sagittal rules, that is, a subset of $\mathcal{R} \times \mathcal{O} \times \mathcal{C} \times \mathcal{C}$.

Let X^* be the set of strings on X and $\mathcal{T}(X, Y)$ be the set of trees whose nodes are labeled in X and whose branches are labeled in Y. The grammar G defines a supercorrespondence between $\mathcal{T}(\Sigma \times \mathcal{C}, \mathcal{R})$ and $(\Sigma \times \mathcal{C})$, as it will be seen in the following sections. Before that, I will exemplify my definition by a grammar which ensures the correspondence between the tree and the string of Fig. 2.

Let us consider $G_0 = (\Sigma_0, \mathcal{C}_0, \mathcal{R}_0, \mathcal{O}_0, \Delta_0)$ with:
- $\Sigma_0 = \{\text{Peter, bean, eat, red}\}$;
- $\mathcal{C}_0 = \{V, N, A\}$;[8]
- $\mathcal{R}_0 = \{subj, obj, mod\}$;
- $\mathcal{O}_0 = \{<, >\}$;[9]
- $\Delta_0 = \{(subj, <, V, N), (obj, >, V, N), (mod, <, N, A)\}$.

---

[8] The set of categories considered here is very simple (and limited to the part of speech). A real size grammar for natural language must consider richer categories. Such categories can be expressed with feature structures. In this case, as it is done in most of contemporary formalisms, categories must be combined by unification rather than identity.

[9] An atomic dependency grammar with $\mathcal{O} = \{>, <\}$ only permits to specify the position of a node towards its governor—before ($<$) or after ($>$)—and not the relative position of codependents of a node. This problem can be solved by indicating the relative distance of the different dependents of a node towards it (see solutions with $\mathcal{O} \subset \mathbf{Z}$, the set of integers, in [19], [7], [15]).

The sagittal rule $(subj, <, V, N)$ says that, for all lexical units X and Y such that X is a V(erb) and Y is a N(oun), the syntactic dependency $X - subj \rightarrow Y$ *corresponds* to the linear order $Y < X$. In the synthesis direction, this means that for all lexical units X and Y such that X is a V and Y is an N, IF $X - subj \rightarrow Y$, THEN it is POSSIBLE to have $Y < X$. And in the analysis direction, it means that for all lexical units X and Y such that X is a V and Y is an N, IF $Y < X$, THEN it is POSSIBLE to have $X - subj \rightarrow Y$. See Fig. 3 for the conventional representation of such a rule in MTT. The symbol $\Leftrightarrow$ indicates the correspondence between two pieces of structures; $\alpha \Leftrightarrow \beta$ is interpreted by $\alpha \Rightarrow \beta$ and $\beta \Rightarrow \alpha$, where $\alpha \Rightarrow \beta$ means IF α, THEN β IS POSSIBLE.

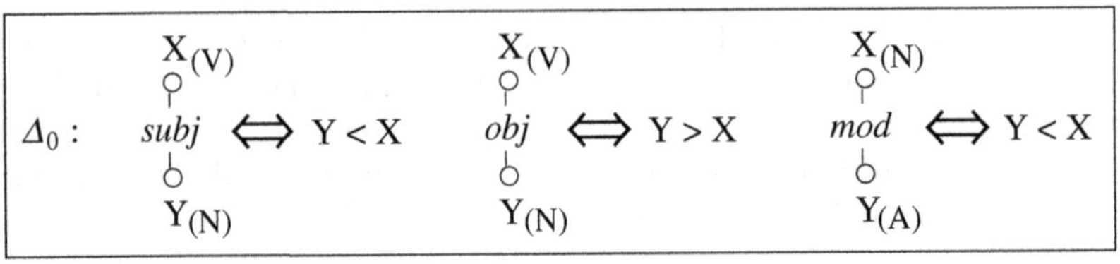

Fig. 3. The rules of Δ_0 in the MTT style

We will see now how a supercorrespondence can be defined. Different strategies are possible. We will study several solutions, in this and the following section.

But first, a remark: the correspondence rules, which only associate pieces of structures, are generally not sufficient to encode all the properties of the product structure, and some *global rules* must be stated. This is the case here, for the syntactic-morphology correspondence, where it is necessary to ensure a property such as projectivity for the product structures.[10] The projectivity is a property of compatibility between a tree and a linear order, that is a property of a linearly ordered tree. A linearly ordered tree is said to be *projective* if no branch crosses another branch and no branch covers the root ([17], [11]).

3.3   Transductive Presentation in the Synthesis Direction

As we have said, an atomic dependency grammar $G = (\Sigma, \mathcal{C}, \mathcal{R}, \mathcal{O}, \Delta)$ defines a supercorrespondence between the trees of $\mathcal{T}(\Sigma \times \mathcal{C}, \mathcal{R})$ and the strings of $(\Sigma \times \mathcal{C})^*$. In the synthesis direction, an atomic dependency grammar ensures the linearization of trees. The synthesis starts with a given tree $T \in \mathcal{T}(\Sigma \times \mathcal{C}, \mathcal{R})$.

---

[10] It is well-known that many linguistic constructions are not projective (unbounded extractions, German scrambling, Dutch cross serial dependencies, Czech clitics ...). Nevertheless, even in these cases, the word order is far to be free and it must be controlled by some global property, weaker than the projectivity. Note that the projectivity is also considered in the phrase structure frameworks where it corresponds to the continuity of the constituents.

A derivation[11] processes is as follows. For each branch of T labeled r whose governor is of category C_1 and whose dependent is of category C_2, a sagittal rule $(r, \omega, C_1, C_2) \in \Delta$ is triggered off and the label $\omega \in \{>, <\}$ is attached to the branch. A string $s = X_1 \ldots X_n \in \Sigma^*$ corresponds to T if T has exactly n nodes labeled $X_1, \ldots, X_n$ and if for each dependency $X - r \rightarrow Y$ of T the label ω attached by the sagittal rule is compatible with the order of X and Y in s, that is, $Y < X$ if $\omega = <$ and $Y > X$ if $\omega = >$. Moreover, the ordered tree $T \times s$ must be projective. See an example of derivation Fig. 4.

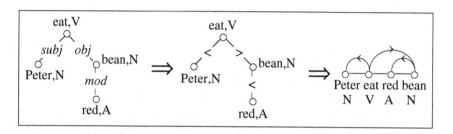

Fig. 4. G_0 used as transductive grammar in the synthesis direction

The process fails if no rules can apply to an element of T. Several orders can be obtained with one derivation, in particular if some codependents are positioned on the same side of their governor, their respective order being free in this case. To obtain all the strings corresponding to a tree T, all the combinations of rules must be tried.

The process proposed here is quite declarative, no order being proposed in the application of the different rules. In fact, the order is free and the derivation could be top-down, in the fashion of the context-free rewriting grammar, or incrementally, following the linear order of the nodes (cf. Section 4).

3.4   A Transductive Grammar in the Analysis Direction

The analysis starts with a given string $s = X_1 \ldots X_n \in \Sigma^*$. The derivation processes as follows. For each couple of nodes (X, X') of categories (C, C') with $X < X'$, a sagittal rule $(r, >, C, C')$ or $(r, <, C', C) \in \Delta$ is triggered off and a branch labeled r from X to X' or from X' to X is introduced. A tree T corresponds to s if T has exactly n nodes labeled $X_1, \ldots, X_n$ corresponding to the nodes of s and if each branch of T corresponds to one of the branches added to s of same extremities and same label. Moreover, the ordered tree $T \times s$ must be projective. See an example of derivation Fig. 5.

Note that the derivation does not need that a sagittal rule can be triggered off for each couple of nodes of s. Conversely, even if more than $n-1$ sagittal rules

---

[11] Although the process described here is not generative, I prefer using the term *derivation* of the generative framework rather introducing a new term.

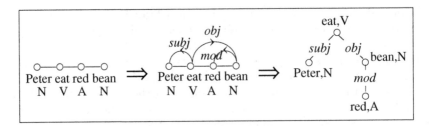

Fig. 5. G_0 used as transductive grammar in the analysis direction

apply, it is not sure that a tree can be extracted from the graph obtained by the application of the rules. Different algorithms permit to extract a projective tree from such a graph; see, for instance, [2], [3].[12]

The process proposed here is still quite declarative. It is possible to constrain the derivation further. For instance, it is possible to produce the tree by reading the string from the left to the right. In this case, the grammar acts as a push-down automaton. We will see that more precisely later. An atomic dependency grammar $G = (\Sigma, \mathcal{C}, \mathcal{F}, \mathcal{O}, \Delta)$ can be associated to a push-down automaton $M = (\Sigma, \mathcal{Z}, \Lambda)$ with a stack alphabet $\mathcal{Z} = \mathcal{C} \times \{+, -\} \times \mathbf{N}$ and a set of transitions $\Lambda \subset \mathcal{U} \times \mathcal{Z}^* \times \mathcal{Z}^* \times \mathcal{W}$, where $\mathcal{U} = \{\varepsilon\} \cup (\Sigma \times \mathcal{C})$ and $\mathcal{W} = (\Sigma \times \mathcal{C} \times \mathbf{N}) \cup (\mathbf{N} \times \mathbf{N} \times \mathcal{R}))$. A tree in $\mathcal{T}(\Sigma \times \mathcal{C}, \mathcal{R})$ can be encoded as a subset of $\mathcal{W}$: a triple $(X, C, i) \in \Sigma \times \mathcal{C} \times \mathbf{N}$ means that the i-th node of the tree is labeled (X, C) and a triple $(i, j, r) \in \mathbf{N} \times \mathbf{N} \times \mathcal{F}$ means that the i-th node governs the j-th node one by a dependency labeled r.

The idea is to stack the nodes which are produced and to remove from the stack the nodes that can no longer have links with other nodes (see [18] for a similar idea). The signs $+$ and $-$ of stack symbols mean that the corresponding node is or is not yet governed. A transition $\lambda = (x, \alpha, \beta, y) \in \Lambda$ is interpreted as follows: the element x of s is read (if nothing is read, $x = \varepsilon$), the string α of stack symbols is removed from the stack, the string β of stack symbols is stacked and the tree description y is produced. Λ is build as follows:

- each couple $(X, C) \in \Sigma \times \mathcal{C}$ yields a *stacking transition* $((X, C), \varepsilon, [C, -, i],$ $(X, C, i))$ reading the i-th node (X, C) of the string, stacking $[C, -, i]$ and producing the node of the tree (X, C, i);

- each sagittal rule $(r, <, C_1, C_2) \in \Delta$ yields a *left dependent linking transition* $(\varepsilon, [C_2, -, i][C_1, -, j], [C_1, -, j], (j, i, r))$ producing the dependency (j, i, r) and removing $[C_2, -, i]$ from the stack, because, due to the projectivity, (X_2, C_2, i) cannot be linked to a node at the right of its governor (X_1, C_1, j);

- each sagittal rule $(r, >, C_1, C_2) \in \Delta$ yields a *left governor linking transition* $(\varepsilon, [C_1, \pm, i][C_2, -, j], [C_1, \pm, i][C_2, +, j], (j, i, r))$ producing the dependency

---

[12] The grammar considered by Blache in [3] is a context-free phrase structure grammar, but this grammar is in fact used exactly in the present way.

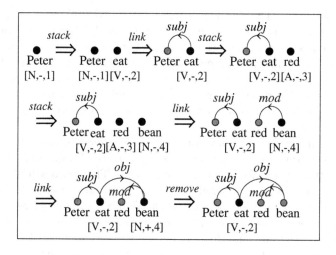

Fig. 6. G_0 used as a push-down automaton

(j, i, r) and replacing $[C_2, -, j]$ by $[C_2, +, j]$ in the stack, because the node (X_2, C_2, j) is now governed;

- at last, each $C \in \mathcal{C}$ yields a *removing transition* $(\varepsilon, [C, +, i], \varepsilon, \varepsilon)$ removing $[C, +, i]$ from the stack, which is possible, because the i-th node is governed.

The stack is empty at the beginning. The process can only stop when the stack content is reduced to a slot $[C, -, i]$. This ensures that there is only one non governed node, that is, that we have produced a tree, whose i-th node is the root. Moreover, our process ensures that no links can cross each other and that the root is not covered by a link, i.e., the tree is projective. Fig. 6 presents the parsing of (1) by the automaton associated to the grammar G_0. A black node represents a node in the stack and a grey node, one that has been removed from the stack. Note that the indexes i in the stack symbols are only useful for the production of the tree corresponding to the read string.

4 Transductive Grammars and Generative Grammars

In the narrow sense, a generative grammar is a formal device which allows to generate a formal language, i.e., a set of linearly ordered string. I will call *generative grammar* every formal device which allows to generate a set of structures, strings being a particular case. In this wide sense of the notion of generative grammars, a transductive grammar can be seen as a generative grammar, as we will see.

4.1 Transductive Grammars as Generative Grammars

Remember that the supercorrespondence defined by a transductive grammar G between two sets of structures $\mathcal{S}$ and $\mathcal{S}'$ is mathematically equivalent to a set of product structures $(S, S', \varphi_{(S,S')})$, with $S \in \mathcal{S}$, $S' \in \mathcal{S}'$ and $\varphi_{(S,S')}$ a correspondence between the pieces of partitions of S and S'. Therefore, a transductive grammar can be seen as a generative grammar generating a supercorrespondence. For instance, an atomic dependency grammar G defines a set of linearly ordered trees, that is, products of a tree and a linear order on a same set of nodes. In a generative interpretation of a transductive grammar, the correspondence rules are seen as pieces of product structures which are assembled to generate the product structures.

Let us see more precisely how an atomic dependency grammar can be used as a generative grammar. Each rule is seen as a piece of a linearly ordered tree. The sagittal rules introduce ordered dependencies. The nodes will be introduced by the nodal rules, which were not considered until now, because they trivially associate a node with a node of same label. We use the conventions of representation of [26]: the nodes, which are really introduced by the rules are in black and the requirements are in white. If we use the terminology of rewriting systems, we can say that black elements are terminal and white elements are non terminal. The rules are combined by unification of nodes: two black elements cannot unify, a black and a white node yields a black node and two white nodes yields a white node. The final structure must be entirely black. A derivation simply consists generating a set of rules and combining them, provided that the resulting structure is a projective linearly ordered tree.

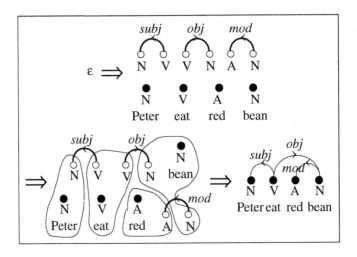

Fig. 7. G_0 used as generative grammar

Although it is not necessary, it is possible to specify an order on the operations of derivation. For instance, we can follow the tree structure and process top-down: a first nodal rule is triggered off generating the root of the tree; after that, a sagittal rule whose governor can unify with the root is triggered off, then a nodal rule that can unify with the requirement of the previous rule and so on (Fig. 8). Cf. [8] for dependency grammars of this kind.

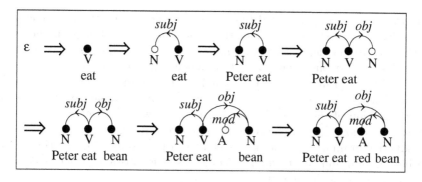

Fig. 8. G_0 used as tree-driven generative grammar

An atomic dependency grammar used as a tree-driven generative grammar is very similar to a context-free rewriting system. This similarity can be brought to the fore: the grammar G_0 can be simulated by the rewriting system $G_0' = (\Sigma_T, \Sigma_{NT}, \bar{V}, \mathcal{R})$, with the terminal alphabet $\Sigma_T = \Sigma_0 \cup \mathcal{R}_0 \cup \{(,),:\}$, the non terminal alphabet $\Sigma_{NT} = \bar{\mathcal{C}}_0 = \{\bar{V}, \bar{N}, \bar{A}\}$ and the set of rewriting rules $\mathcal{R}$:

$$\bar{V} \to (\bar{N} : subj)\bar{V} \quad \bar{V} \to \bar{V}(\bar{N} : obj) \quad \bar{N} \to (\bar{A} : mod)\bar{N}$$
$$\bar{V} \to (\text{eat}, V) \quad \bar{N} \to (\text{Peter}, N) \quad \bar{N} \to (\text{bean}, N) \quad \bar{A} \to (\text{red}, A)$$

We can derive, beginning with $\bar{V}$, a sequence which encodes the product of the structures of Fig. 2: $((\text{Peter}, N) : subj)(\text{eat}, V)(((\text{red}, A) : mod)(\text{bean}, N) : obj)$. This derivation is very similar to the derivation of Fig. 8. In particular, a non terminal symbol $\bar{X}$ is similar to the label of a white node, while a terminal symbol X is similar to the label of a black node.

4.2   Generative Grammars as Transductive Grammars

Contrary to the fact that a transductive grammar can be seen as a generative grammar, I think that most of the generative grammars used for modeling natural languages can be seen as transductive grammars.

Let us consider the basic case of context-free grammars. Such grammars generate a set of sentences, but associate to each derivation of a sentence a derivation tree, which is interpreted as the syntactic structure of the sentence. In other words, a context-free grammar can be seen as a transductive grammar that defines a correspondence between sentences and constituency trees. Nevertheless, this is not a correspondence in the MTT sense, because the constituency tree contains both the syntactic structure of the sentence and the sentence itself (with its linear order).[13] However, a context-free grammar can also be seen as

---

[13] Many linguists think in the analysis direction and they do not find any problem to associate a string of words to a richer structure containing the string of words with more information. But such a view on language is absurd as soon as you are thinking in the synthesis direction. When you want to express a meaning, you cannot suppose

a transductive grammar that defines a correspondence between sentences and non ordered constituency trees. In this case, the context-free grammar is not far from an atomic dependency grammar (see [9] for conditions on context-free grammars to be strongly equivalent to a dependency grammar). It is the case of the context-free grammar G'_0 which simulates the atomic dependency grammar G_0 (Section 4.1). But as we have seen, G'_0 corresponds to a particular procedural implementation of the transductive grammar G_0, where the generation is tree-driven generation. This can be generalized: context-free grammars can be seen as transductive grammars including a tree-driven procedure of generation (which can be unuseful and constraining in some cases, for instance when we want to use the grammar for analysis).

More recent models of language also define product structures, like LFG (morphological string + c-structure + f-structure), TAG (morphological string + derived tree + derivation tree), HPSG (morphological string + syntactic-semantic feature structure) ... It is not the case of whatever generative grammar; for instance, it seems difficult to interpret a Turing machine as a transductive grammar, because it is not clear which structure associates with a string generated by the machine.

I nevertheless must insist on the fact that even the generative grammars that can be interpreted as transductive grammars do not clearly consider two levels of representations that are in correspondence and the fact that they define a (super)correspondence is in fact a side effect. For instance, for the rewriting grammars, it is the process of derivation itself which is interpreted as a representation and not the result of the derivation (although this vision has evolved with tree-rewriting system such as TAG).

I will finish this discussion on transductive and generative grammars with a point which seems very important to me, even if I miss elements to support it. I think that the notion of *strong generative capacity* is related to the fact that the grammars devoted to the description of natural language are in fact hidden transductive grammars. It can be considered that two grammars are *strongly equivalent* if they are equivalent as transductive grammars, that is, if they generate the same supercorrespondence.

4.3   Equative Grammars

To conclude my presentation I present a third way of defining a supercorrespondence with a transductive grammar, in a complementary way to transductive and generative ways. As we have seen, the main difference between a transductive and a generative presentation of a transductive grammar G is that the former presupposes that one of the two sets of corresponding structures is available (G producing the other one), while the latter considers that G produces directly both ones.

---

that you already known the word order. If it were the case, there would be nothing to compute!

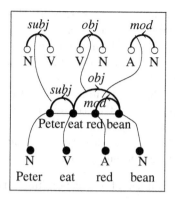

Fig. 9. G_0 as an equative grammar

The third way of defining the supercorrespondence, the *equative* approach, presupposes that both sets of structures are available: the process consists to filter all the couples of structures which correspond to each other. The correspondence rules are used as a set of equations or constraints to be met (as does, for instance, HPSG). From a purely mathematical viewpoint, this is the simplest definition of the correspondence and it is also the least procedural one: a product structure is given and each piece of the structure must be validated by a correspondence rule. For instance, we can verify that the two structures of Fig. 2 are associated with our atomic dependency grammar G_0; for that, we must verify that each element (node or branch) of the product structure (the linearly ordered tree) is validated by a correspondence rule (Fig. 9).

In other words, the equative presentation is the *declarative* presentation of a transductive grammar, i.e., a grammar relating two set of structures. Nevertheless, such a presentation is not very useful for computational applications, because, in such cases, meaning and text are never available together. And, in fact, another device is needed which generates couples of structures, the equative grammar being only used to filter the couples of structures that really correspond to each other.

5   Conclusion

There is now a consensus about the fact that grammars describing natural languages must relate meaning and text. However, few formalisms describe languages as correspondences between meanings and texts explicitly. For that, I have proposed a general mathematical notion of grammars defining a (super)correspondence between two sets of structures.

I have focused my discussion on an elementary family of transductive grammars, the atomic dependency grammars, defining a supercorrespondence between dependency trees and linear strings. I think that these grammars are the simplest grammars to define such a supercorrespondence, because they handle only atoms of structure: nodes and edges. Clearly, this formalism does not permit to describe all the linguistic phenomena and various extensions are possible (cf., for instance, [15]). This simple formalism has been only introduced in order to show that, even with a very simple grammar defining a very little fragment of language, there is many ways to define the language from the grammar. (It appears that atomic dependency grammars may also be a formalism of reference for dependency grammars, just as context-free grammars are a formalism of reference for phrase structure grammars.)

If you accept that a language is a correspondence between meanings and texts, only three directions are possible to describe a language with a grammar:

1. to produce directly couples of corresponding structures (generative approaches);
2. to produce structures corresponding to a given structure (transductive approaches);
3. to filter couples of corresponding structures (equative or declarative approaches).

From a computational point of view, as well as, from a cognitive point of view, we need transductive approaches, i.e., we need to get a meaning from a text (analysis or reading) or to get a text from a meaning (synthesis or speaking).

References

1. Aho Alfred & Ullman Jeffrey, 1972, *The Theory of Parsing, Translation and Compiling, Vol. I: Parsing*, London: Prentice-Hall.
2. Arnola Harri, 1998, "On parsing binary dependency structures deterministically in linear time", in Kahane & Polguère (eds), *Workshop on dependency-based grammars, COLING-ACL'98*, Montreal, 68-77.
3. Blache Philippe, 1998, "Parsing ambiguous structures using controlled disjunctions and unary quasi-trees", *Proc. COLING-ACL'98*, Montreal, 124-130.
4. Boyer Michel & Lapalme Guy, 1985, "Generating paraphrases from Meaning-Text semantic networks", *Comput. Intell.*, *1*, 103-117.
5. Brody Michael, 1997, *Lexico-Logical Form: A Radically Minimalist Theory*, Cambridge: MIT Press.
6. Chomsky Noam, 1957, *Syntactic Structure*, Cambridge: MIT Press.
7. Courtin Jacques & Genthial Damien, 1998, "Parsing with Dependency Relations and Robust Parsing", in Kahane & Polguère (eds), *Workshop on dependency-based grammars, COLING-ACL'98*, Montreal, 95-101.
8. Dikovsky Alexander & Modina Larissa, 2000, "Dependencies on the other side of the Curtain", in S. Kahane (ed.), *Grammaires de dépendance, T.A.L.*, *41:1*.
9. Gaifman Haïm, 1965, "Dependency systems and phrase-structure systems", *Information and Control* **8**, 304-337; Rand Corporation Techn. Report RM-2315, 1961.
10. Gladkij Aleksej & Mel'čuk Igor, 1975, "Tree grammars: A Formalism for Syntactic Transformations in Natural Language", *Linguistics, 150*, 47-82.
11. Iordanskaja Lidija, 1963, "O nekotoryx svojstvax pravil'noj sintaksičeskoj struktury (na materiale russkogo jazyka)" [On some properties of the correct syntactic structure (on the basis of Russian)], *Voprosy jazykoznanija, 4*, 102-12.

12. Iordanskaja Lidija & Polguère Alain, 1988, "Semantic processing for text generation", in *Proc. First International Computer Science Conf. - 88*, Hong Kong, 310-18.
13. Jackendoff Ray S., 1977, *X' Syntax : A Study of Phrase Structure*, Linguistic Inquiry Monograph, MIT Press.
14. Kahane Sylvain, 1997, "Bubble trees and syntactic representations", in Becker & Krieger (eds), *Proc. 5th Meeting of the Mathematics of Language (MOL5)*, Saarbrücken: DFKI.
15. Kahane Sylvain, 2001, "A fully lexicalized grammar for French based on the Meaning-Text theory", this issue.
16. Kahane Sylvain & Mel'čuk Igor, 1999, "Synthèse des phrases à extraction en français contemporain (Du graphe sémantique à l'arbre de dépendance)", *T.A.L.*, *40:2*, 25-85.
17. Lecerf Yves, 1961, "Une représentation algébrique de la structure des phrases dans diverses langues naturelles", *C. R. Acad. Sc. Paris, 252*, 232-234.
18. Kornaï Andreás & Tuza Zsolt, 1992, "Narrowness, pathwidth, and their application in natural language processing", *Disc. Appl. Math, 36*, 87-92.
19. Mel'čuk Igor, 1967, "Ordre des mots en synthèse automatique des textes russes", *T.A. Informations, 8:2*, 65-84.
20. Mel'čuk Igor, 1988, *Dependency Syntax: Theory and Practice*, Albany, NY: State Univ. of New York Press.
21. Mel'čuk Igor, 1997, *Vers une Linguistique Sens-Texte*, Leçon inaugurale au Collège de France, Paris: Collège de France.
22. Mel'čuk Igor, 1993-2000, *Cours de morphologie générale, Vol. 1, 2, 3, 4 & 5*, Montreal: Presses de l'Univ. Montreal / Paris: CNRS.
23. Mel'čuk Igor & Pertsov Nikolaj, 1987, *Surface Syntax of English. A Formal Model within the Meaning-Text Framework*, Amsterdam: Benjamins.
24. Mel'čuk Igor *et al.*, 1984, 1988, 1992, 1999, *Dictionnnaire explicatif et combinatoire du français contemporain, Vol. 1, 2, 3, 4*, Montreal: Presses de l'Univ. Montreal.
25. Milićević Jasmina, 2001, "A short guide to the Meaning-Text linguistic theory", in Alexander Gelbukh (ed.), *Computational Linguistics and Intelligent Text Processing, Colección en Ciencias de Computación*, Fondo de Cultura Económica - IPN - UNAM, Mexico.
26. Nasr Alexis, 1995, "A formalism and a parser for lexicalised dependency grammars", *4th Int. Workshop on Parsing Technologies*, State Univ. of NY Press.
27. Polguère Alain, 1997, "Meaning-Text Semantic Networks as a Formal Language", in L. Wanner (ed.), *Recent Trends in Meaning-Text Theory*, Amsterdam/Philadelphia: Benjamins.
28. Pollard Carl & Sag Ivan A., 1994, *Head-Driven Phrase Structure Grammar*, CSLI series, Chicago : Univ. of Chicago Press.
29. Žolkovskij Aleksandr & Mel'čuk Igor, 1965, "O vozmožnom metode i instrumentax semantičeskogo sinteza" [On a possible method an instruments for semantic synthesis (of texts)], *Naučno-texničeskaja informacija* [Scientific and Technological Information], 6, 23-28.
30. Žolkovskij Aleksandr & Mel'čuk Igor, 1967, "O semantičeskom sintez" [On semantic synthesis (of texts)], *Problemy kybernetiki* [Problems of Cybernetics], 19, 177-238. [Fr. transl. : 1970, *T.A. Information, 2*, 1-85.]

A Fully Lexicalized Grammar for French
Based on Meaning-Text Theory

Sylvain Kahane

CNRS & Lattice-Talana, Université Paris 7, UFRL, case 7003,
2, place Jussieu, 75251 Paris Cedex 05, France
sk@ccr.jussieu.fr
http://www.linguist.jussieu.fr/~skahane

Abstract. The paper presents a formal lexicalized dependency grammar based on Meaning-Text theory. This grammar associates semantic graphs with sentences. We propose a fragment of a grammar for French, including the description of extractions. The main particularity of our grammar is it that it builds bubble trees as syntactic representations, that is, trees whose nodes can be filled by bubbles, which can contain others nodes. Our grammar needs more complex operations of combination of elementary structures than other lexicalized grammars, such as TAG or CG, but avoids the multiplication of elementary structures and provides linguistically well-motivated treatments.[1]

1 Introduction

Meaning-Text theory (MTT) has been developed since more than thirty years, but no complete formalization of the model has been achieved. Our main goal in this paper is to propose a formal grammar based on MTT. We insist on the fact that our grammar in any case is a 'kosher' implementation of MTT.

Following the MTT postulates ([16]: 53), we consider that 1) a grammar[2] is a formal system which ensures the bidirectional correspondence between texts and meanings (= semantic representations) and that 2) intermediate levels of representation—a morphological level and a syntactic level—must be considered and that a grammar consists of several modules which establish correspondence between representations of adjacent levels. Our grammar is composed of three modules: the morphological module ensures the correspondence between sentences and morphological representations, the syntactic module ensures the correspondence between morphological and syntactic representations and the semantic module ensures the correspondence between syntactic and semantic representations.

In section 2, we present the different levels of representation, in section 3, the syntactic module and in section 4, the semantic module. Our formalism will be exemplified by a fragment of French grammar. Extractions, which need extensions of the formalism, will be treated separately in section 5.

---

[1] I want to thank Jasmina Miliçeviç, as well as two anonymous referees, for many valuable comments and corrections.

[2] The term grammar is used in its Chomskian sense of 'linguistic model'.

A. Gelbukh (Ed.): CICLing 2001, LNCS 2004, pp. 18-31, 2001.
© Springer-Verlag Berlin Heidelberg 2001

2   Different Levels of Representation of a Sentence

A *morphological representation* of a sentence is the sequence of the morphological representations of the words of the sentence; the morphological representation of a word is *surface lexical unit* accompanied with a list of *surface grammemes*. Consider the sentence:

(1)   *Zoé a parlé à un type étrange.*
       Zoé has talked to a guy strange
       'Zoé has talked to a strange guy'

The morphological representation of (1) is:

(2) $ZOÉ_{sg}\ AVOIR_{ind,présent,3,sg}\ PARLER_{part\_passé}\ À\ UN_{masc,sg}\ TYPE_{sg}\ ÉTRANGE_{masc,sg}$

The *syntactic representation* of a sentence is a non ordered *dependency tree* similar to the surface syntactic trees of MTT ([16]) or the stemmas of Tesnière ([23]). The nodes of the structure are labeled with surface lexical units, each being accompanied with a list of *surface grammemes,* and the dependencies are labeled with (surface) *syntactic relations.*

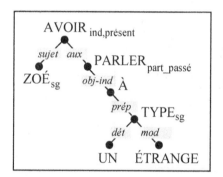

Fig. 1. *Syntactic representation of (1)*

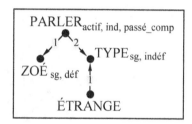

Fig. 2. *The semantic representation of (1)*

The *semantic representation* of a sentence is a directed graph whose nodes are labeled by deep lexical units, each being accompanied by a list of deep grammemes. A *deep lexical unit* corresponds to a surface lexical unit or a group of surface lexical units making an idiom. A *deep grammeme* is a grammeme with a meaning (including voice grammemes, which do not exactly express a meaning, but depend on semantic communicative choices). A deep grammeme can correspond to a surface grammeme or a complex expression including surface lexical units: that is the case of the French *passé composé* ($AVOIR_{ind,présent}$ + $V_{art\_passé}$) or the French passive voice (ÊTRE + $V_{part\_passé}$). A deep lexical unit acts like a predicate and is linked to its arguments by arrows pointing on them. The different arrows emerging from a deep lexical unit are numbered from 1 to n following the increasing syntactic salience of the arguments. Such an arrow, representing a predicate-argument relation, is called a *semantic dependency*; the predicate is *the semantic governor* and its argument, the *semantic dependent.* Our semantic representation is a compromise between the semantic and deep syntactic representations of MTT. On the one hand, the nodes of our semantic representation are labeled with deep lexical units, rather than by semantemes (= the meaning of a deep lexical unit)[3]. On the other hand, a hierarchy on the nodes is superimposed to the graph structure; this hierarchy, which expresses the communicative importance of the meanings expressed in the sentence, is called the *communicative dependency*, following [21][4]. In our figures, the communicative hierarchy is expressed by placing a communicative governor above its communicative dependents. Therefore, a downward arrow indicates semantic and communicative dependencies in the same direction, the (communicative and semantic) dependent being an *actant* (or argument), while a upward arrow indicates semantic and communicative dependencies in opposite directions, the communicative dependent (and semantic governor) being a *modifier*. With this hierarchy, our semantic representation is close from a TAG derivation tree (cf. [2] for a comparison between TAG and MTT).

In the previous example, every communicative dependency is superimposed with a semantic dependency, which allows us to indicate the communicative dependencies with the upward or downward direction of the semantic dependencies. Relative clauses are more complex. Consider:

(3)   *Zoé connaît la dame sur le mari de laquelle je pense que tu peux compter.*
       Zoé knows the woman on the husband of whom I think you can count
       'Zoé knows the woman whose husband I think you can count on'

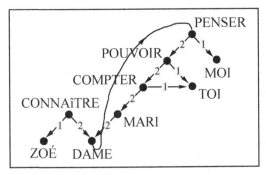

Fig. 3. *The semantic representation (without grammemes) of (3)*

A relative clause modifies its antecedent and therefore communicatively depends on it, but there is generally no semantic dependency between the antecedent (here DAME 'woman') and the communicative top node of the relative clause (here PENSER 'think'). Consequently the communicative dependency must be represented by an own link (the light arrow without label). Moreover, the antecedent fills a semantic

---

[3] The initial objective of the MTT semantic representation is to be a semantic invariant of a set of paraphrases, which requires attributing two synonymous lexical units to the same sememe. We prefer considering that there is one-to-one correspondence between deep lexical units and semantemes and the replacement of a lexical unit by a synonymous lexical unit is a paraphrase rule (see Mel'čuk 1992 for a presentation of these rules).

[4] In the MTT tradition, only the communicative top nodes of some sub-graphs (such as the rheme and the theme) are indicated. The communicative top node (= the dominant node of Polguère 1990) of a phrase is the node which "summarizes" its meaning (cf. Zwicky 1985). For instance, *un verre à vin* 'a wine glass' is a glass and its top node is *verre* 'glass', while *un verre de vin* 'a glass of wine' is wine and its top node is *vin* 'wine'. Note that in both cases *verre* 'glass' is the semantic governor of *vin* 'wine'.

position in the relative clause (here as argument of MARI 'husband') and is consequently communicatively dominated by the top node of the relative clause. Our semantic description is based on [12] (see Fig. 3).

3   Syntactic Module

The formalism of our syntactic module is based on Nasr's formalism ([19], [20]), itself inspired by the TAG formalism ([7]). It is a *lexicalized grammar*, that is, a formal grammar that has the form of a lexicon: each lexical unit is associated with a set of elementary structures which describe its possible syntactic environments. The correspondence between a morphological and a syntactic representation is ensured by a combination of elementary structures associated with the lexical unit labeling both representations.

3.1   Elementary Structures

An elementary structure is a portion of a syntactic representation enriched with some features on the labeling. Each element, node or dependency, receives a feature `type`. Elements of `type:1` elements are said black and elements of `type:0`, white. Intuitively, black elements are the elements really introduced by the elementary structure, while white elements are requirements.

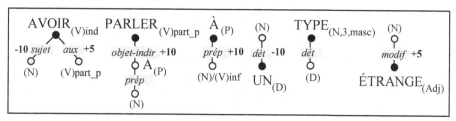

Fig. 4. *Elementary structures (AVOIR 'have', PARLER 'speak', À 'to', UN 'a', TYPE 'guy', ÉTRANGE 'strange')*

Moreover, each node a feature for the part of speech and some morphological features (gender, person...). Each dependency receives a feature `weight` for expressing the linear position of the dependent vis-à-vis its governor (see below). Some features can be not instantiated. (Black and white dependencies are represented by bold and light lines.)

3.2   Morphology-to-Syntactic Correspondence

Elementary structures are combined by merging of one or more elements; two elements can be merged if their labels can be unified. Note that the merging of a black and a white element gives a black element, while the merging of two white elements gives a white element; two black elements cannot be merged ($0 \cup 0 = 0$, $0 \cup 1 = 1$ and $1 \cup 1 = $ `failure`).

A morphological representation M and a syntactic representation S *correspond* to each other if the nodes of M and S are labeled by the same lexical units and if it is possible to associate with each lexical unit an elementary structure such that the combination of the elementary structures gives a structure X subsuming both M and S. A morphological string M is subsumed by X if the nodes of X can be ordered respecting both the projectivity[5] and the local order constraints given by the weights on the dependencies, assuming that the sign of the weight (- or +) indicates if the dependent is before or after the governor and the absolute value of the weight indicates the relative distance between the dependent and the governor (see [15], [4] for similar ideas).

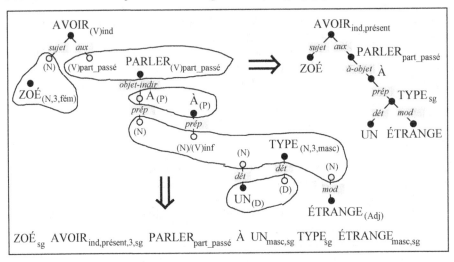

Fig. 5. *Combination of elementary structures and correspondence*

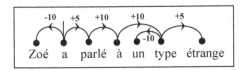

Fig. 6. *Projectivity and local order constraints*

Before seeing how our formalism can be enriched to take into account other phenomena, let us note that our formalism allows us to build non-lexicalized grammars equivalent to our lexicalized grammar. For instance, we can decide that an elementary structure contains only one black element; an elementary structure with a black node will be called *nodal* and an elementary structure with a black dependency, *sagittal* (lat. *sagitta* = arrow). A lexicalized elementary structure can be got back by merging of nodal and sagittal elementary structures (Fig. 7).

The partition of the rules into nodal and sagittal rules is equivalent to the partition of the grammar (= linguistic model) into lexicon and grammar (in the true sense). A nodal structure indicates the subcategorization pattern of a lexical unit, while a sagittal structure indicates the properties of a syntactic relation, such as linearization or agreement. Although our formalism is different from traditional MTT formalism ([18]), a sagittal structure is equivalent to an MTT surface syntactic correspondence rule.

---

[5] A linearly ordered tree is said *projective* if no dependencies cross each other and no dependency covers the root.

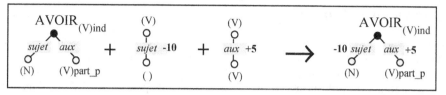

Fig. 7. *Combination of nodal and sagittal structures giving a lexicalized structure*

3.3   Quasi-Dependency

The biggest problem of all the lexicalized grammars we know (essentially TAG and the Categorial Grammars) is the combinatorial explosion of the number of structures associated with a lexical unit. This problem is generally due to a bad repartition of the linguistic information between the elementary structures. This repartition depends on the answer of questions such as the following: which of two words decides if they can combine? which decides how they are positioned towards each other? etc.

The first example we will study is the attributive and predicative use of an adjective. Compare *ce livre étrange* 'this strange book', *ce livre est étrange* 'this book is strange' et *Pierre trouve ce livre étrange* 'Pierre finds this book strange'. In all these constructions, LIVRE 'book' is the semantic argument of ÉTRANGE 'strange'. Moreover, in French, in all these cases the adjective must agree with the noun, which could be a problem for predicative adjectives, if they are not linked to it. Therefore, we will introduce in the elementary structure of a copulative verb a sort of dependency we will call a *quasi-dependency*. Quasi-dependencies are distinguished from real dependencies by the fact they have no role in the linearization (and consequently they do not bear a weight). Nevertheless, they bear a syntactic relation and a type. Formally, dependencies and quasi-dependencies will be differentiated by a + or - value of an ad hoc feature `quasi`. Quasi-dependencies are represented by broken arrows.

A *modif(icative)* quasi-dependency from the adjective to the noun modified is introduced in the elementary structure of copulative verbs. The same elementary structure can now be used for the attributive and predicative uses of an adjective, provided a dependency can merge with a quasi-dependency to give a dependency (Fig. 8).

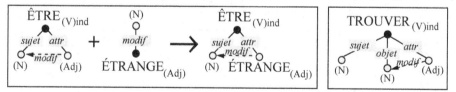

Fig. 8. *Combination of the copula (ÊTRE 'be') and the adjective (ÉTRANGE 'strange'). Elementary structure for the predicative verb(TROUVER 'find')*

The same ideas can be used for control and raising verbs (section 4). Quasi-dependencies will be also used for argument in non-canonical position (section 5).

4   Semantic Module

The semantic rules are of two types: lexical rules for the expression of deep lexical units and grammatical rules for the expression of deep grammemes.

A *lexical semantic rule* indicates the correspondence between a deep lexical unit and a configuration of surface lexical units. The correspondence between semantic actants and syntactic nodes is indicated by the variables *x*, *y*, etc. The deep grammemes that must be translated by grammatical rules are simply copied out in the syntactic configuration (right part of the rule) and preceded by an arrow ($\rightarrow$) indicating that they must be translated by grammatical rules; for a French verb, it is the m(ood), the t(ense) and the v(oice). A special feature, symbolized by *, indicates that a node cannot be modified.

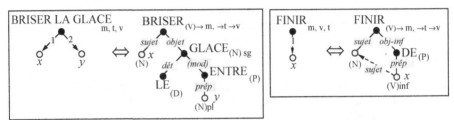

Fig. 9. *Lexical semantic rules for the idiom BRISER LA GLACE 'break the ice' and the raising verb COMMENCER 'begin'*

A *grammatical semantic rule* translates a deep grammeme into a surface grammeme or a more complex configuration. For instance, the inf(initive) mood is expressed by the surface grammeme inf and the transformation of the subject (Fr. *sujet*) dependency into a quasi-dependency. The passive (Fr. *passif*) voice (Fr. *passif*) is expressed by ÊTRE + -é, while the object (Fr. objet) node becomes subject and the subject node becomes an optional prepositional complement introduced by the prepositions PAR 'by' (in the default case). Note that the grammatical semantic rules are not correspondences between a semantic and a syntactic configuration, but between two syntactic configurations. The order in which the grammatical rules are applied does not matter; the notation ($\rightarrow$)m corresponds to both $\rightarrow$m and m depending to the fact that a rule translating m has been yet applied.

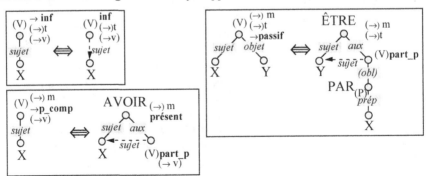

Fig. 10. *Grammatical semantic rule for the infinitive mood, the passive voice and the passé composé tense.*

5   Extractions

This section is devoted to the description of extractions (topicalization, relativization, interrogation, clefting...). Extractions are problematic for at least two reasons. First, the ordered dependency tree of a sentence with an extraction is generally not projective (Fig. 11). Second, since Ross' work ([22]), it is well known that the extractions are subject to a lot of constraints. These two problems can be solved simultaneously.

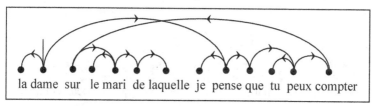

Fig. 11. *The (non projective) syntactic dependency tree of (3)*

5.1   Description of Extractions

Our description of extraction is based on a new linguistic concept, the *nucleus*, which has been introduced in [8] and used in [12]. Some groups of words, which we will call nuclei, can behave like a single word from the viewpoint of various phenomena including extraction. We consider two types of nuclei:

- A *verbal nucleus* is a string of verbs or equivalent forms (copula+adjective, light verb+predicative noun...): *un livre que Pierre **lit, a commencé à lire, a envie de lire, a l'air de trouver facile à lire, pense que** Zoé **devrait lire**...* 'a book that Pierre is reading, began to read, feels like reading, looks to find easy to read, thinks that Zoé should read...'

- A *nominal nucleus* is a string of nouns including prepositions and determiners: *une dame **sur laquelle** tu comptes, **sur le mari de laquelle** tu comptes*... 'a woman on whom you count, on whose husband you count...'

The exact nature of nuclei depends on the language: for instance, in English, contrary to French, a preposition can end a verbal nucleus (preposition stranding: *the girl you are talking to, *la fille que tu parles à*). The nature of nuclei also depends on the linguistic phenomena: for instance, the strings *V que V* 'V that V', possible for extractions or gapping coordination, are more difficult for the negation: *la personne à qui Jean **veut que** tu **parles** '*the person to who Jean wants that you speak'; **Jean veut qu'on appelle** la police et Zoé les pompiers '*Jean wants that one calls the police and Zoé, the fire department; *[??]Jean ne **veut que** tu **parles** à personne '*Jean does not want that you speak to anyone'*).

It is possible to integrate the nucleus in the syntactic representation (Fig. 12). Nuclei are represented by bubbles. The resulting structure is called a *bubble tree* ([8]). Bubbles trees are trees whose nodes can be filled by bubbles, which can contain others nodes which can, in their turn, be filled by bubbles or have their own dependents.

There are some advantages to consider nuclei and represent them by bubbles:

- Some phenomena can be accounted for more easily with the use of nuclei. For instance, relativization can be described as follows: 1) the wh-word must belong to a nominal nucleus governed by a verbal nucleus, itself governed by the antecedent of the relative; 2) the nominal nucleus must be positioned at the beginning of the relative clause. [6]

- While extraction clauses generally have a non-projective dependency tree, their bubble tree is projective[7]. The projectivity of the bubble tree allows us to ensure the linearization with only *local* linearization rules, that is, with weights on the dependencies.

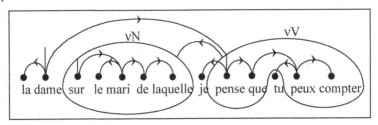

Fig. 12. *A (projective) bubble tree for (3)*

5.2   Elementary Structures for Relative wh-Words

In order to satisfy the constraints on extraction, a relative wh-word will introduce in its elementary structure a nominal nucleus and a verbal nucleus, the wh-word belonging to the nominal nucleus, the nominal nucleus depending on the verbal nucleus and the verbal nucleus depending on a nominal node. In other words, the whole information concerning the structure of a relative clause is encoded in the elementary structure of the wh-word, that is the constraints on extraction and the fact that a relative clause modifies a noun. We will now see how to solve the problem of the word order (and the non-projectivity).

In a lexicalized grammar such as TAG, actants are positioned in the elementary structure of their governor, whether they are in a canonical or non-canonical position.[8] This means a combinatorial explosion of the number of elementary structures. To avoid, this problem, in our grammar, only actants in canonical position are positioned in the structure of their governor. An actant in a non-canonical position will ensure its own positioning in its elementary structures. This can be done by introducing in the elementary structure associated with a lexical unit L in a non-canonical position a quasi dependency that will unify with the dependency between L and its governor and thus void the weight on it, L being positioned by another dependency bearing an appropriate weight. Such a situation occurs in the case of relativization, where the nominal nucleus (or, more exactly, its top node) is in a non-canonical position. Therefore the dependency between the verbal nucleus and the nominal nucleus in the elementary structure of a relative wh-word will in fact be a quasi-dependency. This will

---

[6] Cases where the wh-word is not the top node of the nominal nucleus are called cases of *pied-piping*.

[7] A bubble tree is said *projective* if no dependencies and no bubbles cross each other and if no dependency and no bubble covers the top node.

[8] The term *position* refers to the linear position (in the morphological string). A position in the syntactic tree is called a syntactic position.

ensure that the top node of the nominal nucleus will not be positioned with respect to its syntactic governor. But how is the nominal nucleus positioned? A solution would be to add a dependency between the verbal nucleus and the nominal nucleus bearing a negative weight. We will adopt another solution, linguistically more motivated.

As Tesnière said, the relative wh-word, besides its pronominal role in the relative clause, has a subordinating role, allowing a clause to modify a noun. The relative wh-word transfers (Fr. *translater*) the verb into an adjective, that is, it masks the verb, allowing it to modify a noun and to occupy a syntactic position traditionally occupied by an adjective.[9] For this reason, Tesnière treats a wh-word as a split node, one part dominating the main verb of the clause, the other part filling a position in the clause.

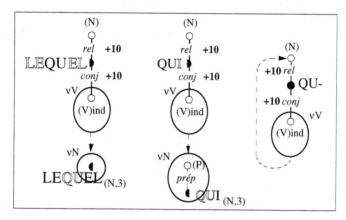

Fig. 13. *Elementary structures for LEQUEL 'which', QUI 'who' and QU- 'that'*

Our elementary structures reflect Tesnière's analysis, the wh-word being split into two semi-nodes. The linearization processes is as follows: the QU- part of the wh-word which dominates the verbal nucleus must be positioned before the verbal nucleus (due to the weight on the dependency linked them); the two part of the wh-word, which forms a single word, must be adjacent; the positioning of the nominal nucleus is conditioned by the positioning of the pronominal part of the wh-word, which belongs to it. Note that the elementary structure of a wh-word combines with three elementary structures: the antecedent noun, the syntactic governor of the wh-word in the relative clause (the governor of the "gap") and the main verb of the relative clause (moreover the wh-words constrains this verb to bear the indicative mood).

Some further information about French relative wh-words. First, the wh-word LEQUEL can be used in all syntactic positions, although the subject and direct object positions are only possible in non-restrictive relative clause (the combination À LEQUEL and DE LEQUEL give the contracted form *auquel* and *duquel*). Second, French has a parallel series of wh-word: QUI_1 for the subject position, QUE for the

---

[9] The grammemes of past participle and present participle are other "translators" of verbs into adjectives: *le livre acheté par Pierre* 'the book bought by Pierre'; *la personne achetant un livre* 'the person buying a book'. On the contrary, the infinitive and the subordinating conjunction *que* 'that' transfers the verb into a noun, allowing it to occupy an actantial position: *Pierre souhaite le départ de Marie/partir/que Marie parte* 'Pierre wishes the departure of Marie/to leave/that Marie leaves'.

direct object position and QUI₂ after a preposition. Clearly, QUI₁ and QUI₂ are two different words because the second denotes only a human.

(4) a. *la personne/le chien qui dort*
      'the person/the dog that is sleeping'
   b. *la personne/le chien que tu regardes*
      'the person/the dog that you are watching'
   c. *la personne/*le chien à qui j'ai parlé*
      'the person/the dog to who I spoke'

Some works since [13] seem to indicate that QUI₁ and QUE are two forms of a same wh-word, which we will call QU-, and that this wh-word is in fact the same word as the subordinating conjunction QUE (exactly like THAT in English). The best argument in favor of this hypothesis is the *qui/que* alternation in case of long distance dependencies:

(5) a. *la personne que je pense qui dort*
      'the person that I think (that) is sleeping'
   b. *la personne que je pense que tu regardes*
      'the personne that I think that you are watching'

Indeed, contrary to what could be expected, in (5a), a case of long distance extraction of the subject, the relative wh-word (which as usual introduces the relative clause) is *que* since the subordinating conjunction is *qui* (which is very unusual, see (5b)). This alternation can be solved by saying that it is still the same word QU- which takes the *qui* form when the verb it subordinates has its subject extracted and takes the *que* form in all other cases (see a formal solution in TAG [10]).

5.3 Operations of Combination with Bubbles

The elementary structures with bubbles combine by unification of nodes and dependencies, like the other elementary structures. There is nevertheless a complication: what happens to the dependents of a node that is positioned in a bubble? Three cases are possible:1) the dependent goes outside the bubble (the default case), 2) the dependent goes inside the bubble as its governor or 3) the dependent is promoted to the bubble. Three different rules of combination, called R1, R2 and R3, will be introduced. Before presenting these rules, we will presents the mechanism which controls their possible application.

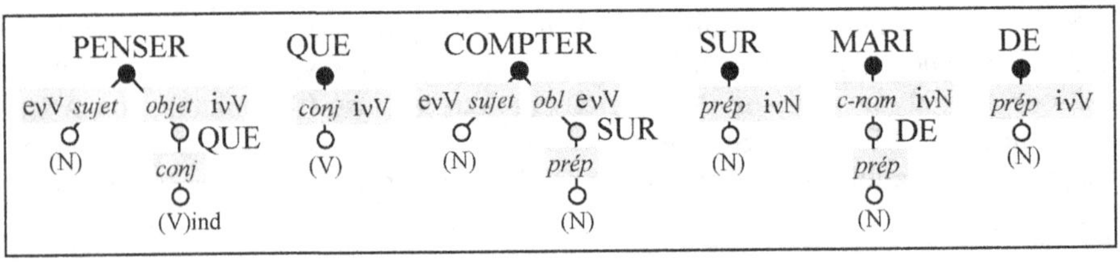

Fig. 14. *Elementary structure with labeling for intra- and extranuclear dependencies*

The fact that a dependency can be positioned inside a bubble or be promoted to a bubble is marked by the value of a feature nucleus. We have considered two types of bubbles, nominal and verbal nuclei, henceforth designated vN and vV. A dependency which can be inside a nucleus of type v receives the `value nucleus:iv` (i for intranuclear). A dependency which can be promoted to a nucleus of type v receives the `value nucleus:ev` (e for extranuclear) (Fig. 14).Now, when a node A' merges with a node A of a bubble v, the nodes linked to A' are positioned by default outside v (Rule R1, Fig. 15). However, the membership of v can be propagated to whatever node B' linked to A' with an intranuclear dependency iv (Rule R2, Fig. 16). Finally, every node B' linked to A' with an extranuclear dependency ev can be promoted to the nucleus v (Rule R3, Fig. 17).

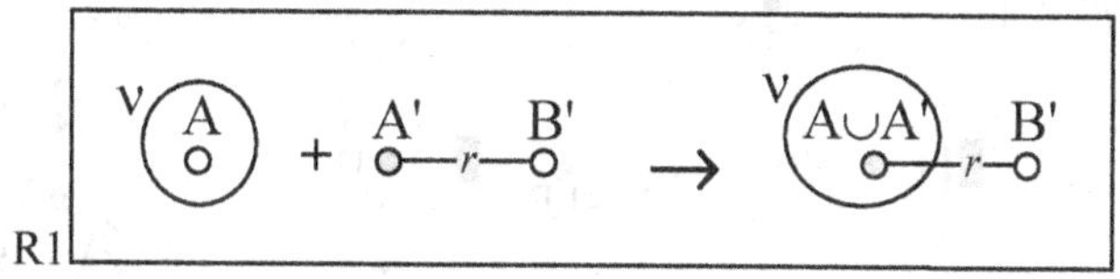

Fig. 15. *R1: Positioning by default of a dependent of a node of a nucleus v*

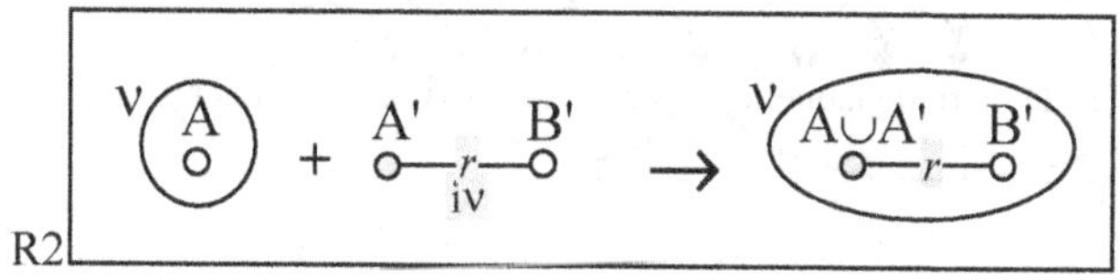

Fig. 16. *R2: Propagation of the membership of a nucleus v*

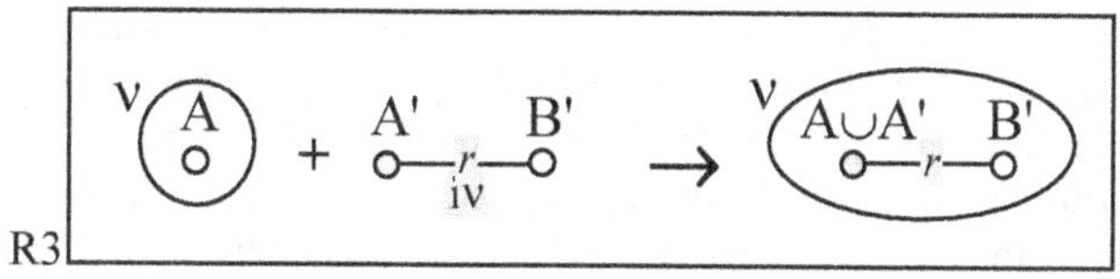

Fig. 17. *R3: Promotion of a dependent to a nucleus v*

We can now explain how the correspondence between the morphological and syntactic representations of (3) is obtained (Fig. 18). The only point that we think needs a comment is the *obl* dependency between COMPTER 'count' and SUR 'on'. This dependency is labeled evV, therefore when COMPTER is positioned in the vV bubble (= the verbal nucleus), it can be promoted to the vV bubble and then unify with the quasi dependency introduced by the elementary structure of LEQUEL.

We achieve a more or less exhaustive description of relativization in French. Other case of extraction cannot be developed here but we hope that we have convinced the reader that they can be described exactly in the same way.

5.4   Comparison with Other Formalisms

In our analysis, the nominal nucleus is promoted from its syntactic governor to the verbal nucleus. For instance, in the analysis of (3), the nominal nucleus *sur le mari de laquelle* does not depend on *compter* but on the verbal nucleus *pense que (tu) peux compter*. In terms of immediate constituents, we see that the projection of the verbal nucleus dominates directly the projection of the nominal nucleus (= the extracted phrase) and the projection of the main verb (the clause with a gap). Our analysis can

30

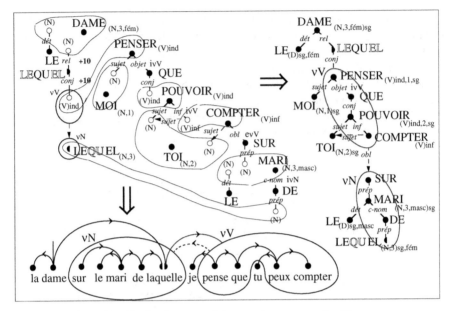

Fig. 18. *Combination of elementary structures for (3)*

therefore be compared of the X' Syntax's analysis ([3], [6]), where the relative clause corresponds to a node S' dominating a node COMP for the extracted phrase and a node S for the rest of the clause. Moreover, our operations can be compared to the movement of the X' Syntax or the slash technique of HPSG: the rule R3 is equivalent to the introduction of a non local (or slash) feature, while the rule R2 corresponds to the propagation of this feature. Several analyses in dependency grammar frameworks use devices equivalent to the slash feature, allowing lifting the extracted phrase on the main verb ([5], [14], [11]). Our analysis differs on at least one point: we do not propagate the content of the nominal nucleus (or extracted phrase) but we simply attach it to verbal nucleus and we propagate the membership of the verbal nucleus.

6 Conclusions

We have proposed a mathematical formalism for the implementation of grammars based on MTT. First, this formalism allows us to write fully lexicalized grammars, which are more efficient for the natural language processing, without bringing about the combinatorial explosion of the elementary structures. Second, our formalism can be extended in order to treat extractions, which are the corner stone of most of the formalisms developed since 25 years. This analysis is based on a linguistic concept, the nucleus, that we think plays a fundamental role in non-local phenomena such as extraction, coordination or negation. Moreover, this linguistic concept is not simply superimposed to the traditional syntactic representation, but it is encoded as a primitive concept, the bubble, associated to a set of geometric properties, such as the projectivity of bubble trees.

References

1. Abeillé Anne, *Une grammaire lexicalisée d'Arbres Adjoints pour le français*, Thèse de Doctorat, Univ. Paris 7 (1991).
2. Candito Marie-Hélène & Kahane Sylvain, "Can the TAG Derivation Tree Represent a Semantic Graph ? An answer in the Light of Meaning-Text Theory", TAG+4 Workshop, Philadelphie (1998) 21-24.
3. Chomsky Noam, "On Wh-movement", in P. Culicover et al. (eds), *Formal Syntax*, Dordrecht : Reidel (1977).
4. Courtin Jacques & Genthial Damien, "Parsing with Dependency Relations and Robust Parsing", in Kahane S. & Polguère A. (eds), *Workshop on dependency-based grammars, COLING-ACL'98*, Montréal (1998) 95-101.
5. Hudson Richard A., "Discontinuity", in S. Kahane (ed.), *Grammaires de dépendance, T.A.L., 41.1* (2000) 15-56.
6. Jackendoff Ray S., *X' Syntax : A Study of Phrase Structure*, Linguistic Inquiry Monograph, MIT Press (1977).
7. Joshi Aravind K., "Introduction to Tree Adjoining Grammar", in Manaster Ramer (ed.), *The Mathematics of Language*, Amsterdam:Benjamins (1987) 87-114.
8. Kahane Sylvain, "Bubble Trees and Syntactic Representations", in Becker T. & Krieger H.-U. (eds), *Proc. MOL'5*, Saarbrücken : DFKI (1997) 70-76.
9. Kahane Sylvain, "How to solve some failures of LTAG", *TAG+5 Workshop*, Paris (2000) 123-28.
10. Kahane Sylvain, Candito Marie-Hélène, de Kercadio Yannick, "An alternative description of extractions in TAG", *TAG+5 Workshop*, Paris (2000) 115-22.
11. Kahane Sylvain, Nasr A. & Rambow Owen, "Pseudo-Projectivity: a Polynomially Parsable Non-Projective Dependency Grammar", *COLING-ACL'98*, Montréal (1998) 646-52.
12. Kahane Sylvain & Mel'čuk Igor, "La synthèse des phrases à extraction en français contemporain. Du réseau sémantique à l'arbre syntaxique", *T.A.L, 40 : 2* (1999) 25-85.
13. Kayne Richard, *French Syntax : the Transformational Cycle*, Cambridge : MIT Press (1975).
14. Lombardo Vincenzo & Lesmo Leonardo, "Formal Aspects and Parsing Issues of Dependency Theory", *COLING-ACL'98*, Montréal (1998) 787-93.
15. Mel'čuk Igor, "Ordre des mots en synthèse automatique des textes russes", *T.A. Information, 2* (1967) 65-84.
16. Mel'čuk Igor, *Dependency Syntax: Theory and Practice*, NY : SUNY Press (1988).
17. Mel'čuk Igor, "Paraphrase et lexique: la Théorie Sens-Texte et le Dictionnaire Explicatif et Combinatoire", in Mel'čuk et al., *Dictionnaire Explicatif et Combinatoire, 3* (1992) 10-57.
18. Mel'čuk Igor & Pertsov Nicolas, *Surface syntax of English – A Formal Model within the Meaning-Text Framework*, Amsterdam : Benjamins (1987).
19. Nasr Alexis), "A Formalism and a Parser for Lexicalised Dependency Grammars", *4th Int. Workshop on Parsing Technologies*, SUNY Press (1995).
20. Nasr Alexis, *Un modèle de reformulation automatique fondé sur la Théorie Sens-Texte – Application aux langues contrôlées*, Thèse de Doctorat, Univ. Paris 7 (1996).
21. Polguère Alain, *Structuration et mise en jeu procédurale d'un modèle linguistique déclaratif dans un cadre de génération de texte*, Thèse de Doctorat, Univ. Montréal (1990).
22. Ross John, *Constraints on Variables in Syntax*, PhD Thesis, MIT (1967); *Infinite syntax !*, Dordrecht : Reidel (1985).
23. Tesnière Lucien, *Eléments de syntaxe structurale*, Paris: Kliencksieck (1959).
24. XTAG Research Group, *A Lexicalized TAG for English*, Technical Report IRCS 95-03, Univ. of Pennsylvania (1995) updated version on the web.

Modeling the Level of Involvement
of Verbal Arguments

Leo Ferres

Institute of Interdisciplinary Studies &
School of Linguistics and Applied Language Studies, Carleton University,
Ottawa, Ontario, K1S 5B6 – Canada.
lferres@chat.carleton.ca

Abstract. The purpose of this paper is to discuss the output of a neural network based on a linguistic model for recognizing the levels of involvement of different verbal arguments, assuming the non-discreteness of thematic relations and their non-primitiveness in linguistic theory. The network's output called for hypothesizing that, contrary to the received view, there is no equal level of involvement in verbal arguments, one having to be always more invovoved than the others, even when having the same number of Proto-Agent and Proto-Patients contributing properties.

1 Introduction: Some Reflections on Argument Structure

Apart from information about their syntactic environment, verbal entries also entail information of a semantic nature; namely, information about the roles (henceforth, θ-roles) that their lexicalized arguments will play in the utterance. Thus, in the example below (see (1)), the verbal entry 'buy' subcategorizes syntactically for two obligatory noun phrases (NP_1 and NP_2) and, in turn, it entails that for those two noun phrases, the roles 'buyer' (for NP_1) and that of 'thing_bought' (for NP_2) will be assigned. In more formal terms;

1.　　*buy*
$$\begin{bmatrix} subcat < NP_1, NP_2 > \\ role < buyer, thing\_bought > \end{bmatrix}$$

where [subcat $\Leftrightarrow$] stands for the entry's syntactic subcategorization and [role $\Leftrightarrow$] stands for the θ-roles that the obligatory arguments will bear in the utterance. Of course, even if we change the 'surface' grammatical construction that realizes (1) above, the θ-roles assigned to those arguments still hold. Take (2a) and (2b) below:

2.　　a. Peter bought a house.
　　　　b. A house was bought (by Peter).

Although grammatical relations have changed (e.g., [Peter]$_{NP}$ is not the grammatical subject of (2b) anymore), (2a) and (2b) would be specified in the same way in argument structure, perhaps along the following lines:

A. Gelbukh (Ed.): CICLing 2001, LNCS 2004, pp. 32–42, 2001.
© Springer-Verlag Berlin Heidelberg 2001

3.   *Peter bought a house/A house was bought (by Peter)*

$$\begin{bmatrix} lexis < Peter_1, a\_house_2 > \\ subcat < NP_1, NP_2 > \\ roles < buyer_1, thing\_bought_2 > \end{bmatrix}$$

where [lexis $\diamond$] stands for the lexical realization of the empty symbols demanded by the entry in both the [subcat $\diamond$] and the [roles $\diamond$] lists. As we see, at this level of description, there is no difference between (2a) and (2b). The entity referred to by [Peter]$_{NP}$ is still the 'buyer' and the entity referred to by [a house]$_{NP}$ is the thing that gets bought.

So far so good. However, I am of the view that discrete functional labels for the roles that fill the [role $\diamond$] list will not do. Labels like 'buyer', 'thing-bought', 'writer', 'thing_written', etc. do not seem to have any semantic content in contemporary linguistic theory [1]. This "functionalist" practice of differentiating θ-roles proves useful when we have to keep track of the entity that initiates -or carries out- the action (versus the entity that is affected by the action) across a variety of grammatical realizations like passives or topicalizations (see (3) above). In spite of this, it is clear that by adopting this approach, we lose loads of information about the real level of involvement of verbal arguments.

Before going into the evidence for the claim above, let me distinguish between two kinds of θ-role descriptions that permeate the linguistic literature. First, there are those authors who take θ-role to be mere labels derived from the name of the verb, with no other information associated to it. I will call this θ-role tokens (henceforth, R_{to}). Some examples of R_{to} are: 'writer' derived from the verb 'write', 'undergoer', derived from the verb 'undergo', 'thing_undergone' from 'undergo', 'thing-bought' from 'buy', etc. [2, 1]. Second, there are those authors who think that θ-roles belong to a somewhat more general category than R_{to}. For example, both R_{to}'s 'buyer' and 'undergoer' would belong to the higher-order category AGENT, while 'thing_bought' and 'thing_undergone' would belong to the higher-order category PATIENT, or something like that [3, 4, and all the literature about roles derived from these authors]. I will call this higher-order category θ-role types (henceforth, R_{ty}). These accounts are, of course, compatible, insofar as θ-roles are taken to be discrete in nature. However, this demand for θ-roles to be discrete is exactly the problem with these two accounts. Now, let me go back to my main point; namely, the claim that by labeling θ-roles in the [roles $\diamond$] list, we lose information about the nature and the degree of involvement of verbal arguments.

Take, first, the case of roles understood as R_{to}. Consider the following two verbal entries and their respective syntactic and semantic information, portrayed in (4a) and (4b) below:

4.   a. *write*

$$\begin{bmatrix} subcat < NP_1, NP_2 > \\ role < writer_1, written_2 > \end{bmatrix}$$

b. *undergo*

$$\left[\begin{array}{l} \text{subcat} < NP_1, NP_2 > \\ \text{role} < \text{undergoer}_1, \text{thing\_undergone}_2 > \end{array} \right]$$

By comparing these two cases, it becomes quite evident that in this approach we fail to formally differentiate the R_{to} 'writer' from the R_{to} 'undergoer'. And the difference is not a minor one. The R_{to} 'undergoer' is not the entity that performs the action in (4b) above, like the R_{to} 'writer' in (2a). Rather, the R_{to} 'undergoer' is the entity that is affected by the event named by the verb, exactly the opposite of the R_{to} 'writer'. Therefore, it seems that an account like this would not really do: The R_{to} approach fails to capture important differences, mostly because we do not know what these labels stand for. Essentially, the same kind of argument holds for the R_{ty}. In categories like AGENT or PATIENT, we still seem to lose information about the level of involvement of the verbal arguments. Take, for instance, the verbs 'frighten' and 'murder', in the following sentences:

5.   a. *scare*

$$\left[\begin{array}{l} \text{subcat} < NP_1, NP_2 > \\ \text{role} < AGENT_1, PATIENT_2 > \end{array} \right]$$

b. *murder*

$$\left[\begin{array}{l} \text{subcat} < NP_1, NP_2 > \\ \text{role} < AGENT_1, PATIENT_2 > \end{array} \right]$$

Here again, an analysis like this would not really do. The levels of involvement of the arguments associated with the grammatical subject of active sentences with these verbs are quite different. Take the following two sentences derived from these two verbs:

6.   a. Peter scared Jon.
        b. Peter murdered Jon.

in (6a), Peter's action of scaring Jon might have been purely accidental, without Peter planning it. This analysis is not possible in sentence (6b) above. Peter, in fact, *wanted* to kill Jon for whatever reason. Thus, in sentence (6b) below, Peter seems to be more involved in the action denoted by the verb than what he seems to be in (6a). The difference being, in this particular case, some sort of 'volitional involvement' on the part of Peter in sentence (6b). As in R_{to} approaches, the R_{ty} approach fails to capture important differences, mostly because we do not know what the labels AGENT and PATIENT stand for, except for the general, received view, that they stand for the entity that initiates an action and the entity that is affected by an action, respectively.

2   θ-roles as Non-primitive Concepts in Linguistic Theory

To be able to calculate the real level of involvement of each of the arguments of a given verb, we have to somehow know what the functional tags 'putter', 'writer', 'undergone', etc. stand for. The solution I propose is simple: θ-roles are not primitives in linguistic theory [5, 6, 7, 8]. Thus, our next logical step is to reduce these functional tags (both of the style R_{to} (e.g. 'putter' and of the style R_{ty} (e.g. AGENT) to a list of contributing properties of some sort. In the best possible scenario, these properties should be grounded in the human perceptual systems, though this is not a topic to discuss in these pages.

For reasons that I have discussed elsewhere [9], I will consider θ-roles to be 'cluster' concepts [10], defined by a set of contributing properties [8, 6, 7]. Dowty [8] argues for the existence of two role-like concepts *proto-agent* (PA) and *proto-patient* (PP). These two concepts delimit a continuum of activity (within which all different θ-roles would fall) and are in turn decomposed in a set of five contributing properties each: for the PA-role, the contributing properties are: a) volitional involvement in the event or state; b) sentience and/or perception; c) the causation of an event or change of state in another participant; d) movement (relative to the position of another participant); e) an existence independent of the event stated by the verb. Set-theoretically,

7. $PA=\{v,s,c,m,e\}$

In turn, the contributing properties for the PP-role are whether the patient: f) undergoes change of state; g) has an incremental theme; h) is causally affected by another participant; i) is stationary (not moving) relative to movement of another participant; j) does not exist independently of the event, or not at all.

8. $PP=\{ch,af,it,st,de\}$

In Dowty's theory [8], for each of its obligatory arguments, a predicate entails some or all of both sets of contributing properties (for a fuller discussion on this topic, see [9]). It is the different combinations of these properties that will determine the level of involvement of each of the verb's obligatory argument in the event named by that verb. Take the following two hypothetical one-place predicates and their entailments:

9.   a. $X(3_{v,s,m}0)$
        b. $Y(1_{v}0)$

where the subindices stand for the contributing properties of both PA and PP roles introduced as sets above. Thus, while predicate X entails three properties of PA (volitional involvement, sentience and the causation of an event) and no PP properties for its only argument, Y only entails one PA property for its argument (volitional involvement) and no PP properties [6].

It is perhaps the case that both arguments in predicates X and Y will ultimately be the AGENT of the utterance in question (and will maybe both lexicalize the subject in surface structure). However, we can be fairly confident that the levels of involvement that the predicates entail for the arguments in (9a) versus (9b) are quite different. The argument in (9a) seems to be playing a 'more agentive' role than that of (9b), and it does so in virtue of the number of proto-agentive properties it has. This is exactly the kind of information that I want to provide a computer with; namely, an account of the level of involvement of an argument as entailed by the verb in question.

This approach, of course, explains the difference between the verbal entries 'scare' and 'murder'. In these cases, the description of the [role ◇] lists associated with these verbs will show the difference. In our standard terminology:

10.   a. *scare*

$$\begin{bmatrix} \text{subcat} < \text{NP}_1, \text{NP}_2 > \\ \text{role} < (1c0)_1, (1s1ch)_2 > \end{bmatrix}$$

b. *murder*

$$\begin{bmatrix} \text{subcat} < \text{NP}_1, \text{NP}_2 > \\ \text{role} < (2v, c0)_1, (1s1ch)_2 > \end{bmatrix}$$

where inside the parentheses you find the descriptions of the level of involvement of the different verbal arguments. In (10a) and (10b), we see how the arguments associated with the direct object (in a traditional terminology) are the same (both having just one property associated to the PA role (sentience) and one property associated to the PP role (change of state)). The reader can actually deny this and give the argument a different description. That would be fine with me, the new description would not, in fact, jeopardize the main argument of this paper. This is so, because it is clear that, at least, the PA properties entailed by the verbal entry for the argument that will lexicalize the subject (in a traditional terminology) **are** different. In one of them (the case of 'murder' in (10b) above), the verbal entry entails a 'volitional involvement' for the argument associated with the grammatical subject, again in a traditional terminology. In (10a), in turn, this is not the case. We can surely find a situation in which the event named by the verb 'scare' was purely accidental.

3   Calculating the Level of Involvement of Verbal Arguments

Obviously, if we reduce θ-roles to two sets of five contributing properties each, we have 2^{10} possible combinations. Implementing all possible combinations in a traditional symbolic system of the style IF ...THEN would be a tedious task and the resulting model would end up being too deterministic to be really interesting, given its totally predictable behavior (I take up this issue in more detail in §4 below). Thus, I have opted to implement the above description of the degree of involvement of verbal arguments in a simple feed-forward neural network that learns by backpropagation.

Neural networks (or connectionist or PDP models) are, basically, a set of interacting processing units [11]. These units interact by transmitting and receiving signals to and from neighboring units by means of a set of weighted connections [12]. The task we have at hand is to pair a set of input values (which contributing properties are set to 'on' in the [roles <>]) list to a set of correct output values (whether the input leans towards a more PA or a more PP involvement). By calculating the difference between the expected result minus the observed result, we can adjust the connections weights so as to approximate the best function to the expected output (a learning algorithm called *backpropagation*, see [13]).

Let me now discuss the general architecture of the neural network. This network, remember, will implement a model for calculating the level of involvement of different verbal arguments. As I said before, this network is a perceptron that learns by backpropagation. The first five input units (i1-i5) stand for the five PA contributing properties mentioned in (7) above. The second five units stand for the PP contributing properties described in (8) above. The two output nodes (o1 and o2) stand for the two opposite sides of the continuum (the PA side and the PP side).

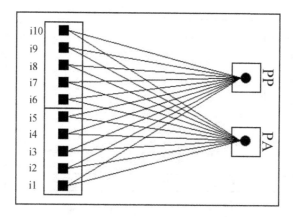

Figure 1: The network's general architecture

The network was trained for fifty thousand sweeps on a training environment consisting of a data file with forty-two random combinations of contributing properties, plus an "expected output results" (teacher) file, consisting of a pair of ideal values for the PA and PP role combination. Essentially, I take contributing properties to be 'on' or 'off'. Each contributing property set to 'on' is represented by a '1' in the relevant input unit. For example, a complete training example of the form [0100101101] means that there are five contributing properties set to 'on'. Moreover, since the input units are ordered (the first five correspond to the PA contributing properties and the second five correspond to the PP contributing properties), then we know that there are two activated input units for the PA role and three activated input units for the PP role. Finally, and again because the units are ordered as in the sets in (7) and (8) above, we know that the properties of being sentient (s) and the property of existing independent of the state named by the verb (e) are the ones set to 'on' for the PA role, while incremental theme (it), causally affected (af) and an existence dependent on the event denoted by the verb (de) are the ones set to 'on' for the PP role.

After the network was trained, an analysis of its error (see figure 2 below) shows that it had learned the task at hand. Obviously, we don't expect perfect performance (RMS=0), but it did seem to have stabilized at a good level of performance (RMS<0.1).

A more reliable way to show that the network has learned is to examine the results the network has produced for each output node after the 50,000 training sweeps. Here, I will just show some examples of activation of the two output nodes (PA and PP), with the corresponding activation of certain input units.

As we can see in Figure 3A above, when we have three PA input nodes activated (white squares), the level of involvement of the verbal argument increases, though it is not yet full involvement (notice the grey area surrounding the PA output node). In Figure 3B, all the input units associated with the PA role have been set to 'on'. As a result, we see how the output unit associated to the PA role is fully involved in the event stated by the verb (no grey area around it). It is evident now that an argument

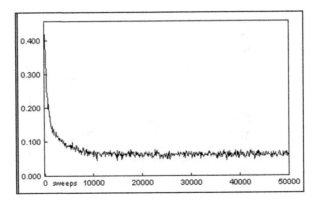

Figure 2: RMS after 50,000 sweeps

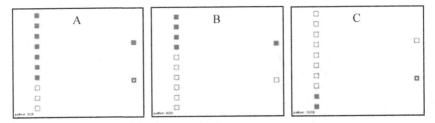

Figure 3: Activations for patterns [1110000000], [1111110000] and [0011111111].

with five PA properties has a higher level of involvement than an argument with just three PA properties. With regards to the units associated to the PP role, in Figure 3A none of the contributing properties are 'on'. Therefore, there is no activation of the PP output node. In Figure 3B, there is activation of just one PP property versus five activated PA properties. As expected, the network will output a full activation of the PA unit versus a very small activation of the PP output unit (0.66 versus 0.918 for the PA output unit). In figure 3C, we find the opposite case. All PP properties have been set to 'on' and therefore the output unit associated with the PP role is very active (0.898), versus a not-so-active PA role (with a value of 0.642), where only three PA contributing properties have been set to 'on'. For an exhaustive comparison of expected and output results, see figure 4 below.

In these two graphs, we can see how the network did a really good job in approximating to the "ideal" values after the extensive training. Notice that for mathematical reasons that need not concern us here, the network does not reach perfect learning, that is why the black line in the graph does not touch floor (axisY=0 in Figure 4 above) or ceiling (axisY=1) or exactly the "idealized" value (axisY=any value between 0 and 1, with increments of 0.2). Thus, it seems the network has learned the different levels of involvement for the training set. However, there are still 982 instances that the network has not been trained on. Does the network generalize to new instances, based on its previous experience? Let's analyze a set of ten random PA and PP property activations that the network has not been trained on (detailed in Table 3 below).

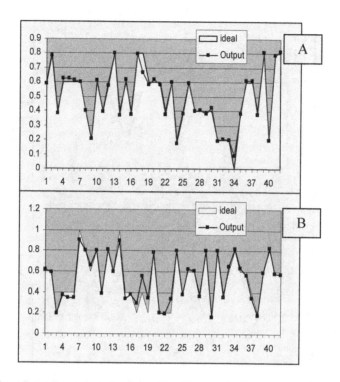

Figure 4: Exhaustive comparison between the "ideal" values (white area) and the values that the network actually output (black line) for each instance (X axis). Figure 4A shows the ideal and actual activations for the PA role and Figure 4B shows the ideal and actual activations for the PP role.

Table 3: Network generalizations after 50K sweeps

No.	New instances	PA value	PP value
1	1 1 0 0 1 0 0 0 1 0	0.583	0.211
2	0 1 1 1 0 0 0 0 1 0	0.623	0.168
3	0 1 0 1 1 0 1 1 1 1	0.643	0.808
4	0 1 1 1 0 0 1 0 1 0	0.636	0.343
5	1 0 0 0 0 1 1 1 1 1	0.182	0.914
6	0 1 1 1 1 1 0 1 0 1	0.817	0.562
7	1 0 0 0 0 1 0 0 1 1	0.166	0.616
8	0 0 1 1 1 0 0 0 0 1	0.647	0.162
9	0 1 0 1 1 1 0 0 0 0	0.618	0.194
10	0 0 1 1 1 0 1 0 0 0	0.662	0.167

What I have instructed the network to do is to generalize from the representation of the training set to some novel combinations of contributing properties. Again, as we can see in Table 3 above and, more intuitively in Figure 5 below, the network has done quite a good job at generalizing its knowledge to novel instances.

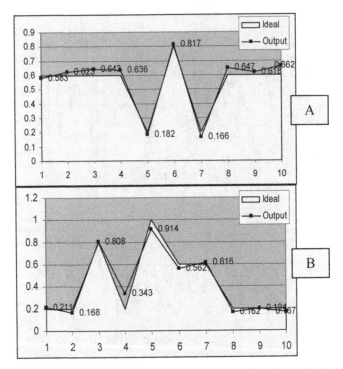

Figure 5: Exhaustive comparison between the expected values (white area) and the values the network output for the novel data (black line) for each instance (X axis). Figure 5A shows the ideal and actual activations for the PA role and Figure 5B shows the ideal and actual activations for the PP role.

We can see how the network's generalizations are quite correct in general. In fact, after averaging out the ten novel values, the network output a value of 0.557 for the PA node (when the ideal value would have been 0.54). Similarly, the network's output for the PP node was 0.414 when the ideal value would have been 0.42.

4 Discussing the Model

There are, obviously, many interesting issues to discuss about the networks performance. However, I would like to, presently, focus on one particular point: the case in which the number of PA and PP properties is the same.

As I have shown, the network seems to have learned the task and is able, based on prior experience, to generalize to new instances. The interesting issue is that, contrary to symbolic systems; the values assigned to the PA and the PP nodes are sometimes quite different, even if they would, in traditional symbolic systems, have exactly the same value. Take, for example, the following novel instance presented to the network after it was trained for 50,000 sweeps.

11. [0011100111]

Although this is not the case, suppose for a minute that we had coded, in a symbolic system, all possible combinations of contributed properties and their associated output values. We could have coded this system, maybe, along the following lines:

12. IF [0011100111] THEN PA=0.6 & PP=0.6.

If so, the symbolic system's output values would be, of necessity, mere idealizations that we provided it with. In return for the discrete coding, when we query the system for some level of involvement, we are able to get the values we provided it with, and those values only. For instance, take the case of (11) with a rule like (12), a symbolic system would output a value of 0.6 for the PA node and a value of 0.6 for the PP node. And we cannot expect anything else.

In neural networks, these output idealizations are not the case because of two important reasons: first, because we did not provide the network with that particular instance of contributing properties, and second, even thought we provided the network with ideal values with which to approximate the function towards the training data, none of the networks outputs was really specified a priori. For example, for case (11) above, the network output a value of 0.644 for the PA node and a value of 0.571 for the PP node. We sure did not provide the network with these two values (we did not even provide the system with that particular instance of contributing properties!). That means that based on previous experience, the network takes always one (and only one) of the sides of the continuum (in this case the PA node) to be slightly more active than the other end (the PP node).

At this point I would like to propose the following hypothesis: even if an argument has an equal number of PA and PP contributing properties (like (11) above), one of the proto-roles will always be favored, yielding either the PA or the PP role to be more activated in any one circumstance, but not both. And this, in turn, means that just one of them wins the grand prix for the level of involvement problem, and just one of them gets to lexicalize either the subject or object, later during derivation.

5 Conclusion

In its current state, this relatively simplistic model gives an account of the different levels of involvement of verbal arguments in one-place predicates. Most interestingly, the network generalizes to novel instances in a way that allows us to solve a riddle with regards to the level of involvement of verbal arguments that possess an equal number of PA and PP contributing properties. This will prove crucial when, in future work, I expand the network to also give an account of two- and three-place predicates and the interaction with NPs of different sorts. It will be crucial because, given the choice, the system will output just one of the arguments as lexicalizing any given R_{ty} (with more naturally-resulting linguistic generalizations). Thanks to the simple implementation discussed in this paper, there are no arguments that are equally involved in the event stated by the verb anymore, and I truly believe this to be an important conclusion to be watched carefully in intelligent text processing as well as in human sentence processing.

References

1. Wechsler, S.: The Semantic Bases of Argument Structure. CSLI Publications, California: USA (1995)
2. Pollard, C., Sag, I.: Head-Driven Phrase Structure Grammar. Center for the Study of Language and Information, Stanford, CA, USA. (1994)
3. Gruber, J.: Studies in Lexical Relations. MIT Dissertation, Cambridge, MA, USA (1965)
4. Fillmore, C.: The Case for Case. In E. Bach & R. Harms, eds., Universals in linguistic theory. New York: Holt, Rinehardt & Winston (1968) 1-88
5. García, E.: The Role of Theory in Linguistic Analysis: The Spanish Pronoun System. North Holland Publishing Company: The Netherlands (1975)
6. Castel, V.: Paquetes de Clíticos del Español: Cálculo de la Correlación entre Roles Semánticos y Propiedades Morfológicas e Implementación en una Gramática Categorial de Unificación. Doctoral dissertation, Université Blaise Pascal à Clairmont-Ferrand, Clairmont-Ferrand: France (1994)
7. Castel, V., Rossi, D.: Proyección de Roles Semánticos en Funciones Sintácticas: Una Formalización del Principio de Selección Argumental de Dowty. Revista Argentina de Lingüística, vol. 10. Mendoza: Argentina (1994) 1-15
8. Dowty, D.: Thematic Proto-Roles and Argument Selection. Language, vol. 6, number 3, USA (1991) 547-619.
9. Ferres-Trahtenbroit, L.: Thematic Proto-Roles and Argument-Predicate Interaction. In: Gelbukh, A. (ed.): Proceedings of CICLing-2000, Mexico City, Mexico (2000) 68-87.
10. Rosch, E., Mervis, C.: Family Resemblances: Studies in the Internal Structure of Categories. Cognitive Psychology (8) (1975) 382-439
11. Stein, D. and Ludik, J.: Neural Networks and Psychopathology: Connectionist Models in Practice and Research. Cambridge University Press, Cambridge, UK (1998)
12. McClelland, J., Rumelhart, D., Hinton, G.: The Appeal of Parallel Distributed Processing. In McClelland, J., Rumelhart, D. and the PDP Research Group: Parallel Distributed Processing: Explorations in the Microstructure of Cognition, Volume 1: Foundations. MIT Press, Cambridge, MA, USA (1986) 3-45
13. Plunkett, K. and Elman, J.: Exercises in Rethinking Innateness: A Handbook for Connectionist Simulations. MIT Press, Cambridge, MA, USA. (1997)

This paper was written while the author was holding a Jose Estenssoro Scholarship, awarded by the Fundacion YPF, Buenos Aires, Argentina, an Antorchas Scholarship, awarded by the Fundacion Antorchas, Buenos Aires, Argentina, a Carleton University Scholarship, awarded by Carleton University, Ottawa, Canada and the generous support (both in time and resources) of Mitercom Inc., Nepean, Ontario, Canada. The author would like to thank all these institutions and especially Andrew Brook, at Carleton University, for his constant support and his always finding the time to go over versions of this paper on a very short notice.

Magical Number Seven Plus or Minus Two: Syntactic Structure Recognition in Japanese and English Sentences

Masaki Murata, Kiyotaka Uchimoto, Qing Ma, and Hitoshi Isahara

Communications Research Laboratory, MPT,
2-2-2 Hikaridai, Seika-cho, Soraku-gun, Kyoto, 619-0289, Japan,
{murata,uchimoto,qma,isahara}@crl.go.jp,
http://www-karc.crl.go.jp/ips/murata

Abstract. George A. Miller said that human beings have only seven chunks in short-term memory, plus or minus two. We counted the number of bunsetsus (phrases) whose modifiees are undetermined in each step of an analysis of the dependency structure of Japanese sentences, and which therefore must be stored in short-term memory. The number was roughly less than nine, the upper bound of seven plus or minus two. We also obtained similar results with English sentences under the assumption that human beings recognize a series of words, such as a noun phrase (NP), as a unit. This indicates that if we assume that the human cognitive units in Japanese and English are bunsetsu and NP respectively, analysis will support Miller's 7 ± 2 theory.

1 Introduction

George A. Miller suggested in 1956 that human beings have only seven chunks[1] in short-term memory, plus or minus two [6]. We counted the number of *bunsetsus* (phrases) whose modifiees are undetermined in each step of an analysis of the dependency structure of Japanese sentences and which therefore must be stored in short-term memory, using the Kyoto University corpus [3]. (The Kyoto University corpus is a syntactic-tagged corpus collected from editions of the Mainichi newspaper.) The number was roughly less than nine, that is, the upper bound of Miller's 7 ± 2 rule. This result supposes that bunsetsus whose modifiees are not determined are stored in short-term memory. For the Kyoto University corpus, the number of stored items was less than nine. This result supports Miller's theory. We made a similar investigation of English sentences using a method described by Yngve [8]. We assumed that human beings recognize a series of words, such as a noun phrase (NP), as a unit and found that the required capacity of short-term memory is roughly less than nine.

---

[1] A chunk is a cognitive unit of information.

A. Gelbukh (Ed.): CICLing 2001, LNCS 2004, pp. 43–52, 2001.

2   Short-Term Memory and the 7 ± 2 Theory

Miller said that human beings have only seven chunks in short-term memory, plus or minus two, because the results of various experiments on words, tones, tastes, sight organs indicated approximately seven. The "plus or minus two" indicates an individual-based variation[2].

Although the research on the 7 ± 2 theory belongs to the field of psychology, it can be applied to the field of engineering. In sentence generation, for example, a sentence that exceeds the seven plus or minus two capacity of short-term memory is difficult to understand, so sentences are generated that do not exceed this upper limitation [8]. In human-interface systems, only about seven plus or minus two objects are displayed at one time because if more pieces of information are given, humans have trouble recognizing the images. Research on the 7 ± 2 theory is useful not only for the scientific investigation of human beings, but also for the engineering of things used in daily life.

3   Investigation of Japanese Sentences

In this work, we consider the process of sentence understanding as the analysis of the syntactic structure of a sentence, and we assume that those items which must be stored in short-term memory when understanding a sentence are bunsetsus whose modifiees are not determined. ("Bunsetsu" is a Japanese technical grammatical term. A bunsetsu is like a phrase in English, but it is a slightly smaller component. *Eki-de* "at the station" is a bunsetsu, and *sono*, which means "the" or "its," is also a bunsetsu. A bunsetsu is roughly a unit referring to an entity. So a bunsetsu is thought to be an appropriate unit of recognition.) Figure 1 is an example of calculating the number of bunsetsus whose modifiees are not determined in each step when analyzing the syntactic structure of the following sentence from left to right.

> *sono shounen-wa chiisai ningyou-wo motteiru.*
> (the)   (boy)   (small)   (doll)   (have)
> The boy has a small doll.

---

[2] Note that the following descriptions are not directly related to Miller's 7 ± 2 theory, but to short-term memory. Lewis's work, "Magical number two or three," discussed linguistic features related to short-term memory [4]. The work discussed the number of center-embedded sentences and theorized that in English only one main clause sentence and one center-embedded sentence, for a total of two sentences, are allowed. In Japanese, one main clause sentence and two center-embedded sentences, for a total of three sentences, are allowed. These limitations are caused by the constraints of short-term memory, and have been discussed in English in principle four, "Two sentences", of Kimball's Seven Principles [2]. This research suggests that the reason for the limited number of center-embedded sentences is the limited capacity of human short-term memory.

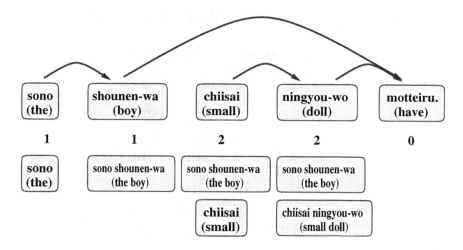

Fig. 1. How to estimate the number of bunsetsus whose modifiees are not determined

Arrows in the figure indicate the dependency structure. The number indicates the number of bunsetsus whose modifiees are not determined, and the lower part indicates the elements which must be stored in short-term memory. At the beginning, when *sono* (the) is input, its modifiee has not been determined yet, so it must be remembered. It is then stored in short-term memory as a bunsetsu whose modifiee is not determined. When *shounen* (boy) is input, *sono* (the) is found to modify *shounen* (boy). So *sono* (the) will not be used in the syntactic analysis after that, and it does not need to be remembered independently. *Sono* (the) is recognized to be attached to *shounen* (boy) in the form of *sono shounen* (the boy). As a result, only one element, *sono shounen* (the boy), whose modifiee is not determined, is stored in short-term memory. Next, *chiisai* (small) is input. This time, the dependency structure is not changed, and *sono shounen* (the boy) and *chiisai* (small) are stored in short-term memory. Next, when *ningyou* (doll) is input, *chiisai* (small) is recognized to modify *ningyou* (doll). *Chiisai* (small) will not be used in later analysis, because it is recognized to be attached to *ningyou* (doll) in the form of *chiisai ningyou* (small doll). Only the two elements *sono shounen* (the boy) and *chiisai ningyou* (small doll) are stored. Finally, *motteiru* (have) is input. Here, all the relationships of the dependency structure are determined and the number of bunsetsus with undetermined modifiees is 0. All the elements which were stored in short-term memory are cleared.

We assume that all human beings understand sentences the above way. The results are shown in Table 1. The number in the "bunsetsu" column is the number of bunsetsus having the given number of undetermined modifiees among all the bunsetsus of the Kyoto University corpus, (19,954 sentences and 192,352 bunsetsus). The number in the "sentence" column is the number of sentences having the given number of undetermined modifiees. In this table, only three

Table 1. Number of bunsetsus which undetermined modifiees

Bunsetsus with un-	Frequency	
determined modifiees	Bunsetsu	Sentence
0	19954	90
1	52751	1352
2	59494	5022
3	38465	6823
4	15802	4468
5	4488	1593
6	1143	480
7	195	102
8	47	17
9	10	5
10	3	2

bunsetsus exceeded the upper bound of Miller's 7 ± 2 rule. The result supports Miller's theory.

4   Investigation of English Sentences

In the investigation of the Japanese corpus in the previous section we estimated the upper bound of the short-term memory required for sentence understanding. This section describes a similar investigation of an English corpus.

Yngve described a method for estimating the short-term memory capacity required in the syntactic analysis of an English sentence [8]. This method supposes that the nonterminal symbols, i.e., S and NP, which are stored in a stack when analyzing a sentence in a top-down fashion by using a push-down automaton, are those which need to be stored in short-term memory, and it counts the number of symbols stored in the stack. Figure 2 shows how the number of nonterminal symbols stored in a stack is counted in the analysis of the sentence, "The boy has a small doll," in a push-down automaton. Boxes in the lower part of Figure 2 indicate the state of the stack as the sentence is parsed. For example, at the beginning of the sentence, "The" is input first. When the sentence is analyzing in a top-down fashion, S is given first. Next, S is transformed into (NP VP). When VP is remembered, NP is transformed into (DT N). When N is remembered, DT is recognized to be "The"[3]. As a result, the two non-terminal symbols, VP

---

[3] Yngve's method has the following two problems. The first is, in Figure 2, we can select two possible patterns, (DT N) and (DT J N), in transforming NP, and we cannot select one of them when "The" is input. The other is that, by changing the grammar used in a corpus, the structure of a syntactic tree is changed and the result is changed. Despite these problems, we used Yngve's method because it is very easy to count with.

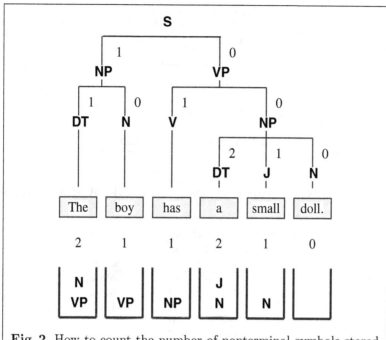

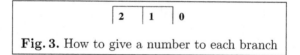

Fig. 2. How to count the number of nonterminal symbols stored in stacks

| 2 | 1 | 0 |

Fig. 3. How to give a number to each branch

and N, need to be stored in a stack while "The" is processed. Similarly, the non-terminal symbols which need to be stored for each stack are shown in Figure 2. The numbers of symbols in the stacks for each word are 2, 1, 1, 2, 1, and 0. Yngve also proposed an easy method of counting the number of nonterminal symbols stored in a given stack. In this method a number is assigned to each branch of a tree as shown in Figure 3. The sum of the numbers in the path from S to a word is considered as the number of symbols stored in a stack at that word. For example, at the word "The", "1, 1" is in the path of S, NP, DT, and "The", so the sum is 2, which matches the number of symbols stored in the stack.

Using this method, Sampson analyzed the SUSANNE corpus (130,000 words) and obtained the results shown in Table 2(a) [7]. "Frequency (words)" means the frequency of words with the corresponding number of nonterminals stored in a stack. With this method of analysis many sentences exceeded the upper bound of 7 ± 2, i.e., 9. Sampson counted again, changing the number of each branch, as in Figure 4. With this new method, when A is recognized, B, C, D, and E

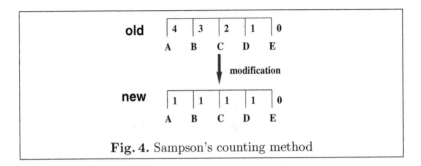

Fig. 4. Sampson's counting method

Table 2. Number of nonterminals stored in a stack (SUSANNE corpus)

(a)Yngve's method

Stack	Frequency (words)
0	7851
1	30798
2	34352
3	26459
4	16753
5	9463
6	4803
7	2125
8	863
9	313
10	119
11	32
12	4
13	1

(b)Sampson's method

Stack	Frequency (words)
0	55866
1	64552
2	12164
3	1274
4	76
5	4

are not remembered independently, but as one set of B, C, D, and E. Using this method, Sampson obtained the results shown in Table 2(b). This result showed that none of the sentences exceeded the lower bound of 7 ± 2, i.e., 5, therefore does not conflict with Miller's 7 ± 2 theory.

We followed the same methods in an analysis of the corpus of The Wall Street Journal of Penn Treebank [5]. We did not use the SUSANNE corpus because its structure is complicated, it is smaller than the Penn Treebank corpus, and it has already been studied by Sampson. The results for the Penn Treebank corpus are shown in Table 3. "Words" means the frequency of words having a given number of nonterminals stored in the stack. "Sentences" means the frequency of sentences having a given number of nonterminals stored in the stack. This time, we eliminated symbols such as periods, and we counted by changing the number of each branch in a coordination clause as in Figure 5, because the Penn

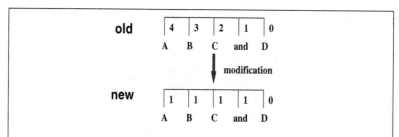

Fig. 5. How to modify the number of each branch in a coordination clause

Treebank corpus is constructed such that the extra number of nonterminals in a coordination clause is counted. The results in Table 3 were found to match those in Table 2(a). Again, many sentences exceed the upper bound of seven plus or minus two. We also counted using Sampson's method. The results are shown in Table 4. Although the number of nonterminal symbols of the SUSANNE corpus did not exceed five, the Penn Treebank corpus included words with up to seven nonterminal symbols.

Table 3. Number of nonterminals stored in a stack (Penn Treebank corpus)

Yngve's method in a word

Stack	Frequency	
	Words	Sentences
0	49208	132
1	377740	772
2	309255	3921
3	213294	9528
4	103864	13324
5	44274	11163
6	16478	6158
7	5750	2719
8	1939	981
9	661	338
10	243	111
11	92	29
12	43	17
13	15	14
14	1	1

Table 4. Number of nonterminals stored in a stack (Penn Treebank corpus)

Sampson's method in a word

Stack	Frequency	
	Words	Sentences
0	49208	132
1	485849	1956
2	414945	13367
3	140611	22966
4	28317	9124
5	3616	1518
6	283	133
7	28	12

Table 5. Number of nonterminals stored in a stack (Penn Treebank corpus)

Yngve's method in a NP

Stack	Frequency	
	NPs	Sentences
0	69820	4546
1	102337	7634
2	74126	16847
3	30025	11489
4	11432	5780
5	3336	2020
6	963	633
7	273	187
8	76	51
9	29	13
10	13	8

We also developed a new counting method for an English corpus which is different from Yngve's and Sampson's methods. Our method is based on an idea that we should not use, as a cognitive unit, words but phrases, which corresponds to bunsetsus, which are the units for counting in Japanese. We assume that human beings recognize NPs all at once instead of dividing them into words, and count the number of nonterminals stored in a stack at the NP level. In other words, we counted by using the sum of the numbers in the path from S to NP. The results shown in Table 5, are very similar to the results for Japanese sentences, shown in Table 1, and contain sentences with eight and nine NPs, which correspond to the plus-two part of Miller's 7 ± 2 theory. These results show our method to be effective.

Yngve's method did not obtain results that agree with Miller's 7 ± 2 theory, but Sampson's method and our method did. However, our method has the following two advantages over Sampson's method.

- Our counting method in English, which uses bunsetsu-corresponding NPs as the unit for counting, is based on our counting method for Japanese. (It is plausible for several languages to have the same level of cognitive units.)
- Although Sampson's method does not result in sentences with eight or nine nonterminal symbols, which is the upper bound of the 7 ± 2 theory, our method produced results that did. (Since "± 2" indicates an individual-based variation, a method that does not result in sentences with eight or nine nonterminals for a large corpus is very unnatural.)

5 Conclusion

We investigated Miller's 7 ± 2 theory using Japanese and English corpora. New information obtained in this paper is shown here.

- When bunsetsus were used as the cognitive unit, the results of the investigation of Japanese syntactic recognition agreed with Miller's 7 ± 2 theory.
- When NPs were used as the cognitive unit, the results of the investigation of English syntactic recognition agreed with Miller's 7 ± 2 theory. This indicates that NPs are likely to be the cognitive unit. It seems natural that the NP level is the cognitive unit, because it is the same level as the Japanese cognitive unit, bunsetsu[4].
- If we suppose that bunsetsus and NPs are the cognitive units, the analyses in Japanese and English support Miller's 7 ± 2 theory and also support Yngve's theory [8], which is that the number of items stored in short-term memory does not exceed 7 ± 2 in language understanding and generation. These analyses support Miller's 7 ± 2 theory and Yngve's theory. From the standpoint of natural language processing, if Yngve's assertion is right, the assertion that "the number of items stored in short-term memory does not exceed 7 ± 2" can be used in the construction of an practical NLP system.

References

[1] Charles J. Fillmore. The case for case. In Emmon Bach and Robert T. Harms, editors, *Universals in Linguistic Theory*, pages 1–88. Holt, Rinehart and Winston, Inc., 1968.
[2] John Kimball. Seven principles of surface structure parsing in natural language. *Cognition*, 2(1):15–47, 1973.

---

[4] A cognitive unit is thought to be a case element [1] or a unit taking the case element in the transformation process from short-term memory to the semantic network of long-term memory. So it seems natural that the cognitive unit is the same level of phrase in Japanese and English.

[3] Sadao Kurohashi and Makoto Nagao. Kyoto University text corpus project. pages 115–118, 1997. (in Japanese).

[4] Richard L. Lewis. Interference in Short-Term Memory: The Magical Number Two (or Three) in Sentence Processing. *Psycholinguistic Research*, 25(1):93–115, 1996.

[5] Mitchell P. Marcus, Beatrice Santorini, and Mary Ann Marcinkiewicz. Building a large annotated corpus of English: the Penn Treebank. *Computational Linguistics*, 19(2):310–330, 1993.

[6] George A. Miller. The magical number seven, plus or minus two: Some limits on our capacity for processing information. *The Psychological Review*, 63:81–97, 1956.

[7] Geoffrey Sampson. Depth in English grammar. *Journal of Linguistics*, 33:131–151, 1997.

[8] Victor H. Yngve. A Model and an Hypothesis for Language Structure. *the American Philosophical Society*, 104(5):444–466, 1960.

Spatio-temporal Indexing in Database Semantics

Roland Hausser

Universität Erlangen-Nürnberg
Abteilung Computerlinguistik (CLUE)
rrh@linguistik.uni-erlangen.de

Abstract In logic, the spatio-temporal location of a proposition is characterized precisely within a Cartesian system of space and time coordinates. This is suitable for characterizing the truth value of propositions relative to possible worlds, but not for modeling the spatio-temporal orientation of natural cognitive agents.[1]
This paper presents an alternative approach to representing space and time. While on the same level of abstraction as the logical approach, it is designed for an analysis of spatio-temporal inferences in humans. Such an analysis is important for modeling natural language communication because spatio-temporal information is constantly coded into language by the speaker and decoded by the hearer.
Starting from the spatio-temporal characterization of direct observation in cognitive agents without language, the speaker's coding of spatio-temporal information into language is analyzed, followed by the hearer's reconstruction of this location. These procedures of transferring spatio-temporal information from the speaker to the hearer are embedded in the general structure of database semantics.

Overview

The goal of database semantics is a computational model of natural communication. The transfer of information from the speaker to the hearer is based on representing the knowledge of speaker and hearer, respectively, in the form of databases. Natural language communication is successful if a certain database content, coded by the speaker into natural language signs, is reconstructed analogously in the database of the hearer.

A special aspect of analogous reconstruction is the coding and transfer of spatio-temporal information. This aspect is integrated deeply into the system of database semantics, for which reason the general structural principles for transferring propositional content are described first (Section 1–3).

Then, the spatio-temporal indexing of direct observations in cognitive agents without language is analyzed (Section 4). In this analysis, the cognitive representation of time is based on the order in which propositions enter the cognitive agent's database. The chain of incoming propositions is structured naturally by observations of cyclical events like

---

[1] The analysis of time in tensed predicate calculus (TPL) is critically reviewed in Kamp & Reyle 1993, Vol. 2, p. 483–510. Their own approach, called discourse representation theory (DRT), however, has "no conclusive answers to these questions, and presumably there are no clear, non-stipulative answers to be had" (op. cit. p. 666). From the viewpoint of database semantics, this is not surprising because DRT is itself a variant of model-theoretic semantics.

A. Gelbukh (Ed.): CICLing 2001, LNCS 2004, pp. 53–68, 2001.

day and night. Such observations serve as landmarks which provide the basis for spatio-temporal reasoning.

Finally, the transfer of spatio-temporal information from the speaker to the hearer is addressed. This raises two questions: (i) How can the spatio-temporal location of a propositional content in the speaker's database be inferred by the hearer (Section 5) and (ii) how should this location, once it is inferred, be represented in the database of the hearer (Section 6)?

It is shown that the answers depend on the distinction between fleeting and permanent signs and between immediate and mediated reference. These distinctions result in four basic types of natural language communication (Section 7). A question-answer example illustrates that landmark-based spatio-temporal reasoning in database semantics is similar to that of humans (Section 8).

1   Intuitive Outline of Database Semantics

In theoretical linguistics, tree structures are assigned to individual sentences in accordance with certain intuitions (constituent structure). Roughly similar intuitions are also used in database semantics, specifically with regard to the functor-argument structure of simple sentences and the composition of complex sentences from simple ones.

However, in database semantics the representation of linguists' intuitions by means of trees turned out to be an unsurmountable obstacle for realizing a functional theory of natural language communication.Instead, the grammatical structures needed for the transfer of information from the speaker to the hearer must be coded in a distributed manner into an abstract data structure.

This data structure may be explained intuitively by the following analogy:

> Consider two girls who store their books in different houses. They are avid readers with an ample budget and continuously add new books to their libraries. Furthermore, they each always finish their current book before they start reading the next one.
>
> To keep track of their reading, they have the habit of writing the author and title of the current book, the book read previously, and the book to be read next on a card and putting it into the current book. Once in a while, they also note the date on the card, thus anchoring the sequence to a temporal landmark. The books with the cards are stored in their libraries in the alphabetical order of the authors' names.
>
> When one of the girls goes on holiday, she keeps up her card-making habit. Furthermore, each time she goes to a new place, she notes it on the card of the current book, thus anchoring the sequence to a spatial landmark. After reading an interesting sequence of books, she sends copies of her cards to her friend. Her friend obtains the books, puts the copied cards into them, and sorts the books alphabetically into her library – keeping the first book in the sequence for immediate reading. When it is finished, she uses its card to go to the next book, etc.

The communication of reading sequences between the two girls is based on (i) structure-based storage and retrieval, (ii) internal chaining, and (iii) landmark anchoring. These principles may be described as follows:

1.1   Structural Principles for Solving the Update Task

1. **Structure-based storage and retrieval** is used in well-organized private libraries. The books in the shelves are ordered alphabetically according to the author's name. Several books by the same author are ordered in their sequence of acquisition. In this way, the storage position of new books is determined uniquely, while the retrieval position of old books is sufficiently narrow.
2. **Internal chaining** is a method for establishing relations between books based on keeping notes in them. Each note describes the book in which it is contained and its relations to other books. By specifying local relations between books A and B, B and C, C and D, etc., arbitrarily long chains may result. By specifying both the preceding and the following book, these chains may be followed forward as well as backward.
3. **Landmark anchoring** is based on (2) internal chaining and makes it possible to connect several items to the same landmark by marking only the initial item in the sequence. For example, if an item in an internal chain is connected to landmark X, e.g. a certain place, then all subsequent unmarked items are assumed to be connected to landmark X as well. As soon as an item in the chain is marked for another landmark Y, however, the following items are connected to Y, etc.

Structure-based storage and retrieval has the advantage that no index has to be constructed and maintained. This is in contrast to catalog-based indexing, as used in public libraries.[2] Database semantics solves the update task of natural language communication without the use of a catalog-based index in order to be compatible with the cognitive evolution of natural agents.

2   Structure-Based Storage and Retrieval

The copies of the cards that are passed between the girls stand for the content words (surfaces), while the corresponding books stand for their meanings. The relation between words and their meaning is established by the lexicon. The meanings in the database are structurally connected into *concatenated propositions*.

Technically, a proposition is represented as a set of feature structures, called proplets. As feature structures, proplets are special in that they use internal chaining to express intra- and extrapropositional relations between proplets.

The intrapropositional relations are expressed as follows: the proplet of an argument specifies the associated functor, the proplet of a functor specifies the associated argument(s), and similarly for modifiers. Proplets belonging to the same proposition share a common proposition number.

---

[2] Such a catalog consists of cards, each describing (i) a book in terms of its author's name and its title, and (ii) the physical storage location of the book in a certain shelf. While the filing cards are ordered alphabetically according to their respective keywords, the choice of the storage locations is free. Once a given book has been assigned a certain location and this location has been noted in the catalog, however, its address is fixed. In this way, the catalog serves as an index which guides the retrieval of the item desired from a specified storage location.

   Another example of catalog-based indexing is a relational database, where several indices, called tables, are used in combination.

The extrapropositional relations are of two types, conjunction and identity. The proplets of functors contain the attribute cnj which specifies the functor of another proposition and the conjunctional relation between them, for example temporal order expressed by '>'. The proplets of arguments contain the attribute id which specifies the identity or non-identity with other arguments.

For example, the concatenated propositions *Peter leave house. Then Peter cross street.* are represented in database semantics by the following proplets:

2.1   Representation of Two Concatenated Propositions

$$
\begin{bmatrix} \text{arg: Peter} \\ \text{FUNC: leave} \\ \text{id: 1} \\ \text{prn: 54} \end{bmatrix}
\begin{bmatrix} \text{func: leave} \\ \text{ARG: Peter house} \\ \text{cnj: } > \text{cross}_{55} \\ \text{prn: 54} \end{bmatrix}
\begin{bmatrix} \text{arg: house} \\ \text{FUNC: leave} \\ \text{id: 2} \\ \text{prn: 54} \end{bmatrix}
$$

$$
\begin{bmatrix} \text{arg: Peter} \\ \text{FUNC: cross} \\ \text{id: 1} \\ \text{prn: 55} \end{bmatrix}
\begin{bmatrix} \text{func: cross} \\ \text{ARG: Peter street} \\ \text{cnj: leave}_{54} > \\ \text{prn: 55} \end{bmatrix}
\begin{bmatrix} \text{arg: street} \\ \text{FUNC: cross} \\ \text{id: 3} \\ \text{prn: 55} \end{bmatrix}
$$

Each proplet is an autonomous, self-contained item which specifies relevant relations to other proplets by means of attributes.[3] The proplets in 2.1 constitute an unordered set.

This coding depends neither on the graphical means of tree structures, as used in theoretical linguistics, nor on the linear ordering of symbols, as used in logic. Therefore proplets can be stored in accordance with the requirements of any type of database.

For structure-based storage and retrieval, each concept type (corresponding to an author's name) is listed in an alphabetically ordered column. Different proplets with the same concept are sorted in a row behind their concept type. Such a row, called a token line, corresponds intuitively to a shelf with books by the same author.

This is the data structure of a record-based classical network database. It defines a 1:n relation between two kinds of records, the owner records and the member records. The following example shows the sorting of proplets into a network database, whereby the types are the owner records and the proplets are the member records.

2.2   Sorting Proplets into a Network Database

TYPES   PROPLETS

$$
\begin{bmatrix} \text{concept: cross} \\ \text{role: functor} \end{bmatrix}
\quad \cdots \quad
\begin{bmatrix} \text{func: cross} \\ \text{ARG: Peter street} \\ \text{cnj: leave}_{54} > \\ \text{prn: 55} \end{bmatrix}
$$

$$
\begin{bmatrix} \text{concept: house} \\ \text{role: argument} \end{bmatrix}
\quad \cdots \quad
\begin{bmatrix} \text{arg: house} \\ \text{FUNC: leave} \\ \text{id: 2} \\ \text{prn: 54} \end{bmatrix}
$$

---

[3] The first specifies the proplet concept, characterizing it as a functor or an argument. The second (in upper case), called continuation predicate, specifies the intrapropositional relation(s). The attributes cnj, id, and prn stand for conjunction, identity and proposition number, respectively.

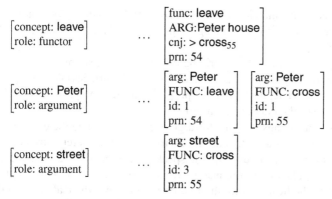

The structure of a network database supports the filing of proplets in their proper positions and their retrieval without the need of building and maintaining a catalog. Compared to structure-based storage and retrieval in a private library, a network database has the advantage of 'flexible shelves,' i.e., a token line may become arbitrarily long.

A network database for proplets is called a *word bank*. Compared to a standard network database, a word bank is special in the following three respects: First, intrapropositional functor-argument structures and extrapropositional relations between proplets are specified by means of continuation predicates (internal chaining). Second, these continuation predicates support an autonomous navigation through the propositional content, whereby the navigation is powered by a motor algorithm. Third, word banks are embedded in cognitive agents.

A navigation through the speaker's word bank and the appropriate filing of proplets in the hearer's word bank may be illustrated as follows:

2.3 Transfer of Information from the Speaker to the Hearer

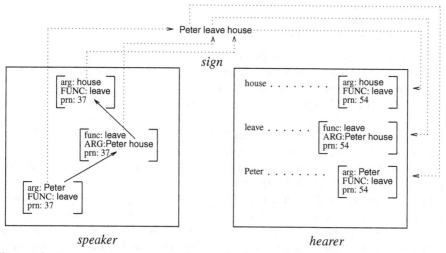

The speaker's navigation starts with the proplet *Peter*, which specifies the continuation proplet *leave*. From *leave*, the navigation continues to the proplet *house*. The navigation serves as the conceptualization and basic serialization of language production. The content of the database is coded into language simply by uttering the surfaces of the proplets traversed (cf. *sign*).

The hearer's interpretation consists in deriving a corresponding set of proplets. This procedure is based on (i) assigning lexical proplets to the sign's surfaces and (ii) copying proplet names into appropriate slots of other proplets during the syntactic-semantic analysis (reconstruction of the internal chaining).

In this way, the word meanings, the functor-argument structure, and the extrapropositional relations of the speaker's content are reconstructed by the hearer. Furthermore, the time-linear order of the sign induced by the speaker's navigation is eliminated, allowing storage of the proplets in accordance with the principles of the data structure in question. Apart from the hearer's prn, the interpretation is exactly analogous to the original structure in the speaker's database.

3   Alternative Realizations of Propositional Content

The representation of content in a word bank is of a universal, language-independent nature. All content is represented in the form of elementary propositions which may be concatenated in only two ways. One is the concatenation of functors via conjunctions. The other is the concatenation of arguments via identity. Using graphical means, this basic structure may be illustrated as follows:

3.1   'Railroad System' Provided by two Propositions

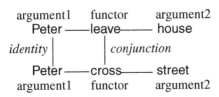

The two propositions in 3.1 correspond to those in 2.1 and 2.2. Language production, based on a navigation through such a universal representation of content, has to take care of the following properties of natural language:

First, there are the language-dependent properties of lexicalization, word order, inflection, and the realization of function words. For example, the underlying navigation *Peter leave house* (cf. 2.3) must be supplied with language-specific surfaces,[4] possibly modified to a different language-dependent word order, provided with inflectional forms (here leave+s), and supplied with function words (here the). The result for English would be Peter leaves the house.

Second, there is the distinction between forward and backward navigation through a given propositional content. For example, an intrapropositional forward navigation through the first proposition is realized as Peter leaves the house, while a corresponding backward navigation is realized as The house is left by Peter. Similarly,

---

[4] The proplet names in 3.1 as well as 2.1 – 2.3 are really language-independent.

a forward navigation through the two propositions illustrated in 2.1, 2.2, and 3.1 is realized as Peter leaves the house. Then Peter crosses the street., while a corresponding backward navigation is realized as Peter crosses the street. Before that Peter leaves the house.

Third, there is hypotactic (embedding) navigation – in addition to the paratactic (conjoining) navigation illustrated above – from one proposition to the next. A hypotactic navigation based on a conjunction results in an adverbial clause, as in Peter, after he leaves the house, crosses the street. or Peter, before crossing the street, leaves the house. A hypotactic navigation based on identity, on the other hand, results in a relative clause, as in Peter, who leaves the house, crosses the street.

Fourth, there is repeated reference – when a navigation returns to a referent previously traversed. This may be reflected in some languages by using an appropriate pronoun, as in Peter leaves the house. Then he crosses the street., and in others by omitting the repeated referent completely.

Fifth, there are abbreviating navigation types through propositional content. One is reduced coordination as in Peter leaves the house and crosses the street. Another is ellipsis and telegraphic style, as in Leaves! Crosses!

Six, there is metaphor, as when the speaker refers to Peter as the old fox.

In successful communication, these different ways of the speaker's navigating through a propositional content and realizing the navigation in a given natural language must all be reversed back to the original propositional content by the hearer. For example, proper understanding requires that the old fox is identified with Peter, that Leaves! is provided with the arguments intended by the speaker, that a hypotactic navigation must be disentangled, etc. The more completely the language sign is reversed by the hearer into the original language-independent content, the better the understanding.

The different possibilities of coding a propositional content are utilized by the speaker to aid the hearer's decoding. When the hearer changes into a speaker, he or she must in turn select one of the possible types of formulation to maximize the transfer of the content in question. This choice is made relative to the current rhetorical goal and the current utterance situation. Sometimes the proper interpretation has to be negotiated between the speaker and the hearer in a dialog.

4   Spatio-temporal Indexing of Direct Observation

The description of database semantics so far has concentrated on the transfer of propositional content without taking its spatio-temporal location into account. Turning now to the analysis of the latter, we begin with direct observations.

Direct observation is a cognitive agent's keeping track of recognitions and actions in the task environment. Direct observation is one of two methods of reading propositional content into a word bank, the other being based on media such as language.

In terms of evolution, the reading-in of propositional content by means of direct observation is prior to the reading-in by means of language. Furthermore, communicating direct observation is one of the basic uses of natural language.

The modeling of direct observation in an artificial cognitive agent requires that static propositional content be related to a continuously evolving present moment and location.[5] For example, *fridge contain cold can of beer* is a static fact stored in memory, but its relevance for the cognitive agent depends on its temporal (is it there now?) and spatial (can I get to it?) relation to the present.

The temporal indexing of direct observations requires no more than the system's keeping track of the sequencing of incoming observations.[6] This is expressed by the proposition numbers, which are used as a parameter for temporal order (in addition to expressing which proplets belong to the same proposition). Pauses between two subsequent observations may be expressed by propositions characterizing the pause.

Based on internal chaining, the system can navigate forward, e.g., 54, 55, 56, etc., and backward, e.g. 54, 53, 52, etc., through the propositions with these numbers. This forward and backward navigation is the basis of temporal inferencing. As an example consider the two propositions *one can of beer put in fridge* and *one can of beer consumed*. Depending on their order in the database, they render different conclusions as to whether or not there is currently one can of beer available.

The sequencing of propositional content is structured by cyclical external events stored in memory, such as the change of day and night, the phases of the moon, the changing seasons, the daily round of the milkman, etc. These cyclical events are used as temporal landmarks and serve as the basis for further inferences.

For example, if a content's proposition number, e.g. 2054, is positioned between two propositions with the content *It is night* and the proposition numbers, e.g. 2045 and 2075, respectively, and no other propositions of this content are intervening between 2045 and the present, then the direct observation expressed by proposition 2054 occurred yesterday. After one more day, there will be an additional night's proposition number, e.g. 2098, between the content in question and the present moment, leading to the conclusion that the observation now occurred the day before yesterday, etc.[7]

Cyclical events are also used for structuring the future, as when telling a child: *You have to sleep three more nights and then it will be your birthday*. Applying temporal inferencing learned from analyzing the past, the child can extrapolate into the future.

What has been said about temporal indexing and inference applies mutatis mutandis to spatial inference as well. The current location of the cognitive agent is indicated by the observation of appropriate landmarks. These observations appear in the sequence of propositions and serve as the basis of spatial inferences.

For example, if a sequence of propositions contains the observations *Going from kitchen to living room* and *Going from living room to kitchen*, then all direct observations between them are located in the living room. Thus spatial inference is analyzed

---

[5] In this sense, our approach corresponds to McTaggart's B-series. See P. Ludlow 1999.

[6] This is in contrast to postulating events as basic entities of one's semantic ontology. For example, in their attempt to avoid the problems of TPL, Kamp & Reyle 1993 introduce events as basic entities, but admit that events treated in this way are problematic as well: "Their identity criteria are ill-defined; it is difficult to know under which conditions there exists, for two or more distinct events, a single new 'sum' event which has those events for its parts; and it is not clear how events are related to other entities, such as, for instance, times." (op. cit. p. 666). The crucial role of ontology for semantic interpretation is shown in Hausser 2001.

[7] Another inference applies to cooccurrence. For example, if events A and B both have proposition numbers which are lower than last night and higher than the night before, then A and B must have occurred on the same day, namely yesterday.

just like temporal inference on the basis of landmarks which are accessed by navigating forward or backward through the sequence of propositions. The similarity between temporal and spatial reasoning is in concord with the fact 'that prepositions of time are on the whole identical to spatial expressions and that temporal prepositional phrases are attached to sentences in the same way as prepositional phrases of location.[8]

In modern society, temporal inference is supported by an external system of clocks and calendars. A realistic model of human cognition should not postulate an absolute internal clock, however, which would provide functor proplets with a time stamp, e.g. [Thursday, Oct. 19 2000, 9:45:24]. This is shown by situations in which the usual cyclical events are missing. For example, being locked up in an empty cell without a watch and without access to daylight causes a painful loss of temporal orientation in humans.

Similarly, spatial inference is supported by an external system of signs and road maps characterizing the relations and distances between places. However, just as temporal inferencing can do without an absolute internal clock, spatial inferencing can do without an absolute positioning system which constantly updates the cognitive agent's location on an internal map representing the external environment.

5 Reconstructing Spatio-temporal Location

In natural language communication, the spatio-temporal location of the speaker's propositional content must be reconstructed by the hearer. This reconstruction is based on three potentially distinct spatio-temporal locations. They are

1. the ST_{prop}, i.e. the spatio-temporal location of the propositional content,[9]
2. the STAR point, i.e. the parameters of the sign's origin in terms of Space, Time, Author, and intended Recipient,[10] and
3. the ST_{inter}, i.e. the spatio-temporal location of the interpretation.

The hearer's analogous reconstruction requires (i) inferring a content's ST_{prop} in the speaker's word bank and (ii) expressing this ST_{prop} in the hearer's word bank.

Inferring a content's ST_{prop} consists of two parts. First, the hearer must proceed from the ST_{inter} to the sign's STAR point. Second, the hearer must interpret the sign by decoding the sign's content and reconstructing its ST_{prop} relative to the STAR point.

---

[8] Jackendoff 1983, p. 189.

[9] The T-value of ST_{prop} corresponds to the 'point of the event' by Reichenbach 1947, p. 288.

[10] For characterizing the origin of a sign's token, spatio-temporal indexing is necessary, but not sufficient. In addition, the author and the intended recipient of the sign must be defined. The author may be distinct from the speaker, as when a letter from far away is being read aloud to the whole family. The intended recipient may be distinct from the hearer, as when a person is forced to overhear other people's conversation on a train.

The STAR point is an extension of the 'point of speech' by Reichenbach 1947, p. 288, which refers to the temporal parameter T only and is terminologically restricted to spoken language. The STAR point was first described in Hausser 1989, p. 274 f. See also Hausser 1999, p. 93 f.

In line with current practice in the field, we will continue to use 'speaker' in the sense of author and 'hearer' in the sense of intended recipient or unintended interpreter, unless clarity requires the correct terms. The current, medium-specific terminology may be understood charitably as emphasizing the primacy of the spoken over the written medium.

For example, a speaker observes on Monday *Peter leave house* (T-value of ST_{prop} = Monday) and expresses this fact on Tuesday (T-value of STAR point = Tuesday) by writing **Yesterday Peter left the house** on a piece of paper. A hearer reads the sign on Wednesday (T-value of ST_{inter} = Wednesday).

The communication is successful if the hearer's word bank stores the sign's content with an ST_{prop} relating to Monday. For this, the hearer must reconstruct the ST_{prop} of the sign's content (i) by inferring the sign's STAR point and (ii) by interpreting the sign's tense and temporal adverb relative to this STAR point.

While the speaker's ST_{prop} of a sign's content and the STAR point of a sign's origin are defined once and for all, there may be many possible ST_{inter} of a sign's interpretation. For example, the above note might be read again by another hearer on Thursday (T-value of ST_{inter} = Thursday). The two different interpretations of the sign are successful only if they use the same STAR point.

The relation between the hearer's ST_{inter} and the sign's STAR point is characterized by the distinction between fleeting and permanent signs.[11]

5.1 Fleeting and Permanent Signs

[+fs] is the use of fleeting signs, which requires the hearer to be present[12] during the sign's production. This presence causes the spatio-temporal location of the interpretation point to equal the STAR point,
formally written as   [+fs]: STAR point = ST_{inter}.

[-fs] is the use of permanent signs, which allows the hearer to be absent during the sign's production. This absence causes the spatio-temporal location of the interpretation point to differ from the STAR point,
formally written as   [−fs]: STAR point $\neq$ ST_{inter}.

When the hearer has no direct access to the situation in which a permanent sign originated ([−fs]), the STAR point must be explicitly coded into the sign's type in order to ensure successful communication.

For example, a standard letter specifies the values of S and T in the dateline, of A in the signature, and of R in the greeting. If different copies are made of such a letter, either by writing or by a copying machine, these copies are additional tokens of the letter's type. Each of these tokens may be interpreted correctly because the STAR point has been explicitly coded into the associated type.

The relation between the speaker's ST_{prop} and the sign's STAR point is characterized by the distinction between *immediate reference* and *mediated reference*,[13] formally expressed by the binary feature [± ir].

---

[11] Permanent signs are used in written language. Recordings of fleeting signs are permanent signs as well. Therefore, recordings of language usually indicate the STAR point explicitly, either by stating place, date, author, and intended recipient at the beginning of the recording, or by specifying this information on the cassette.

[12] An exception created by modern technology is telephone conversations. Their signs are fleeting, yet STAR point and interpretation point differ in their S values, necessitating that spatial information be interpreted accordingly.

[13] See also Hausser 1999, p. 73 f.

5.2   Immediate and Mediated Reference

[+ir] is the speaker's reference to objects in the current task environment, which causes the spatio-temporal location of the propositional content to equal the sign's STAR point,
formally written as   [+ir]: ST_{prop} = STAR point.

[−ir] is the speaker's reference to objects not in the current task environment,[14] which causes the spatio-temporal location of the propositional content to differ from the sign's STAR point,
formally written as   [−ir]: $ST_{prop} \neq$ STAR point.

The pivot of natural language communication is a sign's STAR point. It stands between the speaker's ST_{prop} and the hearer's ST_{inter}. The speaker characterizes the content's ST_{prop} relative to the sign's STAR point and the hearer reconstructs the content's ST_{prop} relative to it. The sign's type and the STAR point of the sign's token jointly determine the ST_{prop} of the sign's content for arbitrary ST_{inter}.

6   Expressing Spatio-temporal Location

The next question is how to express a content's ST_{prop} in the hearer's word bank once it has been inferred. More specifically, given the hearer's spatio-temporal system based on proplets stemming from direct observation, where should the proplets stemming from language content be stored?

Proplets stemming from direct observation have a two-fold temporal characterization. One is by means of internal chaining which relates propositional content to temporal landmarks (cf. Section 4). The other is by means of the proplets' order in their token lines, which reflects the temporal sequence of their arrival.

Consider a proposition P which is stored in the speaker's word bank as a direct observation, but in the hearer's word bank as a language-based content. Does analogous reconstruction require that the storage of P in the hearer's word bank reflect temporal order in exactly the same way as the storage of P in the speaker's word bank? In other words, should proplets stemming from language-based content be sorted into the hearer's token lines to express their temporal location in terms of the token-line-ordering? This would have several disadvantages.

First, it would be difficult to find the position in the token line which would correctly express the temporal location of the language proplet in question. Second, the content of a word bank would have to be constantly restructured to accommodate the temporal interpretation of incoming language proplets. Third, this method cannot be extended to express the spatial location of language-based content.

---

[14] For example, J.S. Bach (1685–1750) as as a database referent has no counterpart in the current real world. The same is true when a speaker talks about future events.

In mediated reference, the ST_{prop} is usually indicated by a suitable spatio-temporal landmark, e.g. a specific date and place. Such landmarks serve as the 'point of reference' in the sense of Reichenbach 1947, p. 288, providing a fixed point for the time structures coded into the language sign.

Therefore, language proplets are sorted in at the end of the token lines in their order of arrival, just like proplets stemming from direct observation. In other words, the ordering of language proplets in a token line characterizes the temporal location of their ST_{inter}, and not of their STAR point or their ST_{prop}. The spatio-temporal location of language-based content is expressed solely by means of internal chaining, which relates the propositional content to suitable landmarks.

For example, based on direct observation the hearer's word bank contains the proposition *It's Monday* with the proposition number, e.g., 23. On Wednesday, the hearer interprets the sign Yesterday Peter left the house, deriving the content *Peter leave house* with the proposition number, e.g., 54. Based on the ST_{inter} and the STAR point, the hearer determines that the ST_{prop} of proposition 54 has Monday as its T-value.

To express this ST_{prop} in the hearer's word bank, proposition 54 is related to the temporal landmark constituted by proposition 23. This is done by extending the leave-proplet of proposition 54 to the attribute cnj: [54 $=_{time}$ 23], meaning that propositions 54 and 23 occurred at the same time. The spatial location of a language-based propositional content is expressed in a similar manner by anchoring it to a spatial landmark.

7   Four Basic Types of Natural Language Communication

Because the [± ir] distinction characterizes the relation between the speaker's ST_{prop} and the sign's STAR point, and the [± fs] distinction characterizes the relation between the sign's STAR point and the hearer's ST_{inter}, there result four basic types of natural language communication. These may be characterized as follows:

7.1   Basic Relations between ST_{prop} and ST_{inter}

(i):   [+ir, +fs]: ST_{prop} = STAR point = ST_{inter}

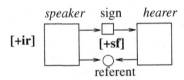

Speaker and hearer are together and talk about objects in their common task environment. This allows the use of fleeting signs and ensures that the ST values of the propositional content agree with the sign's STAR point and the hearer's ST_{inter}. Consequently, the language-based information may be stored by the hearer just like direct observation, without any need to establish spatio-temporal relations to stored landmarks.

(ii):   [+ir, –fs]: ST_{prop} = STAR point ≠ ST_{inter}

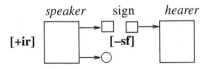

The ST values of the propositional content agree with the sign's STAR point, as in (i). However, the situations of utterance and interpretation are distinct, requiring the use of permanent signs. Therefore, the hearer must determine the STAR point and relate the propositional content to landmarks corresponding to the STAR point.

(iii):   [−ir, +fs]: $ST_{prop} \neq$ STAR point = ST_{inter}

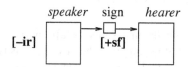

Speaker and hearer are present in the same situation, allowing the use of fleeting signs. However, because of mediated reference the ST values of the propositional content do not agree with the sign's STAR point. Therefore, the hearer must determine the spatio-temporal relation of the content in the speaker's database to the STAR point, and relate the content to suitable landmarks in his or her own database.

(iv):   [−ir, −fs]: $ST_{prop} \neq$ STAR point $\neq ST_{inter}$

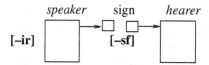

The situations of utterance and interpretation are distinct, requiring the use of permanent signs. Furthermore, the ST values of the propositional content do not agree with the sign's STAR point. Therefore, the hearer must determine both the STAR point and the relation of the content to the STAR point. This jointly determines the spatio-temporal location of the content for the hearer.

The four types constitute only the most basic distinctions. They are based solely on whether the ST values of propositional content, STAR point, and interpretation point are equal or not. There are many kinds of nonequality, however.

One set of additional distinctions arises from nonequality between the ST values of the propositional content and the STAR point ($ST_{prop} \neq$ STAR point). The nonequality may consist in reference to events in recent past, distant past, near future, distant future, to objects which are spatially near, spatially distant, above, below, in front of or behind the speaker or a certain landmark,[15] to structures outside of time and space, like mathematical laws, etc. All these distinctions are reflected in natural language and must be decoded by the hearer with reference to the STAR point.

Another set of additional distinctions arises from non-equality between the ST values of the interpretation and the STAR point (STAR point $\neq ST_{inter}$). This requires

---

[15] For a summary of ego-centered, object-centered, and environment-centered frames of spatial description see MacWhinney 1999, p. 221 f.

the hearer to determine the STAR point, which may be specified explicitly by reference to external landmarks, like date and place in a letter, or left implicit, necessitating inference. In the case of the latter, the question arises as to how far the ST values of interpretation and STAR point are apart, how precisely the STAR point has to be inferred for proper understanding, etc.

8 Spatio-temporal Questions and Answers

Corresponding to the distinction between fleeting signs ([+fs]) and permanent signs ([−fs]) there is the distinction between dialog and text. Thereby dialog is type i and iii, while text, including books, letters, notes, emails, etc., is of type ii and iv.

In text, the relation between speaker and hearer is STAR point $\neq$ ST_{inter}. Therefore, reactions of the hearer (reader) are either not fed back to the speaker (author) at all, or take a considerable amount of time and effort, as in a reply letter. Furthermore, common ground cannot be negotiated between the speaker and the hearer. Instead, it is up to the hearer to infer the intention of the speaker on his or her own.

In dialog, the relation between speaker and hearer is STAR point = ST_{inter}. Therefore, the intended recipient as well as third parties present in the utterance situation[16] can react immediately by taking over the role of speaker (turn taking), including the possibility of negotiating the common ground between the parties involved. This is particularly relevant for type iii communication, where $ST_{prop} \neq$ STAR point.

Even if the possibility of immediate reaction may seem to favor questions, answers, and commands in dialog, while the absence of this possibility may seem to favor statements in text, these different uses of language all occur in both dialog and text. For example, a dialog may contain statements – just as a text, e.g. a letter, may contain questions, answers, and commands. Apart from the distinction between STAR point $\neq$ ST_{inter} and STAR point = ST_{inter}, the production and interpretation of statements, questions, answers, and commands function the same in texts and dialogs.

As an example, consider a dialog in which a user asks the word bank 2.2 When did Peter cross the street? Because STAR point = ST_{inter}, problems of narrowing the relevant temporal interval do not arise. In order to respond, the system can go immediately through the following three steps:

First, the system's syntactic-semantic interpretation assigns to the sign a 'query proplet' as its semantic representation:

8.1 Query Proplet Representing When Did Peter Cross the Street?

$$
\begin{bmatrix}
\text{func: cross} \\
\text{ARG: Peter street} \\
\text{cnj: } ?_{time} \\
\text{prn: } ?
\end{bmatrix}
$$

---

[16] A special case are telephone conversations, where third parties may take part in the utterance situation, in the interpretation situation, or in both.

A query proplet contains variables (here characterized by '?') which turn it into a pattern. The pattern is used to find suitable variable values in the word bank.

Second, the system uses the query proplet pattern to search the associated token line, here that of cross. Beginning at the end, the pattern is tried on one proplet after the next until it finds the first (and here only) one matching the arguments Peter and street. The matching proplet binds the variable of the prn to 55.

Third, starting from proposition 55, the system navigates either forward, e.g. to 56, 57, 58, etc., or backward, e.g. 54, 53, 52, etc. Given that the proposition numbers of proplets stemming from direct observation reflect temporal order, any one of them would serve as a suitable basis for an answer.

In our example, the preceding proposition is *Peter leave house* with the prn 54. Because 54 < 55, the system answers After Peter left the house.

This is the kind of vague answer one might expect from a human. As a reaction, the user could ask When was it exactly? or What time was it? A word bank with more propositional content than 2.2 might try a more precise response by looking for a temporal landmark like It was before I looked at my watch and saw that it was 10am.

Searching through propositions in order to adequately answer adverbial wh-questions requires that the system can recognize temporal landmarks in the case of temporal questions, spatial landmarks in the case of spatial questions, causal landmarks in the case of causal questions, etc. However, given proper lexical analysis, this is not a difficult problem, especially when inferences are supplied in addition.

Technically, the navigation through the token line and subsequently through the propositional chain is handled like all navigation in database semantics, namely by suitable LA-grammars. The detailed formal treatment of the navigations realizing the search initiated by when- and where-questions is similar to that of yes/no- and who-questions presented in Hausser 1999, p. 491f.

9   Conclusion

In our approach, the spatio-temporal location of propositional content is specified without the usual reference to a precise, objective, external Cartesian coordinate system. Instead, spatio-temporal location is characterized cognitively by the order of direct observations entering the database of a cognitive agent. The sequence of propositions is structured by observations of cyclical events, serving as temporal landmarks, and by observations of the environment, serving as spatial landmarks.

This analysis works for cognitive agents with and without language. Modeling the former, however, poses the additional task of communicating the spatio-temporal location of propositional content (in addition to the propositional content itself) from the speaker to the hearer. For this, a propositional content's spatio-temporal location is (i) characterized in the database of the speaker, (ii) coded into language signs, (iii) reconstructed by hearer, and (iv) and represented in the hearer's database.

Spatio-temporal inferences are handled on the basis of navigating forward or backward through the sequence of concatenated propositions. The purpose is finding a suitable spatio-temporal landmark. The result of these inferences is shown to be similar to that of humans.

In artificial agents, spatio-temporal localization can be made more powerful by using technical devices such as on-board clocks, geo-stationary satellite positioning systems, indexing and retrieval tools of databases, etc. Instead of replacing the 'soft' system described above, however, technology should only complement it in a way that maintains the basis for a natural understanding between artificial and human cognitive agents.

References

Hausser, R. (1989) *Computation of Language, An Essay on Syntax, Semantics and Pragmatics in Natural Man-Machine Communication*, Springer-Verlag, Symbolic Computation: Artificial Intelligence, Berlin, New York.

Hausser, R. (1999) *Foundations of Computational Linguistics*, Springer-Verlag, Berlin, New York.

Hausser, R. (2001) 'The Four Basic Ontologies of Semantic Interpretation,' in H. Kangassalu et al. (eds.) *Information Modeling and Knowledge Bases XII*, IOS Press Ohmsha, Amsterdam.

Jackendoff, R. (1983) *Semantics and Cognition*, The MIT Press, Cambridge, Mass.

Kamp, H. & U. Reyle (1993) *From Discourse to Logic*, Part 2, Kluwer Academic Publishers, Dordrecht, Holland.

Ludlow, P. (1999) *Semantics, Tense, and Time: An Essay in the Metaphysics of Natural Language*, The MIT Press, Cambridge, Mass.

MacWhinney, B. (1999) "The Emergence of Language from Embodiment," in B. MacWhinney (ed.) 1999.

MacWhinney, B. (ed.) (1999) *The Emergence of Language*, Lawrence Erlbaum Associates, Mahwah, New Jersey.

Reichenbach, H. (1947) *Elements of Symbolic Logic*, The Free Press, New York.

Russellian and Strawsonian Definite Descriptions in Situation Semantics

Roussanka Loukanova

[1] Illinois Wesleyan University,
Department of Mathematics and Computer Science,
P.O. Box 2900, Bloomington, IL 61702-2900, USA
rloukano@titan.iwu.edu
[2] Department of Math. Logic and Applications,
Faculty of Mathematics and Computer Science,
Sofia University, 1126 Sofia, Bulgaria

Abstract. In this paper I give two alternatives for representing the definite descriptions – Russellian and Strawsonian approaches realized in situation semantics. I show how the Russellian treatment of the definites can be made "referential", while preserving its original generalized quantifier mode. The Strawsonian representation is substantially referential with presuppositional effect of the restriction imposed over the parametric representative of the potential referent of the definite description. The situation theoretical *restricted parameters, speakers' reference functions* in particular contexts of utterances, and the notion of a *resource situation* for evaluating NPs are the key formal tools used. This work does not reject any of the two accounts in favor of the other, but shows how both approaches give better results in a theory which models partiality of the linguistic information, discourse dependency and in particular, speakers' references. In both approaches, the prototypical definite NPs get appropriate "parametric" interpretations.

Introduction

The natural language expressions, when taken out of any context of use, express semantical information which is partial, parametric and often ambiguous. Even when the expressions are considered unambiguous, their linguistic meanings are normally parameterized in sense that they have constituents that are abstractions from any particular denotations in one or other context of use. For example, an utterance of the sentence MARIA IS READING THE BOOK can be used for describing a situation in which an individual named Maria is reading a particular and definite book. The speaker uses the NP THE BOOK to refer to a particular object by using its having the property of being a book. Out of any context, this sentence is still meaningful but expresses parameterized semantical information, i.e. the described situation, the subject and the object of reading are indeterminate. They can be represented as parameters restricted to satisfy the minimal linguistic information expressed by the sentence components: the

A. Gelbukh (Ed.): CICLing 2001, LNCS 2004, pp. 69–79, 2001.

agent of reading is a parameter for an individual with a restriction to be named Maria, while the parameter for the object of reading is restricted to be the unique book which is to be referentially defined by the potential speaker. In a particular context of use, the parameters are anchored to particular objects satisfying the corresponding restrictions.

By a definite NP the speaker refers to an object by using some of its properties expressed by the noun description. The speaker relies on the listeners' knowledge of the object and/or its properties so that they are able to single out the referent on the base of its having those property. Shared knowledge does not require that the speaker and the listener are literally able to identify the referent, only that its identification is a cognitive potentiality. This can be modeled by using the notion of *resource situation*, which is a situation to which the speaker refers and in which, the referent of the definite description is the unique object having the property expressed by the noun of the definite NP, i.e. the property of being a book in the above example. What is shared by the speaker and the listener is the knowledge of the resource situation uniquely identifying the referent. The resource situation might have been introduced by the previous discourse or taken from the common life experience. Generally, it can be different from the situation described by the whole sentence. For example, by an utterance of the sentence THE MATH TEACHER FROM MY HIGH SCHOOL IS SWIMMING. the speaker is describing a situation in which a particular individual is swimming. The swimmer is referred to by using a resource situation, which is the speaker's high school situation different from the swimming situation and in which the referent is the unique individual having the property of being a math teacher. There is no requirement for the listener to know or be able to recognize the swimmer. Neither there is such a requirement for the speaker, which is more explicit in using a sentence like, THE MATH TEACHER FROM MY SISTER'S HIGH SCHOOL IS SWIMMING. Therefore, for a particular interpretation of an utterance with respect to the listener and/or the speaker, the referent of a definite description might be a particular indeterminate object, i.e. a semantic parameter imposed to represent an unique object satisfying the definite description in the resource situation.

Situation theory, see Barwise and Perry (1983), Barwise (1987), Devlin (1991), is a formal system for modeling the partiality and intensionality of the information and meaning relations. One of the ways it represents the partiality of the information about the objects designated by language units is by introducing primitive and complex restricted parameters – the restrictions over a parameter represent information currently available about the "partially known" object represented by the parameter. I.e. the parameters are semantical designators of indeterminate objects and can be used to represent the parametric character of linguistic meanings in abstraction of any context of use. The restrictions over parameters impose conditions on anchoring the parameters to appropriate particular interpretations in specific discourses. In this way, the parametric situational objects provide tools for twofold semantical representation: linguistic meanings in an abstraction of usage, and interpretations in one or other context. The interpretations themselves also can be parametric and have restricted parameters as discussed above. Aczel-Lunnon lambda abstraction operator, see Aczel-Lunnon (1991), gives the computational tool for getting the abstract types needed to represent the abstract linguistic meanings and the restrictions over parameters. The corresponding application operator is the formal tool for anchoring the argument roles of the abstract types to particular objects provided by the circumstances. For a formal overview of higher order logic and functional types, see Leivant (1994).

Situation semantics can accommodate two approaches toward definite NPs: Russellian definite descriptions, and Strawsonian referential definites. The Russellian definite NPs are represented as generalized quantifiers constrained to express unique existence. In the Strawsonian account, a restricted parameter represents the potential referent denoted by the definite NP. The parameter is restricted to be anchored to the unique object satisfying the description denoted by the noun component of the NP. In this way the restriction has presuppositional effect on the particular interpretations in particular contexts of usage, not over the abstract linguistic meaning.

1 Speakers' References and Generalized Quantifiers in Situation Semantics

The NPs formed by quantitative determiners such as A, SOME, NO, EVERY, FEW, MANY, ... and numerals ONE, TWO, ..., can be treated as generalized quantifiers by representing the determiners as two place relations between types of individuals, see Barwise and Cooper (1981), Barwise (1986), Cooper (1993), Loukanova (1991, 2000), Cooper and Ginzburg (1996). Meaning constraints associated with the particular quantities can be defined by using the notion of an extension of a type – for this notion, see Barwise and Perry (1983), and Loukanova (2000). The definite NPs formed with the determiner THE can also be represented as generalized quantifiers expressing existence of a unique object. Russell (1905) was the first to suggest this approach to THE in a non-typed system. Later, Henkin (1950) and Mostowski (1957) represented quantificational NPs in higher order logic. Montague was the first to use this suggestion for a computational semantics of NL by unifying all NPs, including the proper names and the pronouns, as generalized quantifiers, which is widely in use in the treatment of the determiners in contemporary type logic semantics.

In a higher-order type system, Russellian representation of the determiner THE is the term $\lambda P \lambda Q \exists x (\forall y (P(y) \leftrightarrow x = y) \wedge Q(x))$. The abstraction over P is what has to be contributed by the noun of the definite NP, while Q is for the VP predicate. For example, the NP THE DOG is translated to the term $\lambda Q \exists x (\forall y (dog(y) \leftrightarrow x = y) \wedge Q(x))$, and the sentence THE DOG IS SWIMMING gets translated to the formula

$$\exists x (\forall y (dog(y) \leftrightarrow x = y) \wedge swim(x)).$$

By this, the translation treats the NP THE DOG as expressing unique existence. One of the problems associated with such treatment of the definite article THE is that it is diverging from the intuitions about how the definite descriptions are generally used – for referring to particular individuals rather then for claiming unique existence. This approach is well suited in model-theoretic approaches for which the models are total and every sentence has to be truth evaluated. For example, the sentence THE DOG IS SWIMMING is evaluated as being false in a model where there is no unique dog, either because there is no dog or there is more than one dogs. In this way, the treatment of the definites is loosing the referential effect while promoting unique existence. Indeed, referring to a particular individual presupposes existence of that individual, and it has to be unique, but rather than in the total world, it has to be unique in the "small" situation that is relevant for the act of reference – the resource situation for evaluating the definite NP. For example, in the situation described by the above sentence there might be several dogs swimming, while the speaker refers to exactly one of them, the one the discourse has been about. The gap between the constraint for unique existence and referentiality is a consequence of the totality of the models which does not give enough finely grained notion of reference and distinction between extensionality and intensionality of the semantical objects.

1.1   Utterance Components and Speakers's References

The concept of language reference encompasses at least three components: a language expression, an object (real or abstract) referred to (called the referent of the expression) and a discourse/utterance situation. The third component contributes various subcomponents most important of which are the speaker, the speaker's act of reference, the space-time location of the discourse and the listener. The speaker's act of reference can be modeled as a function the arguments of which are language units, while the values are the objects referred to. The reference function itself is dependent on the discourse. In situation theory the utterance components can be modeled in the following way by using *restricted parameters* and type abstraction:

1. The fact of an utterance of an expression φ in a situation u, called *utterance situation*, can be modeled by the proposition:

   $$pu(u, l, x, z, \varphi) = (u \models \ll tells{-}to, x, z, \varphi, l; 1 \gg).$$

   The utterance situation u, the space-time location l, the speaker x, the listener z and the expression uttered φ are parameters, but in particular utterance of a particular expression all these are particular objects.

2. The type of an utterance situation:

   $$ru(l, x, z, \varphi) = [u/pu(u, l, x, z, \varphi)].$$

3. The type of an individual to be the speaker in an utterance situation u:

$$rsp(u, l, z, \varphi) = [x/pu(u, l, x, z, \varphi)].$$

4. The type of an individual to be the listener in an utterance situation u:

$$rlst(u, l, x, \varphi) = [z/pu(u, l, x, z, \varphi)].$$

5. The type of an object to be an utterance location:

$$rdl(u, x, z, \varphi) = [l/pu(u, l, x, z, \varphi)].$$

6. The type of an object to be referred to by the expression φ:

$$r_\varphi(u, l, x, z, \varphi, s_{res}) = [y/q(u, l, x, z, y, \varphi)], \text{ where}$$

$$q(u, l, x, z, y, \varphi) =$$
$$(u^{ru(l,x,z,\varphi)} \models \ll refers\text{--}to\text{--}by, x^{rsp(u,l,z,\varphi)}, y, \varphi, l^{rdl(u,x,z,\varphi)}; 1 \gg).$$

The last proposition expresses that the speaker x^{rsp} refers to y by using the expression φ. Thus, the act of referring is part of the utterance situation u.

7. Generally, the type of an object to be referred to by the expression φ is an abstraction over all discourse components:

$$tr_\varphi(u, l, x, z, \varphi, s_{res}) = \lambda u, x, z, l[y/q(u, l, x, z, y, \varphi)].$$

The linguistic meaning of a proper name, like MARIA, has to capture the way the names are used normally, for reference to particular individuals. That can be represented with the complex conjunctive restriction r over a parameter y^r, where

$r = r_1 \wedge r_2$, with types r_1 and r_2 as follows:
$r_1 = [y/(u \models \ll named\text{--}Mary, y; 1 \gg)],$
$r_2 = [y/(u \models \ll refers\text{--}to\text{--}by, x^{rsp}, y, \text{MARIA}, l^{rdl}; 1 \gg)].$

Another way the linguistic meaning, i.e. the intension of a name to be represented is by a discourse abstraction over that restricted parameter, i.e. by: $\lambda u, l^{rdl} y^r$, where u is a parameter for an utterance situation, l is a parameter for its space-time location, and r is as defined above. Thus, the utterance situation defines a reference function called *speaker's references (connections)* and denoted by c. It is defined over expressions and its values can be either particular individuals and properties or parameters for such. The speaker's reference function extends to assignments of objects to the semantic parameters in the linguistic meanings of the expressions.

If we want to represent the fact that an individual can be referred by a name, no matter whether she is actually named by it, we can use the restriction r_1' instead of r_1.

$$r_1' = [y/(u \models \ll believes, x^{rsp},$$
$$(s^{rsit} \models \ll named-Mary, y; 1 \gg),$$
$$l^{rdl(u,x,z,\alpha)}; 1 \gg)]$$

1.2 Quantifiers in Situation Semantics

In what follows, I shall briefly mention some of the notions needed for the Russellian treatment of the definites in situation semantics, for more on these, see Loukanova (2000).

Let $\sigma(x,l)$ be a parametric infon with x and l among its parameters. This infon can be the linguistic information contributed by a sentence. In such a case, the linguistic meaning of that sentence, in abstraction of any particular utterance, is the type $T = \lambda s, l[x/(s \models \sigma(x,l))]$, where s is a parameter for the situation described by the utterance of the sentence and l is a parameter for a space-time location. In other words, the type T represents the intension of the sentence. The components of the infon $\sigma(x,l)$ are contributed by the linguistic meanings of the sentence subexpressions. For example, the linguistic meanings of the verb IS READING and the common noun BOOK are represented, respectively, by the following types:

$$t_{read} = \lambda s, l\lambda x[y/(s \models \ll read, y, x, l^{[l/lol^{rdl}]}; 1 \gg)].$$

$$t_{book} = \lambda s, l[x/(s \models \ll book, x, l; 1 \gg)],$$

A particular utterance of an expression defines the speaker's reference function c, which is the assignment function over the parameters of the types that are meanings of the subexpressions. Generally, the *extension* of a type T with respect to the assignment c is denoted by $\mathcal{E}(T,c)$ and is defined to be the set of all objects of type T in the described situation:

(1.1) $\mathcal{E}(T,c) = \{c'(x)/$ the proposition $(c(s) \models c'(\sigma(x)))$ is true, where c' is an assignment different from c only possibly for $x\}$.

For example, the extension of the type of objects being a book in a situation $c(s)$ is the set of all books in that situation $c(s)$, where $c(s)$ and $c(l)$ are, respectively, a situation and a location referred to by the speaker:

$$\mathcal{E}(t_{book}, c) = \{b/c(s_2) \models \ll book, b, c(l_2); 1 \gg\}.$$

The extension of the type of objects being read by the individual referred to by the name MARIA (see previous section) in the same context of use is:

$$\mathcal{E}(t_{read}, c) = \{a/c(s_1) \models \ll read, c(y^r), a, c(l_1^{[l/lol^{rdl}]}); 1 \gg\}.$$

English determiners SOME and A, can be taken to have the same meaning as AT LEAST ONE and as such, when combined with common nouns in NPs, can be treated as generalized quantifiers:

(1.2) $\lambda s \lambda T_1 \, [T_2/(s \models \ll exist, T_1, T_2; 1 \gg)]$.

After putting together[1] the semantical representations of the subparts of the sentence (1.3) given bellow, the propositional content of its linguistic meaning is expressed by the type (1.4):

(1.3) MARIA IS READING A BOOK.

(1.4) $[s, s_1, s_2, l_1, l_2/(s \models \ll exist, [x/(s_2 \models \ll book, x, l_2; 1 \gg)],$
$$[x/(s_1 \models \ll read, y^r, x, l_1^{[l/lol^{rdl}]}; 1 \gg)]; 1 \gg)]$$

In a given context, the proposition expressed by an affirmative utterance of (1.3) is true iff:

(i) $c(s) \models \ll exist, [x/(c(s_2) \models \ll book, x, c(l_2); 1 \gg)]$
$$[x/(c(s_1) \models \ll read, c(y^r), x, c(l_1^{[l/lol^{rdl}]}); 1 \gg)]; 1 \gg,$$

and if the situation $c(s)$ is informative (i.e., represents the actuality), then

(ii) $\mathcal{E}(t_{book}, c) \bigcap \mathcal{E}(t_{read}, c) \neq \emptyset$.

While the indefinite quantitative determiners are used to separate a quantity of indefinite, i.e. unspecified objects in a domain of quantification denoted by the noun of the corresponding NP, the major semantic characteristics of the definites and in particular of the determiner THE, is that they are used for referring to objects. The generic usages of the definite descriptions differ from the referential ones only by being abstractions over any particular referents.

2   Russellian Account of Definites

In a Russellian style, the definite article THE, can be treated as a primitive two-argument relation between types. Thus, its linguistic meaning can be represented by the following abstraction:

(2.2) $[\![THE]\!] = \lambda s \lambda T_1 \, [T_2/(s \models \ll the, T_1, T_2; 1 \gg)]$,

where T_1 and T_2 are parameters for types of the same king, for example, types of individuals, and *the* is a primitive higher order relation between types. The NP THE BOOK and the sentence (2.2) bellow have linguistic meanings represented, respectively, by the type (2.3) and the quantificational abstract proposition (2.4):

---

[1] For a compositional grammar, see Cooper and Ginzburg (1996) and Loukanova (1991)

(2.2) MARIA IS READING THE BOOK.

(2.3) $[\![\text{THE BOOK}]\!] = \lambda s\,[T_2/(s \models\!\!\ll the, [x/(s_2 \models\!\!\ll book, x, l_2; 1 \gg)], T_2; 1 \gg)],$

(2.4) $[s, s_1, s_2, l_1, l_2/(s \models\!\!\ll the, [x/(s_2 \models\!\!\ll book, x, l_2; 1 \gg)],$
$$[x/(s_1 \models\!\!\ll read, y^r, x, l_1^{[l/lol^{rdl}]}; 1 \gg)]; 1 \gg)].$$

In a given utterance u of the sentence (2.2) the speaker's references define an assignment function c over the referential argument roles of the abstractions and the free parameters in (2.4). The interpretation of (2.3) is obtained from (2.2) by filling up the argument roles and substitution of the parameters with their values with respect to c:

(2.5) $(c(s) \models\!\!\ll the, [x/(c(s_2) \models\!\!\ll book, x, c(l_2); 1 \gg)]$
$$[x/(c(s_1) \models\!\!\ll read, c(y^r), x, c(l_1^{[l/lol^{rdl}]}); 1 \gg)]; 1 \gg).$$

In a Russellian treatment of definites as generalized quantifiers, the proposition (2.5) carries the information that there is a unique book read by Maria. This is formalized by using the notion of extension of a type and an appropriate meaning constraint associated with the definite article THE. The meaning constraint of the relation *the* contributes the following information for a particular utterance of (2.2). The proposition (2.5) is true in a given context, i.e. for given speaker's references, iff:

(2.6)

(i) $c(s) \models\!\!\ll the, [x/(c(s_2) \models\!\!\ll book, x, c(l_2); 1 \gg)]$
$$[x/(c(s_1) \models\!\!\ll read, c(y^r), x, c(l_1^{[l/lol^{rdl}]}); 1 \gg)]; 1 \gg,$$

and if the situation $c(s)$ is informative (i.e., represents the actuality), then

(ii) $\mathcal{E}(t_{book}, c) \bigcap \mathcal{E}(t_{read}, c) \neq \emptyset$, and

(iii) $\mathcal{E}(t_{book}, c) = \{c(z_1)\}$, where $c(z_1)$ is the speaker's referent for the NP THE BOOK, i.e.:

(2.7) $u \models\!\!\ll refers\text{–}to\text{–}by, z^{speaker(u, l^{rdl})}, c(z_1), \text{THE BOOK}, l^{rdl}; 1 \gg.$

As before, the constituent $c(y^r)$ is the individual to which the speaker z refers to by the name MARIA.

There are two important advantages of the Russellian treatment of definites in situation semantics in comparison to its realization in classical higher order systems (like Montague grammars):

- The requirement 2.6 (ii) expresses the existence, i.e. there exists a book which is read by Maria.

- The requirement 2.6 (iii) encompasses the uniqueness condition, but is also consistent with the referential use of the definite articles i.e. 2.6 (iii) replaces the traditional uniqueness condition for the Russellian definites: $|\mathcal{E}(t_{book}, c)| = 1$.

- 2.6 (iii) is also consistent with prototypical usages of some definite NP, as for example in an utterance of the sentence, THE BOOK IS A SOURCE OF KNOWLEDGE. There is no particular referent of the NP THE BOOK. The value of the speaker's assignment function $c(z_1)$ is not one or other particular book, but just a parameter $c(z_1) = z_1$ – situation theory permits parametric assignments. The situational assignments $c(s_1)$ and $c(s_2)$ are also parameters in such utterances.

3   Strawsonian Account of Definites in Situation Semantics

In a Strawsonian style, the linguistic meaning of the definite article THE can be given by the following abstraction over a restricted parameter:

(3.1) $[\![THE]\!] = \lambda s, l\lambda T\, x^{[x/T(x)\wedge(s\models\ll unique, x, T; 1\gg)]}$, where:

(i) The abstraction is over the parameters s and l, respectively for a resource situation and a location for evaluating the NP formed by using the definite article.

(ii) The primitive higher order relation *unique* between an individual and a type satisfies the next meaning constraint: the proposition
$(c(s) \models\ll unique, c(x), T; 1 \gg)$
is true in a given context supplying a reference function c iff $|\mathcal{E}(T, c)| = \{c(x)\}$. Hence, there must be exactly one object of type T in the resource situation $c(s_2)$ – the speaker's referent $c(x)$.

The linguistic meaning of the NP THE BOOK is:

(3.2) $[\![THE\ BOOK]\!] = \lambda s, l([\![THE]\!](s, l)([\![BOOK]\!](s, l))) = \lambda s, l\, x^q$, where q is the following type:

(3.3) $q = [x/(s \models \ll book, x, l_2; 1 \gg \wedge \\ \ll unique, x, [x/(s_2 \models \ll book, x, l_2; 1 \gg)]; 1 \gg)]$.

Then the linguistic meaning of the sentence[2] (2.2) is represented by the parametric proposition:

(3.5) $\lambda s_1, s_2, l_1, l_2(s_1 \models\ll read, y^r, x^q, l_1^{[l/lol^{rdl}]}; 1 \gg)$,

---

[2] The grammar rules given in Loukanova (1991, 1999) will fit for the Strawsonian treatment of the definite descriptions too.

where the restrictions r and q are as above. The proposition (3.5) is true in a given context with respect to speaker's references c, iff the situation $c(s_1)$ described by the utterance of (2.2) is of the type (3.5), i.e. iff:

(3.6) $c(s_1) \models \ll read, c(y^r), c(x^q), c(l_1^{[l/lol^{rdl}]}); 1 \gg.$

The restrictions r and q must be satisfied by the individuals referred to by the speaker, which means that the next propositions must be true in addition to (3.6):

(3.7) $(c(s_2) \models \ll book, c(x), c(l_2); 1 \gg),$
(3.8) $(c(s_2) \models \ll unique, x, [x/(s_2 \models \ll book, x, l_2; 1 \gg)]; 1 \gg),$ and
(3.9) $(u \models \ll refers{-}to{-}by, z^{speaker(u, l^{rdl})}, c(y), \text{MARIA}, l^{rdl}; 1 \gg)$

The restrictions r and q over the parameters have a presuppositional effect for particular parameter assignments and interpretations of the proposition (3.5) in one or other context of use of the sentence (2.2). Out of any context, the restricted parameters x^q and y^r, and the proposition (3.5) are well defined situational objects, i.e. (3.5) is a legitimate situational type representing a parametric proposition independently of any truth values of the propositional contents of the type restrictions r and q. Truth values can be assigned only in particular context of use and with respect to particular reference functions.

A particular interpretation, i.e. a claim that a situation $c(s_1)$ is of the type (3.5) is either true or false with respect to a particular reference function c. In case that some of the propositions (3.7), (3.8) and (3.9) are not true for the given context and the assignment function c, the assignments $c(y^r)$ and/or $c(x^q)$ are not well-defined and hence, the situational "infon"

$$\ll read, c(y^r), c(x^q), c(l_1^{[l/lol^{rdl}]}); 1 \gg$$

is not well defined object too. Thus (3.6) does not make sense. In such case though, the situation $c(s_1)$ is not of type (3.5) with respect to c, and the proposition that $c(s_1)$ is of type (3.5) with respect to c is false.

In case that all required presuppositions, including (3.7), (3.8) and (3.9) are true, the proposition that the situation $c(s_1)$ is of type (3.5) may be true or false depending on whether (3.6) is the case. In both cases, the truth of the proposition (3.8) implies the existence of the unique referent $c(x)$ which, by 3.1 (ii), is the unique book in the resource situation $c(s^2)$. In this way the traditional problem with the Strawsonian iota ι operator is not available in such situation semantical approach.

References

[1991]Aczel, P. and R. Lunnon. 1991. *Universes and Parameters.* In Seligman J. and D. Westerstahl, eds. *Situation Theory and Its Applications. Vol. 1.* CSLI Lecture Notes Number 37. Stanford: CSLI Publications.

[1981]Barwise, J. and R. Cooper. 1981. *Generalized Quantifiers and Natural Language.* Linguistics and Philosophy 4 (1981):159-219.

[1983]Barwise, J. and J. Perry. 1983. *Situations and Attitudes.* Cambridge, MA:MIT Press. Republished in 1999 by The David Hume Series of Philosophy and Cognitive Science Reissues.

[1986]Barwise, J. 1986. *Noun Phrases, Generalized Quantifiers and Anaphora.* Generalized Quantifiers, ed. P. Gärdenfors. Studies in Language and Philosophy. Dordrecht: Reidel Publishing Company.

[1987]Barwise, J. 1987. *The situation in Logic.* CSLI Lecture Notes Number 17. Stanford: CSLI Publications.

[1993]Cooper, R. 1993. *Generalized Quantifiers and Resource Situations.* in Aczel, P., D. Israel, Y. Katagiri, and St. Peters, eds. *Situation Theory and Its Applications. Volume 3.* CSLI Lecture Notes Number 37. Stanford: CSLI Publications.

[1996]Cooper, R. and J. Ginzburg. 1996. *A Compositional Situation Semantics for Attitude Reports.* in Seligman, J., and D. Westerstaahl, eds. *Logic, Language and Computation. Volume 1.* CSLI Lecture Notes Number 58. Stanford: CSLI Publications.

[1991]Devlin, K. 1991. *Logic and Information.* Cambridge University Press, Cambridge, UK.

[1950]Henkin, L. 1950. *Completeness in the theory of types.* Journal of Symboli Logic. 15:81-91.

[1994]Leivant, D. 1994. *Higher Order Logic.* In Dov M. Gabbay (ed.), Handbook of Logic in Artificial Intelligence. Oxford University Press. 230-321.

[1991]Loukanova, R. 1991. *Situation Semantical Analyses of the Natural Language.* Ph.D. dissertation. Moscow State University and Saratov State University.

[1999]Loukanova, R. 1999. *Semantical Storage: a sample situational grammar.* Indiana University. draft

[1999]Loukanova, R. and R. Cooper. 1999. *Some Situation Theoretical Notions.* Annuaire de l'Universite de Sofia "St. Kliment Ohridski", Faculte de mathematiques et informatique, tome 87(1993), livre 1 - mathematiques, 297–306.

[2000]Loukanova, R. 2000. *Nominal Scope in Situation Semantics.* CICLing-2000 Proceedings: Computational linguistics and Intelligent Text Processing by IPN Publishing House. Mexico.

[1957]Mostowski, A. 1957. *On a generalization of quantifiers.* Fundamenta Mathematicae 44:12-36.

[1905]Russell, B. 1905. *On denoting.* Mind 14:479-493.

Treatment of Personal Pronouns
Based on Their Parameterization

Igor A. Bolshakov

Center for Computing Research
National Polytechnic Institute
Mexico City, Mexico
igor@pollux.cic.ipn.mx

Abstract. Personal pronouns of several European languages are re-demarcated and parametrized by means of their morphological, syntactic, and semantic features. A universal semantic representation of personal pronouns as vectors of few semantic components is proposed. The main semantic components are implied by syntactic features: grammatical person, number, and gender. The results of parameterization are applied to morpho-syntactic and semantic agreement, translation of pronouns from one language to another, and disambiguation of several verbal constructions.

Key words: personal pronouns, inflectional categories, syntactic features, semantic components, agreement, translation, disambiguation.

1 Introduction

Personal pronouns (P-pronouns) play important role in natural language. Their *deictic* function is to determine persons participating in a given speech act, while their *anaphoric* function is to replace nouns occurred in a same text and thus to create references to the corresponding entities.

For purposes of automatic processing of texts containing pronouns, it is necessary to formally describe (parametrize) those features of P-pronouns, which are relevant on different levels of linguistic representation:

- In order to recognize specific forms of pronominal lexemes in texts, it is necessary to know inflectional properties of P-pronouns, which, in European languages, are more complicated than for nouns.
- In order to recognize morpho-syntactic agreement of pronouns with syntactically related verbs in finite forms, it is necessary to know the so-called syntactic features implying the agreement.
- In order to resolve pronoun-antecedent relations (anaphoric links), it is necessary to determine those semantic features of P-pronouns and corresponding nouns, which admit such relations.
- If P-pronouns have semantic features irrelevant for deictic and anaphoric functions, they should be fully inventoried.

A. Gelbukh (Ed.): CICLing 2001, LNCS 2004, pp. 80-92, 2001.
© Springer-Verlag Berlin Heidelberg 2001

- In order to utilize all information about a given pronominal lexeme, which can occur two or more times in the same text in different forms, it is sometimes necessary to re-demarcate pronominal lexemes by means of their re-demarcation and subdivision, as compared with usual grammars.
- For purposes of automatic translation from one language (or dialect) to another, it is quite topical to study what semantic features of P-pronouns are interlingually universal and what are not.

The comparative study of P-pronouns is the task of general linguistics. The classical research touched upon main properties of P-pronouns in several European and non-European languages, even if without a high formality. Another deficiency of classical study is its orientation mainly to morphology and syntax.

Among popular books on computational linguistics [1], [5], [14], [16], [17], only [14] contains a short study of anaphoric links. It is performed for English – the main object of applied research so far. Meantime, semantics is encoded in English P-pronouns in a straightforward manner, different from most other languages, and morphology of P-pronouns is rather poor in English.

This paper studies features P-pronouns of languages belonging to Standard Average European languages, i.e. subfamily of Indo-European family including Romance, Germanic, Slavic, and Baltic languages. However, examples are given only for two languages: Serbo-Croatian (Slavic language) and Spanish (Romance language).

Our study is based on description of P-pronouns given in classical monographs [2], [3], [8], reference books [15] and [4], encyclopedias [7], few modern books [6], [10], [11], and papers [12], [13], [18], [19]. We do not introduce new facts about P-pronouns, but rearrange known facts in a systematic manner, with the stress to semantics. Our objective is to meet requirements of modern text processing, as well as to reveal features that were not yet properly realized and can be used in text processing later.

As to our method of elaboration, several explanations and reservations are needed.

- The Meaning ⇔ Text Theory (MTT) by I. Mel'čuk [9], [10], [11], is taken as the main source of terminology. However, we are no bound with all subtleties of the MTT and our results might evidently have theory-independent interpretation.
- Common principles of division of sets of pronominal word-forms to lexemes for all languages under consideration are accepted. Namely, we suppose that all P-pronouns of a given language have the same sets of inflectional categories, syntactic features, and semantic components. At the same time, any P-pronoun should differ from the other at least in one of these parameters.
- All languages are considered only in their written form.

2   Inflectional Categories, Co-occurrence Parameter, and Syntactic Features

Inflectional categories characterize a 'system of inner coordinates' of a lexeme as a set of word-forms. Each part of speech (POS) has its own set of inflectional categories; usually they are the same for all lexemes of a given POS. Values of the categories are called grammemes.

Two inflectional categories are sufficient for P-pronouns:

- **Grammatical case (*GrCase*)** has the set of at least two values. One of them gives a standard dictionary form used for subjects of sentences. This case is referred to as *nominative*. All other cases are called *oblique*. Case is not semantically induced. It serves surface syntactic purposes only and is ignored on the deeper levels.
- **Tonicity.** The P-pronouns of several languages have short unstressed (= clitic) forms as opposed to tonic (= full) forms. We consider clitics autonomous word-forms, even if they are pasted to verbs in writing (Spanish, Italian), cf. [10], [13], [19]. According to [12], the **Tonicity** category is introduced for P-Pronouns with the values {*clitic, tonic*}.

Co-occurrence variation parameter characterizes influence of a nearest phonetic context of a P-pronoun in several languages. Since P-pronouns are influenced by a juxtaposed word-form belonging to a limited list, we refer the variation parameter as **Neighbor**. Specific pronominal word-form is selected, depending on the neighbor's presence. For example, the Spanish *le* and *les* change to *se* when form *lo, la, los* or *las* occurs to the right. For another example, the French *je, me, te* change to *j', m', t'*, if the neighbor verb starts with a vowel. **Neighbor** values are {+, −}, for availability and absence of the influential neighbor correspondingly. If **Neighbor** is relevant for a given language, but not for a given P-pronoun and a given combination of other grammemes, the value *n/a* 'not applicable' is used.

Syntactic features subcategorize each lexeme of a specific POS with regard to its combinability with other words. Syntactic features of P-pronouns are:

- **Grammatical person (*GrPer*)** with the value set {1, 2, 3};
- **Grammatical number (*GrNum*)** with the value set {*sing*(ular), *plur*(al)};
- **Gender** existing in many European languages has the two {*masc*(uline), *fem*(inine)} or the three values {*masc, fem, neut*(er)}. The value *irrel*(evant) is used when gender relevant for this language, but is irrelevant for a given P-pronoun.

3   Semantic Components

The main semantic components of P-pronouns are connected with syntactic features, though not always straightforwardly. The other components are determined immediately by a given lexeme.

Person & number combination (*SemP&N*). For reasons explained below, it is reasonable to subdivide all combinations of number and person to six distinct options, introducing the component **SemP&N** to cover them all. Following are the values of this component, with corresponding comment.

- *1_sing*: 'I' = 'the person who is speaking now in a given speech act'.
- *2_sing*: "your$_{sing}$' (Old Eng. 'thou') = 'the addressee in a given speech act'.

- *3_sing*: 'any person neither "I" nor "thou", or any thing'. In European languages, P-pronouns covering entirely *3_sing* are unknown: two or three pronouns are used for this purpose, e.g., *he*, *she*, and *it* in English. The standard demarcation between them is performed according to other semantic components.
- *1_plur*: 'we' = 'a group of person the speaker points out, to which he or she belongs'. *We* is not plural of *I*, and this is a reason in favor of person & number combining.
- *2_plur*: 'your$_{plur}$' = 'a group of person including the addressee of a given speech act.' Again, 'you$_{plur}$' is not plural of 'you$_{sing}$'.
- *3_plur*: 'they' = 'a group of persons that does not include any participant of a given speech act, or a set of things'. The *3_plur* value seems to be plural of *3_sing*. However, *3_sing* is always represented by several P-pronouns, and it is not certain to what P-pronoun of the available pair or triple a given *3_plur* pronoun corresponds. Moreover, the *3_plur* pronoun can be not unique, depending on other semantic features. Thus, we consider all P-pronouns of *3_sing* and of *3_plur* separately, as different lexemes.

According to [18], 'I' and 'thou' are primitive semantic elements (semes). It seems not certain, but we cannot propose a consistent semantic decomposition of the **SemP&N** values.

Person vs. thing opposition (SemP/T). This component is introduced to characterize the dichotomy {*Person, Thing*}, where *Person* reflects a human or an entity likened to humans in language, and *Thing* is any other entity. For our purposes, the value *Person* should be subdivided according to the semantic gender, i.e. sex: *Person = Male/Female*, where / denotes disjunction. In Spanish language, the value *Thing* is additionally dichotomized as *Thing = Physobj/Abstr*, where *Physobj* is a physical object, and *Abstr* is an abstraction. As a result, **SemP/T** can be considered four-valued {*Male, Female, Physobj, Abstr*}. These values can be used individually or constitute formulas like *Person* or *Female/Thing* – for pronouns denoting single entities, or like *allFs* = 'all are females' – for groups of entities (see below).

Esteem. This component is relevant for some languages and has the value set {*Famil*(iar), *Formal*} to reflect a grade of esteem to a person referenced by a given pronoun. It is usually relevant for *2_sing* or *2_plur*. When a language considers this component, but it is not relevant for a given P-pronoun, the value *Ir_estm = Famil / Formal* is used. Similarly to **SemP/T**, values of **Esteem** can be used individually or can constitute logical formulas (see below).

Focus is a binary semantic component of words or word combinations, which discerns elements of the so-called communicative structure of an utterance. If **Tonicity** is relevant for a given language, it should be used somehow to determine **Focus**. However, general linguistics did not suggest so far how Focus is to be turned into account in text processing. Hence we will have nothing to say more about **Focus**.

4   Formulas for Features of Plural

Any value of the **SemP/T** component can be given in an explicit logical form. It is especially instructive for plural. Introducing the variable p_i for ith participant of the group pointed with a P-pronoun, the following equivalences are obtained:

$$allFs \equiv \text{'all are females'} \equiv \forall_{n>1} \bigwedge_{i=1}^{n} (p_i = Female) \tag{1}$$

$$not\ allFs \equiv \text{'not all are females'} \equiv \forall_{n>1} \sim \bigwedge_{i=1}^{n} (p_i = Female) \equiv \forall_{n>1} \bigvee_{i=1}^{n} (p_i = \tag{2}$$

Male)

The leftmost parts of these equations are denotations used in the tables below, the second parts are their verbal interpretations, then go equivalent logical expressions. The conjunction of (1) and (2) covers all options possible for animate participants of the pointed groups:

$$allPers \equiv \text{'any combination of persons'} \equiv \forall_{n>1} \bigwedge_{i=1}^{n} (p_i = Person) \equiv \text{'all are} \tag{3}$$

$$\text{females or not females'} \equiv \forall_{n>1} \bigwedge_{i=1}^{n} (p_i = Female) \vee \forall_{n>1} \sim \bigwedge_{i=1}^{n} (p_i = Female)$$

The options (1) – (3) proved to be sufficient for all languages under consideration. Thus, the correlation between grammatical and semantic gender is not straightforward in plural, depending on language. A fairly complicated semantic formula can correspond to each value of grammatical gender.

Esteem component sometimes regulates the attitude to a human group in the manner similar to that of the sex distinguishing. For example, the Castilian pronoun *nosotros* 'you$_{plur,familiar}$' can be used only when all participant of the addressed group are considered familiar:

$$allFas \equiv \text{'all are familiar'} \equiv \forall_{n>1} \bigwedge_{i=1}^{n} (p_i = Famil). \tag{4}$$

For the complementary situation

$$not\ allFas \equiv \text{'not all are familiar'} \equiv \forall_{n>1} \sim \bigwedge_{i=1}^{n} (p_i = Famil) \equiv \forall_{n>1} \bigvee_{i=1}^{n} (p_i = Formal) \tag{5}$$

the pronoun *ustedes* 'you$_{plur,formal}$' is used in this dialect. Irrelevance of **Esteem** for a given P-pronoun in plural can be represented as

$$Ir\_estm \equiv allFas \vee not\ allFas. \tag{6}$$

The options (4) – (6) proved to be sufficient for all languages under consideration.

Thus, the tendency of natural language is as follows. If a two-valued category is to be expressed for a group of entities, one value is considered more 'standard' and is applied when at least one member of the group, taken separately, corresponds to the standard value. Otherwise, the supplementary value is applied to the group.

5   Serbo-Croatian Pronouns

Serbo-Croatian pronouns seem the most diversified among Slavic languages. They have the following properties:

- There are three P-pronouns for *3_sing* (ON, ONA$_1$, ONO) and three for *3_plur* (ONI, ONE, ONA$_2$) differing in **Gender** (*masc, fem, neut* correspondingly). Based on the semantic differences, the six distinct lexemes are introduced. Note that ONI 'they$_{masc}$' can cover any number of ONA$_1$ 'she/it' and at least one ON 'he/it', i.e. it is not plural of ON.
- There are six values of **GrCase**. **Tonicity** is relevant for four case values: *nom*(inative), *gen*(itive), *dat*(ive), and *acc*(usative).
- **Neighbor** is relevant only for accusative clitic of ONA$_1$. The influential neighbor stays immediately to the right and is the clitic of the verb BITI 'to be' or of the same pronoun ONA$_1$ with a different coreferential noun.
- **Esteem** is relevant for *2_sing*. To reflect this component, strictly homonymic pronouns VI$_1$ 'you$_{plur}$' and VI$_2$ 'you$_{sing,formal}$' are introduced, while 'you$_{sing,familiar}$' is expressed by TI.

Morphology of Serbo-Croatian P-pronouns is given below, with oblique forms only for ONA$_1$:

WFrm	Lexeme	GrCs	Toni	Nei	WFrm	Lexeme	GrCs	Toni	Nei
ja	JA 'I'	nom	tonic	n/a	nju	ONA$_1$	acc	tonic	n/a
ti	TI 'you$_{sg,famil}$'	nom	tonic	n/a	ju	ONA$_1$	acc	clitic	+
vi	VI$_2$ 'you$_{sg,form}$'	nom	tonic	n/a	je	ONA$_1$	acc	clitic	−
on	ON 'he or it'	nom	tonic	n/a	ono	ONO 'it'	nom	tonic	n/a
ona	ONA$_1$ 'she/it'	nom	tonic	n/a	mi	MI 'we'	nom	tonic	n/a
nje	ONA$_1$	gen	tonic	n/a	vi	VI$_1$ 'you$_{plur}$'	nom	tonic	n/a
je	ONA$_1$	gen	clitic	n/a	oni	ONI 'they$_{masc}$'	nom	tonic	n/a
njoj	ONA$_1$	dat	tonic	n/a	one	ONE 'they$_{fem}$'	nom	tonic	n/a
joj	ONA$_1$	dat	clitic	n/a	ona	ONA$_2$ 'they$_{neut}$'	nom	tonic	n/a

The syntactic features are person, number, and gender:

Lexeme	GrPers	GrNum	Gender
JA	1	sing	irrel
TI	2	sing	irrel
VI$_2$	2	plur	irrel
ON	3	sing	masc
ONA$_1$	3	sing	fem
ONO	3	sing	neut

Lexeme	GrPers	GrNum	Gender
MI	1	plur	irrel
VI$_1$	2	plur	irrel
ONI	3	plur	masc
ONE	3	plur	fem
ONA$_2$	3	plur	neut

The following table gives the semantic decomposition:

Lex.	SemP&N	SemP/T	Esteem	Lex.	SemP&N	SemP/T	Esteem
JA	1_sing	Person	Ir_estm	MI	1_plur	allPers	Ir_estm
TI	2_sing	Person	Famil	VI$_1$	2_plur	allPers	Ir_estm
VI$_2$	2_sing	Person	Formal	ONI	3_plur	(not allFs) /allThings	Ir_estm
ON	3_sing	Male/Thing	Ir_estm				
ONA$_1$	3_sing	Female/Thing	Ir_estm	ONE	3_plur	allFs/allThings	Ir_estm
ONO	3_sing	Thing	Ir_estm	ONA$_2$	3_plur	allThings	Ir_estm

6   Spanish Pronouns

Spanish P-pronouns are rather typical for Romance languages. They are taken in two dialects, Castilian and Mexican, whose distinctions are instructive for our purposes. The following properties of Spanish P-pronouns should be mentioned:

- **Gender** is relevant for all pronouns in plural, as well as for the polite form *usted* 'you$_{sing,masc,formal}$'. Based on the semantic differences, the lexemes NOSOTROS *vs.* NOSOTRAS ('we' of different genders), VOSOTROS *vs.* VOSOTRAS ('you$_{plur}$' of different genders, exist in Castilian dialect only), USTEDES$_1$ *vs.* USTEDES$_2$ (both 'you$_{plur,formal}$'), and USTED$_1$ *vs.* USTED$_2$. (both 'you$_{sing,formal}$') are introduced.

- **Tonicity** is relevant, but is strictly connected with **GrCase**: *nom, acc, dat* or *prep*(ositive). If **GrCase** is equal to *nom* or *prep*, then **Tonicity** is *tonic* else *clitic*. That is why **Tonicity** does not appear in the corresponding table.

- The form *ello* 'it' does not conform to the standard values of **Gender** {*masc, fem*} and is considered *neuter*. Based on semantics, we introduce the lexemes ÉL, ELLA, and ELLO for *3_sing*.

- **Neighbor** is relevant for dative forms of ÉL, ELLA, ELLO, ELLOS, and ELLAS. They alter to *se* when the neighbor at the right is the clitic accusative form of the same pronouns. The two neighboring clitics should have different coreferential nouns.

- **Esteem** is relevant for Spanish, and polite forms of the 2nd person are grammatically the 3rd person in both numbers.

The paradigms of Spanish pronouns are given in the following table:

Word form	Lexeme	GrCase	Neig	Word form	Lexeme	GrCase	Neig
	Both dialects			se	ELLA	dat	+
yo	YO 'I'	nom	n/a	ello	ELLO 'it'	nom/ prep	n/a
me	YO	dat/acc	n/a				
mí	YO	prep	n/a	lo	ELLO	acc	n/a
tú	TÚ	nom	n/a	le	ELLO	dat	–
	'you$_{sing,famil}$'			se	ELLO	dat	+
te	TÚ	dat/acc	n/a	usted	USTED$_1$	nom/ prep	n/a
ti	TÚ	prep	n/a		'you$_{sing,masc,form}$'		
él	ÉL 'he/it'	nom/ prep	n/a	lo	USTED$_1$	acc	n/a
				le	USTED$_1$	dat	–
lo[1]	ÉL	acc	n/a	se	USTED$_1$	dat	+
le	ÉL	dat	–	usted	USTED$_2$	nom/ prep	n/a
se	ÉL	dat	+		'you$_{s-}$		
ella	ELLA 'she/it'	nom/ prep	n/a		ing,fem,formal'		
				la	USTED$_2$	acc	n/a
la	ELLA	acc	n/a	le	USTED$_2$	dat	–
le	ELLA	dat	–	se	USTED$_2$	dat	+
				nosotros	NOSOTROS 'we$_{masc}$'	nom/ prep	n/a

---

[1] We ignore the variation *lo* vs. *le* in Castilian.

Word form	Lexeme	GrCase	Neig
nos	NOSOTROS	dat/acc	n/a
nosotras	NOSOTRAS 'we$_{fem}$'	nom/ prep	n/a
nos	NOSOTRAS	dat/acc	n/a
ellos	ELLOS 'they$_{masc}$'	nom/ prep	n/a
los	ELLOS	acc	n/a
les	ELLOS	dat	–
se	ELLOS	dat	+
ellas	ELLAS 'they$_{fem}$'	nom/ prep	n/a
las	ELLAS	acc	n/a
les	ELLAS	dat	–
se	ELLAS	dat	+
Castilian			
vosotros	VOSOTROS 'you$_{plur,masc,famil}$'	nom/ prep	n/a

Word form	Lexeme	GrCase	Neig
vosotras	VOSOTRAS 'you$_{plur,fem,famil}$'	nom/ prep	n/a
ustedes	USTEDES$_1$ 'you$_{plur,masc,form}$'	nom/ prep	n/a
ustedes	USTEDES$_2$ 'you$_{plur,fem,form}$'	nom/ prep	n/a
Mexican			
ustedes	USTEDES$_1$ 'you$_{plur,masc}$'	nom/ prep	n/a
los	USTEDES$_1$	acc	n/a
les	USTEDES$_1$	dat	–
se	USTEDES$_1$	dat	+
ustedes	USTEDES$_2$ 'you$_{plur,fem}$'	nom/ prep	n/a
las	USTEDES$_2$	acc	n/a
les	USTEDES$_2$	dat	–
se	USTEDES$_2$	dat	+

The syntactics of Spanish pronouns are:

Lexeme	GrPer	GrNum	Gender
Both dialects			
YO	1	sing	irrel
TÚ	2	sing	irrel
ÉL	3	sing	masc
ELLA	3	sing	fem
ELLO	3	sing	neut
USTED$_1$	3	sing	masc
USTED$_2$	3	sing	fem
NOSOTROS	1	plur	masc
NOSOTRAS	1	plur	fem

Lexeme	GrPer	GrNum	Gender
ELLOS	3	plur	masc
ELLAS	3	plur	fem
Castilian			
VOSOTROS	2	plur	masc
VOSOTRAS	2	plur	fem
USTEDES$_1$	3	plur	masc
USTEDES$_2$	3	plur	fem
Mexican			
USTEDES$_1$	3	plur	masc
USTEDES$_2$	3	plur	fem

The following table gives semantic decomposition:

Lexeme	Sem-P&N	Sem-P/T	Esteem
Both dialects			
YO	1_sing	Person	Ir_estm
TÚ	2_sing	Person	Famil
ÉL	3_sing	Male/ Physobj	Ir_estm
ELLA	3_sing	Female /Thing	Ir_estm
ELLO	3_sing	Abstr	Ir_estm
USTED$_1$	2_sing	Male	Formal
USTED$_2$	2_sing	Female	Formal
NOSOTROS	1_plur	not allFs	Ir_estm
NOSOTRAS	1_plur	allFs	Ir_estm
ELLOS	3_plur	notallFs/ allThings	Ir_estm

Lexeme	Sem-P&N	Sem-P/T	Esteem
ELLAS	3_plur	allFs/ allThings	Ir_estm
Castilian			
VOSOTROS	2_plur	not allFs	allFas
VOSOTRAS	2_plur	allFs	allFas
USTEDES$_1$	2_plur	not allFs	not allFas
USTEDES$_2$	2_plur	allFs	not allFas
Mexican			
USTEDES$_1$	2_plur	not allFs	Ir_estm
USTEDES$_2$	2_plur	allFs	Ir_estm

7   Morpho-syntactic and Semantic Agreement

The morpho-syntactic agreement between P-pronouns and predicative verbs in finite forms is well known. It is performed based on syntactic features *GrPers*, *GrNum*, and *Gender* (the latter is taken into account, e.g., in Russian past tense).

The semantic agreement is not so evident. For languages without gender (e.g., English), nouns and coreferenced P-pronouns agree in their semantic components. This is relevant for humans. For example, the proper name *Mary* can be substituted with *she* since *Mary* has semantic representation NAME(*Female*, *Mary*), whereas SHE = [*3_sing, Female*].

For languages with gender the semantic agreement persists for humans. In most cases, gender for human-designating nouns corresponds to sex, hence both types of agreement coincide. However, examples from various languages permit to reveal strictly semantic agreement.

- Several German nouns of neuter reflecting female persons, e.g., *Mädchen* 'girl' or *Weib* 'woman', are substitutes by the pronoun of feminine gender, with the *Female* semantic component.
- Several Russian nouns of neuter are applicable both to males and females, e.g., *sozdanie* 'creature' or *sokrovišče* 'treasure.' Adjectives agree with them in neuter, whereas the corresponding pronouns usually reflect the sex of the person.
- In Spanish, sentences like *Su Alteza está disgustado* 'His Highness is displeased' show that the noun of feminine gender can imply the nominal part of the predicate in masculine and can be replaced by the masculine P-pronoun *él*, which agrees with *Su Alteza* semantically.

8   Translation

When a pronoun is translated mentally from one language (dialect) to another, all abovementioned semantic components are intuitively taken into account. This process can be automated. For this purpose, the component vector should be taken for the given P-pronoun in the source language, and vectors "similar" to the latter in the target language is to be searched.

Three options can then occur.

Equivalence. The two vectors are equal in their dimensions and values in each position, or the dimensions are different, but can be equalized by means of the default components. Then unique and usually correct translation is reached. Following are examples (the subindex $_{Spanish}$ denotes any dialect of Spanish):

$\text{TÚ}_{Spanish}$ = [*2_sing, Person, Famil*] = TU_{French}

$\text{USTED}_{2\,Castilian}$ = [*2_plur, Female, Formal*] = $\text{USTED}_{2\,Mexican}$

$\text{I}_{English}$ = [*1_sing, Person*] = [*1_sing, Person, Ir_estm*] = $\text{YO}_{Spanish}$

Implication. After replenishing of default coordinates (if necessary), the semantic component vector in the source language in some cases proves to be the logical antecedent of the vector in the target language. In other words, these two vectors can be connected by operation of logical implication from the source to the target. That is the scope of the source vector is narrower than of the target one. Then unique translation is possible. Following are examples (the sign $\rightarrow$ denotes logical implication):

$\text{VOSOTROS}_{\text{Castilian}} = [2\_plur, \ not \ allFs, \ allFas] \rightarrow [2\_plur, \ not \ allFs, \ Ir\_eteem]$
$= \text{USTEDES}_{1 \ \text{Mexican}}$

$\text{NOSOTRAS}_{\text{Spanish}} = [1\_plur, \ allFs, \ Ir\_estm] \rightarrow [1\_plur, \ allPers] = \text{WE}_{\text{English}}$

$\text{TÚ}_{\text{Spanish}} = [1\_sing, \ Person, \ Famil] \rightarrow [1\_sing, \ Person] = \text{YOU}_{1 \ \text{English}}$

Ambiguity. The scopes of the source and target vectors sometimes intersect in different manner. In particular, the target could be inverse implication of the source. Then the unique translation is unreachable, and it is only possible to determine all vectors with intersecting scope. Following are examples (the sign $\leftarrow$ denotes inverse implication):

$\text{USTEDES}_{2 \ \text{Mexican}} = [2\_plur, \ allFs, \ any(Fas/Fos)]$
$\leftarrow [2\_plur, \ allFs, \ allFas] = \text{VOSOTRAS}_{\text{Castilian}}$
$\leftarrow [2\_plur, \ allFs, \ not \ allFas] = \text{USTEDES}_{2 \ \text{Castilian}}$

$\text{WE}_{\text{English}} = [1\_plur, \ allPers]$
$\leftarrow [1\_plur, \ not \ allFs, \ Ir\_estm] = \text{NOSOTROS}_{\text{Spanish}}$
$\leftarrow [1\_plur, \ allFs, \ Ir\_estm] = \text{NOSOTRAS}_{\text{Spanish}}$

In some cases, morphological homonymy or an omission in the target language can neutralize the ambiguity. E.g., English *We like...* can be translated to Spanish *Queremos...*, and English *us* = WE(*oblique*), to the Spanish *nos,* independently of whether NOSOTROS or NOSOTRAS is implied in the target text. Nevertheless, in general case the total parsing is necessary.

The comparison of component vectors is just the same as unification used in computational linguistics mainly for parsing [1]. The search of possible translations of a P-pronoun corresponds to the following idea:

Having at input a component vector of a P-pronoun in the source language, select among component vectors belonging to the target language those unifiable with the input vector.

The target set of vectors is never empty.

9   Disambiguation and Finer Specification of Spanish Pronouns

Many Spanish sentences use the same pronoun twice, but in different case and tonicity. In the sentence *Me gustan los vecinos a mí* 'I like the neighbors', uniting two pronominal forms effectively does not contribute anything to the deep syntactic structure. Indeed, the clitic *me* is YO(*acc/dat*), and the tonic *mí* is YO(*prep*). Considering possible valencies of the verb *gustar* 'to like', which requires a clitic in dative and/or a phrase with the preposition *a* for its indirect object, a parser resolves the morphological ambiguity "*acc/dat*" to dative and then eliminated the redundant clitic.

In the sentence *A mí, me vea Juan* 'Juan sees me', the verb *ver* requires a direct object, so the parser resolves the ambiguous forms *me* = YO(*acc/dat*) to accusative and then eliminates redundant clitic in favor of the tonic forms *mí*.

In the sentences

$$\text{Le gustan los vecinos a él 'He likes the neighbors'} \tag{7}$$
$$\text{Le gustan los vecinos a ella 'She likes the neighbors'} \tag{8}$$

the clitic *le* is ÉL(*dat*) or ELLA(*dat*) or USTED$_1$(*dat*) or USTED$_2$(*dat*). Accounting for valency properties of the verb *gustar*, the parser selects ÉL in (7) and ELLA in (8), again without a remnant in the deep-level representation.

Meantime, in the sentences

$$\text{La veo a usted lit. 'Her I see you}_{\text{sing,fem,formal}}\text{'} \tag{9}$$
$$\text{Lo veo a usted lit. 'Him I see you}_{\text{sing,masc,formal}}\text{'} \tag{10}$$

the ambiguity USTED$_1$(*prep*) *vs.* USTED$_2$(*prep*), after the unification, is resolved as USTED$_2$ in (9) and USTED$_1$ in (10). The reason is that *la* has only USTED$_2$(*acc*) among its morphological analyses, and *lo* has only USTED$_1$(*acc*). It can be noticed that just the subdivision to the lexemes USTED$_1$ *vs.* USTED$_2$ has permitted to express the refined knowledge directly through separate lexemes.

The semantic decomposition proves to be useful also for Spanish sentences like *Estoy cansada* '[I] am tired$_{\text{fem,sing}}$' o *Soy golpeada por Juan* '[I] am bitten$_{\text{fem,sing}}$ by Juan', where P-pronoun is omitted, according to the norms of Spanish. In these examples, the analysis first requires the restoration of the corresponding P-pronoun, and then the elimination of the grammemes of number and gender expresses for the adjective or participle. Indeed, these grammemes play purely syntactic role. During the restoration of the pronoun on the basis of the grammeme combination (*1, sing*) belonging to the finite verb form, the component vector [*1_sing, Person*] = YO is determined. Further refinement is possible based on the grammeme *fem* of the adjective or participle. This gives the vector [*1_sing, Female*] finer than YO. It has no strict lexical correspondence, but serves semantic purposes more adequately.

For the proposed set of Spanish pronominal lexemes, the sentence can be processed equally well by introduction of a separate predicate reflecting the sex of YO or by replacement of the lexeme by the finer component vector immediately at the deep syntactic level. As a next alternative, the subdivision of lexemes could be continued by introducing two homonymous lexemes, YO$_1$ = [*1_sing, Male*] and YO$_2$ = [*1_sing, Female*].

Analysis of the Russian sentence *Ja ustala* 'I [am] tired$_{\text{fem,sing}}$' necessitates restoring the zero copula and the further accounting for the grammeme *fem* of the verb in past tense. This leads to the same finer vector [*1_sing, Female*].

10   Conclusions

Personal pronouns of European languages constitute a homogeneous lexical group and can be described in the same morphological, syntactic, and semantic terms. On morphological level, inflectional categories of case and tonicity are sufficient. On the syntactic level, person, number, and gender are relevant.

Semantics of P-pronouns is never empty. The main semantic components reflecting person & number combination and person vs. thing opposition are related with syntactic features. In several languages there exists an additional component called esteem. Just it implies discordance between syntactic and semantic features in some languages. E.g., the Spanish polite forms of the 2nd person of both numbers are grammatically the 3rd person.

English P-pronouns were not given among examples, since features relevant for it turned to be minimal. Hence, English cannot be taken as a pattern for the parameterization of P-pronouns. Separate study of Russian P-pronouns shows that Serbo-Croatian P-pronouns are quite typical for Slavic languages. Analogously, Spanish P-pronouns are typical for Romance languages: Portuguese, French, and Italian.

Reckoning on semantic differences, we have proposed to subdivide P-pronominal lexemes of several languages more finely than it is commonly accepted. For example, all Spanish P-pronouns of plural were split to masculine and feminine counterparts. This facilitates syntactic disambiguation with determination of sex. Sometimes even the deeper subdivision seems to be necessary, since the syntactic analysis leads to a combination of semantic components which cannot be expressed by P-pronouns in their accepted definition. For example, no language distinguishes the *1_sing* pronoun 'I' in masculine *vs.* feminine variants, whereas Spanish or Russian texts sometimes evidently distinguish such variants.

At morpho-syntactic levels, P-pronouns agree with finite-form verbs and participle in grammatical person, number, and gender. However, the agreement with substituted nouns is semantic.

All revealed features of P-pronouns could be easily arranged to the structures operated in the standardization project EAGLES [20] primarily oriented to the same family of languages.

Acknowledgement. I am very grateful to Jasmina Milićević and Igor Mel'čuk for their bitter criticism and last-ditch attempts to save me from serious ideological errors. The remaining errors are totally on me.

References

1. Allen, J. *Natural Language Understanding.* Amsterdam/Bonn/Sidney: Benjamin/Cummings Publ., 1995.
2. Benvenist, Emil. *Problèmes de linguistique général.* Paris: Gallimard, 1966.
3. Bloomfield, Leonard. *Language.* NY/Chicago/ San Francisco/Toronto: Holt, Rinehart, and Winston, 1964.
4. *Diccionario de dudas de Manuel Seco.* Madrid: Espasa Calpe Edit. 1998.
5. Grishman, R. *Computational linguistics. An introduction.* Cambridge University Press, 1986.
6. Klavans, J. *On Clitics and Clitization: The Interaction of Morphology, Phonology, and Syntax.* NY/London: Garden Publ., 1987.
7. *Linguistic encyclopedic dictionary* (V.N. Yarsteva ed.) Moscow: Soviet Encyclopedia Publ. (in Russian), 1990.
8. Lyons, John. *Introduction to Theoretical Linguistics.* Cambridge University Press, 1972.
9. Mel'čuk, Igor. *Dependency Syntax: Theory and Practice.* New York: SUNY Press, 1988.

10. Mel'čuk, Igor. *Cours de morphologie général.* Vol. 1. Montréal/Paris: Les Presses de l'Université de Montreal, 1993.
11. Mel'čuk, Igor. *Cours de morphologie général.* Vol. 2. Montréal/Paris: Les Presses de l'Université de Montreal, 1994.
12. Milićević, Jasmina. *Pronominal and verbal clitics in Serbian: A morphological description.* Wiener Slavistischer Almanach, V. 43, pp. 231-256., 1999
13. Monachesi, Paola. *A lexical analysis of Italian clitics.* Proc. VEXTAL'99 Conference, San Servolio, V.U.I., Italy, 22-24 November, 1999, pp. 57-65.
14. Pollard, C., I. A. Sag. *Head-driven Phrase Structure grammar.* Chicago/London: CSLI Publ., University of Chicago Press, 1994
15. Real Academia Española. *Esbozo de una Nueva Gramática de la Lengua Española.* Madrid, 1973.
16. Sag, I. A., T. Wasow. *Syntactic theory: Formal Introduction.* Chicago/London: CSLI Publ., 1997
17. Sell, P. *Lectures on Contemporary Syntactic Theories.* Chicago/London: CSLI Publ., 1985.
18. Wierzbicka, Anna. *The Semantics of Modality.* Folia linguistica, V. 21, No. 1, 1987, pp. 25-43.
19. Zwicky, A. and G. Pullum. *Clitization vs. inflection: English n't.* Language V.59, No. 3, 1983, pp. 502-513.
20. EAGLES. Synopsis and comparison of morpho-syntactic phenomena encoded en lexicons and corpora. A common proposal and application to European languages. Technical Report EAG-LWG-Morphsyn, ILC-CNR, Pisa, Italy. Available at: http://www/icl.pi.cnr.it/EAGLES96/morphsyn/morphsyn.html

Modeling Textual Context
in Linguistic Pattern Matching

Slim Ben Hazez

CAMS/LaLIC, UMR du CNRS,
96 Boulevard Raspail, 75006 Paris, France
Slim.Ben-Hazez@paris4.sorbonne.fr

Abstract. We present a model to describe linguistic patterns regarding their textual contexts. The description of contexts takes into account all the information about text structure and contents. The model is an algebra that manipulates arbitrary regions of text. We show how to use the model to describe linguistic patterns and contextual rules in order to identify semantic information among parts of text.

Recent methods for filtering information from large volumes of texts (information extraction, information retrieval, text summarization, etc.) extract topic data on some of interest to a user from a corpus of texts. In many current systems using NLP techniques (e.g. information extraction systems [7]), most of the text analysis of filtering tasks is performed by matching the text against a set of patterns (regular expressions) based on the technology of finite state automata and transducers.

Describing *textual context* by using regular expressions or applying contextual probability or local grammar rules is not practicable. Using local context (such as in syntactic parsers [3], [4]) to identify the semantics of the textual categories involved in a text is totally inadequate [5]. We rely on linguistic works that identify linguistic markers and their combination, to lend meaning to textual units. We designed a model called **Ltext** that contains means for describing linguistic patterns regarding their textual contexts. The description of the contexts takes accounts for all the information about the text structure and contents. We use this model to describe contextual rules and to represent the linguistic knowledge for the Filtext project [8]. This project aims to identify the semantics of textual or discourse categories involved in texts by using a contextual exploration method [5], [6]. Several tasks in this project (such as identification of causal actions or relations, definitions, relations between concepts, thematic announcements, recapitulations, etc) describe how to use context to identify semantic information. These tasks capture specific information in order to build an abstract or a network of terms.

The Ltext language is an operational algebra over sets of regions. Linguistic patterns and their textual contexts are described in terms of regions expressions. Each region represents a set of disjoint segments. A text segment is a contiguous portion of the text. Set of text segments are described in terms of operations, which combine regions to yield new ones, and primitive regions defined either by a text parser (predefined region) or by the user (user-defined region). Operators take regions as arguments and generate a region as the result. They can be classified by type, such as

A. Gelbukh (Ed.): CICLing 2001, LNCS 2004, pp. 93-95, 2001.

structure operators, relational operators (like before, after, contains, in, starts_with, ends_with, etc.) and composition set operators (intersection, union, difference and complement). Primitives describe three region types:

1. Linguistic units (morphemes, words, phrases, propositions, etc.) defined by patterns. Linguistic patterns are defined in terms of word sequences, part-of-speech, syntactic features, orthographic features (e.g., capitalization), etc.
2. Structural components (sections, paragraphs, titles, etc) obtained by parsing the text, by following markup tag, etc.
3. Named regions generated by a set of patterns defined in the linguistic database.

The algebra can be used not only for text queries but also for structure definition and contextual text analysis. Contextual rules entail the identification of specific linguistic indicators to trigger semantic decisions. The semantic analysis process of a linguistic unit search others linguistic clues by exploring the textual context in order to solve ambiguities caused, for example, by the phenomenon polysemy. A contextual rule of a filtering task is described by a query which combines four region expressions: (i) trigger regions containing or matching linguistic patterns (linguistic indicators which are relevant clues for the task); (ii) region constraints which identify and explore the textual context of the pattern in order to perform action. Various kinds of contexts can be described by region expressions (such as contextual word meaning, expression location in the sentence, sentence or paragraph location in the text, structural level of text, etc) and relations among regions; (iii) selected regions which describe the set of segments to be labeled; (iv) value regions referenced by the action which constructs an attribute-value structure and labels the selected region. We describe an example of a French contextual rule (defined in the Filtext automatic summarization task) that captures conclusive sentences. This rule can be described by combination of some region expressions:

1. Class of linguistic indicators of conclusive sentences: `$expr = pour résumer|en guise de conclusion|titre de conclusion|...`
2. Region to be selected: `($sentence contains $expr)`
3. Contextual constraints: for example, locate the indicators (referenced by `$expr`) in the first or last section of the text to be sure that these conclusions are global compared with the author's argumentation: `(($sections[1] or $sections[2]) contains $expr)`. The associated action assign the "*concluion*" label to the selected sentence. The sentence to be selected is not the default one that contains the indicators. For example, "***Ceci est notre** troisième* **conclusion**" (*That is our third conclusion*), is a conclusive sentence, but gives no information about the conclusion itself. In this case, the preceding sentence (`$sentence before $expr`) can be selected because the clue "*ceci*" is located at the beginning of the sentence `(($sentence contains $expr) startswith "ceci")`.

We do not intend to define a query language accessed by a final user, but a model for describing and structuring linguistic knowledge in terms of region expressions. The textual filtering tasks using this linguistic knowledge are performed by matching the text against a database of linguistic patterns and contextual rules. This model and the software architecture provide a linguistic development environment to manage linguistic knowledge database and create linguistic resources for capturing specific semantic information [2].

Our model has several important advantages over other systems limited to regular expression patterns or to local grammar rules. Region expressions permit conjunctions of patterns, references to context and operations on text structure. The cost of this expressiveness is efficiency. Ltext prototype is linear in most operations, but the structure index is kept in memory. Region expressions are implemented using efficient set intervals representation. The actual evaluation time of region expressions varies according to the complexity of the expression and the size of its intermediate results. Other models have been proposed for querying structured text databases, such as Proximal Nodes [9], PAT expressions [10]. A survey of structured query languages is found in [1], [9]. These models address different goals, but not the modeling of contextual knowledge in semantic text filtering. Textual processing tasks should select the most efficient model supporting them.

References

1. Baeza-Yates, R. and Navarro, G.: Integrating contents and structure in text retrieval. ACM SIGMOD Record 25, 1 (1996) 67-79.
   ftp://sunsite.dcc.uchile.cl/pub/users/gnavarro/sigmod96.ps.gz
2. Ben Hazez, S. and Minel, J.-L.: Designing tasks for identification of complex linguistic expressions used for semantic text filtering. In RIAO'2000, Paris, (2000) 1558-1566.
3. Brill, E.: Automatic Grammar Induction and Parsing Free Text: A Transformation-Based Approach. In Proceeding 31st Meeting of the Association of Computational Linguistics, Columbus, (1993). ftp://cs.jhu.edu/pub/brill
4. Church, K.: A stochastic parts program and noun phrase parser for unrestricted text. Acts 2nd Conference on Applied Natural Language Processing, Austin, Texas, (1988) 136-143.
5. Desclés, J.-P., Cartier, E., Jackiewicz, A., Minel, J.-L.: textual processing and contextual exploration method. In CONTEXT'97, rio de janeiro, brésil, (1997).
6. Desclés, J.-P., Jouis, C., Hum-Ghum O., Danièle Maire Reppert.: Exploration Contextuelle et sémantique : un système expert qui trouve les valeurs sémantiques des temps de l'indicatif dans un texte. In Knowledge modeling and expertise transfer, D. Herin-Aime, R. Dieng, J.-P. Regourd, J.P. Angoujard (éds), Amsterdam, (1991) 371-400.
7. Grishman, R.: Information Extraction: Techniques and Challenges. In M.T. Pazienza, (Ed.), Information extraction, Lecture Notes in Artificial Intelligence, Vol. 1299. Springer-Verlag, Berlin Heidelberg New York, (1997) 10–27.
8. Minel, J-L., Desclés, J.-P., Cartier, E., Crispino, G., Ben Hazez, S., Jackiewicz, A.: Résumé automatique par filtrage sémantique d'informations dans des textes. Présentation de la plate-forme FilText , to appear in TSI, (2000).
9. Navarro, G. and Baeza-Yates, R.: Proximal Nodes: A Model to query Document Databases by Contents and Structure. Trans. Info. Sys. Record 15 (4), (1997) 400-435. ftp://-sunsite.dcc.uchile.cl/pub/users/gnavarro/sigmod96.ps.gz
10. Salminen, A. and Tompa, F.: PAT expressions: an algebra for text search. In COMPLEX'92 (1992) 309-332.

Statistical Methods
in Studying the Semantics of Size Adjectives

Valentyna Arkhelyuk

Chernivtsi National University, Ukraine
arvalentina@mail.ru

Abstract. The present study deals with a statistical analysis of the lexico-semantic group of size adjectives (*great, big, large, little, small*, and the like). The statistical procedures and methods, as well as the mathematical formulae used, reveal the integrative and differential semes, along with the lexico-semantic links found in the microsystem.

1 Introduction

By understanding language processes in procedural terms, we can give computer systems the ability to interpret natural language messages [1]. This study was born of necessity - as a response to the lack of current satisfactory work performed in lexicography. Using as a starting point the theories presented in [3, 8, 9], as well as the new computational approaches [2, 5, 6, 7], this study explores the way in which words combine in a given text. We chose 30 literary works taken from a variety of texts—British as well as American—written during the 19th and 20th centuries. The corpora consist of more than 2.5 million word combinations of size adjectives and noun subclasses.

2 Paradigmatic Relations between Size Adjectives

We used "chi-square" (χ^2) as a test of significance [4] to compare frequency counts across corpora. The measure of the relations between sizes was calculated with the help of the coefficient of "mutual association" *K*. In addition, we used correlation analysis to investigate the paradigmatic relationships between size adjectives and computer statistical programs to tally all possible occurrences within the above-mentioned texts.

2.1 The Results of the Correlation Analysis

Our results support Shaikevich's [8] conclusion that the more the characteristics of the words that are combined coincide, the more these words will be connected

A. Gelbukh (Ed.): CICLing 2001, LNCS 2004, pp. 96–97, 2001.

semantically (direct proportional dependency). However, our investigation offers both direct and inverse proportional dependencies between the sizes of correlation. Thus, the minimum statistically significant coefficient is 0.46 (P=0.05), or 0.58 (P=0.01). As a result, the correlation of the words with a coefficient lower than 0.46 is "weak", from 0.46 to 0.58 is "average", and more than 0.58 is "strong". The results with such coefficients have statistical meanings, indicating the essential correlation between the combinations of size adjectives. For example: *high-narrow* (r=0.95); *small-narrow* (r=0.87); *little-high* (r=0.86); *tall-wide* (r=0.86); *tall-broad* (r=0.86). 65% of positively-correlated pairs of adjectives show a high degree of correlation (from 0.58 to 0.98). Synonyms (such as *big-large* (r=0.97), *wide-broad* (r=0.94) as well as the antonyms (such as *big-small* (r=0.98) and *large-small* (r=0.95) show the best correlation and have similar distribution. The correlation between the synonyms *great-big, great-large* (r=0.34) and the antonyms *tall-low* (r=0.43) has low statistical significance. The size adjectives *great, tall,* and *long* are negatively correlated. This means that, unlike the rest of the adjectives studied, there are more differences than similarities in their distribution. This confirms the linguistic fact that polysemantic words have insignificant paradigmatic relations, a great number of synonyms, and a high frequency of usage.

References

[1] Grishman, Ralph. *Computational Linguistics*. Cambridge, Mass: CUP, 1986.

[2] Jurafsky, Dan. *Speech and Language Processing: An Introduction to Natural Language Processing, Computational Linguistics*. Upper Saddle River, N.J: Prentice Hall, 2000.

[3] Levitsky, Viktor V. *Statisticheskoye izucheniye leksicheskoi semantiki*. Kiev: UMK BO, 1989.

[4] Lorenz, Gunter R. *Adjective Intensification - Learners versus Native Speakers: A Corpus Study of Argumentative Writing*. Amsterdam: Rodopi, 1999.

[5] Manning, Christopher D., and Hinrich Schütze. *Foundations of Statistical Natural Language Processing*. Cambridge: MIT Press, 1999.

[6] Mel'cuk, Igor Aleksandrovich. Lexical Functions: A Tool for the Description of Lexical Relations in a Lexicon. *Lexical Functions in Lexicography and Natural Language Processing*. Ed. Warren Leo. Amsterdam: John Benjamins, 1996.

[7] Saint-Dizier, P., and E. Viegas. *Computational Lexical Semantics*. Cambridge: CUP, 1995.

[8] Shaikevich A. *Raspredeleniye slov v tekste i vydeleniye semanticheskih polei. Inostrannyye yazuki v Shkole*. Moscow: Rosvuzizdat, Vyp. 2, 1963.

[9] Zipf, George K. *Human Behavior and the Principle of Least Effort*. Cambridge, MA: Addison-Wesley, 1949.

Numerical Model of the Strategy for Choosing Polite Expressions

Tamotsu Shirado and Hitoshi Isahara

Communications Research Laboratory,
2-2-2 Hikaridai Seikacho, Kyoto 619-0289, Japan
{shirado, isahara}@crl.go.jp

Abstract. Japanese speakers often use different expressions having the same meaning but with different levels of politeness when speaking to different listeners. Brown and Levinson proposed a theory to explain how the expression to use is selected, but it is only qualitative. We propose a numerical model, constructed using the quantification-I method and multiple regression analysis, for predicting the expressions selected in various relationships such as familiarity and relative social power between speaker and listener. The politeness of each expression is quantified by the method of paired comparison.

1 Introduction

In Japan, politeness plays important roles in social activities, especially in conversations. Japanese speakers often use different expressions having different politeness but similar meanings (speech intentions) when persons concerned with conversation are changed. There are few languages which politeness has so developed as Japanese in the world[1].

Politeness is the recognition of relationships such as relative social power and social distances among speakers, listeners, and topic persons. Let us call such relationships **"politeness-relationship,"** and assume a situation where only one speaker and one listener are concerned is assumed in our present study.

In speech acts, the speaker choose specific expressions among expressions which can deliver his speech intentions to the listener. At this time, the face of the listener may be threaten if too impolite expressions are chosen. On the other, the face of the speaker himself may be threaten if he choose too polite expressions. So, the speaker is required to choose appropriate expressions which can keep balance between the magnitude of threat to the speaker's face and those to the listener's face. There have been many studies on such speech strategy for choosing polite expressions (let us call "politeness-strategy") .

A theory proposed by Brown and Levinson (let us call "BL theory") is a famous study on the politeness-strategy by linguistics approach[2]. The BL theory draws how the expressions are chosen by combination of several factors concerning speech situations. However, the BL theory is only conceptual, no ideas are included in the theory for constructing practical models.

A. Gelbukh (Ed.): CICLing 2001, LNCS 2004, pp. 98–109, 2001.

As engineering approach, a automatic generation program of polite expressions has been developed[3]. This program can generate polite expressions based on heuristic rules when original polite expressions and some parameters on politeness are given. As the heuristic rules depend on linguistic intuition of programmer, the program lacks of commonality and universality.

As mathematical approach, Mizutani proposed a theory for modeling politeness by algebra and class logic[4]. As the theory is not based on psychological experiments, the applicability of the theory to practical speech situations is doubtful.

In our previous study, we proposed a computational model for politeness of expressions. The model, however, was devoted to predict the changes of politeness through the addition of word endings[5].

We propose a numerical model of politeness-strategy based on psychological experiments. In our study, two kinds of regression models with the dependent variable: politeness of expressions (scalar values), the independent variables: two factors (nominal values) are proposed. The method of Hayashi's quantification-I[6] and the linear regression method were applied to data obtained by psychological experiments. The politeness of expressions were also obtained by psychological experiments.

The proposed models are constructed by the psychological experiments and statistical methods, so the models are superior than previous models described above in commonality and applicability.

2   Politeness-Relationship

Our study refers to the BL theory partially. Three factors concerning speech situations:

1. the social distance (ex. familiarity) between a speaker and a listener,
2. the relative social power (ex. age difference) between a speaker and a listener, and
3. the ranking of impositions (the magnitude of threat of the speech intentions to the listener's face[7])

are introduced to explain the politeness-strategy in the BL theory. The theory said that the more the magnitudes of these factors, the more the polite of expressions to be chosen. However, the weight among these factors and the politeness of the expressions are only qualitatively described in the theory.

We assume that the politeness-relationship can be expressed by the combination of the social distance D between a speaker and a listener and the the relative social power P of the listener from the speaker. In detail, let us define values of $D = D_1$: "close friend", D_2: "friend", D_3: "acquaintance", D_4: "first meeting", and $P = P_1$: "very younger", P_2: "younger", P_3: "almost same age", P_4: "older", P_5: "very older or social standing of the listener is (guessed) very high".

The other factor described in the BL theory: ranking of impositions is not included in our model because the factor depends on speech intentions. So the model parameters are estimated for each speech intention in our study.

The remaining sections of this paper are comprised of quantification of politeness of expressions and ANOVA (ANalysis Of VAriance)[9] for data obtained by psychological experiments (section 3-5), proposal of our model and evaluation (section 6 and 7).

3   Politeness Value

Ogino showed that Japanese expressions having similar speech intentions can be sorted in a one-dimensional psychometrical space of politeness. We assume the characteristics is fulfil in the present study, then the magnitudes of politeness of expressions can be obtained by the method of paired comparison and Thurstone's scaling[10]. Let us call the politeness of an expression $\mathbf{e}$ measured by these methods the "politeness value $v(\mathbf{e})$."

The procedures for obtaining the politeness values of expressions $\mathbf{e}_1, \mathbf{e}_2, .., \mathbf{e}_n$ are as follows.

3.1   The Method of Paired Comparison

All pairs of $\mathbf{e}_i$ and $\mathbf{e}_j (i,j{=}1,..,n,\ i{\neq}j)$ are presented one by one to subjects. Subject are required to answer which expression in each pair is more polite.

3.2   Thurstone's Scaling

Let us denote the standard deviation and the mean of single discriminal process for the expression $\mathbf{e}_i$ by σ_i and μ_i, and those for the expression $\mathbf{e}_j$ by σ_j and μ_j. Here, we assume that the Thurstone's case V: $\sigma_i{=}\sigma_j\ (=\sigma)$ and there is no correlation between these two discriminal processes. Then we get the following equation:

$$\mu_i - \mu_j = z_{ij}\sqrt{2}\sigma, \tag{1}$$

where z_{ij} represents the z(or standard) score[11] of $p_{ij}{=}(N_{ij}{+}N'_{ij}/2)/N$, where N, N_{ij}, and N_{ij} are the number of all subjects, the number of subjects which answer that $\mathbf{e}_i$ is more polite than $\mathbf{e}_j$, and the number of subjects which answer that $\mathbf{e}_i$ is polite as $\mathbf{e}_j$, respectively.

We can determine each μ_i as the relative value from the minimum among $\mu_i(i{=}1,..,n)$ by using the Eq (1). Let us define μ_i by unit of $\sqrt{2}\sigma$ as the politeness value for $\mathbf{e}_i$.

As mentioned above, each politeness value is obtained by data of all subjects, so it represents the average impressions of politeness for expressions over subjects. Furthermore, we must notice it is meaningless to compare the politeness values among the expression belonging to different speech intentions because the politeness values represent the relative values in each expression group corresponding to each speech intention.

4 Experiments

Paired comparison experiments by the method of paired comparison and expression selection experiments were executed for several speech intentions, speech situations and expression groups corresponding to speech intentions.

4.1 Speech Intentions

Ten speech intentions showed in Table 1 were assumed in psychological experiments.

Table 1. Speech intentions

title	speech intention	situation
TIME	"what time is it now?"	on the road
CLEAR WAY	"clear my way"	on the road
HELP ME	"help me for loading my baggage"	in train
OFFER HELP	"may I help you?"	listener is looking for something on the floor
LEFT BEHIND	"is it your umbrella?"	listener is leaving behind his umbrella
APOLOGIZE	"I'm sorry"	speaker's hand touched to shoulder of listener
NO SMOKING	"smoking is inhibited here"	listener is smoking in no smoking area
STOP	"is this train will stopping at XX?"	listener is not crew
PHOTOGRAPH	"take my picture?"	on the road
SEAT	"make a seat for me by sit close"	in the train

Correspond to each speech intention in Table 1, expression group comprised of twenty expressions with different politeness were prepared. Table 2 shows such a expression group corresponding to speech intention **TIME**.

Paired comparison experiment and expression selection experiment were performed on each expression group.

4.2 Paired Comparison Experiment

One hundred-forty males and females whose age range from teen to sixty participated in the paired comparison experiment.

All pairs of expressions included in same expression group were presented one by one to subjects. Subject were required to answer which expression in each pair is more polite or both expressions had same politeness. Politeness values were calculated by Thurstone's scaling.

Table 2. The expression group corresponding to speech intention **TIME** (In parentheses: rough meanings of words)

1: *nanji?*
    (what time)
2: *ima-nanji-kana?*
    (now)-(what time)-(an interrogative)
3: *ima-nanji?*
    (now)-(what time)
4: *jikan-wakaru?*
    (time)-(do you know)
5: *jikan-osiete*
    (time)-(inform me)
6: *jikan-osiete-kureru?*
    (time)-(inform me)-(an interrogative)
7: *chotto-jikan-osiete*
    (excuse me {not so polite})-(time)-(inform me)
8: *chotto-jikan-osiete-kureru?*
    (excuse me {not so polite})-(time)-(inform me)-(an interrogative)
9: *ima-nanji-deshou?*
    (now)-(what time)-(an interrogative {polite})
10: *chotto-jikan-o-osiete-kudasai*
    (excuse me {not so polite})-(time)-*-(inform me)-(an interrogative {polite})
11: *chotto-jikan-o-osiete-itadakemasu*
    (excuse me {not so polite})-(time)-*-(inform me)-(an interrogative {very polite})
12: *chotto-jikan-o-ukagatte-mo-yorosiideshouka?*
    (excuse me {not so polite})-(time)-*-(ask {polite})-*-(may I {very polite})
13: *sumimasen, ima-nanji-deshou?*
    (excuse me {polite}), (now)-(what time)-(an interrogative {polite})
14: *sumimasen, chotto-jikkan-o-osiete-kudasai*
    (excuse me {polite}), (excuse me {not so polite})-
    (time)-*-(inform me)-(an interrogative)
15: *sumimasen, chotto-jikkan-o-osiete-itadakemasu?*
    (excuse me {polite}), (excuse me {not so polite})-
    (time)-*-(inform me)-(an interrogative {very polite})
16: *sumimasen, chotto-jikkan-o-ukagatte-mo-yorosiideshouka?*
    (excuse me {polite}), (excuse me {not so polite})-
    (time)-*-(ask {polite})-*-(may I {very polite})
17: *situreidesuga, ima-nannji-deshou?*
    (excuse me {very polite}), (now)-(what time)-(an interrogative {polite})
18: *situreidesuga, chotto-jikan-o-osiete-kudasai*
    (excuse me {very polite}), (excuse me {not so polite})-
    (time)-*-(inform me)-(an interrogative)
19: *situreidesuga, chotto-jikan-o-osiete-itadakemasu?*
    (excuse me {very polite}), (excuse me {not so polite})-
    (time)-*-(inform me)-(an interrogative {very polite})
20: *situreidesuga, chotto-jikan-o-ukagatte-mo-yorosiideshouka*
    (excuse me {very polite}), (excuse me {not so polite})-
    (time)-*-(ask {polite})-*-(may I {very polite})

4.3   Expression Selection Experiment

One hundred-eighty males and females whose age range from teen to sixty participated in the expression selection experiment. Subjects were divided into six groups of different sex (male, female) and age brackets (young: under thirty, middle: thirty to forty nine, or old: over fifty), therefore each subject group is comprised of thirty persons.

Speech strategy may depend on the listener's sex which speaker assume because sex differences have been observed in various aspects of social activities[12]. So, we adopt also the listener's sex as stimulus variation addition to the politeness-relationships. Totally, forty combinatorial conditions of listener's sex (two kinds) and politeness-relationship (twenty kinds) were prepared as speech conditions.

Each subject was required to answer all the expressions which he feels "adequate" to use for each speech condition. He also required to answer the "most adequate" expression when he feels several expressions as "adequate".

5   Statistical Analysis

Politeness value of the most "adequate" expression (or only a expression) for each speech condition was used for statistical analysis.

5.1   Dependency on the Listener's Sex

Two way ANOVA (listener's sex × politeness-relationship) with no repeated measure were performed at significance level 1% for each speech intention, each subject.

The main effects of listener's sex were not significant for all speech intentions on the one hundred-twenty subjects (67%) out of one hundred-eighty subjects. The main effects were significant for 18 % out of ten intentions in average on other (sixty) subjects.

These results reveals that the politeness-strategy hardly depends on the listener's sex which speakers assume. Therefore, we ignore the variation on listener's sex after here, instead we regard the average of politeness values over listener's sex as representative value on each politeness-relationship.

5.2   Dependency on Speaker's Sex, Speaker's Age Bracket, and Politeness-Relationships

Three way ANOVA (speaker's sex × speaker's age bracket × politeness-relationship) with repeated measure of thirty subjects (subjects in each group) were performed at significance level 1% for each speech intention.

The results showed that

- interaction among three factors were not significant on all (ten kinds) speech intentions.

- interaction between speaker's sex and speaker's age bracket were significant on 8 (80%) speech intentions.
- interaction between speaker's age bracket and politeness-relationship were significant on 9 (90%) speech intentions.
- interaction between speaker's sex and politeness-relationship were significant on 7 (70%) speech intentions.
- main effects of speaker's sex were significant on 6 (60%) speech intentions.
- main effects of speaker's age bracket and politeness-relationship were significant on all speech intentions.

These results suggest that we cannot ignore the interaction between any factors out of speaker's sex, speaker's age bracket, or politeness-relationship. So it is suggested that politeness-strategy may differ among six subject groups.

5.3   Interaction Between Social Distance D and Relative Power P

Two way ANOVA (social distance D × relative power P) with repeated measure of thirty subjects were performed at significance level 1% for each subject group, for each speech intention.

The results showed that interaction between social distance D and relative power P were not significant on fifty-two cases (87%) out of sixty combinatorial cases of subject group (six groups) and intentions (ten kinds).

This results suggests that the social distance D and the relative power P contribute to politeness-strategy independently on most cases assumed in our present experiments.

6   Numerical Model of Politeness-Strategy

It was suggested in the previous section that the social distance D and the relative power P contribute to politeness-strategy independently. So let us assume that the determination process of the politeness value v of the "most adequate" expression (or only a expression) for each politeness-relationship $D×P$ can be described by some regression models independent variable: v, dependent variable D, P. Concretely, we propose two kind of models: a model based on the Hayashi's quantification-I and a model based on the linear regression analysis.

6.1   Quantification-I Model

The variable D and P having nominal values D_i (i=1,..,4) and P_j (j=1,..,5) are treated as categorical variables in the quantification-I model. The politeness value v of the expression to be chosen for the politeness-relationship $D×P$ is calculated by Eq. (2) .

$$v = \sum_{i=1}^{4} w_i x_i + \sum_{j=1}^{5} z_j y_j + c, \qquad (2)$$

where x_i, y_j represent dummy variables having 0 or 1 corresponding to D_i, P_j respectively, w_i, z_j, and c are regression coefficients to be estimated by data obtained psychological experiments. The goodness of fitting of the model to the data can be evaluated by the coefficients of determination defined in quantification-I theory[6].

6.2   Linear Regression Model

As described above, D_i and P_j are nominal values. However, we can arrange them in magnitude order such as $D_1, D_2,.., D_4$ and $P_1, P_2,.., P_5$ respectively. So let the interval scaling apply to D_i and P_j by assigning the value i to D_i (let us denote the variable representing such values d) and the value j to P_j (let us denote the variable representing such values p). Then v is calculated by linear combination of d and p (Eq. (3)).

$$v = w_d d + w_p p + c, \tag{3}$$

where w_d, w_p, and c are regression coefficients to be estimated by data obtained psychological experiments. The goodness of fitting of the model to the data can be evaluated by coefficients of determination defined in linear regression analysis[13].

The interval scaling performed in the liner model is not always assured to be valid generally, so the quantification-I model may be superior than the linear regression model in this point. However, linear regression model is superior than quantification-I model in applicability because the politeness value v is determined continuously by the continuous variables in the regression model, on the other v is determined discretely by the categorical variables in the quantification-I model.

7   Evaluation

7.1   The Goodness of Fitting

Model parameters and the coefficients of determination were calculated for all data (one hundred-eighty subjects), for each speech intentions. As mentioned in the previous section, politeness-strategy may differ among six subject groups. So, model parameters and the coefficients of determination were also calculated for data (thirty subjects) in each subject group. Table 3 shows the coefficients of determination averaged over speech intentions (values in parentheses represent the standard deviations).

No significant difference were observed between the mean value of six groups and the value for all data at significant level 1%.

These results suggests that

1. fitting of the both models to the data were not good (especially for the linear model), and

Table 3. Coefficients of determination averaged over speech intentions

sex	age bracket	Quantification-I	Linear
male	young	0.71(0.07)	0.47(0.08)
male	middle	0.71(0.06)	0.48(0.08)
male	old	0.68(0.05)	0.45(0.06)
female	young	0.72(0.07)	0.51(0.09)
female	midle	0.75(0.06)	0.55(0.09)
female	old	0.69(0.06)	0.46(0.09)
mean		0.71(0.06)	0.49(0.08)
all data		0.69(0.06)	0.46(0.07)

2. fitting of the both models to the data were not improved by division of all subjects into six subject groups of different sex and age bracket.

However, the coefficients of determinations were greater than 0.9 for both models when we use the data averaged over subjects for each politeness-relationship. This suggests that the politeness-strategy of the average subject can be expressed well by both models. So, the results 1. and 2. mentioned above probably due to the characteristics:

1. dispersion among subjects were large, and
2. the magnitude of the dispersion did not depend on sex and age bracket

7.2 Prediction

In this section, precision of the prediction by the present models are devaluated. Model parameters were estimated for each data mentioned above. Politeness value was calculated by Eq. 2 (or Eq. 3) for each politeness-relationship, each speech intention (let us denote the politeness value $\tilde{v}$). The expression having politeness value closest to $\tilde{e}$ is extracted as predicted expression. We regarded the predicted expression as "hit" to the answer of a subject for a politeness-relationship if the expression coincides any expression which the subject answer "adequate" (including also "most adequate"). Average hit ratios were calculated over politeness-relationships and subjects. The definition of "hit" may not be strict because only the "most adequate" expressions were used for parameter estimations. However, it is properly meaningful for engineering purpose if we can predict the expression which most subjects feel "adequate" to use for the politeness-relationship.

The problem of the definition of "hit" described above is that the larger the number of answer for each politeness-relationship, the larger hit ratios even if the prediction is not precise. So, two kind of prediction method were introduced for comparative discussions on precision.

Prediction Method 1: Prediction by Linear Model with Equivalent Weight This method is almost same as prediction by linear regression model described above except that the parameters w_d, w_p, c are determined such that d and p equivalently contribute to v. Concretely, w_d, w_p, c are determined such that the line $v = w_d d + w_p p + c$ through the points $(1,1,0)$ and $(4,5,max)$ in the three- dimensional space of $d(=1,..,4) \times p(=1,..,5) \times v(0,..,max)$, where max represents the maximum of politeness values among concerning expressions.

So, this method use politeness values obtained by the paired comparison experiments, but ignore the results of the expression selection experiments.

Prediction Method 2: Random Prediction The prediction value $\tilde{v}$ are given as uniform random numbers range 0 to max, where max is same defined in the prediction method 1.

So, this method do not use any results of the psychological experiments performed in the present study.

The appearance ratio of each expression in answer of subjects (i.e. the percentage of subjects which answered the expression as "adequate") was calculated for each speech intentions, for each politeness-relationship. The maximum value of appearance ratios gives the upper limit of hit ratios because the hit ratio become best when the predicted expression coincides to the expression which appears most frequently in subjects answers.

The hit ratios by methods mentioned above and the upper limit were calculated for the data as used for parameter estimations.

Table 4 shows the hit ratios and upper limits averaged over speech intentions (values in parentheses represents the standard deviations).

Table 4. Hit ratios and upper limits averaged over speech intentions

sex	age bracket	Quantification-I	Linear	Equiv. weight	Random	Upper limit
male	young	0.48(0.05)	0.49(0.04)	0.21(0.06)	0.24(0.1)	0.66(0.04)
male	middle	0.41(0.06)	0.40(0.04)	0.26(0.06)	0.18(0.1)	0.61(0.05)
male	old	0.30(0.05)	0.30(0.04)	0.21(0.06)	0.14(0.06)	0.44(0.04)
female	young	0.41(0.07)	0.41(0.06)	0.21(0.08)	0.19(0.09)	0.66(0.05)
female	middle	0.40(0.04)	0.40(0.05)	0.25(0.08)	0.17(0.1)	0.65(0.06)
female	old	0.38(0.07)	0.37(0.06)	0.30(0.08)	0.16(0.11)	0.60(0.06)
mean		0.40(0.06)	0.39(0.05)	0.24(0.07)	0.18(0.09)	0.60(0.05)
all data		0.37(0.04)	0.39(0.03)	0.24(0.06)	0.18(0.09)	0.56(0.05)

The hit ratios by quantification-I and linear model were both around 0.4 for all cases. The best upper limits was 0.66 .

No significant differences were observed between the hit ratio by quantification-I and those by linear model for all cases, and hit ratios by both methods were significantly larger than those by method of equivalent weight and random prediction at significant level 1%. Furthermore, no significant differences were observed between mean hit ratios of six groups and those of all data by quantification-I and also by linear model. This result suggests that the hit ratios do not improved by division of all subjects into six subject groups of different sex and age bracket.

The reason of such low hit ratio around 0.4 probably due to same reason as described above that the dispersion among subjects were large, and the magnitude of the dispersion did not depend on sex and age bracket.

However, the present models may be useful for listing only the promising candidate expressions in the initial process of some system to predict the appropriate expressions for politeness-relationship if the dispersion among subject concentrates around the predicted politeness value $\tilde{v}$. To confirm such the characteristics of dispersion is fulfilled in the present study, we extracted n candidates one by one in reverse order of the $|\tilde{v}-c|$, where c represents the politeness value of the candidate expression. We regarded the candidate expression as "quasi-hit" to the answer of a subject for a politeness-relationship if the expression coincides any expression which the subject answer "adequate" (including also "most adequate").

Fig .1 shows the quasi-hit ratio averaged over all (one hundred-eighty) subjects, all (ten) speech intentions, and politeness-relationships for n(the number of candidates)=1,..,9 for all data.

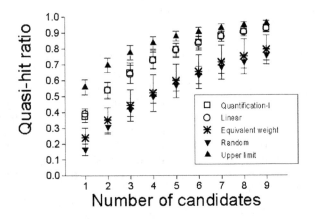

Fig. 1. Quasi-hit ratios when the number of candidate expressions is n

The values by quantification-I and those by linear model have no significant differences from the upper limit, but significantly larger than those by equivalent weight and random prediction at significant level 1% when $n\geq7$.

The results suggest that the characteristics of dispersion mentioned above is fulfilled in the present study.

8   Conclusion

We proposed the two kinds of numerical model of strategy for choosing the expressions in various relationships such as familiarity and social power differences between speaker and listener. The experimental results showed that 1. such strategy do not depend on the listeners sex which speakers assume, and 2. dispersion among subjects is large, and 3. the magnitude of the dispersion do not depend on sex and age bracket.

The both of the present model cannot predict subjects answers precisely, but useful for listing only the promising candidate expressions in the initial process of some system to predict the appropriate expressions for politeness-relationship.

The factors other than speakers sex, listeners sex, speakers age bracket, social distance, relative social power are required to incorporate in model for predicting each subjects answers more precisely.

Acknowledgements

We would like to thank Prof. Dr. Alexander Gelbukh and Dr. Masaki Murata for their comments on our paper.

References

1. Kikuchi Y.: Politeness (in Japanese), Koudan-Sha Tokyo(1997).
2. Brown P., and Levinson S.: Politeness - Some universals of language usage -, Cambridge London(1987).
3. Tanaka S et. al: Nihongo-sin-kouza(in Japanese), Asakura-shoten Tokyo(1983).
4. Mizutani S.: A theory of politeness(in Japanese), keiryou keikaku Laboratory(1995).
5. Shirado T. and Isahara H.: A computational model for politeness of expressions - changes of politeness through the addition of word endings -, International Symposium on Linguistic Politeness '99(1999).
6. Hayashi C.: On the prediction of phenomena from qualitative data and the quantification of qualitative data from the mathematicostatistical point of view, Ann. Inst. Statist. Math. Vol. 3 (1952) 121–143.
7. Goffman E.: Interaction ritual: essays on face to face behavior, Garden City New York(1967).
8. Ogino T: Social linguistic research on polite expressions, Nihongo-gaku   Vol. 5 (1986) 55–64(in Japanese).
9. Stapleton J.H: Linear statistical models, Wiley New York(1995).
10. Thurstone L.L., Measurement of values, Univ. of Chicago Press Chicago(1959).
11. Baird J.C. and Noma E.: Fundamentals of scaling and psychophysics, Wiley New York(1978).
12. Canary D.J. and Emmers-sommer T.M.: Sex and gender differences in personal relationships, The Guilford Press, New York(1997).
13. Montgomery, D.C. et al. 1992. Introduction to linear regression analysis. Wiley, New York.

Outstanding Issues in Anaphora Resolution

Ruslan Mitkov

School of Humanities, Languages and Social Studies
University of Wolverhampton
Stafford Street, Wolverhampton WV1 1SB
United Kingdom
R.Mitkov@wlv.ac.uk

Abstract. This paper argues that even though there has been considerable advance in the research in anaphora resolution over the last 10 years, there are still a number of outstanding issues. The paper discusses several of these issues and outlines some of the work underway to address them with particular reference to the work carried out by the author's research team.

1   Anaphora Resolution: Where Do We Stand Now?

Anaphora accounts for cohesion in text and is a phenomenon of active study in formal and computational linguistics alike. The correct interpretation of anaphora is vital for Natural Language Processing. For example, anaphora resolution is a key task in natural language interfaces, machine translation, automatic abstracting, information extraction, and in a number of other NLP applications.

After considerable initial research, and after years of relative silence in the early eighties, anaphora resolution attracted the attention of many researchers in the last 10 years and much promising work on the topic has been reported. Discourse-orientated theories and formalisms such as DRT and Centering have inspired new research on the computational treatment of anaphora. The drive towards corpus-based robust NLP solutions has further stimulated interest, for alternative and/or data-enriched approaches. Last but not least, application-driven research in areas such as automatic abstracting and information extraction has independently identified the importance of (and boosted the research in) anaphora and coreference resolution.

Much of the earlier work in anaphora resolution heavily exploited domain and linguistic knowledge ([9], [11], [57], [58]), which was difficult both to represent and process, and required considerable human input. However, the pressing need for the development of robust and inexpensive solutions to meet the demands of practical NLP systems encouraged many researchers to move away from extensive domain and linguistic knowledge and to embark instead upon knowledge-poor anaphora resolution strategies. A number of proposals in the 1990s deliberately limited the extent to which they rely on domain and/or linguistic knowledge ([6], [15], [31], [35], [38], [51], [65]) and reported promising results in knowledge-poor operational environments.

The drive towards knowledge-poor and robust approaches was further motivated by the emergence of cheaper and more reliable corpus-based NLP tools such as POS taggers and shallow parsers, alongside the increasing availability of corpora and other

A. Gelbukh (Ed.): CICLing 2001, LNCS 2004, pp. 110-125, 2001.

NLP resources (e.g. ontologies). In fact the availability of corpora, both raw and annotated with coreferential links, provided a strong impetus to anaphora resolution with regard to both training and evaluation. Corpora (especially when annotated) are an invaluable source not only for empirical research but also for automated learning methods (e.g. Machine Learning methods) aiming to develop new rules and approaches, and provide also an important resource for evaluation of the implemented approaches. From simple co-occurrence rules ([15]) through training decision trees to identify anaphor-antecedent pairs ([3]) to genetic algorithms to optimise the resolution factors ([53]), the successful performance of more and more modern approaches was made possible through the availability of suitable corpora.

Whereas the last 10 years have seen considerable advances in the field of anaphora resolution, there are still a number of outstanding issues that remain either unsolved or need further attention and, as a consequence, represent major challenges to the further development of the field. One significant problem for automatic anaphora resolution systems is that the accuracy of the pre-processing is still too low and as a consequence the performance of such systems is still far from ideal. As a further consequence, only a few anaphora resolution systems operate in fully automatic mode: most of them rely or manual pre-processing or use pre-analysed corpora. One of the impediments for the evaluation or for the employment of Machine Learning (ML) techniques is the lack of widely available corpora annotated for anaphoric or coreferential links. More research into the factors influencing the performance of the resolution algorithm is necessary; so too is work towards the proposal of consistent and comprehensive evaluation.

This paper discusses some of the outstanding issues in anaphora resolution and outlines some of the work underway to address them with particular reference to the work carried out by the author's research team.[1] The paper covers the task of anaphora resolution and not that of coreference resolution even though some of the issues raised apply to both tasks. In anaphora resolution the system has to determine the antecedent of the anaphor; for identity-of-reference nominal anaphora any preceding NP which is coreferential with the anaphor, is considered as the correct antecedent. On the other hand, the objective of coreference resolution is to identify all coreferential chains.

2   Pre-processing and Dully Automatic Anaphora Resolution

A real-world anaphora resolution system vitally depends on the efficiency of the pre-processing tools that analyse the input before feeding it to the resolution algorithm. Inaccurate pre-processing could lead to a considerable drop in the performance of the system, however accurate an anaphora resolution algorithm may be. In the pre-processing stage a number of hard pre-processing problems such as morphological analysis / POS tagging, named entity recognition, unknown word recognition, NP extraction, parsing, identification of pleonastic pronouns, selectional constraints, etc. have to be dealt with. Each one of these tasks introduces error and thus contributes to a reduction of the success rate of the anaphora resolution system. The accuracy of

---

[1] Research Group in Computational Linguistics, School of Humanities, Languages and European Studies, University of Wolverhampton (http://www.wlv.ac.uk/sles/compling/).

today's pre-processing is still unsatisfactory from the point of view of anaphora resolution. Whereas POS taggers are fairly reliable, full or partial parsing are not. Name
entity recognition is still a challenge (with the development of a product name recogniser being a vital task for a number of genres), gender recognition is still inaccurate
and the identification of non-anaphoric pronouns and definite NPs and term recognition have a long way to go. For instance, the best accuracy reported in robust parsing
of unrestricted texts is around the 87% mark ([13]); the accuracy of identification of
non-nominal pronouns normally does not exceed 80% ([18], [19]).[2] Other tasks may
be more accurate but still far from perfect. The state of the art of NP chunking which
does not include NPs with post-modifiers, is 90-93% recall and precision. The best-
performing named entity taggers achieve an accuracy of about 96% when trained and
tested on news about a specific topic, and about 93% when trained on news about on
topic and tested on news about other topic ([25]).

Whereas *'standard' pre-processing programs* such as part-of-speech taggers,
shallow parsers, full parsers etc. are being constantly developed and improved (however, there could be formidable problems in getting hold of public domain software!),
anaphora resolution *task-specific pre-processing tools* such as programs for identifying non-anaphoric pronouns or definite NPs, or programs for animacity or gender
recognition, have received considerably less attention. The Research Group in Computational Linguistics at the University of Wolverhampton has already addressed the
problems of identification of pleonastic pronouns and animacity recognition (see
below) and is currently working on name entity recognition as well as term identification.

In pronoun resolution only the anaphoric pronouns have to be processed further,
therefore non-anaphoric occurrences of the pronoun *it* as in 'It must be stated that
Oskar behaved impeccably'[3] have to be recognised by the program.[4] Several algorithms to pleonastic pronoun recognition have been reported in the literature so far.
Lappin and Leass' ([32]) and Denber's ([17]) algorithms operate on simple pattern
matching but they have not been described in detail or evaluated. Paice and Husk's
([54]) approach is more sophisticated in that it proposes a number of patterns based
on data from the LOB corpus[5] and prior grammatical description of *it* and, in contrast
to the above two approaches, applies constraints during the pattern matching process.
With a view to ensuring a wider coverage, we developed a new approach that identifies not only pleonastic pronouns but also any non-nominal occurrences of *it* ([18],
[19]).[6] In this approach each occurrence of *it* is represented as a sequence (vector) of
35 features that classify *it* as pleonastic, non-nominal or NP anaphoric. These features, whose values are computed automatically, include the location of the pronoun
as well as features related the surrounding material in the text, for instance the proximity and form of NPs, adjectives, gerunds, prepositions and complementisers. The

---

[2] However, Paice and Husk ([54]) reported 92% for identification of strictly pleonastic *it* in a
    narrow domain.
[3] Thomas Keneally, Schindlers List, p.165. BCA: London, 1994.
[4] Such occurrences are termed *pleonastic* ([42]).
[5] LOB stands for Lancaster-Oslo-Bergen.
[6] These include instances of *it* whose antecedents are constituents other than noun phrases such
    as verb phrases, sentences etc.

approach benefits from training data extracted from the BNC[7] and Susanne corpora consisting of approximately 3100 occurrences of *it* (1025 of which non-nominal) annotated for these features. A TiMBL's memory based learning algorithm ([14]) maps each pronoun *it* into a vector of feature values, computes similarity between these and the feature values of the occurrences in the training data and classifies the pronoun accordingly. The accuracy of the new approach was found to be 78.68%, compared with that of 78.71% for Paice and Husk's method over the same texts.

A program identifying animate entities could provide essential support in employing the gender constraints. Denber ([17]) and Cardie and Wagstaff ([10]) use Word-Net (see below) to recognise animacity. At Wolverhampton we proposed a method combining FDG Parser, WordNet, a first name gazetteer and a small set of heuristic rules to identify animate entities in English texts ([20]). The study features extensive evaluation and provides empirical evidence that in supporting the application of agreement constraints, animate entity recognition contributes to the better performance in anaphora resolution.[8]

As a result of the above limitations, the *majority of anaphora resolution systems do not operate in fully automatic mode.* In fact, research in anaphora resolution has so far suffered from a bizarre anomaly in that until recently hardly any fully automatic operational systems had been reported: almost all described approaches relied on some kind of pre-editing of the text which was fed to the anaphora resolution algorithm;[9] some of the methods were only manually simulated. As an illustration, Hobbs' naïve approach ([28], [29]) was not implemented in its original version. In [3], [15], [16], and [31] pleonastic pronouns were removed manually[10], whereas in [38] and [21] the outputs of the POS tagger and the NP extractor/partial parser were post-edited in a similar way to [32] where the output of the Slot Unification Grammar parser was corrected manually. Finally, Ge at al's ([23]) and Tetrault's approaches ([60]) made use of an annotated corpus and thus did not perform any pre-processing.

In addressing this challenge, we implemented a fully automatic anaphora resolution system based on Mitkov's ([35], [38]) knowledge-poor approach for English ([53])[11] as well as its fully automatic Bulgarian ([59]) and French ([42]) versions. In addition, for the purpose of evaluation we implemented fully automatic versions of Baldwin's as well as Kennedy and Boguraev's approaches ([7]; see also section 4). Finally, we developed and implemented a fully automatic anaphora resolution system for Japanese ([22]). In a further response to 'the automatic resolution challenge', we

---

[7] British National Corpus.

[8] The experiment was carried out on the pronoun resolution system MARS (see below).

[9] Note that we refer to anaphora resolution systems and do not discuss the coreference resolution systems implemented for MUC-6 and MUC-7.

[10] In addition, Dagan and Itai ([16]) undertook additional pre-editing such as removing sentences for which the parser failed to produce a reasonable parse, cases where the antecedent was not an NP etc.; Kennedy and Boguraev ([31]) manually removed 30 occurrences of pleonastic pronouns (which could not be recognised by their pleonastic recogniser) as well as 6 occurrences of *it* which referred to a VP or prepositional constituent.

[11] The implementation, referred to as MARS in recent publications, was carried out by Richard Evans. MARS incorporated additional antecedent indicators such as parallelism of syntactic functions, due to the ability of the FDG supper tagger used for pre-processing, to return the syntactic functions of the words.

optimised Mitkov's approach using genetic algorithms and benefiting from corpora that we had annotated for coreferential links ([53]).

Our results provide compelling evidence that fully automatic anaphora resolution is more difficult than previous work has suggested. By fully automatic anaphora resolution we mean that there is no human intervention at any stage: such intervention is sometimes large-scale, such as manual simulation of the approach and sometimes smaller-scale, as in the cases where the evaluation samples are stripped of pleonastic pronouns or anaphors referring to constituents other than NPs.

The evaluation of the fully automatic system MARS was carried out on a corpus built on texts from computer manuals. The success rate of 54.65% (323 pronouns out of 591 were resolved correctly) shows that fully automatic anaphora resolution is a very difficult task indeed and is still far from achieving high success rates, mainly due to pre-processing errors (MARS' performance on perfectly analysed input is as high as 90%). After optimisation, the success rate rose to 62.44% (369/591). The success rate was higher for Bulgarian (72.6%, 75.7% after optimisation) and Japanese (75.8%). One possible explanation for the better results in Bulgarian and Japanese is that Bulgarian is much more gender-discriminative and a considerable number of anaphors were resolved after applying gender constraints; the Japanese approach benefited from verb hierarchical structures which pointed with higher reliability to the antecedent.

3   The Need for Annotated Corpora

Since the early 1990s, research and development in both anaphora[12] and coreference resolution[13] has been benefiting from the availability of corpora, both raw and annotated. However, raw corpora have so far made only a limited contribution to the process of anaphora resolution with only Dagan and Itai ([15], [16]) reporting use of them for the purpose of extracting collocation patterns.

Corpora annotated with anaphoric or coreferential links are not widely available, despite being much needed for different methods in anaphora/coreference resolution systems. Corpora of this kind have been used in the training of machine learning algorithms [3]) or statistical approaches ([23]) to anaphora resolution. In other cases, they were used for optimisation of existing approaches ([53]) and their evaluation ([46]). The automatic training and evaluation of anaphora resolution approaches require that the annotation cover anaphoric or coreferential chains and not just single anaphor-antecedent pairs, since the resolution of a specific anaphor would be considered successful if any preceding non-pronominal element of the anaphoric chain associated with that anaphor, is identified. Unfortunately, as aforementioned, anaphorically or coreferentially annotated corpora are not widely available, and those that do exist are not of a large size. The most significant of such resources are the *Lancaster*

---

[12] *Anaphora* is the linguistic phenomenon of pointing back to a previously mentioned item in the text as opposed to *coreference*, which is the act of referring to the same referent in the real world. Note that not all varieties of anaphora have a referring function, such as verb anaphora.

[13] Whereas the task of anaphora resolution has to do with tracking down an antecedent of an anaphor, coreference resolution seeks to identify all coreference classes (chains).

Anaphoric Treebank, a 100 000 word sample of the Associated Press (AP) corpus ([33]), annotated with the UCREL anaphora annotation scheme and featuring a wide variety of phenomena ranging from pronominal and NP anaphora to ellipsis and the generic use of pronouns,[14] and the *annotated data produced for the MUC coreference task* which amounts to approximately 65 000 words[15] and lists coreferential chains from newswire reports on subjects such as corporate buyouts, management takeovers, airline business and plane crashes[16], have been by no means sufficient for the anaphora resolution research community. In 1999, the Research Group in Computational Linguistics at the University of Wolverhampton embarked upon an initially small-scale, but steadily expanding project aiming to partially satisfy this need ([47]).

The need for *annotated corpora* is an outstanding issue which brings about additional issues. The act of annotating corpora follows a specific *annotation scheme*, an adopted methodology as to how to encode linguistic features in a text. The annotation scheme ideally has to deliver wide coverage and should be clear and simple to use: it appears, however, that wide coverage and reliable mark-up are not compatible desiderata. Once an annotation scheme has been proposed to encode linguistic information, user-based tools (referred to as *annotating tools*) have to be developed to apply this scheme to corpus texts, making the annotating process faster and user-friendlier. Finally, the process of annotation will be more efficient if a specific *annotation strategy* is employed.

To address the above challenges fully, we have developed annotating tools for marking coreference ([52]) and put forward an annotation strategy ([47]). One of the annotating tools developed, ClinKA, offers a user-friendly annotation environment for marking coreferential chains and can operate in a semi-automatic mode. The annotation strategy includes guidelines as to which constituents are markables and which are not, and also puts forward suggestions for improving the interannotators' agreement. The annotation scheme adopted is a modified version of the MUC-7 scheme ([27]) that, despite its limitations, appears to be practical enough for our project. Given the complexity of the anaphora and coreference annotation task, we have decided to adopt a less ambitious but clearer approach as to what variety of anaphora to annotate. This move is motivated by the fact that (i) annotating anaphora and coreference in general is a very difficult task and (ii) our aim is to produce annotated data for the most widespread type of anaphora which is the main focus in NLP: that of identity-of-reference direct nominal anaphora featuring a relation of coreference between the anaphors (pronouns, definite descriptions or proper names) and any of their antecedents (non-pronominal NPs).[17] We annotate identity-of-reference direct nominal anaphora, which can be regarded as the class of single-document identity coreference and which includes relationships such as specialisation, generalisation and synonymy, but excludes

---

[14] The Lancaster Anaphoric treebank has not been made publicly available as its production was commercially funded.

[15] This figure is based on data/information kindly provided to us by Nancy Chinchor.

[16] Some of the articles are also about reports on scientific subjects. Management of defence contracts is covered and there are also reports on music concerts, legal matters (lawsuits, etc.) and broadcasting business.

[17] Since the task of anaphora resolution is considered successful if any element of the anaphoric (coreferential) chain preceding the anaphor is identified, our project addresses the annotation of whole anaphoric (coreferential) chains and not only *anaphor-closest antecedent* pairs.

part-of and set membership relations that are considered instances of indirect anaphora. Whilst we are aware that such a corpus will be of less interest in linguistic studies, we believe that the vast majority of NLP work on anaphora and coreference resolution (and all those tasks which rely on it) will be able to benefit from this corpus by using it for evaluation and training purposes. Therefore, we believe that the trade-off of a wide coverage, but complicated and potentially error-prone annotation task with low-consistency across annotations for a simpler, but more reliable annotation task with a NLP-orientated end product is a worthwhile endeavour. The size of the annotated corpora so far amounts to 30 504 words for fully annotated texts (all coreferential chains are marked) and 41 778 for partially annotated data.

In our work we discovered that the interannotators' agreement is a major issue that needs further attention. At one point at the beginning of our project, our two experience annotators scored as little as 65% agreement! A well-thought annotation strategy is a key prerequisite for better agreement, but additional efforts are needed to further improve the other two components of the annotation process: the annotating scheme and the annotating tool.

4 The Resolution Algorithm Issue: Factors in Anaphora Resolution

Despite the extensive work on anaphora resolution so far, there are a number of outstanding issues associated with the factors that form the basis of anaphora resolution algorithms. To start with, we do not know yet if it is possible to propose a core set of factors used in anaphora resolution and if there are factors that we are not fully aware of. Factors are usually divided into *constraints* and *preferences* ([9]) but other authors (e.g. [36]) argue that all factors should be regarded as preferential, giving higher preference to more restrictive factors and lower preference to less "absolute" ones, calling them simply *factors* ([56]), *symptoms* ([34]) or *indicators* ([38]). Mitkov ([42]) shows that the borderline between constraints and preferences is sufficiently blurred and that treating certain factors in an "absolute" way may be too risky.

The impact of different factors and/or their co-ordination have also been investigated by Carter ([12]). He argues that a flexible control structure based on numerical scores assigned to preferences allows greater co-operation between factors as opposed to a more limited depth-first architecture. His discussion is grounded in comparisons between two different implemented systems - SPAR ([11]) and the SRI Core Language Engine ([1]).

In addition to the impact of each factor on the resolution process, factors may have impact on other independent factors. An issue that needs further attention is the "(mutual) dependence" of factors. Dependence/mutual dependence of factors is defined ([36]) in the following way: given the factors x and y, y is taken to be *dependent* on factor x to the extent that the presence of x implies y. Two factors will be termed mutually dependent if each depends on the other. [18]

---

[18] In order to clarify the notion of (mutual) dependence, it would be helpful to view the factors as "symptoms" or "indicators" observed to be "present" or "absent" with the candidate in a certain discourse situation. For instance, if *gender agreement* holds between a candidate for an anaphor and the anaphor itself, we say that the symptom or indicator *gender agreement* is present with this the candidate. Similarly, if the candidate is in a subject position, we say that

The phenomenon of (mutual) dependence has not yet been fully investigated, but we feel that it can play an important role in the process of anaphora resolution, especially in algorithms based on the ranking of preferences. Information on the degree of dependence would be especially welcome in a comprehensive probabilistic model and would be expected to lead to more precise results.

More research is needed to give precise answers to questions such as: "Do factors hold good for all genres?" (which factors are genre specific and which are language general?) and "Do factors hold good for all languages?" (which factors seem to be multilingual and which are restricted to a specific language only?). One tenable position is that factors have general applicability to languages, but that languages will differ in the relative importance of factors, and therefore on their relative weights in the optimal resolution algorithm.[19] For some discussion on these topics see [36] and [42].

Finally, while a number of approaches use a similar set of factors, the "computational strategies" for the application of these factors may differ. The term "computational strategy" refers here to the way factors are employed, i.e. the formulae for their application, interaction, weights etc. Mitkov ([36]) showed that it is not only the optimal selection of factors that matters but also the optimal choice of computational strategy.

5   Evaluation in Anaphora Resolution

There have been a few interesting recent proposals related to the evaluation in anaphora resolution ([5], [8], [37], [39], [40]). Bagga ([5]) proposed a methodology for evaluation of coreference resolution systems that can be directly transferred to anaphora resolution. He classified coreference according to the processing required for resolution, and proposes that evaluation be carried out separately for each of the following classes (listed in ascending order of processing): appositives, predicate nominals, proper names, pronouns, quoted speech pronouns, demonstratives, exact matches, substring matches, identical lexical heads, synonyms and anaphors that require external world knowledge for their resolution.

Byron ([8]) is concerned that most pronoun resolution studies do not detail exactly what types of pronouns (e.g. personal, reflexive, gendered, singular pronouns etc.) they resolve. Therefore, she proposes that the *pronoun coverage* be explicitly reported. Next, she would like to see more information on which types of pronouns have been *excluded* from a specific experiment. Byron explains that it has been common to exclude (i) difficult constructions involving set constructions which are required to interpret pronouns with a split antecedent or cataphora, (ii) pronouns with

---

the symptom *subjecthood* is present. As an illustration consider the example "Mary invited John to the party. He was delighted to accept." In this discourse the symptoms subjecthood, number agreement, entities in non-adjunct phrases are present (among others) with the candidate *Mary*, the symptoms gender agreement, number agreement, entities in non-adjunct phrases are observed with the candidate *John* and finally number agreement and recency are present with the candidate *the party*.

[19] If a specific factor is not applicable to a language, then its importance or weight for this language will be 0.

no antecedents in the discourse such as deictic and generic pronouns, (iii) pronouns which have antecedents different from NPs such as clauses or pronouns representing examples of indirect anaphora[20] and (iv) pronouns excluded due to idiosyncratic reasons imposed by the domain/corpus. In addition to making explicit the pronoun coverage and exclusion categories, Byron suggests that all evaluations of pronoun resolution methods should provide details on the evaluation corpus, on the evaluation set size, and report not only recall/precision but also resolution rate. She proposes that this information be presented in a concise and compact format (table) called standard disclosure ([8]).

We have argued ([40]) that the evaluation of anaphora resolution algorithms and anaphora resolution systems should be carried out separately: it would not be fair to compare the performance of a fully automatic anaphora resolution system with that of an algorithm operating on manually analysed data. Secondly, we have shown ([40]) that recall and precision are imperfect as measures for anaphora resolution algorithms and have proposed the 'clearer' measure of success rate which is computed as the number of correctly resolved anaphors divided by the numbers of all anaphors in the text. In addition, we have also proposed an evaluation package for anaphora resolution approaches and systems consisting of (i) performance measures (ii) comparative evaluation tasks and (iii) component measures ([37], [39], [40]). The performance measures are *success rate, non-trivial success rate* and *critical success rate*. The comparative evaluation tasks include evaluation against *baseline models,* comparison with *similar approaches* and comparison with *classical, 'benchmark' algorithms*. The measures applied to evaluate separate components of the algorithm are *decision power* and *relative importance*.

In order to secure a fair, consistent and accurate evaluation environment, we developed an *evaluation workbench for anaphora resolution* that allows the comparison of anaphora resolution approaches sharing common principles (e.g. POS tagger, NP extractor, parser). The workbench enables the 'plugging in' and testing of anaphora resolution algorithms on the basis of the *same* pre-processing *tools* and *data*. The current version of the evaluation workbench[21] employs one of the best available 'super-taggers' in English - Conexor's FDG Parser ([61]). The workbench also incorporates Evans' ([18], [19]) program for identifying and filtering instances of non-nominal anaphora. The workbench incorporates an automatic scoring system that operates on an SGML input file where the correct antecedents for every anaphor have been marked.

Three approaches that have been extensively cited in the literature were first selected for comparative evaluation by the workbench: Kennedy and Boguraev's parser-free version of Lappin and Leass' RAP ([31]), Baldwin's pronoun resolution method Cogniac which uses limited knowledge ([6]) and Mitkov's knowledge-poor pronoun resolution approach ([38]). All three of these algorithms share a similar pre-processing methodology: they do not rely on a parser to process the input and use instead POS taggers and NP extractors; none of the methods make use of semantic or real-world knowledge. The overall success rate calculated for the 426 anaphoric pronouns found in the texts was 62.5% for MARS, 59.02% for Cogniac and 63.64% for

---

[20] Some of the original terms used by Byron have been replaced with equivalent terms introduced in Chapter 1.

[21] Implemented by Catalina Barbu.

Kennedy and Boguraev's method. In addition to the evaluation system, the workbench also incorporates a basic statistical calculator of the anaphoric occurrences in the input file. The parameters calculated are: the total number of anaphors, the number of anaphors in each morphological category (personal pronoun, noun, reflexive, possessive), the number of inter- and intrasentential anaphors and average number of candidates per anaphor. More details on the current implementation of the evaluation workbench are reported in ([7]).

In spite of the recent progress, we feel that the proposals still fall short of providing a comprehensive and clear picture of the evaluation in anaphora resolution. There are still a number of outstanding issues related to the reliability of the evaluation results that need further attention and one such issue is the statistical significance. We are currently experimenting not only with the selection of random samples, but also with selecting them in such a way that no two anaphors are located within a window of 100 sentences. The question as to how reliable or realistic the obtained performance figures are largely depends on the nature of the data used for evaluation. Some evaluation data may contain anaphors which are more difficult to resolve, such as anaphors that are (slightly) ambiguous and require real-world knowledge for their resolution, or anaphors that have a high number of competing candidates, or that have their antecedents far away both in terms of sentences/clauses and in terms of number of 'intervening' NPs etc. Therefore, we suggest that in addition to the evaluation results, information should be provided as to how difficult the anaphors are to resolve in the evaluation data.[22] To this end, we are working towards the development of suitable and practical measures for quantifying the average 'resolution complexity' of the anaphors in a certain text. For the time being, such measures include simple statistics such as the number of anaphors with more than one candidate, and more generally, the average number of candidates per anaphor, or statistics showing the average distance between the anaphors and their antecedents. We believe that these quantifying measures would be more indicative of how 'easy' or 'difficult' the evaluation data is, and should be provided in addition to the information on the numbers or types of anaphors (e.g. intrasentential vs. intersentential) occurring in the evaluation data.

In addition, most evaluation results are *relative* rather than *absolute*. They are relative either with regard to a specific evaluation data, or relative with regard to the performance of other approaches. It would be helpful to have absolute results too, but this is more difficult to achieve. Evaluation on all naturally occurring texts is an impossible task, but evaluation on the basis of representative or balanced corpora, or suitable sampling, appear to be more realistic. With regard to representativeness it is important that the evaluation corpus be sufficiently balanced and representative from the point of view of each type of anaphora. Even if the approach was developed to process one type of anaphora only, how can one be sure that most anaphors are not always in a similar syntactic or semantic relation to the antecedent and that most anaphors are not resolved after applying one particular rule only?

---

[22] To a certain extent, the critical success rate ([37]) addresses this issue in the evaluation of anaphora resolution algorithms by providing the success rate for the anaphors that are more difficult to resolve.

6   Other Outstanding Issues

Other outstanding issues include the fact that *most people still work mainly on pronoun resolution* despite the fact that there have been good progress in the resolution of NP anaphora ([48], [62], [63]). Also, apart from identity-of-reference direct nominal anaphora and zero anaphora (mainly for Japanese) there has been little work reported for other types of anaphora. However, there have been a few recent attempts to tackle indirect anaphora ([24], [49], [50], [55]).

Another issue that deserves further attention and emerges from the *multilingual context* of recent NLP work as a whole is the development of multilingual anaphora resolution systems. Against the background of a growing interest in multilingual NLP, multilingual anaphora/coreference resolution has gained considerable momentum in the last few years ([2], [4], [26], [43], [45]). One of the challenges in the era of multilingual language processing is to exploit the benefit of multilingual tools and resources for enhancing the efficiency of NLP tasks or applications. The Wolverhampton multilingual anaphora resolution projects include not only adapting a specific approach to other languages as in the case of Mitkov's approach for French ([42]), Bulgarian ([59]), Polish and Arabic ([41]), or developing a new approach for Japanese ([22]), but also include exploiting the strengths of the approach in one language to enhance the performance in another ([44]). The latter is best seen by our 'mutually enhancement strategy' for bilingual pronoun resolution in English and French. It is motivated among other things, by the fact that whereas gender discrimination plays a prominent role in filtering gender-incompatible candidates in French, this is not the case in English. As an illustration, without access to collocation patterns or subcategorisation knowledge, the majority of anaphora resolution approaches would have problems with examples such as 'John puts the cassette in the videoplayer and rewinds it', with the system wrongly selecting the cassette as the antecedent.[23] On the other hand, an anaphora resolution system for French would not have problems processing the equivalent French example 'Jean insère la cassette dans le magnétoscope et la rebobine' and identifying *la cassette* (the cassette) as the correct antecedent of the pronoun *la* - since the other candidate *le magnétoscope* does not match the pronoun in gender. We have developed a bilingual (English/French) anaphora resolution system that features a strategy for mutual enhancement of performance, in that the output of the French module is used to improve resolution in English and vice versa. The 'mutually enhancing' algorithm exploits cases where the English pronoun has been translated as a lexical noun phrase in French or vice versa[24], the gender discrimination in French can help the English module, the English pronoun is resolved reliably by means of intrasentential constraints, the confidence with which antecedents are proposed for each of the languages etc. The English module of the system is the latest

---

[23] The reason why many approaches would prefer the wrong candidate *the cassette* to the correct one *the videoplayer* is because indirect objects and noun phrases that are contained in adverbial prepositional phrases are usually penalised ([32], [38]). Similarly, centering theory regards direct objects as more salient than indirect objects ([64]).

[24] Parallel bilingual English-French corpora are produced in most cases either on the basis of translating an original English text into French or on the basis of translating original French text into English.

implementation of Mitkov's ([38]) knowledge-poor approach to anaphora resolution, referred to as MARS.[25] The French module is an adaptation of Mitkov's aforementioned approach for French which was specially developed for this project. The system operates on bilingual English and French corpora aligned at word level.

Finally, the work on anaphora resolution should provide a suitable *service to the research community*. More has to be done in the way of facilitating researchers working in this field; experience, software and data produced should be readily shared. By way of example, against the background of scarce annotated data, it would be particularly important if the existing resources were shared by the anaphora community. Anaphora resolution programs should be freely available for testing and for integration in larger NLP systems. It should be noted that to date, there are even no anaphora resolution demos yet with the exception of 3 demos set up by the Wolverhampton team. Also, the preparation of a computational archive of papers on anaphora resolution can be regarded as a positive example of service to the community. A preliminary list of downloadable papers is now available at (the list is updated on a regular basis) http://www.wlv.ac.uk/~le1825/download.htm.

7   A Pessimistic Note: Four Traps

NLP in general is very difficult but after working hard on anaphora resolution we have learned that it is *particularly* difficult. We shall briefly outline several traps which deserve special attention and which illustrate the formidable challenges that researchers have to address.

Trap No. 1   Evaluation is conducted against a corpus that is annotated by humans. How reliable can be the evaluation figure if the evaluation corpora cannot be annotated reliably?

Trap No. 2   Inaccurate pre-processing is a chain reaction: usually inaccurate POS tagging affects NP extraction which in turns affects parsing which in turns deteriorates anaphora resolution. If pre-processing is unreliable, is accurate automatic anaphora resolution possible?

Trap No. 3   The resolution of bridging (indirect) anaphora requires semantic or world-knowledge. The lexical or domain resources available are still insufficient.[26]

Trap No. 4   Centering and other discourse theories often rely on anaphora resolution; anaphora resolution relies on them as well.

---

[25] MARS was implemented by Richard Evans ([53]).
[26] Practically with exception of WordNet and EuroWordNet.

8   An Optimistic Voice: The Future Is Not Bleak

The area is difficult but not intractable. Anaphora and coreference resolution have enjoyed increasing attention and have produced promising results (see section 1 of this paper). The growing interest has been demonstrated clearly over the last 5-6 years through the MUC coreference task projects and at a number of related fora. The Discourse Anaphora and Anaphora Resolution Colloquiums (DAARC'96, DAARC'98, DAARC-2000), the successful ACL'97/EACL'97 workshop on operational factors in practical, robust anaphora resolution for unrestricted texts, the strong interest in the COLING'98/ACL'98 tutorial on anaphora resolution, the recent ACL'99 workshops (coreference and its applications; discourse/dialogue structure and reference; towards standards and tools for discourse tagging), the special issues of the journals *Computational Linguistics* and *Machine Translation* and the fact that major NLP conferences over the last few years have featured a number of papers on anaphora resolution (5 papers on anaphora resolution were presented at ACL'2000 only) are only a few of the many examples that serve as evidence.

The promising results obtained so far from implemented systems and the increasing volume of supporting resources and tools will definitely provide distinct opportunities for further advances in the field. All we have to do is work more and hope for slow, but steady progress. We just have to be patient!

References

1. Alshawi, H.: Resolving quasi logical forms. Computational Linguistics, 16:3 (1990)
2. Aone, C., McKee, D.: A language-independent anaphora resolution system for   understanding multilingual texts. In: Proceedings of the 31st Annual Meeting of the ACL (ACL'93), (1993) 156-163
3. Aone, C., Bennett, S.: Evaluating automated and manual acquisition of anaphora resolution rules. In: Proceedings of ACL'95, (1995) 122-129
4. Azzam, S., Humphreys, K., Gaizauskas, R.: Coreference resolution in a multilingual information extraction. In: Proceedings of the Workshop on Linguistic Coreference. Granada, Spain (1998)
5. Bagga, A.: Evaluation of coreferences and coreference resolution systems. In: Proceedings of the Second Colloquium on Discourse Anaphora and Anaphor Resolution (DAARC2), Lancaster, UK (1998) 28-33
6. Baldwin, B.: CogNIAC: high precision coreference with limited knowledge and linguistic resources. In: Proceedings of the ACL'97/EACL'97 workshop on Operational factors in practical, robust anaphora resolution Madrid, Spain (1997) 38-45
7. Barbu, C., Mitkov. R.: Evaluation environment for anaphora resolution. In: Proceedings of the International Conference on Machine Translation and Multilingual Applications (MT2000), Exeter, UK. (2000) 18.1-18.8
    8. Byron, D.: A proposal for consistent evaluation of pronoun resolution algorithms. (2001) (forthcoming)
9. Carbonell, J., Brown R.: Anaphora Resolution: a Multi-Strategy Approach. In: Proceedings of the 12. International Conference on Computational Linguistics (COLING'88), Vol.I, Budapest, Hungary (1988) 96-101
10. Cardie, C.,Wagstaff, K: Noun phrase coreference as clustering. In: Proceedings of the 1999 Joint SIGDAT conference on Empirical Methods in NLP and Very Large Corpora (ACL'99) University of Maryland, USA. (1999) 82-89

11. Carter, D.: Interpreting Anaphora in Natural Language Texts. Ellis Horwood, Chichester (1987)
12. Carter, D.: Control issues in anaphor resolution. In: Journal of Semantics, 7, (1990) 435-454
13. Collins, M.: Three generative, lexicalised models for statistical parsing. In: Proceedings of the 35th Annual Meeting of the ACL (ACL'97) Madrid, Spain (1997) 16-23
14. Daelemans, W., Zavarel, J., van der Slot, K., van den Bosch, A.: Timbl: Tilburg Memory Based Learner, version 2.0. Reference guide, ilk technical report ILK, Tilburg University (1999) 99-01
15. Dagan, I. and Itai, A.: Automatic processing of large corpora for the resolution of anaphora references. In: Proceedings of the 13th International Conference on Computational Linguistics (COLING'90), Vol. III, 1-3, Helsinki, Finland (1990) 1-3
16. Dagan, I., Itai, A.: A statistical filter for resolving pronoun references. In: Y.A. Feldman, Y.A, Bruckstein, A (eds): Artificial Intelligence and Computer Vision, Elsevier Science Publishers B.V. (North-Holland) (1991) 125-135
17. Denber, M.: Automatic resolution of anaphora in English. Internal Report. Eastman Kodak Co. (1988)
18. Evans, R.: A Comparison of Rule-Based and Machine Learning Methods for Identifying Non-nominal It. In: Natural Language Processing-NLP2000, Second International Conference Proceedings, Lecture Notes in Artificial Intelligence, Springer-Verlag, (2000) 233-242
19. Evans, R.: Applying machine learning toward an automatic classification of it. In: Literary and Linguistic Computing (2001) (forthcoming)
20. Evans, R, Orasan, C.: Improving anaphora resolution by identifying animate entities in texts. In: Proceedings of the Discourse, Anaphora and Reference Resolution Conference (DAARC2000). Lancaster, UK. (2000)
21. Ferrandez, A., Palomar. M., Moreno L.: Slot unification grammar and anaphora resolution. In: Proceedings of the International Conference on Recent Advances in Natural Language Proceeding (RANLP'97) Tzigov Chark, Bulgaria (1997) 294-299
22. Fukumoto, F.,Yamada, H, Mitkov, R.: Resolving overt pronouns in Japanese using hierarchical VP structures. In: Proceedings of Corpora and NLP Monastir, Tunisia. (2000) 152-157
23. Ge, N., Hale, J., Charniak, E.: A statistical approach to anaphora resolution. In: Proceedings of the Workshop on Very Large Corpora. Montreal. Canada. (1998) 161-170
24. Gelbukh, A., Sidorov G.: On Indirect Anaphora Resolution. In: Proceedings of PACLING-99, Waterloo, Ontario, Canada, (1999) 181-190
25. Grishman, R.: Information extraction. In: Mitkov R., Oxford Handbook of Computational Linguistics, Oxford University Press (2001) (forthcoming)
26. Harabagiu, S., Maiorano, S. J: Multilingual Coreference Resolution. In: Proceedings of ANLP-NAACL2000 (2000) 142-149
27. Hirschman, L.: MUC-7 coreference task definition. Version 3.0 (1997)
28. Hobbs, J. R.: Pronoun resolution. Research Report 76-1. New York: Department of Computer Science, City University of New York (1976)
29. Hobbs, J. R.: Resolving pronoun references. Lingua, 44 (1978) 339-352.
30. Kameyama, M.: Recognizing referential links: an information extraction perspective. In: Proceedings of the ACL'97/EACL'97 workshop on Operational factors in practical, robust anaphora resolution Madrid, Spain (1997) 46-53
31. Kennedy, C. Boguraev, B.: Anaphora for everyone: pronominal anaphora resolution without a parser. In: Proceedings of the 16th International Conference on Computational Linguistics (COLING'96) Copenhagen, Denmark (1996) 113-118
32. Lappin, S., Leass, H.: An algorithm for pronominal anaphora resolution, Computational Linguistics, 20(4), (1994) 535-561
33. Leech, G. and Garside, R.: Running a grammar factory: the production of syntactically analysed corpora or "treebanks". In: Johannsson, S., Stenstrom, A. (eds.), English Com-

puter Corpora: Selected Papers and Research Guide. Mouton De Gruyter, Berlin (1991) 15-32

34. Mitkov, R.: An uncertainty reasoning approach for anaphora resolution. In: Proceedings of the Natural Language Processing Pacific Rim Symposium (NLPRS'95), Seoul, Korea (1995) 149-154

35. Mitkov, R.: Pronoun resolution: the practical alternative. Paper presented at the Discourse Anaphora and Anaphor Resolution Colloquium (DAARC), Lancaster, UK (1996). Also appeared in: Botley, S., McEnery, T. (eds): Corpus-based and computational approaches to discourse anaphora. John Benjamins, Amsterdam/Philadelphia (2000)189-212

36. Mitkov, R.: Factors in anaphora resolution: they are not the only things that matter. A case study based on two different approaches. In: Proceedings of the ACL'97/EACL'97 workshop on Operational factors in practical, robust anaphora resolution, Madrid, Spain (1997) 14-21

37. Mitkov, R.: Evaluating anaphora resolution approaches. In: Proceedings of the Discourse Anaphora and Anaphora Resolution Colloquium (DAARC'2). Lancaster, UK (1998)

38. Mitkov, R.: Robust pronoun resolution with limited knowledge. In: Proceedings of the 18.th International Conference on Computational Linguistics (COLING'98)/ACL'98 Conference Montreal, Canada (1998) 869-875

39. Mitkov, R.: Towards more consistent and comprehensive evaluation in anaphora resolution. In: Proceedings of LREC'2000, Athens, Greece, (2000) 1309-1314

40. Mitkov, R.: Towards more consistent and comprehensive evaluation of robust anaphora resolution algorithms and systems. Invited talk. In: Proceedings of the Discourse, Anaphora and Reference Resolution Conference (DAARC2000), (forthcoming). Lancaster, UK (2000)

41. Mitkov, R.: Multilingual anaphora resolution. Machine Translation. (2000) (forthcoming)

42. Mitkov, R.: Anaphora resolution. Longman (2001) (forthcoming).

43. Mitkov, R., Stys, M.: Robust reference resolution with limited knowledge: high precision genre-specific approach for English and Polish. In: Proceedings of the International Conference "Recent Advances in Natural Language Proceeding" (RANLP'97) Tzigov Chark, Bulgaria (1997) 74-81

44. Mitkov, R., Barbu, C.: Improving pronoun resolution in two languages by means of bilingual corpora. In : Proceedings of the Discourse, Anaphora and Reference Resolution Conference (DAARC 2000), Lancaster, UK. (2000)

45. Mitkov, R., Belguith, L., Stys, M.: Multilingual robust anaphora resolution. In: Proceedings of the Third International Conference on Empirical Methods in Natural Language Processing (EMNLP-3) . Granada, Spain (1998) 7-16

46. Mitkov, R., Orasan, C., and Evans, R.: The importance of annotated corpora for NLP: the cases of anaphora resolution and clause splitting. In: Proceedings of "Corpora and NLP: Reflecting on Methodology Workshop". TALN'99, Corsica, France (1999) 60-69

47. Mitkov, R., Evans, R., Orasan, C., Barbu, C., L. Jones, L., Sotirova, V.: Coreference and anaphora: developing annotating tools, annotated resources and annotation strategies. In: Proceedings of the Discourse, Anaphora and Reference Resolution Conference (DAARC2000). Lancaster, UK. (2000)

48. Munoz, R., Palomar, M.: Processing of Spanish definite description with the same head. In: Proceedings of NLP'2000, Patras, Greece (2000) 212-220

49. Munoz, R., Saiz-Noeda, M., Suárez, A., Palomar, M.: Semantic approach to bridging reference resolution. In: Proceedings of the International Conference Machine Translation and Multilingual Applications (MT2000) Exeter, UK. (2000) 17-1-17-8

50. Murata, M., Nagao, M.: Indirect reference in Japanese sentences. In: Botley, S., McEnery, T. (eds): Corpus-based and computational approaches to discourse anaphora. John Benjamins, Amsterdam/Philadelphia (2000) 211-226

51. Nasukawa, T.: Robust method of pronoun resolution using full-text information. In: Proceedings of the 15th International Conference on Computational Linguistics (COLING'94) Kyoto, Japan (1994) 1157-1163
52. Orasan, C.: CLinkA – a coreferential links annotator. In: Proceedings of the Second International Conference on Language Resources and Evaluation (LREC'2000), Athens, Greece (2000)
53. Orasan C., Evans R., and Mitkov R.: Enhancing Preference-Based Anaphora Resolution with Genetic Algorithms, In Proceedings of NLP'2000, Patras, Greece (2000) 185-1
54. Paice, C.D., Husk, G.D.: Towards the automatic recognition of anaphoric features in English text: the impersonal pronoun 'it'". In: Computer Speech and Language, 2, (1987) 109-132
55. Poesio, M., Vieira, R., Teufel, S.: Resolving bridging references in unrestricted text. In: Proceedings of the ACL'97/EACL'97 workshop on Operational factors in practical, robust anaphora resolution, Madrid, Spain (1997) 1-6
56. Preuß S., Schmitz, B., Hauenschild, C., Umbach, U.: Anaphora Resolution in Machine Translation. Studies in Machine Translation and Natural Language Processing. In: Ramm, W.(ed) : (Vol. 6 "Text and content in Machine Translation: Aspects of discourse representation and discourse processing"): Luxembourg: Office for Official Publications of the European Community (1994) 29-52
57. Rich, E., LuperFoy S.: An Architecture for Anaphora Resolution. In: Proceedings of the Second Conference on Applied Natural Language Processing (ANLP-2), Austin, Texas, U.S.A. (1988) 18-24
58. Sidner, C.: Toward a computational theory of definite anaphora comprehension in English. Technical report No. AI-TR-537. MIT Press, Cambridge, Massachussetts (1979)
59. Tanev, H., Mitkov, R.:LINGUA - a robust architecture for text processing and anaphora resolution in Bulgarian. In: Proceedings of the International Conference on Machine Translation and Multilingual Applications (MT2000), Exeter, UK. (2000) 20.1-20.8.
60. Tetreault, J. R.: Analysis of Syntax-Based Pronoun Resolution Methods. In: Proceedings of the 37th Annual Meeting of the Association for Computational Linguistics, Maryland, USA. (1999) 602-605
61. Tapanainen, P., T. Jarvinen, T.: A non-projective Dependency Parser. In: Proceedings of the 5th Conference of Applied Natural Language Processing, ACL, USA. (1997) 64-71
62. Vieira, R., Poesio, M.: Processing definite descriptions in corpora In: Botley, S., McEnery, T. (eds): Corpus-based and computational approaches to discourse anaphora. John Benjamins, Amsterdam/Philadelphia (2000a) 189-212
63. Vieira, R., Poesio, M.: An empirically-based system for processing definite descriptions. In: Computational Linguistics (2000b) 26(4).
64. Walker, M., Joshi, A., Prince, E.: Centering in naturally occurring discourse: an overview. In: Walker, M., Joshi, A., Prince, E. (eds): Centering theory in discourse. Clarendon Press, Oxford (1998)
65. Williams, S., Harvey, M., Preston, K.: Rule-based reference resolution for unrestricted text using part-of-speech tagging and noun phrase parsing. In: Proceedings of the International Colloquium on Discourse Anaphora and Anaphora Resolution (DAARC), Lancaster, UK. (1996) 441-456

PHORA: A NLP System for Spanish

Manuel Palomar, Maximiliano Saiz-Noeda, Rafael Muñoz, Armando Suárez,
Patricio Martínez-Barco, and Andrés Montoyo

Dpto. Lenguajes y Sistemas Informáticos, Universidad de Alicante, Spain
{mpalomar,max,rafael,armando,patricio,montoyo}@dlsi.ua.es

Abstract. In this paper we present a whole Natural Language Processing (NLP) system for Spanish. The core of this system is the parser, which
uses the grammatical formalism Lexical-Functional Grammars (LFG).
The system uses the Specification Marks Method in order to resolve the
lexical ambiguity. Another important component of this system is the
anaphora resolution module. To solve the anaphora, this module contains a method based on linguistic information (lexical, morphological,
syntactic and semantic), structural information (anaphoric accessibility
space in which the anaphor obtains the antecedent) and statistical information. This method is based on constraints and preferences and solves
pronouns and definite descriptions. Moreover, this system fits dialogue
and non-dialogue discourse features. The anaphora resolution module
uses several resources, such as a lexical database (Spanish WordNet) to
provide semantic information and a POS tagger providing the part of
speech for each word and its root to make this resolution process easier.
Keywords: Anaphora resolution, semantics, LFG grammar and parsing,
EuroWordNet, WSD.

1   Introduction

It is necessary to have adequate information sources in order to develope a
suitable mechanism for anaphora resolution. In the course of the last years,
numerous researches have concentrated their efforts on solving the problem of
lexical and morphological analysis. Also, they have been worked on the obtaining
of universal information sources to provide the information adapted to each
problem. With reference to the addition of semantic information in the resolution
of linguistic phenomena, it is not easy to find references and resources that
provide succesfull results.

The system presented in this work combines a set of tools (taggers, parser)
and uses a combination of information sources to anaphora resolution (linguistic
and structural information).

Summarizing, we propose a NLP system that counts on as much information
sources as possible for the anaphora resolution. We think that the base of the
language processing is the information used for it.

Next section shows the main aspects of the anaphora phenomenon. Following,
the paper gives a detailed description of the NLP system and all the processes

A. Gelbukh (Ed.): CICLing 2001, LNCS 2004, pp. 126–139, 2001.

and resources related to it. After that, the constraint-based mechanism for the anaphora resolution and the required information sources are explained. Finally, some conclusions of this work and the work in progress are presented.

2   The Problem

We commonly use different expressions to refer to a person, an object, an event, a place or a process. These expressions usually used in this way are, among others, pronouns and definite descriptions[1]. But, the latter not always make reference to a linguistic entity previously mentioned. In this case, the definite description introduces a new entity into the discourse.

This new entity (person, object, event, place or event) is called *candidate* of the next anaphoric expressions. The candidates are noun phrases, verbal phrases, full sentences or text fragments. According to Eckert and Strube [6], if the antecedent is a noun phrase then the anaphora is classified as *individual anaphora*, otherwise, the anaphora is classified as *abstract anaphora*.

Moreover, different kinds of relations can be found between the antecedent and the anaphoric expression (pronoun and definite description). These relations can be *parts of*, *sct-subsct* and *set-member* for definite descriptions and *identity* for both pronouns and definite descriptions. Another difference between pronouns and definite descriptions is the *accessibility space* (see section 4.5) used to solve the references. Pronouns use a shorter accessibility space than definite description because the former don't provide semantic information.

In this paper we only treat identity relations between the antecedent and the anaphoric expression, particularly those whose antecedent is a noun phrase (individual anaphora).

Pronouns and definite descriptions can be classified into different types. Pronouns are divided into personal, demonstrative, reflexive and omitted pronouns (zero-pronouns) in third person in Spanish. Personal and demonstrative pronouns are classified according to whether they are included in a prepositional phrase (PP) or not and whether they are complement personal pronouns. Moreover, the antecedents (noun phrases) can be divided into intrasentential and intersentential. Definite descriptions are divided into non-anaphoric and anaphoric definite descriptions. The former introduce a new entity discourse while the latter refers to a previous antecedent. A complete classification of definite description has been developed by several authors, such as Hawkins [8], Christopherson [3] for English language and Muñoz et al. [17] for Spanish language.

The following examples give a short view of the different types of anaphora above mentioned:

– *Complement personal pronoun.*
  Ana abre la puerta y la cierra tras de sí.
  Ana opens the door and closes it after herself.

---

[1] Rusell [19] called definite descriptions to definite noun phrases. That is, noun phrases headed by definite article or demonstratives, such as *the newspaper* or *this journal*

- *Personal pronouns not included in a PP.*
  <u>Andrés</u> es mi vecino. <u>Él</u> vive en el segundo.
  Andrés is my neighbor. He lives on the second floor.
- *Personal pronouns included in a PP.*
  <u>Juan</u> debe asistir pero Pedro lo hará por <u>él</u>.
  Juan must attend but Pedro will do it for him.
- *Demonstrative Pronoun not included in a PP.*
  <u>Pedro</u> está enfadado con Antonio. <u>Éste</u> no le habla.
  Pedro is angry with Antonio. He doesn't speak to him.
- *Demonstrative Pronoun included in a PP.*
  Ana vive con <u>Paco</u> y cocina para <u>él</u> cada día.
  Ana lives with Paco and cooks for him everyday.
- *Reflexive Pronoun.*
  <u>Ana</u> abre la puerta y la cierra tras de <u>sí</u>.
  Ana opens the door and closes it after herself.
- *Omitted pronoun (zero pronouns).*
  <u>Ana</u> abre la puerta y <u>Ø</u> la cierra tras de sí.
  Ana opens the door and closes it after herself.
- *Definite description with the same head its antecedent.*
  <u>La casa</u> de la playa es preciosa ... Era <u>la casa</u> de un médico.
  The house in the beach is beutifull .. It was the house of a doctor.
- *Bridging reference[2].*
  <u>Los soldados</u> irrumpieron en la ciudad. <u>Esos bravos hombres</u> mataron a los luchadores de la guerrilla.
  The soldiers burst into the town. Those brave men killed the guerrilla fighters.

Next section shows the different resources used by the PHORA system.

3   Resources

The system uses the following resources:

- **EuroWordNet.** WordNet (WN), as described by Miller et *al.* [13], is an electronic dictionary that stores sets of synonyms. Each set of synonyms - synset - describes a semantic concept and contains a list of pairs (word - sense number) and several pointers to others synsets as semantic relations. So, meanings of a word are stored in WordNet as synsets, one per sense. Furthermore, each synset can have a definition or gloss, like conventional dictionaries.
  EuroWordNet (EWN) [23] is a recent development based on the English WordNet 1.5. Briefly, EWN consists of a set of different WordNets for various languages (English, Dutch, Spanish, Italian, German, French, Czech

---

[2] Clark [4] called bridging descriptions to definite descriptions that either have an antecedent denoting the same discourse entity, but using a different head noun (synonym, hypernym or hyponym) or are related by other relation than identity

and Estonian) and an inter-lingual index that links the synsets of each language with the synsets in the English WN. In most cases, these synsets have the same meaning. Recently, WordNets in other languages have been developed. Like WN1.5, each WN in EWN maintains a set of pointers between synsets as a representation of heterogeneous semantic relations like hypernym/hyponym between nouns. Moreover, the hyper/hyponimy relation establishes a basic ontology (Top Ontology) common to all the languages, classifying the synsets in a conceptual category.

EuroWorNet will be used as a base resource for semantic tagging in order to apply semantic knowledge to the anaphora resolution process through semantic patterns and semantic constraints an preferences.

- **WSD module.** In order to help many NLP tasks, particularly anaphora resolution, a WSD Module is being used. This module follows the proposal of Montoyo and Palomar [14], which consist of a method for the automatic disambiguating of nouns in texts, using the notion of Specification Marks and employing the noun taxonomy of the spanish WordNet lexical knowledge base [12]. The method resolves the lexical ambiguity of nouns in any sort of text, and although it relies on the semantic relations (Hypernymy and Hyponymy) and the hierarchic organization of WordNet, it does not, however, require any sort of training process, no hand-coding of lexical entries, nor the hand-tagging of texts.

- **Parser.** The parser takes different input sources. On the one hand, it receives the output of a POS tagger that provides, for each word in the analysed corpus, its morphological features (gender, number, person, verbal tense,...). On the other hand, the parser takes as input the output of the semantic tagger. The parser uses the grammatical formalism LFG for the analysis process.

- **LFG Grammar.** Dalrymple *et al* [5] say that LFG assumes two syntactic levels of representation. Constituent structure (c-structure) encodes phrasal dominance and precedence relations, and is represented as a phrase structure tree. Functional structure (f-structure) encodes syntactic predicate-argument structure, and is represented as an attribute-value matrix.

F-structure consists of a collection of attributes, such as PRED, SUBJ, OBJ or IOBJ, whose values can be other f-structures. In this paper, we present the structures suitable for pronouns and definite descriptions, which are the required components for the anaphora resolution.

Figure 1 shows the output of the parser using the gramatical formalism LFG.

- **The anaphoric accessibility space.** NLP researchers have proposed a lot of mechanisms to solve the anaphora problem focusing their interest in the choice of the adequate antecedent among a list of candidates. However, there is a lack of studies performing a proposal about anaphoric accessibility space, that is the space where the system can found this list of candidates in each kind of anaphora. This definition has a great importance in the remaining process because definitions of anaphoric accessibility space which are too short cause the removal of valid antecedents for the anaphor. On the other hand, definitions of anaphoric accessibility space which are too large

Sentence: *"Portugal ha vivido en torno a su equipo"*

```
S[ aTree : "[[ProperNoun]NP
            [AuxVerb MainVerb]VC
            [Preposition
                [[[PossessiveAdj]Det]
                 Determine Noun]NP
            ]PP
    ]S",

adjunct : <:
    PP[
        head : Noun[
                exp : "equipo",
                lex : LexMorph,
                infl : InflMorph[
                        number : #143=Singular,
                        gender : #141=Masculine]],
        mod : ADJP,
        prep : Preposition[
                exp : "en_torno_a"],
        spec : Determine[
                number : #143,
                gender : #141,
                det : Det[
                        number : #143,
                        gender : #141,
                        head : PossessiveAdj[
                                exp : "su",
                                lex : LexMorph,
                                infl : InflMorph[
                                        number : #143,
                                        gender : #141]]],
                postdet : Null,
                predet : Null]]:>,
head : VC[
        tense : #293=Present,
        number : #283=Singular,
        mod1 : AuxVerb[
                exp : "haber",
                infl : InflMorph[
                        tense : Present,
                        person : Third,
                        number : Singular,
                        mood : Indicative]],
        head : MainVerb[
                exp : "vivir",
                lex : LexMorph[
                        subcat : #252=Transitive],
                infl : InflMorph[
                        tense : #293,
                        number : #283,
                        mood : Participle]],
        cat : #252],
subject : NP[
        number : #283,
        head : ProperNoun[
                exp : "portugal"]]]
```

Fig. 1. *Parser output*

cause large candidate lists, where failure probabilities in anaphora resolution increase.

Anaphora resolution systems based on linguistic knowledge usually define an accessibility space using n previous sentences to the anaphor, where n is variable according to the kind of anaphora. However, this definition is arbitrary and there are not structural reasons for it.

In Martínez-Barco and Palomar [10], a study about the anaphoric accessibility space is presented. This study shows that antecedents of pronominal and adjectival anaphors in Spanish can almost always be found in the set of noun phrases taken from the anaphoric accessibility space, defining this space according to an structure based on adjacency pairs and topics.

According to Fox [7] the first mention of a referent in a sequence is done with a full noun phrase. After that, by using an anaphor the speaker displays an understanding that sequence has not been closed down. The author shows that two different sequences generate most of the anaphors to be found in dialogues: the adjacency pair and the topic scope. The former generates references to any local noun phrase, and the latter generates references to the main topic of the dialogue.

Based on this, the anaphoric accessibility space is proposed as the set of noun phrases taken from:

- the same adjacency pair as the anaphor, and
- the previous adjacency pair to the anaphor, and
- another adjacency pair including the anaphor adjacency pair, and
- the noun phrase representing the main topic of the dialogue.

According to this study, 95.9% of the antecedents were located in the proposed anaphoric accessibility space. Remaining antecedents (4.1%) were estimated to be located in subtopics of the dialogues.

Besides, this study shows the importance of defining the adequate anaphoric accessibility space for each kind of anaphora, and also for each kind of discourse.

4 PHORA System

PHORA system is a whole Natural Language Processing system made up by three main modules as shown in figure 2. The core of this system is the parser which uses the grammatical formalism Lexical-Functional Grammars (LFG). Another important component of this system is the anaphora resolution module. To solve the anaphora, this module contains a method based on linguistic information (lexical, morphological, syntactic and semantic), structural information (anaphoric accessibility space in which the anaphor obtains the antecedent) and statistical information. This method is based on constraints and preferences and solves pronouns and definite descriptions. Moreover, this system fits dialogue and non-dialogue discourse features.

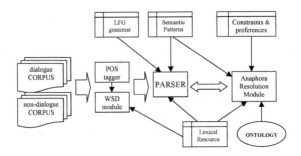

Fig. 2. *PHORA System Architecture*

4.1 Method with Specification Marks to WSD

Our method consists basically of the automatic sense-disambiguating of nouns that appear within the context of a sentence and whose different possible senses are quite related. Its context is the group of words that co-occur with it in the sentence and their relationship to the noun to be disambiguated. The disambiguation is resolved with the use of the Spanish WordNet lexical knowledge base.

The intuition underlying this approach is that the more similar two words are, the more informative the most specific concept that subsumes them both will be. In other words, their lowest upper bound in the taxonomy. (A "concept" here, corresponds to a Specification Mark (SM)). In other words, the more information two concepts share in common, the more similar they obviously are, and the information commonly shared by two concepts is indicated by the concept that subsumes them in the taxonomy.

The input for the WSD module will be the group of words $W = \{W_1, W_2, ..., W_n\}$. Each word wi is sought in WordNet, each one has an associated set $Si = \{S_{i1}, S_{i2}, ..., S_{in}\}$ of possible senses. Furthermore, each sense has a set of concepts in the IS-A taxonomy (hypernymy/Hyponymy relations). First, the concept that is common to all the senses of all the words that form the context is sought. We call this concept the Initial Specification Mark (ISM), and if it does not immediately resolve the ambiguity of the word, we descend from one level to another through WordNet´s hierarchy, assigning new Specification Marks. The number of concepts that contain the subhierarchy will then be counted for each Specification Mark. The sense that corresponds to the Specification Mark with highest number of words will then be chosen as the sense disambiguation of the noun in question, within its given context.

To illustrate graphically how the word (W_1) is disambiguated, in Figure 1 the word (W_1) has four different senses and several word contexts.

In the above figure, it can be seen that the Initial Specification Mark does not resolve the lexical ambiguity of the word W_1 since it appears in three subhierarchies with different senses. The Specification Mark with the symbol (*) however, contains the highest number of words from the context (three) and

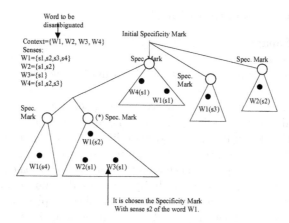

Fig. 3. *Intuitive example of Specification Marks algorithm.*

will therefore be the one chosen to resolve the sense S_2 of the word W_1. The words W_2 and W_3 are also disambiguated by choosing their respective senses S_1. W_4 has not been successfully disambiguated, as it lies outside the scope of the application of the heuristics.

Improvement At this point, we should like to point out that after having evaluated the method, we subsequently discovered that it could be improved, providing even better results in disambiguation. We therefore define three heuristics:

– Heuristic of Hypernym: This heuristic solves the ambiguity of those words that are not directly related in WordNet but the word that is forming the context, is in some composed synset of a hypernymy relationship for some sense of the word to be disambiguated. To disambiguate a given word, all of the other words included in the context in the hypernyms synsets of each of its senses are checked, and a weight is assigned to it in accordance with its depth within the sub-hierarchy, and the sense that carries the greater weight is chosen. In the case of there being several senses with the same weight, we apply the following heuristic.
– Heuristic of Common Specification Mark: With this heuristic, the problem of fine-grainedness is solved. To disambiguate the word, the first Specification Mark that is common to the resulting senses of the above heuristic is checked. As this is the most informative of the senses, it is chosen. By means of this heuristic one it is tried to solve the problem of the fine grainedness of WordNet´s sense distinguishes, since in most of the cases, the senses of the words to be disambiguated differ very little in nuances, and as the context is a rather general one it is not possible arrive at the most accurate sense.

4.2   Anaphora Resolution Module

Our method of anaphora resolution within this module, is based on constraints and preferences that are extracted from linguistic and structural sources. The method solves the anaphora phenomena both in dialogue and non-dialogue discourses.

The method uses an anaphoric accessibility space in order to extract the list of possible candidates to be the solution of the anaphor. This anaphoric accessibility space varies depending on the kind of discourse (dialogue or non-dialogue) and the kind of anaphora (pronoun or definite description). Anaphora resolution in dialogues uses an anaphoric accessibility space based on the dialogue structure. However, the anaphoric accessibility space used in non-dialogue discourse is based on a window of sentences when it is applied to pronouns and is based on the previous full text when applied to definite descriptions [11].

Next, we will describe our sets of constraints and preference that are defined for each kind of discourse and for each kind of anaphor. Finally, the system that manages these sets will be shown.

The sets of constraints and preferences are based on different kinds of knowledge, excepting the discourse structure-based knowledge that requires not only semantic knowledge but also word knowledge and an almost perfect parsing [1].

Like in the known systems that are based in constraints and preferences, the former eliminate all the candidates that disagree with the anaphor, while the latter treats to establish the preference order among the candidates that have been "survived" to the constraints. Next subsections describe the constraints and the preferences used in the system.

Constraints

- *Morphological constraints:* Morphological constraints establish gender, number and person parallelisms that demand the compatibility or agreement between the antecedent and the anaphoric pronoun. If the anaphoric expression is a definite description this constrain is not applied because the correct antecedent and the definite description can have different morphological structure.
- *Syntactic constraints:* Syntactic constraints are based on the well-known non-coreference conditions by Lappin and Leass [9]. We propose conditions for NP-pronoun non-coreference adapted for Spanish. A pronoun is non-coreferential with a noun phrase (NP) if any of the non-coreference conditions are fulfilled. These conditions relate reflexive, demonstrative and personal pronouns with their syntactic role and position in the sentence, as can be seen in Palomar *et al* [18].
- *Semantic constraints:*
  Semantic knowledge is applied for the anaphora resolution method in two different ways. On the one hand, for pronoun resolution, from the semantic features associated to each antecedent NP, semantic constraints eliminate those candidates that are not compatible with the verb of the sentence in

which the anaphoric expression appears. So, in this case, the compatibility is not determined directly by the anaphoric expression, but by the verb that it accompanies. Subsection 4.3 makes a further detailed explanation of the pattern learning method that is used to determine the verb compatibility.

On the other hand, semantic relations such as synonym, hypernym, hyponym and meronym are applied between both antecedent and definite description in order to provide the candidates.

Preferences According to the kind of discourse and the kind of anaphor a subset of preferences will be applied.

- **Repetition.** Candidates with the same head noun as their definite description and with the same pre and post-modifiers. This preference is used to solve references produced by definite descriptions. The preferences used to solve definite description can be seen in Muñoz et al. [15] and Muñoz and Palomar [16].
- **Same Head.** Candidates with the same head noun as their definite description and with pre and post-modifiers semantically related. This preference is used to solve references produced by definite descriptions.
- **Related Semantically Head.** Candidates with a head noun semantically related with the head noun of definite description. This preference is used to solve references produced by definite descriptions.
- **Role Agent.** Candidates that are related with the verb of the sentence in which the definite description appears. If this relationship is direct, then candidates with a subject syntactic function are preferred. Otherwise, if this relationship is indirect, then those with a complement function are preferred. This preference is used to solve references produced by definite descriptions.
- **Same Adjacency Pair.** Candidates that are in the same AP as the anaphor. This preference is used to solve references produced by pronouns in dialogues.
- **Previous Adjacency Pair.** Candidates that are in the previous AP to the anaphor. This preference is used to solve references produced by pronouns in dialogues.
- **Nested Adjacency Pair.** Those candidates that are in the most recent unclosed AP. This preference is used to solve references produced by pronouns in dialogues.
- **Same Position with reference to the verb.** Those candidates that are in the same position with reference to the verb as the anaphor (before or after). This preference is used to solve references produced by pronouns.
- **Same Syntactic Position.** Those candidates in the same syntactic position as the anaphor. This preference is used to solve references produced by pronouns.
- **Closest.** Nearest candidate. This preference is used by any kind of anaphoric expression and discourse. Moreover, this preference guarantees that only one candidate will be selected at the end of the process. This candidate will be the antecedent proposed.

4.3   Pattern Learning Method

For defining the semantic structure of a sentence, we have considered a set of patterns formed by the semantic concepts associated to the main elements in the aforesaid sentence. This way, the objective of this method is to extract a set of *subject noun-verb* and *verb-complement noun* patterns from each sentence. The patterns will be formed by the semantic or ontological concepts of the noun phrase head (subject or complement) and predicate verbal phrase head. For the pattern construction, the Spanish version of the lexical resource WordNet, within the EuroWordNet proyect described by Vossen [23] has been chosen. WordNet provides a main level of ontological concepts to describe all the words contained in the knowledge base. These concepts are 25 for nouns and 15 for verbs and they get the main semantic characteristic of each word sense. These concepts are:

- *Nouns*: act, animal, artifact, attribute, body, cognition, communication, event, feeling, food, group, location, motive, object, person, phenomenon, plant, possession, process, quantity, relation, shape, state, substance and time
- *Verbs*: body, change, cognition, communication, competition, consumption, contact, creation, emotion, motion, perception, possession, social, stative and weather

For the pronoun resolution system, it is important to define the concept of compatibility between a noun (subject or complement) and a verb. This compatibility will allow choosing the correct antecedent of an anaphora among a group of noun phrases, being the correct antecedent the one with the highest compatibility degree. For example, taking the verb comer(*to eat*) and two noun phrases la piedra (*the stone*) and el león (*the lion*), the patterns generated by both nouns and the verb are *object-consumption* and *animal-consumption*. Intuitively, we can deduce that the second pattern defines elements as semantically more compatible. So, if both noun phrases comprise an antecedent list of an anaphoric expression with the verb comer, it is possible to say that, from the semantic point of view, el león can be the correct antecedent because of its compatibility.

4.4   Anaphora Resolution Process

The anaphora resolution module uses as input the output of the parser. This output is made up by different kind of information (morphological, syntactic and semantic) for each word and for each group of word (chunks). The anaphora resolution module uses this information to apply a set of constraints and preferences. Depending on the kind of discourse (dialogue or non-dialogue) and the kind of anaphoric expression (pronoun or definite description), the module uses a different set of constraints and preferences. But, the method to be applied is the same without bearing this difference in mind.

Once the morphological, syntactical and semantic constraints have been applied, if there is only one candidate left, it is chosen as the correct antecedent of the pronoun.

Otherwise, a set of preferences are applied to provide the antecedent of anaphora. In this line, we can remark the use of a set of semantic criteria based on the semantic patterns and the semantic structure above mentioned is applied.

The use of these patterns is double. We can use this semantic information as a constraint and also as a preference. It depends on the compatibility degree between the anaphora and the antecedent. It is considered that a compatibility degree of 0% can be used as a constraint. In case of a lower compatibility degree the candidates will "compete" with their compatibility degree for being the correct antecedent.

This semantic information will allow the selection of the antecedent that is conceptually most compatible. Some results concerning to the use of these patterns in Spanish and English texts can be seen in Saiz-Noeda et al. [22, 21] respectively, while another apporach to apply semantic information from an ontology instead of WordNet can be found in Saiz-Noeda and Palomar [20].

5 Conclusions

General-purpose Natural Language Processing (NLP) systems that can be applied to any domain are nowadays more and more sought after. Also, these systems need to use heterogeneous information sources to achieve optimal results. It means, the use of different kind of information is necessary in the treatment of Natural Language.

In this work, we have presented a general Natural Language Processing system with a module to solve a discourse phenomenon (anaphora) that can be applied to different applications, such as, Machine Translation (MT), Information Retrieval (IR) or Information Extraction (IE).

We have developed this anaphora resolution module based on constraints and preferences and it can be applied to solve the anaphora in dialogue and non-dialogue texts. Moreover, the system can solve different types of anaphoric expressions such as pronouns and definite descriptions.

Last years, many research efforts have been focused on anaphora resolution in this kind of expressions achieving satisfactory results for Spanish. Nowadays, we are developing tools to link all information sources in an only independent multi-platform system[3] to be used in any application.

References

[1] S. Azzam, K. Humphrey, and R. Gaizauskas. Evaluating a Focus-Based Approach to Anaphora Resolution. In *Proceedings of the 36th Annual Meeting of the Association for Computational Linguistics and 17th International Conference on Computational Linguistics (COLING-ACL'98)*, pages 74–78, Montreal (Canada), August 1998.

---

[3] More information about these tools can be seen at http://gplsi.dlsi.ua.es

[2] Dimitris N. Christodoulakis, editor. *Second International Conference on Natural Language Processing, NLP'2000*, volume 1835 of *Lectures Notes in Artificial Intelligence*, Patras, Greece, June 2000. Springer-Verlag.

[3] P. Christopherson. *The Articles: A study of their theory and use in English.* E. Munksgaard, Copenhagen, 1939.

[4] H. H. Clark. Bridging. In P. Johnson-Laird and P Wason, editors, *Thinking: readings in cognitive science*, pages 411–420. Cambridge University Press, London New York, 1977.

[5] M. Dalrymple, J. Lamping, F. Pereira, and V. Saraswat. Quantifiers, Anaphora, and Intensionality. *Journal of Logic, Language, and Information*, (6):219–273, 1997.

[6] M. Eckert and M. Strube. Resolving Discourse Deitic Anaphora in Dialogues. In *Proceedings of 9th Conference of the European Chapter of the Association for Computational Linguistics (EACL'99)*, pages 37–44, Bergen, Norway, 1999.

[7] B. Fox. *Discourse Structure and Anaphora*. Written and conversational English. Cambridge Studies in Linguistics. Cambridge University Press, Cambridge, 1987.

[8] J. A. Hawkins. *Definiteness and indefiniteness*. Humanities Press, Atlantic Highlands, New Jersey, 1978.

[9] S. Lappin and H. Leass. An algorithm for pronominal anaphora resolution. *Computational Linguistics*, 20(4):535–561, 1994.

[10] P. Martínez-Barco and M. Palomar. Empirical study of the anaphoric accessibility space in Spanish dialogues. In *Proceedings of the Fourth Workshop on the Semantics and Pragmatics of Dialogue (GOTALOG'2000)*, Göteborg, Sweden, June 2000.

[11] P. Martínez-Barco and M. Palomar. Structure-based Anaphoric Accesibility Space. *Computational Linguistics*, 2000. Submitted.

[12] G. Miller, R. Beckwith, C. Fellbaum, D. Gross, and K. Miller. WordNet: An online lexical database. *International journal of lexicography*, 3(4):235–244, 1990.

[13] G. Miller, R. Beckwith, C. Fellbaum, D. Gross, and K. Miller. Five Papers on WordNet. *International journal of lexicography*, Special Issue(3), 1993.

[14] A. Montoyo and M. Palomar. Word Sense Disambiguation with Specification Marks in Unrestricted Texts. In *Proc. 11th International Workshop on Database and Expert Systems Applications (DEXA 2000)*, pages 103–107, Greenwich, London, UK, September 2000. IEEE Computer Society.

[15] R. Muñoz and A. Ferrández. Definite Descriptions Resolution in Spanish. In *Proceeding of ACIDCA'2000: Corpora and Natural Language Processing*, pages 140–145, Monastir, Túnez, Marzo 2000.

[16] R. Muñoz and M. Palomar. Processing of Spanish Definite Descriptions with the Same Head. In Christodoulakis [2], pages 212–220.

[17] R. Muñoz, M. Palomar, and A. Ferrández. Processing of Spanish Definite Descriptions. In O. Cairo and E. L. Sucar and F. J. Cantu, editor, *Proceeding of Mexican International Conference on Artificial Intelligence*, volume 1793 of *Lectures Notes in Artificial Intelligence*, pages 526–537, Acapulco, Mexico, April 2000. Springer-Verlag.

[18] M. Palomar, A. Ferrández, L. Moreno, P. Martínez-Barco, J. Peral, M. Saiz-Noeda, and R. Muñoz. An algorithm for Anaphora Resolution in Spanish Texts. *Computational Linguistics (submitted)*, 2000.

[19] B. Russell. Descripciones. In Luis Ml. Valdés Villanueva, editor, *La búsqueda del significado: Lecturas de filosofía del lenguaje*, pages 46–56. Tecnos, 1919.

[20] M. Saiz-Noeda and M. Palomar. Semantic Knowledge-driven Method to Solve Pronominal Anaphora in Spanish. In Christodoulakis [2], pages 204–211.

[21] M. Saiz-Noeda, J. Peral, and A. Suárez. Semantic Compatibility Techniques for Anaphora Resolution. In *Proceeding of ACIDCA'2000: Corpora and Natural Language Processing*, pages 43–48, Monastir, Túnez, Marzo 2000.

[22] M. Saiz-Noeda, A. Suárez, and J. Peral. Propuesta de incorporación de información semántica desde WordNet al análisis sintáctico parcial orientado a la resolución de la anáfora. *Procesamiento del Lenguaje Natural*, 25:167–173, 1999.

[23] P. Vossen. EuroWordNet: Building a Multilingual Database with WordNets for European Languages. *The ELRA Newwsletter. K.Choukri, D.Fry, M. Nilsson (des). ISSN:1026-8200*, 3(1), 1998.

Belief Revision on Anaphora Resolution

Sandra Roger

Departamento de Informática y Estadística, Facultad de Economía y Administración,
Universidad Nacional del Comahue, Buenos Aires 1400 - Neuquén. Argentina
sroger@uncoma.edu.ar

Abstract. The aim of this article is to describe a new approach for solving anaphora problem. We focus on anaphora resolution by means of *belief revision* process.

Introduction Anaphora resolution [1][3] is a very important problem to solve in any system that intends to work with natural language, e.g. information extraction, machine translation, etc. The *belief revision* process[2] works with belief change. Our beliefs will be considered as the possible antecedents to the anaphora. Whenever is possible, the process of belief revision of these antecedents w.r.t. the anaphora will give as result the right anaphora.

Belief Revision When learning new information[1], a human will try to accommodate it in such a way that this new knowledge does not damage the knowledge he already has. However, in many cases, the task of incorporating new information to a knowledge set will require previously maintained beliefs to be discarded. In other words, when an agent learns new information it is possible that this information conflicts with his belief set. When a contradiction exists, it is necessary to eliminate old beliefs in order to consistently incorporate the new information. On the other hand, when no conflict exists, the reasoner can simply add the new information to his set of beliefs. This process is known as *belief revision*.

An Outline of Our Approach In this section we will introduce the main concepts related to the process used for determining the anaphora antecedent, which is governed by morphological, syntactical, semantic and pragmatic information by using belief revision.

In the process of anaphora resolution, we have to identify the antecedents of anaphors. Following this, attributes have been defined for the anaphora expressions and possible antecedents. These attributes include the linguistic information for the belief revision process mentioned above. In order to describe this process it is necessary to define what will be considered belief and belief base. In our opinion, both anaphora attributes and possible antecedents attributes will be interpreted as *belief*. In addition, only the set of the possible antecedent

---

[1] it's also called knowledge

A. Gelbukh (Ed.): CICLing 2001, LNCS 2004, pp. 140–141, 2001.
© Springer-Verlag Berlin Heidelberg 2001

attributes, will be called *belief base*. The process of belief revision consists of the following steps:

- Identifying the anaphora to be solved.
- Obtaining the resulting set of the belief revision applied to the belief base w.r.t. the anaphora. If this set is a singleton, then its element will be the antecedent. If this set has more elements, then the information given will not be enough.

In this sense, we still need to define the concept of consistence: we say that a belief α is consistent w.r.t. a belief base K if and only if for all belief β in K, $attributes_i(\alpha) == attributes_i(\beta)$ for all $1 \leq i \leq n$ where n is the number of attributes. We define what $attributes_i(\alpha) == attributes_i(\beta)$ w.r.t. the attributes type:

- Suppose that $attributes_1$ identify the morphological attribute: *gender*, then

$$attribute_1(Maria) == attribute_1(ella)\text{iff}$$

$$attribute_1(Maria) = {}^2attribute(ella) = (femenino)$$

- Now suppose that "Maria" is in the clause number one, "ella" es in the clause numbre two and $attributes_2$ identify the pragmatic attribute: *clause distance*, then

$$attribute_2(ella) = (2, different) \quad attribute_2(Maria) = (1). \qquad (1)$$

$$attribute_2(Maria) == attribute_2(ella) \text{ iff}$$

$$different(attribute_2(Maria), first(attribute_2(ella)))$$

In the above example, $attribute_2(ella)$ (1) has more information than *attribute₂ (Maria)*: the clause of the first attribute has to be different from the second attribute.

Conclusions and Future Research Most of the recent development in anaphora resolution has been based on several approaches. Our approach can be seen as an "iterative method" in the sense that we can add different attributes without order restrictions. Informally it is feasible to assume that we have found a method easily adaptable to many other languages. In comparison to previous approaches, our work still needs to be refined.

References

1. Ferrández, Antonio: Tesis Doctoral. Universidad de Alicante. España (1998)
2. Gärdenfors, Peter: Belief Revision. Department of Philosophy. Lund University. Cambridg University Press (1992).
3. Mitkov, Ruslan: Anaphora resolution: the state of the art. Working paper (Based on the COLING'98/ACL'98 tutorial on anaphora resolution). University of Wolverhampton, Wolverhampton (1999)

---

[2] " $=$ " represent the logical operator

A Machine-Learning Approach to Estimating the Referential Properties of Japanese Noun Phrases

Masaki Murata, Kiyotaka Uchimoto, Qing Ma, and Hitoshi Isahara

Communications Research Laboratory, MPT,
2-2-2 Hikaridai, Seika-cho, Soraku-gun, Kyoto, 619-0289, Japan,
{murata,uchimoto,qma,isahara}@crl.go.jp,
http://www-karc.crl.go.jp/ips/murata

Abstract. The referential properties of noun phrases in the Japanese language, which has no articles, are useful for article generation in Japanese-English machine translation and for anaphora resolution in Japanese noun phrases. They are generally classified as generic noun phrases, definite noun phrases, and indefinite noun phrases. In the previous work, referential properties were estimated by developing rules that used clue words. If two or more rules were in conflict with each other, the category having the maximum total score given by the rules was selected as the desired category. The score given by each rule was established by hand, so the manpower cost was high. In this work, we automatically adjusted these scores by using a machine-learning method and succeeded in reducing the amount of manpower needed to adjust these scores.

1   Introduction

To estimate the referential property of a noun phrase (NP) in the Japanese language, which does not have any articles, is one of the most difficult problems in natural language processing [5]. The referential property of a noun phrase represents how the noun phrase denotes the referent and is classified into the following three types:

- An indefinite NP — denotes an arbitrary member of the class of the noun phrase.
  (Ex.) There are three <u>dogs</u>.

- A definite NP — denotes a contextually non-ambiguous member of the class of the noun phrase.
  (Ex.) <u>The dog</u> went away.

- A generic NP — denotes all members of the class of the noun phrase or the class itself of the noun phrase.
  (Ex.) <u>Dogs</u> are useful.
  Note that "dogs" in this sentence denotes general dogs and are classified generic.

A. Gelbukh (Ed.): CICLing 2001, LNCS 2004, pp. 142–154, 2001.

Estimating the referential properties of noun phrases in Japanese sentences is useful for (i) generating articles when translating Japanese nouns into English and (ii) estimating the referents of noun phrases.

(i) Article generation in machine translation

In the process of generating articles, when a noun phrase is estimated to be indefinite, it is given the indefinite article, "a/an", when it is singular, but is given no article when it is plural. When a noun phrase is estimated to be definite, it is given the definite article, "the". When a noun phrase is estimated to be generic, usage in terms of articles is generated by a method used for generic noun phrases (a generic noun phrase can be given a definite or an indefinite article or no article, and may also be in the plural form.)[1] For example, *hon* (book) in the following sentence is a generic noun phrase.

> *hon-toiunowa   ningen-no   seichou-ni kakasemasen*
> (book)   (human being) (growth) (be necessary)   (1)
> (Books are necessary for the growth of a human being.)

So it can be translated as "a book," "books," or "the book" in English. Note that in the following sentence, *hon* (book) is a definite noun phrase.

> *kinou   boku-ga kashita hon-wa yomimashitaka*
> (yesterday) (I)   (lend) (book)   (read)   (2)
> (Did you read the book I lent you yesterday?)

It can thus be translated as "the book" in English.

(ii) Anaphora resolution

Only a definite noun phrase can refer to a previous noun phrase and this is very useful in anaphora resolution [6]. For example, in the following example, *hon* (book) in the second sentence is a generic noun phrase, so it cannot be referring to *hon* (book) in the first sentence.

> *hon-wo   omiyage-ni   kaimashita.*
> (book) (as a present)   (buy)
> (I bought books as a present.)
>
> *hon-toiunowa   ningen-no   seichou-ni kakasemasen*
> (book)   (human being) (growth) (be necessary)
> (Books are necessary for the growth of a human being.)

(3)

As in the above explanation, the referential properties of noun phrases, i.e., generic, definite, and indefinite, are useful for article generation and anaphora resolution, and estimating them is a serious problem in natural language processing.

---

[1] Bond et al. have actually used the referential properties of noun phrases in generating articles [1].

In the conventional estimation of referential properties [5], heuristic rules (made by hand) using surface clue words are used for estimation. For example, in sentence (1) above the referential property is estimated to be generic by using a Japanese clue word *toiu-nowa*; in sentence (2), the referential property of a noun phrase, *hon* (book), is estimated to be definite since the noun phrase is modified by an embedded sentence, *kinou boku ga kashita* (I lent you yesterday). In their work, 86 heuristic rules were created. When plural rules conflicted and the rule used in estimation was ambiguous, the conflict was solved by using the scores given in the rules. These scores needed to be adjusted by hand in order to properly resolve conflicts.

In the current work, to reduce human costs of previous research, we have used a machine-learning method to automatically adjust these rules. We selected the maximum entropy method (which is robust for sparse data problems) as the machine-learning method.

2   How to Estimate Referential Property

2.1   Method Used in Previous Research

The previous research gave each referential property two evaluation values, *possibility* and *value*, by using heuristic rules and estimated the referential property according to these values. Here, *possibility* is logically conjuncted and *value* is added. As a result, the referential property whose *possibility* is 1 and whose *value* is maximum is estimated to be the desired one.

Heuristic rules are given in the following forms:

(*condition for rule application*)
$\Longrightarrow$ { indefinite (*possibility, value*)
    definite (*possibility, value*)
    generic (*possibility, value*) }

A surface expression, which contains a clue word for estimating the referential property, is written in *condition for rule application*. *Possibility* has a value of 1 when the categories indefinite, definite and generic are possible in the context checked by the condition. Otherwise, the *possibility* value is 0. *Value* means that a relative possibility value between 1 and 10 (an integer) is given according to the plausibility of the condition that the *possibility* is 1. A larger value means the plausibility is high.

Several rules can be applicable to a specific noun in a sentence. In this case, the possibility values for the individual categories are added, and the category for the noun is decided as the category with the highest sum of possibility values.

86 rules were created. Some of the rules are given below.

(1) When a noun is modified by a referential pronoun, *kono* (this), *sono* (its), etc., then {indefinite $(0, 0)^2$ definite $(1, 2)$ generic $(0, 0)$}
kono hon-wa omoshiroi.
(this) (book) (interesting)
(This book is interesting.)

(2) When a noun is accompanied by a particle, *wa*, and the predicate is in the past tense, then {indefinite $(1, 0)$ definite $(1, 3)$ generic $(1, 1)$}
inu-wa mukou-he itta.
(dog) (away there) (went)
(The dog went away.)

(3) When a noun is accompanied by a particle, *wa*, and the predicate is in the present tense, then {indefinite $(1, 0)$ definite $(1, 2)$ generic $(1, 3)$}
inu-wa yakunitatsu doubutsu desu.
(dog) (useful) (animal) (is)
(Dogs are useful animals.)

When there are no clues, "indefinite" is assigned as the default value.
Let us look at an example of a noun to which several rules apply, *kudamono* (fruit) as used in the following sentence.

wareware-ga   kinou   tsumitotta kudamono-wa aji-ga   iidesu.
(we)   (yesterday) (picked)   (fruit)   (taste) (be good) (4)
(The fruit that we picked yesterday tastes delicious.)

All the rules were applied and the condition only satisfied the following seven rules which were then used to determine the degree of the definiteness of the noun.

(a) When a noun is accompanied by *wa*, and the corresponding predicate is not in the past tense
(*kudamono-wa aji-ga iidesu*), then
{indefinite $(1, 0)$ definite $(1, 2)$ generic $(1, 3)$}

(b) When a noun is modified by an embedded sentence which is in the past tense
(*tsumitotta*),
then
{indefinite $(1, 0)$ definite $(1, 1)$ generic $(1, 0)$}

(c) When a noun is modified by an embedded sentence which has a definite noun accompanied by *wa* or *ga* (*wareware-ga*), then
{indefinite $(1, 0)$ definite $(1, 1)$ generic $(1, 0)$}

(d) When a noun is modified by an embedded sentence which has a definite noun accompanied by a particle (*wareware-ga*), then
{indefinite $(1, 0)$ definite $(1, 1)$ generic $(1, 0)$}

(e) When a noun is modified by a phrase which has a pronoun (*wareware-ga*),
then
{indefinite $(1, 0)$ definite $(1, 1)$ generic $(1, 0)$}

---

2 (a, b) means *possibility* (a) and *value* (b).

(f) When a noun has an adjective as its predicate (*kudamono-wa azi-ga iidesu*),
then
{indefinite (1, 0) definite (1, 3) generic (1, 4)}
(g) When a noun is a common noun (*kudamono*),
then
{indefinite (1, 1) definite (1, 0) generic (1, 0)}

By using the scores from these rules, total *possibilities* and *values* were calculated. The overall *possibilities* for all three categories were 1 because all three categories carried *possibilities* of 1 for all of these rules. The total *values* for all three categories were 1, 9, and 7, respectively, because the results of aggregating the *values* of all of these rules were $1 (= 0 + 0 + 0 + 0 + 0 + 0 + 1)$, $9 (= 2 + 1 + 1 + 1 + 1 + 3 + 0)$, and $7 (= 3 + 0 + 0 + 0 + 0 + 4 + 0)$, for the respective categories. A final score of {indefinite (1, 1) definite (1, 9) generic (1, 7)} was obtained, and the system judged, correctly, that the noun here is "definite."

Each noun, from left to right, in the sentence was estimated according to (a) - (g) above. This process allows the decision process to make use of referential properties that has already been determined (see (c) and (d), for example).

In the method used in the previous work *possibility* and *value* had to be adjusted in order to estimate referential properties properly, and this required much work by human. Although gathering the clue words by hand might be effective, *possibility* and *value* can be adjusted by a certain machine-learning method. In this paper, we report on our use of the machine-learning method described in the next section. to verify this possibility,

2.2   The Machine-Learning Method

A machine-learning method was applied to the estimation of referential properties. We used the maximum entropy method as a machine-learning method, which is robust against data sparseness, because it is difficult to make a large corpus tagged with referential properties. By defining a set of features in advance, the maximum entropy method estimates the conditional probability of each category in a certain situation of the features, and it is called *the maximum entropy method* since it maximizes entropy when estimating a probability. The process of maximizing entropy can make the probabilistic model uniform, and this effect is the reason that the maximum entropy method is robust against data sparseness. We used Ristad's system [8, 9] as the maximum entropy method. The three probabilities, generic, definite, or indefinite, are calculated from the output of Ristad's system. The category having the maximum probability is judged to be the desired one.

To use the maximum entropy method, we must choose the features used in learning. We used the conditions of the 86 rules that had been used in the previous work. 86 features are thus used in learning.

If we use, for example, rules 1, 2, and 3 as described in Sec. 2.1, only condition parts are detected and the following three features are obtained.

1. Whether or not a noun is modified by a referential pronoun, *kono* (this), *sono* (its), etc.
2. Whether or not a noun is accompanied by a particle *wa*, and the predicate is in the past tense.
3. Whether or not a noun is accompanied by a particle *wa*, and the predicate is in the present tense.

Now, we use the last example from the previous section to explain how the referential property is estimated by the maximum entropy method.

> *wareware-ga   kinou   tsumitotta kudamono-wa aji-ga   iidesu.*
> (we)   (yesterday) (picked)   (fruit)   (taste) (be good)   (5)
> (The fruit that we picked yesterday tastes delicious.)

We again look at *kudamono* (fruit). The same seven rules are again applied. The value assigned to each of the referential properties for each rule indicates the conditional probability of that category being correct when only that rule is applied and they are calculated by the maximum entropy method. The values written here were obtained in our experiment of "Machine-Learning 2" described in Sec. 3.

(a) When a noun is accompanied by *wa* and the corresponding predicate is not in the past tense,
(*kudamono-wa aji-ga iidesu*), then
{indefinite 0.31   definite 0.29   generic 0.40}
(b) When a noun is modified by an embedded sentence which is in the past tense (*tsumitotta*),
then
{indefinite 0.31   definite 0.49   generic 0.19}
(c) When a noun is modified by an embedded sentence which has a definite noun accompanied by *wa* or *ga* (*wareware-ga*), then
{indefinite 0.19   definite 0.61   generic 0.19}
(d) When a noun is modified by an embedded sentence which has a definite noun accompanied by a particle (*wareware-ga*), then
{indefinite 0.01   definite 0.80   generic 0.18}
(e) When a noun is modified by a phrase which has a pronoun (*wareware-ga*),
then
{indefinite 0.20   definite 0.44   generic 0.37}
(f) When a noun has an adjective as its predicate (*kudamono-wa azi-ga iidesu*),
then
{indefinite 0.13   definite 0.80   generic 0.07}
(g) When a noun is a common noun (*kudamono*),
then
{indefinite 0.72   definite 0.15   generic 0.14}

In the maximum entropy method the values assigned by the above rules are multiplied, the values in each category are normalized, and the category with

the highest value is judged to be the desired one. In this case, we multiplied and normalized the values of all the rules and obtained the following results:
{indefinite 0.001, definite 0.996, generic 0.002}
"Definite" had the highest value and was thus judged to be the desired category.

3   Experiment and Discussion

Morphological and syntactic information are used as features in estimating referential properties. Before estimating the referential property, morphology and syntax were analyzed [4, 3]. We used the same learning set and test set as had been used in previous work.[3] The 86 rules had been made by examining the learning set by hand. In the previous work, the values written in the 86 rules had been adjusted by checking the accuracy rates in the learning set.

Firstly, we carried out the following two experiments.

- Manual Adjustment — The estimation was made by using the method described in Sec 2.1. (This result is identical to the result of the previous work.)
- Machine-Learning 1 — The estimation was made by using the method described in Sec 2.2.

The results are listed in Tables 1 to 4. "Other" in the tables indicates that the referential property is ambiguous; such cases can be neglected here since they were few.

The accuracy rate obtained by Manual Adjustment (Table 2) in the test set was 68.9% and that of Machine-Learning 1 (Table 4) was 72.1%. The machine-learning method was thus more accurate than Manual Adjustment method. But, as can be seen in Tables 2 and 4, all the categories of Manual Adjustment are about 70% and the method did not have a bad-accuracy category. However, the result from Machine-Learning 1 of the "generic" category was low (5.2%). We cannot therefore conclude that Machine-Learning 1 reliably gives good results[4].

We felt that the reason for this low accuracy in estimating the "generic" category is that the frequency of "generic" terms is low and machine learning is biased toward "definite" terms, which have higher frequency than "generic" terms. We therefore carried out the following further experiments.

- Machine-Learning 2 — When machine learning is performed by using the maximum entropy method, the number of events in each category of the

---

[3] The learning set: "Usage of the English Articles"[2], a folktale "The Old Man with a Wen" [7], and an essay *tensei jingo*. The test set: a folktale *turu no ongaeshi* [7], an essay *tensei jingo*, "Pacific Asia in the Post-Cold-War World" (A Quarterly Publication of The International House of Japan Vol. 12, No. 2 Spring 1992).

[4] Here, we assume that not producing a bad-accuracy category was more important than having the highest total accuracy rate. We then constructed Method 2 as described in the following passages. However, if we assume that having the highest total accuracy rate is more important than not producing a bad-accuracy category, Method 1 is, in fact, better.

Table 1. Manual Adjustment (learning set)

	indef	def	gen	other	total
Usage of the Articles (140 sentences, 380 nouns)					
correct	96	184	58	1	339
incorrect	4	28	8	1	41
% of correct	96.0	86.8	87.9	50.0	89.2
The Old Man with a Wen (104 sentences, 267 nouns)					
correct	73	140	6	1	222
incorrect	14	27	4	0	45
% of correct	83.9	84.0	60.0	100.0	83.2
an essay *tensei jingo* (23 sentences, 98 nouns)					
correct	25	35	16	0	76
incorrect	5	14	3	0	22
% of correct	83.3	71.4	84.2	—	77.6
average					
% of appearance	29.1	57.7	12.8	0.4	100.0
% of correct	89.4	84.0	84.2	66.7	85.5

Table 2. Manual Adjustment (test set)

	indef	def	gen	other	total
a folktale *Turu* (263 sentences, 699 nouns)					
correct	109	363	13	10	495
incorrect	38	160	6	0	204
% of correct	74.2	69.4	68.4	100.0	70.8
an essay *tensei jingo* (75 sentences, 283 nouns)					
correct	75	81	16	0	172
incorrect	41	60	10	0	111
% of correct	64.7	57.5	61.5	—	60.8
Pacific Asia (22 sentences, 192 nouns)					
correct	21	108	11	2	142
incorrect	17	31	2	0	50
% of correct	55.3	77.7	84.6	100.0	74.0
average					
% of appearance	25.6	68.4	4.9	1.0	100.0
% of correct	68.1	68.7	69.0	100.0	68.9

Table 3. Machine Learning 1 (learning set)

	indef	def	gen	other	total
Usage of the Articles (140 sentences, 380 nouns)					
correct	95	199	32	0	326
incorrect	5	13	34	2	54
% of correct	95.0	93.9	48.5	0.0	85.8
The Old Man with a Wen (104 sentences, 267 nouns)					
correct	71	151	1	0	223
incorrect	16	18	9	1	44
% of correct	81.6	89.4	10.0	0.0	83.5
an essay *tensei jingo* (23 sentences, 98 nouns)					
correct	21	46	5	0	72
incorrect	9	3	14	0	26
% of correct	70.0	93.9	26.3	—	73.5
average					
% of appearance	29.1	57.7	12.8	0.4	100.0
% of correct	86.2	92.1	40.0	0.0	83.4

Table 4. Machine Learning 1 (test set)

	indef	def	gen	other	total
a folktale *Turu* (263 sentences, 699 nouns)					
correct	104	408	0	0	512
incorrect	43	115	19	10	187
% of correct	70.8	78.0	0.0	0.0	73.3
an essay *tensei jingo* (75 sentences, 283 nouns)					
correct	72	108	2	0	182
incorrect	44	33	24	0	101
% of correct	62.1	76.6	7.7	—	64.3
Pacific Asia (22 sentences, 192 nouns)					
correct	21	130	1	0	152
incorrect	17	9	12	2	40
% of correct	55.3	93.5	7.7	0.0	79.2
average					
% of appearance	25.6	68.4	4.9	1.0	100.0
% of correct	65.5	80.5	5.2	0.00	72.1

Table 5. Machine Learning 2 (learning set)

	indef	def	gen	other	total
Usage of the Articles (140 sentences, 380 nouns)					
correct	97	188	57	0	342
incorrect	3	24	9	2	38
% of correct	97.0	88.7	86.4	0.0	90.0
The Old Man with a Wen (104 sentences, 267 nouns)					
correct	80	137	6	0	223
incorrect	7	32	4	1	44
% of correct	92.0	81.1	60.0	0.0	83.5
an essay *tensei jingo* (23 sentences, 98 nouns)					
correct	26	40	17	0	83
incorrect	4	9	2	0	15
% of correct	86.7	81.6	89.5	—	84.7
average					
% of appearance	29.1	57.7	12.8	0.4	100.0
% of correct	93.6	84.9	84.2	0.0	87.0

Table 6. Machine Learning 2 (test set)

	indef	def	gen	other	total
a folktale *turu* (263 sentences, 699 nouns)					
correct	112	360	13	0	485
incorrect	35	163	6	10	214
% of correct	76.2	68.8	68.4	0.0	69.4
an essay *tensei jingo* (75 sentences, 283 nouns)					
correct	79	88	14	0	181
incorrect	37	53	12	0	102
% of correct	68.1	62.4	53.9	—	64.0
Pacific Asia (22 sentences, 192 nouns)					
correct	25	110	10	0	145
incorrect	13	29	3	2	47
% of correct	65.8	79.1	76.9	0.0	75.5
average					
% of appearance	25.6	68.4	4.9	1.0	100.0
% of correct	71.8	69.5	63.8	0.0	69.1

learning set is multiplied by the inverse of its occurrence. For example, in this paper, we multiplied 4, 2, and 9 by the frequencies of "indefinite," "definite," and "generic."

In other words, since generic noun phrases only made up 2/9 of definite noun phrases, we changed the frequencies of data as if definite noun phrases had occurred twice as often as in the actual data and generic noun phrases had occurred nine times more often than in the actual data. We found that this change made the frequencies of the three referential properties uniform and did not bias the analysis towards definite noun phrases. The change produced the following result. Machine-Learning 1 applies a general method of learning and learns data in order to maximize the following equation.

$$\text{evaluation function} = [\% \text{ of correct in overall the data}] \qquad (6)$$

On the other hand, Machine-Learning 2 uses the frequencies of the referential properties and learns data in order to maximize the following equation.

$$
\begin{aligned}
&\text{evaluation function} \\
&= \text{the average of} \\
&\quad [\% \text{ of correct in "indefinite"}], \\
&\quad [\% \text{ of correct in "definite"}] \text{ and} \\
&\quad [\% \text{ of correct in "generic"}]
\end{aligned}
\qquad (7)
$$

The results for Machine-Learning 2 are listed in Tables 5 and 6.

The accuracy rate of Machine-Learning 2 on the test set was 69.1%. This is nearly equal to the 68.9% obtained by using the Manual Adjustment. It was found that the accuracy rates for all three referential properties were about 70%. Since even for the worst category, "generic," 63.8% was achieved, it is clear that Machine-Learning 2 was able to quite precisely estimate the referential properties.

As the above results show, we found that manual adjustment for estimating referential properties was not necessary and therefore human costs were decreased.

We also examined the values of the rules as given by the maximum entropy method used in Machine-Learning 2. We examine some of the rules as listed below. In each of the rules in the list, (i) the condition parts, (ii) values assigned by hand, and (iii) values assigned by Machine learning 2 are included.

1. Rules for indefinite noun phrases
   (a) When a noun is accompanied by a particle, *ga* (new-topic marker), then
   {indefinite (1, 2) definite (1, 1) generic (1, 0)}
   {indefinite 0.62,   definite 0.21,   generic 0.17}

   In general, a noun accompanied by a particle, *ga*, one function of which is to indicate a new topic, roughly tends to be indefinite. The highest value is thus assigned to "indefinite" when manual adjustment is used. The value of "indefinite" as determined by Machine-Learning 2 is also the highest. In manual adjustment, the possibilities of all categories are set to 1, so any of the three categories can be the answer. In Machine-Learning 2, since the value of "indefinite" is not terribly high, (not, e.g., 0.99), any of the three categories can also be the answer.

(b) When a noun is modified by an adjective *aru* (a certain ∼), then
{indefinite (1, 2)   definite (0, 0)   generic (0, 0)}
{indefinite 0.99, definite 0.0001, generic 0.0001}

Generally, a noun modified by *aru* (a certain ∼) is indefinite. The values for *possibility* of the other categories are thus set to 0 in manual adjustment. The values used in Machine-Learning 2 are 0.0001, which is also a very small value. The value of "indefinite" is extremely high in Machine-Learning 2. We find that Machine-Learning 2 can judge that the category of a noun modified by *aru* is almost certainly indefinite.

2. Rules for definite noun phrases
   (a) When a noun is a pronoun, then
   {indefinite (0, 0)   definite (1, 2)   generic (0, 0)}
   {indefinite 0.005,   definite 0.99, generic 0.005}
   When a noun is a pronoun, it is always definite, so the values of *possibility* of the other categories are manually set to 0. The values assigned to the other categories by Machine-Learning 2 are also very small.

   (b) When a noun is modified by an embedded sentence which has a definite noun accompanied by *wa* or *ga* (nominative-case particle), then
   {indefinite (1, 0)   definite (1, 1)   generic (1, 0)}
   {indefinite 0.19,   definite 0.61,   generic 0.19}
   Although such a noun is not always definite, it is likely to be definite. The value of "definite" in Machine-Learning 2 is the highest of the three, but is not extremely high.

3. Rules for generic noun phrases
   (a) When a noun is followed by a particle *wa*, which does not have a modifier, then
   {indefinite (1, 0)   definite (1, 1)   generic (1, 1)}
   {indefinite 0.03,   definite 0.26,   generic 0.71}

   The particle *wa*, which is a topic marker, is an expression which is likely to accompany either a definite noun phrase or a generic noun phrase. The *possibility values* of the two categories are both set to 1 by Manual Adjustment. Machine-Learning 2 found that the values assigned to "definite" and "generic" are higher than that assigned to "indefinite," but "generic" is assigned a higher value than "definite." This is because there are many rules for estimating that a noun phrase is "definite," so a word can be estimated as "generic" if no other clue words appear.

   (b) When a noun is followed by a particle *wa* and it modifies an adjective, then
   {indefinite (1, 0)   definite (1, 3)   generic (1, 4)}
   {indefinite 0.13,   definite 0.80,   generic 0.07}

Although "generic" is assigned the highest value by Manual Adjustment, "definite" is assigned the highest value by Machine-Learning 2. This is because of (i) a wrong estimate by Machine-Learning 2 due to a small learning set, (ii) the influence of other rules, such as the previous rule, or (iii) incorrect manual adjustment in the earlier work. If the actual reason is (i), then making the learning set larger should improve the results.

As stated above, the values assigned by Machine-Learning 2 tended to be similar to those obtained by hand, and they demonstrated some degree of linguistic intuition.

4   Conclusions

We have succeeded in creating a system for automatically giving rules values for solving conflicts when estimating the referential properties of noun phrases. We have thus shown that the cost in terms of human time of manually adjusting values is not unavoidable. We also found that, in machine learning, making the frequencies of the categories uniform can help to make their accuracy rates more uniform. Finally, we examined the values produced for rules by applying the Machine-Learning method, and confirmed that they were consistent with linguistic intuition.

References

[1] Francis Bond, Kentaro Ogura, and Satoru Ikehara. Countability and Number in Japanese to English Machine Translation. In *COLING '94*, pages 32–38, 1994.

[2] Akihisa Kumayama. *Usage of the English Articles*. Taishukan Publisher, 1985. (in Japanese).

[3] Sadao Kurohashi and Makoto Nagao. A Method of Case Structure Analysis for Japanese Sentences based on Examples in Case Frame Dictionary. *IEICE Transactions on Information and Systems*, E77–D(2):227–239, 1994.

[4] Sadao Kurohashi and Makoto Nagao. *Japanese Morphological Analysis System JUMAN version 3.5*. Department of Informatics, Kyoto University, 1998. (in Japanese).

[5] Masaki Murata and Makoto Nagao. Determination of referential property and number of nouns in Japanese sentences for machine translation into English. In *Proceedings of the 5th TMI*, pages 218–225, 1993.

[6] Masaki Murata and Makoto Nagao. An estimate of referent of noun phrases in Japanese sentences. In *COLING '98*, pages 912–916, 1998.

[7] Kiyoaki Nakao. *The Old Man with a Wen*, volume 7 of *Eiyaku Nihon Mukashibanashi Series*. Nihon Eigo Kyouiku Kyoukai, 1985.

[8] Eric Sven Ristad. Maximum Entropy Modeling for Natural Language. ACL/EACL Tutorial Program, Madrid,, 1997.

[9] Eric Sven Ristad. Maximum Entropy Modeling Toolkit, Release 1.6 beta. http://www.mnemonic.com/ software/memt, 1998.

The Referring Expressions in the Other's Comment

Tamara Matulevich

Surgut State Teacher Training College
Surgut, Russia
tmatulev@hotmail.com

Abstract. The linguistic facts required for artificial intelligence to be able to distinguish between text and metatext include expressions referring to 'text about text' insertions. Such data can be provided by discourse linguistics. The present paper offers a list of expressions used to identify text about text in the current conversation and outlines other semantic and pragmatic phenomena which may constitute the individual profile of the system designed to process the other's comment containing those expressions.

Seen as a language unit, the other's comment is a sentence possessing certain semantic properties. It refers to the speaker's (commentor's) immediate discourse partner's preceding utterance and specifies the latter in terms of speech acts and strategies: *This is blasphemy, Dorian!* (O.Wilde); *It's a lie!* (E.O'Neill); *That's a promise to your old mother.* (J.Priestley); *Now, that's evasion!* (T.Hardy); *Even that's a contradiction.* (J.Heller); etc. The 'other' in this case is the person estimating his interlocutor's replicas in the current dialogue (cf: [1]):

(a) „No. I like it best when I don't know anybody."
   „That's a compliment for some of us. However – I know what you mean. [...]"
   (D. Lawrence)

The preceding adjacent utterance in (a) is categorized as a compliment, although it hardly qualifies for that. This deliberate misattribution has a humorous effect.

Together with the quasi-comment describing the commentor's own immediately preceding or following text and the comment proper describing the commentor's own preceding distanced utterance, the other's comment forms a class of meta-units performing a number of various functions explored by discourse linguistics.

The interpretation of this kind of text about text insertions is a challenging proposition for artificial intelligence and a matter of future achievements. The other's comment carries a communicative value description, and the latter must be processed and taken for what it is - quite a specific sort of message about an instance of the semiotic system employment. The linguistic data required to fulfill this task in programming include the types of expressions referring to the utterance generated prior to the last turn-taking. This paper pursues a goal to offer a list of such expressions derived from the 19th-20th century British and American prose.

When commenting it is indispensable to make known which of the many utterances produced in the given conversation is being talked about. The referring

A. Gelbukh (Ed.): CICLing 2001, LNCS 2004, pp. 155-156, 2001.
© Springer-Verlag Berlin Heidelberg 2001

expressions identifying the other's preceding utterance are divided here into four groups:

1. The demonstrative *that, this*, the personal pronoun *it*.
2. Substantive phrases with an illocutionary or strategy-describing noun and a demonstrative or possessive pronoun in them: *that remark, your refusal*.
3. Clauses specifying the current position of the utterance in the discourse through indicating its connection with the present moment: *what you have just said, what you are saying*.
4. A combination of some of the above and a paraphrase of the propositional content: *your last remark as to the possibility of there being an understanding between the burglar and the servant, and this being a note of appointment from one to the other* (C.Doyle) (a substantive phrase with an illocutionary noun, position in the discourse, a paraphrase of the propositional content).

The commentor favours one referring expression of all – the pronoun *that* – which may be explained as a manifestation of „emotional distance" [2].

If artificial intelligence were to process the other's comment, it would require some specific semantic and pragmatic data. The individual profile of the system has been partially outlined in 1. – 4. The reference of the pronouns in this case is domain-restricted. The other classes of words involved would be illocutionary and strategy-describing nouns. The system would need knowledge of strategies and speech acts with their felicity conditions, too. The relevant pragmatic data would also include the utterances commented on and their contexts represented in terms of felicity conditions. The challenging task for artificial intelligence modeling the natural language user understanding would be to tell the correct classification of the utterance from the incorrect (like in (a)) one and to comprehend the true communicative value of the utterance commented on and of the other's comment itself.

References

[1] Bakhtin, M.M. Problema rechevykh zhanrov. In *Estetika Slovesnogo Tvorchestva*. Izdaniye vtoroye. Moskva, Iskusstvo, 1986.
[2] Lyons, Ch. *Definiteness*. Cambridge, Cambridge University Press, 1999.

Appendix: Sources

Hardy, T. *Far from the madding crowd.*
Heller, J. *Catch-22.*
Lawrence, D. *Kangaroo.*
O'Neill, E. *Long day's journey into night.*
Priestley, J. *Angel Pavement.*
Wilde, O. *The picture of Dorian Gray.*

Lexical Semantic Ambiguity Resolution with Bigram-Based Decision Trees

Ted Pedersen

University of Minnesota Duluth, Duluth, MN 55812 USA
tpederse@d.umn.edu,
http://www.d.umn.edu/~tpederse

Abstract. This paper presents a corpus-based approach to word sense disambiguation where a decision tree assigns a sense to an ambiguous word based on the bigrams that occur nearby. This approach is evaluated using the sense-tagged corpora from the 1998 SENSEVAL word sense disambiguation exercise. It is more accurate than the average results reported for 30 of 36 words, and is more accurate than the best results for 19 of 36 words.

1   Introduction

Word sense disambiguation is the process of selecting the most appropriate meaning for a word, based on the context in which it occurs. For our purposes it is assumed that the set of possible meanings, i.e., the sense inventory, has already been determined. For example, suppose *bill* has the following set of possible meanings: a piece of currency, pending legislation, or a bird jaw. When used in the context of *The Senate bill is under consideration,* a human reader immediately understands that *bill* is being used in the legislative sense. However, a computer program attempting to perform the same task faces a difficult problem since it does not have the benefit of innate common–sense or linguistic knowledge.

In the last decade, natural language processing has turned to *corpus–based* methods. These approaches use techniques from statistics and machine learning to induce models of language usage from large samples of text. These models are trained to perform particular tasks, usually via supervised learning. This paper describes an approach where a *decision tree* is learned from some number of sentences where each instance of an ambiguous word has been manually annotated with a sense–tag that denotes the most appropriate sense for that context.

Prior to learning, the sense–tagged corpus must be converted into a more regular form suitable for automatic processing. Each sense–tagged occurrence of an ambiguous word is converted into a feature vector, where each feature represents some property of the surrounding text that is considered to be relevant to the disambiguation process. Given the flexibility and complexity of human language, there is potentially an infinite set of features that could be utilized. However, in corpus–based approaches features usually consist of information that can be

A. Gelbukh (Ed.): CICLing 2001, LNCS 2004, pp. 157–168, 2001.

extracted directly from the text, without relying on extensive external knowledge sources. These typically include the part–of–speech of surrounding words, the presence of certain key words within some window of context, and various syntactic properties of the sentence and the ambiguous word. The approach in this paper relies upon a feature set made up of *bigrams*, two word sequences that appear in a text. The context in which an ambiguous word occurs is represented by some number of binary features that indicate whether or not a particular bigram has occurred in the sentence containing the ambiguous word, or in its immediate predecessor.

This paper continues with a discussion of our methods for identifying the bigrams that should be included in the feature set for learning. Then the decision tree learning algorithm is described, as are some benchmark learning algorithms that are included for purposes of comparison. The experimental data is discussed, and then the empirical results are presented. We close with an analysis of our findings and a discussion of related work.

2   Building a Feature Set of Bigrams

We define bigrams simply as two word sequences that occur consecutively in text. Given the sparse and skewed distributions of bigram data, it is important to choose a statistical test or measure appropriate for this kind of data. We explore two alternatives, the power divergence family of goodness of fit statistics and the Dice Coefficient, an information theoretic measure related to Mutual Information.

Figure 1 shows an example of a 2×2 contingency table used for storing bigram counts. We use this representation and notation in the following discussion. The value of n_{11} shows how many times the bigram *big cat* occurs in the corpus. The value of n_{12} shows how often bigrams occur where *big* is the first word and *cat* is not the second. The counts in n_{+1} and n_{1+} indicate how often words *big* and *cat* occur as the first and second words of any bigram in the corpus. The total number of bigrams in the corpus is represented by n_{++}.

	cat	¬cat	totals
big	$n_{11}=10$	$n_{12}=20$	$n_{1+}=30$
¬big	$n_{21}=40$	$n_{22}=930$	$n_{2+}=970$
totals	$n_{+1}=50$	$n_{+2}=950$	$n_{++}=1000$

Fig. 1. Representation of Bigram Counts

2.1   The Power Divergence Family

[3] introduce the power divergence family of goodness of fit statistics. A number of well known statistics belong to this family, including the likelihood ratio statistic G^2 and Pearson's X^2 statistic.

These measure the divergence of the observed (n_{ij}) and expected (m_{ij}) sample counts, where m_{ij} is calculated assuming that the the words in the bigram have no relationship or association to one another.

$$m_{ij} = \frac{n_{i+}\, n_{+j}}{n_{++}}$$

Given this value, G^2 and X^2 are calculated as:

$$G^2 = 2 \sum_{i,j} n_{ij} \log \frac{n_{ij}}{m_{ij}}$$

$$X^2 = \sum_{i,j} \frac{(n_{ij} - m_{ij})^2}{m_{ij}}$$

[5] argues in favor of G^2 over X^2, especially when dealing with very sparse and skewed data distributions. However, [3] show that there are cases where Pearson's statistic is more reliable than the likelihood ratio and that there is no reason to always prefer one over the other. In light of this, [10] presented Fisher's exact test as an alternative.

We have developed an approach to deciding which of these tests to use based on the observation that they should all produce the same result when the sample counts stored in the contingency table are not violating any of the distributional assumptions that underly the goodness of fit statistics. We compute values for X^2, G^2, and Fisher's exact test for each bigram. If they differ, then this is a case where the distribution of the bigram counts is causing at least one of the tests to become unreliable. When this occurs we rely upon the value from Fisher's exact test since it does not depend upon assumptions about the underlying distribution of data. Since Fisher's exact test can be computationally complex, a practical shortcut is to run both X^2 and G^2 and see if they differ. If they produce comparable results then they are likely reliable and Fisher's test can be omitted.

For the experiments in this paper, we identified the top 100 ranked bigrams that occur more than 5 times in the training corpus associated with a word. Given that low frequency bigrams are excluded, there are no cases where G^2, X^2, and Fisher's exact test disagreed. All of these statistics produced the same rankings, so hereafter we make no distinction among them and simply refer to them generically as the power divergence statistic.

2.2   Dice Coefficient

The Dice Coefficient is a descriptive statistic that provides a measure of association among two words in a corpus. It is similar to pointwise Mutual Information, a widely used measure that was first introduced for identifying lexical relationships in [2]. Since Mutual Information is so well-known, we describe it first so as to make the relationship between it and the Dice Coefficient clear. Pointwise Mutual Information can be defined as follows:

$$MI(w_1, w_2) = log_2 \frac{n_{11} * n_{++}}{n_{+1} * n_{1+}}$$

where w_1 and w_2 represent the two words that make up the bigram, n_{11} represents the number of times the two words occur together as a bigram, n_{+1} and n_{1+} are the number of times the words occur as the first and second words of a bigram, and n_{++} represents the total number of bigrams in the corpus.

Mutual Information quantifies how often a word occurs in a bigram (the numerator) relative to how often it occurs overall in the corpus both in and out of the bigram (the denominator). However, there is a curious limitation to pointwise Mutual Information. A bigram w_1w_2 that occurs n_{11} times in the corpus, and whose component words w_1 and w_2 also occur n_{11} times (i.e., the only time the component words occur is together in the bigram), will result in increasingly strong measures of association as the value of n_{11} decreases. Thus, the greatest possible pointwise Mutual Information value is attained when the frequencies of the bigram and its component words are all 1. This causes rankings to be dominated by very low frequency bigrams that may not be especially useful for the disambiguation process.

The Dice Coefficient overcomes this limitation, and can be defined as follows:

$$Dice(w_1, w_2) = \frac{2 * n_{11}}{n_{+1} + n_{1+}}$$

When $n_{11} = n_{1+} = n_{+1}$ the value $DC(w_1, w_2)$ will be 1 for any value of n_{11}. When the values of n_{11} is less than either of the marginal totals (the more typical case) the rankings produced by the Dice Coefficient are similar to those of Mutual Information. The relationship between Mutual Information and the Dice Coefficient is also discussed in [12].

3   Learning Decision Trees

Decision trees are among the most widely used machine learning algorithms. They perform a general to specific search of a feature space, adding the most informative features to a tree structure as the search proceeds. The objective is to select a minimal set of features that efficiently partitions the feature space into classes of observations and assemble them into a tree. In our case, the observations are manually sense–tagged examples of an ambiguous word in context and the partitions correspond to the different possible senses.

Each feature selected during the search process is represented by a node in the learned decision tree. Each node represents a choice point between a number of different possible values for a feature. Learning continues until all the training examples are accounted for by the decision tree. In general, such a tree will be overly specific to the training data and not generalize well to new examples.

Therefore learning is followed by a pruning step where some nodes are eliminated or reorganized to produce a tree that can generalize to new circumstances.

Test instances are disambiguated by finding a path through the learned decision tree from the root to a leaf node that corresponds with the observed features. In effect an instance of an ambiguous word is disambiguated by passing it through a series of tests, where each test asks if a particular bigram occurs nearby.

We also include three benchmarks in this study: the majority classifier, decision stumps, and the Naive Bayesian classifier.

The *majority classifier* assigns the most common sense in the training data to every instance in the test data. A *decision stump* is a one node decision tree[6] that is created by stopping the decision tree learner after the single most informative feature is added to the tree.

The *Naive Bayesian classifier* [4] is based on certain blanket assumptions about the interactions among features in a corpus. There is no search of the feature space performed to build a representative model as is the case with decision trees. Instead, all features are assumed to be relevant to the task at hand and are assigned weights based on their frequency of occurrence in the training data. It is most often used with a *bag of words* feature set, where every word in the training examples is represented with a binary feature that indicates whether or not it occurs in some proximity to the ambiguous word.

We have developed Perl software to identify bigrams and convert the text into feature vectors for input to a learning algorithm, and have made this freely available at our WWW site. We use the Weka [14] implementations of the C4.5 decision tree learner (known as J48), the decision stump, and the Naive Bayesian classifier.

4   Experimental Data

Our empirical study utilizes the training and test data from the 1998 SENSEVAL evaluation of word sense disambiguation systems. Ten teams participated in the supervised learning portion of this event. Additional details about the exercise, including the data and results referred to in this paper, can be found at the SENSEVAL web site and in [7].

We included all 36 tasks from SENSEVAL for which training and test data were provided. Each task requires that the occurrences of a particular word in the test data be disambiguated based on a model learned from the sense–tagged instances in the training data. Some words were used in multiple tasks as different parts of speech. For example, there were two tasks associated with *bet*, one for its use as a noun and the other as a verb. Thus, there are 36 tasks involving the disambiguation of 29 different words.

The words and part of speech associated with each task are shown in Table 1 in columns 1 and 2. Note that the parts of speech are encoded as *n* for noun, *a* for adjective, *v* for verb, and *p* for words where the part of speech was not provided. The number of test and training instances for each task are shown in columns 3 and 5. Each instance consists of the sentence in which the ambiguous word occurs as well as either the preceding or succeeding sentence. In general the total context available for each ambiguous word is less than 100 surrounding words. The number of senses that exist in the test data for each task is shown in column 4.

5 Experimental Method

The following process is repeated for each task. Capitalization and punctuation are removed from the training and test data. Two feature sets are selected from the training data based on the top 100 ranked bigrams according to the power divergence statistic and the Dice Coefficient. The bigram must have occurred 5 or more times to be included as a feature. The training and test data are converted to feature vectors where each feature represents the occurrence of one of the bigrams that appears in the feature set. This representation of the training data is the actual input to the learning algorithms. There are two different decision tree and decision stump learning processes, one based on the feature set determined by the power divergence statistic and another from the feature set identified by the Dice Coefficient. The majority classifier does not use a feature set, but rather simply determines the most frequent sense in the training data and assigns that to all instances in the test data. The Naive Bayesian classifier is based on a feature set where every word that occurs 5 or more times in the training data is included as a feature.

The learned decision tree is then used to disambiguate the test data. The test data has been kept completely out of the process until now. It is not used to select bigram features nor is it used in any phase of decision tree learning. We employ a fine grained scoring method, where a word is counted as correctly disambiguated only when the assigned sense tag exactly matches the true sense tag. No partial credit is assigned for near misses.

6 Experimental Results

The accuracy attained by each of the learning algorithms is shown in Table 1. Column 6 reports the accuracy of the majority classifier, columns 7 and 8 show the best and average accuracy reported by the 10 participating SENSEVAL teams. The evaluation at SENSEVAL was based on precision and recall, so we converted those scores to accuracy by taking their product. However, the best precision and recall may have come from different teams, so the best accuracy shown in column 7 may actually be higher than that of any single participating SENSEVAL system. The average accuracy in column 8 is the product of the average precision and recall reported for the participating SENSEVAL teams. Column 9 shows the accuracy of the decision tree using the J48 learning algorithm and the features identified by power divergence statistic. Column 11 shows the accuracy of the decision tree when the Dice Coefficient selects the features. Columns 10 and 12 show the accuracy of the Decision Stump based

Table 1. Experimental Results

(1)	(2)	(3)	(4)	(5)	(6)	(7)	(8)	(9) j48	(10) stump	(11) j48	(12) stump	(13) naive
word	pos	test	senses	train	maj	best	avg	pow	pow	dice	dice	bayes
accident	n	267	8	227	75.3	87.1	79.6	85.0	77.2	83.9	77.2	83.1
behaviour	n	279	3	994	94.3	92.9	90.2	95.7	95.7	95.7	95.7	93.2
bet	n	274	15	106	18.2	50.7	39.6	41.8	34.5	41.8	34.5	39.3
excess	n	186	8	251	1.1	75.9	63.7	65.1	38.7	60.8	38.7	64.5
float	n	75	12	61	45.3	66.1	45.0	52.0	50.7	52.0	50.7	56.0
giant	n	118	7	355	49.2	67.6	56.6	68.6	59.3	66.1	59.3	70.3
knee	n	251	22	435	48.2	67.4	56.0	71.3	60.2	70.5	60.2	64.1
onion	n	214	4	26	82.7	84.8	75.7	82.7	82.7	82.7	82.7	82.2
promise	n	113	8	845	62.8	75.2	56.9	48.7	63.7	55.8	62.8	78.0
sack	n	82	7	97	50.0	77.1	59.3	80.5	58.5	80.5	58.5	74.4
scrap	n	156	14	27	41.7	51.6	35.1	26.3	16.7	26.3	16.7	26.7
shirt	n	184	8	533	43.5	77.4	59.8	46.7	43.5	51.1	43.5	60.9
amaze	v	70	1	316	0.0	100.0	92.4	58.6	12.9	60.0	12.9	71.4
bet	v	117	9	60	43.2	60.5	44.0	50.8	58.5	52.5	50.8	58.5
bother	v	209	8	294	75.0	59.2	50.7	69.9	55.0	64.6	55.0	62.2
bury	v	201	14	272	38.3	32.7	22.9	48.8	38.3	44.8	38.3	42.3
calculate	v	218	5	249	83.9	85.0	75.5	90.8	88.5	89.9	88.5	80.7
consume	v	186	6	67	39.8	25.2	20.2	36.0	34.9	39.8	34.9	31.7
derive	v	217	6	259	47.9	44.1	36.0	82.5	52.1	82.5	52.1	72.4
float	v	229	16	183	33.2	30.8	22.5	30.1	22.7	30.1	22.7	56.3
invade	v	207	6	64	40.1	30.9	25.5	28.0	40.1	28.0	40.1	31.0
promise	v	224	6	1160	85.7	82.1	74.6	85.7	84.4	81.7	81.3	85.3
sack	v	178	3	185	97.8	95.6	95.6	97.8	97.8	97.8	97.8	97.2
scrap	v	186	3	30	85.5	80.6	68.6	85.5	85.5	85.5	85.5	82.3
seize	v	259	11	291	21.2	51.0	42.1	52.9	25.1	49.4	25.1	51.7
brilliant	a	229	10	442	45.9	31.7	26.5	55.9	45.9	51.1	45.9	58.1
floating	a	47	5	41	57.4	49.3	27.4	57.4	57.4	57.4	57.4	55.3
generous	a	227	6	307	28.2	37.5	30.9	44.9	32.6	46.3	32.6	48.9
giant	a	97	5	302	94.8	98.0	93.5	95.9	95.9	94.8	94.8	94.8
modest	a	270	9	374	61.5	49.6	44.9	72.2	64.4	73.0	64.4	68.1
slight	a	218	6	385	91.3	92.7	81.4	91.3	91.3	91.3	91.3	91.3
wooden	a	196	4	362	93.9	81.7	71.3	96.9	96.9	96.9	96.9	93.9
band	p	302	29	1326	77.2	81.7	75.9	86.1	84.4	79.8	77.2	83.1
bitter	p	373	14	144	27.0	44.6	39.8	36.4	31.3	36.4	31.3	32.6
sanction	p	431	7	96	57.5	74.8	62.4	57.5	57.5	57.1	57.5	56.8
shake	p	356	36	963	23.6	56.7	47.1	52.2	23.6	50.0	23.6	46.6
win-tie-loss						23-7-6	19-0-17	30-0-6	28-9-3	14-15-7	28-9-3	24-1-11

on the power divergence statistic and the Dice Coefficient respectively. Finally, Column 14 shows the accuracy of the Naive Bayesian classifier based on a bag of words feature set.

The most accurate method is the decision tree based on a feature set determined by the power divergence statistic. The last line of Table 1 shows the win-tie-loss score for the decision tree/power divergence method. A win means it was more accurate than the method in the column, a loss means it was less accurate, and a tie means it was equally accurate. This approach was more accurate than the best reported SENSEVAL results for 19 of the 36 tasks, and more accurate for 30 of the 36 tasks when compared to the average reported accuracy. The decision stumps also fared well, proving to be more accurate than the best SENSEVAL results for 14 of the 36 tasks.

There are 6 tasks where the decision tree / power divergence approach is less accurate than the SENSEVAL average; promise-n, scrap-n, shirt-n, amaze-v, bitter-p, and sanction-p. The most dramatic difference occurred with amaze-v, where the SENSEVAL average was 92.4% and the decision tree accuracy was 58.6%. However, this was an unusual task where every instance in the test data belonged to a single sense that was not even the majority sense in the training data.

7   Analysis of Experimental Results

The characteristics of the decision trees and decision stumps learned for each word are shown in Table 2. Columns 1 and 2 show the word and part of speech. Columns 3, 4, and 5 are based on the feature set selected by the power divergence statistic while columns 5, 6, and 7 are based on the Dice Coefficient. Columns 3 and 6 show the node selected to serve as the decision stump. Columns 4 and 7 show the number of leaf nodes in the learned decision tree relative to the number of total nodes. Columns 5 and 8 show the number of bigram features selected to represent the training data.

This table shows that there is little difference in the decision stump nodes selected from feature sets determined by the power divergence statistics versus the Dice Coefficient. However this is to be expected since the top ranked bigrams for each measure are consistent, and the decision stump node is generally chosen from among those.

However, the power divergence statistic and Dice Coefficient do result in different sets of features overall, and this is reflected in the different sized trees that are learned from these feature sets. The number of leaf nodes and the total number of nodes for each learned tree is shown in columns 4 and 7. The number of leaf nodes shows how many unique paths from the root of the tree to a sense distinction/leaf node exist. The number of total nodes is the sum of the leaf nodes and the internal nodes. Since a bigram feature can only appear once in the decision tree, the number of internal nodes represents the number of bigram features selected by the decision tree learner. This acts as a second level of feature selection, further reducing the original feature set selected by

Table 2. Decision Tree and Stump Characteristics

(1) word	(2) pos	power divergence			dice coefficient		
		(3) stump node	(4) leaf/node	(5) features	(6) stump node	(7) leaf/node	(8) features
accident	n	by accident	8/15	101	by accident	12/23	112
behaviour	n	best behaviour	2/3	100	best behaviour	2/3	104
bet	n	betting shop	20/39	50	betting shop	20/39	50
excess	n	in excess	13/25	104	in excess	11/21	102
float	n	the float	7/13	13	the float	7/13	13
giant	n	the giants	16/31	103	the giants	14/27	78
knee	n	knee injury	23/45	102	knee injury	20/39	104
onion	n	in the	1/1	7	in the	1/1	7
promise	n	promise of	95/189	100	a promising	49/97	107
sack	n	the sack	5/9	31	the sack	5/9	31
scrap	n	scrap of	7/13	8	scrap of	7/13	8
shirt	n	shirt and	38/75	101	shirt and	55/109	101
amaze	v	amazed at	11/21	102	amazed at	11/21	102
bet	v	i bet	4/7	10	i bet	4/7	10
bother	v	be bothered	19/37	101	be bothered	20/39	106
bury	v	buried in	28/55	103	buried in	32/63	103
calculate	v	calculated to	5/9	103	calculated to	5/9	103
consume	v	on the	4/7	20	on the	4/7	20
derive	v	derived from	10/19	104	derived from	10/19	104
float	v	floated on	24/47	80	floated on	24/47	80
invade	v	to invade	55/109	107	to invade	66/127	108
promise	v	promise to	3/5	100	promise you	5/9	106
sack	v	return to	1/1	91	return to	1/1	91
scrap	v	of the	1/1	7	of the	1/1	7
seize	v	to seize	26/51	104	to seize	57/113	104
brilliant	a	a brilliant	26/51	101	a brilliant	42/83	103
floating	a	in the	7/13	10	in the	7/13	10
generous	a	a generous	57/113	103	a generous	56/111	102
giant	a	the giant	2/3	102	a giant	1/1	101
modest	a	a modest	14/27	101	a modest	10/19	105
slight	a	the slightest	2/3	105	the slightest	2/3	105
wooden	a	wooden spoon	2/3	104	wooden spoon	2/3	101
band	p	band of	14/27	100	the band	21/41	117
bitter	p	a bitter	22/43	54	a bitter	22/43	54
sanction	p	south africa	12/23	52	south africa	12/23	52
shake	p	his head	90/179	100	his head	81/161	105

the power divergence statistic or the Dice Coefficient. In general the number of features included in the decision tree is quite a bit less than the original number of features. Note that the smallest decision trees are functionally equivalent to other classifiers. A decision tree with 1 leaf node and no internal nodes (1/1) acts as a majority classifier. A decision tree with 2 leaf nodes and 1 internal node (2/3) has the structure of a decision stump.

For most words the top ranked 100 bigrams constitute the feature set that is used to represent the training data. If there were ties in the top 100 then there may be more than 100 features, and if the there were fewer than 100 bigrams that occurred more than 5 times then feature selection reduces to choosing all of those bigrams.

8   Discussion

One of our long-term objectives is to identify a simple set of features that will be useful for disambiguating a wide class of words using both supervised and unsupervised methodologies. The results of this paper suggest that bigrams may be an appropriate starting point. Our interest in extending these methods to unsupervised approaches motivated the decision to include bigrams that did not include the ambiguous word as one of the components. Thus, many of the bigrams that were included in the decision trees are bigrams that can be selected without the aid of sense–tagged text.

We hypothesize that accurate decision trees of bigrams will generally include a relatively small number of bigram features. The decision stump results tend to support this view, showing that high accuracy is attainable with just a single bigram feature. Thus, we set the initial criteria for identifying bigram features to include at most the top 100 ranked bigrams and implement an aggressive pruning strategy during the decision tree learning stage. As a result, there were no decision trees that used all of the bigram features, and most of them discarded a considerable number of features. The number of features included in each decision tree can can be seen in Table 2 by taking the difference between the node and leaf counts in columns 4 or 7 and comparing that to the number of features shown in columns 5 or 8.

Decision trees have the considerable advantage that intuitive and understandable rules for disambiguation can be easily extracted from the tree structure. Each path from the root to a leaf node represents a series of binary choices based on whether or not a particular bigram occurs in the text being disambiguated. These rules can be used to discover more general principles of disambiguation and potentially identify features that are useful for a broad class of words.

We found that the feature sets selected by the power divergence statistic tended to result in more accurate decision trees than those selected by the Dice Coefficient. We hypothesize that this is due to the fact that the *gain ratio* used by the decision tree learner J48 to select nodes is based on Mutual Information and as such is closely related to the Dice Coefficient. We believe that this overly biases the feature selection processes towards Mutual Information and results in a feature set that is skewed towards that measure and not optimal for classification.

9   Related Work

Bigrams have been used as features for word sense disambiguation, particularly in the form of collocations where the ambiguous word is one component of the bigram (e.g., [1], [9], [16]). While some of the bigrams we identify are collocations that include the word being disambiguated, there is no requirement that this be the case. This makes our approach less dependent on sense–tagged text and suggests that it may extend more easily to environments where the amount of sense–tagged text is smaller or does not exist.

Decision trees have been used in supervised learning approaches to word sense disambiguation, and have fared well in a number of comparative studies (e.g., [8], [11]). In the former they were used with the bag of word feature sets and in the latter they were used with a mixed feature set that included part-of-speech, morphological, and collocation features. The approach in this paper is the first time that decision trees based strictly on bigram features have been employed.

The decision list is a closely related approach that has also been applied to word sense disambiguation (e.g., [15], [13], [17]). Rather than building and traversing a tree to perform disambiguation, a list is employed. In the general case a decision list may suffer from less fragmentation during learning than decision trees. However, we believe that fragmentation also reflects upon the feature set used to represent the training data. Our feature set is based on 100 binary features. This is a relatively small feature space and not as likely to suffer from fragmentation as a larger space.

10   Conclusions

This paper shows that bigrams are powerful features for performing word sense disambiguation. Our findings show that a simple decision tree where each node tests whether or not a particular bigram occurs near the ambiguous word results in accuracy comparable with state–of–the–art methods. This is demonstrated via an empirical comparison using data from the 1998 SENSEVAL word sense disambiguation exercise that shows the decision tree approach is more accurate than the best SENSEVAL results for 19 of 36 words.

11   Acknowledgments

This work has been supported by a Grant–in–Aid of Research, Artistry and Scholarship from the Office of the Vice President for Research and the Dean of the Graduate School of the University of Minnesota. I would like to thank the SENSEVAL organizers and participants for putting the data and results of the 1998 event in the public domain.

References

1. R. Bruce and J. Wiebe. Word-sense disambiguation using decomposable models. In *Proceedings of the 32nd Annual Meeting of the Association for Computational Linguistics*, pages 139–146, 1994.

2. K. Church and P. Hanks. Word association norms, mutual information and lexicography. In *Proceedings of the 28th Annual Meeting of the Association for Computational Linguistics*, pages 76–83, 1990.

3. N. Cressie and T. Read. Multinomial goodness of fit tests. *Journal of the Royal Statistics Society Series B*, 46:440–464, 1984.

4. R. Duda and P. Hart. *Pattern Classification and Scene Analysis*. Wiley, New York, NY, 1973.

5. T. Dunning. Accurate methods for the statistics of surprise and coincidence. *Computational Linguistics*, 19(1):61–74, 1993.

6. R. Holte. Very simple classification rules perform well on most commonly used datasets. *Machine Learning*, 11:63–91, 1993.

7. A. Kilgarriff and M. Palmer. Special issue on SENSEVAL: Evaluating word sense disambiguation programs. *Computers and the Humanities*, 34(1–2), 2000.

8. R. Mooney. Comparative experiments on disambiguating word senses: An illustration of the role of bias in machine learning. In *Proceedings of the Conference on Empirical Methods in Natural Language Processing*, pages 82–91, May 1996.

9. H.T. Ng and H.B. Lee. Integrating multiple knowledge sources to disambiguate word sense: An exemplar-based approach. In *Proceedings of the 34th Annual Meeting of the Society for Computational Linguistics*, pages 40–47, 1996.

10. T. Pedersen. Fishing for exactness. In *Proceedings of the South Central SAS User's Group (SCSUG-96) Conference*, pages 188–200, Austin, TX, October 1996.

11. T. Pedersen and R. Bruce. A new supervised learning algorithm for word sense disambiguation. In *Proceedings of the Fourteenth National Conference on Artificial Intelligence*, pages 604–609, Providence, RI, July 1997.

12. F. Smadja, K. McKeown, and V. Hatzivassiloglou. Translating collocations for bilingual lexicons: A statistical approach. *Computational Linguistics*, 22(1):1–38, 1996.

13. Y. Wilks and M. Stevenson. Word sense disambiguation using optimised combinations of knowledge sources. In *Proceedings of COLING/ACL-98*, 1998.

14. I. Witten and E. Frank. *Data Mining - Practical Machine Learning Tools and Techniques with Java Implementations*. Morgan–Kaufmann, San Francisco, CA, 2000.

15. D. Yarowsky. Decision lists for lexical ambiguity resolution: Application to accent restoration in Spanish and French. In *Proceedings of the 32nd Annual Meeting of the Association for Computational Linguistics*, 1994.

16. D. Yarowsky. Unsupervised word sense disambiguation rivaling supervised methods. In *Proceedings of the 33rd Annual Meeting of the Association for Computational Linguistics*, pages 189–196, Cambridge, MA, 1995.

17. D. Yarowsky. Hierarchical decision lists for word sense disambiguation. *Computers and the Humanities*, 34(1–2), 2000.

Interpretation of Compound Nominals Using WordNet

Leslie Barrett,[1] Anthony R. Davis,[1] and Bonnie J. Dorr [2]

[1] AnswerLogic, Inc.
1111 19th St. NW, suite 600, Washington, DC 20036 USA
{lbarrett,tdavis}@answerlogic.com

[2] Dept. of Computer Science
Univ. of Maryland, College Park, MD 20740 USA
bonnie@umiacs.umd.edu

Abstract. We describe an approach to interpreting noun-noun compounds within a question answering system. The system's lexicon, based on WordNet, provides the basis for heuristics that group noun-noun compounds with semantically similar words. The semantic relationship between the nouns in a compound is determined by the choice of heuristic for the compound. We discuss procedures for selecting one heuristic in cases where several can apply to a compound, the effects of lexical ambiguity, and some initial results of our methods.

1   Introduction

We describe an approach to interpreting noun-noun compounds (henceforth NNC) under development for use within a question-answering system. Because there is no explicit linguistic indication of the semantic relationship between the nouns in a compound, this is both a difficult problem and a task better suited to computational semantic methods than purely grammatical ones. Our approach uses a set of heuristics for classifying compounds according to the nouns in them, and associates each heuristic with a type of relationship between two entities. We determine which heuristics apply to a given compound by the classes of nouns specified in each heuristic and by a comparison of heuristics to choose the one that fits best according to criteria of semantic similarity. The WordNet system (Fellbaum (1998), http://www.cogsci. princeton.edu/~wn/) furnishes both a lexical database and a basis for computing measures of semantic similarity among nouns.

We believe that this work is important because it draws on a widely-used lexical resource and combines it with a pragmatic and implementable approach to interpreting NNCs. Apart from its usefulness in estimating semantic similarity, WordNet offers some direct advantages as a basis for interpretation, such as its hyponymy links, which mirror the relationships between the nouns in some compounds (e.g., 'elm tree', 'turtleneck sweater'). We assign a heuristic, and then a semantic relationship, to an NNC by choosing the heuristic that is "semantically closest" to the compound. This two-stage process is desirable because most of the heuristics are designed to cover a specific semantic domain, but the same relationship may hold in NNCs form quite different domains (e.g., both 'wine glass' and 'bird cage' would be assigned the

A. Gelbukh (Ed.): CICLing 2001, LNCS 2004, pp. 169–181, 2001.

same semantic relationship, but would be covered by different heuristics). We have tested different measures of semantic distance, supplemented with frequency information for different senses of ambiguous nouns. The latter is important because many nouns are ambiguous and this interacts with the heuristic choice. We have tested our ideas on a set of several hundred NNCs found in text, using a set of over a hundred heuristics and about 25 semantic relationships. Though our implementation remains incomplete, we report some preliminary results that indicate promise.

Following a brief discussion of our goals and the problems we confront in reaching them, we compare our work with two other approaches to interpreting NNCs. One, due to Vanderwende (1995), posits a relatively small number of relationships that can be assigned to the nouns in a compound. We have found that, in the context of our system, this set is smaller and less precise than what we require. On the other end of the spectrum is the abduction-based view of interpretation advocated in Hobbs et al. (1993), in which the range of possible relationships is potentially limitless and complex, but which depends on extensive knowledge representation and inference mechanisms that we strive to avoid. We take an intermediate position on the number and extensibility of relationships that are useful for interpreting most NNCs (again, in the context of our question-answering system), and then explain how our WordNet-based heuristics are formulated. We close the paper with a discussion of our results and suggestions for further research.

2   Challenges of the Task

Interpretation of NNCs is known to be difficult. As noted by Finin (1980), "...there can be arbitrarily many possible relationships between the nouns, each appropriate for a particular context." In brief, there is little explicit linguistic information to be exploited with no clearly predefined target set of relationships that we can assume. Also, compounds range from completely lexicalized to novel, on-the-fly, context-dependent formations, and from highly idiosyncratic semantically to more or less compositional; compounds may contain several nouns, bracketed ambiguously, and the individual lexical items in them are also frequently ambiguous. In this paper we do not address all of these matters. We confine ourselves to NNCs containing just two nouns, and we are concerned with semantically transparent ones, rather than the lexicalized, non-compositional ones (which we have lexicalized in numerous cases).

Some work on the problem has supposed a fairly small set of relations, somewhat like thematic roles or broad relationships of time and location. We have found this unsatisfactory for our purposes, however. There is no obvious set of discrete, distinct relations "out there" in the world, and we prefer not to define a set of relationships from abstract principles, but to be guided by potential usefulness in the domain of our system. At one extreme we could create a unique semantic relation between each pair of noun senses, but not all differences between relations are important. Deciding which ones are is a task that tends to be domain and application dependent, and we have let our intuitions guide us in developing the set of relations we use. Inevitably, this will result in cases that are hard to classify. Should 'shortwave broadcast' be regarded as a relationship of instrument, medium, or something else between 'short-wave' and 'radio'? We leave open the possibility of defining our relations so that more than one applies. Sometimes, as in this case, a unique interpretation isn't clear (and we may not want to be forced to choose one). Because our goal is to improve a question-answering and document retrieval system, we wish to find relationships that are similar enough to be useful. Thus a mention of radio broadcasts in a question should be interpreted using a relation that is identical to, or allows us to infer, the relation between, say, 'program' and 'radio', in a document mentioning "radio programs" or "programs on the radio". In contrast, the relationship between the nouns in 'shortwave frequencies' is sufficiently different from that between 'radio' and 'broadcast' that we would not wish to assign the same relation to it.

Aside from making choices in individual cases, and deciding what degree of overlap can be allowed, we also are concerned with the inventory of heuristics as a whole. The challenge involved in creating an optimal inventory of heuristics is to satisfy the criteria of accuracy and generality simultaneously. That is, each NNC encountered by the system needs to be classified into a semantic relationship that is both narrow enough to be informative, and broad enough to extend beyond the single encountered example.

3   Some Recent Approaches to Noun-Noun Compound Interpretation

Recent classification proposals for NN compounds address these issues from two perspectives. Vanderwende (1995) bases a set of diagnostics for NNCs on the basis of WH-word classifications. That is, the function of the relation between two nouns in a compound is to match question types. Each 'class', under this analysis, corresponds to a WH-word. For example, the NNC 'garden party' is assigned to the 'Where' class, because it answers the question: "Where is the party?" Effectively, then, this is a way of saying that the relationship between the members of the compound is that the location of the head ('party') is given by the modifier ('garden'). Vanderwende's classifications are applied according to the following criteria:

1. Rule Type – this can be either:
   a. Modifier-based, if the semantic feature of the attribute (i.e. the defining feature of the compound) is on the modifier N
   b. Head-based, if the semantic feature of the attribute is on the head N
   c. Head-deverbal, if the semantic feature of the attribute is found on the verb corresponding to the noun
2. Modifier feature – the semantic features that are tested for the modifier noun
3. Head feature – the semantic features that are tested for the head noun

For example, the NNC 'pacifist vote' has the following analysis under Vanderwende's system:

Class: Who/What?
Rule Type: Head-based (because the semantic focus, being the class-correspondent in this case is 'vote')
Modifier feature: +HUMAN (because 'pacifist' represents a human)
Head Feature: +SPEECH ACT (because 'vote' represents a speech act)

The descriptive apparatus used here basically says that the NNC 'pacifist vote' is a 'speech-act' type N modified by a 'human' type N which can be used as an answer to the question 'Who' or 'What'. The advantage of such an approach is the ability to provide a complete semantic classification of each noun in the compound, and, in turn, to associate such classification with question types. Such an approach could be considered a 'holistic' approach to NNC classification in that the external relations of the compound as a whole are the focus rather than the internal relations (i.e. the relationship which N1 has to N2).

Vanderwende's classification relies on the varieties of WH-words in the language in order to determine relationships assigned to NNCs. It is unclear that there is a necessary, deep, and tight connection between these two domains (except in the broadest sense, in which any modifier can be considered an answer to the question: "What kind?"). We have furthermore found in our work on question answering systems that more specific domain-dependent relationships between nouns prove useful in interpreting NNCs. Thus, restricting the set of relationships to the fairly broad ones associated with WH-words is not ideal for our purposes, though it provides a good starting point.

The analysis presented in Hobbs et al (1993) takes a different approach. This analysis starts with the assumption that the salient problem involved in compound nominal resolution is defining the relationship between N1 and N2.[1] The representational apparatus chosen to represent NN relations is a first-order logic simulation whereby variables are mapped to noun-compounds. For the NNC 'oil sample', for example, the representation is the following:

$$(\forall x,y)sample(y,x) \rightarrow nn(x,y)$$

This handles the case where the head noun (x) is a relational noun, and the modifying noun fills one of its roles. Where the head noun is not inherently relational, three propositions are used, one for each noun, and one for the relation between them. For example, in the NNC 'turpentine jar', Hobbs et al. give the following formula:

$$(\exists x,y)turpentine(y) \wedge jar(x) \wedge nn(y,x)$$

The authors argue that proving the statement nn(y,x) constitutes determining the implicit relation between the nouns. This determination, in turn, is dependent upon knowing and representing the salient features of the conjuncts 'turpentine' and 'jar'. In addition, our real-world knowledge, which tells us that jars can contain turpentine, is related to the fact that jars can contain liquid. The problem of representing this connection, however, is based upon the fact that the pragmatic inference relating 'turpentine' to 'liquid' in this case goes the wrong way. That is, we know that jars can contain liquids, and one of the ways that a liquid can manifest itself in the world is to be turpentine. That is, what we would like to describe the pragmatic effect of 'turpentine' in the NNC 'turpentine jar' is the following:

$$(\forall x)liquid(x) \supset turpentine(x)$$

---

[1] Since Hobbs et al. (1993) discuss NN compounds with two members or more, their relation holds between N(n) and (n-1)

This, however, would be saying that all liquids in the world are turpentine. To say that all liquids with certain properties (not specified in the context given) can be turpentine, Hobbs et al. use the predicate 'etc':

$$(\forall x)\text{liquid}(x) \wedge \text{etc}(x) \supset \text{turpentine}(x)$$

One way that the authors express the meaning of the (etc) predicate is to apply an inference that they refer to as 'weighted abduction'. This amounts to saying that the cost of interpreting elements with a low semantic contribution is high. By the same token, high semantic-contributors have correspondingly high worth for their cost. Thus, saying that something is a liquid only helps us slightly in assuming that it may be turpentine, and therefore the term 'liquid' in the above proof would be given a lower value than the term 'etc.', which represents the particular properties of such a liquid.

Since we also know that 'liquids' are 'contained' in 'jars', this same formula can be applied to the NNC to express the idea that a containment relation holds in NNCs:

$$(\forall e',x,y) \text{ contain}'(e',x,y) \supset \text{nn}(y,x)$$

The system proposed in Hobbs et al. (1993) differs from the analysis in Vanderwende (1995) in that the primary concern is to represent the relation between N1 and N2 in NNCs, as is ours. It shares with Vanderwende's system the exhaustive semantic representation of each individual NN component. While this makes the system highly extensible and appropriate for knowledge representation, it is not well suited for systems of a practical size and speed. Some of the same ideas of class inclusion are captured in the WordNet hierarchy and representable in our system without the need to state them as proofs. Thus, for example, we represent an NNC like 'elm tree' with the relation Hyponym, because 'elm' is a type of tree. The relation of hyponymy is already encoded in Wordnet. Furthermore, all the other types of things that share properties of elms, like 'oak' or 'pine' will be listed in a WordNet 'synset' and therefore will fall under the same relation.

4   Using WordNet in Determining NN Relationships

Our operational definition of interpreting an NNC consists of two things: first, choosing the correct senses of each noun, which is but a part of the general lexical disambiguation problem, and second, selecting among our set of predefined relationships the one (or possibly more) that best captures how the two senses should be related.

Which relationships we choose to represent depends on how deep and detailed our system's analysis needs to be. Using only some sort of uniform "mystery relation" (like Hobbs et al's high-cost *nn* relation) between the nouns in any compound is unlikely to be useful, as is assuming a unique relationship for every distinct compound. Vanderwende suggests that the number of useful relationships can be fairly small, but again this question has application and domain dependent answers. For a medical domain, a system might make use of many relationships between disease conditions or disease causing organisms and their host, while a single umbrella relationship might suffice for these in another domain. We have approached this issue in a less *a priori* fashion, seeking to find and distinguish relations where it seems important to do so, and leaving the inventory of relationships open-ended. Our inventory of relationships can be extended and enriched for specific domains, though once we have decided on a set it cannot be changed at run time. The relationships are not necessarily mutually exclusive, and one might imply others. In the latter case, we would consider a correct result to be selecting the most specific relationship that applies. For example, a relationship of EquipmentBrand (e.g., 'Trek bicycle') implies the broader relationship MadeBy (covering 'artisan jewelry' and 'beaver dam' as well as 'Trek bicycle'). EquipmentBrand would then be the correct relationship for 'Trek bicycle'. Note also that these relationships are intended to cover not only compound nominals, but also prepositional modifiers of noun phrases and other constructions where two entities are related. Thus our system should yield an interpretation of 'bicycle made by Trek' that will match 'Trek bicycle'.

Some additional examples of noun-noun relationships and compounds they are intended to apply to may be useful at this point. Much like Vanderwende, we have relations signifying that N1 is the Location of N2 ('bedroom window' or, more abstractly, 'network traffic') and the rarer inverse ('account domain'), that N1 is the Time of N2 ('afternoon meeting', 'Renaissance art'), that N1 is the Purpose of N2 ('user interface', 'adjustment screw'), that N1 is the Means or Instrument of N2 ('dialup connection', 'radio broadcast'), and so on. We also have relations that are tied to syntactic relations of verbs, which are useful for NNCs headed by nominalizations: Subject ('insect flight', 'computer crash'), Object ('waste disposal'), and others. Additional relations, not so obviously corresponding to Vanderwende's inventory, are Copular ('target zone', 'child actor') and Hyponymic ('elm tree', 'tuna fish'). This is not intended to be a complete list; in all, we have about thirty such relationships.

Our lexicon is based on WordNet, but has been considerably expanded and revised. For the purposes of this paper, though, most of these modifications can be ignored. We use WordNet as a classification of noun senses[2] and as a rough measure of the semantic distance between senses. The latter is particularly important here, as our strategy for hypothesizing noun-noun relationships relies on the following assumption:

Suppose we have an NNC in which the first noun has the sense S1 and the second has the sense S2. If S1 bears the relationship R to S2 and S1' is a sense semantically "close" to S1 (via links in WordNet), then the same relationship may well hold between the nouns in a compound with S1' as the sense of its first noun and S2 for the second. Similarly, the same relationship may well hold for a compound in which an S2' semantically close to S2 is substituted. A clear set of examples is plant names; alongside 'elm tree' we have 'oak tree', 'pine tree', 'palm tree', and, changing both nouns: 'berry bush', 'cherry tree', 'grape vine', and 'tomato plant'. Troublesome counterexamples to our assumption exist, naturally (compare 'mosquito net' and 'butterfly net'), but it is a good initial strategy.

---

[2] WordNet distinguishes separate senses of nouns, organizing synonymous senses into *synsets*, which are connected to one another with various types of links. For example, 'woodchuck' and 'groundhog' have senses that are in the same synset. In this paper, we discuss only one type of link, that expressing hyponymy/hypernymy ('woodchuck' is a hyponym of 'rodent'). Other types of WordNet links, such as part-whole links, might also prove useful in interpreting NNCs.

Starting with a prototype NNC, we can allow for similar compounds, with semantically close nouns, to be assigned the same relationship by specifying a region of the WordNet hierarchy around each noun sense. Our rule will then be that if we have another compound with first and second noun senses in the same region as the prototype's, the relationship in that compound (between N1 and N2) will be the same. We allow any subtree of WordNet noun senses to be designated as a region. We treat a heuristic for assigning a relationship as an ordered pair of sense IDs (or as a pair of WordNet *synsets*). A heuristic *applies* to an NNC iff there exists a usage of the first noun in the same synset as the heuristic's first sense ID or in a hyponym of that synset, and a usage of the second noun in the same synset as the heuristic's second sense ID or in a hyponym of that synset. Every heuristic is associated with one of the noun-noun relationships we posit. In general, there will be several heuristics associated with a noun-noun relation, because there are different portions of the WordNet hierarchy from which the nouns in semantically similar NNCs are found.

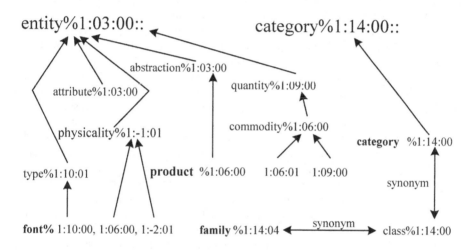

Fig. 1. Two possible NN candidates to match the heuristic 'relCategoryOf' : *'product category'* and *'font family'*. Word senses with direct hyponym and synonym paths shown in bold.

In Figure 1, the possible applications of the heuristic relCategoryOf to the NNCs 'product category' and 'font family' are shown. For the first case, 'product category', at least *one path* from each sense of each word in the compound will reach the correct heuristic. For 'font family', there are several senses of both 'font' and 'family' to consider, but we simplify here by taking only one sense of 'family'; the three senses of 'font' all meet the criterion of the heuristic, which requires only that the first noun of an NNC be a hyponym of entity%1:03:00::, the root of the noun hierarchy. Naturally, the chance of a match is inversely proportional to the specificity of the heuristic.

Each of our heuristics is associated with one of the noun-noun relationships discussed earlier. There may be compounds containing nouns from several areas of the WordNet hierarchy, which we need to cover with different heuristics, but which we wish to assign the same relationship. For example, the Copular relation plausibly applies to compounds in which the first word refers to some kind of indicator or target ('target zone', 'goal area', 'indicator light') and to tree names ('elm tree', 'ponderosa pine'). We have two heuristics to handle these two sets of compounds, but both are associated with the same Copular relation. Since the coverage of individual heuristics is governed not so much by principles as by quirks of WordNet's organization and of English, it makes sense to keep them separate from the relationships used in interpretations.

The strategy of treating compounds with semantically close words alike, though obviously not foolproof, is flexible because it allows for any number of heuristics and noun-noun relationships to be defined, for more than one relationship to hold between the nouns in a compound, and for incremental changes in the lexicon and the heuristics that are used for determining which relationship(s) are applicable.

We will now address two questions that arise from this approach. When more than one relationship might be postulated for a compound, how do we decide which one(s) to choose? And how does lexical ambiguity of the nouns in a compound affect and interact with choosing an interpretation for the compound?

In practice, we have addressed the first issue by checking which heuristics apply, and then choosing one of those according to metrics (computed from the WordNet hierarchy) of how specific a heuristic is (the more specific, the better) or how close the synsets in the heuristic are to those in the compound (the closer, the better). Other algorithms are possible; for example, the set of heuristics might simply be applied in a fixed order, and the first one that applies would be chosen. We will discuss below some of the refinements we have tested with the specificity and closeness metrics.

The specificity metric we have used is to add the number of synsets that are descendents of the two synsets in the heuristic. While this is a crude measure of how specific the synsets in a heuristic are, it seems preferable to, say, summing the path lengths from the root to the two synsets, as these are more dependent on individual arbitrary decisions about the arrangement of noun senses in the hierarchy. Using our specificity metric, more specific heuristics will have smaller numbers, because they have fewer descendent synsets. In a descendent synset, we consider the descendent nodes to be dominated by the parent node. Often, a single parent node will directly dominate multiple child-nodes, creating a "bushy" tree. We consider such a parent node to be less specific than one that directly dominates fewer nodes.[3] Again, the essential motivation behind this measure is to choose specialized heuristics with narrow applicability over broader ones, because we can provide a more accurate noun-noun relationship for a narrower range of compounds than we could for a broader one.

Table 1 shows the calculation of a rough specificity measure for heuristics, determined by summing the distances between root node of the noun hierarchy and the two synsets specified by the heuristic. (In practice, we measure specificity by calculating the number of descendent synsets.) The closeness metric (not shown in Table 1) we define by counting the number of hyponym links on the shortest path from a synset containing a noun usage to the synset in the heuristic, for both the first and second nouns and heuristic synsets. Smaller numbers therefore indicate heuristics that are "closer" to the compound. Here, the motivation is that we prefer heuristics with synset

---

[3] For simplicity, the distance relations shown in the chart below simply count the distance in links (the less desirable measure mentioned in the text), rather than the sum of the number of descendent synset nodes of the two heuristic synsets.

pairs that are close to the senses of the nouns in the compound, again because we can provide a more accurate guess at the noun-noun relationship than we can with a more distant heuristic.

Figure 2 below shows a scenario in which there are two senses of two nouns in a compound. In this example, the closeness and specificity measures yield different results, as shown in Table 2.

Table 1. Sample set of five heuristics showing senseIDs for N1 and N2, the distance between N1, N2 and their respective unique beginners (i.e. root nodes) in the Wordnet hierarchy, and the sum of the distance of N1 and N2 to their respective unique beginners. This measure of specificity is an alternative to the one discussed in the text, which totals the number of synset nodes *dominated by* the two synsets in the heuristic.

Heuristic	N1 synset	N2 synset	Dist. root to N1 syn-set	Dist. root to N2 syn-set	Sum of dist.
relAttrOfBcgd	display%1:06:01	back-ground%1:06:01	7	7	14
relConnTo_2	entity%1:03:00	connec-tion%1:24:00	1	2	3
rel-CommForFnctOf	act%1:03:00	publica-tion%1:10:00	1	4	5
relMemberOf	group%1:03:00	member%1:18:00	1	5	6
relPartOf_15B	pro-gram%1:10:02	area%1:07:00	5	4	9

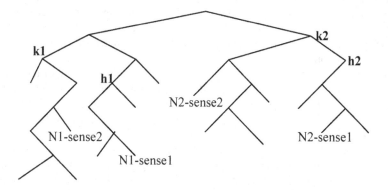

Fig. 2. Two heuristics and their application to an NNC, in which each noun has two senses.

Table 2. Choice of heuristics for an NNC in which each noun has two senses. The two heuristics 'h' and 'k' apply to the NNC for some, but not all, of the possible combinations of senses. When the specificity metric is used to select a sense, heuristic 'h' is chosen, but when the closeness metric is used, 'k' is chosen Here, specificity is calculated using the number of synsets dominated by the synsets in the heuristic.

N1 sense	N2 sense	Specificity h	Specificity k	Closeness h	Closeness k
N1S1	N2S1	*	n.a.	6	n.a.
N1S1	N2S2	n.a.	n.a.	n.a.	n.a.
N1S2	N2S1	n.a.	*	n.a.	7
N1S2	N2S2	n.a.	*	n.a.	5

In the diagram and table above, the results of applying the specificity measure are compared to the results of applying the closeness measure with both senses of each noun in the compound (i.e. for both senses of N1 and N2). The specificity measure chooses heuristic 'h' over heuristic 'k', for any sense combination that is applicable, since the synsets of 'h' dominates fewer nodes than those of 'k' for the combination (and since 'h' dominates both Ns, a necessary precondition for applying the heuristic). The closeness measure, on the other hand, computes a path of length 6 for 'h' when considering sense 1 of N1 and sense 1 of N2 (i.e. 3 nodes for each N) and will not calculate 'k', since 'k' does not dominate N1S1 (note: the table abbreviates "sense" as "S"). But, for a combination of N1 sense 2 and N2 sense 2, since 'h' does not apply, 'k' has a path-length of 4, less than the length for any either heuristic with any other combination of senses. This means that, under the closeness metric, heuristic 'k' is selected, along with the sense 2 for N1 and sense 2 for N2.

Combining these two measures is also a possibility. They are not truly comparable in the form we have just stated them, but we can modify the specificity metric so that it is combinable with the closeness metric. Rather than using the raw number of descendent synsets, we can use the log of this number, which is related to the average length of a path to a leaf node in the hierarchy from that point. Since the branching factor in the WordNet noun hierarchy is approximately 4, we use the log base 4 of the number of descendant synsets as the revised specificity measure (summing the two numbers, one for each element of the heuristic). This can then be added to the number obtained for the closeness metric. Weighting of the two metrics forming the combined measure can of course be varied.

Another parameter that we will explore is the relative importance of the specificity or closeness measures for the head and modifier nouns in a compound. Summing these numbers weights them equally, but this too could be varied, so that if a particular heuristic applies, its closeness measure might depend heavily on the head, rather than the modifier.

Now we need to address how lexical ambiguity interacts with these metrics. Many of the nouns we encounter in compounds are multiply ambiguous. This is sometimes an artifact of WordNet, but most often it reflects genuine lexical ambiguity. The problem this poses should be clear; when we consider all the senses of the nouns in a compound, rather than just the intended ones, various heuristics may apply to these irrelevant senses, and some of them may have better measures than the correct heuristic does applying to the correct sense. We can circumvent this problem to the extent that we can disambiguate the nouns successfully before attempting to interpret the compound they form, but this is not always feasible. A simple strategy for weeding out rare senses of nouns that are unlikely to be the ones used in the compound, is to boost the score of the most common sense (we have at our disposal usage counts for each sense from which we can determine the most common sense). Since lower scores are better ones for specificity and closeness, this translates into subtracting some points from the score of a heuristic when it applies to a compound and one or both of the nouns is assumed to used in the most common sense. Other, more sophisticated uses of the usage count information can be imagined, but this is the one we have explored so far.

5   Results

We have tested our methods on a set of 388 NNCs, for the most part selected from source documents used in implementations of our question-answering system. We developed our heuristics in tandem with this set, so there is admittedly a danger of cheating; that is, of tailoring our heuristics to account for the compounds in our test set but failing to ensure that they handle new data well. Preliminary results on a test set of 1,219 additional NNCs shows promising results, however. Approximately 85% of the compounds were assigned a heuristic. While this is not as high as the assignment percentage of the run discussed here (which is above 93%), this corpus is over three times as large, so some decline in assignment percentage is expected. Further evaluation of these results is currently underway. In this section we report some early results we have obtained using the specificity and closeness metrics and the enhanced version of WordNet that our lexicon is based on. For each compound we decided which senses of the nouns and which heuristic are correct (and hence which noun-noun relationship is the correct one). We then applied the specificity and closeness metrics for ordering the heuristics (there are about 150 of them) to our set of NNCs. For 27 of the NNCs, no heuristic was applicable; for the remaining 361 at least one heuristic applies.

Generally, the results favor the closeness metric over the specificity metric (we have not yet examined the effects of combined metrics). Results with the specificity and closeness metrics appear in the following table (percentages are of the total 388, not the 361 assigned a heuristic, so they do not include the 27 (6.95%) of cases in which no heuristic applied):

Table 3. Comparison of specificity and closeness metrics in assigning correct heuristics to NNCs.

Specificity		Closeness	
correct	incorrect	correct	incorrect
113 (29.1%)	248 (63.9%)	161 (41.5%)	200 (51.5%)

These numbers are lower than we wish them to be, of course, but it is worth bearing in mind that even when an erroneous heuristic is chosen, it may be associated to the same noun-noun relationship as the correct one. For example, 'connection period' was incorrectly assigned the heuristic relTimeTakenBy under the closeness metric, instead of relActionPeriod, but both of these heuristics are associated with the relationship MeasureOf, so no harm is done. Similarly, for 'newsgroup discussion', the incorrect relActionInLocation_1 is closer than relInLocation_2, but both are associated with the relationship Location. Thus the effective performance is somewhat higher than these figures indicate.

There was considerable overlap in the behavior of the specificity and closeness metrics but also noticeable differences. For 98 of the compounds in our sample, both metrics chose the correct heuristic, while in 185 cases neither did. There were 63 cases in which the closeness metric chose the correct heuristic and the specificity metric did not, but only 15 in which the specificity metric chose correctly and the closeness metric did not. One such case is 'human eye', for which the heuristic relAbilityOf won out on the closeness measure over the correct relOrganismBodyPart. This happened because there is a sense of 'eye' meaning "discernment" (as in: "She has an eye for fresh talent.") which is just three links away in WordNet from the sense of 'ability' used in the relAbilityOf heuristic, and the intended sense of 'eye' ("organ of sight") is also three links away from 'body part'. However, there is a sense of 'human' that happens to have a short path to 'entity' (the first synset of the pair used in relAbilityOf), but which has a rather long path to 'organism' (the first synset of the pair used in relOrganismBodyPart), because each larger taxonomic category ('hominid', 'primate', 'mammal', 'vertebrate', etc.) adds a link in this path. For organisms not classed as 'sentient entities' in our version of WordNet, the short path to 'entity' will not exist, and the correct heuristic would likely be chosen under both metrics. This example shows some of the challenges faced when estimating semantic distance from a structure like WordNet; certain hyponymy links, such as those relating biological taxonomic categories, should perhaps be weighted less than others, but tuning the weights would involve a large amount of effort. Another possibility is to penalize the less common discernment sense of 'eye' involved in the erroneous heuristic assignment. This method can be at least partly implemented using existing information on relative frequencies of word senses, but whether it would compensate for the long path from 'human' to 'organism' is questionable.

6   Conclusion

We have explored methods for interpreting NNCs based on the structure of WordNet. We have formulated heuristics to capture the likely similarity among compounds with nouns that lie in the same WordNet region. Each heuristic is associated with broader noun-noun relationships that are employed throughout the rest of our system. We have examined two metrics for choosing the best heuristic in situations where multiple heuristics can apply to an NNC, and presented some preliminary results.

We believe that this approach can capture many of the same benefits of the very robust system presented in Hobbs et al. (1993) in our system without creating a system dependent on intractable amounts of knowledge representation and inferencing. Such systems prove difficult for practical application (see Hobbs et al.'s discussion of Reiger 1974). At the same time we are able to provide more coverage than the system argued for in Vanderwende (1995).

Acknowledgements. We would like to thank Marti Hearst for extensive discussions, George Krupka and Stephan Greene for crucial assistance in implementing the ideas presented here, and Jamie Hamilton and Paul Jacobs for their support of these efforts.

References

1. Finin, T.W. (1980). *The Semantic Interpretation of Compound Nominals*, Ph.D. dissertation, University of Illinois, Urbana-Champaign
2. Fellbaum, Christiane (ed.) (1998). *WordNet: An Electronic Lexical Database*, The MIT Press, Cambridge, MA.
3. Hobbs, Jerry R., Mark E. Stickel, Douglas E. Appelt, and Paul Martin (1993). "Interpretation as Abduction", *Artificial Intelligence*, 63:1-2, pp. 69-142.
4. Rieger, C.J. III (1974). "Conceptual Memory: A Theory and Computer Program for Processing the Meaning Content of Natural Language Utterances". Memo AIM-233, Stanford Artificial Intelligence Laboratory, Stanford University.
5. Vanderwende, Lucretia H. (1995). *The Analysis of Noun Sequences using Semantic Information Extracted from Online Dictionaries*, Ph.D. dissertation, Dept. of Linguistics, Georgetown University.
6. WordNet website: http://www.cogsci.princeton.edu/~wn/

Specification Marks for Word Sense Disambiguation: New Development

Andrés Montoyo and Manuel Palomar

Department of Software and Computing Systems, University of Alicante, Alicante, Spain
{montoyo, mpalomar}@dlsi.ua.es

Abstract. This paper presents a new method for the automatic resolution of lexical ambiguity of nouns in English texts. This new method is made up of three new heuristics, which improve the previous Specification Marks Method. These heuristics rely on the use of the gloss in the semantic relations (hypernym and hyponym) and the hierarchic organization of WordNet. An evaluation of the new method was done on both the Semantic Concordance Corpus (Semcor)[7], and Microsoft 98 Encarta Encyclopaedia Deluxe. The percentages of correct resolutions were Semcor 66.2% and Encarta 66.3% respectively. These percentages show that successful results can be obtained with different domain corpus, and therefore our proposed method can be applied successfully on any corpus.

1 Introduction

In [8], we present a method that requires the knowledge of how many of the words in the context are grouped around a Specification Mark, which is similar to a semantic class in the WordNet taxonomy. The word-sense in the sub-hierarchy that contains the greatest number of words for the corresponding Specification Mark will be chosen for the sense-disambiguating of a noun in a given context. This is called Specification Marks Method. Moreover, we used three heuristics that improved the results. These heuristics are denominated Hypernym, Definition and Common Specification Marks. In order to improve the results of the above method, we define three new heuristics denominated Hyponym, Gloss Hypernym and Gloss Hyponym.

In this paper we present a new development of the Specification Marks Method and its heuristics. Finally, we show the results obtained when applying these new heuristics.

1.1 Other Approaches

Most of the recent research done in the field of WSD has been carried out with the knowledge-driven method. Lesk in [4], proposes a method for deciphering the sense of a word in a given context by counting the number of over-laps that appear between each dictionary definition and the context. Cowie in [2] describes a method for lexical disambiguation of texts that uses the definitions given in the machine-readable version

A. Gelbukh (Ed.): CICLing 2001, LNCS 2004, pp. 182-191, 2001.

of the Longman's Dictionary of Contemporary English (LDOCE), as in the Lesk method, but also uses simulated annealing for greater efficiency.

Yarowsky in [17] derives different classes of words, starting from the common categories of words in Roget's Thesaurus. Wilks in [16] uses co-occurrence data, extracted from the LDOCE, for constructing word-context vectors and, thus, word-sense vectors. Voorhees in [15] defines a form of construction, called a *hood* that represents different sense categories in the WordNet noun hierarchy. Sussna in [14] defines a meter-based measurement that takes the semantic distance between the different nouns in a given text into account. It assigns weights, based on its type of relation (synonymy, hypernymy, etc) to WordNet links, and counts the number of arcs of the same type leaving a node, as well as the total depth of the arcs. Resnik in [10] computes the commonly shared *information content* of words, which serve as measurement of the Specification of the concept that subsumes the words included in the WordNet IS-A hierarchy. Agirre in [1] presents a method for the resolution of lexical ambiguity of nouns, using the WordNet noun taxonomy and the notion of conceptual distances among different concepts. Rigau in [12] combines a set of un-supervised algorithms that can accurately disambiguate word senses in a large, completely untagged corpus. Hale in [3] presents the results obtained from using a combination of Roget's International Thesaurus and WordNet as taxonomies, in a measurement of semantic similarity (four-similarity metrics). Stetina in [13] introduces a general supervised word-sense disambiguating method, based on a relatively small syntactically parsed and semantically tagged training corpus. This method exploits a complete sentence-context and all the explicit semantic relations that occur in a sentence. Resnik in [11] presents a measure of semantic similarity in an IS-A taxonomy, based on the notion of commonly-shared information content, as well as introducing algorithms that exploit taxonomic similarity in resolving syntactic and semantic ambiguity. Mihalcea in [6] suggests a method that attempts to disambiguate all of the nouns, verbs, adverbs and adjectives in a given text by referring to the senses provided by WordNet.

2 Specification Marks Method [8, 9]

The Specification Marks Method consists basically of the automatic sense disambiguating of nouns that appear within the context of a sentence and whose different possible senses are quite related. Its context is the group of words that co-occur with it in the sentence and their relationship to the noun to be disambiguated. The disambiguation is resolved with the use of the WordNet lexical knowledge base (1.6).

The input for the WSD module will be the group of words $W=\{W_1, W_2, ..., W_n\}$. Each word w_i is sought in WordNet, each one has an associated set $S_i=\{S_{i1}, S_{i2}, ..., S_{in}\}$ of possible senses. Furthermore, each sense has a set of concepts in the IS-A taxonomy (hypernym/hyponym relations). First, the concept that is common to all the senses of all the words that form the context is sought. We call this concept the Initial Specification Mark (ISM), and if it does not immediately resolve the ambiguity of the word, we descend from one level to another through WordNet's hierarchy, assigning new Specification Marks. The number of concepts that contain the subhierarchy will then be counted for each Specification Mark. The sense that corresponds to the Specification Mark with highest number of words will then be chosen as the sense disambiguation of the noun in question, within its given context.

The following tables show the percentages obtained when the method is applied with the base algorithm.

%	Correct	Incorrect	Ambiguous
Base Method (Semcor)	52.5%	28%	19.5%
Base Method (Encarta)	55.2%	26.7%	18.1%

2.1 Heuristics

The first approach of the Specification Marks Method had the following three heuristics.

Heuristic of Hypernym: This heuristic solves the ambiguity of those words that are not directly related in WordNet (i.e. plant and leaf). But the word that is forming the context is in some composed synset of a hypernym relationship for some sense of the word to be disambiguated (i.e. leaf#1 → plant organ). To disambiguate a given word, all of the other words included in the context in the hypernyms synsets of each of its senses are checked, and a weight is assigned to it in accordance with its depth within the sub-hierarchy, and the sense that carries the greater weight is chosen. In the case of there being several senses with the same weight, we apply the following heuristic.

Heuristic of Definition: With this heuristic, the word sense is obtained using the definition (gloss used in WordNet system) of the words to be disambiguated (i.e. sister, person, musician). To disambiguate the word, all of the other words that belong to the context in the gloss of WordNet for each of the synsets, are checked, and the weight of each word that coincides is increased by one unit. The sense that finally has the greatest weight is chosen. If several senses have the same weight, the following heuristic is then applied.

Heuristic of Common Specification Mark: With this heuristic, the problem of fine-grainedness is solved (i.e. year, month). To disambiguate the word, the first Specification Mark that is common to the resulting senses of the above heuristic is checked. As this is the most informative of the senses, it is chosen. By means of this heuristic it tries to resolve the problem of the fine grainedness of WordNet. Since in most of the cases, the senses of the words to be disambiguated differ very little in nuances, and as the context is a rather general one it is not possible to arrive at the most accurate sense.

3   Specification Marks Method: New Development

In this section, we present a new development to the Specification Marks Method formed by three new heuristics.

3.1 New Heuristics

At this point, we should like to point out that after having evaluated the Specification Marks Method with the Hypernym, Definition and Common Specification Mark heuristics, we subsequently discovered that it could be improved, providing even better results in disambiguation. We therefore define these new heuristics:

Heuristic of Gloss Hypernym: This heuristic solves the ambiguity of those words that are neither directly related in WordNet nor are in some composed synset of a hypernym relationship for some senses of the word to be disambiguated. To solve this problem we use the gloss of each synset of a hypernym relationship. To disambiguate a given word, all of the other words are included in the context in some gloss of a hypernyms relationship of WordNet, each of its senses are checked, and a weight is assigned to it, therefore the sense that carries the greatest weight is chosen. In the case of there being several senses with the same weight, we apply the following heuristic. For example:

Context: *plane, air*
Word non-disambiguated: *plane*
Senses: *plane#1, plane#2, plane#3, plane#4, plane#5.*

For Plane#1: → Weight = **1**

airplane, aeroplane, plane -- (an aircraft that has fixed a wing and is powered by propellers or jets; "the flight was delayed due to trouble with the airplane")
    => aircraft -- (a vehicle that can fly)
      => craft -- (a vehicle designed for navigation in or on water or **air** or through outer space)
        => vehicle -- (a conveyance that transports people or objects)
          => conveyance, transport -- (something that serves as a means of transportation)
            => instrumentality, instrumentation -- (an artifact (or system of artifacts) that is instrumental in accomplishing some end)
              => artifact, artefact -- (a man-made object)
                => object, physical object -- (a physical (tangible and visible) entity; "it was full of rackets, balls and other objects")
                  => entity, something -- (anything having existence (living or nonliving))

For Plane#2: → Weight = **0**

plane, sheet -- ((mathematics) an unbounded two-dimensional shape; "we will refer to the plane of the graph as the X-Y plane"; "any line joining two points on a plane lies wholly on that plane")
    => shape, form -- (the spatial arrangement of something as distinct from its substance; "geometry is the mathematical science of shape")
      => attribute -- (an abstraction belonging to or characteristic of an entity)
        => abstraction -- (a general concept formed by extracting common features from specific examples)

For Plane#3: → Weight = **0**

plane -- (a level of existence or development; "he lived on a worldly plane")
  => degree, level, stage, point -- (a specific identifiable position in a continuum or series or especially in a process; "a remarkable degree of frankness"; "at what stage are the social sciences?")
    => state -- (the way something is with respect to its main attributes; "the current state of knowledge"; "his state of health"; "in a weak financial state")

In this example the best sense is **plane#1**, because it has the greatest weight.

Heuristic of Hyponym: This heuristic solves the ambiguity of those words that are not directly related in WordNet (i.e. sign and fire). But the word that is forming the context is in some composed synset of a hyponym relationship for some sense of the word to be disambiguated (i.e. sign#3→ Visual signal → watch fire). To disambiguate a given word, all of the other words included in the context in the hyponyms synsets of each of its senses are checked, and a weight is assigned to it in accordance with its depth within the sub-hierarchy, and the sense that carries the greater weight is chosen. When several senses have the same weight, we apply the following heuristic. For example:

Context: *ground, fire, sign, activity*
Word non-disambiguated: *sign*
Senses: *sign#1, sign#2, sign#3,..., sign#9, sign#10*

For Sign#2→ weight=**0**

  => scoreboard
  => poster, placard, notice, bill, card
    => show bill, show card, theatrical poster
    => flash card
  => street sign
    => address
  => signpost, guidepost
    => fingerpost, fingerboard

For Sign#3→ weight=(1/2)+(1/2)+(1/3) =**1.33**

  => recording
    => bologram, bolograph
    => chromatogram
    => oscillogram
    => spirogram
...

    => fire alarm
    => foghorn, fogsignal
...

=> visual signal
  => watch **fire**
  => light

...

  => rocket, skyrocket
  => beacon, beacon **fire**
    => signal **fire**, signal light

For Sign#4 → weight=**0**

=> billboard, hoarding
  => sandwich board
  => shingle

Therefore, in this example the best sense is **sign#3**, because it has the greatest weight.

Heuristic of Gloss Hyponym: This heuristic solves the ambiguity of those words that are neither directly related in WordNet nor are in some composed synset of a hypo-nymy relationship for some sense of the word to be disambiguated. To resolve this problem we use the gloss of each synset of a hyponym relationship. To disambiguate a given word, all of the other words included in the context in some gloss of a hypo-nyms relationship of WordNet of each of its senses are checked, and a weight is as-signed to it, and the sense that carries the greatest weight is chosen. In the case of there being several senses with the same weight, we apply the following heuristic. For example:

Context: *action, court, ward, cost, servant, criticism, jury*
Word non-disambiguated: *cost*
Senses: *cost#2, cost#3*

For Cost#1 → weight = 1/5+1/6+1/6+1/3+1/3 = **1.2**

  => expense, disbursal, disbursement -- (amounts paid for goods and services that may be currently tax deductible (as opposed to capital expenditures))
    => business expense, trade expense -- (ordinary and necessary expenses incurred in a taxpayer's business or trade)
    => lobbying expense -- (expenses incurred in promoting or evaluating legislation; "many lobbying expenses are deductible by a taxpayer")

....

    => relief -- ((law) redress awarded by a **court**; "was the relief supposed to be protection from future harm or compensation for past injury?")
    => actual damages, compensatory damages, general damages -- ((law) compen-sation for losses that can readily be proven to have occurred and for which the injured party has the right to be compensated)
    => nominal damages -- ((law) a trivial sum (usually $1.00) awarded as recogni-tion that a legal injury was sustained (as for technical violations of a contract))

=> punitive damages, exemplary damages, smart money -- ((law) compensation in excess of actual damages (a form of punishment awarded in cases of malicious or willful misconduct))

=> double damages -- (twice the amount that a **court** would normally find the injured party entitled to)

=> treble damages -- (three times the amount that a **court** would normally find the injured party entitled to)

=> atonement, expiation, satisfaction -- (compensation for a wrong; "we were unable to get satisfaction from the local store")

=> counterbalance, offset -- (a compensating equivalent)

=> reparation -- (compensation exacted from a defeated nation by the victors)

=> refund -- (money returned to a payer)

=> rebate, discount -- (a refund of some fraction of the amount paid)

=> rent-rebate -- ((British) a rebate on rent given by a local government authority)

=> conscience money -- (payment made voluntarily to reduce guilt over dishonest dealings)

=> support payment -- (a payment made by one person for the support of another)

=> palimony -- (support paid by one half of an unmarried partnership after the relationship ends)

=> alimony, maintenance -- (**court**-ordered support paid by one spouse to another after they are separated)

=> child support -- (**court**-ordered support paid by one spouse to the other who has custody of the children after the parents are separated)

=> reward -- (payment made in return for a service rendered)

....

For Cost#2→ weight=**0**

=> average cost -- (total cost for all units bought (or produced) divided by the number of units)

=> marginal cost, incremental cost, differential cost -- (the increase or decrease in costs as a result of one more or one less unit of output)

=> expensiveness -- (the quality of being high-priced)

=> costliness, dearness -- (the quality possessed by something with a great price or value)

=> lavishness, luxury, sumptuosity, sumptuousness -- (the quality possessed by something that is excessively expensive)

=> assessment -- (the market value set on assets)

=> tax assessment -- (the value set on taxable property)

=> inexpensiveness -- (the quality of being affordable)

=> reasonableness, moderateness, modestness -- (the property of being moderate in price; "the store is famous for the reasonableness of its prices")

=> bargain rate, cheapness, cut rate, cut price -- (a price below the standard price)

In this example, the best sense is **cost#1**, because it has the greatest weight.

4   Empirical Results

We tested this method on sentences taken from the Semantic Concordance corpus (Semcor) and from Microsoft's electronic encyclopaedia (Microsoft Encarta 98 Encyclopaedia Deluxe). With texts that were chosen at random, 90 sentences and 619 nouns for the Semcor and 90 sentences and 697 nouns for the encyclopaedia. The evaluation of the method was carried out twice, first without and later with the heuristics, to demonstrate the percentage of improvement that these heuristics provide.

The following tables show the percentages obtained when the method is applied with the base algorithm and with the heuristics employed here. These results demonstrate that when the method is applied with the heuristics, the percentages of correct resolutions increases, thereby improving word-sense disambiguation. These tables provide some statistics for comparing the improvements obtained for the individual application of each heuristics.

For Semcor:

%	Correct	Incorrect	Ambiguous
Base Method	52.5%	28%	19.5%
H. Hypernym	53%	29.7%	17.3%
H. Definition	53.5%	30.2%	16.3%
H. Hyponym	53.6%	30.8%	15.5%
H. Gloss Hypernym	54.9%	31.8%	13%
H. Gloss Hyponym	56.8%	32.1%	10.9%
H. Synset Common	66.2%	32.3%	1.5%

For Encarta:

%	Correct	Incorrect	Ambiguous
Base Method	55.2%	26.7%	18.1%
H. Hypernym	56.4%	27.2%	16.4%
H. Definition	58.3%	27.5%	14.2%
H. Hyponym	59.7%	28.2%	12%
H. Gloss Hypernym	60.5%	28.9%	10.4%
H. Gloss Hyponym	62.4%	30.4%	7.1%
H. Synset Common	66.3%	32.5%	1.1%

Regarding the above data, we should like to point out that the appearance of 1.7% and 1.1% of ambiguous words is due to the fact that no common synsets are obtained for ambiguous nouns.

5   Conclusion and Further Work

In this paper, we have presented three new heuristics that improve the Specification Marks Method. This new development does not require any training process nor any hand-tagging. Its use allows us to automatically obtain the sense of a given word in a context-independent environment.

This approach tackles the problem found in the Specification Marks Method, which depends on the hierarchical structure of WordNet. There are words that should be related semantically, but WordNet does not reflect such relationships. However, in WordNet the gloss of a noun synset provides a context for the word to be disambiguated, i.e. the possible nouns occurring in the context of that particular word. We have applied the glosses in our new development in the same way a corpus is used.

These three new heuristics are used for resolving the ambiguity of those words that are not directly related in WordNet. To solve this problem we used the gloss of each synset referred to any hypernym/hyponym relationships.

We think that the results obtained are promising, considering the difficulty of the task carried out. We used free-running texts with a great number of senses for each of its words in WordNet. Furthermore, texts suffered from a considerable lack of context.

In further work we intend to modify the method by using more and better semantic relationships from WordNet, and by adding more lexical categories for disambiguating, such as verbs, adjectives and adverbs. This should not only give the method more context information but also further relate such information, in line with the proposal of McRoy in [5], that fledged lexical ambiguity resolution should combine several information sources. More information from other lexical sources, both dictionaries and thesaurus, is also required. The most important innovation, however, is probably the combination of syntactic relationships with other techniques and resources, to produce an overall better word-sense disambiguation.

6   Acknowledgements

We will like to thank German Rigau and Eneko Agirre for revising and discussing this paper.

References

1. Agirre E. and Rigau G. (1996) *Word Sense Disambiguation using Conceptual Density.* Proc. 16th International Conference on COLING. Copenhagen.
2. Cowie J., Guthrie J. and Guthrie L. (1992) *Lexical disambiguation using simulated annealing.* Proc. DARPA Workshop on Speech and Natural Language. 238-242. New York.
3. Hale, Michael L. Mc. A comparison of WordNet and Roget's taxonomy for measuring semantic similarity.
4. Lesk, M. (1986) *Automatic sense disambiguation using machine readable dictionaries: How to tell a pine cone from an ice cream cone.* Proc. 1986 SIGDOC Conference, ACM 24-26, New York.
5. McRoy S. (1992) *Using Multiple Knowledge Sources for Word Sense Discrimination.* Computational Linguistics 18 (1).
6. Mihalcea R. and Moldovan D. (1999) *A Method for word sense disambiguation of unrestricted text.* Proc. 37th Annual Meeting of the ACL 152-158, Maryland, Usa.
7. Miller G., Leacock C., Randee T. and Bunker R. (1993) *A Semantic Concordance.* Proc. 3rd DARPA Workshop on Human Language Tecnology, 303-308, Plainsboro, New Jersey.
8. Montoyo, A. and Palomar M. (2000) *Word Sense Disambiguation with Specification Marks in Unrestricted Texts.* Proc. 11th International Workshop on Database and Expert Systems Applications (DEXA 2000). 103-108, Greenwich, London, UK.

9. Montoyo, A. and Palomar M. (2000) *WSD Algorithm applied to a NLP System*. 5th International Conference on Application of Natural Language to Information Systems (NLDB´2000). Versailles (France).

10. Resnik P. (1995) *Disambiguating noun groupings with respect to WordNet senses*. Proc. Third Workshop on Very Large Corpora. 54-68.Cambridge, MA.

11. Resnik P. (1999) *Semantic similarity in a taxonomy: an information-based measure and its application to problems of ambiguity in natural lenguage*. In Journal of Artificial Intelligence Research 11. 95-130.

12. Rigau G., Atserias J. and Agirre E. (1997) *Combining Unsupervised Lexical Knowledge Methods for Word Sense Disambiguation*. Proc. 35th Annual Meeting of the ACL, 48-55, Madrid, Spain.

13. Stetina J., Kurohashi S. and Nagao M. (1998) *General word sense disambiguation method based on full sentencial context*. In Usage of WordNet in Natural Language Processing. COLING-ACL Workshop, Montreal, Canada.

14. Sussna M. (1993) *Word sense disambiguation for free-text indexing using a massive semantic network*. Proc. Second International CIKM, 67-74, Airlington, VA.

15. Voorhees E. (1993) *Using WordNet to disambiguation word senses for text retrieval*. Proc. 16th Annual International ACM SIGIR Conference on Research and Development in Information Retrieval. 171-180, Pittsburgh, PA.

16. Wilks Y., Fass D., Guo C., McDonal J., Plate T. and Slator B. (1993) *Providing Machine Tractablle Dictionary Tools*. In Semantics and the lexicon (Pustejowsky J. Ed.) 341-401.

17. Yarowsky D. (1992) *Word Sense disambiguation using statistical models of Roget's categories trainined on large corpora*. Proc. 14th COLING, 454-460, Nantes, France.

Three Mechanisms of Parser Driving
for Structure Disambiguation

Sofía N. Galicia-Haro, Alexander Gelbukh, and Igor A. Bolshakov

Natural Language Processing Laboratory. Center for Computer Research,
National Polytechnic Institute. Juan de Dios Batiz s/n 07738 México D.F.
{sofia, gelbukh, igor}@cic.ipn.mx

Abstract. Structural ambiguity is one of the most difficult problems in natural language processing. Two disambiguation mechanisms for unrestricted text analysis are commonly used: lexical knowledge and context considerations. Our parsing method includes three different mechanisms to reveal syntactic structures and an additional voting module to obtain the most probable structures for a sentence. The developed tools do not require any tagging or syntactic marking of texts.

1 Introduction

Structural ambiguity while parsing takes place because the syntactic information alone does not suffice to make a unique structure assignment. Researchers use now knowledge-intensive techniques for disambiguation. These techniques required a lot of manually coded information. Thus, they could be inapplicable to unrestricted texts.

Probabilistic context-free grammars (CFG), being introduced for choosing between alternative parses gave disappointing results too, which can be explained by the fact that these grammars do not reveal dependencies between words. In research introducing lexical dependencies, some approaches towards disambiguation have been recently tried: basic noun phrase chunking and bigrams [1], mutual information to obtain lexical attraction between content words [2], etc. But the former approach remains ambiguity in the basic noun phrase, while the latter approach misses the prepositional links to previous words. In this paper we propose a model for syntactic analysis and disambiguation based on three different methods.

2 Overview of the Model

We mainly consider two kinds of disambiguation mechanisms: the first referred to as *lexical* regards dependencies between predicative words and their arguments, and the second uses a *local context* in order to solve syntactic disambiguation that is mainly constituted by adjunct arguments.

In the examples

1. *Juan lanzó una pelota sobre el puente* 'Juan threw a ball onto the bridge'
2. *Juan admitió una plática sobre el puente* 'Juan admitted a communication on the bridge,'

A. Gelbukh (Ed.): CICLing 2001, LNCS 2004, pp. 192-194, 2001.
© Springer-Verlag Berlin Heidelberg 2001

the prepositional phrase *sobre el puente* is attached to the verb *lanzó* or to the noun *plática*. The difference is due to lexical preference. The Spanish verb *admitir* does not accept preposition *sobre,* whereas the verb *lanzar* does.

In the examples

3. *Juan bebe licores con menta* 'Juan drinks spirits with mint'
4. *Juan bebe licores con sus amigos* 'Juan drinks spirits with his friends'

the phrase *con menta* is attached to the noun *licores,* while the phrase *con sus amigos* 'with his friends,' to the verb *bebe* 'drinks.' The disambiguation could be resolved by the local context, i.e., by the fact that 'mint' is semantically closer to 'spirits' and 'friends' is closer to 'drink'. In our model both mechanisms are used in parallel.

For syntactic ambiguity resolution we propose the voting between of the outputs of different syntactic structure assignment subsystems. The overall system is presented in Figure 1. Each module gives a set of weighted variants. Those weights are based on the satisfied characteristics in each method. So, each module gives a quantitative measure of the probability of each syntactic structure in a dependency structure format.

The quantitative character gives the advantage for combining several methods as it is shown in Figure 1.

Three Mechanisms. The system includes government pattern (subcategorization frame) module, semantic proximity module, and extended CFG module. The three mechanisms require the compilation of several linguistic resources: the advanced government pattern (PMA) dictionary [3], the semantic network [4], and the extended CFG rules.

Advanced Government Patterns. This mechanism considers the linguistic knowledge contained in the so-called syntactic valences. It is the main mechanism of the model. It is the most practical to resolve most of the structure ambiguities, but does not suffice for all of them. The knowledge in this module is the lexical information about valences of verbs, adjectives, and nouns [5]. We developed a statistical version of this approach [6].

Extended CFG. It is the simplest method to compile parsing tools. We have created an extended CFG for Spanish language with agreement in gender and number and then have implemented it in a chart parser. We assumed equally weighted variants for the CFG module.

Semantic Proximity considers local context knowledge. When several structures are quite possible or adjuncts attachment is ambiguous the semantic proximity, i.e., the concepts more close related to the words in the possible constituents, could help to disambiguate structure variants. The idea behind the semantic proximity is finding the shortest paths between constituents obtained from the CFG module. For this purpose we assign different weights to relations, hierarchy concepts links and implicit relations.

Voting Module. To disambiguate syntactic structures, the module uses the weights assigned in each module, voting for the maximum among variants. The result is a ranked list of the syntactic variants.

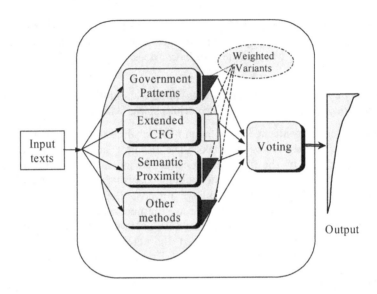

Figure 1. The model for syntactic disambiguation.

3   Conclusions

We propose three mechanisms for syntactic structuring and a voting disambiguation module for quantitative comparison of results. Each mechanism is realized as a module outputting a set of weighted parsed variants. The output is a ranked set of variants in a dependency structure format. The experiment on a corpus of 100 sentences confers the 1st rank to the correct parsing variant in 35% of cases.

References

1. Collins, M.: Head-driven Statistical Models for Natural language parsing. Ph.D. thesis. University of Pennsylvania. (1999) http:// xxx.lanl.gov/ find/cmp-lg/
2. Yuret, D.: Discovery of Linguistic Relations Using Lexical Attraction. Ph. D. thesis. Massachusetts Institute of Technology. (1998) http:// xxx.lanl.gov/ find/cmp-lg/9805009
3. Galicia-Haro, S. N, A. Gelbukh, I.A. Bolshakov: Advanced Subcategorization Frames for Languages with Relaxed Word Order Constraints. Natural Language Processing VEXTAL. (1999) 101- 110.
4. Gelbukh, A. F.: Lexical, syntactic, and referential disambiguation using a semantic network dictionary. Technical report. CIC, IPN (1998)
5. Mel'čuk, I.: Dependency Syntax: Theory and Practice. State University of New York Press (1988)
6. Gelbukh, A. F.: Extracción de un Diccionario de PMA http://www.cic.ipn.mx/ ~gelbukh/REDII/REDII-99

Recent Research in the Field of Example-Based Machine Translation

Michael Carl

Institut für Angewandte Informationsforschung,
Martin-Luther-Straße 14,
66111 Saarbrücken, Germany
carl@iai.uni-sb.de

Machine Translation (MT) is a multi-disciplinary, fast evolving research domain, which makes use of almost all computational methods known in artificial intelligence. Paradigms as different as logic programming, case-based reasoning, genetic algorithms, artificial neural networks, probabilistic and statistic methods have all been employed for the translation task. However, none of the proposed methods has yet led to overall satisfactory results and given birth to a universal machine translation engine. Instead, the search for what translation quality and what coverage of the system one would realistically need, what methods and knowledge resources are required for that end and how much one is willing to invest, is a research domain in itself.

Until the end of the eighties, MT was strongly dominated by rule-based systems which deduce translations of natural language texts based on a bilingual lexicon and a grammar formalism. Source language sentences were analyzed with a monolingual grammar and the source language representation was mapped into the target language by means of a transfer grammar. The target representations were then refined and adapted to the target language requirements.

Since the beginning of the nineties, huge corpora of bilingual translated texts have been made available in computer-readable format. This empirical knowledge has given raise to a new paradigm in machine translation, that of corpus-based machine translation. Corpus-based machine translation (CBMT) systems make use of reference translations which are assumed to be ideal with respect to text type and domain, target reader and its intention.

The first CBMT-systems using pre-translated reference texts were purely statistic. Translation was considered to be a stochastic process that relied on a number of random variables which all could be instantiated by careful investigation of the reference text. However, it quickly turned out that both the knowledge of the reference translations and linguistic knowledge of the source and the target language would complement each other.

With the emergence of example-based machine translation (EBMT), empirical and 'rationalist' knowledge resources were used in one machine translation system. Each of the EBMT systems extracts translation relevant knowledge from the reference text which is used in combination with other pre-defined knowledge resourced for translation. The degree to which these systems should learn representations from the reference text, and the way in which the knowledge

A. Gelbukh (Ed.): CICLing 2001, LNCS 2004, pp. 195–196, 2001.

learned is to be combined with rationalist knowledge, are still open questions in EBMT-systems.

In this context, the principal achievements in the field of research for Example-Based Machine Translation include:

- An analysis of the complexity of the search space in EBMT. Formulation of heuristics to reduce this search space and implication for translation results are researched.
- The modularization of example-based translation. The modules include bilingual alignment, bilingual grammar inference and the actual example-based translation task.
- The coupling of morphological and shallow syntactic knowledge with numeric knowledge, probabilities of translation patterns and probabilities of word translations. It is examined how the combined knowledge can be efficiently used for alignment, grammar inference and example-based translation.
- The formulation of constraints on a bilingual grammar to be induced from data. It is examined whether the use of particular constraint grammars can enhance the translation results.
- The possibilities/limits of a linkage of different MT-systems - such as rule-based and example-based systems - whether such a linkage is reasonable and feasible and under what conditions it can enhance the translation quality and the coverage of the integrated system.

References

[1] R. D. Brown. Adding linguistic knowledge to a lexical example-based translation system. In *TMI'99*, 1999.
[2] R. D. Brown. Example-Based Machine Translation at Carnegie Mellon University. *The ELRA Newsletter*, 5(1):10–12, 2000.
[3] M. Carl. Inducing Translation Templates for Example-Based Machine Translation. In *MT-Summit VII*, 1999.
[4] M. Carl. Tackling the complexity of context-free representations in example-based machine translation. In *NLPRS 99*, 1999.
[5] M. Carl. Combining invertible example-based machine translation with translation memoy technology. In *AMTA 2000*, 2000.
[6] B. Collins. *Example-Based Machine Translation: An Adaptation-Guided Retrieval Approach*. PhD thesis, Trinity College, Dublin, 1998.
[7] R. Frederking and S. Nirenburg. Three heads are better than one. In *Proceedings of ANLP-94*, Stuttgart, Germany, 1994.
[8] H. A. Güvenir and I. Cicekli. Learning Translation Templates from Examples. *Information Systems*, 23(6):353–363, 1998.
[9] S. Vogel and H. Ney. Construction of a hierarchical translation memory. In *Coling 2000*, 2000.
[10] H. Watanabe, S. Kurohashi, and E. Aramaki. Finding Structural Correspondences from Bilingual Parsed Corpus for Corpus-Based Translation. In *Coling 2000*, 2000.
[11] A. Way. A hybrid architecture for robust MT using LFG-DOP. *Journal of Experimental & Theoretical Artificial Intelligence*, 1999.

Intelligent Case Based Machine Translation System

Wang JianDe, Chen ZhaoXiong, and Huang HeYan

Computing Institute of Technology, Chinese Academic of Science
Beijing China 100081
wangjiande@sina.com

Abstract. Interactive Hybrid Strategies Machine Translation (IHSMT) system has just been designed to solve the translation problems. It forms a nice interdependent cooperation relation between human and machine by interaction. The system achieves hybrid strategy translation by synthesizing the rule-based reasoning and case-based reasoning, and therefore overcomes the demerits of single strategy. This paper has done some work on learning mechanism of this system and proposes a learning model of human-machine tracking and memorizing (HMTM). This model can store the information of human-machine interaction into memory base as case of machine learning, and then gradually accumulate knowledge to improve the intelligence of MT system.

1. Introduction

With the growth of international communication and Internet, the language barrier is becoming a serious problem. The grown-up of Machine Translation (MT) brings a good chance to solve this problem. It has taken on great significance in academic research and good prospect in applications, as diverse as below: translation of business letters and reports, translation of technical documents and articles, and speech-to-speech translation for business and travel. MT has become one of the international drastic competing areas of high technology.

Until now, MT has developed for almost half a century. During these five decades, all kinds of MT application systems, such as on-line MT, domain-restricted MT and machine-aided MT, have come forth to accommodate information processing and network developing. But from the point of view of a great deal of demand and the low quality of translation, these systems are far from practicality. The problems are:

1. The quality of direct MT translation is so low that human has to do heavy and difficult work after that.
2. Machines cannot collect experiences and not enhance the power of it, so always makes the same mistakes.

The case based MT or example based MT [1,2,5,6,9] can memorize the sentence or chunk, and use them to improve the MT system, but they cannot use them effectively.

A. Gelbukh (Ed.): CICLing 2001, LNCS 2004, pp. 197–205, 2001.

2.   IHSMT System

Until now, there are no machine translation system can finish the language translation like human. Although the automatic translation is the aim of Machine Translation, the interaction between human and computer is necessary and emphasis nowadays. Interactive Hybrid Strategies Machine Translation—IHSMT system has just been designed to solve these problems. It forms a nice interdependent cooperation relation between human and machine, which not only helps solve the inherent problems of MT, but also makes the feedback learning possible. At the same time, IHSMT achieves hybrid strategy translation by synthesizing the Rule-based Reasoning and Case-based Reasoning, and therefore overcomes the demerits of single strategy. This paper has done some work on learning mechanism of this system and proposes a learning model of human-machine tracking and memorizing (HMTM) from the point of view of cognitive psychology. This model can store the information of human-machine interaction into memory base as analogous case by machine learning, and then gradually accumulate knowledge to improve the intelligence of MT system.

The system consists of six[3] parts: Knowledge Base, CBAMT (Case-based Analogy MT), RBMT (Rule-based MT), Human-Computer Interactive Interface, PostEdit Interface, Model Knowledge Acquisition Interface.

CBAMT (Case-based Analogy MT). With the feature abstraction from sentence and analogically matching in Case Base, the most analogical result is found. The results of translation are produced from the case.

RBMT (Rule-based MT) [7]. With the Rule-based Reasoning and knowledge, the sentence is analyzed, and the result is produced.

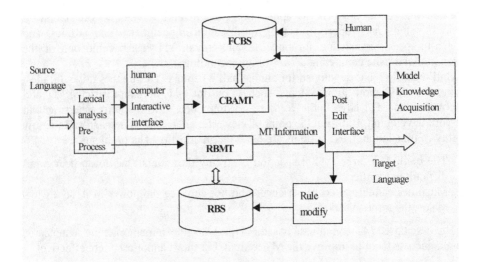

Fig. 1. Framework of IHSMT System.

Knowledge Base. Feature Case Base (FCBS), which is word aligned, store all kinds of bilingual language models in natural language sentence and translation result.

Rule Base (RBS) stores the syntax rules and lexical rules of the RBMT method.

Human-Computer Interactive Interface. The interface is Object-Orient and visualized. Human can analyze the sentence, select the target model, get the result of translation with computer interactively.

Model Knowledge Acquisition. When the English sentence is input into the system, the language model in the base is retrieved at first. If the same sentence or model exists, the analogical result can be obtained. Otherwise, the RBMT is used to translate the sentence. After that, the result can be edited with the bilingual mapping information. The source- target translation template is constructed, and added into the FCBS.

Comparing with the single-strategy Machine Translation, IHSMT has the opening knowledge base, can learn from the human-machine interaction and enhance the intelligence of the system.

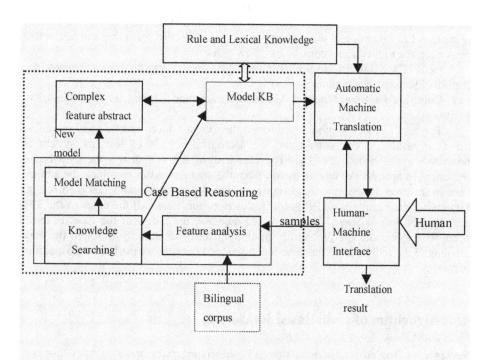

Fig. 2. HMTM Learning Model.

3.   Lazy Learning (LL) Strategy and HMTM Learning Model

With the algorithm of Lazy Learning, analogous cases in memory are compared, classified [10], and then memorized. After that, cases have different abstract levels including functional words of syntax and semantic, which is used in comparing and retrieving similar cases. Furthermore, they are also used to the generation of cases with Complex Features from concrete cases. It not only extends the application of concrete cases, but also reduces the memory size of system. The "Useful-life" of cases is used to limit the growth of memory base.

Lazy learning is one kind of analogy machine learning. The cases are stored into the TM in classes. Because the rule and the decision tree are not used, the method is simple. When a new model is input, according to the distance of the examples, the most similar sample is found.

In the Lazy Learning, every sample has its own property matrix, which forms a model space. The similar samples belong to the same model space. And the similarity can be measure by the distance between the matrixes.

Machine learning is the main problem of Artificial Intelligence, which can apply the knowledge to the similar conditions. The machine learning mechanism of the system is used to accumulate the knowledge and experience, and form the Knowledge Base that can be used to improve the translation. The method reduces the interception of human. Lazy learning of the system is used the case based reasoning and analogical reasoning, the model frame consists of below parts:

CBR (Case Based Reasoning) Model: these models can analysis and search the feature of the sentence model;

Complex Feature Abstract Model: abstract models from the TM (Translate Memory).

The result of MT is modified through the Orient-Object interface and output as the final result. At the same time, the analogical sample of learning system is produced, and sent into the TM. The classifier of the system use the case based reasoning to abstract the feature matrix from the samples. After searching the similar case in the case database, if the distance is over the value of analogical then return. Otherwise, the sample is added into the cluster of the class. All the cases in the TM are obtained in this way. When the cases increase, the radius of the case database becomes bigger, and the probability of finding result is more. So through the lazy learning, the intelligence of machine increased, and the work of the human post edit is reduced.

4.   Algorithm of Case Based Reasoning

Sentence 1: *It is easy to identify some simple writing rules and strategies that can improve the performance of MT system.*
Sentence 2: *It is easy to identify some simple writing rules that can improve the performance of almost any general-purpose MT system.*

These two sentences are similar, if they are all saved in the case database, the store space is wasted, and the performance of the search is low, so we can take the model from the sentence case:

Model: *It is easy to identify NP (ABS) that can improve the performance of NP MT system.*

ABS represents the feature of NP, which is an abstract noun.

There are two ways to acquire the Complex Feature

2.   Automatic case based learning;
3.   With the help of expert.

To keep the stability and efficiency in the CFS, we design the limited rule of grammar, which can prevent the bad or explicit expression.

The algorithm consists of: lexical learning algorithm LexLearning(), phrase or sentence learning algorithm SentLearning().

Algorithm 1. Lexical learning function[1]

```
LexLearning(Inst)
Input - analogical sample;
BEGIN
while (SearchWordMemory(Inst, patt)==1) {
    /* if find the similar model pattern :patt */
    if (WordDist (Inst, patt)==0) then
      /* distance between Inst and patt is 0 (equal) */
      1 is added to the probability of patt;
    else {
      if (patt.LivingTime > Live_Time)
           delete the pattern patt; search next model;
      if (WordDist (Inst, patt) < 1) {
         /* same word, different property */
         Add the property of Inst into the patt
              to TM (Translation Memory);
      return;
      }
}
}
Add Inst to TM
END
```

Algorithm 2. Sentence learning function:[2]

```
SentLearning(Inst)
Input Inst - analogical sample;
Variable
    AbsFea - Abstract property of sentence in Inst;
    DiffArray - Difference array stores the difference of
                the Inst and the model in the database;
    FeaCollect - The result of search;
    Distance - Distance between Inst and patt;
    Threshold - The threshold of property distance;
```

---

[1] WordDist (Inst, patt) is the distance of Inst and patt.

[2] Match (Inst, patt, DiffArray) calculates the distance of Inst and patt,
  AbstractFeat (AbsFea, Inst) abstracts the sample feature of Inst.

```
BEGIN
AbstractFeat(AbsFea, Inst);
/* abstract the property in Inst*/
i=0;
FeaCollect=SearchSentMemory(Inst, AbsFea)
if (FeaCollect Is Empty)
    Build a new class A,
    add Inst into Class A,
    and return
while (FeaCollect Is not Empty) {
    Find the analogical model patt in the TM
    Excute the fuzzy matching,
    calculate the distance of the property distance,
    and add the result to the DiffArray
    if (patt.LivingTime>Live_Time)
      Delete the model patt,
      search the next model;
      Distance=Match (Inst, patt, DiffArray);
    if(Disatance==0)
      1 is added to probability property of patt, i++;
}
Find the shortest distance D in DiffArray, and
map into the respond sample model
if (D > Threshold)
    build a new class A, add Inst to class A, return;
if (i > 5 and
    all values are less than the value of threshold
    and the human-machine returns YES) {
    if (AbsFeatPattern(NewPatt, DiffArray)==success)
      Replace all class in patt with NewPatt;
    else
      Add the inst into the class of patt
}
else
    Add Inst into the class of patt
END
```

There is a group of samples: 'He studies in Beijing University.' 'He studies in my school.' 'I study in Beijing. '

First the CFS function abstract the common feature: 'Study in' and they are different places: 'he' and 'I' 'Beijing University 'and 'my school 'and 'Beijing'

Then reduce in the above difference, get the difference of CFS $A(x)$ and $A(y)$ (A represent the grammatical class , x and y represent their semantic property). At last get the CFS: $A(x)$ study in $A(y)$.

Case-based reasoning is realized as matching analogy that obtains function words, syntax features of compared case. Retrieves the best case through measuring similarity. As to matching algorithm, a hybrid method based on multi-function levels and word-driven is described. While performing the matching, it builds the function of difference between compared cases. Matching results show that this kind of analogical matching can reflect not only the surface similarity of characters but also the deep similarity between cases. So it can reach the high accuracy but low complexity. Furthermore, according to the multi-levels structure of memory base, this

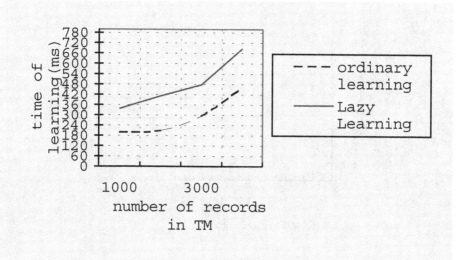

time of learning (ms)

780
720
660
600
540
480
420
360
300
240
180
120
60
0

--- ordinary learning

—— Lazy Learning

1000   3000
number of records
in TM

Fig. 3. Compare the original learning and lazy learning

paper also suggests a restricted retrieving method to speed up the retrieval on the abstract features of cases.

5.   Experiment and Evaluation of the Leaning Algorithm

With respect to the construction of case-based analogical MT, we propose and implement a similar translation building method by setting up the direct transfer operators between the case and target translation. The experiments show that this method can avoid building syntax tree of target language so that it performs simply and gets good results when similarity is larger than 80%.

1. **Time of feature abstraction.** We have select 300 typical sentences whose length is not equal. The time of model feature abstractions includes that of sentence of pre-process and lexical analysis. From Chart 1, the time of feature abstraction increases when the number of word increase, and the Lazy Learning method is quick than ordinary one.
2. **The efficiency of learning in system.** To evaluate the efficiency of learning properly, by regulating the function of learning, we test and analyze the time and accuracy of classification.

We have built TM (Translation Memory) of 1000 sentences, and the number of the test sentences is 200. We have tested the time spent in leaning without classification that is stored into TM directly, and Lazy learning which is store into different clusters.

With the increasing of case data in the TM, the time used in learning is more and more. Comparing with the simple learning, Lazy Learning can spend time 40% more.

To evaluate the precision, we test the TM with 3000 sentence, and the threshold is 80% and 60%, the precision of system is below.

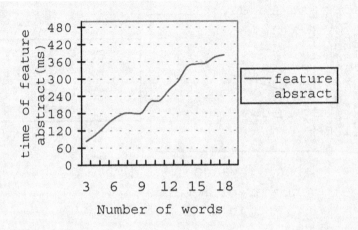

Fig. 4. Time Curve of Model Feature Abstraction

Table 1. Learning result of system

Threshold	Error of Cluster, %	Error of classification, %
80%	9.78%	6.32%
60%	12.4%	8.63%

The capacity of TM can affect the time of translation. If the size of TM increases, the time spent in translation will be longer. When there are 3000 sentences, the time of translation is 0.5 s, and when the number increases to 10000, the time is 0.7s.

According to the performance of IHSMT system, the learning model of tracking and memorizing, which is combined, with strategies of case-based analogical reasoning and rule-based reasoning, effectively improves the translation quality of ordinary MT system. The larger the memory base is, the less user interaction is involved, and more intelligent the MT system is.

References

1. David B. Leake, CBR in Context: the Present and Future, Case-Based Reasoning Experiences, Lessons, & Future Directions, AAAI press / the MIT press.
2. Hideo Watanable, A Similarity-Driven Transfer system, COLING-92, pp. 770-774.
3. Huang Heyan, Chen Zhaoxiong, Song Jiping. The Design and Implementation Principle of an Interactive Hybrid Strategies Machine Translation System: HISMTS. Proceedings of the International conference in Machine Translation & computer language Information processing, Beijing, June 1998, pp. 270-276.

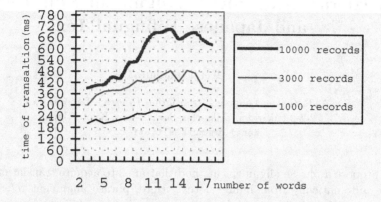

Fig. 5. Size of TM affect the time of translation (threshold is 80%)

4. Lambros Cranicas, Harris Papageorgiou, Stelios Piperidis, A Matching Technique In Example-Based Machine Translation, COLING-94, pp. 100-104.
5. Matthias Heyn, Integrating Machine Translation into Translation Memory Systems, In: EAMT Workshop(1996), pp. 111-124.
6. S. Sato, Example-Based Machine Translation, Ph.D. Thesis, Kyoto University, 1991.
7. Sergei Nirenburg, Jaime Carbonell, Masaru Tomita, Kenneth Goodman, Machine Translation: a Knowledge-based Approach, Morgan Kaufmann Publishers, 1992.
8. Sergei Nireburg. Two Approaches to Matching in EBMT, TMI-93, pp. 47-50.
9. Shlomo Argamon, Ido Dagan, and Yuval Krymolowski. A Memory-Based Approach to Learning Shallow Natural Language Patterns, http://xxx.lanl.gov/find/cmp-lg/9806011, 1998.
10. Wilpon J. & L. Rabiner, A Modified k-Means Clustering Algorithm for Use in Isolated Word Recognition, IEEE ASSP-33.
11. Walter Daelemans, Memory-Based Lexical Acquistion and Processing, http://xxx.lanl.gov/find/cmp-lg/9405018, 1994.
12. Riesbeck C., Schank R., Inside Case-Based Reasoning, Lawrence Erlbaum Associates, 1989.

A Hierarchical Phrase Alignment from English and Japanese Bilingual Text

Kenji Imamura

ATR Spoken Language Translation Research Laboratories
2-2-2 Hikaridai, Seika-cho, Soraku-gun, Kyoto, Japan
kenji.imamura@slt.atr.co.jp

We propose a phrase alignment method that aims to acquire translation knowledge automatically from bilingual text. Here, phrase alignment refers to the extraction of equivalent partial word sequences between bilingual sentences. We used the term phrase alignment since these word sequences include not only words but also noun phrases, verb phrases, relative clauses, and so on. We consider English and Japanese as the target languages.

For example, in the case of the following sentence pair, the phrase alignment method should extract the word sequence pairs of *n ($n = 1, 2, 3, 4$).

English	(*1 I would like to (*2 book (*3 a flight (*4 to Sydney)))).
Japanese	(*1 (*2 (*3 (*4 Sydney made no) hikoki) wo yoyaku-shi) tai no desu ga).

We assume that if the word sequences of the bilingual text have the same semantic information, and the phrase types are equal, the sequences are regarded as equivalent phrases even though they involve historically different languages. In this method, word sequences are hierarchically identified as follows.

1. Tag and parse an English sentence and a Japanese sentence, respectively.
2. Extract equivalent content words by word alignment. We assume N word pairs are extracted. A lot of word alignment methods have been proposed, but we do not discuss this in this paper.
3. Select i word pairs from among all of the pairs ($1 < i \leq N$), get all of the syntactic nodes that include the pairs, and exclude all other word pairs in the leaves from a parsed English tree and Japanese tree.
4. Compare the types of all English and Japanese nodes. When identical node types are found, regard the leaves of the nodes as equivalent word sequences.
5. Try processes 3. and 4. for all word pair combinations.

In the above procedure, when the structures between two languages are different, this method generates few correspondences that are mostly unnatural short phrases. In the case of the following sentence pair, there are two equivalent word pairs (*1 and *2). However, because same phrase types are not found individually, the verb phrase *3 is identified first as equivalent.

English	Single rooms (*3 are (*1 fully/ADV) (*2 booked/V)).
Japanese	single room ha (*3 (*2 yoyaku/N) de (*1 ippai/N) desu).

A. Gelbukh (Ed.): CICLing 2001, LNCS 2004, pp. 206–207, 2001.
© Springer-Verlag Berlin Heidelberg 2001

The idea that partial trees are aligned on the basis of equivalent word pairs is the same as Kaji's [1], Kitamura's and Meyers'. However, a common problem with these methods is the use of a parser. That is, the accuracy of the phrase alignment depends on the accuracy of the parsing.

Parsing errors are roughly classified into two types. One is when the parsing result contains ambiguities and the parser selects wrong candidates. The other is when the parsing process fails because of incomplete grammar (lack of production rules). Our method solves these problems by utilizing following three features and techniques.

Solution 1. The two languages are made to correspond to eliminate ambiguities that occur during the individual parsings. For example, the PP attachment modifyee in English is itself disambiguous when the equivalent Japanese phrase has only one structure. Then, the equivalent node count is maximized. We set an evaluation function that selects the candidate having the maximum number of equivalent nodes when parsing results are ambiguous.

Solution 2. Results are obtained by combining the partial trees if the parsing process fails due to a lack of production rules. Because it is known that an enormous amount of time is necessary to examine all combinations of partial trees, we developed a forward DP backward depth-first search algorithm to avoid this problem; this algorithm is from the forward DP backward A^* algorithm used in morphological analysis [2]. This algorithm obtains the best partial tree sequence (or some same-score sequences) in $O(n)$ time without pruning.

Solution 3. Parsing ambiguities are not completely solved by using the above solutions. Accordingly, node correspondent patterns are constructed with the non-correspondent leaves and phrase types of correspondent daughter nodes to select a final candidate. Then, the frequency of each pattern in the corpus is calculated, and finally, the parser selects the structure constructed with the most frequent patterns and outputs the structure as the parsing and alignment result.

We evaluated the precision of this phrase alignment with 289 sentences translated from Japanese travel dialogues to English by human translators. The evaluation used the following three levels: A (correct), B (not wrong in this sentence, but depends on the context), and C (incorrect). In the case of manual word alignment, the precision rate of A was 86%, and in the case of automatic word alignment (with a precision rate of 82%, and recall rate of 67%), the precision rate of A was 82%. Therefore, this phrase alignment method is able to extract equivalent phrases, and even if word alignments are partially incorrect, the method generates few incorrect correspondences.

References

1. Kaji, H., Kida, Y. and Morimoto, Y.: Learning Translation Templates from Bilingual Text. Proc. of COLING-92 (1992) 672–678
2. Nagata, M.: A Stochastic Japanese Morphological Analyzer Using a Forward-DP Backward-A* N-Best Search Algorithm. Proc. of COLING-94 (1994) 201–207

Title Generation Using a Training Corpus

Rong Jin and Alexander G. Hauptmann

Language Technology Institute, School of Computer Science, Carnegie Mellon University
5000 Forbes Ave., Pittsburgh, PA 15213, U.S.A
{rong+,alex+}@cs.cmu.edu

Abstract. This paper discusses fundamental issues involved in word selection for title generation. We review several methods for title generation, namely extractive summarization and two versions of a Naïve Bayesian, and compare the performance of those methods using an F1 metric. In addition, we introduce a novel approach to title generation using the k-nearest neighbor (KNN) algorithm. Both the KNN method and a limited-vocabulary Naïve Bayesian method outperform the other evaluated methods with an F1 score of around 20%. Since KNN produces complete and legible titles, we conclude that KNN is a very promising method for title generation, provided good content overlap exists between the training corpus and the test documents.

1   Introduction

To create a title for a document is to engage in a complex task: One has to understand what the document is about, one has to know what is characteristic of this document with respect to other documents, one has to know how a good title sounds to catch attention and how to distill the essence of the document into a title of just a few words. Title generation is very desirable and useful because it produces a compact representation of the original document, which helps people to quickly understand the important information contained in a document. For research, title generation is a very difficult problem from the viewpoint of machine learning and natural language processing.

Historically, the title generation task is strongly connected to traditional summarization [2][3] because it can be thought of extremely short summarization. Traditional summarization has emphasized the extractive approach, using selected sentences or passages from the document to provide a summary [4][5][6]. The weakness of this extraction approach is that it usually can't produce headline-sized summaries since the selected units are either complete sentences or passages.

More recently, some researchers have moved toward "learning approaches" that take advantage of training data for generating headlines. The learning paradigm is different from traditional text summarization in that the system is exposed to a set of training documents and their corresponding titles before being asked to generate titles for new documents. By learning the some kind of association between documents and corresponding titles, a learning system is able to come up with reasonable titles for new, previously unseen documents. Witbrock and Mittal [1] have tried one form of "learning approach" for title generation. They assume that a document word can only

A. Gelbukh (Ed.): CICLing 2001, LNCS 2004, pp. 208-215, 2001.

generate a title word with the same surface string, and then compute the probability that a document word will appear in the title. These probabilities are applied to all words in a new document to generate title words for that document. Even though the assumption (that a document word and its generated title word must have the same surface string) seems quite strong, our experiments show that it is a very useful restriction. Kennedy and Hauptmann [12] relax this constraint and allow all document words to participate in generating a title word. Their approach maps the title generation problem to a machine translation problem by treating documents as a verbose language and titles as a concise language. Generating titles is equivalent to translating from the verbose into the concise language.

In this paper, we compare the performance of different title generation methods, by examining the following learning approaches:

1. *Extractive summarization* which selects the "best" sentence from the document as a title. This approach uses a term frequency and inverse document frequency (tf.idf) based approach [9] to weighting individual sentences. Extractive summarization is used by MicroSoft Word as part of the "*AutoSummarize*" feature.
2. *Naïve Bayesian* approach *with limited vocabulary*. In this approach we compute the probability of generating a title word given a document word with the restriction that the title word and the document word are identical, that is they are both represented by the same surface string ($w_t = w_d$).. This closely mirrors the experiments reported in [1].
3. *Naïve Bayesian* approach *with full vocabulary*. In this approach, we compute the probability of generating a title word given a document word for all words in the training data, not just those that where the document word is same as the title word. As a result, the search space becomes much larger, but the principles are the same as in [1].
4. *KNN (k nearest neighbor)* approach which treats title generation as a special classification problem. When we consider the titles in the training corpus to be a fixed set of labels, then the task of generating a title for a new document is essentially the same as selecting an appropriate label (title) from the fixed set of training labels. The task reduces to finding the document in the training corpus, which is most similar to the current document to be titled. Standard document similarity vectors can be used [9]. The new document title will be set to the title for the training document that is most similar to the current new document. One drawback of this approach is the assumption that any new document will be appropriately titled by an existing title in the training dataset, which does not change over time.

2   The Contrastive Title Generation Experiment

In this section we describe the experiment and present the results. Section 2.1 describes the data. Section 2.2 discusses the evaluation method. Section 2.3 gives a detailed description of all the methods that were compared. Results and analysis are presented in section 2.4.

2.1 Data Description

The experimental dataset comes from a CD of 1997 broadcast news transcriptions published by Primary Source Media [13]. There were a total of 50,000 documents and corresponding titles in the dataset. The training dataset was formed by randomly picking four documents-title pairs from every five pairs in the original dataset and the leftover one pair was placed into the held-out test collection. The size of training corpus was therefore 40,000 documents with corresponding titles. The size of the test collection was 10,000 documents (with their titles used as 'truth'). By separating training data and test data in this way, we ensure strong overlap in topic content between training dataset and test dataset, which gives the learning algorithms a chance to play a significant role in the headline generation.

2.2 Evaluation

We evaluate title generation using the F1 metric [9]. For an automatically generated title T_{auto}, F1 is measured against correspondent human assigned title T_{human} as follows:

$$F1 = \frac{2 \times \text{precision} \times \text{recall}}{\text{precision} + \text{recall}} \tag{1}$$

Precision and recall is measured as the number of identical words in T_{auto} and T_{human} over the number of words in T_{auto} and the number of words in T_{human} respectively. Obviously, the sequential word order of the generated title words is ignored by this metric. There are several other metrics that take this ordering information into consideration: string edit distance (DTW) [12] and maximal sub-string [1]. Since we are focusing here on the choice of appropriate title words, F1 is the most appropriate measure for this purpose. Thus we do not evaluate those parts of each title generation approach which order generated title words into a 'sentence'. To be fair to each approach, we only generate 6 title words, which is the average number of title words in the training corpus. Stop words were removed from both documents and titles throughout training and testing.

2.3 Description of the Compared Approaches

The symbols used throughout this paper are defined in Table 1.

Table 1. Symbols used throughout the paper

Symbol	Definition
doc_tf(w, i)	Term frequency of word w in i-th document
doc_tf(w)	Term frequency of word w in the new document
title_tf(w, i)	Term frequency of word w in i-th title
N	Number of document-title pairs in training dataset
max_tf	Maximum term frequency in a document
tf	Term frequency of a word in a document
df	The number of documents that a word occurs in a collection

2.3.1   Naïve Bayesian Title Generation with Limited Vocabulary (NBL).
Essentially, this algorithm duplicates the work in [1], which tries to find out which
document words are likely to appear in the title and which are not. The following
processing steps are performed:

1. From the training corpus, count the occurrence of each document-word-title-word
   pair whose document word and title word is the same. C_w represents the occurrence
   of such a pair when both document word and title word are w. C_w is expressed as:

$$C_w = \sum_{j=1}^{N} doc\_tf(w,j) \times title\_tf(w,j)$$

(2)

The sum goes over all document-title pairs in the training corpus. The conditional
probability P(titleword w | documentword w) is obtained as :

$$P(\text{titleword } w \mid \text{documentword } w) = \frac{C_w}{\sum_{j=1}^{N} doc\_tf(w,j)}$$

(3)

2. To generate a title for a new document, we compute the generation probability P_w
   for each word w in the new document:

$$P_w = doc\_tf(w) \times P(\text{titleword } w \mid \text{documentword } w)$$

(4)

Here, doc_tf(w) is the term frequency of word w in the new document. Those title
words with the largest generation probability P_w will be chosen to form the title.

2.3.2   Naïve Bayesian Approach with Full Vocabulary (NBF). In the previous
approach, we counted only the cases where the title word and the document word are
the same. This restriction is based on the assumption that a document word is only
able to generate a title word with same surface string. The constraint can be easily
relaxed by counting all the document-word-title-word pairs. In detail:

1. C(dw, tw) represents the occurrence of document-word-title-word pairs when the
   document word is dw and the title word is tw. C(dw, tw) can be computed from the
   training corpus as:

$$C(dw,tw) = \sum_{j=1}^{N} doc\_tf(dw,j) \times title\_tf(tw,j)$$

(5)

The sum goes over all the document-title pairs in the training dataset. Then we can
compute the conditional probability of generating the title word tw given a
document dw as follows:

$$P(tw \mid dw) = \frac{C(dw,tw)}{\sum_{tw} C(dw,tw)}$$

(6)

2. To generate a title for a new document, we compute the generation probability P_{tw} for each possible title word tw in the new document as follows:

$$P_{tw} = \sum_{dw} P(tw \mid dw) \times doc\_tf(dw) \tag{7}$$

Here, $doc\_tf(dw)$ is the term frequency of word dw in the new document and the sum in the above equation goes over all the words in the new document. Those title words with maximum generation probability P_{tw} will be chosen for the title. This full vocabulary version of Naïve Bayesian approach can be compared directly with the limited vocabulary version to see the importance of the vocabulary restriction.

2.3.3   Extractive Summarization Approach Using TF/IDF (TF.IDF). We have mentioned the similarity between title generation and story summarization. In this paper we include a sentence-based summarization method [3] for a baseline comparison. The extraction of the title sentence is based on tf.idf information. The details are as follows:

1. Compute the idf (inverse document frequency [9]) values for all words in the documents of the training corpus. Ignore the titles.
2. Decompose the new document into sentences. Compute the average tf.idf value for each sentence. If an unknown word occurs in a sentence, assign zero to the idf of that word. Use the sentence with highest average tf.idf as the title.

2.3.4   K Nearest Neighbor Approach (KNN). This algorithm is similar to the KNN algorithm applied to topic classification in [8]. It treats the titles in the training corpus as a set of fixed labels. For each new document, instead of creating new title, it tries to find an appropriate "label", which is equivalent to searching the training document set for the closest related document. This training document title is then used for the new document. The algorithm proceeds as follows:

1. Index the documents in the training corpus using the SMART document retrieval system [10] using the standard stop word list. The SMART document weighting schema used was "ATC", which is:

$$A : \frac{tf + 0.5}{max\_tf + 1.0} \tag{7}$$

$$T : \log(\frac{collection\_size}{df})$$

$$C : \text{Euclidian vector length normalization}$$

2. For each new document, compute its similarity to all the documents in the training corpus by SMART and output the title of the one document (K=1) in the training corpus most similar to the new document as the title for the new document.

2.4   Results and Observations

The results are shown in Figure 1. An example of an original title and machine-generate title keywords by the various methods is shown in Table 2. The extractive summarization approach based on TF.IDF performs worst at F1 = 3.2%, while the K-nearest neighbor (KNN) and Naïve Bayesian with limited vocabulary (NBL) approaches select the best title words at 20.04% and 20.2% respectively. The NBF approach is in the middle with 13.6%. The results of an 'oracle' approach using each method are also plotted. The oracle approach assumes that the correct title is known. In the KNN (62%) approach, the oracle will select the best title from the training corpus that matches the test title. In NBL (81.6%) and NBF (74%), the oracle selected all words from the respective vocabulary that were matches in the current title. In the TF.IDF (41%) extractive summarization approach, that sentence from the document, which most closely matches the desired title, is selected.

Sentence-based extractive summarization performs poorly. TF.IDF extractive summarization will work well if there is much redundancy in the data and the summarization does not approach less than 10% of the document size [11]. This reflects the limited ability of the TF.IDF measure to select important words.

Table 2. An example of human assigned title vs. machine generate title words for a document on the trial of Oklahoma City bombing suspect Terry Nichols.

Human assigned title	NICHOLS TRIAL: PROSECUTION CLOSE TO COMPLETING CASE
Title generated by KNN	EMOTION RUNS HIGH ON SECOND DAY OF NICHOLS TRIAL
Title generated by NBL	nichols bombing terry jury trial death
Title generated by NBF	trial nichols mcveigh news 1997 bombing
Title generated by TF.IDF	REYES' FATHER TONY ALSO A HUD EMPLOYEE WAS KILLED

KNN works surprisingly well. KNN generates titles for a new document by choosing from the titles in the training corpus. This works fairly well because the training set and test sets were constructed to guarantee good overlap in content coverage. We conclude that KNN will be good candidate for title generation if there is strong overlap in coverage between the training and test data. If consideration of human readability matters, which our F1 scores did not reflect, we would expect KNN to out-perform all the other approaches since it is guaranteed to generate human readable title.

NBF performs much worse than NBL. The difference between NBF and NBL is that NBL assumes a document word can only generate a title word with the same surface string. Intuitively, this very strong assumption ignores much information. However, the results tell us that some information can be safely discarded. In NBF, nothing distinguishes between important words and trivial words, and the co-occurrence between all document words and title words is measured equally. This lets frequent, but unimportant words dominate the document-word-title-word correlation.

As an extreme example, stop words show up frequently in every document. However, they have little effect on choosing title words.

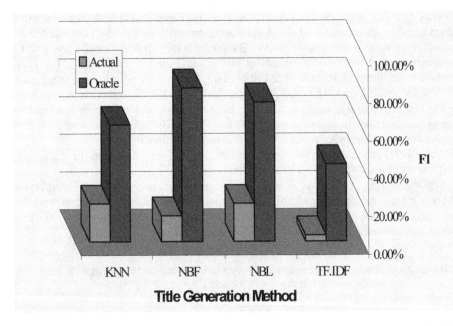

Fig. 1. Comparison of four Title Generation Approaches on a held-out test corpus of 10000 documents using the F1 score. Oracle scores represent the best possible score an approach could receive if given perfect knowledge.

3   Conclusion and Future Work

From the analysis discussed in previous section, we draw the following conclusions:

1. Applying pure extractive summarization approaches to title generation is not good idea because extractive summarization fails to make use of potential training information and restricts the title candidates to the sentences of the original document. Even optimal (oracle) sentence selection provides limited performance.
2. The KNN approach works well especially when there is large content overlap between the training data set and the test collection. By exploiting the WWW, in informal experiments we easily obtained large, relevant training corpora of documents with titles, so that there is always a good chance of finding an appropriate title in the training corpus for new, unseen documents. KNN is also simple in terms of implementation. Another big advantage of KNN is that it always produces human readable titles.
3. The comparison between performance of NBF and NBL shows that we need treat important words and trivial words differently to limit the noise introduced by frequent, but trivial words.

In this paper, we actually implement KNN approach as the single nearest neighbor (K=1). This has no flexibility to form new titles and restricts any new title to be identical to one in the training pool. Our future work will be choosing K (K>1) most similar documents in the training pool and form a new title based on the K chosen titles. This may create a more appropriate title for a new document. The trade-off would be that the title may not be human readable anymore since the new title is synthetically composed.

References

1. M. Witbrock and V. Mittal: Ultra-Summarization: A Statistical Approach to Generating Highly Condensed Non-Extractive Summaries. In Proceedings of SIGIR 99, Berkeley, CA, August 1999
2. J. Kupiec, J. Pedersen, and F. Chen: A trainable document summarizer. In Proceedings of ACM/SIGIR'95, pages 68-73. ACM
3. J. Goldstein, M. Kantrowitz, V. Mittal, and J. Carbonell: Summarizing Text Documents: Sentence Selection and Evaluation Metrics. In Proceedings of SIGIR 99, Berkeley, CA, August 1999.
4. T. Strzalkowski, J. Wang, and B. Wise: A robust practical text summarization system. In AAAI Intelligent Text Summarization Workshop, pp. 26-30, Stanford, CA, March, 1998.
5. G. Salton, A. Singhal, M. Mitra, and C. Buckley: Automatic text structuring and summary. Info. Proc. And Management, 33(2):193-207, March, 1997.
6. M. Mitra, A. Sighal, and C. Buckley: Automatic text summarization by paragraph extraction. In Proceedings of the ACL'97/EACL'97 Workshop on Intelligent Scalable Text Summarization, Madrid, Spain.
7. Y. Yang, C. G. Chute: An example-based mapping method for text classification and retrieval. ACM Transactions on Information Systems (TOIS),12(3):252-77. 1994.
8. V. Rjiesbergen: Information Retrieval. Chapter 7. . Butterworths, London, 1979.
9. G. Salton (ed): The SMART Retrieval System: Experiments in Automatic Document Proceeding. Prentice Hall, Englewood Cliffs, New Jersey. 1971.
10. V. Mittal, M. Kantrowitz, J. Goldstein and J. Carbonell: Selecting Text Spans for Document Summaries: Heuristics and Metrics. *AAAI-99.*
11. H. Nye: The Use of a One Stage Dynamic Programming Algorithm for Connected Word Recognition. IEEE Transactions on Acoustics, Speech and Signal Processing, Vol. AASP-32, No 2, pp. 262-271, April 1984.
12. P. Kennedy and A.G. Hauptmann: Automatic Title Generation for the Informedia Multimedia Digital Library. ACM Digital Libraries, DL-2000, San Antonio Texas, May 2000, in press.
13. Primary Source Media, Broadcast News CDROM, Woodbridge, CT, 1997

A New Approach in Building a Corpus
for Natural Language Generation Systems

Mª del Socorro Bernardos Galindo[1] and Guadalupe Aguado de Cea[2]

[1] Laboratorio de Inteligencia Artificial,
Facultad de Informática, Universidad Politécnica de Madrid.
Campus de Montegancedo, s/n. 28660 Boadilla del Monte, Spain.
sgalindo@delicias.dia.fi.upm.es

[2] Departamento de Lingüística Aplicada a la Ciencia y a la Computación,
Facultad de Informática, Universidad Politécnica de Madrid.
Campus de Montegancedo, s/n. 28660 Boadilla del Monte, Spain.
lupe@fi.upm.es

Abstract. One of the main difficulties in building NLG systems is to produce a good requirement specification. A way to face this problem is by using a corpus to show the client the features of the system to be developed. In this paper we describe a method to elaborate that corpus and how can be used for a particular system. This method consists of five steps: text collection, input determination, text and input analysis, corpus construction, and pattern extraction.

1   Introduction

The development of an NLG system involves the performance of multiple tasks, such as the study of the linguistic phenomena to be handled, the design of its architecture, the construction of a grammar, to mention just a few. One of the main tasks (and among the first to face) is to make a requirements analysis in order to yield an initial specification of the requirements of the system. There are general techniques, applied in software engineering [13], that can be used here, but using specific methods for NLG can be much more interesting. One of the most representative ones is described in [14], where the developer uses a corpus to describe the user the system under construction. Its advantage is that it is much easier to talk about the functionality of the system with the users showing them examples than speaking about NLG in a more abstract way, especially because many users do not have previous experience with NLG technology. In this paper a method to elaborate a corpus based on that approach is introduced.

Before describing the method, it is convenient to explain what is understood by the term "corpus". According to [6] a corpus is a "closed set of texts established according to specific structural criteria" It can be considered as the result of an empirical process of linguistic data collection combined with the author's own capacity of elicitation and introspection. Taking this definition as a base, and adding some nuances specific to the NLG field (taken from [5]), a corpus can be defined as

A. Gelbukh (Ed.): CICLing 2001, LNCS 2004, pp. 216–225, 2001.

"a set of examples of output texts and input data that specify the functionality of the NLG system to be developed".

The reason to include the input data is that it is senseless to have texts in the corpus that will never be generated, i. e. corresponding to no input.

The relevance of the corpus does not lie only in its usefulness to specify the requirements of the systems, but also in its use as a resource to study the linguistic phenomena the system has to handle.

2   Method

The process to elaborate a corpus for an NLG system presented here consists of five steps: output text collection, input determination, text and input analysis, corpus construction and pattern extraction. The first four steps help to build the corpus. We start by collecting a set of possible output texts and input data. Then an analysis of both sets is made and finally, that analysis is used to construct the corpus, where each output text has an input associated. The last step, pattern extraction, is useful only if the reuse of the work is intended.

2.1   Output Text Collection

In this phase, the aim is to obtain a set of texts, belonging to the application domain, that cover the complete range of the texts the system is expected to produce. We can use several sources to get this set of texts: reference books, experts in the domain, and documents or reports written in the past.

It is important in this stage to have gathered a great number of texts. Their final usefulness is less interesting than to have a sample as complete as possible of all the possibilities that can be presented as output text.

2.2   Input Determination

The goal of this step is to determine the kind of inputs the NLG system has to face.

Based on our experience, the input of an NLG system has been identified by four components: the communicative goal to achieve, the model of the user to whom the text is addressed, the history of the discourse that has already taken place, and the user request.

A *communicative goal* can be defined as what one intends to express and what it is for. Communicative goals direct the generation process: they determine what should be selected from the information source, how the text should be structured, what words should be used, etc. These goals can have different complexity levels, some are simple, such as providing information about some contents of the knowledge or data base, but others are quite complex, such as trying to persuade someone to do something.

The *user model* is a characterization of the recipient (reader) of the text. Among the several aspects than can be included in a user model are: the information about the user's expertise level, his/her preferences and the task he/she intends to do. This enables the customization of the text.

The *discourse history* is a model of all the previous interactions between the user and the system. It is used so that the output text can be generated counting on what has already been discussed on previous occasions.

The *user request* is what the user enters in the system in a particular interaction. It can vary widely depending on the sort of system. For instance, in a document generation system, it would be the request for a particular document (such as the meteorological report of a day, a week or a month, etc.); in an information retrieval system, the concrete query, for example.

All these components are not necessarily present in every system. There can be systems that do not care about the user, or do not mind repeating what has already been said, or they always have the same goal, etc.

Unlike in the text collection step, we do not use concrete data, specially because the amount of user requests can be huge. Here we are interested in the possible kinds of requests. It will be later, when we associate the input data to their corresponding output text (see Sec. 2.4), when we will need the concrete combination of the different components of the input and also their concrete value.

This phase, input determination, can be carried out previously or simultaneously to the text collection.

2.3   Text and Input Analysis

The aim of this phase is to get a detailed understanding of the correspondences between the output texts and the data of the available information source (data base, knowledge base, etc.), and between the output texts and the input data.

The first thing can be achieved analysing the content of the texts. To do so, the clauses of the text can be classified into the categories proposed by Reiter and Dale [14]:

- *Unchanging text*: A textual fragment that is always present in the output texts.
- *Directly-available data*: Text that presents information that is available directly in the input data or an associated information source.
- *Computable data*: Text that presents information that can be derived from the input data via some computation or reasoning.
- *Unavailable data*: Text that presents information that is not present in or derivable from the input data.

This last kind of texts cause the most problems, since the information needed to generate them can not be obtained. This can be solved by making more information available to the system, changing the text to eliminate the affected parts, and expecting the human to write such text.

As for the second thing, the study of the relations between the output texts and the inputs would be useful to establish not only the correspondences between both of them, but also to find out those texts without an associated input and vice-versa.

Finally, the form of the texts has to be analyzed too. It is necessary to investigate if for a given input there are several texts with the same content and very different style (e. g., because they belong to different experts) and to study what these styles are like.

In addition, the non-optimal texts (e. g., because they are difficult to understand) and the ones that can be improved have to be detected.

2.4   Corpus Construction

Based on the analysis done in the previous phase, and the criteria established by the clients and the developers, it is time to determine the corpus in which the texts the NLG system will be able to generate and the inputs related to them are included.

There are several tasks that can be done in this process:

- Rejecting or modifying the texts that refer to unavailable data when the solutions mentioned above are technically impossible or prohibitively expensive to adopt any of them.
- Simplifying texts that are difficult or impossible to generate.
- Adding inputs to the texts that do not correspond to any input or removing them.
- Adding output texts to the inputs that do not correspond to any text or removing them.
- Modifying texts that are difficult to understand or can be improved.
- Solving conflicts, as the ones caused by different experts.

For a better result, it is advisable to make the corpus in close collaboration with the experts (linguistic and domain ones) and the clients, each contribution should take place at the appropriate moment. Experts will ensure that it is correct (both grammatically and in the domain) and discussion with the clients will be useful to take decisions about eliminating, including or modifying an input or a text.

Quite often, the corpus obtained will not be the final one, because the little experience in the NLG field makes it difficult to establish from the beginning what can be done, i.e., what linguistic phenomena will be handled.

2.5   Pattern Extraction

After the corpus is elaborated, the patterns of the texts to be generated can be designed.

First of all, the structures of the texts have to be determined replacing the domain words with general ones, such as concept, property, etc. The resulting texts can be thought of as the "skeletons" of the texts. Next, a notation to represent the patterns has to be decided. Finally the different skeletons are united using the notation.

This phase is useful only in case the system is intended to be as independent of the application domain as possible, so that it can be reused. In these situations the use of patterns as the base of generation will be useful so that text with the same structure, even belonging to different domains, can be generated correctly.

The idea is that the patterns can help the developers to see if there are similar texts generated for other projects. Once the corpus is finished they can examine the patterns produced in other projects and study if they can be applied to the texts of their project. After that, they can reuse the previous results for similar texts whenever it is possible and convenient. In this way, time and effort can be saved.

As we have already said, the corpus is very likely to suffer from continuous modifications throughout the development of the system. In those cases in which the patterns have been extracted, the most advisable thing is to make the modifications in the patterns. In this way, besides keeping the intended independence, some repetitive work is avoided: the modification of the texts and the reflection of those changes in the patterns.

3   Elaboration of a Corpus in the ONTOGENERATION Project

The method described above was applied in the ONTOGENERATION project [1] but adapting it to the specific situation. The aspects that had more influence in the corpus were:

- The information source was predetermined, namely, the *Chemicals* ontology [7]. This fact caused the range of texts to be quite limited and even in the first moments a lot of useless material had to be rejected.
- The result was intended to be reused with other information sources, basically other ontologies.

Let us look at how the process to elaborate the corpus was carried out.

3.1   Text Collection

First of all, several books on Chemistry, such as [8][10], were examined in order to collect the texts referring to the chemical elements and their properties.

But these texts were considered to be very long and they included a lot of information that was not, and would never be[1], present in the *Chemicals* ontology. That was the reason why it was decided not to use those texts as they were but rather eliminate some parts and create new ones from others instead[2].

Each member of the team prepared a group of possible texts and then a new set was created jointly from those groups. Since the texts were not exactly those appearing in the books, an expert was consulted to validate its suitability and correctness in the chemical domain.

3.2   Input Determination

Once the text collection was finished, the following input was determined, taking into account the aspects mentioned in 2.2.:

- *Communicative goal*: The system had a single aim: to provide all the information requested by the user. Since there was only one, there was no need to make it explicit.

---

[1] The contents of these texts were so clearly out of the requirements of *Chemicals* that it was out of discussion their inclusion in the ontology.

[2] This is a very superficial purge for which it is not necessary a detailed analysis (carried out later), it just helps to save time in posterior phases.

- *User model*: There were no variations in the texts due to the differences between the users.
- *Discourse history*: Every time a new query was made, it was supposed to be isolated from the others, so there was not a real discourse history.
- *User request*: This component consisted of all the queries the user could make to the NLG system. These queries could be about anything included in the *Chemicals* ontology (concepts, instances, attributes, axioms and functions).

As the reader can deduce, the input to the generation system had only one component, the query made by the user. This part was studied more deeply in this step, so that different kinds of queries could be determined.

First, the queries were divided into five categories:

- Chemical group descriptions
- Formula descriptions
- Chemical element descriptions
- Chemical element comparisons
- Chemical element property descriptions

These categories were refined later and we got a total of thirteen types classified according to them. For example: the class "chemical group description" included "concept classification", "concept definition", concept decomposition", "concept properties", "concept examples" and "concept synonyms".

The concrete queries were not determined until the correspondences between the output texts and the inputs were established.

3.3   Input and Text Analysis

In this phase, there was a discussion about which of the collected texts should be included as an answer to each kind of query. Each text could be associated to more than one query. Thus, the sentence "Non transition metals are divided in alkalines and alkalineterreus", corresponded to concept classification, concept definition and concept decomposition.

On the other hand, the analysis of the content of the texts showed that, according to Reiter and Dale's classification [14], the texts showed the following characteristics:

- Unchanging text: Complete utterances were not always present in the same way.
- Directly available and computational data: No computations are needed except for those expressions that refer to information stored in the description of the ontology terms, i. e. those containing data that are not related to chemical properties as in "Argon was discovered by Lord Rayleigh and Sir William Ramsay in 1894" or "Arsenium is poisonous

Note that the texts that contain these clauses are not included as an answer to any of the inputs determined previously.

- Unavailable data: There are texts like "Reactiveless elements are classified according to its metallic feature, thus, there are non metals, semi-metals and metals", that are impossible to generate because the ontology does not have concept attributes.

Other unavailable data were detected in clauses that expressed the qualitative value of a property as in "The electronegativity of the bromum is high". This is because *Chemicals* does not provide data useful to state if a value is high, medium or low.

There was nothing special to report on the form of the texts.

3.4   Corpus Construction

The first corpus that was built had the texts collected in the first step, classified according to the kinds of queries determined in the second step, and also based on the analysis of the third step, in which the following clauses were eliminated:

- Those that referred to concept attributes. The inclusion of concept attributes clashed with the requirements of *Chemicals*, so we decided to remove those texts referring to that kind of attributes.
- Those that had computable data related to the description field. Several options were studied for this situation; e. g., canned text and text analysis. The first was impossible since the description was in English and our system generated text in Spanish. The effort involved for the second did not make it advisable.

According to the analysis made, clauses expressing qualitative values could present some problems too. After studying the ontology and the different options, the decision was to include a "scale mechanism" that supported the generation of this kind of expressions.

3.5   Pattern Extraction

Since one of the goals of the project was that the final result was as source-independent as possible, patterns of the texts were created so that the sentences could be generalized to other information sources different from *Chemicals*.

Using the notation reflected in **Table 1**, 95 patterns were defined, most of them corresponding to more than one sentence. For instance[3]:

> *Concept-name {, concept-name}$_0^n$ and *concept-name* [**make up** *article* |**are included in** *article* |**are called**] *concept-name.*

can refer to:

> "First transition series, second transition series, third transition series and actinides make up non transition metals."

and

> "Halogens are included in the metals class."

among many others.

---

[3] This pattern has been adapted from the real one, to make it simpler and understandable for non-Spanish speakers.

A → B	A has the same structure as B
[A]	Optional elementl
[A | B | C]	A or B or C, al least one of them
$\{A\}^m_n$	A is repeated between n and m times
A → B | C	A has the same structure as B or C
bold	fixed words
italics	variable words

Table 1. Pattern notation

3.6   Corpus Evolution

The first modification made to the corpus was organizational and it was due to the tool used for the development of the grammar[4] and the generation, namely KPML [3]. KPML only produces sentences, not paragraphs[5]. So patterns were classified in two groups: sentences and paragraphs. Paragraphs were correspondingly divided into sentences. The generation of those sentences can be thought of as an intermediate goal to get the target text.

Other changes were due to the relation between the texts and the queries. At the beginning a text could be associated to several queries. To simplify the planning of the texts, this situation was changed and a pattern could only correspond to a single query.

The last modifications consisted in a reduction of the corpus so that the project could be finished within the time established at the beginning of the project. We examined the corpus and selected three patters at most for each type of query.

It is worth pointing out that the modifications on the corpus were done in continuous interaction with the domain experts, so that they could state the things they disagreed with or could be improved.

To sum it up, the changes made in the initial corpus were due to:

- Design decisions.
- Expert corrections.
- Time planning.

All the changes were done directly on the patterns.

The final corpus contains 10 kinds of queries (classified in four groups) and 28 patterns. It can be seen in [12]; [4] and [11] show the corpus at different moments of the project.

---

[4] The grammar was developed according to Halliday's functional grammar [9].
[5] For the purpose of this project, we understand 'paragraph' as the units of written language that begin with a capital letter and end with a full stop. The next paragraph begins on a new line.

4   Conclusions and Future Work

A method to build a corpus in the area of NLG has been presented. This method systematizes the task of the analysis of the requirements related to the input data and the output texts of an NGL system in five steps: text collection, input determination, text and input analysis, corpus construction and pattern extraction. The result of the process (the corpus) is not only useful as the system requirements but also as a resource for the analysis and the design of the system.

The main contributions of the method described here are:

- There is a phase in which the input data are determined. These data are associated with the corresponding output texts in a later phase. In this way the corpus will never have texts the system will never generate. To help the developers to carry out this step, the components of the input have been identified: communicative goal, user model, discourse history and user request.
- There is a special emphasis on reusing software components and resources. The use of patterns can help to reuse the different products in other projects with similar features.

Each phase has been explained and some guidelines to perform them have been given. Note that the ideas expressed here are general and will have to be adapted to the particular application, as has been shown for the ONTOGENERATION project.

There remains to study to what extent this method can be applied to other NLG systems different from ONTOGENERATION, and see which modifications are needed. With that in view, other NLG projects are being considered. Those projects are intended to produce the same kind of texts as ONTOGENERATION to find out the real usefulness of the extracted patterns.

References

1. Aguado, G., Bañón, A., Bateman, J., Bernardos, S., Fernández, M., Gómez, A., Nieto, E., Olalla, A., Plaza, R., Sánchez. A.: Ontogeneration: Reusing Domain and Linguistic Ontologies for Spanish Text Generation. Workshop on Applications of Ontologies and Problem Solving Methods, ECAI'98, Brighton (1998)
2. Bañón, A.: Modelo de generación multisentencial EPRS. Trabajo Fin de Carrera, Facultad de Informática, Universidad Politécnica de Madrid, Madrid (1999)
3. Bateman, J. A.: Enabling Technology for multilingual natural language generation: the KPML development environment. In Natural Language Engineering, Vol. 1. Cambridge University Press, Cambridge (1997) 1-42
4. Bernardos, S.: GUME: Extensión de la Ontología GUM para el Español. Trabajo Fin de Carrera, Facultad de Informática, Universidad Politécnica de Madrid. Madrid (1997)
5. Dale, R. and Reiter, E.: Tutorial on Building applied Natural Language Generation Systems. ANLP-97 (1997)
6. Francis, W.N.: Language Corpora B.C. in J. Svartvik (ed) Directions in Corpus Linguistics. Proceedings of the Nobel Symposium 82. Berlin. Mouton de Gruyter (1992)
7. Fernández, M.: *Chemicals*: Una Ontología de Elementos Químicos, Trabajo Fin de Carrera, Facultad de Informática, Universidad Politécnica de Madrid (1996)
8. Fernández M. A. *et al:* Ciencias Naturales GAIA. Vincens-Vives. Barcelona. España (1995)

9. Halliday, M. A. M.: An Introduction to Functional Grammar. Edward Arnold, London (1985)

10. Lasheras, A. L. and Carretero, M.P. Física y Química. POSITRON Vincens-Vives. Barcelona. España (1987)

11. Nieto, E.: Metodología para adaptar una gramática sistémica-funcional para la generación en castellano. TFC, Facultad de Informática, Universidad Politécnica de Madrid (1999)

12. Olalla.A.: Sistema de GLN basado en ontologías: Ontogeneration. Trabajo Fin de Carrera, Facultad de Informática, Universidad Politécnica de Madrid (1999)

13. Pressman, R.: Software Engineering: A Practitioner's Approach. McGraw-Hill (1994)

14. Reiter E., and Dale, R.: Building Applied Natural language Generation Systems. Journal of Natural Language Engineering, 3(1). (1997). 57-87

A Study on Text Generation
from Non-verbal Information on 2D Charts

Ichiro Kobayashi

Hosei University, Faculty of Economics,
4342 Aihara-machi, Machida-shi, Tokyo, 194-0298, Japan
koba@mt.tama.hosei.ac.jp

Abstract. This paper describes a text generation method to explain
non-verbal information with verbal information, i.e., natural language.
We use as non-verbal information, two dimensional numerical information, is explained its behavior with natural language. To bridge the gap
between non-verbal information and verbal information, I apply fuzzy
sets theory to translate quantitative information into qualitative information. The proposed method is verified by showing the generation process of some example texts which explain the behavior of a line chart.

1 Introduction

There are many works that study to handle multimodal information in the both
fields of human interface and text generation technologies[1]-[4]. Many of them
are related to the development of a system which can integrate multimodal
information so that it can provide users with the most suitable information.
To generate multimodal documents, there are many tasks; for example, content
selection, automated layout of media, tailoring multimedia output, multimedia
integration method, multimedia interfaces, etc. Those tasks are basically one
of approaches to achieving the purpose that the same propositional content can
often be expressed in multiple, intermixed, different kinds of modalities. However,
the task of translating a modality into the different kind of modality is not
normally included in the tasks. If the meaning of a modality can be expressed
with another modality, it would increase the information to be used, moreover,
we will be able to easily understand the meaning of a modality regarded as
difficult to be understood as it is. For example, by displaying numerical data
with a graph, we can understand an overview of what numerical data suggest.
This is one of the cases for such translation. Therefore, in this paper, I would like
to show an approach to translating a modality into a different kind of modality,
in particular, focusing on that non-verbal information is explained with verbal
information, i.e., natural language.

We can often see that there are many cases where multimodal information
is explained with natural language. This means that non-verbal information can
be described with natural language, thought it cannot be said that every piece
of non-verbal information can completely be described with natural language.

A. Gelbukh (Ed.): CICLing 2001, LNCS 2004, pp. 226–238, 2001.

However, to some degree non-verbal information can be described with natural language. This is because there should exist common parts in meaning which can be shared by several modalities through the meanings covered by natural language. According to this fact, in this paper, I attempt to propose a method to describe non-verbal information with verbal information; concretely, I show a method to describe numerical data figured as a line chart with natural language that explains the behavior of the line chart. In the process, I explain how fuzziness functions to bridge the gap between non-verbal information and verbal information. The basic idea of text generation in this paper comes from the idea of systemic functional linguistics (SFL) [5] and text generation based on the linguistics [6]-[8], therefore, the way of analyzing a text shown below also follows the ideas.

2   Analysis of a Line Chart and Accompanying Text

Fig. 1 shows an example of a financial article[1] with a line chart figure.

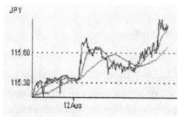

Tokyo The Yen Dropped Upon Reaching The Level of 116 Yen to The Dollar Temporarily
At 12:00 GMT (17:00 pm, EST) *The yen rate in Tokyo dropped. The dollar was quoted at 115.66-69 yen, below 114.68 at the same time the day before in Tokyo.* In the morning, with reports that the U.S. stocks and bonds market had stabilized, *the dollar buying had gone ahead.* Afterwards, *it leveled off.* In the afternoon, as trading began to slack off in the market, *the dollar was shifting in the range of 115 yen level.* After 15:00 pm. *the dollar buying by European investigators was promoted, the range which the yen dropped was slightly wider, and the yen was temporarily quoted at 115.82 yen.* After 17:00, *the yen was temporarily dropped back to 116 yen level.* (Aug.12,1999)

Fig. 1. This article with a line chart reports the real behavior of foreign exchange rate between Japanese yen and the U.S. dollar on August 12, 1999.

As we see Fig. 1, the behavior of the line chart is explained with natural language with some additional explanations on the trends of the financial market. It is impossible to express all the behaviors of a line chart with natural language, however, we can see that natural language aggregates important information and functions to make us recognized the points where we should focus on.

---

[1] The text analyzed in this paper is a Japanese financial article. The text in Fig. 1 was translated into English by the author.

2.1   Analysis of the Characteristics of a Line Chart

In order to analyze the relation between a line chart and an accompanying text.
First of all, I analyze the components of a line chart. The behavior of a line chart
is explained with natural language, focusing on some points of its behavior. Those
focused points of a line chart are summarized as shown in Fig. 2.

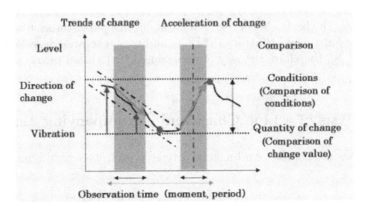

Fig. 2. Focused points of a line chart

An accompanying text with a line chart is composed to explain the conditions
of some focused points shown in Fig. 2. The behavior of a line chart is recognized
by mathematically understanding its shape. An example of the recognized shape
of a line chart and its mathematical expressions is shown in Table 1.

Table 1. Focused points of a line chart

Images	Mathematical Interpretation	
	• quantity of change (difference between the values in a particular period) $\Delta y = \|y(t_1) - y(t_0)\|$ • width of change $\Delta y(t) = y'(t) - y''(t)$ where, y'(t) is the upper approximate line y''(t) is the lower approximate line • change value: β is defined as follows: $\beta = \int_{t_0}^{t_1} \Delta y(t) dt$	• change value of trend Change value of trend: γ is defined as follows: $\gamma = \frac{\Delta y(t_1) - \Delta y(t_0)}{t_1 - t_0}$ where, $\Delta y(t_0) = y'(t_0) - y''(t_0)$ $\Delta y(t_1) = y'(t_1) - y''(t_1)$

In order to know how a text explaining the behavior of a line chart is composed by reflecting the observed aspects of the chart, the relation between the
line chart components and a text explaining the behavior of a line chart showing

the trend of foreign exchange rate changes is analyzed. The analysis result is summarized with system network shown in Fig. 3. This network expresses the whole possible components to describe the behavior of a line chart, related to a text explaining the behavior of the line chart.

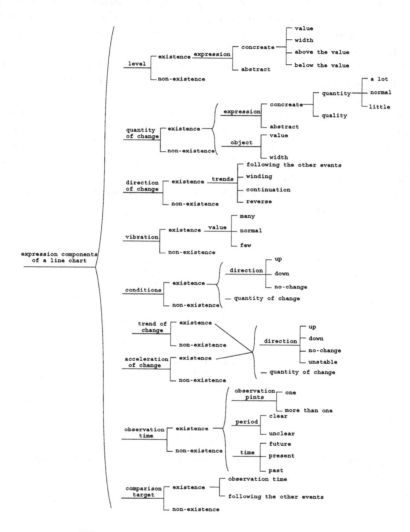

Fig. 3. System of a line chart's components

2.2 Lexico-Grammatical Analysis

When representing phenomena with natural language, we use word, clause, or clause complex to describe the phenomena. Here, focusing on the organization of a Japanese clause, according to SFL, a clause can be broken down into three functional constituents: *Process* (it corresponds to predicate part), *Participants* in the process (it can be described in terms of various participant roles such as Actor, Agent, Goal, Carrier, Sayer, etc.), and *Circumstances* associated with the process (it can be described as several types of circumstances such as Spatial, Temporal, Manner, Cause, Matter, etc.). The Process is the core of a clause, and in case of a Japanese clause, it is divided into four basic process types: material, mental, verbal, and relational [10]. Each process type has its own grammatical constraints, therefore, once a process type is decided, Participants and Circumstances are also limited by the process type in terms of how they appear in a clause.

Fig. 4 shows a part of Japanese linguistic system used in this work to generate texts explaining the behavior of line charts. The square box under each clause type is called 'realization statement' which expresses semantic and lexico-grammatical constraints on realizing a text. The semantic constraints decide what lexico-grammatical characteristics should appear in participant and circumstance. In other words, once a process type is determined, the structure of a clause will be automatically determined.

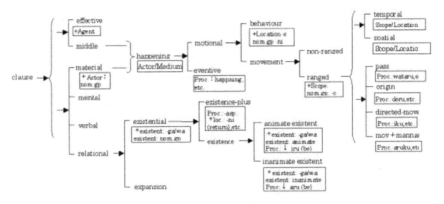

Fig. 4. A part of Japanese grammar system used to describe the behavior of a line chart

2.3   Lexical Characteristics and Line Chart Aspects

Generally speaking, in terms of expressing a phenomenon with natural language, lexical selection is one of the most difficult problems [11]. This is because it is difficult to select the most appropriate single word for a given information. Moreover, it is also difficult for dividing a phenomenon with several words. In case of explaining a line chart verbally, it is important to decide which part of the shape of a line chart is particularly expressed. Depending on the views to a line chart, a way of explaining a line chart behavior would be different. This means that the words included in a generated text should be selected on the basis of the focused aspects of the chart. And also since each word has its own meaning to express the line chart aspects, therefore, there exist some constraints for the usage of the words.

Since the domain for generating a text is related to a financial article on foreign exchange rate changes, there are words often used to explain the behavior of line charts showing the trends of foreign exchange rate changes in a generated text, I have analyzed the relation between the variety of the words appeared in financial articles and the line chart aspects. Table 2 shows some example words used for describing the aspects of a line chart[2].

As we see on Fig. 2, a line chart is characterized by nine aspects such as *observation level, observation time, conditions, trends of change, acceleration of change, quantity of change, direction of change, vibration, comparison.* A text explaining the behavior of a line chart should contain words expressing some of these aspects in themselves. These nine aspects[3] are recognized quantitatively or qualitatively through mathematical interpretation of two dimensional numerical information figured as a line chart. Therefore, the values of those aspects can frequently be expressed with vague linguistic expressions, i.e., linguistic fuzzy values. To express the values of the aspects with fuzzy linguistic values is useful for relatively identifying the meaning of each word.

Table 2. Relation between words and aspects of a line chart

process	level	direction	observation time	conditions	trends of change	change value
hanraku-suru (drop in reaction)		+ → −	middle-long		$|a_0| > |a_1|$	
tsukeru (is quoted)	(p_0)		very short			
senkou-suru (go ahead)		$|y_0| < |y_1|$	very short (*focused*)			
(sage/age)-siburu (hang back)		+/−	middle-long		$|a_0| > |a_1|$	
suii-suru (shift)			long			
fukuramu (promote)						$|y(t_0) - p_0| < |y(t_1) - p_0|$
kakudai-suru (be wider)				$|y(t_0) - p_0|$ is sort of big		$|y(t_0) - p_0| < |y(t_1) - p_0|$
geraku-suru (drop)		−		$|y(t_0)| > |y(t_1)|$		

---

[2] In this paper, since Japanese texts are handled, Table 2 deals with the meaning of only Japanese words, especially appeared as predicates.

[3] In the case of the aspects of a line chart listed in Table 2, two aspects: *acceleration of change* and *vibration* were omitted from Table 2 because they do not characterize the predicates shown in Table 2.

An example of how the sense of a word is characterized based on the aspects of a line chart is shown as follows:

Given a word w_i, its word sense is characterized by the values of the aspects of the word.

Aspects	A_{i1}	A_{i2}	$\cdots$	A_{in-1}	A_{in}
Values	$\|a_0\| < \|a_1\|$	$+$	$\cdots$	big	high

Here, A_{ij} indicates the *jth* aspect of a line chart. '$\|a_0\| < \|a_1\|$' indicates a fuzzy relation. '$+$' indicates the direction of the trends expressed by qualitative value. 'big' and 'high' are expressed by fuzzy values.

With a formal expression, w_i is defined as follows:

$$w_i \leftarrow \bigwedge_{j=1\sim n} A_{ij}(X) \tag{1}$$

where, $A_{ij}(\cdot)$: the *jth* aspect of word w_i

X : values expressed as either fuzzy relation, fuzzy values, or qualitative values

In general, there are quite a few words that allow us to verbally express a particular non-verbal modality. Each word should have its own meaning and a word sense to express the non-verbal information. Considering what makes difference among those words in terms of word sense, generally speaking, the words which are able to be expressed verbally can be characterized by some aspects shared with the particular non-verbal modality and verbal modality, i.e., natural language. In the case of explaining a line chart with natural language, the words to be included in a generated clause are selected based on the values of the aspects which characterize the source modality, that is, in case of this paper, two dimensional graphical information. To sum up, we can say that fuzziness functions to distinguish the differences among words and also to bridge the gaps between two different kinds of modalities.

2.4   Constraints on the Usage of Words

There should exist constraints on the usage among words in a clause. This is because if one word expresses a particular aspect of an observed line chart, the remaining aspects of the line chart have to be described by the other words in a clause. Table 3 shows the relation between some verbs appeared in Fig. 1 and their lexical constraints to the other words in a clause.

Table 3. Lexical constraints

process	examples
drop in reaction (*hanraku-suru*)	• The yen rate in Tokyo dropped in reaction.
• 'drop in reaction' contains the meaning of *direction*. • Exchange becomes the subject of a clause.	
is quoted (*tsukeru*)	• The dollar is quoted at 115.66-69 yen, below 114.68 at the same time yesterday in Tokyo. • yen was temporary quoted at 115.82 yen.
• 'is quoted at' accompanies a word expressing *level*.	
go ahead (*senkou-suru*)	• dollar buying was going ahead.
• *direction* appears as the subject in a clause. • A particular time is clearly described in a clause.	
hang back ((*sage/age*)-*siburu*)	• dollar buying hanged back. • yen temporary hanged back to 119.77 yen.
• Exchange becomes the subject of a clause. • *level* tends to appear in the same clause.	
shift (*suii-suru*)	• dollar was shifting at 115 yen levels. • The yen rate in Tokyo was shifting in a bullish tone at the latter half of 120 yen levels.
• Exchange becomes the subject of a clause. • *level* tends to appear in the same clause. • A modifier such as adverb often accompanies in order to tell how exchange shifts. • *comparison* is sometimes mentioned in the same clause.	
promote (*fukuramu*)	• dollar buying by European investigators was promoted.
• *direction* appears in the subject in a clause.	
be wider (*kakudai-suru*)	• the range yen dropped was slightly wider.
• 'be wider' basically takes *direction* as its target.	
drop (*geraku-suru*)	• yen was temporary dropped to 116 yen levels.
• *level* tends to appear in a clause. • *comparison* is sometimes mentioned in a clause.	

3   The Process of Text Generation

Since the composition of a clause is constituted of process part for predicate, participant part for subject and goal, and circumstance part for temporal and spatial expressions of a clause, as an approach to generating a text for describing the behavior of a line chart, it is checked that the aspects of the behavior of a line chart appears in which part of a clause, i.e., process, participant, and circumstance part.

Since the lexico-grammatical characteristics of a clause is determined by process part, first of all, we decide which lexicon for predicate part is the most suitable for describing the behavior of a line chart[4], and then as next step, we decide words for participants, following the lexico-grammatical characteristics given by the decided process type. Finally we express the remaining parts of the

---

[4] Here, 'the most suitable' lexicon means that a lexicon whose meaning includes the aspects of a line chart as many as possible.

observed aspects of the line chart's behavior with circumstantial words. The text
generation process is summarized as the following steps.

step1. Input of focus on chart

Input information for text generation corresponds to focuses on the aspects
which a user wants to describe the behavior of the line chart with natural
language. As Fig. 5 shows, input information is given by arrows, points, areas
marked on the image of a line chart.

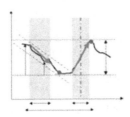

Fig. 5. An example of input information

step2. Distribution of input information to the aspects of a line chart

The focused aspects of a line chart are distributed to the elements in the
system network of the composition of a line chart shown in Fig. 3, and they
are converted into two dimensional numerical information through mathematical interpretation.

step3. Identification of the state to each chart component

The aspects of a line chart observed as quantitative value is recognized with
the linguistic label of either a fuzzy value or a fuzzy relation. The different
value of the aspects of a line chart reflects the different sense of words expressing the behavior of a line chart. Therefore, we can identify the most
suitable lexicon to describe a line chart.

step4. Identification of a lexicon for predicate

Since the syntactic structure of a clause is determined by process types, a
lexicon for predicate which can describe as many aspects of a line chart as
possible is chosen.

In the same way of Table 2 shown above, the lexicons for predicate are listed
in a dictionary in which each lexicon is defined by the values of the aspects
of a line chart.

step 5. Identification of process type

Which process type the lexicon for predicate selected at *step 4* belongs to
is identified at this step. It is revealed by the information in the dictionary
that holds the relation between lexicons and the process types.

step 6. Identification of participants based on the identification of syntactic structure

Based on the realization statements the identified process type has, lexico-grammatical characteristics is made clear. By this, it can be clear which aspects of the line chart are expressed as participants of a clause.

step 7. Identification of circumstances

The aspects of the line chart which have not yet been realized as lexicons by *step 6* do not have grammatical constraints provided by the realization statements of the identified process type. They normally correspond to temporal and comparative aspects of a line chart, and are realized as circumstantial words in a clause.

Fig. 6 shows an algorithm to generate a clause expressing the behavior of a line chart.

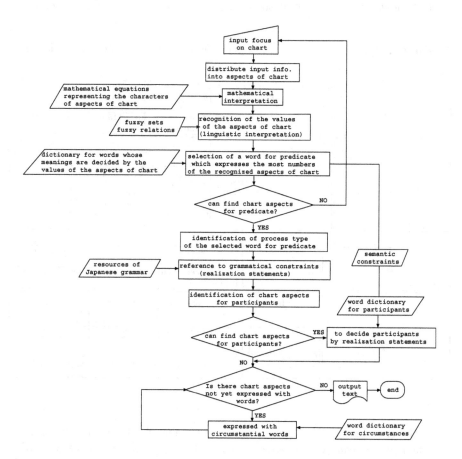

Fig. 6. This is the algorithm to generate a clause expressing the behavior of a line chart.

The relation of how the aspects of a line chart can be realized by process, participant, and circumstance depends on how much a simple sentence can express the aspects of the line chart and also on the semantic constraint the selected lexicon has.

It cannot be said that the lexico-grammatical constraints provided by the realization statements produce all Japanese clauses, as in there are many cases where lexical selection is not uniquely taken place especially at *step 4, step 6, step 7* mentioned above. To solve this problem, using the semantic constraints, I provide unique matching between the lexicons and the charts' aspects to avoid the failure of lexical selection. In this sense, we can say that the text generation method suggested in this paper is template-based text generation method.

4   Examples: A Line Chart and Generated Clauses

Table 4 shows examples of how the aspects of a line chart appear in a clause.

Table 4. Examples of how the aspects of a line chart appear in a clause

(1)

Image	doru wa	zenjitu kurabete	98-sen yasu-doru taka no	en 1 doru = 115-en 66- sen wo	tsuketa
	The dollar	below 114.68 at the same time yesterday		at 115.66-69 yen	was quoted
(chart)	Actor	Circ.	Range		Proc.:mat.: happ.:event: alter
	Medium	Proc.	Medium		Proc.
		comparison: observation time	quantity of change concrete: qualitative	level : concrete:value	

(2)

Images	15 ji sugini	en no sage-haba ga	yaya	kakudai-sita
	After 15:00 pm	The ranged yen dropped	slightly	was wider
(chart)	Circ.	Actor	Circ.	Proc.:mat. happ.:event: alter
	Circ.	Medium	Circ.	Proc.
	time: particular period	level:width direction:negative	change rate: qualitative	quantity of change: qualitative

In the example (1), the focused points of the line chart are the current *level*, and *quantity of change compared* to the values at the same time yesterday. Therefore, those aspects are distributed into a clause. The predicate '*tuketa* (was quoted)' must accompany *level*, therefore, it is expressed as '*was quoted at*

115.66-69 yen' in English. *Quantity of change* is expressed, compared to the previous observation time, as '*below 114.68 at the same time yesterday'*. The subject of the predicate is expressed as '*The dollar'*. Then, a clause is generated as '*The dollar was quoted at 115.66-69 yen below 114.68 at the same time yesterday.'*

In the example (2), the focused points of the line chart are *particular period, level:width, direction of change, change rate,* and *quantity of change*. The predicate '*kakudai-sita* (was wider)' itself expresses *quantity of change* and basically takes *level:width* and *direction* as its target. In this case, both *level:width* and *direction* are expressed as '*The range* yen *dropped'*. *Change rate* is expressed as a circumstantial word, '*slightly'*. *Particular period* is expressed as circumstantial words, '*After 15:00 pm'*. Then, a clause is generated as '*After 15:00 pm, the range yen dropped was slightly wider.'*

5   Conclusions

A line chart behavior can be explained using natural language phrase, however, there has not been a clear method of how to generate a text for such graphical information. I have proposed a method to describe non-verbal information with natural language. In the proposed method, fuzziness plays an important role to bridge the gaps between non-verbal information and verbal information in that the meanings of words to express non-verbal information are characterized based on fuzzy values and fuzzy relations. While generating a clause which explains the behavior of a line chart, it is important to consider how the aspects of a line chart are distributed into a generated clause and how a clause is worded. Wording functions provide a variety of ways of expressing, which means that even if we observe the same phenomenon, the way of expressing the phenomenon should be different by taking a different view at the phenomenon. Although natural language description of a phenomenon cannot always be justified, it can provide us with a new piece of knowledge that we cannot find from a single modality viewpoint. This fact can lead us to the development of new methods for data mining and knowledge discovery.

References

1. Maybury, M.T. (ed.): Intelligent Multimedia Interfaces, AAAI Press/The MIT Press (1993)
2. Maybury, M.T., Wahlster,W (eds.):Readings in Intelligent User Interfaces, Morgan Kaufmann Publishers, Inc. (1998).
3. Maybury,M.T.: Research in Multimedia and Multimodal Parsing and Generation, In: Kevitt, P.M. (ed.): Integration of Natural Language and Vision Processing (Volume II) Intelligent Multimedia, Kluwer Academic Publishers (1995), 31–55
4. Kevitt, P.M. (ed.): Integration of Natural Language and Vision Processing, (Volume II) Intelligent Multimedia, Kluwer Academic Publishers (1995)
5. Halliday, M.A.K.: An Introduction to Functional Grammar, Edward Arnold (1985)
6. Matthiessen,C., Bateman, J.: Text Generation and Systemic-Functional Linguistics: Experiences from English and Japanese, Pinter (1991)

7. Matthiessen, C., Kobayashi,I. Zeng, L., Cross,M.: The Modelling of Multimodal Resources and Processes for Defense, In: Proc. of Artificial Intelligence in Defense Workshop, 8th Australian Artificial Intelligence Conference (1995) 91-108

8. Matthiessen, C. Zeng, L., Cross, M., Kobayashi, I., Teruya, K. Canzhong, W.: The Multex generator and its environment: application and development, In: Proc. of the 9th International Workshop on Natural Language Generation (INLG-98) (1998) 228–237

9. Hovy, E.H., Arens,Y.: On the Knowledge Underlying Multimedia Presentations, In: Maybury, M.T. (ed.): Intelligent Multimedia Interfaces, AAAI Press/The MIT Press (1993)

10. Teruya, K.: An exploration into the world of experience: a systemic-functional interpretation of the grammar of Japanese, Ph.D thesis, Macquarie university (1998)

11. Cole, A.R. (ed.): Survey of the State of the Art in Human Language Technology (1995)

12. Kobayashi, I.: Toward Text Based Information Processing: with An Example of Natural Language Modeling of A Line Chart, In: Proc. of IEEE-SMC'99, Vol. 5 (1999) 202–207

13. Kobayashi, I.: Natural Language Modeling of the Behavior of a Line Chart In Proc. of Asian Fuzzy Systems Symposium 2000 (2000) 341-346

14. Gunther, K., van Leeuwen, T.: Reading Images The Grammar of Visual Design, Routledge (1996)

Interactive Multilingual Generation

José Coch and Karine Chevreau

LexiQuest
261, rue de Paris
93556 Montreuil Cedex, FRANCE
jose.coch@lexiquest.fr, karine.chevreau@lexiquest.fr

Abstract. The paper presents interactive multilingual generation, which in most cases is a viable alternative to machine translation and automatic generation. The idea is to automatically produce a preliminary version of the text, and allow the user to modify it in his native language. The software then produces the other languages following the user's modifications. This technique has been used in an international project and validated in operation on a dozen European sites.

1 Introduction

The need for high-quality text production in several languages is considerable. Apart from human writing (relatively expensive and long), several techniques such as machine translation or automatic generation can help to satisfy this need. In this paper, we propose a new technique, interactive multilingual generation, which combines automatic generation (of a first version of the text), with a particular type of controlled translation.

Our approach combines the advantages of automatic generation (no source language to analyse, and then no errors) with the richness of human writing.

In the second section we introduce and compare the techniques to produce texts in several languages. In the third section we describe the technical details of interactive generation. Finally, in the fourth section, we describe an in-use system where our approach has been applied.

2 To Produce Texts in Several Languages

The need for producing and maintaining high-quality texts in several languages is nowadays common.

The cost of a human translation of a document is around US$50 per page on an average. As million of pages are produced each day in the world, this market is enormous.

Documents written in a technical, precise domain can now be produced (or translated in other languages) using several automatic techniques. Basically, these techniques are until now machine translation and automatic text generation. We propose a

A. Gelbukh (Ed.): CICLing 2001, LNCS 2004, pp. 239-250, 2001.

new approach derived from automatic text generation: interactive multilingual generation.

2.1 Machine Translation

We do not think it would be useful here to describe this well-known technique. Documents in one or more target languages are obtained from a "master" document in a source language. When the goal is to obtain a high-quality text in the target language(s), even if the analysis of the source language is very robust, the text produced can have errors, is generally poor or over-literal, and as a consequence, it has to be revised by a human translator.

2.2 Automatic Text Generation

Automatic generation means production of texts (by a software system) from some language-neutral data. The existing industrial automatic-generation systems are based on this principle. For example, *FoG* (Goldberg et al. 1994) generates weather forecasts from conceptual messages coming from the forecaster's workstation. *PLANDoc* (McKeown et al. 1994) generates reports from data coming from a route-planning system. *AlethGen* (Coch 1996) generates customised commercial letters from a customer database.

However, one can observe that the need for text production is enormous when there are only a few in-use automatic generation systems. The point here is that often the data (that would be necessary to generate the required documents) do not exist or are not precise or complete enough.

Symbolic authoring. No available data implies that automatic generation is impossible. To solve this problem, some authors have developed a technique called *Symbolic Authoring*. The human "author" writes (often helped by a graphical user interface) symbolic, language-neutral representations of the document to generate in several languages. *Exclass* (Caldwell & Korelsky 1994) generates job descriptions from graphical conceptual representations entered by the user. *Drafter* (Paris & Vander Linden 1996) generates software manuals from procedures descriptions entered by the human author.

The problem with this approach is that human authors usually find the conceptual language and even the graphical user interface hard to interpret and use (see Scott et al. 1998).

WYSIWYM. WYSIWYM or "What You See Is What You Meant" (Scott et al. 1998, Power & Scott 1998) is a technique for natural symbolic authoring. For creating a conceptual representation, the starting point is a kind of empty generic sentence (for example "Do this action by using these methods"). Some parts of the sentence are mouse-sensitive (or "clickable"). In other words, a pop-up menu can be opened, from which a concept may be selected. Then the text generator produces a new version of the text containing the selected concept. Iterating this action, the final text can be obtained.

Here is an example from the domain of technical software manuals (Scott et al. 1998):

1. Do this action[1] by using these methods
2. Schedule this event by using these methods
3. Schedule the appointment by using these methods
4. To schedule the appointment:
    Before starting, perform this task.
    Then proceed as follows:
        Do this action by using these methods
5. To schedule the appointment:
    Before starting, open the Appointment Editor window by using these methods.
    Then proceed as follows:
        Do this action by using these methods
6. (etc.)

Other problems of automatic generation. Even when the input data are available, two problems can subsist:

1. generated texts seem to need a kind of "human touch", not really a correction but perhaps a detail, a subjective aspect,
2. automatic generation produces also the source text, the text that the human writer normally writes: the system can be a competitor for the human writer.

Of course, concerning point 1, one can think that the techniques will be able in the future to take into account "subjective" knowledge bases, etc., but it is obvious that this kind of modelling is hard to develop and maintain.

Concerning point 2, the technical advantage of being able to produce also the "source" language, can be, in fact, a psychological and social negative aspect of the generation in most cases, where human writers see the program as the automatic "thing" that will replace them.

2.3 Interactive Multilingual Generation

The technique that we propose starts with a first automatic generation based on (possibly incomplete) available input data. This first text can be complete or not. It is generated in a set of languages, but it is displayed to the human user only in his or her mother tongue.

The Interactive Generation GUI allows the user to read the generated text, and to click in the part of the text he wishes to modify. A pop-up menu then opens, proposing a set of alternative concepts, and a set of modifiers (related with probability, phase,

---

[1] Underlined text indicates the sequence on which the user clicked to obtain the next step. "Do this action" is replaced by "Schedule this event", etc.

etc.). The following picture shows an example of this technique in the Meteorology domain (MultiMeteo software, Meteo-France version).

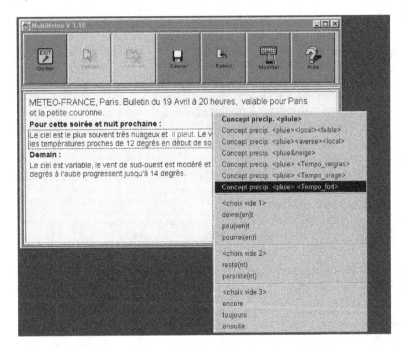

Fig. 1.

In this example, after clicking on "il pleut" (it will rain), a pop-up menu opens with several groups of options. The first group contains a set of alternative concepts derived from "rain", like light rain, showers, temporarily heavy rain, etc. The second group contains modifiers related to probability (which are represented by "should be", "can be", and "could be"). The third and fourth groups deal with the evolution of the concept (phases, repetitions, "still", "always", etc.). The content of this menu is the result of the specifications done by Météo-France. It is a subset of the potential possibilities, which could concern also the category of the selection (noun phrase or finite sentence), the tense of the verb, the style telegraphic or not, temporal and other modifiers, etc.

In the example, the user takes the alternative concept "<pluie>, <tempo fort>" ("<rain>, <temporarily heavy>").

The system then modifies the sentence and the new French version is: *"Le ciel est généralement très nuageux et des pluies parfois violentes se produisent" (literally "the sky [will] generally [be] very cloudy and temporarily heavy rain [will] take place").*

Once the user saves the result, the system takes into account the modifications for all the selected languages. For example the final English version of the text contains the sentence: *"It will be mostly overcast and rain will be heavy for a time".*

Other possible modifications can concern titles, comments (adding general remarks like "Tomorrow: nice weather", etc.) and links (changing "et" to "avec" implies a new generation of the next group as a noun phrase: "et il pleut" becomes "avec de la pluie").

Advantages of the Interactive multilingual generation. Key benefits of the Interactive multilingual generation can be outlined as follows:

- Feasibility even in case of incomplete input data
    - this point is relatively similar to the WYSIWYM approach,
- Higher quality of generated texts
    - taking into account the human modification (the "human touch") not only in the "source" language, but also in the target languages in a controlled way (without typical machine translation problems),
- Cost effective maintenance and adaptability
    - thanks to "reasonable" knowledge bases, because the more subjective or highly conceptual knowledge can be added by the human user,
- Acceptability by the human users
    - the system is not seen as an automatic competitor but as a tool which allows people "to write in foreign languages",
- Around 2 seconds per text and per language, to be compared with around 10 minutes per text and per language for a human translation.

This is why we think that in many cases, Interactive Generation is a viable alternative to Machine Translation.

3   Interactive Generation: Technical Description

3.1   Overview

Our approach is based on the standard NLG architecture, with a Planner, and a Realisation module, or more exactly, a set of Realisation modules (one per language). The Planner produces a conceptual representation, which is independent from the language. In fact this representation is a type of interlingua, object-oriented, based on Events. It contains not only the conceptual representation of the text to be realised, but also a large set of alternatives of each concept, link, etc.

The Interactive Generation GUI module takes at the same time the interlingua and the realised text, displays the text, and allows the user to click on the text to change it, adding modifiers, comments, modifying concepts, links, etc. The following picture shows the integration of the modules:

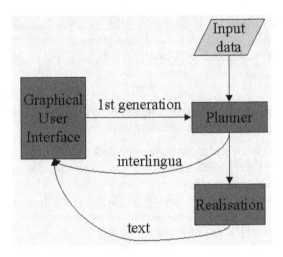

Fig. 2.

The main point here is that the user has the impression that he is modifying the text, but in fact, he is editing the interlingua. The Interactive Generation GUI is an interlingua editor, but the interface only shows clickable and modifiable texts in the language of the user. After each modification, the Realisation module is used to update the displayed text, as shown in Fig. 3 below.

3.2 Description of the Interlingua

The central element of the interlingua is the Event. An Event is a conceptual object associated to a fact or a situation. It is realised as text in each language. The Event is calculated by the Planning module.

There are two types of Events, atomic and molecular. Atomic Events are used for simple situations and have only one value (*Value* attribute). Molecular Events are used for complex situations (several parameters, evolution, etc.) and have at least two values (*Value0* and *Value1*), and a global predicate implying both values (*Operator* attribute).

As our goal here is not to describe exhaustively the Events, but to show multilingual modeling for the interactive generation, we only describe atomic Events.

Example of atomic *Event*. Suppose that in a meteorological database a cloud covering from 90 to 100% of the sky is represented by the code 3 in the column "cloud covering". In this case the model of the *Event* representing that situation could be:

```
Event_CloudCovering3: Event {
       Value = ClassCloudCovering_code3;
}
```

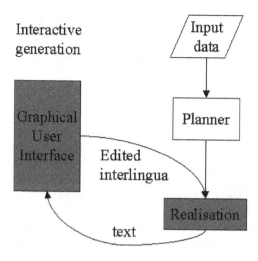

Fig. 3.

The value of this *Event* is a class, or in other words a set of concepts, here the class `ClassCloudCovering_code3`. This class contains the concepts associated to the code 3, which can be `Overcast`, `No-Sun`, `VeryCloudy-Overcast`. These concepts have themselves a set of corresponding terms in each language.

When producing a weather forecast from a code 3 cloud-covering situation, the Planning module produces the *Event* and selects one of the three concepts of the class, the rest of them remaining inactive. The interactive generation GUI then allows the human forecaster to click on the text (written in his mother tongue) that he wants to modify, and to take a different concept (from the list of three possible concepts of code 3). The software then re-generates all the languages following the modification.

In addition, a set of modifiers can be added to the *Event*. As a consequence, the realisation in each language of the *Event* can change. The modifiers can be for example:

- PROBA, the probability (1, 0.7, 0.5, 0.2)
- PHASE (BEGIN, CONT, END),
- PERIOD of the Event,
- CAT, the global category (PROP for proposition with a finite verb, NP for noun phrase, ADJP for adjectival phrase).

For example, if our Event has the modifiers

```
PROBA = 0.7,
CAT = PROP, and
PERIOD = MORNING,
```

the text in French can be "Le ciel devrait être couvert le matin", in Spanish "El cielo estará probablemente cubierto por la mañana", in English "The sky should be overcast during the morning".

Note that the terms are selected and realised in an autonomous manner in each language and the result is not necessarily the exact translation (or the literal translation) of a virtual source language. The interlingua contains the concept, but not the term, which belongs to a given language. In addition, even in the same language, a concept can be realised by different terms.

3.3 The First Step of the Realisation

The linguistic realisation process is inspired by the Meaning-Text theory (MTT). It is divided into 5 steps: Conceptual, Semantic, Deep Syntax, Surface Syntax, and Morphology. The Conceptual step has been added to the MTT for the processing of the Event and the production of the Semantic Representation.

The Conceptual sub-module takes as elementary input the Event produced by the Planning module and produces the Semantic Representation (SemR) in each language. The SemR is formed by Semantic units ("Usems") as nodes and predicative relations (Rel1, Rel2, Rel3, Rel4) as arcs.

Construction of the SemR: principles. The construction of the SemR of an Event depends on the selected concepts and on its modifiers.

A concept can be realised by different terms, even in the same language. The selection of a term is one of the first tasks of the Conceptual sub-module.

In the knowledge base, a canonical SemR represents each term. In other words, each term is represented by Usems and predicative relations. Examples of French terms for the concepts Overcast and Very Cloudy-Overcast are shown in Table 1.

Here "Rel1" stands for the relation between a predicate and its first argument (semantic relation "1" in the MTT, Mel'cuk 1988).

Table 1.

French term	Canonical SemR
Ciel_couvert	Usem1 = ciel1Sem Usem2 = couvert1Sem Usem2 -> Rel1 -> Usem1
Couvert	Usem=couvert1Sem
Ciel très nuageux	Usem1 = ciel1Sem Usem2 = très1Sem Usem3 = nuageux1Sem Usem3 -> Rel1 -> Usem1 Usem2 -> Rel1 -> Usem3

3.4   List of Transformations with Respect to the Canonical SemR

Realisation of a term as an NP or a PROP. In our example, the French term Ciel_couvert can be realised as the NP "ciel couvert" or as the PROP "le ciel est couvert" with the verb *être*. In other cases, the head of the SemR can correspond to a predicative noun, for example as in "renforcement du vent". In this case, the PROP is obtained by the (a) verb associated to the same predicate as the noun, in our case "le vent se renforce".

Realisation of terms which SemR is a single Usem with support verb. In this case the PROP is obtained using the support verb associated to the Usem, for example in French ("averses" ➔ "des averses se produisent") or in Spanish ("vientos" ➔ "soplan vientos").

Realisation of terms which SemR is a single Usem with impersonal verb. ("rain" ➔ "it will rain").

4   A Real-World Application

4.1   Production of Weather Forecasts

MultiMeteo is a weather-forecast production system based on the interactive multilingual generation technique. The goal of MultiMeteo is to offer an automatic and customisable multilingual generation system to be used by weather information providers.

This system is currently used by European organisations to produce weather forecasts in several languages from structured data.

Thanks to MultiMeteo, it is possible to obtain automatically high-quality weather forecast texts:

- For a specified area,
- In a defined time interval (for example tomorrow, next week),
- Taking into account the more recent forecast data, typically coming from the Weather Service's mathematical models,
- Following a selected profile (city, sports, seaside, agriculture, road, etc.),
- In the target languages, currently French, Spanish, English, German, Dutch, Catalan and Galician.
- Around 2 seconds per text and per language

In the table below you will find an example of forecast paragraph automatically produced by MultiMeteo in the "per provinces" style of the INM (Spain) in 7 languages: German, French, English, Dutch, Spanish, Catalan, and Galician.

German :
Stark bewölkter Himmel mit verbreitet mäßigen Regenschauern. Spürbarer Temperaturrückgang. Schwacher Wind aus Südwest der auf Nordwest dreht. Höchsttemperatur : 18 Grad. Tiefsttemperatur : 13 Grad.

French :
Ciel très nuageux avec des averses modérées généralisées. Températures en chute importante. Léger vent de sud-ouest s'orientant au nord-ouest. Température maximale : 18 degrés, minimale : 13 degrés.

English :
Very cloudy sky, with widespread moderate showers of rain. Noticeable drop in temperatures. Gentle south-westerly winds turning north-westerly. High: 18 degrees Celsius. Low: 13 degrees Celsius.

Spanish :
Cielo muy nuboso con chubascos moderados generalizados. Temperaturas en descenso notable. Viento flojo del Suroeste tendiendo al Noroeste. Máximas: 18 grados. Mínimas: 13 grados.

Catalan :
Cel molt ennuvolat amb xàfecs moderats generalitzats. Temperatures en descens notable. Vent feble del sud-oest tendint al nord-oest. Màximes: 18 graus. Mínimes: 13 graus.

Galician :
Ceo moi nuboso con chuvascos moderados xeneralizados. Temperaturas en descenso notable. Vento suave do sudoeste tendendo ó noroeste. Máximas: 18 graos. Mínimas: 13 graos.

Dutch :
Zwaar bewolkte lucht met matige buien op de meeste plaatsen. Belangrijke temperatuursdaling. Zwakke winden uit het zuidwesten die naar het noordwesten draaien. Maximumtemperatuur : 18 graden. Minimumtemperatuur : 13 graden.

4.2 Validation

Several types of evaluations have been performed in a dozen European cities: "operational" (focusing on the software quality), "literary", and "meteorological" (coherence between the input data and the content of the generated texts).

Operational validation. Concerning software integration in the operational sites, the main conclusions are that MultiMeteo is user-friendly (is "easy to use"), and is accepted by the forecasters (some modifications has been suggested and have been implemented).

This point is important because rejection by the forecasters had been identified as a major risk for MultiMeteo.

Literary evaluation. Blind tests on randomly selected sets of weather forecasts (both produced by MultiMeteo and written by human forecasters) have shown that the quality of the generated texts is good, and comparable to the human-written weather forecasts. Human texts appear to be richer and to have more information, while MultiMeteo texts are more understandable.

Conceptual (Meteorological) validation. Meteorological evaluation gives acceptable results. Selected forecasters were invited to examine a set of weather forecasts (also both MultiMeteo-generated and human-written) and give a score related to the coherence between the meteorological situation and the text. The MultiMeteo average was 14.5/20 while the human-written average was 12.5/20.

4.3 Exploitation

As a consequence, Météo-France has acquired 15 licences for the software, which was used notably in 1999 to produce weather forecasts during the Rolland Garros tennis championship. It will be used for a set of other applications from the middle of 2001. INM (Spain) offers weather forecasts daily on its Web site in four languages for all the provinces of Spain (http://www.inm.es/wwi/MultiMeteo/ Multimeteo.html). ZAMG (Austria) plans to start operational exploitation of MultiMeteo beginning 2001.

5 Conclusion

Interactive multilingual generation is an interesting alternative to machine translation and automatic generation, notably in the cases that satisfy these conditions:

- need for high-quality texts,
- risk of rejection by the human writers, who can see a purely automatic system as a competitor,
- formalisation of the domain, even if the available data are incomplete.

The real-world software described in section 4 is a very good example of application of interactive multilingual generation, and its evaluation shows very encouraging results.

Acknowledgements. Our thanks go to the European Commission (DGXIII), Météo-France, Instituto Nacional de Meteorología (Spain), Royal Meteorological Institute (Belgium), and Zentralanstalt für Meteorologie und Geodynamik (Austria).

References

1. Caldwell, David E.; Korelsky, Tatiana (1994): *Bilingual generation of job descriptions from quasi-conceptual forms*, Proceedings of the 4th Conference on Applied Natural Language Processing (ANLP-94), Stuttgart, Germany, pp. 1-6.
2. Coch J. (1996). *Evaluating and comparing three text-production techniques.* Proceedings of the 16th Conference of Computational Linguistics, Coling 96, Copenhagen, Danmark.
3. Coch J. (1998). *Interactive generation and knowledge administration in MultiMeteo.* Proceedings of the Ninth International Workshop on Natural Language Generation. Niagara-on-the-lake, Ontario, Canada.
4. Goldberg, E., Driedger N., Kittredge R. (1994). *Using natural-language processing to produce weather forecasts.* IEEE Expert, 9(2):45-53.
5. Kerpedjiev S., Noncheva V. (1990). *Intelligent handling of weather forecasts.* Proceedings of the 13th Conference of Computational Linguistics, Coling 90, Helsinki.
6. McKeown, Kathleen; Kukich, Karen; Shaw, James (1994): *Practical Issues in Automatic Documentation Generation*, Proceedings of the 4th Conference on Applied Natural Language Processing (ANLP-94) Stuttgart, Germany, pp. 7-14.
7. Mel'cuk I. (1988). Dependency Syntax: Theory and Practice. State University of New York Press, Albany, NY, USA.
8. Paris, C. and Vander Linden, K.(1996): *DRAFTER: An Interactive Support Tool for Writing Multilingual Manuals.* IEEE Computer, Vol. 29, No. 7. Special Issue on Interactive Natural Language Processing, July 1996, pp. 49-56.
9. Polguère A. (1998): *La Theorie Sens-Texte*, Dialangue, 8-9, Université du Québec à Chicoutimi, pp.9-30, Canada.
10. Polguère A. (1997): *Engineering text generation*, Tribune des Industries de la Langue et de l'Information Electronique, N°23-24, pp. 21-29. Paris, France.
11. Power, R., Scott, D. (1998): *Multilingual authoring using feedback texts.* Proceedings of the 36th annual meeting of the Association for Computational Linguistics and 17th international conference on Computational Linguistics, Coling-ACL'98, Vol. II, pp. 1053-1059. Montréal, Canada.
12. Scott, D., Power, R., Evans, R. (1998): *Generation as a solution to its own problem.* Proceedings of the Ninth International Workshop on Natural Language Generation. Niagara-on-the-lake, Ontario, Canada.
13. Sigurd B., Willners C., Eeg-Olofsson M., Johansson C. (1992). *Deep comprehension, generation and translation of weather forecasts (Weathra).* Proceedings of the 14th Conference of Computational Linguistics, Coling 92, Nantes.
14. Sigurd B., Lastow B., Vävargård T. (1996). *Computer generation of weather overviews.* Proceedings of the ECAI 96 Workshop Gaps and Bridges: New directions in Planning and Natural Language Generation.
15. Tiafang Y., Dongmo Z., Qian W. (1998): *Multilingual weather forecast generation system* in Proceedings of the Ninth International Workshop of Natural Language Generation, Niagara-on-the-lake, Ontario, Canada.
16. Vavargard T. (1997) *RiPP; Autotext and symbol* in Proceedings of the 3rd European Conference on Applications of Meteorology, Lindau, Germany.

A Computational Feature Analysis for Multilingual Character-to-Character Dialogue

Charles Callaway

North Carolina State University
Department of Computer Science
P.O. Box 7534   Raleigh, NC 27695
cbcallaw@eos.ncsu.edu
http://multimedia.csc.ncsu.edu/imedia/index.html

Abstract. Natural language generation systems to date have concentrated on the tasks of explanation generation, tutorial dialogue, automated software documentation, and similar technical tasks. A largely unexplored area is *narrative prose generation,* or the production of texts used in stories such as novels, mysteries, and fairy tales. We present a feature analysis of one complex area of NLG found in narrative prose but not in technical generation tasks: character-to-character dialogue. This analysis has enabled us to modify a surface realization system to include the necessary features that dialogue requires and thus to write the types of texts found in narratives.

1   Introduction

Recent years have witnessed an intense interest in the use of interactive language technologies in educational and entertainment applications. Their successful integration requires a number of support technologies that are currently under development in order to effectively engage learners and game players. Character-to-character dialogue in particular is one of the support technologies necessary for the realization of interactive multiagent education and entertainment. By creating computational models of these phenomena, it becomes possible to create intelligent systems for both literacy tutoring and producing interactive drama and novels. Furthermore, the capability of multilingual dialogue would allow those systems to reach a much wider audience.

Creating an interactive literacy tutoring system would be a key step in achieving software that could have a significant impact on the education of large numbers of children. First, such a system could function as a one-on-one reading tutor [15]. By allowing students to select key aspects of a story's content, those students could be immersed in a narrative world of their own origination. Such a world might contain their own characters, props, and action sequences. By allowing students to make such directorial choices, they will be more interested in the resulting outcome and more likely to avidly read what they have helped to create.

A. Gelbukh (Ed.): CICLing 2001, LNCS 2004, pp. 251–264, 2001.

Second, students could engage in *exploratory narration* [11,22]. For example, if a student had access to the raw materials for their favorite Jack London novella, they could request the same story content, but in a different style, such as Ernest Hemingway's choppiness, or James Joyce's stream-of-consciousness style. This kind of capability encourages students to approach text in a different way, to understand the difference between content and presentation, and to want to create their own literary works with an appreciation for the world of potential design choices.

Third, students could engage in a new form of foreign language education. Students could elect to generate the narrative prose in any of a number of languages [1,2], inviting them to make comparisons between different language versions of the same story. With conversational capability, this kind of interactive narrative system would enable students to have a one-on-one foreign language tutor.

Finally, this type of real-time interactive communication opens the way for intelligent tutors to actively explore 3D learning environments with students. Current such knowledge-centered learning environments [13,21] interact with learners by sequencing prerecorded audio files. Once appropriate responses are determined, the corresponding audio files containing the pieces of spoken text are put into the proper order and sent to the audio device. The vast time and space requirements this method requires can be avoided by instead using a narrative prose generation system in combination with a high-quality voice synthesizer with prosody control [4,6].

Although character-to-character dialogue is found in both spoken and written forms, the research described here discusses only the computational aspects of written dialogue, *i.e.*, the range of linguistic phenomena that comprise it and a computational feature analysis which will enable the creation of feature-based grammars for the generation of character dialogue. The phenomena of direct character-to-character dialogue is comprised of five major parts: the structure and function of the quoted material, the structure and function of the external elements, the utterer of the dialogue, the utterance matrix relation, and the orthography of dialogue punctuation. Although several of these elements have been discussed in the literature, no effort has yet been made to integrate them and thus create a comprehensive computational model of character dialogue.

The computational feature analysis of multilingual character-to-character dialogue described here is part of a long-term research program into educational and entertainment applications that make use of knowledge-based learning environments, natural language generation, and animated 3D agents in immersive 3D worlds. The model of dialogue described here has been implemented in a narrative prose generation system [3] which writes Little Red Riding Hood stories (cuentos de Caperucita Roja). By combining all of these technologies, we will be able to create 3D environments populated with engaging animated 3D characters capable of teaching literacy skills. This paper describes our model of character-to-character dialogue as part of the natural language generation module of such a literacy tutor.

2   Character-to-Character Dialogue

Written character-to-character dialogue is an aspect of narrative that takes the form of turn-taking conversational interactions between one or more agents. The written form lacks prosodic and accentual features found in spoken dialogue; instead, the substitution of orthographic punctuation marks serves as clues allowing the reader to reconstruct the spoken conversation.

Aside from the topic of narration, several researchers have worked on the topic of punctuation in (computational) linguistics, including Quirk *et al.*'s book [18] governing distribution of punctuation in discourse, Geoffrey Nunberg's book [16], Christine Doran's dissertation [8] that discuss the theory of punctuation in regard to particular grammatical theories, and Bernard Jones' dissertation [10] that uses distributional and frequency analysis to describe a functional model of punctuation incorporating both syntax and semantics. Other researchers such as Longacre [14] discuss conversational dialogue without reference to punctuation or its computational analysis.

However with regard to narration, there is very little extant research. Christine Doran [7] discusses reported speech in newspaper article corpora, provides a preliminary structural analysis, and describes how an LTAG grammar can be augmented for parsing applications. However, newspaper articles rarely contain true turn-taking conversational dialogue and are usually so formal that they do not contain as wide a range of variation as that found in fictional narratives (novels, mysteries, short stories, etc.)

In order for literacy education, conversational tutoring, or interactive fiction to become a reality, we must ensure that the conventions found in literature can be followed by natural language generation systems. Thus if particular linguistic phenomena are found in actual short stories and novels, they need to be computationally reproducible. The first stage in this process is to analyze in detail character-to-character dialogue that occurs naturally, then to model the phenomena (via the definition of features and rules that govern them in the case of functional systemic natural language generation grammars), and finally to write a grammar that uses the newly defined features in the actual production of narrative prose. In addition, if we wish our system to be *multilingual* so that it applies to as broad an audience as possible, we must repeat this process for each desired language.

Typical English Dialogue Patterns. Written English dialogue in direct form[1] has a small set of realizable forms, consisting of four main types: `Utterance-Only` where the speaker and the manner of speech must be inferred, `Utterance-Speaker` where the identity of the speaker follows the quoted material, `Speaker-Utterance` where the opposite is true, and `Utterance-Speaker-Utterance` where the utterances are either a single sentence split along an appropriate linguistic

---

[1] Note that we present here only positive examples of direct speech, ignoring ungrammatical cases. For instance, the utterer sequence "said he" is considered to be archaic. These cases are discussed elsewhere in the literature.

boundary or are separate sets of (possibly multiple) sentences. Each utterance may be a statement, an exclamation, or a question; each speaker includes a relation and an optional modifying clause describing how the utterance was delivered by the speaker. Additionally, utterances may be complete sentences, or split where one half of a coordinated phrase is in one utterance while the other half plus an optional sentential component are in the other half. A representative sample is shown below.

- "<sentence>.?!"
  (1) "That scarf belongs to Patty."

- "<nounphrase>,?!" John said <adverbial-manner>.
  (2) "I couldn't catch up to him," John said breathlessly.

- "<sentence–np1>," John said <time-manner>, "and <np2>.?!"
  (3) "I usually drink coffee," John said when he got up, "and orange juice."

- John smiled, "<sentence>.?!" (nonverbal speaking relation)
  (4) John smiled, "Were you always so ticklish?"

- "<sentence>.?! <sentence>.?! ..."
  (5) "I think it's great. But you have to decide for yourself."

- "<sentence>,?!" John said slowly, "<sentence>.?!"
  (6) "Get out of here," John said slowly, "I want to be alone."

- "<sentence1>," John said dryly, "but <sentence2>. <sentence3>."
  (7) "It'll do," John said dryly, "but I don't like it. It smells bad."

- "<nounphrase>.?!"   "<prepphrase>.?!"   ...   (In answer to a question.)
  (8) "The table."   "On the shelf?"   "Now!"

- "<np1>," John said, "and <np2>.?!"
  (9) "A hammer," said John, "and nails."

- "<interjection>,?!" John yelled, "<sentence>.?!"
  (10) "No!" John yelled, "It's mine!"

- "<circumstantial>,?!" John spoke up suddenly, "<sentence>.?!"
  (11) "Before the sun goes down," John spoke up suddenly, "Get some matches!"

- "<sentence>,?!" John exclaimed, "<preposition>.?!"
  (12) "I want the garage door up," John exclaimed, "up."

Typical Spanish Dialogue Patterns. Written Spanish dialogue in direct form[2] is for the most part similar to English except in punctuation and style (determinable by distributional statistics) and that due to verb morphology, the

---

[2] Again, only grammatical examples are considered here. Spanish also has idiosyncrasies which I have not been able to find described in the literature. For example, the utterer sequence "Marcelo dijo" seems to be dispreferred.

identity of the speaker can be more easily inferred than in English by examining its ending. Spanish uses the long dash rather than quotation marks, and it only functions as a delimiter when a linguistic boundary must be given (*c.f.* examples (1) and (13)). A representative sample of Spanish character-to-character dialogue is shown below.

- – ¿¡<sentence>.!?
  (13) –Anoche acabé mi nuevo invento.   –¡Ya vamos, papá!   –¿Ahora?

- – ¿¡<sentence>!?–dijo Juan.
  (14) –Está a punto de prueba–dijo, muy orgulloso.
  (15) –¿Cuál es la sorpresa?–quiso saber Juan.

- –¿¡<sentence>!?–dijo Juan <manner>.
  (16) –Os dejasteis la puerta sin cerrar–dijo Juan, entrando en la tienda.
  (17) –¿Qué querran los ladrones?–comentó Juan, mirando el desorden.

- –¿¡<sentence>!?–dijo Juan–. ¿¡<sentence>.!?
  (18)–¡Espere, espere!–pidió Juan, intentando tranquilizar a la asustada ancianita–. ¿No vive aquí ningún hombre?
  (19) –Está bien–dijo Juan en voz alta–. ¡Veamos qué hacéis con ellos!
  (20) –Ésta es la calle de la Nuez–dijo Juan, al volver una esquina–. El número dieciséis se halla en la acera de enfrente.

- –¿¡<sentence-part>–dijo Juan–<sentence-remainder>!?
  (21) –¿Por qué–preguntó Juan, cogiéndole el horario–has rodeado todas las clases de Diego con corazoncitos?

- –¿¡<sentence-part>–dijo Juan–, <sentence-remainder>.!?
  (22) –La policía está trabajando ahí dentro–dijo la señora Martinez–, y nos han pedido que esperásemos fuera.

- Juan sonreió y dijo–: ¿¡<sentence>.!?
  (23) Pero Juan le hizo una seña y cuchicheó–: No te pelees con ellos.

By comparing the requirements for multilingual direct character-to-character dialogue in a feature-based way, we can create a single natural language generation system capable of composing dialogue in a multitude of languages.

3 Features of Character-to-Character Narrative Dialogue

A computational feature analysis for some linguistic phenomenon begins with an analysis of its overall variability (or coverage). Once commonalities in the data can be observed, it becomes possible to assign a finite set of features and values which those features can take on. For example, one feature for nouns is *gender*, whose values can be *masculine*, *feminine*, or *neuter*. For character-to-character dialogue there are six relevant high-level features:

- The structure and function of the quoted material
- The utterer (speaker) of the dialogue
- The utterance matrix clause
- The structure and function of the surrounding paragraphs
- Whether it is direct or indirect
- The orthography of dialogue punctuation

We discuss each of these in turn.

3.1   The Quoted Material

Basic direct quotations can be of any syntactic structure: **S, NP, PP**, etc. (*c.f.* 1 and 8), especially when the quotation is a direct response to a previous question in the dialogue. However, there are several modifications to the basic sentential structure that authors may employ:

- *Interjections*: To express shock, surprise, and pain among a number of other feelings, characters will frequently utter interjections such as "Oh!", "Aha!", or "Ouch!". These interjections are frequently fronted inside a complete sentence.
  (24) "Ouch, you must have just come from the dentist!"
  (25) "Oh my, perhaps you should sit down."

- *Addressee*: In face to face dialogue, characters will frequently address each other by name, nickname, or some other appellation:
  (26) "Carol, don't forget to pick up some milk."
  (27) "My dear, all the better to see you with!"

- *Written stylistic effects*: In order to show emotions and have characters express themselves in nonstandard ways, authors write dialogue that includes onomatopoeiatic effects, simulated yelling, regional dialects, ellipsis, vocal handicaps, or vowel lengthening. Current surface realizers are ill-equipped to deal with these types of textual effects.
  (28) "Ewwww, I can't believe you just did that!"
  (29) "Mom, you CAN'T do that!"
  (30) "I'd really 'preciate it if you'd be gettin' along now."
  (31) "But Molly ..."
  (32) "B-b-but, it's so s-s-scary!"
  (33) "Nooooooo!"

- *Combinations*: Furthermore, these modifications to traditional sentential structures can be used in combination:
  (34) "Wow, John, you REALLY hit that ball!"

Before a traditional grammar can be used to generate narratives that contain these types of utterances, its sentence-level syntactic category must be augmented to include interjections and addressees, and surface realizers that are accustomed to producing only precisely grammatical utterances must be modified to create the types of stylistic effects that are commonly found in existing narrative corpora.

Finally, these types of effects must be available in a multilingual environment. Natural language researchers must come to realize that some types of effects are available in some languages but not possible in others. In addition, these effects should be expressed semantically to allow surface realizers to produce their best syntactic interpretation for a specific language.

3.2   The Utterer and Matrix Clause

Although direct quotes can stand alone (and often do in fast-fire exchanges), more frequently they are accompanied by another unquoted clause which specifies the speaker and the manner in which the speaker conveyed the utterance. In these cases, the particular language (English, Spanish, etc.) strongly affects the way the utterer and matrix clause can be realized. There are six major features that influence these possibilities:

- *Communicative Act Ordering*: There are four positions (in English) that the utterer and the communicative relation can appear in comparison to the quoted dialogue: `utterance-only` as in *"<sentence>"*, `preposed` as in *John said, "<sentence>"*, `postposed` as in *"<sentence>," John said.* and `interposed` as in *"<sentence1>," John said, "<sentence2>."*
- *Utterer Ordering*: There are two positions (in English) that the utterer and the communicative relation can appear in comparison to each other: `utterer-first` as in *"<sentence>," John said.* and `utterer-second` as in *"<sentence>," said John.* Also see [18, Section 14.29]. The former possibility is not available in Spanish unless it is followed by a nonverbal relation immediately coordinated with the matrix clause (*c.f.* example 23). Also, certain combinations are not allowed in modern English, *e.g.*, *Said John, "I don't think so."*
- *Utterance Manner*: The matrix relation in pure dialogue is often modified with a manner phrase indicating accompanying action or style in which the communicative act was delivered (besides connotative nuances of the communicative relation itself), such as `adverbial` in *"<sentence>," John said hurriedly,* with a `prepositional phrase` as in *"<sentence>," John said with aplomb,* with a `gerundive clause` as in *"<sentence>," John said fidgeting with his tie,* or with a `co-event clause` as in *"<sentence>," John said as he pressed the button.* Our informal corpora analyses indicate that these modifications occur more frequently in Spanish in texts that have been translated from English rather than written originally in Spanish.
- *Utterance relation semantics*: The utterance relation is not restricted to the traditional notion of purely communicative acts. For example, emotive verbs

are frequently used as in *"That's my favorite," John smiled.* Additionally, the utterance manner can be indicated by the connotation of the utterance relation, *e.g., John whispered, "Do you think so?"* It is not clear from the available evidence however that the relation semantics should be a top level feature rather than some combination of low-level features; more investigation into similar phenomena in other languages is required.

- *Use of Pronouns*: English requires a speaker in direct speech if a communicative act is used; because Spanish verbs include person and number, a distinct speaker or pronoun is unnecessary. In addition, if a pronoun is used after a communicative act in English in direct speech, it is considered archaic; a postposed pronoun in indirect speech is prohibited. These restrictions must be considered by a surface realizer when creating text.
- *Segmentation*: Most notably in replies to questions [14], quoted dialogue does not need to be a complete sentence. There are a large number of utterances that are fragmentary phrases due to the informal nature of dialogue [18, Chapter 11]. For example, *"On the chair," said John, "and near the door."*

3.3   The Surrounding Paragraphs

Necessarily, turn-taking dialogue interacts with expository text in a narrative and with dialogue initiated by a different character in the story. In addition, narrative passages are told from a particular point of view, either that of a particular character or some narrator who is not a participating character. Whenever an author switches between embodied characters or narrators in a turn-taking dialogue, there is a required paragraph break, which functions as a whitespace delimiter. Consider the following example from a recent Harry Potter book [20]:

> The Dursleys often spoke about Harry like this, as though he wasn't there — or rather, as though he was something very nasty that couldn't understand them, like a slug.
> "What about what's-her-name, your friend — Yvonne?"
> "On vacation in Majorca," snapped Aunt Petunia.
> "You could just leave me here," Harry put in hopefully.
> Aunt Petunia looked as though she'd just swallowed a lemon.

On the other hand, when an author switches between dialogue and expository text where the same character is both the speaker and main actor, the author may choose either to delimit via a paragraph break or not. In addition, a particular author or publisher will almost always follow a consistent editing scheme in a particular publication. The following example demonstrates the choice of delimiting between expository text and dialogue when the actor and speaker are the same:

> "What's this?" he asked Aunt Petunia. Her lips tightened as they always did if he dared ask a question.
> "Your new school uniform," she said.
> Harry looked in the bowl again.
> "Oh," he said, "I didn't realize it had to be so wet."

3.4   Direct vs. Indirect Speech

An author has a wide range of choices concerning the choice between characters'
use of direct and indirect speech[3]. The text can range from pure exposition
(with no communicative acts) to exposition with indirect communication to fully
interleaved exposition and direct dialogue to pure dialogue. Longacre [14] cites
examples along this range, some of which are adapted slightly here:

- *Pure Dialogue*:
  "It's a beautiful night, Mary," John said.
  "Yes, John, and how softly the moon is lying on the water," replied Mary.
  "I love you, Mary," John said.
  "At your age, John?" Mary asked.
- *Interleaved Exposition and Dialogue*:
  It was a beautiful night. The moon lay softly on the water. Then John said
  to Mary, "I love you." But Mary said, "At your age, John?"
- *Exposition and Indirect Dialogue*:
  It was a beautiful night. The moon lay softly on the water. Then John told
  Mary that he loved her. She said she couldn't believe he would ask her such
  a thing.
- *Exposition with No Communicative Acts*:
  It was a beautiful night. The moon lay softly on the water. Then John talked
  with Mary about his love for her. Mary refused to believe him.

In addition, the entire narrative can contain a mixture of these four types of
character interactions as the author sees fit, taking into account various stylistic
factors.

3.5   Orthography

The actual rules used to insert punctuation into direct character-to-character
dialogue vary highly by language, as shown in the previous enumeration of English and Spanish examples. For English, Christine Doran's work [7,8] on the
incorporation of punctuation into lexicalized tree-adjoining grammar describes
how this can be accomplished at the deep structure level. However, her work
does not investigate the complete range of coverage found in narrative texts.
The features we found necessary are:

- Quotation marks: The actual orthographical punctuation marks expressed in
  the text, and whether they are used as delimiters or not. These are typically
  different for different languages.
- Capitalization inside quotations: In English, when a question or exclamation
  occurs as one part of the direct quotation, it is treated as one entire sentence
  and is capitalized accordingly; in Spanish, the question or exclamation is
  marked and not capitalized:
  "Well, boy, do you know what I'm telling you?"
  –Bueno, muchacho, ¿sabes qué te digo?

---

[3] See [8] for more details on indirect speech.

- Modifications to terminal punctuation: There are important differences between punctuation in quoted dialogue and punctuation within expository text. First, normally terminating punctuation such as question marks and exclamation points can become nonterminal if they do not end the utterance, as in *"Hey!" John yelled.* However in English, periods always remain terminal and must be replaced with a comma if they do not terminate the utterance, regardless of whether the termination is for the communicative relation or the quoted text. Also see [8].
- Multiple sentences in one quotation: Multiple sentences within the same dialogue turn are combined into one large paragraph where adjacent quotation marks or other dialogue delimiters are removed.

4   NLG Aspects

The rules of character-to-character dialogue described above must be integrated into a natural language generation system in order to allow it to create narrative texts. Previous NLG systems have focused on explanation generation [12], tutorial systems [19], and automatic software documentation [17] among other domains. Deep-level NLG systems typically have a pipelined architecture where semantic input specifications are processed successively until text is finally produced (Figure 1).

The process begins when the system receives a high-level semantic specification to communicate information. In the case of writing narratives with characters and a plot, the source is usually a high-level narrative planner. Once a narrative plan is received, a *sentence planner* maps out which conceptual elements should be sentential subjects, sentential objects, verbal relations, locations, etc. The concepts are then assigned those roles, instantiated into a deep structure, and lexicalized by retrieving the appropriate items from the lexicon.

Because thematic roles map well across multiple languages, it is relatively easy to perform a "direct" translation by replacing lexical items at all levels of the deep structure produced by the sentence planner. The main key is to ensure that the interface between the sentence planner and the surface realizer is constant across all supported languages and to ensure that the surface realizer accepts semantic rather than syntactic input. However, it is not necessarily the case that the direct translation is the best translation.

Typically every element of the pipeline from the sentence planner on down concentrates solely on individual sentences. Thus, the features described in the previous section should be divided into two categories: those that are extrasentential, which require some knowledge on the part of the narrative planner to model, and those that are intrasentential, which can be handled solely by the lower levels of the NLG system. However, since many surface features of the previously described phenomena concern punctuation that must be integrated with the surface realization phase, it is usually easier for the narrative planner to supplement the sentential planner with enough additional semantic information to make informed choices about extrasentential phenomena.

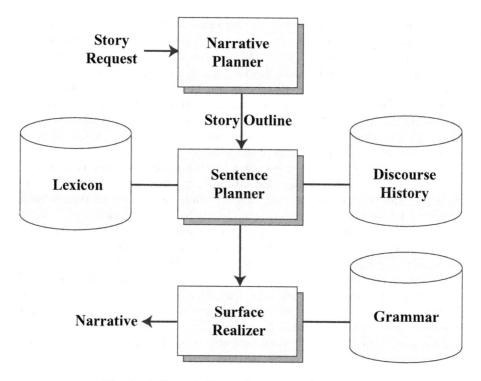

Fig. 1. A Generic Deep Generation Architecture

5   Implementation

The linguistic phenomena of narrative character-to-character dialogue and the model described above have been implemented in the full-scale narrative prose generator STORYBOOK, described in [3]. STORYBOOK takes a linearized narrative plan produced by a simple LISP based narrative planner and, using knowledge of character-to-character dialogue along with more traditional expository natural language generation techniques, writes publishable-quality narratives complete with formatting. The "rules" that the narrative planner uses to create the plot are currently hand-coded in a standard knowledge representation language. STORYBOOK uses the publically available FUF/SURGE [9] surface realization system with modifications to its systemic-functional grammar to implement the low-level dialogue features described in the previous section:

- Paragraph formatting
- Interjections
- Addressee
- Communicative Act Ordering
- Utterer Ordering
- Utterance Manner

In addition to these features, our implementation of the additions to the
FUF/SURGE English grammar allows for the proper low level punctuation that
readers expect from narrative prose. As an example, consider the following excerpt from the grammar for dealing with punctuation in dialogue consisting of
two of the five necessary alternative branches. The first branch governs the case
when only a direct utterance is given (marked as utt1) but no speaker or utterance relation is given. In all such cases, the grammar capitalizes the first word,
adds a quotation mark before the sentence, and the terminal punctuation and a
second quotation mark to the end of the sentence.

The second branch governs the case when the direct quotation consists of a
single utterance and the speaker and utterance relation are expressed with the
quote preceding the speaker and utterance relation. In this case, as the grammar
shows, if the terminal punctuation for the quote is the period, it is replaced
with a comma. Additionally, the grammar expresses the constraint that the
linearization module must force the quote to appear before the remainder of the
sentence. Other branches of the main grammar add the terminal punctuation to
the utterance relation. The additional three branches of the quotation module of
the grammar deal with cases where the quotation follows the utterance relation,
the utterance relation is surrounded by two quoted elements, or the default case
where no quotation is expressed. As a final note, the Spanish grammar version
contains similar branches for dealing with quotations but with rules, constraints,
and lexicalizations particular to the Spanish language.

```
(alt ordering
     (((sayer none) (utt2 none) (utt1 given) (pattern (utt1))
      (utt1 ((alt (((cat clause) (mood \#(under interrogative))
                    (mood given) (question-mode direct)
                    (punctuation ((before ") (capitalize yes)
                                  (after ?"))))
                   ((punctuation ((before ") (capitalize yes)
                                  (after ."))))
                   ((punctuation ((before ") (capitalize yes)
                                  (after !"))))))))))
     ((sayer given) (utt1 given) (utt2 none)
      (sayer ((order second))) (pattern (utt1 sayer))
      (utt1 ((alt (((cat clause) (mood #(under interrogative))
                    (mood given) (question-mode direct)
                    (punctuation ((before ") (after ?")
                                  (capitalize yes))))
                   ((punctuation ((before ") (after ,")
                                  (capitalize yes))))
                   ((punctuation ((before ") (after !")
                                  (capitalize yes))))))))))
     . . .
```

The modifications to the FUF/SURGE grammar described here are used by
the STORYBOOK implementation to write 2 to 3 page fairy tales in the Little Red

Riding Hood domain [3]. A sample of STORYBOOK's narrative prose is shown
below.

```
     The road to grandmother's house led through the dark
forest.  Little Red Riding Hood was not afraid, instead she
was quite happy.  Birds sang her their sweetest songs while
squirrels ran up and down tall trees.  Now and then, a
rabbit would cross her path.  She had not gone far when she
met a wolf.   "Hello," greeted the wolf.

     The wolf was a cunning looking creature.  He asked,
"Where are you going?"

     "I am going to my grandmother's house," replied Little
Red Riding Hood.

     "Well then, take care.  There are many dangers."
```

6   Conclusion

Natural language generation systems to date have concentrated on the more
technical aspects of text: explanation generation, tutorial dialogue, and automated software documentation, among other areas. One relatively unexplored
area is *narrative prose generation*, or the production of texts used in stories
such as novels, mysteries, and fairy tales. We have presented a feature analysis
of character-to-character dialogue, which is extensively used in narrative texts.
This analysis has enabled us to modify a widely-used surface realization system
to include the necessary features that dialogue requires. This surface realizer was
used in an implemented system that wrote fairy tales in the domain of Little Red
Riding Hood. The resulting narrative prose displayed the correct punctuation
and formatting expected of human-produced narrative prose.

References

1. Bateman, J., Sharoff, S.: Multilingual grammars and multilingual lexicons for multilingual text generation. In Proceedings of the ECAI Workshop on Multilinguality
   in the Lexicon-II. Brighton, UK (1998) 1–8
2. Callaway, C., Daniel, B., Lester, J.: Multilingual Natural Language Generation for
   3D Learning Environments. In Proceedings of the 1999 Argentine Symposium on
   Artificial Intelligence. Buenos Aires, Argentina (1999) 177–190
3. Callaway, Charles: Narrative Prose Generation. Ph.D. Dissertation. North Carolina
   State University. Raleigh, NC (2000)
4. Cassell, J., Stone, M., Yan, H.: Coordination and Context-Dependence in the Generation of Embodied Conversation. International Natural Language Generation
   Conference. Mitzpe Ramon, Israel (2000)

5. Dale, Robert: Exploring the Role of Punctuation in the Signalling of Discourse Structure. In Proceedings of the Workshop on Text Representation and Domain Modelling. T. U. Berlin (1991) 110–120
6. Daniel, B., Bares, W., Callaway, C., Lester, J.: Student-Sensitive Multimodal Explanation Generation for 3D Learning Environments. In Proceedings of the Sixteenth International Conference on Artificial Intelligence. Orlando, FL (1999) 114–120
7. Doran, Christine: Punctuation in Quoted Speech. In Notes of the ACL Workshop on Punctuation in Computational Linguistics. Santa Cruz, CA (1996) 9–18
8. Doran, Christine: Incorporating Punctuation into the Sentence Grammar: A Lexicalized Tree Adjoining Grammar Perspective. Ph.D. Dissertation. University of Pennsylvania. Philadelphia, PA (1998)
9. Elhadad, Michael: Using Argumentation to Control Lexical Choice: A Functional Unification Implementation. Ph.D. Dissertation. Columbia University. New York, NY (1992)
10. Jones, Bernard: What's the Point? A (Computational) Theory of Punctuation. Ph.D. Dissertation. The University of Edinburgh. Edinburgh, Scotland (1996)
11. Laurel, Brenda: Toward the Design of a Computer-Based Interactive Fantasy System. Ph.D. Dissertation. The Ohio State University. Columbus, OH (1986)
12. Lester, James C., Porter, Bruce W.: Developing and Empirically Evaluating Robust Explanation Generators: The KNIGHT Experiments. Computational Linguistics **23** 1:65–101 (1997)
13. Lester, James C., Stone, Brian A.: Increasing Believability in Animated Pedagogical Agents. In Proceedings of the First International Conference on Autonomous Agents. Marina del Rey, CA (1997) 16–21
14. Longacre, Robert E.: The Grammar of Discourse. Plenum Press, New York, NY (1983)
15. Mostow, J., Aist, G.: The Sounds of Silence: Towards Automated Evalutation of Student Learning in a Reading Tutor that Listens. In Proceedings of the Fourteenth National Conference on Artificial Intelligence. Providence, RI (1997) 355–361
16. Nunberg, Geoffrey: The Linguistics of Punctuation. Center for the Study of Language and Information. Stanford, CA (1990)
17. Paris, Cécile L., Vander Linden, Keith: Building Knowledge Bases for the Generation of Software Documentation. In Proceedings of the 16th International Conference on Computational Linguistics. Copenhagen, Denmark (1996) 734–739
18. Quirk, R., Greenbaum, S., Leech, G., Svartvik, J.: A Comprehensive Grammar of the English Language. Longman Publishers, London (1985)
19. Rosenblum, James A., Moore, Johanna D.: Participating in Instructional Dialogues: Finding and Exploiting Relevant Prior Explanations. In Proceedings of the World Conference on AI and Education. August (1993)
20. Rowling, J. K.: Harry Potter and the Sorcerer's Stone. Scholastic, Inc. (1998)
21. Towns, S., Callaway, C., Voerman, J., Lester, C.: Coherent Gestures, Locomotion, and Speech in Life-Like Pedagogical Agents. Proceedings of the Fourth International Conference on Intelligent User Interfaces. San Francisco, CA (1998) 13–20
22. Walker, Marilyn A., Cahn, Janet E., Whittaker, Stephen J.: Improvising Linguistic Style: Social and Affective Bases of Agent Personality. Proceedings of the First International Conference on Autonomous Agents. Marina del Rey, CA (1997)

Experiments on Extracting Knowledge from a Machine-Readable Dictionary of Synonym Differences

Diana Zaiu Inkpen and Graeme Hirst

Department of Computer Science, University of Toronto, Toronto, Ontario, Canada, M5S 3G4
{dianaz,gh}@cs.toronto.edu

Abstract. In machine translation and natural language generation, making the wrong word choice from a set of near-synonyms can be imprecise or awkward, or convey unwanted implications. Using Edmonds's model of lexical knowledge to represent clusters of near-synonyms, our goal is to automatically derive a lexical knowledge-base from the *Choose the Right Word* dictionary of near-synonym discrimination. We do this by automatically classifying sentences in this dictionary according to the classes of distinctions they express. We use a decision-list learning algorithm to learn words and expressions that characterize the classes DENOTATIONAL DISTINCTIONS and ATTITUDE-STYLE DISTINCTIONS. These results are then used by an extraction module to actually extract knowledge from each sentence. We also integrate a module to resolve anaphors and word-to-word comparisons. We evaluate the results of our algorithm for several randomly selected clusters against a manually built standard solution, and compare them with the results of a baseline algorithm.

1 Near-Synonyms

Near-synonyms are words that are almost synonyms, but not quite. They are not fully inter-substitutable, but rather vary in their shades of denotation or connotation, or in the components of meaning they emphasize; they may also vary in grammatical or collocational constraints. Examples of near-synonymic variations are given in Table 1 (Edmonds 1999).

There are very few absolute synonyms, if they exist at all. The so-called "dictionaries of synonyms" actually contain near-synonyms. This is made clear by dictionaries such as *Webster's New Dictionary of Synonyms* (Gove 1984) and *Choose the Right Word* (Hayakawa 1994), which list clusters of similar words and explicate the differences between the words in the each cluster. They are in effect dictionaries of near-synonym discriminations. Writers often turn to such resources when confronted with a choice between near-synonyms, because choosing the wrong word can be imprecise or awkward, or convey unwanted implications. These dictionaries are made for human consumption and they are available only on paper.

DiMarco, Hirst, and Stede (1993) analyzed the type of differences adduced in dictionaries of near-synonym discriminations. They found that only a limited number of types were used, making it possible to formalize the entries in a computational form (DiMarco and Hirst 1993).

A. Gelbukh (Ed.): CICLing 2001, LNCS 2004, pp. 265–280, 2001.

Table 1. Examples of near-synonymic variations

Type of variation	Example
Collocational	*task* : *job*
Stylistic, formality	*pissed* : *drank* : *inebriated*
Stylistic, force	*ruin* : *annihilate*
Expressed attitude	*skinny* : *thin* : *slim*
Emotive	*daddy* : *dad* : *father*
Continuousness	*seep* : *drip*
Emphasis on different subcomponents	*enemy* : *foe*
Fuzzy boundary	*woods* : *forest*

We hypothesize that the language of the entries contains enough regularities to allow automatic extraction of knowledge from them. The dictionary of near-synonym differences that we use is *Choose the Right Word* (Hayakawa 1994) (hereafter CTRW).[1] A page from this dictionary is presented in Figure 1.

2   The Clustered Model of Lexical Knowledge

Edmonds (1999) and Edmonds and Hirst (2000) show that current models of lexical knowledge used in computational systems cannot account well for the properties of near-synonyms.

The conventional view is that the denotation of a lexical item is represented as a concept or a structure of concepts (i.e., a word sense is linked to the concept it lexicalizes), which are themselves organized into an ontology. The ontology is often language-independent, or at least language-neutral, so that it can be used in multilingual applications. Words that are nearly synonymous have to be linked to their own slightly different concepts. Hirst (1995) showed that such a model entails an awkward taxonomic proliferation of language-specific concepts at the fringes, thereby defeating the purpose of a language-independent ontology. Such a model defines words in terms of necessary and sufficient truth-conditions; therefore it cannot account for indirect expressions of meaning or for fuzzy differences between near-synonyms.

Edmonds and Hirst (2000) modify this model to account for near-synonymy. The meaning of each word arises out of a context-dependent combination of a context-independent denotation and a set of explicit differences from its near-synonyms. Thus the meaning of a word consists of both necessary and sufficient conditions that allow the word to be selected by a lexical choice process and a set of nuances of indirect meaning that may be conveyed with different strengths. In this model, a conventional ontology is cut off at a coarse grain and the near-synonyms are clustered under a shared concept, rather than linking each word to a separate concept. The result is a *clustered model of lexical knowledge*. Each cluster has a core denotation that represents the essential shared denotational meaning of its near-synonyms. The internal structure of each cluster is complex, representing semantic (or denotational), stylistic, and expressive (or attitudinal) differences between near-synonyms. The differences or lexical nuances are

---

[1] We are grateful to HarperCollins Publishers, Inc. for permission to use CTRW in our project.

abjure. Do not confuse the verb *abjure* (renounce under oath) with the verb *adjure* (urge solemnly).

abrogate. Do not confuse the verb *abrogate* (cancel or repeal) with the verb *arrogate* (claim a power, privilege, etc., unduly).

absorb

assimilate
digest
imbibe
incorporate
ingest

These verbs, all relatively formal, indicate the taking in of one thing by another. **Absorb** is slightly more informal than the others and has, perhaps, the widest range of uses. In its most restricted sense it suggests the taking in or soaking up specifically of liquids: the liquid *absorbed* by the sponge. In more general uses *absorb* may imply the thoroughness of the action: not merely to read the chapter, but to *absorb* its meaning. Or it may stress the complete disappearance of the thing taken in within the encompassing medium: once-lovely countryside soon *absorbed* by urban sprawl. **Ingest** refers literally to the action of taking into the mouth, as food or drugs, for later absorption by the body. Figuratively, it designates any taking in and suggests the receptivity necessary for such a process: too tired to *ingest* even one more idea from the complicated philosophical essay she was reading. To **digest** is to alter food chemically in the digestive tract so that it can be *absorbed* into the bloodstream. In other uses, *digest* is like *absorb* in stressing thoroughness, but is even more emphatic. [You may completely *absorb* a stirring play in one evening, but you will be months *digesting* it.]

Assimilate is even more emphatic about the thoroughness of the taking in than either *absorb* or *digest*—in both its specific physiological and general uses. Physiologically, food is first *digested*, then *absorbed* by the bloodstream, and then *assimilated* bit by bit in each cell the blood passes. In more general uses, *assimilate*, unlike the previous verbs, often implies a third agent beside the absorber and the absorbed—an agent that directs this process: architects who *assimilate* their buildings to the environment. The process, furthermore, often implies the complete transformation of the absorbed into the absorbing medium. *Assimilate* also suggests a much slower process than *digest* and certainly than *absorb*, which can be nearly instantaneous: It would take the city generations to *assimilate* the newcomers into the patterns of a strange life.

Incorporate is the only verb here that does not have a specific use pertaining to the taking in of liquids or of food, meaning literally embody. It resembles the aspect of *assimilate* that stresses the loss of separate identity for the absorbed quantity: *incorporating* your proposals into a new system that will satisfy everyone. It is unlike *assimilate* in lacking that verb's suggestion of necessarily careful, time-consuming thoroughness.

Imbibe, while capable of uses comparable to those for *assimilate*, is mainly rooted still to its specific use for the taking in of liquids. Even this use, and certainly any others, now sound slightly archaic and excessively formal: Do you *imbibe* alcoholic beverages? See EAT.

Antonyms: *disgorge, disperse, dissipate, eject, emit, exude.*

abstain

forbear
refrain

The verb **abstain** means withhold oneself from an action or self-indulgence. [There were six votes in favor, two against, and two *abstaining*: She *abstained* from drinking.] **Refrain** has to do with withholding an action temporarily, or checking a momentary desire: He *refrained* from scolding his child until the company left. To **forbear**, in its intransitive sense, is to exercise self-control, often out of motives of patience or charity. [Though impatient, the customer *forbore* to upbraid the harried sales clerk: The teacher *forbore* to report Johnnie's misbehavior to his parents.] See FORGO, FORSWEAR.

Antonyms: BEGIN, PERMIT.

Fig. 1. A page from *Choose the Right Word* by S.I. Hayakawa. Copyright ©1987. Reprinted by arrangement with HarperCollins Publishers, Inc.

expressed by means of peripheral concepts (for denotational nuances) or attributes (for nuances of style and attitude).

In this model, a cluster includes the following fields:

1. `syns` — A list of near-synonyms in the cluster.
2. `core` — The core denotation, or essential shared meaning of the near-synonyms in the cluster. It is represented as a configuration of concepts.
3. `periph` — A set of peripheral concepts that extend the core denotation, and pertain to the differentiation of the near-synonyms.
4. `distinctions` — The actual distinctions between near-synonyms.

For example, the (slightly simplified) structure for the near-synonyms of the word *error*, built by hand by Edmonds (1999), is shown in Figure 2.

Building such representations by hand is difficult and time-consuming, and Edmonds completed only nine of them. We want to automatically extract the content of all the entries in the CTRW dictionary of near-synonyms. In order to build a practical lexical knowledge-base, we use a simplified form of Edmonds's representation for the content of a cluster.

3   Preprocessing CTRW

After OCR scanning and error correction, we used XML markup to segment the text of the dictionary into: cluster name, cluster identifier, members (the near-synonyms in the cluster), entry (the actual description of the meaning of the near-synonyms and of the differences among them), cluster's part-of-speech, cross-references to other clusters, and antonyms list. The markup is quite complex, but only part of it is relevant for the purpose of this paper. An example of segmented content from Figure 1 is given in Figure 3.

In the text of the entry for a cluster, the first occurrence of a synonym is in bold face, and all the other occurrences are in italic. We marked each occurrence with the tag `<near_syn>`. This is useful when we want to extract general patterns, when we don't care what the near-synonym is but just need to know that it is a near-synonym.

We determine sentence boundaries and clearly label examples, which will not presently be considered. We use general heuristics to detect the end of sentences, plus specific heuristics for this particular dictionary; e.g., examples are in square brackets or after a colon. The tag `<s>` marks sentences which describe the nuances of meaning, and the tag `<eg>` marks examples using the near-synonyms. The `<s>` tags have the attribute `punctuation`, taking as value the punctuation mark ending the sentence (full stop, question mark, exclamation mark, etc.). If the value is ':', that means that the sentence ended, but one or more examples immediately follow. Examples are of two kinds: those that follow a colon, and those contained between square brackets. Therefore, the `<eg>` tag has, besides the attribute `punctuation`, the attribute `type` (':' or ']').

4   Relating CTRW to Edmonds's Representation

From each sentence of the dictionary we need to extract the information relevant to the representation. We rely on the relative regularity of the language of the entries.

```
(defcluster error_C
    :syns (error_1 mistake_1 blunder_1 slip_1 lapse_1 howler_1)
    :core (ROOT Generic-Error)
    :periph ((P1 Stupidity)
             (P2 Blameworthiness)
             (P3 Criticism (ATTRIBUTE (P3-1 Severity)))
             (P4 Misconception)
             (P5 Accident)
             (P6 Inattention))
    :distinctions
    (
    (blunder_1 usually medium implication P1)
    (mistake_1 sometimes medium implication (P2 (DE-
GREE 'medium)))
    (blunder_1 sometimes medium implication (P2 (DE-
GREE 'high)))
    (mistake_1 always medium implication (P3-1 (DEGREE 'low)))
    (error_1 always medium implication (P3-1 (DEGREE 'medium)))
    (blunder_1 always medium implication (P3-1 (DEGREE 'high)))
    (mistake_1 always medium implication P4)
    (slip_1 always medium implication P5)
    (mistake_1 always low implication P5)
    (lapse_1 always low implication P5)
    (lapse_1 always medium implication P6)
    (blunder_1 always medium pejorative)
    (blunder_1 high concreteness)
    (error_1 low concreteness)
    (mistake_1 low concreteness)
    (howler_1 low formality)
    )
)
```

Fig. 2. Simplified cluster for *error, mistake, blunder, slip, lapse, howler.*

4.1   Core Denotation

Usually, the first sentence in a CTRW entry expresses the core meaning shared by all members of the family. An example is: *These verbs all refer to rather forceful communications between a speaker and another person.* In some entries, this information is skipped, and the first sentence is about the first near-synonym in the cluster.

4.2   Denotational Distinctions

Near-synonyms can differ in the frequency with which they express a component of their meaning (e.g., ***hard up** often implies only a temporary shortage of money; Occasionally, **invasion** suggests a large-scale but unplanned **incursion***), in the indirectness of the expression of the component (e.g., ***Test** strongly implies an actual application*

```
<s punctuation="."> These verbs, all relatively formal, indicate
   the taking in of one thing by another </s>
<s punctuation="."> <near_syn><b>Absorb</b></near_syn> is
   slightly more informal than the others and has, perhaps, the
   widest range of uses </s>
<s punctuation=":"> In its most restricted sense it suggests the
   taking in or soaking up specifically of liquids </s>
<eg type=":" punctuation="."> the liquid <near_syn><i>absorbed
   </i></near_syn> by the sponge </eg>
<s punctuation=":"> In more general uses <near_syn><i>absorb</i>
   </near_syn> may imply the thoroughness of the action </s>
<eg type=":" punctuation="."> not merely to read the chapter,
   but to <near_syn><i>absorb</i></near_syn> its meaning </eg>
<s punctuation="."> To <near_syn><b>digest</b></near_syn> is to
   alter food chemically in the digestive tract so that it can be
   <near_syn><i>absorbed</i></near_syn> into the bloodstream </s>
<s punctuation="."> In other uses, <near_syn><i>digest</i>
   </near_syn> is like <near_syn><i>absorb</i></near_syn> in
   stressing  thoroughness, but is even more emphatic </s>
<eg type="]" punctuation="."> You may completely <near_syn><i>
   absorb </i></near_syn> a stirring play in one evening, but you
   will be months <near_syn><i>digesting</i></near_syn> it </eg>
```

Fig. 3. Example of text from CTRW with XML markup

of these means), and in fine-grained variations of the idea itself (e.g., **Paternalistic** *may suggest either benevolent rule or a style of government determined to keep the governed helpless and dependent*).

For *denotational distinctions* we extract tuples of the form `near-synonym frequency strength indirectness peripheral-concept`. The `indirectness` takes the values `suggestion`, `denotation`, `implication`. It is signaled by many words in CTRW, including the obvious words *suggests*, *denotes*, *implies*, and *connotes*. `Strength` takes the values `low`, `medium`, `high`, and it is signaled by words such as *strongly* and *weakly*. `Frequency` takes the values `always`, `usually`, `sometimes`, `seldom`, `never` and is signaled by the corresponding English words, among others. `Peripheral-concepts` form the basic vocabulary of fine-grained denotational distinctions. In Edmonds (1999) they are structures of concepts defined in the same ontology as the core denotations. Every peripheral concept extends the core denotation in some way, but they represent non-necessary and indirect aspects of meaning. In DiMarco and Hirst (1993) peripheral concepts can be a binary, continuous, or discrete dimension. However, in our first stage of extracting knowledge, we treat the peripheral concepts as strings, without analyzing them more deeply. From a sentence fragment such as **precipice** *usually suggests danger*, we can extract `precipice usually medium suggestion danger`. Default values are used when `strength` and `frequency` are not specified in entry.

4.3   Attitudinal Distinctions

A word can convey different attitudes of the speaker towards an entity of the situation. The three attitudes represented in the model are pejorative, neutral, and favorable. Examples of sentences in CTRW expressing attitudes are: ***Blurb*** *is also used pejoratively to denote the extravagant and insincere praise common in such writing* and ***Placid*** *may have an unfavorable connotation in suggesting an unimaginative, bovine dullness of personality*. Both contain information about the pejorative attitude, though they also contain information about denotational distinctions.

The information we extract for attitudinal distinctions has the form near-synonym frequency strength attitude, where strength and frequency have the same values and significance as in the case of denotational distinctions. Edmonds (1999) has an extra element, a pointer to the entity the attitude is directed towards.

We are not always able to extract from the beginning absolute values for the strength of the feature, because they are presented as comparisons between near-synonyms in the cluster, which must be resolved after extraction. The initial information extracted may have the form near-synonym frequency strength comparison-term attitude near-synonym. For example, from the sentence ***Sycophantic*** *is sometimes used interchangeably with **obsequious**, but is more strongly pejorative* we extract sycophantic usually more pejorative obsequious. After the comparison is resolved (see Section 7.3) this becomes sycophantic usually high pejorative.

4.4   Stylistic Distinctions

In the absence of a comprehensive theory of style, the representation uses a basic approach to representing the stylistic variation of near-synonyms. The information we need to extract from CTRW about stylistic variations has the form near-synonym strength stylistic-feature, where the stylistic feature has the values formality, force, concreteness, floridity, and familiarity (Hovy 1990). The strength has the values low, medium, high, indicating the level of the stylistic attribute.

Because the stylistic attributes are expressed by adjectives (or nouns derived from these adjectives), the information is rarely absolute, but is relative to the other near-synonyms in the cluster. Comparatives and superlatives are very frequent. So, in the first phase we may extract information of the form near-synonym comparison-term stylistic-feature near-synonym. From a sentence such as ***Designate*** *is the most formal of all these terms*, the information extracted in the end (after the comparisons are resolved) is designate high formality.

Words that signal formality include *formal, informal, formality*, and *slang*. Concreteness is signaled by words such as *abstract, concrete*, and *concretely*. From the sentence ***Center***, *most concretely, indicates such a point within the circumference of a circle or a sphere*, we should extract center high concreteness. The third kind of stylistic information we extract is force (floridity and familiarity will be dealt with in future work). From the sentence ***Request*** *is considerably weaker* *than any sense of demand*, we should extract `request less force demand`, and in the end `request low force`.

A sentence in CTRW can contain more than one piece of information. Consider the sentence **Coworker** *is the least formal of these and applies as readily to manual labor as to more highly skilled occupations*. We need to extract information both about the stylistic feature `formality` and about the denotations of manual labor and highly skilled occupations.

5   The Class Hierarchy of Distinctions

Following Edmonds's analyses of the distinctions among near-synonyms, we derived the class hierarchy of distinctions presented in Figure 4. The top-level class DISTINCTIONS consists of DENOTATIONAL DISTINCTIONS, ATTITUDE, and STYLE. The last two are grouped together in a class ATTITUDE-STYLE DISTINCTIONS because they present similar behavior from the point of view of this research (see explanation in Section 6).

The leaf classes are those that we classify CTRW sentences into. The leaves of DENOTATIONAL DISTINCTIONS are SUGGESTION, IMPLICATION, and DENOTATION; those of ATTITUDE are FAVORABLE, NEUTRAL, and PEJORATIVE; those of STYLE are FORMALITY, CONCRETENESS, FORCE, FLORIDITY, and FAMILIARITY. All these leaf nodes have the attribute `strength`, which takes the values `low`, `medium`, and `high`. All the leaf nodes except those in the class STYLE have the attribute `frequency`, which takes the values `always`, `usually`, `sometimes`, `seldom`, and `never`.

In order to automatically create near-synonym representations, we must be able to extract relevant portions of the text that are informative about these attributes. Therefore, the goal is to learn for each leaf class in the hierarchy a set of words or expressions in CTRW that characterizes descriptions of the class. When classifying a sentence (or fragment of sentence) we have to decide which leaf class it expresses, and also with what `strength` and what `frequency`. We use a decision-list algorithm to learn sets of words and patterns for the classes DENOTATIONAL DISTINCTIONS and ATTITUDE-STYLE DISTINCTIONS.

6   The Decision-List Learning Algorithm

Unsupervised learning may be used when annotated corpora are not available. Yarowsky's (1995) work on word sense disambiguation using an unsupervised decision-list algorithm inspired many researchers. He classified the senses of a word on the basis of other words that given word co-occurs with. Collins and Singer (1999) classified proper names as `Person`, `Organization`, or `Location` using contextual rules (other words appearing in the context of the proper names). Starting with a few spelling rules (some proper-name features) in the decision list, their algorithm learns new contextual rules; using these rules then it learns more spelling rules, and so on, in a process of mutual bootstrapping. Riloff and Jones (1999) learned domain-specific lexicons and extraction patterns (such as *shot in* $\langle x \rangle$ for the terrorism domain). They used a mutual bootstrapping technique to alternately select the best extraction pattern for a category

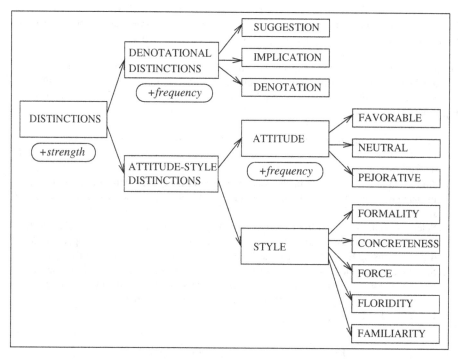

Fig. 4. The class hierarchy of Distinctions (rectangles represent classes, ovals represent attribute a class and its descendents have).

and add its extractions to the semantic lexicon, which is the basis for selecting the next-best extraction pattern.

Our decision-list (DL) algorithm (Figure 5) is tailored for extraction from CTRW. It takes ideas from the previously mentioned work. Like Collins and Singer, we learn two kinds of rules, main rules and auxiliary rules. We also extract patterns and relevant words for the classes DENOTATIONAL DISTINCTIONS and ATTITUDE-STYLE DISTINC-TIONS, similar to the domain-specific lexicon extracted by Riloff and Jones.

In order to obtain input data, we chunk the text with Abney's chunker (1996). The training set E is formed from all the verb phrases, noun phrases, adjectival and adverbial phrases (denoted vx, nx, ax, rx, respectively) that occur more than a threshold t times (where $t = 3$ in our experiments). (We prefer to use a chunker rather than a parser, because the sentences are long and contain lots of coordinations that a parser cannot reliably handle.)

We learn rules of the form: word x is significant for the given class with confidence $h(x)$. All the rules $x \rightarrow h(x)$ for that class form a decision list that allows us to compute the confidence with which new patterns are significant for the class.

We compute the confidence of a word x with the formula:

$$h(x) = \frac{count(x, E') + \alpha}{count(x, E) + k\alpha} \tag{1}$$

Input: Set E of training examples, class, main seed words for class, part-of-speech (pos) for words that are to be in mainDL, and pos for words that are to be in auxDL.

Output: Two decision lists for the given class: main decision list (mainDL) and auxiliary decision list (auxDL), plus list E' of patterns for the class. (Each decision list contains rules of the form $x \rightarrow h(x)$, meaning that the word x is significant for that class with confidence $h(x)$ computed by Equation 1.)

1. Set $N = 10$, the maximum number of rules to be induced at each step.
2. Initialization: Set the mainDL to the set of main seed words (with confidence 0.99). Set E' to empty set.
3. Add to mainDL those words in chunks from E that have the same stem as any words already in mainDL. (For example, if *suggest* is in mainDL, add *suggests, suggesting, suggested, suggestion*.)
4. Select examples (chunks) from $E - E'$ that contain words in mainDL, and add them to E'.
5. Use E' to compute more auxiliary rules. For each word x not in any DL, compute the confidence $h(x)$ using Equation 1. Take the N highest values and add them to auxDL.
6. Select more examples from $E - E'$ using auxDL, and add them to E'. Stop if E' is unchanged.
7. Using the new E', compute more main rules. For each word x not in any DL, compute the confidence $h(x)$. Take the N highest values and add them to mainDL.
8. Go to step 3 unless E' is unchanged.

Fig. 5. The decision-list learning algorithm.

where E' is the set of patterns selected for the class, and E is the set of all input data. Following Collins and Singer (1999), we set $k = 2$, because we partition into two sets (relevant and irrelevant for the class). $\alpha = 0.1$ is a smoothing parameter. So we count how many times x is in the patterns selected for the class versus the total number of occurrences in the training data.

We learn two different types of rules. Main rules are for words that are significant for distinction classes. Auxiliary rules are for frequency words, strength words, and comparison words. Mutual bootstrapping in the algorithm alternates between the two types.

The idea behind the algorithm is that starting with a few main rules (seed words), we can select examples containing them and learn a few auxiliary rules. Using these we can select more examples and learn new main rules. We keep iterating until no more new rules are learned.

We apply the DL algorithm for each of the classes DENOTATIONAL DISTINCTIONS and ATTITUDE-STYLE DISTINCTIONS.

For the class DENOTATIONAL DISTINCTIONS the input to the algorithm is: the set E of all chunks, the main seed words (*suggest, imply, denote, mean, designate, connote*), the restriction that the part-of-speech (pos) for words in main rules be verbs and nouns, and the restriction that the pos for words in auxiliary rules be adverbs and modals.

For the class ATTITUDE-STYLE DISTINCTIONS the input to the algorithm is: the set E of all chunks, the main seed words (*formal, informal, pejorative, disapproval, favorable, abstract, concrete*), the restriction that the pos for words in main rules be adjectives and nouns, and the restriction that the pos for words in auxiliary rules be adverbs.

For example, for the class DENOTATIONAL DISTINCTIONS, starting with the rule *suggest* → 0.99, we select examples such as these (where the numbers give the frequency in the training data):

```
[vx [md can]        [vb suggest]]---150
[vx [rb sometimes]  [vb suggest]]---12
```

We learn auxiliary rules for the words *sometimes* and *can* with confidence factors given by the count of these words in the current set of selected examples compared with the count in the rest of the set of examples. Using the new auxiliary rules for the words *sometimes* and *can*, we select more examples such as these:

```
[vx [md can]  [vb refer]]---268
[vx [md may]  [rb sometimes]  [vb imply]]---3
```

From these we learn new main rules, for the words *refer* and *imply*. Using new main rules we select more auxiliary rules for the word *may*, and so on.

We considered extracting patterns for each leaf class in the hierarchy, but after analyzing part of the text, we reached the conclusion that there are just two kinds of patterns: for DENOTATIONAL DISTINCTIONS and for ATTITUDE-STYLE DISTINCTIONS. That is, patterns are characteristic for each of the two top-nodes in the class hierarchy. The following examples show some of the patterns that describe the DENOTATIONAL DISTINCTIONS class:

```
[vx [rb often]  [vbz suggests]]---65
[vx [md may]    [vb indicate]]---65
[vx [md may]    [rb also]  [vb refer]]---62
```

The auxiliary words that form the pattern (i.e, *often, also, may*) are the same for the subclasses DENOTATION, IMPLICATION, SUGGESTION.

For these examples from the DENOTATIONAL class, we derive main rules that *suggests, indicate,* and *refer* are significant for the class (with a computed confidence). Auxiliary rules say that *often, also,* and *may* are significant for `frequency` or `strength` (with a computed confidence). The decisions for the subclasses are made later.

The ATTITUDE and STYLE classes had to be considered together because both of them use adjectival comparisons. Examples for ATTITUDE-STYLE DISTINCTIONS class are:

```
[ax [rbs most]  [jj formal]]---54
[ax [rb much]   [more more]  [jj formal]]---9
[ax [rbs most]  [jj concrete]]---5
```

For this example, main rules contain the words *formal* and *concrete*, and auxiliary rules *much, more,* and *most*.

7   Extracting Knowledge from CTRW

7.1   Classification

After we run the DL algorithm for the class DENOTATIONAL DISTINCTIONS, the words in the list mainDL are manually split into three classes: SUGGESTION, IMPLICATION, and DENOTATION. Some words can be insignificant for any class (e.g., the word *also*) or for the given class; therefore they are classified in the class OTHER. We repeat the same procedure for *frequencies* and *strengths* with the words in auxDL. The words classified as OTHER and the patterns which do not contain any word from mainDL are ignored in the next processing steps.

After we have run the algorithm for the class ATTITUDE-STYLE DISTINCTIONS, the words in the list mainDL have to be split into two classes: ATTITUDE and STYLE. ATTITUDE is split into FAVORABLE, NEUTRAL, PEJORATIVE. *Frequencies* can be computed from the auxDL list. STYLE is split into FORMALITY, CONCRETENESS, FORCE. *Strengths* will be computed by the module which resolves comparisons.

7.2   Extraction

The knowledge extraction module takes each sentence in CTRW and tries to extract one or more pieces of knowledge from it. It considers what near-synonyms the sentence fragment is about, what the expressed distinction is, and with what frequency and relative strength. If it is a denotational distinction, then the peripheral concept involved has to also be extracted. This module is very minimal for the moment. It relies on tuples ⟨*verb, subject, object*⟩ extracted by the chunker. Simple heuristics are used to correct cases when the information in the tuple is not accurate. When tuples are not available, it relies on patterns for the classes DENOTATIONAL DISTINCTIONS and ATTITUDE-STYLE DISTINCTIONS. Simple heuristics are used to extract the subject and object in this case. In order to decide the leaf class, we use the manual partitions of the rules in the mainDL of the two classes.

For example, consider three sentences from the cluster *imbibe, digest, absorb, ingest, assimilate, incorporate* depicted in Figure 1. The results of extraction at this stage are the following:

```
near_syn(absorb) is slightly more informal than the others and
has, perhaps, the widest range of uses
Patterns:
Tuples:    informal :than others :subj near_syn(absorb)
RESULT: subj: near_syn(absorb) class: FORMALITY(informal)
than: others freq:  degree:

in its most restricted sense it suggests the taking in or
soaking up specifically of liquids
Patterns: [vx [vbz suggests]]
Tuples:    suggests :obj taking :in in :subj it
RESULT: subj: near_syn(absorb) class: SUGGESTION(suggests)
periph: the taking freq:  degree:
```

```
in more general uses near_syn(absorb) may imply the thoroughness
of the action
Patterns: [vx [md may] [vb imply]]
Tuples: imply    :subj thoroughness
RESULT: subj: near_syn(absorb) class: IMPLICATION(imply) periph:
the thoroughness of the action freq: sometimes(may) degree:
```

7.3 Anaphors and Comparisons

The final module resolves anaphors and comparisons. Anaphora resolution is very simplistic. The last-mentioned near-synonym is recorded in a stack. When *it* is a subject, it most probably refers to the near-synonym on top of the stack. There are cases when the sentence is about two or more near-synonyms or is about all the words in a class. There are other anaphoric expressions we need to resolve (such as *both verbs* and *the remaining nouns*).

CTRW often expresses stylistic or attitudinal features relative to other near-synonyms in the cluster (see examples in Sections 4.3 and 4.4). Such comparisons are easy to resolve because we consider only three levels (low, medium, high). We explicitly tell the system which words represent what absolute values of the corresponding feature (e.g., *abstract* is at the low end of CONCRETENESS), and how the comparison terms increase or decrease the absolute value (e.g. *less abstract* could mean medium value of CONCRETENESS).

8   Results and Evaluation

CTRW contains 912 clusters, with a total of 14138 sentences, from which we derive the lexical knowledge base. Our program is able to extract knowledge from 7450 of the sentences.

An example of final results, corresponding to the example in the previous section, is the following:

```
absorb usually low FORMALITY
absorb usually medium SUGGESTION the taking
absorb sometimes medium IMPLICATION the thoroughness of the
action
```

In order to evaluate the final results, we randomly selected 25 clusters. We built by hand a standard solution to be compared with the results of our algorithm and with the results of a baseline algorithm. As the baseline algorithm, we choose the default values whenever it is possible; it is not possible for peripheral concepts (the direct object in the sentence) and for the near-synonyms the sentence is about (the subject in the sentence). The baseline algorithm relies only on tuples extracted by the chunker to extract the subjects and the objects.

The measures we use for evaluating each piece of information extracted from a sentence fragment are *labeled precision* and *labeled recall*. These measures are usually used to evaluate parse trees obtained by a parser (Charniak 1997); they allow for rewarding good partial results. In our case, the results we need to evaluate have four

Table 2. Labeled precision and labeled recall of the baseline and of our algorithm and the error reduction.

	Baseline algorithm		Our algorithm		Error reduction rate	
	Labeled precision	Labeled recall	Labeled precision	Labeled recall	Labeled precision	Labeled recall
All constituents	.40	.23	.61	.43	35%	26%
Class only	.49	.28	.68	.48	37%	28%

constituents (for ATTITUDE-STYLE DISTINCTIONS) and five constituents (for DENO-TATIONAL DISTINCTIONS).

There could be missing constituents (except `strength` and `frequency` which take default values). Labeled precision is the number of correct constituents found (summed over all the sentences in the test set) divided by the total number of constituents found. Labeled recall is the total number of correct constituents found divided by the number of constituents in the standard solution.

For example, for the sentence *artificer still can suggest its earliest meaning of a worker who possesses mechanical facility*, the program obtains: `artificer some-times medium SUGGESTION its earliest meaning`, while the solution is `ar-tificer sometimes medium SUGGESTION a worker who possesses me-chanical facility`. The labeled precision is .80 (4 correct out of 5 found), and the labeled recall is .80 (4 correct out of 5 in the standard solution).

Table 2 presents the evaluation of the 25 randomly selected clusters. The first row of the table presents the results as a whole (all the constituents of the extracted lexical knowledge-base). Our algorithm increases labeled precision by .21 and labeled recall by .20. Because the baseline algorithm has very low values for labeled precision and recall, it is useful to calculate the error reduction rate, defined as the difference of the error of the baseline algorithm and the error of our algorithm, divided by the error of the baseline algorithm. Our algorithm reduces the error rate of the baseline algorithm by 35% in labeled precision and by 26% in labeled recall. The second row of the table gives the results when only the (leaf) class of the distinctions expressed in CTRW is considered. By considering only whether the class is right, we evaluate more directly the results of the DL learning algorithm. In this case our algorithm attains higher labeled precision, and so does the baseline algorithm (probably because the default class DENOTATION is the most frequent in CTRW).

A problem in comparing the knowledge extracted from a sentence with the cor-responding knowledge in the standard solution is the fact that often there are several pieces of knowledge to be aligned with several pieces in the standard solution. Our evaluation method aligns pieces of knowledge that are about the same near-synonym. Because the anaphors are resolved only minimally, sometimes the near-synonym is ex-tracted incorrectly or is missing, misleading the alignment. This is one possible expla-nation of the relatively low figures for recall in Table 2.

A more-realistic evaluation of the lexical knowledge-base would have to be done in the context of a machine translation (or natural language generation) system.

9   Conclusion and Future Directions

This paper presents a first step towards building a lexical knowledge-base by automatically extracting knowledge from a dictionary of near-synonym discriminations.

The methods used in this work still need to be improved. We need to use a more reliable method of extracting subjects and objects from multi-clause sentences. We need to implement better anaphor resolution. We need a better understanding of the nuances of the language of CTRW itself.

One of the next steps is to treat peripheral concepts, to decide what the peripheral concept involved is and what its place in the ontology is.

Another direction of further research is to extend Edmonds's representation to be able to represent all the distinctions adduced in CTRW. Examples of knowledge we cannot fit in the current representation are information about generic versus specific near-synonyms and literal versus figurative meanings of near-synonyms.

Acknowledgments

We thank Suzanne Stevenson for useful discussions and comments on earlier versions of this paper. We are grateful to HarperCollins Publishers, Inc. for permission to use CTRW in our project. Our work is financially supported by the Natural Sciences and Engineering Research Council of Canada and the University of Toronto.

References

[1996]Abney, Steven: Partial parsing via finite-state cascades. Proceedings of the ESSLLI '96 Robust Parsing Workshop (1996)

[1997]Charniak, Eugene: Statistical techniques for natural language parsing. AI Magazine 18(4) (1997) 33–44

[1999]Collins, Michael and Singer, Yoram: Unsupervised models for named entity classification. In Proceedings of Empirical Methods in Natural Language Processing and Very Large Corpora (EMNLP/VLC-99) (1999)

[1993]DiMarco, Chrysanne, Hirst, Graeme and Stede, Manfred: The semantic and stylistic differentiation of synonyms and near-synonyms. Proceedings of AAAI Spring Symposium on Building Lexicons for Machine Translation, Stanford, CA (1993) 114–121

[1993]DiMarco, Chrysanne and Hirst, Graeme: Usage notes as the basis for a representation of near-synonymy for lexical choice. Proceedings of 9th annual conference of the University of Waterloo Centre for the New Oxford English Dictionary and Text Research (1993) 33–43

[1999]Edmonds, Philip: Semantic representations of near-synonyms for automatic lexical choice. Ph.D Thesis, University of Toronto (1999)

[2000]Edmonds, Philip and Hirst, Graeme: Reconciling fine-grained lexical knowledge and coarse-grained ontologies in the representation of near-synonyms. In Proceedings of the Workshop on Semantic Approximation, Granularity, and Vagueness, Breckenridge, Colorado (2000)

[1984]Gove, P.B. (ed.): Webster's New Dictionary of Synonyms. G.&C. Merriam Co. (1984)

[1994]Hayakawa, S.I., Ehrlich Eugene (revising ed.): Choose the Right Word. HarperCollins Publishers, Second edition (1994)

[1995]Hirst, Graeme: Near-synonymy and the structure of lexical knowledge. Working notes, AAAI Symposium on Representation and Acquisition of Lexical Knowledge: Polysemy, Ambiguity, and Generativity, Stanford University (1995) 51–56

[1990]Hovy, Eduard: Pragmatics and language generation. Artificial Intelligence, 43 (1990) 153–197

[1999]Riloff, Ellen and Jones, Rosie: Learning dictionaries for information-extraction by multi-level bootstrapping. In Proceedings of the Sixteenth Conference on Artificial Intelligence (AAAI-99) (1999) 474–479

[1995]Yarowsky, David: Unsupervised word sense disambiguation rivaling supervised methods. In Proceedings of the 33rd Annual Meeting of the Association for Computational Linguistics. Cambridge, MA (1995) 189–196

Recognition of
Author's Scientific and Technical Terms

Elena I. Bolshakova

Laboratorio de Inteligencia Artificial
Centro de Investigación en Computación
Instituto Politécnico Nacional, México
elena@pollux.cic.ipn.mx

Abstract. The intensive use of terms of a specific terminology is admittedly one of the most distinguishing features of scientific and technical (sci-tech) texts. We propose to categorize the terms as either dictionary units of generally accepted terminology or new terms introduced into a sci-tech text to facilitate the description of new author's concepts; we call such terms author's. The paper discusses issues concerned with authors' terms, including frequent ways of their definition and using in sci-tech texts. It is argued that recognition of author's sci-tech terms are important for NLP applications such as computer-aided scientific and literary editing, automatic text abstracting and summarization, or acquiring of expert knowledge. A sketch of the procedure for recognition of author's terms with certain degree of accuracy is given.

1 Introduction

The usage of special terms is the primary feature of the functional style of scientific and technical prose including various genres of documents – papers, theses, monographs, reviews, abstracts, technical reports, etc. Terms are linguistic units, namely, words or words combinations, designating concepts or objects of a highly specialized field of human activity. Collection of terms related with a particular field usually forms a coherent conceptual system known as terminology.

The general theoretical problems of sci-tech terms and terminologies, as well as practical issues of their regularization and standardization, were extensively studied, see, e.g., [9]. Practical terminological work involves describing and denominating concepts of a specialized field, with the ultimate goal to provide high-quality consistent terminology and terminological dictionaries. In order to support wide spectrum of the terminological activity, in particular, to create terminological dictionaries and banks, special computer tools are developed [3].

The valuable amount of scientific papers, as well as technical documents contain terms that are explicitly or implicitly defined by their authors and then are used within their texts. The following text fragment presents an example of author's term explicit definition: *"A set of entities created by the expansion process we call reference markers"*. As opposite to terms of generally accepted terminology fixed in dictionaries, either in computer or on paper, newly introduced terms have a specialty that need to be taken into account for an adequate automatic processing of sci-tech texts.

A. Gelbukh (Ed.): CICLing 2001, LNCS 2004, pp. 281-290, 2001.
© Springer-Verlag Berlin Heidelberg 2001

The first objective of this paper is to substantiate the categorization of terms to *dictionary* vs. *author's* ones and to analyze some theoretical and practical aspects of functioning of author's terms. The second objective is to outline key ideas of computer procedures for recognition of author's terms and their definitions from sci-tech texts, as well as to explain usefulness of these procedures in complex processing of terminological units.

A few recent papers [6], [7] explore the problem of extracting term definitions, primarily aiming at extraction of expert knowledge from it. They consider only highly specialized sci-tech texts, with a limited number of immanent definition patterns, for which surface and local syntactic analysis is sufficient. In [5] similar local context technique for extraction concepts (terms) on the basis of particular lexical units is regarded, but it is appropriate only for sci-tech documents of a specific genre and a narrow domain.

Our work does not touch the extraction of knowledge elements from term definitions. Rather, it considers more widely a problem of detecting author's terms in sci-tech texts including cases when terms are used without any definition. The work originated in an empirical study of sci-tech texts in several fields, mainly in computer science. The study was initially performed for Russian sci-tech texts, and then expanded to English texts. In both languages the principal features of author's terms proved to be the same – this fact emphasizes the international character of scientific prose. For this reason we give in the paper illustrative examples only from English sci-tech texts.

Before describing the characteristics of author's terms, we give a short outline of general features of sci-tech terms and terminologies. Then the importance of recognition of author's terms for various NLP systems are discussed, and the procedure for recognition of author's terms in texts is sketched.

2 Author's Terms in Sci-Tech Texts

2.1 Scientific Terms and Terminology

Sci-tech terminology is a system of terms reflecting mutually related concepts of a particular field. Within the scope of a given terminology, a term has only one specific meaning usually defined on the basis of other terms from the same terminology.

Strictly speaking, the correspondence between a concept and its linguistic form is determined not by meanings of composing words, as for usual lexemes, but by the definition of the concept formulated with acceptable in the field preciseness and conciseness and registered in a terminological dictionary. Thereby, a sci-tech term does not merely denominate a concept, but also defines it logically.

Sci-tech terms present a specific heterogeneous layer of general lexicon, including:

- Special words that are not used in everyday life (for example, *lexeme* in linguistics or *γ-rays* in physics);
- Commonly used words employed as terms (for example, *compiler* in computer science or *root* in mathematics or biology);

- Compound terms, i.e. word combinations composed of special and commonly used words (for example, *goal-based reasoning* in artificial intelligence).

Each language has its own established grammatical types of terminological word combinations. For example, in Russian, the most typical combinations are noun-adjective phrases composed of syntactically connected nouns and adjectives.

Terms are to be distinguished from *nomenclature signs* also used in the sci-tech prose. As opposed to terms, such signs designate particular objects or type of objects (e.g., *IBM-360* denotes a computer series).

Sci-tech terminologies are forming evolutionary, and practical terminological work involves analysis of existing terms, their meanings and linguistic forms, and selection or construction of appropriate variants. Since a term is opposed to a non-term only on semantic level, by its function of designating and defining the corresponding concept, its definition should be properly formulated.

Concerning the cognitive aspect of terminology, it is worthwhile to note that concepts are basic elements of knowledge structure and universal way to form knowledge. Therefore, terms are conceptual and linguistic instrument of scientists.

2.2 Author's *Vs.* Dictionary Terms

When speaking about terms, specialists usually mean terminological words and word combinations of established sci-tech lexicon fixed in terminological dictionaries. They are called **dictionary terms**. Besides this kind of terms, there exist terms introduced by the authors of papers. These terms have only a local scope of applicability. They are created and formulated in the process of scientific research and writing of resulting documents. We will call such terms **author's terms**.

Inevitability of author's terms in sci-tech texts is obvious. Since the purpose of scientific research is producing a new knowledge, author's terms appear in scientific papers, denoting new concepts and ideas and structuring the created knowledge.

Another reason why authors introduce new terms relates to the need to facilitate text understanding via designating certain processes, types of systems, and their parts. The need often arises in technical writing including user's manuals (e.g., for software packages), specifications of systems and devices.

Below we give some examples of author's terms in the context of their definition (they are taken from texts on computer science and computational linguistics).

If the number of descendants is always the same for every tree node except   (1)
*terminal node, that number will be called the **branching factor**.*

*There are two classes of rules. **Morphological rules** express relationships*   (2)
between characters and morphemes within a word.

More examples can be easily found in this paper which proposes new terms *dictionary term* and *author's term*.

Comparing author's terms with dictionary ones, we should point out that the former have the same nominative and definitive functions discussed earlier. Their distinction concerns, in the first place, frequent ways of their introducing into texts and their possible linguistic forms.

In diachronic aspect, there is no well-marked boundary between dictionary and author's terms. Very often, the life of terms began as author's terms. Once appeared in certain scientific paper or document, an author's term usually has more or less long way of evolution until it is entrenched and fixed in a terminological dictionary. The criterion for final conversion of any author's term into a dictionary one is its high frequency in various texts of a given field, with the same specialized terminological meaning and with quite stable linguistic form [8].

2.3 Introducing Author's Terms into Sci-Tech Texts

Since definition of term's meaning is the condition for its correct functioning, each author's term should be defined or explained in the text, preferably on the basis of the other dictionary and author's terms. Corresponding rule is usually given in manuals devoted to technical or scientific writing, for example, in [13]. Regrettably, in practice, the important rules of sci-tech writing are quite frequently violated. The ways used to introduce an author's term into a text essentially vary, and below we give more examples illustrating the way things are:

Such a plan is called a **nonlinear plan** *because it is not composed of a linear sequence of complete subplans.* (**3**)

Many problems can be viewed as **nearly decomposable***, by which we mean that they can be divided into subproblems that have a small amount of interaction.* (**4**)

Each entry contains four fields – a **citation form** *(which is a canonical spelling for the morpheme), a* **phonological form***, a* **syntactic category** *(an unordered set of features as in current unification-style grammars), and a* **semantic structure***, about which we shall say nothing here.* (**5**)

Besides explicit explications given in the examples (1) - (4) for terms *branching factor, morphological rules, nonlinear plan, nearly decomposable* and in (5) for terms *citation form* and *syntactic category*, there exists another way to introduce an author's term. The term is simply somehow displayed, usually in the point when it first occurs in the text, with linguistic or graphical means (such as typographical signs or fonts). This is how terms *phonological form* and *semantic structure* are introduced in the example (5). The absence of definition is undesirable for a reader, though admissible, if the meaning of the displayed term can be derived and understood from its linguistic form, i.e. from the meanings of composing words.

Another undesirable, but rather frequent way of introducing new terms into texts corresponds to cases when terms are used in the texts without any definition and displaying. For example, such a case arises, if a term *flexible key* is extensively used, without any explication, in a paper describing algorithms of string search.

To summarize, there are three different kinds of author's terms depending on how they are introduced into a sci-tech text:

- term is explicitly *defined* (and might be additionally displayed);
- term is left undefined (its definition is absent), but it is visually *displayed*;
- term is neither defined nor displayed, thus, being *hidden*.

In all the cases (defined, displayed, hidden) a new author's term is really formed and used, even if its meaning might be left unexplained. In any way, an appropriate linguistic form of the term, i.e., a word or word combination of a grammatical type acceptable for terms, is created.

For the sake of completeness, it is worthwhile to point out a special case of undefined terms also encountered in texts. A new concept is created, but is expressed in the text periphrastically, i.e. by a long and complicated phrase describing its meaning. For example, *maintenance of logical truth with the aid of assumptions* is used instead of the shorter but yet clear variant *assumption-based truth maintenance* that could be regarded as a term. Therefore, an appropriately concise linguistic form for the concept is not yet created (although needed), and the description is used instead of a term.

2.4 Distinction of Linguistic Forms

Our empirical analysis of texts shows that author's terms are rarely separate words. Usually new terms are created as free word combinations of general and sci-tech lexicons, for example, *coefficient adjustment learning* or *dependency-directed analysis*. However, a tendency of converting the free combinations into stable forms is observed. While dictionary terms are characterized by linguistic forms stable within representative corpus of texts of a given field, word combinations taken for author's terms become more or less stable only within the text in which they were introduced.

The linguistic stability means a limited variety of admissible synonymous or quasi-synonymous transformations of the linguistic form. As a rule, dictionary terminological word combinations are reproduced in texts as invariable collocations, without replacements of composing words (including by synonymy), changes of the fixed word order, and insertions of other words. Such linguistic stability is the necessary condition for completely unambiguous nominating concepts within a text, making the text more easy to understand.

In contrast with dictionary terms, author's terms have relatively wide variety of linguistic transformations, especially for hidden terms. These transformations involve substitutions of synonyms for words of common lexicon, for example, *registration sign* vs. *registration symbol*. The so-called syntactical synonyms are also encountered in sci-tech texts, for example, *line of force* vs. *force line* or *candidate elimination algorithm* vs. *algorithm for elimination of candidates*. Various syntactical synonyms of a term differ only in the part of speech of composing words and syntactic relations between them. For a particular natural language such synonymous and quasi-synonymous changes can be described by a set of syntactic transformation rules similar to those proposed for Russian language in [1].

As to phrases and text fragments defining explicitly author's terms, their observed diversity cannot be reduced to a fixed number of syntactic patterns. Nevertheless, a limited list of definition templates can be compiled, describing typical single-sentence definitions with ordinary lexical units. In English, such lexical units are nouns *term*, *name*, etc., verbs *call, mean, refer, define* and so on. One representative definition template is *<Ph> we [will] call [as] <N>*, where *N* denotes an author's term, and *Ph* is an extended phrase explaining its meaning. The example of term definition given in the introduction of this paper fits this template. At the same time, such templates do not cover the definition given in the example (2).

A preliminary inventory of definition templates derived through the empirical study of Russian sci-tech texts proved to be rather similar to that from [7] considering only term definitions in English texts referred to as well-bounded. Moreover, it seems likely that both languages have nearly the same basic types of definitive templates.

3 Automatic Text Processing and Author's Terms

Term processing plays crucial role in the information retrieval (IR), the oldest field of automatic text processing with basic tools of automatic indexing of texts and queries [10], and, in particular, in the retrieval in full NL text bases, the recent trend of IR.

One direction within the IR field concerns procedures of automatic extraction of key-words (descriptors) regarding them as terms frequently occurred in texts and of forming clusters of related terms on the basis of their co-occurrences in texts. Among another directions of IR, thesauri, i.e. special dictionaries of terms with semantic relations between them, are developed. Besides the well known generic/specific relation, thesauri can include whole/part and tool/instrument relations. A relationship of semantic derivation between terms is also investigated for these purposes [12].

In the best IR systems, the content of a sci-tech text or its parts is reduced to a collection of key dictionary terms and semantic relations between them which are representable in a computer thesaurus. Meantime, our empirical analysis of scientific papers shows that frequently author's terms and corresponding concepts closely concern with the central content of sci-tech documents. This observation is confirmed by independent researches, for example, by the work [8], explaining additionally that it is just the reason why author's terms often appear in titles of scientific papers.

In order to represent the content of a sci-tech text more properly, significant author's terms should be recognized, as well as their relations with the other terms. Therefore, identification of author's terms can be regarded as a basic step of complex processing of terms, required for various NLP applications, in particular, for automatic abstracting and summarizing. Clearly, it is true and for designing artificial intelligence systems aimed at forming coherent conceptual structures of sc-tech texts.

It is worthwhile to note that the task of recognition and extraction of hidden author's terms is quite similar to the problem of identification of expert concepts, arisen in the field of artificial intelligence with the need to acquire a specific knowledge for expert systems. Since very often experts in narrow problem-oriented domains create their own concepts and unconsciously use them without explications in any form, a knowledge engineer has to recognize such concepts while formalizing the expert knowledge. Regretfully, among various methods developed for knowledge acquisition and identification of expert concepts [4], methods of how to recognize concepts and corresponding terms in source expert's NL texts is not practically explored.

Another field of automatic text processing, where term processing become more important, is computer-aided editing and creating of NL texts. Besides development of universal text editors and spellers, such as well-known commercial MS Word, some experimental narrow-oriented computer systems for literary and scientific text editing are yet implemented [2]. Such experimental systems can be regarded as an initial step toward automating the hard work of literary editor of sci-tech texts.

Checkups of terminological consistency and accuracy within a sci-tech document are the essential part of the scientific editing. In particular, undefined author's terms should be recognized, and the text should to be corrected appropriately through suggesting definitions or explications of the author's terms. Hence, new facilities supporting correct use of author's terms (including their detection) are required for further improvement of computer-aided editing systems. For example, it seems rather attractive to have an editing system checking presence of definitions of author's terms in a text, revealing hidden author's terms used in various linguistic forms, and showing them to the user (the author of the text) for inspecting and further elaboration.

4   Automatic Recognition of Author's Terms in Texts

4.1 Basic Assumptions and Key Ideas

We see that procedures for recognizing and extracting of author's terms, as well as procedures for revealing their meaning, are important for development of diverse NLP applications. With respect to different kinds of author's terms discussed above, the following questions seem as relatively independent in their solution:

- How to recognize explicitly defined authors' terms?
- How to extract knowledge conveyed by textual definition of author's terms?
- How to detect author's terms visually displayed (highlighted) in a text?
- How to recognize hidden author's terms?

The first two problems can be solved simultaneously through partial syntactic analysis based on a given inventory of definition templates. Our preliminary inventory for Russian can be regarded as starting point for development more representative inventory tested on a large corpus of texts. However, since this approach permits to identify only limited types of definitions, it should be complemented by other techniques applicable to recognize rather complicated cases of term definitions or at least detect a term as such.

All displayed words can be easily identified in text (via detecting typographical means used for their displaying). The problem is to decide, what displayed units are author's terms, and what are dictionary ones or something else. Thus, additional considerations should be taken into account here.

Hidden terms present the major difficulty. Indeed, syntactic analysis is evidently insufficient, so that elements of semantic or statistical analysis is required for proper recognition. However, having been developed for hidden terms, an extraction procedure could be useful for the other kinds of author's terms as well, enhancing the reliability of recognition.

We believe that certain degree of accuracy in recognition of author's term (as well as in deep text processing in a whole) can be achieved only by using a terminological dictionary and other dictionaries representing semantic and syntactic information and reflecting the specialty of the functional style of sci-tech prose. We also consider that elements of syntactic, semantic or statistic analysis by themselves are insufficient for positive identification of author's terms, and they should be combined to realize rather reliable recognition.

To develop a recognition procedure, we assume that terms once introduced into a text tend to be mentioned many times in it – in opposite case they can not be regarded significant. Their statistical frequencies grow with their significance, and it seems reasonable to extract more frequent words and words combinations as possible author's terms. In order to exclude obvious mistakes, such a method should recognize the other rather frequent lexical units in texts.

According to known researches of scientific lexicon, e.g., [11], the most frequent units in sci-tech texts are just terms, as well as separate words and collocations taken from common sci-tech lexicon (e.g., *idea, main problem* or *developed system*). Technical nomenclature signs and special symbols (e.g. in chemistry or mathematics) are frequent as well. Hence, these groups of lexical units should be omitted in the process of recognizing author's terms. Among the other words and word combinations of the text, those should be selected as potential author's terms, which, on the one hand, have grammatical types allowable for terms in a particular natural language, and on the other hand, have frequencies within the text exceeding some preset threshold, say, seven. In addition, to properly evaluate the frequencies, possible linguistic transformations of author's terms, pointed above, should be taken into account.

Thus, we assume that a text processing system recognizing author's terms should contain several basic components:

- Terminological dictionary with lexical units of a specific domain;
- List of nomenclature signs and special symbols;
- Dictionary of words and words combinations of common scientific lexicon;
- Morphological analyzer converting words to their normalized forms;
- Procedures of partial syntactic analysis revealing word combinations of fixed grammatical types;
- Procedures performing synonymous and quasi-synonymous transformations of word combinations;
- Dictionary of separate words of commonly used lexicon representing synonymy relationship.

4.2 Sketch of the Recognition Procedure

Assuming that necessary dictionaries and procedures are incorporated into the text processing system, the general procedure for recognition author's terms in a sci-tech text has following steps:

1. Identification of dictionary terms, including their abbreviated forms;
2. Recognition of lexical units of general scientific lexicon;
3. Detection nomenclature signs and special symbols (if any);
4. Identification of instances of known definition templates and extracting words or word combinations from the proper places of the instances;
5. Detection of displayed words and word combinations, considering only lexical units unprocessed on the steps 1-3;
6. Extraction of separate words and word combinations of grammatical types allowable for terms in a given natural language;

7. Identification, within a set of word combinations extracted on the step 6, of different linguistic forms of the same terms, according to syntactic transformation rules fixed for a given language;
8. Evaluation of frequencies of lexical units extracted on the step 6, considering different linguistic forms identified on the step 7;
9. Heuristic decision: any term whose frequency exceed the preset threshold is considered an author's term. It is an explicitly defined author's term, if it was extracted on the step 4; it is a displayed author's term, if it was detected on the step 5; otherwise, it is a hidden term.

Each step of procedure, except the steps 7 and 9, corresponds to one scan of the text with sequential processing of sentences in it. Having been recognized on the steps 1 to 3, corresponding lexical units (words and word combinations) are simultaneously converted into items that are not processed on succeeding steps of the procedure. The step 4 also includes checking the correspondence of the extracted words to the allowable grammatical types of terminological word combinations.

It should be noted, that as any automatic procedure based on statistic information, the described procedure might lead to mistakes of two kinds: omission of certain author's term or recognition of a non-term. Therefore, it is reasonable to validate the results of the procedure by asking the user of the overall text processing system.

5   Conclusions and Future Work

We have described main features of author's terms as they can be derived from the empirical study of sci-tech texts. We have also proposed a sketch of the procedure intended to recognize such terms in texts. The procedure uses data from terminological dictionaries and thus processes sci-tech texts in a particular problem domain. Tuning to a new domain can be realized by change of dictionaries.

The presented sketch can serve as a basis for implementation of algorithms recognizing author's terms. For Russian language, the algorithms and necessary dictionaries are already under development. The work is being done within the overall framework of designing computer-aided systems for scientific text editing [2]. We hope, experimental checkup of resulting algorithms on sci-tech texts will permit to evaluate their adequacy and appropriately correct them.

In the further prospect, a procedure which helps authors to properly introduce their terms could be a part of any modern text editor.

For this purpose, the investigation of author's terms in Russian and English languages should be continued. First, we plan to extend the preliminary inventory of definition templates for author's terms, to process potentially extractable multiple-sentences definitions. Second, we intend to refine the set of possible linguistic transformations of author's terms. Third, we mean to handle undefined author's terms in the mentioned case when periphrases are used in a text instead of a term.

References

1. Apresian, Y.D., Cinman L.L. *Computer-aided periphrasing*. In: Semiotics and Informatics, Issue 36, Moscow, 1998.
2. Bolshakova, E.I., Vasilieva N.E. *On the problem of computer-aided literary and scientific editing*. Proceedings of International Workshop on Computational Linguistics and its Applications Dialog2000. Russia, Protvino, 2000.
3. Meyer, I. *Knowledge Management for Terminology-Intensive Applications: Needs and Tools*. In: Lexical semantics and Knowledge Represantation, First SIGLEX Workshop, J. Pustejovsky and S. Bergler (Eds.), Springer, 1991.
4. Olson, J., Rueter H. Extracting expertise from experts: methods for knowledge acquisition. Expert systems, Vol. 4, 1987, No. 4.
5. Paice, C.D., Jones P.A. *The Identification of Important Concepts in Highly Structured Technical Papers*. In: Proc. of the Sixteenth Annual Int. ACM SIGIR Conference on Research and Development in Information Retrieval, Pittsburg, 1993.
6. Pearson, J. *Terms in Context*. In: Studies in Corpus Linguistics. John Benjamins, Amsterdam, Vol. 1, 1998.
7. Penagos, C.R. *Extraction of Knowledge about Terms from Indications of Metalinguistic Activity in Texts*. Proceedings of Int. Conf. On Intelligent text processing and Computational Linguistics CICLing-2000, Mexico, 2000.
8. Pshenichnaya, L.E., Corenga O.N. *Scientific Term in a Dictionary and in a Text*. Nauchno-Texnicheskaya Informatciya (Scientific and Technical Information), 1991, No. 12.
9. Sager, J.C. *A Practical Course in Terminology Processing*. John Benjamins Publ. House, 1990.
10. Salton, G. *Automatic Text Processing: the Transformation, Analysis, and Retrieval of Information by Computer*. Reading, MA: Addison-Wesley, 1998.
11. Senkevich, M.P. *Style of scientific speech and literary editing of scientific works*. Moscow, Vysshaia Shkola, 1976.
12. Skorokhod'ko, E.F. *Semantic Complexity of Word (Term): Network Parameters and Communicative Characteristics*. Nauchno-Texnicheskaya Informatciya (Scientific and Technical Information), 1995, No. 2.
13. Zobel, J. *Writing for Computer Science*. Springer, 1997.

Lexical-Semantic Tagging of an Italian Corpus

Nicoletta Calzolari [1], Ornella Corazzari [2], Antonio Zampolli [1]

[1] Istituto di Linguistica Computazionale (ILC), Via Alfieri, 1
56010 Pisa, Italy
{glottolo, pisa}@ilc.pi.cnr.it

[2] Consorzio Pisa Ricerche (CPR), Piazza A. D'Ancona, 1
56100 Pisa, Italy
corazzar@ilc.pi.cnr.it

Abstract. Semantically tagged corpora are becoming an urgent need for training and evaluation within many applications. They are also the natural accompaniment of semantic lexicons, for which they constitute both a useful testbed to evaluate their adequacy and a repository of corpus examples for the attested senses. It is essential that sound criteria are defined for their construction and a specific methodology is set up for the treatment of various semantic phenomena. We present some observations and results concerning the lexical-semantic tagging of an Italian corpus within the framework of two projects: the ELSNET feasibility study, part of a preparatory phase started with Senseval/Romanseval, and an Italian National Project (TAL), where one of the components is the lexical-semantic annotation of larger quantities of texts for an Italian syntactic-semantic Treebank. The results of the ELSNET experiment have been of utmost importance for the definition of the technical guidelines for the lexical-semantic level of annotation of the Treebank.

1 Introduction

In this paper we present some observations and results concerning the manual lexical-semantic tagging of an Italian corpus performed within the framework of the ELSNET project and of an Italian National Project (TAL).

The ELSNET experimental project, as a feasibility study, was part of a preparatory phase started with the SENSEVAL/ROMANSEVAL initiative [4]. Given its preparatory nature, we decided to focus the lexical-semantic annotation on the predicate-argument part of the sentences, which can be considered the core of a sentence and is crucial for semantic interpretation. The ELSNET corpus is composed of 1000 contexts of 20 verbs (50 contexts for each verb) extracted from the journalistic section of the Italian PAROLE corpus [16]. The semantic annotation of both verb senses and their argument heads allows i) to consider the disambiguation task from the perspective of the semantic relations holding between verb and arguments (e.g. to what extent the disambiguation of one of the two has an impact on the disambiguation of the other), ii) to analyze different aspects of verb semantics (e.g. the possibility to draw a list of typical semantic subjects vs. objects of a verb sense; the influence of the verb sense on the meaning of the subjects and direct

A. Gelbukh (Ed.): CICLing 2001, LNCS 2004, pp. 291-304, 2001.
© Springer-Verlag Berlin Heidelberg 2001

objects which combine with it and vice-versa; the adequacy of the "semantic types" of the reference lexicon with respect to the previous tasks, etc.).

In TAL, a multi-level annotated corpus, the Italian Syntactic-Semantic Treebank (ISST) [15], is now being created. The final and tested version of ISST will be available in 2001. ISST has a three-level structure ranging over syntactic and semantic levels of linguistic description. Syntactic annotation is distributed over two different levels, the constituent structure level and the functional relations level: constituent structure is annotated in terms of phrase structure trees reflecting the ordered arrangement of words and phrases within the sentence, whereas functional annotation provides a characterisation of the sentence in terms of grammatical functions (i.e. subject, object, etc.). The third level deals with lexical-semantic annotation, carried out in terms of sense tagging augmented with other types of semantic information. The three annotation levels are independent of each other, and all refer to the same input, namely a morpho-syntactically annotated (i.e. pos-tagged) text which is linked to the orthographic file with the text and mark-up of macrotextual organisation (e.g. titles, subtitles, summary, body of article, paragraphs). The final resource will be available in XML coding. The multi-level structure of ISST shows a novelty with respect to other treebanks: it combines within the same resource syntactic and lexical-semantic annotations, thus creating the prerequisites for corpus-based investigations on the syntax-semantics interface (e.g. on the semantic types associated with functional positions of a given predicate, or on specific subcategorization properties associated with a specific word sense). ISST corpus consists of about 300,000 word tokens reflecting contemporary language use. It includes two different sections: 1) a "balanced" corpus, testifying general language usage, for a total of about 210,000 tokens; 2) a specialised corpus, amounting to 90,000 tokens, with texts belonging to the financial domain. Finally, information stored in ISST will be used, for "external" evaluation within the TAL project, to improve an automatic Italian-English translation system.

In this paper we focus on: i) the methodology for lexical semantic tagging and the strategies for the treatment of some phenomena relevant to this level of annotation (such as titles, proper nouns, idioms etc.); ii) some interesting aspects emerged from the analysis of the annotated verbs and their argument heads (e.g. the usefulness of using a lexicon enriched with semantic types). Finally, some observations are provided about the limits of lexical-semantic annotation, in other words, about what cannot be expressed through lexical tagging.

2   A Brief Description of the Annotation Strategies

2.1   The ELSNET Experiment

The ELSNET experiment was performed through different steps:

- verb selection: verbs were selected to represent different semantic fields (e.g. speech acts (*chiedere, chiamare*), movement (*entrare, portare*), perception (*vedere*), etc.), and various subcategorization properties (transitive, intransitive, reflexive, etc.);

- verb context selection: contexts were selected to illustrate the different meanings of a verb, and to display a significant variety of argument heads for each verb sense;
- corpus annotation at three different levels of description: morpho-syntactic, functional, lexical-semantic.

At the lexical-semantic level, the corpus annotation was manually performed and consisted in both sense-tagging and semantic-tagging [12]. By sense-tagging we mean the assignment, to corpus occurrences, of the appropriate sense taken from the ItalWordNet(IWN)/EuroWordnet lexicon [2]. By semantic-tagging we mean the assignment, to corpus occurrences, of the appropriate semantic type/concept (such as "human, animal", etc.) as defined within the SIMPLE lexicon [13]. The combined use of both the IWN lexicon and the SIMPLE ontology of semantic types was decided in order to allow future comparisons of the two types of annotation and evaluation of the disambiguating power of the SIMPLE semantic types.

2.2   The ISST Annotation Methodology

In ISST, lexical-semantic annotation consists in the assignment of semantic tags, expressed in terms of attribute/value pairs, to full words or sequences of words corresponding to a single unit of sense (e.g. compounds, idioms). Annotation is restricted to nouns, verbs and adjectives and corresponding multi-word expressions.

ISST semantic tags convey three different types of information:

- sense of the target word(s) in the specific context: IWN is the reference lexical resource used for the sense tagging task;
- other types of lexical-semantic information not included in the reference lexical resource, e.g. for marking of figurative uses;
- information about the tagging operation, mainly notes by the human annotator about problematic annotation cases.

It is worth noting that, through the taxonomic organisation of IWN, an implicit assignment is made also of the semantic types of the IWN top-ontology. In this way, ISST sense tagging can also be seen as implicit semantic tagging, and an evaluation can later be done of the level of granularity needed in an ontology e.g. in order to discriminate between different senses of the same word or to express selection preferences on arguments.

Starting from the assumption that senses do not always correspond to single lexical items, the following typology of annotation units is identified and distinguished:

- **us**: sense units corresponding to single lexical items (nouns, verbs or adjectives);
- **usc**: semantically complex units expressed in terms of multi-word expressions (e.g. compounds, support verb constructions, idioms);
- **ust**: title sense units corresponding to titles of any type (of newspapers, books, shows, etc.). Titles receive a two-level annotation: at the level of individual components and as a single title unit.

As to the annotation methodology, in order to ensure that polysemous words and usc are tagged consistently, the annotation is manually performed 'per lemma' and not sequentially. When more than one IWN sense applies to the context being tagged, arbitrary sense assignments are avoided by resorting to under-specification, expressed in terms of disjunction/conjunction over different IWN senses.

3   Treatment of Some Problematic Cases

It is obviously of utmost importance to set up an annotation strategy for semantic phenomena such as idiomatic expressions, compounds, etc., when a sense does not correspond to one single orthographic word. The ELSNET experiment was useful to highlight the issues to be considered and solved for semantic tagging of the larger ISST corpus. In the specifications of ISST criteria are given for idioms, compounds, figurative uses, evaluative suffixation, proper nouns, foreign words, titles, etc. [18]. For the treatment of these phenomena sense assignment is augmented through specification of lexical-semantic tags conveying information not explicitly included in the reference lexicon.

3.1   Compounds

Compounds are treated as a single unit. This treatment is justified from a linguistic point of view because in most cases they are not semantically compositional or they are only partially compositional (e.g. *un_filo_di_continuità, professore_d'orchestra, compagnia_di_prosa, ombrello_antimissile, alta_moda*).

3.2   Proper Nouns

Proper nouns are assigned a semantic type (such as "human, artifact, institution"), e.g. *Francia* is tagged as "place". Proper nouns composed by two or more lexical items are treated as one entry (e.g. *Pippo_Baudo, Incisa_della_Rocchetta* (proper noun), *Teatro_Stabile_delle_Erbe* (theatrical company/troupe), *Amici_ della_ farsa* (theatrical company/ troupe).

3.3   Titles

Titles composed by more than one lexical item are compositional sequences, and the single components should be semantically annotated to allow e.g. information retrieval queries not only on the titles as such but also on the internal components of the title. In the experimental phase, titles were marked only as single units in order to simplify the annotation strategy, while in ISST they are annotated both at the level of the single components and as a unique sequence, identified by a specific tag. Their identification at the semantic level is desirable at least for the following reasons: i) for linguistic reasons, to obtain more coherent data (e.g. considering the sentence *pubblicare* (publish) *"I fiori del male"*, if titles were not annotated one could draw the wrong conclusion that *pubblicare* can have as object a "flower/natural kind", in addition to "book/title/semiotic artifact"; ii) for translation purposes, because titles frequently have no literal/equivalent translation or are left in their original language. Few corpus examples are: *Ditegli_ sempre_ di_ si* (title of a show), *Si_recita_Feydeau* (title of a show), *Il_Corriere_della_Sera* (title of a newspaper).

3.4   Figurative Uses and Idiomatic Expressions

Figurative uses and idiomatic expressions in general are marked with specific features. Their identification is important at least: i) for machine translation, since in many cases they have no exact lexical and - as far as idioms are concerned - structural equivalents; ii) for linguistic acquisition purposes, to obtain a correct data extraction (e.g. in the sentence *non comprendo la **molla** di una simile violenza* 'I don't understand the reason of such a violence', the extraction of the objects of *comprendere* 'to understand' would lead to the wrong conclusion that one of its typical objects is an "artifact" (*molla* 'spring') of type "product" (some artifacts indeed can be used in this position: *non comprendo i suoi dipinti/libri*, but they are "artwork/semiotic_artifact"); iii) for lexicographic purposes, to extend existing computational lexicons with new idioms, collocations, lexicalized metaphors, and allow studies on them.

Metaphors. Examples from the ELSNET corpus are: *abbandonare la **passerella** dell'alta moda* 'abandon the haute couture', *questo tenore…è arrivato fino alle **vette*** 'this tenor…is arrived till the top', *abbandonare la **strada** dello sport* 'abandon the road of the sport'. The distinction between lexicalized and non lexicalized metaphors was ignored in the experimental project, while it is taken into account in ISST, where the figurative uses are marked with a specific feature (FIG.=metaf). Non lexicalized metaphors are always linked to the literal sense.

Metonymy. Metonymy, that raises the same problems of data interpretation as the other figurative uses, is also marked by a specific feature. For example, in the corpus context *conquistare l'argento* 'to win the silver', *argento* is annotated as metonymy.

Evaluative Suffixation. Similar observations hold for semantic modification conveyed through evaluative suffixation: non lexicalized cases are linked to the relevant sense of the stem word, e.g. *porticciolo* 'small port', *borsone* 'large bag'.

Idiomatic Expressions and Complex Units. Idiomatic expressions are treated as a single word and marked with a specific feature, e.g.: *il processo **entra nel vivo*** 'to enter into the heart of the process', ***cartone animato*** 'cartoon', ***aprire un** nuovo **capitolo** nell'industria* lit.: 'to open a new chapter in the industry', ***tagliare la testa al toro*** lit.: 'to cut the head of the bull'. Corpus annotation also identifies expressions that are not recognized as such in IWN, but behave as semantically complex units. This is the case e.g. of *anni Sessanta* 'the sixties' which, being fully compositional and productive, does not appear in the lexical resource.

Sense assignment combined together with the additional lexical-semantic tags make the ISST annotated corpus more than a mere list of instantiations of the senses attested in the reference lexical resource. The corpus becomes a repository of interesting semantic information (going from titles and proper nouns to non-lexicalized metaphors, metonymies and evaluative suffixation), especially for what concerns non-conventional uses of a word, i.e. those semantic facts which are excluded – either programmatically or just by chance – from the reference lexical resource. Corpus annotation can also shed light on the variability of multi-word expressions - from compounds to support verb constructions and idiomatic expressions -, that are prone to massive variation. The gray areas spotted by the above examples in which corpus annotation either diverges from the lexical resource or further specifies it, can be seen – in perspective – as the starting point for revisions and refinements of both the annotated corpus and the lexicon. In this way, the annotated corpus presents itself as a flexible resource, which is – to some extent – independent from the specific internal architecture of the selected reference lexicon.

4 Some Remarks about the Annotated Verbs and Argument Heads

We report here some observations stemming from the semantic annotation of verbs and their arguments, and we touch issues such as the possibility to characterize typical subjects/objects combining with a given verb sense, the usefulness of a lexicon enriched with semantic types and/or collocations, criteria for disambiguating senses.

4.1 Typical Semantic Arguments of a Verb

From the analysis of the semantically annotated corpus, it turns out that there are various ways of describing - in terms of semantic types - a typical argument of a given verb sense. The arguments combining with a verbal head can be:

- semantically restricted: in this case, it is possible to define the specific semantic types which combine with it (*selection restrictions*);
- semantically completely unrestricted (*no selection restrictions*);
- semantically unrestricted, but it is possible to define which semantic types cannot combine with it (it is particularly relevant when this allows to discriminate between different senses of the same verb) (we could call it a *negative restriction*);
- partially semantically restricted: a list of preferences in terms of semantic types can be defined (*selection preferences*).

Let us consider as illustrative example the verb *arrestare*.

1. In the first sense the verb means 'to stop'. According to the annotated corpus its typical arguments are of the following semantic types:
subj=act; cause_act; natural_substance; purpose_act; time
dobj=non_relational_act; change_of_value; movement_of_thought; act; cause_act; cause_natural_transition; event. In many cases the object has a *negative connotation*.

Summing-up, the sense 'to stop' selects almost unrestricted subjects and direct objects. However, the subject is preferably non-human (it is rarely human, as in *il governo ha arrestato l'inflazione* 'the government stopped inflation'), while the direct object is preferably an "event; act; change;...", but it is usually not a human or human-like (human-group, institution, etc.). Moreover the object has preferably a negative connotation. All this can be broadly expressed in the following way.

Table 1. Arg.s description of *arrestare1*

SUBJ:
preference= non-human;
DOBJ:
preference= event; act; change; phenomenon
preference= negative connotation
negative_restriction= human

2. The second meaning of the verb is 'to arrest'. Semantic types of the arguments are: **subj**= human; human_group; institution; profession, with **domain**=military; law **dobj**=human; agent_of_temporary_activity; agent_of_persistent_activity; kinship; profession; people. In many cases the direct object has a *negative connotation*.

This sense clearly selects a human or human-like subject and direct object. The subject preferably belongs to the military/law domain, while the object preferably has a negative connotation (not always however, e.g. *arrestare un innocente* 'arrest an innocent').

Table 2. Arg.s description of *arrestare2*

SUBJ:
selection_restriction= human or human-like
preference= domain=law, military
DOBJ:
selection_restriction= human
preference= negative connotation

Another example is the verb *percepire*. Its direct objects can be described as follows:

1. The first meaning is 'to perceive'. This sense is marked as a "perception" type. **dobj**= color; group; shape; sign; phenomenon

2. The second sense is 'to receive' and is marked as "change_possession". **dobj**= money; convention; number; amount

3. The third is a figurative use ('to perceive with the intuition', 'to perceive something as if it is something else') and is marked as "perception figurative". **dobj**= unrestricted

This last sense frequently - but not always - occurs with a complement introduced by *come* (e.g. *l'opinione pubblica percepisce il Servizio sanitario nazionale (Ssn) come poco efficiente* 'public opinion perceives the Ssn as not so efficient').

Summing-up, for *percepire* only the second sense seems to have a semantically restricted direct object, while the third meaning is frequently marked by a specific (preferred) syntactic pattern.

4.2   Verb/Arguments Interaction at the Lexical-Semantic Level

The interpretation/disambiguation of the sense of a given argument head may strongly depend on the meaning of the surrounding context, more precisely of the verbal head. Between the verb and its arguments there is a strong interaction from the semantic point of view: the verb meaning may determine (or select) the sense of its subject and/or direct object. For instance *arrestare*, both 'to arrest' and 'to stop', as said above frequently selects direct objects which have themselves, or receive from the verb, a negative connotation, as shown in the corpus examples below.

Table 3. Dobj of the verb *arrestare*

Dobj	Sem.type of Dobj	Conn. Feat.
ladro_1	agent_temp_act	neg
spacciatore_1	agent_temp_act	neg
trafficante_1	agent_temp_act	neg
traffico_2	act	neg
invasione_1	cause_act	neg
massacro_1	cause_nat_trans	neg
inflazione_1	event	neg
pregiudicato_1	human	neg
balordo_1	human	neg
maniaco_1	human	neg
strozzino_1	agent_temp_act	neg

Another example is *comprendere* which, in the meaning of 'to include', selects a specific sense of its subjects. For the lemmas below, the sense marked in the SIMPLE lexicon as "group of entities" (which can therefore 'include' other entities) is selected.

Table 4. Dobj of the verb *comprendere*

Dobj	Sem.type of Dobj
carico_1	group
elenco_1	group
equipaggiamento_2	group
lista_2	group
panorama_1	group
tris_1	group
comune_1	human_group
consiglio_2	human_group
costituente_2	human_group
dossier_1	group

It may also happen that the sense/semantic type of the direct object determines the meaning of the verb. For instance, the semantic type of the objects helps to characterize different possible senses/nuances of meaning of the verb *coprire,* as shown in the tables below.

– *coprire un periodo* 'to cover a period of time':

Table 5. Sem. type of Dobj of *coprire*

Dobj	Sem.type of Dobj
periodo_1	time
1970-1993	time

– *coprire uno spazio* 'to cover a space/a distance':

Table 6. Sem. type of Dobj of *coprire*

Dobj	Sem.type of Dobj
superficie_1	area
territorio_1	area
area_2	area
area_1	area
pista_1	artifactual_area
continente_1	geopolitical_location
80_per_cento	part
35%	part

– *coprire un suono* 'to smother':

Table 7. Sem. type od Dobj of *coprire*

Dobj	Sem.type of Dobj
rumore_1	experience_sound

– *coprire una persona/un reato* 'to hide a crime' :

Table 8. Sem. type of Dobj of *coprire*

Dobj	Sem.type Of Dobj	Conn. Feat.
crimine_1	act	neg
mafioso_2	human	neg
violento_1	human	neg

4.3   Acquisition of Senses and Enhancement of Existing Lexical Resources

The analysis of a semantically tagged corpus allows not only to identify totally new senses, but also to have a more precise and complete view on the semantics of a lemma, and therefore helps to decide on a more sound basis than human intuition which senses to encode for a lemma. Relying on the different semantic types of argument heads that combine with a given verb, it is easier to identify the most general senses of a lemma and to capture the most specific senses or shifts of meaning of the same lemma. One can then decide how to collapse some specific uses into more general, inclusive senses according to:

- different design requirements of the lexical resource to be created/extended/tuned. Indeed, both the number and type of senses to be encoded may strongly depend on the 'apparatus' (information types and representation means) available to describe them, i.e. semantic nets, frames, selection restrictions, ontology, domain, semantic relations, etc.
- different applications of the lexical resource (e.g. MT, IR, etc.). For instance, in an MT environment (bilingual, multilingual resources), it makes sense to treat as independent meanings those that have a different translation (e.g. also the sense number 9 below, among others, for the language pair Italian/English), but not necessarily for IR, where an excessive granularity may create noise.

It is important that corpus analysis does not lead to an excessive granularity of sense distinctions - not desirable for different reasons [4], [9] -, but that it provides ground for decisions based on actual evidence. We give below the example of the verb *abbandonare* 'to abandon/leave', which has at least the following three main senses according to current paper dictionaries: 1) to abandon, to leave forever (e.g. a place), 2) to abandon, to desert (e.g. the children), 3) to give up, to renounce. On the basis of the analysis of the semantic types of direct objects, the following major/minor senses (uses) of *abbandonare* come out:

1. 'to leave a place': dobj= building, geopolitical_location, area
2. 'to get up' (*abbandonare la sedia, un veicolo*): dobj= furniture, vehicle
3. 'to abandon someone'': dobj= kinship, animal, human
4. 'to give up an activity': dobj= act, purpose_act
5. 'to give up an ideology, a dream..': dobj= movement_of_thought, cognitive_fact
6. 'to leave a group, a party, a club..': dobj= institution, human_group
7. 'to abandon a sector, a domain...(sport, biology)': dobj= domain
8. 'to change one's psychological state' (*abbandonare la calma, la prudenza,* lit.: 'to abandon the calm, the caution'): dobj= psych_property
9. 'to drop something' (*abbandonò la divisa a casaccio sulla sedia* 'he dropped the uniform at random on the chair'): in this case the direct object is a "concrete/ inanimate entity" (neither human nor animal). It is worth noting that this specific use of *abbandonare* combines with a particular modifier which cannot occur with the other senses of the verb (e.g. **abbandona la moglie a casaccio* *'he abandoned the wife at random').

These very granular distinctions – even though motivated by textual evidence - can/should be grouped under the three main senses above, however this additional information on the various semantic type preferences can be encoded within each broad sense and may be necessary for the selection of the correct translation in MT.

5   The Complexity of Word Sense

Word sense disambiguation (WSD) can be performed, in different contexts, through the use of various information types at different levels of linguistic description: morphosyntactic/syntactic/semantic and even multilingual [10]. Other projects, such as DELIS [14], stressed the interaction between e.g. morphosyntactic patterns and word meanings. The following are some syntactic and semantic indicators which can sometimes help in the identification of a word-sense. The problem is that they are not at all sure tests: they have only a partial validity, and are not completely discriminating. Moreover it is not easy to predict when to apply which test. Therefore human judgement has still an important part in WSD.

- A specific syntactic pattern may allow selecting a particular sense [14], [5], [1]. This is the case of *comprendere* which co-occurs with a that-clause when it means 'to understand' (and not when it means 'to include'), or *aprire* which occurs with a PP introduced by *a* and with "human" head when it has the meaning of 'to be ready, open, well disposed towards someone' (e.g. *Cossiga apre a La Malfa*).
- The domain of use can help to select a specific word meaning (e.g. *perseguire un reato* 'to prosecute a crim' (domain=law)).
- Even the presence of a specific modifier more often than one could think selects a particular sense [14], [5]: e.g. *perseguire penalmente* 'to prosecute at the penal level', does not mean 'to pursue (a goal)'; *comprendere benissimo* 'to understand very well', does not mean 'to include'.
- A specific semantic type of subjects and/or direct objects and/or indirect objects, etc. can help to select a particular meaning of a word (e.g. a human subject always selects the meaning 'to understand' of the verb *comprendere*).
- Different synonyms and/or antonyms select different senses [7].
- Two different senses of a lemma cannot be selected simultaneously in the same context [7] (e.g. **Leo arresta sia il colpevole che il corso degli eventi* *'Leo arrests both the criminal and the events').

It is clear that the availability of large quantities of semantically tagged corpora may help i) to better analyze the impact of different clues to perform WSD in different contexts, and ii) to study the interaction of clues belonging to different levels of linguistic description, in order to improve WSD strategies.

6   What Cannot Be Easily Encoded
at the Lexical-Semantic Level of Annotation

In a large number of cases, sense interpretation requires appeal to extra-linguistic knowledge (world knowledge, etc.) which cannot be encoded or, to put it that way, captured at the lexical-semantic level of description. We provide below a few examples.

- When the metaphors are not restricted to a single lemma (e.g. *la **chiave** del problema* 'the clue to a problem'), but extended to an entire sequence (e.g.: *l'auto* *verde arriva sul tavolo del governo* lit.: 'the green car arrives on the table of the government').

The sequence means that the "topic" of *auto verde* (the car which does not pollute) will be discussed by the government. However, at the lexical level only *auto*, *verde* and *tavolo* can be marked as figurative uses, whereas the metaphorical sense of the whole sentence will come out only from a violation of the selection restrictions. Indeed, a car (type=vehicle) can arrive (type=move) but not on a table (type=furniture), more probably in a "place/location", while the "topic" of *auto verde* can arrive on the table of the government. This complex sense interpretation of the whole expression cannot be characterized through simple lexical-semantic annotation. It is impossible to imagine the assignment of a label "topic" to *auto* and/or *verde* (everything can indeed be a topic).

– When it is the intention of the author that a sequence is actually ambiguous between two meanings, e.g. *[Titolo]: Nina Vinchi **entra in scena** '[Title]: Nina Vinchi starts/comes on stage' [Sottotitolo]: A 84 anni la signora del Piccolo affronta per 3 ore i giudici.*

In this corpus context the multi-word expression *entrare in scena* has the double meaning of 'to appear/to start' (the idiomatic sense) and 'to come on stage' (the literal sense). In this case, the interpretation of the sequence is based on knowledge about the domain type (domain=theater) and the context type (indeed ambiguities of this kind are frequently used within titles).

– When some words acquire a specific sense, strictly dependent on the context in which they occur, that cannot be encoded at the lexical-semantic level, e.g. *la donna (Pauline Collins), che ha già visto arrestare il marito dai **tedeschi**, ...*

Arrestare usually combines with a subject belonging to the military/law domain. Also in this case *tedesco* has to be interpreted as 'German soldier' (and not any kind of German people). However, in the computational lexicon *tedesco* is obviously marked as "people" and cannot be otherwise. Another example is the verb *chiamare* which sometimes means (is synonymous of) 'to telephone'. In most cases the identification of this sense strongly depends on a complex process of context interpretation (even if there are few cases in which the disambiguation is easy, e.g. when the direct object is not a human but a phone number or an inanimate entity, as in *chiamare il (numero) 113/Buckingham Palace/l'ambulanza*). Examples of difficult interpretation are the following: *E io **chiamo** Craxi per 150 miserabili milioni?* 'And I should call Craxi for 150 miserable millions?', *In gran parte sono bambine dai 6 ai 14 anni. **Chiamano** per lo più da Milano ..* 'In most cases they are girls from 6 to 14 years. They call mostly from Milan ..'.

– At last, we provide the example of *tagliare* 'to cut'. From the table below it is evident the complexity and variety of nuances implied by the verb, according to the type of direct object which co-occurs with it.

Not all these shifts of meanings can/must be captured through lexical-semantic annotation (sense and semantic tagging). For instance, *tagliare il prato* 'to cut the grass' means 'to eliminate/reduce the grass'; *tagliare le gomme* 'to make a hole (to punch) in the pneumatic'; *tagliare i capelli* means also 'to give a nice shape to the hair' (not necessarily to shorten them); *tagliare il mantello* 'to divide the mantle'; *tagliare la legna* 'to cut into pieces the wood'; *tagliare le corolle* 'to detach the corolla of flowers' (to separate the corolla from the flower); on the other hand, *tagliare una fettina* 'to cut a small slice' moves the focus from the whole cut entity to the cut part, etc.

Table 9. Dobj of *tagliare*

Dobj	Sem.type of Dobj	Sem.type of the Verbal Head
prato	area	cause_change_of_state
gomma	artifact	cause_change_of_state
stoffa	artif.material	cause_constitutive_change
lingua	body_part	cause_constitutive_change
testa	body_part	cause_constitutive_change
capello	body_part	cause_change_of_state
mano	body_part	cause_constitutive_change
mantello	clothing	cause_constitutive_change
legna	material	cause_constitutive_change
corolla	part	cause_constitutive_change
fettina	part	cause_constitutive_change
pezzo	part	cause_constitutive_change
cespuglio	plant	cause_constitutive_change
spino	plant	cause_constitutive_change

Also in this case, this collocational information, which not necessarily implies sense distinction, may be of use – as additional, more subtle information of syntagmatic nature encoded within the existing senses - in a multilingual lexicon for translation purposes.

7   Concluding Remarks

Even a rather small experiment of semantic corpus annotation allows to better understand some of the problematic aspects of lexical-semantic corpus annotation and to have a broad overview of possible types of analysis that can be done on a corpus tagged at the lexical semantic level.

The availability of semantically tagged corpora is considered useful, among others, (i) to evaluate the disambiguating power of the semantic types of the lexical resource used for semantic corpus annotation, (ii) to assess the need of integrating computational lexicons with senses and/or phraseology attested in the corpus, (iii) to identify the inadequacy of certain sense distinctions attested in traditional dictionaries or current computational lexicons which are not applicable to actual usage (see [4]), (iv) to check the real frequency of known senses in different text types or *genres* (some of them may in fact be scarcely attested in a specific corpus type, e.g. in a journalistic corpus), (v) to draw a distinction between sense discrimination – that has to be kept "under control" - and additional, more granular information (often of collocational nature, such as lexical co-occurrence or selection preferences on arguments) which can/must be encoded within the broader senses e.g. to help translation.

References

1. Atkins, B.T., Kegl, J., Levin, B.: Anatomy of a Verb Entry: from Linguistic Theory to Lexicographic Practice. International Journal of Lexicography 1 (1988) 84–126
2. Alonge, A., Calzolari, N., Vossen, P., Bloksma, L., Castellon, I., Marti, T., Peters, W.: The Linguistic Design of the EuroWordNet Database. Special Issue on EuroWordNet. Computers and the Humanities 32 (1998) 2-3, 91–115
3. Busa, F., Calzolari, N., Lenci, A., Pustejovski, J.: Building a Lexicon: Structuring and Generating Concepts. In: Proceedings of the Computational Semantics Workshop. Tilburg (1999)
4. Calzolari, N., Corazzari, O.: Senseval/Romanseval: the framework for Italian. Computers and the Humanities 34 (2000) 1-2, 61–78
5. Calzolari, N., Corazzari, O., Monachini, M., Roventini, A.: Speech Act and Perception Verbs: Generalizations and Contrastive Aspects. In: EURALEX-96 Proceedings. Goteborg (1996) 73–83
6. Corazzari, O.: Phraseological Units. ILC, Pisa (1992)
7. Cruse, D.A.: Lexical Semantics. Cambridge University Press, Cambridge (1986)
8. Fass, D.: A Method for Discriminating Metonymy and Metaphor by Computer. Computational Linguistics 17 (1991) 1, 49–90.
9. Fellbaum, C. (ed.): Wordnet, An Electronic Lexical Database. MIT Press, Cambridge, (1998)
10. Gale, A. W., Church, K.W., Yarowsky, D.: A Method for Disambiguating Word Senses in a Large Corpus. Computers and the Humanities 26 (1992) 415–439.
11. Kilgarriff, A.: Dictionary word sense distinctions: An enquiry into their nature. Computers and the Humanities 26 (1993) 365–387
12. Kokkinakis, D., Kokkinakis, S. J.: Sense-Tagging at the Cycle-Level Using GLDB. Göteborg University (1999)
13. Lenci, A., Busa, F., Ruimy, N., Gola, E., Monachini, M., Calzolari, N., Zampolli, A.: Linguistic Specifications. SIMPLE Deliverable D2.1. ILC and University of Pisa (1999)
14. Monachini, M., Roventini, A., Alonge, A., Calzolari, N., Corazzari, O.: Linguistic Analysis of Italian Perception and Speech Act Verbs. DELIS Working Paper. ILC, Pisa (1994)
15. Montemagni, S., Barsotti, F., Battista, M., Calzolari, N., Corazzari, O., Zampolli, A., Fanciulli, F., Massetani, M., Raffaelli, R., Basili, R., Pazienza, M.T., Saracino, D., Zanzotto, F., Mana, N., Pianesi, F., Delmonte, R.: The Italian Syntactic-Semantic Treebank: Architecture, Annotation, Tools and Evaluation. In: Proceedings of the COLING Workshop on "Linguistically Interpreted Corpora (LINC-2000)". Luxembourg (2000) 18–27
16. PAROLE: Preparatory Action for Linguistic Resources Organization for Language Engineering. LE-4017, Pisa (1996).
17. Rodriguez, H., Climent, S., Vossen, P., Loksma, L., Peters, W., Alonge, A., Bertagna, F., Roventini, A. : The Top-Down Strategy for building EuroWordNet: Vocabulary Coverage, Base Concepts and Top Ontology. Special Issue on EuroWordNet. Computers and the Humanities 32 (1998) 2-3.
18. SI-TAL: Specifiche Tecniche di SI-TAL. Manuale Operativo. ILC and CPR, Pisa (2000)

Meaning Sort
— Three Examples: Dictionary Construction, Tagged Corpus Construction, and Information Presentation System —

Masaki Murata, Kyoko Kanzaki, Kiyotaka Uchimoto, Qing Ma, and
Hitoshi Isahara

Communications Research Laboratory, MPT,
2-2-2 Hikaridai, Seika-cho, Soraku-gun, Kyoto, 619-0289, Japan,
{murata,kanzaki,uchimoto,qma,isahara}@crl.go.jp,
http://www-karc.crl.go.jp/ips/murata

Abstract. It is often useful to sort words into an order that reflects relations among their meanings as obtained by using a thesaurus. In this paper, we introduce a method of arranging words semantically by using several types of 'is-a' thesauri and a multi-dimensional thesaurus. We also describe three major applications where a meaning sort is useful and show the effectiveness of a meaning sort. Since there is no doubt that a word list in meaning-order is easier to use than a word list in some random order, a meaning sort, which can easily produce a word list in meaning-order, must be useful and effective.

1 Using Msort

Arranging words in an order that is based on their meanings is called a meaning sort (Msort). The Msort is a method of arranging words by their meanings rather than alphabetically. The method used to list the meanings is described in the next section.

For example, suppose we obtain the following data in a research project:[1]

> an event
>
> a temple, a formal style, an alma mater, to take up one's post, the Imperial Household, a campus, Japan, the Soviet Union, the whole country, an agricultural village, a prefecture, a school, a festival, the head of a school, an established custom, a government official, a celebration, a Royal family

This is a list of noun phrases (NPs), each followed by the word *gyoji* (an event) in the form NP X *no gyoji* (an event of NP X) in Japanese. To find the most useful way to examine the list, we first arrange the NPs alphabetically:

---

[1] We actually obtained this data from the EDR co-occurrence dictionary [1].

A. Gelbukh (Ed.): CICLing 2001, LNCS 2004, pp. 305–318, 2001.

an agricultural village, an alma mater, a campus, a celebration, an established custom, a festival, a formal style, a government official, the head of a school, the Imperial Household, Japan, a prefecture, a Royal family, a school, the Soviet Union, to take up one's post, a temple, the whole country

This list is not easy to use, so we next arrange the NPs by frequency of appearance:

an established custom, a school, a formal style, Japan, a prefecture, the whole country, a temple, an agricultural village, a Royal family, the Soviet Union, a festival, a campus, to take up one's post, a celebration, an alma mater, the Imperial Household, a government official, the head of a school

Yet, even arranged this way, it is too difficult to use the list.

We then use an Msort to arrange the NPs semantically, by using following categories: Human, Organization, and Action:

(Human)   the Imperial Household, a Royal family, a government official, the head of a school
(Organization)   the whole country, an agricultural village, a prefecture, Japan, the Soviet Union, a temple, a school, a campus, an alma mater
(Action)   a celebration, an established custom, a formal style, to take up one's post, a festival

This list is much easier to use than a listing in alphabetical or frequency order. Note that the words in each line are also arranged in an order that reflects relations among their meanings. For example, *Japan* and *the Soviet Union* are listed side by side, as are *a school, a campus,* and *an alma mater.*

Although the list shows a variety of events, we can see at a glance that some are events related to certain special persons, and some are events related to a certain organization, and the others are miscellaneous forms of events.

The Msort is also applicable to other situations as described in later sections. The Msort enables users to more easily and efficiently recognize and examine various types of problems.

2   Implementing Msort

To sort words in an order that reflects relations among their meanings, we first need to determine an order for the meanings. The Japanese thesaurus *Bunrui Goi Hyou* [10], an 'is-a' hierarchical thesaurus, is useful for this. We refer to it as *BGH*. In BGH, each word has *a category number*. In the electronic version of BGH, each word has a 10-digit category number that indicates seven levels of

Table 1. Modified BGH category numbers

Semantic marker	Original code	Modified code
Animal	[1-3]56	511
Human	12[0-4]	52[0-4]
Organization	[1-3]2[5-8]	53[5-8]
Products	[1-3]4[0-9]	61[0-9]
Part of a living thing	[1-3]57	621
Plant	[1-3]55	631
Nature	[1-3]52	641
Location	[1-3]17	657
Quantity	[1-3]19	711
Time	[1-3]16	811
Phenomenon	[1-3]5[01]	91[12]
Abstract relation	[1-3]1[0-58]	aa[0-58]
Human activity	[1-3]58,[1-3]3[0-8]	ab[0-9]
Other	4	d

the 'is-a' hierarchy. The top five levels are expressed by the first five digits, the sixth level is expressed by the next two digits, and the last level is expressed by the last three digits. (Although we have used BGH, Msort can also be used with other thesauri in other languages.)

The easiest way of implementing Msort is to arrange words in order of their category numbers. However, only arranging words semantically does not produce a convenient result. If the items arranged are numbers, the order is clear, but there is no clear order for words. It is thus convenient to insert a mark, as a kind of bookmark, in certain places. We used semantic markers such as *Human*, *Organization* and *Action* as bookmarks.

These markers were created by combining nominal semantic markers in the IPAL verbal dictionary [2] with the BGH classification system. Table 1 shows the modified category numbers obtained by integrating these new markers with the BGH codes. The first three digits of each category number have been changed. For example, the notation [1-3]56 and 511 in the first line means that when the first three digits of the category number are 156, 256, or 356, those digits will be changed to 511. ([1-3] means 1, 2, or 3.)

The process of using an Msort is explained by applying it to the data set listed in Section 1, obtained by the word *gyoji* (an event), as follows:

1. Firstly, we give each word a new category number according to the transformation shown in Table 1, to obtain the results shown in Table 2(a). *A temple* occurs twice, and *a formal style* occurs four times. This indicates that both *a temple* and *a formal style* have multiple meanings. In the BGH thesaurus, *a temple* is defined as having two meanings, and *a formal style* is defined as having four meanings.

Table 2. An example of the Msort process

(a) Examples with BGH category numbers

5363005022	a temple	7118007013	the whole country
5363005021	a temple	5353007012	the whole country
ab18207012	a formal style	5354006033	an agricultural village
ab21509016	a formal style	5355004017	a prefecture
aa11011014	a formal style	5363010012	a school
ab70004013	a formal style	ab46002012	a festival
5363013015	an alma mater	5241023012	the head of a school
ab41201016	to take up one's post	ab18205021	an established custom
5210007021	the Imperial Household	5233004015	a government official
5363010015	a campus	5241101061	a government official
5359001012	Japan	ab14308013	a celebration
5359004192	the Soviet Union	ab46019012	a celebration
continued in the right-hand column		5210007022	a Royal family

2. We then add semantic markers to the set of words in Table 2(a) to get the results shown in Table 2(b).
3. Next, we arrange the items in Table 2(b) in the order of their category numbers to get the results shown in Table 2(c).
4. Finally, we convert the data into a form that is easier to use. For example, when we delete the category numbers, redundant words with the same semantic marker in a line, and semantic markers to which no words correspond, we obtain the data shown in Table 4.

This data is much easier to use than the data shown in the other tables.

3   Msort Using Different Dictionaries

3.1   Msort Using a Different 'is-a' Thesaurus

In Section 2 we described the implementation of an Msort using the BGH thesaurus. This is the most suitable 'is-a' thesaurus for an Msort because each word which contains is assigned a category number. This section examines whether an Msort can be used with an 'is-a' hierarchical thesaurus which has no category numbers, such as the EDR dictionary [1].

It is useful to consider the definition sentence of the concept in each node of an is-a thesaurus as the number of the level. If we do this, it is not necessary to create a new number. For example, the definitions of concepts from the top node to the node of the term "an alma mater" are as shown in Table 3.

When we do a meaning sort using the EDR dictionary, we only have to consider the connections of the hierarchy of meanings "concept: agent: autonomous

Table 2. Example of the Msort process

(b) Adding semantic markers
   for divisions

5100000000	(Animal)
5200000000	(Human)
5300000000	(Organization)
6100000000	(Product)
6200000000	(Part of a living thing)
6300000000	(Plant)
6400000000	(Nature)
6500000000	(Location)
7100000000	(Quantity)
8100000000	(Time)
9100000000	(Phenomenon)
aa00000000	(Abstract relation)
ab00000000	(Human activity)
d000000000	(Other)
5363005022	a temple
5363005021	a temple
ab18207012	a formal style
ab21509016	a formal style
aa11011014	a formal style
ab70004013	a formal style
5363013015	an alma mater
ab41201016	to take up one's post
5210007021	the Imperial Household
5363010015	a campus
5359001012	Japan
5359004192	the Soviet Union
7118007013	the whole country
5353007012	the whole country
5354006033	an agricultural village
5355004017	a prefecture
5363010012	a school
ab46002012	a festival
5241023012	the head of a school
ab18205021	an established custom
5233004015	a government official
5241101061	a government official
ab14308013	a celebration
ab46019012	a celebration
5210007022	a Royal family

(c) Arranging elements in the order
   of their category number

5100000000	(Animal)
5200000000	(Human)
5210007021	the Imperial Household
5210007022	a Royal family
5233004015	a government official
5241023012	the head of a school
5241101061	a government official
5300000000	(Organization)
5353007012	the whole country
5354006033	an agricultural village
5355004017	a prefecture
5359001012	Japan
5359004192	the Soviet Union
5363005021	a temple
5363005022	a temple
5363010012	a school
5363010015	a campus
5363013015	an alma mater
6100000000	(Product)
6200000000	(Part of a living thing)
6300000000	(Plant)
6400000000	(Nature)
6500000000	(Location)
7100000000	(Quantity)
7118007013	the whole country
8100000000	(Time)
9100000000	(Phenomenon)
aa00000000	(Abstract relation)
aa11011014	a formal style
ab00000000	(Human activity)
ab14308013	a celebration
ab18205021	an established custom
ab18207012	a formal style
ab21509016	a formal style
ab41201016	to take up one's post
ab46002012	a festival
ab46019012	a celebration
ab70004013	a formal style
d000000000	(Other)

Table 3. Definitions of concepts from the top node to the node of the term "an alma mater"

concept
agent
autonomous being
organization
educational organization
an organization to provide education, called a school
a school at which a person was or is a student

Table 4. Results of an Msort using the BGH thesaurus

(Human)	the Imperial Household, a Royal family, a government official, the head of a school
(Organization)	the whole country, an agricultural village, a prefecture, Japan, the Soviet Union, a temple, a school, a campus, an alma mater
(Quantity)	the whole country
(Relation)	a formal style
(Action)	a celebration, an established custom, a formal style, to take up one's post, a festival

being: organization: educational organization: an organization to provide education, called a school: a school at which a person was or is a student" as the category number.

Some results of a meaning sort using the EDR dictionary are shown in Table 5[2]. We used the first three definition terms as division markers.

The above analysis demonstrates that a meaning sort can be done using any is-a thesaurus. However, there is a problem in that the order of the branching-point nodes of a hierarchical structure is ambiguous. In the case shown in Table 5, the order is the alphabetical order of the strings in the definition terms. It is better to specify the order manually, but if this is too difficult, it is better to do a meaning sort of the definition terms themselves by using another dictionary or thesaurus, e.g. the BGH thesaurus.

3.2 Msort Using a Dictionary Where Each Word Is Expressed with a Set of Multiple Features

In some dictionaries, each word is expressed with a set of multiple features [5] [12]. For example, the research of the IPAL Japanese generative dictionary [7]

---

[2] This table was obtained by using a Japanese dictionary. In the table, "a temple" and "a prefecture" belong to the category "human being." In Japanese, "a temple" and "a prefecture" have many meanings, including "human being."

Table 5. Results of an Msort using the EDR dictionary

(concept : agent : autonomous being)	a school, a campus, an alma mater, a temple, a prefecture, the Soviet Union, Japan, a Royal family, the Imperial Household, the head of a school, a government official
(concept : agent : human being)	a temple, a prefecture, the head of a school, a government official
(concept : event : action)	a celebration, to take up one's post
(concept : event : phenomenon)	a festival
(concept : matter : event)	a festival, an established custom, a celebration
(concept : matter : thing)	a temple, a school, a prefecture, the head of a school, a government official, a celebration, a formal style
(concept : space : location)	a temple, a school, the whole country, a prefecture, an agricultural village, the Soviet Union, Japan

Table 6. Example of a dictionary in which each word is assigned multiple features

Word	Feature				
	Style	Object	Depth	Size	Material
utsuwa (a container)	—	—	—	—	—
wan1 (a ceramic bowl)	Oriental	—	deep	—	ceramic
wan2 (a wooden bowl)	Oriental	—	deep	—	wooden
yunomi (a Japanese teacup)	Oriental	Japanese tea	deep	—	ceramic
sara (a plate)	—	—	shallow	—	—

gives multiple features to various words having the meaning of the containers in Table 6. In this table, "—" means that the feature value is not specified.

It is possible to do an Msort in the case of such a dictionary. We have only to treat the information as if each feature is equivalent to a level in an imaginary 'is-a' thesaurus. In Table 6, if we assume that the features, from left to right, correspond to the levels, from top to bottom, of an imaginary thesaurus, the levels become *Style, Object, Depth, Size,* and *Material,* and a category number represents *Style:Object:Depth:Size:Material,* which is essentially the same situation as for the EDR data. For example, the category number of *wan2* (*a wooden bowl*) is *Oriental: —: deep: —: wooden.* (Actually in order to do an Msort of feature values, we may change *Oriental, deep,* and *wooden* into the corresponding category numbers in BGH.) We simply do an Msort, assuming that each word has such a category word. The result of this Msort is shown in Table 7.

Table 7. Result of an Msort, from the leftmost feature

Word	Feature				
	Style	Object	Depth	Size	Material
utsuwa (a container)	—	—	—	—	—
sara (a plate)	—	—	shallow	—	—
wan1 (a ceramic bowl)	Oriental	—	deep	—	ceramic
wan2 (a wooden bowl)	Oriental	—	deep	—	wooden
yunomi (a Japanese teacup)	Oriental	Japanese tea	deep	—	ceramic

Table 8. The result of an Msort, from the rightmost feature

Word	Feature				
	Style	Object	Depth	Size	Material
utsuwa (a container)	—	—	—	—	—
sara (a plate)	—	—	shallow	—	—
wan1 (a ceramic bowl)	Oriental	—	deep	—	ceramic
yunomi (a Japanese teacup)	Oriental	Japanese tea	deep	—	ceramic
wan2 (a wooden bowl)	Oriental	—	deep	—	wooden

Table 7 shows the result of an Msort based on the supposition that the leftmost feature is the most important. Which feature is most important is, in fact, not clear. For example, if we suppose that the rightmost feature is the most important and we do an Msort from that feature, we get a different result, as shown in Table 8. From a dictionary with multiple features, we can get various results of Msorts in this wasy, by changing the features which are thought to be most important. This means that users can do an Msort in any order of features that they may be interested in. This kind of dictionary, that is, the kind which provides multiple features, is therefore very flexible.

When a hierarchical thesaurus is used to examine this, there are further interesting results. We can assume that each feature corresponds to a level of the hierarchical thesaurus, so we can construct many kinds of hierarchical thesauri by changing the correspondence between levels and features. For example, we can construct the hierarchical thesaurus shown in Figure 1 from the result of an Msort from the leftmost feature as shown in Table 7. We can construct a hierarchical thesaurus shown in Figure 2 from the result of an Msort from the rightmost feature as shown in Table 8. In the thesaurus of Figure 1, we can see the semanitical similarity between *wan1* (*a ceramic bowl*) and *wan2* (*a wooden bowl*). In the thesaurus of Figure 2, we can understand that *wan1* (*a ceramic bowl*) and *wan2* (*a Japanese teacup*) are semantically similar in that they are both ceramic. Such construction of multiple thesauri has led to further research into a multi-dimensional thesaurus. The necessity for a multi-dimensional thesaurus

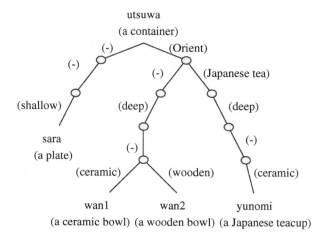

Fig. 1. Hierarchical thesaurus of meaning sort
from the leftmost feature

was discussed in Kawamura's paper [3]. Kawamura's paper argued that if we
divide *a bird* and *an airplane* into other categories at a relatively higher level
of a hierarchy than the level at which entries are divided according to whether
the item can fly or not, we will not be able to see that *a bird* and *an airplane*
are semantically similar in that they can both fly. Therefore a dictionary with
multiple features, which can be flexibly reconfigured into hierarchical thesauri of
many kinds, would be very useful, and the construction of such a dictionary is
necessary for reasons of practicality. Also, we have our doubts as to whether it
is necessary to make a word dictionary in the form of a hierarchical thesaurus.
Looking at Table 6, because all the features of *utsuwa* (*a container*) are "—"
representing no specification of feature values, we are able to see that *utsuwa* (*a
container*) is super-ordinate to the other words by looking at the information on
the multiple features. We can estimate super-ordinate and subordinate relation
from the inclusion relationships of features, so construction of a hierarchical
thesaurus as such is not necessary. A dictionary with multiple features is all
that is necessary. Furthermore, a dictionary with multiple features has a further
advantage in that we can define the similarity of two words in terms of the
proportion of features that are the same for both words. Although a high-order
predicative logic and a natural language sentence can be thought of as the true
semantic descriptions of words, we think that a dictionary using multiple features
would be useful in that it can be handled by existing natural language processing
techniques, and can handle various multi-dimensional thesauri.

If such a dictionary is constructed, it would be convenient for meaning sort,
since it would allow users to do interest-based meaning sort.

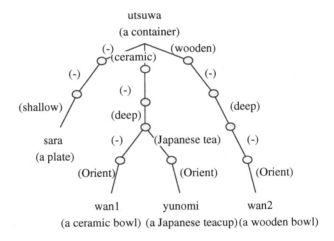

Fig. 2. Hierarchical thesaurus of meaning sort
from the rightmost feature

4   Three Examples of Using an Msort

In this section, we describe three major applications for which an Msort is useful.

4.1   Dictionary Construction

Table 9 shows the construction of a case frame for the verb *eat* according to data
in a noun-verb relational dictionary as an example. The table shows the results
of an Msort of NPs which may be taken as case elements of *eat*. It is easy to
manually construct a case-frame dictionary from such data, as shown in Table 9.
The nominative case of *eat* consists of agents, such as animals and people, and
the objective case consists of various NPs mainly meaning foods. Regarding the
optional case, various phrases such as *by myself*, *in an office*, and *in a meeting*
are also included.

The construction of a verbal case-frame dictionary is one example of the
potential applications of an Msort. A similar construction process can also be
easily applied to copulas and other kinds of relationships among words. An Msort
is not only useful for constructing dictionaries, but also for examining data and
extracting important information in language investigation. An Msort is also
useful for examining data in the process of knowledge acquisition.

4.2   Tagged Corpus Construction (Related to Semantic Similarity)

Recently, various corpora have been under construction [6, 1, 4, 11], and the investigation of corpus-based learning algorithms is attracting much attention [8].

Table 9. Example construction of a case frame of the verb *eat*

(a) Results of an Msort of terms in the nominative case

(Animal)	cattle, a calf, fish
(Human)	we, us, all, myself, babies, a parent, a sister, a customer, a Japanese, a nurse, a writer

(b) Results of an Msort of terms in the objective case

(Animal)	an animal, shellfish, plankton
(Product)	prey, a product, a material, food, feed, Japanese food, Japanese-style food, Western food, Chinese food, a rice ball, gruel, sushi, Chinese noodles, macaroni, sandwiches, a pizza, a steak, a barbecued dish, tempura, fried food, cereals, rice, white rice, Japanese rice, barley, kimchi, sugar, jam, a confection, a cake, a cookie, ice cream
(Body part)	the mortal remains, the liver
(Plant)	a gene, a plant, grass, a sweet pepper, chicory, a mulberry, a banana, a matsutake mushroom, kombu
(Phenomenon)	a delicate flavor, snow
(Relation)	the content
(Activity)	breakfast, lunch, dinner, supper

(c) Results of an Msort of terms in the optional cases
(In Japanese, "in", "on", and "by" are expressed by
the same word, so, we cannot divide data according to "in" or "by")

(Human)	(by) myself
(Organization)	(in) an office, (in) a restaurant, (in) a hotel
(Product)	(by) soy sauce, (in) a dressing room, (in) bed, (on) a table
(Location)	(on) the spot, (in) the whole area, (on) a train
(Quantity)	(by) two persons, (at) a rate, (by) many people
(Activity)	(at) work, (in) a meeting

In this section, we demonstrate how an Msort can be useful in the construction of corpora.

Suppose that we want to disambiguate the meanings of *of* in NP X *of* NP Y by using the example-based method [9]. In this case, we need a tagged corpus for semantic analysis of the noun phrases in NP X *of* NP Y. We attach semantic relationships such as *Part-of* and *Location* to each example of the noun phrases. When we do an Msort of these phrases, similar examples are grouped together and the tagging of semantic relationships by hand is made easier.

Table 10 shows part of a manually tagged corpus. In this example we have supposed that NP X in NP X *of* NP Y will be the more important NP, so we first did an Msort of NP X, and then did one of NP Y. Although the technical terms representing the semantic relationships in the table are specialized, it can be seen that the examples which are grouped together by this Msort often have

Table 10. Construction of a manually tagged corpus for the semantic analysis of noun phrases in "NP X of NP Y"

NP X	NP Y	Semantic Relation
an affair	Panama	Location
an affair	a junior high school	Location
an affair	an army	Location
an affair	an album	Indirect-determiner
an affair	a tanker	Indirect-determiner
an affair	the worst	Adjective-feature
an affair	the largest	Adjective-feature
a property	the circumference	Location
items	both countries	Object-agent
items	documentary records	Field-determiner
items	a general meeting	Object-agent
a provision	the Upper House	Field-determiner
a provision	a new law	Field-determiner
a provision	a treaty	Field-determiner
a provision	an agreement	Field-determiner

the same relationship. Also, when semantically similar examples are grouped together like this, the cost of tagging is decreased.

In the example-based method, the tag attached to the example that is the most similar to the input phrase is judged to be the result of the analysis. An Msort performs the function of grouping similar examples. The example-based method and the Msort both use word similarity, and this is an advantage of both techniques.

In this section, we noted that using the Msort is an efficient way to construct a noun-phrase corpus. In addition, when a certain corpus uses words, we can also use an Msort for the construct of it.

4.3   Information Retrieval

Information retrieval activity has increased with the growth of the Internet. An Msort can also easily be applied to this area.

For example, in research conducted by Tsuda and Senda, the features of a document database were displayed to users by using multiple keywords [13]. For example, assume that the document database we want to display has the following set of keywords.

> retrieval, a word, a document, construction, candidate, a number, a keyword

Displaying the list of words in a random order is not very convenient for users. However, if we do an Msort of the keywords, we can obtain the following list:

(Quantity)	a number
(Abstract relation)	candidate
(Human activity)	retrieval
	a document, a keyword, a word,
	construction

(Here, we have displayed words with the same first three-digit BGH category number on the same line.) This method provides a more useful perspective for users.

In some cases we may display many keywords and ask the users to select the appropriate ones [13]. In such a case, if we do not have another way of arranging the words in an appropriate order, it is convenient for users if we use an Msort.

5   Conclusion

In summary, we have introduced a useful method of arranging words semantically and shown how to implement it by using thesauri. We gave three major examples of the applications of an Msort (dictionary construction, tagged corpus construction, and information presentation).

Since there is no doubt that a word list in a meaning-order is easier to use than a word list in a random-order, the Msort, which can easily produce a word list in a meaning-order, must be useful and effective.

The Msort is a very useful tool for natural language processing, and NLP research can be made more efficient by applying it.

References

[1] EDR. *EDR Electronic Dictionary Technical Guide.* EDR (Japan Electronic Dictionary Research Institute, Ltd.), 1993.

[2] IPA. (Information–Technology Promotion Agency, Japan). *IPA Lexicon of the Japanese Language for Computers IPAL (Basic Verbs)*, 1987. (in Japanese).

[3] Kazumi Kawamura and Masahiro Miyazaki. Multi-dimensional thesaurus with various facets. In *Information Processing Society of Japan, the 48th National Convention, 3Q-2*, pages 75–76, 1994. (in Japanese).

[4] Sadao Kurohashi and Makoto Nagao. Kyoto University text corpus project. pages 115–118, 1997. (in Japanese).

[5] P.N. Johnson Laird. *Mental models.* Cambridge Univ. Press, 1983.

[6] Mitchell P. Marcus, Beatrice Santorini, and Mary Ann Marcinkiewicz. Building a large annotated corpus of English: the Penn Treebank. *Computational Linguistics*, 19(2):310–330, 1993.

[7] Kenichi Murata, Naoko Ishida, Ryoya Okabe, Masaki Hosoi, Wakako Kashino, and Hajime Iizuka. R&D for IPAL (SURFACE/DEEP). *Proceedings of the 17th IPA Technological Meeting*, pages 149–158, 1998. (in Japanese).

[8] Masaki Murata, Kiyotaka Uchimoto, Qing Ma, and Hitoshi Isahara. Bunsetsu identification using category-exclusive rules. In *COLING 2000*, pages 565–571, 2000.

[9] Makoto Nagao. A Framework of a Mechanical Translation between Japanese and English by Analogy Principle. *Artificial and Human Intelligence*, pages 173–180, 1984.

[10] NLRI. (National Language Research Institute). *Word List by Semantic Principles*. Syuei Syuppan, 1964. (in Japanese).

[11] RWC. RWC text database, second edition. (in Japanese), 1998.

[12] John R. Taylor. *Linguistic Categorization*. Oxford University Press, 1989.

[13] Koji Tsuda and Shuuji Senda. Query formulation support by automatically generated term-to-term links. In *Information Processing Society of Japan, the 48th National Convention, 4E-6*, pages 157–158, 1994. (in Japanese).

Converting Morphological Information Using Lexicalized and General Conversion

Mitsuo Shimohata and Eiichiro Sumita

ATR Spoken Language Translation Research Laboratories
{mshimoha,sumita}@slt.atr.co.jp

Abstract. Today, many kinds of tagged corpora are available for research use. Often a different morphological system is used in each corpus. This makes it difficult to merge different types of morphological
information, since conversion between different systems is complex and
necessitates a understanding of both systems.
This paper describes a method of converting morphological information
between two different systems by using lexicalized and general conversion. The difference between lexicalized and general conversion is the
existence or absence of a lexicalized condition. Which conversion is applied depends on the frequency of segments.

1 Introduction

Corpus-based NLP research is becoming more and more active with the increase
in the available number of text corpora. Large corpora are necessary for research
on statistical methods. In the Japanese language, tagged corpora such as the Kyodai corpus [Kurohashi 1997], the RWC corpus [Isahara 1997], the ATR Dialog
Database [Morimoto 1994], and the EDR [EDR 1995] corpus are available.

Since these corpora are each tagged using a different morphological system, it
is necessary to convert morphological information, e.g., part of speech (POS) and
conjugation, to use any combination of the corpora together. However, because
there are large differences between the morphological system, it is laborious to
make conversion rules by hand. In the English language, the AMALGAM project
[AMALGAM] has been investigating and developing methods of automatic mapping between a range of different syntactic annotation schemes.

In this paper, we describe a method of converting morphological information between different morphological systems. In order to disambiguate target
[1] information, we use decision tree learning, giving the information of the morpheme to be converted [2] and neighboring morphemes as features. Decision tree
learning allows target information to be estimated when some values of features
are unknown. A corpus with morphological information of two systems is used
for training data.

---

[1] "source" is converted to "target".

[2] We refer to this morpheme as the "focus morpheme".

A. Gelbukh (Ed.): CICLing 2001, LNCS 2004, pp. 319–331, 2001.

Our conversion method features lexicalized conversion and general conversion. Which conversion is selected depends on the frequency of segments. Lexicalized conversion has a lexicalized condition in its rules and is applied only to frequent morphemes. General conversion has no lexicalized condition and can be applied to any morphemes.

Morphological information conversion enables not only the conversion of tagged corpora but also the utilization of a morphological analyzer for tagging in other morphological systems. It can be easily implemented by attaching a conversion process to the end of a morphological analyzer.

2 Problems in Morphological Information Conversion

There are two major problems in converting morphological information. One is ambiguity in target information. That is many POS in a source system can take various POS in the target system. The other problem involves at word boundaries. Since word boundaries do not appear in the Japanese language and there is no universal policy on word separation, each system has its own policy on word separation. Methods for resolving these problems are described below.

Table 1. POS correspondences between the Kyodai corpus and the RWC corpus

Kyodai	RWC (THiMCO)								
(JUMAN)	*noun*	*verb*	*adj.*	*adv.*	*prt.*	*aux.*	*adn.*	*conj.*	*pref.*	*interj.*
noun	305,088	637	23	283	215	13	18	10	1,942	-
verb	508	47,978	57	146	81	28	45	34	5	1
adj.	886	9	7,881	298	4	33	315	1	1	-
adv.	3,006	19	9	7,558	10	-	4	386	37	-
prt.	203	69	-	56	232,881	499	-	200	-	-
aux.	774	2	3	1	243	1,614	-	-	-	-
adn.	1	24	3	2	1	1	713	-	3	-
conj.	5	4	-	22	-	-	-	3,265	-	1
pref.	351	2	-	-	-	-	1,027	-	4,023	-
interj.	32	4	-	2	-	-	-	29	-	10
demo.	2,584	3	-	802	-	-	4,580	23	-	-
cop.	4	6	-	-	997	3,958	-	-	-	-
suf.	30,935	14,563	1392	-	144	6,935	-	-	187	-

2.1 Ambiguity in Target POS

When two different morphological systems are compared, it is often the case that the same POS between the two systems do not represent the same concepts, or specific POS exist on both systems. Table 1 shows POS correspondences between the Kyodai corpus and the RWC corpus (the details of both corpora are given in Sect. 4).

The Kyodai corpus is tagged in the JUMAN system, and the RWC corpus is tagged in the THiMCO system. The POS common to both corpora are the noun(*noun*), verb(*verb*), adjective(*adj.*), adverb(*adv.*), particle(*prt.*), auxiliary verb(*aux.*), adnominal(*adn.*), conjunction(*conj.*), prefix(*pref.*) and interjection (*interj.*) The Kyodai corpus has specific POS, i.e., demonstrative(*demo.*), copula(*cop.*) and suffix(*suf.*).

In seven of the 10 common POS, cases that use the same POS in both systems occur frequently. In particular, *prt.* represents that both systems have similar concepts; the other correspondences rarely occur. However, the POS with the highest correspondence in the THiMCO system *adn.* is not *adn.* but *demo.* in the JUMAN system. Suffixes in the JUMAN system have a broad concept. Suffixes correspond to *noun*, *verb*, *adj.*, and *aux.* parts in the THiMCO system. In our conversion method, the POS and conjugation of focus morphemes and the POS of neighboring morphemes are used for disambiguating the target POS.

2.2 Discrepancies at Word Boundaries

Discrepancies at word boundaries pose a difficult problem. More specifically, some source words must be lengthened and others shortened, and these length changes must be consistent. To avoid this problem, conversion is performed by not "word" but "segment". A segment is a part of a text separated by word boundaries; this is common to both systems. Word boundary changes are confined to segments, and the source and target segments do not differ in length. A segment contains one morpheme or several morphemes. An example of segment division is shown in Fig. 1. The text in the figure is divided into five segments.

	Seg.1	Seg.2	Seg.3	Seg.4	Seg.5
JUMAN	全国 | *noun*	的に | *suffix*	拡大 | *noun*	して | *verb*	きた | *suffix*
THiMCO	全国 | *noun*	的 - に | *noun - prt.*	拡大 | *noun*	し - て | *verb - prt.*	き - た | *verb - aux.*

Fig. 1. Example of Division into Segments

Segments 2, 4, and 5 contain one morpheme in the JUMAN system(source) and two morphemes in the THiMCO system(target). We call segments containing multiple morphemes "MM-segments". These word boundary differences are converted by the segment conversion. An example of an MM-morpheme conversion rule including a word boundary changes is shown in Fig. 2.

source seg. : して (*verb*)   ⟹   target seg. : し (*verb*) + て (*prt.*)

Fig. 2. Conversion Rule Including a Word Boundary Change

3   Conversion Method

Although there is wide diversity in the POS correspondences shown in Table 1, most individual segments [3] in a source system have only one or two kinds in the target system. Therefore, it is effective for conversion rules to involve lexicalization. In other words, it is effective for conversion to be done for each segment.

For statistic confidence, sufficient data is needed for the generation of rules. Accordingly, the lexicalized conversion rule is applied only to frequent segments. Infrequent segments are integrated as general data and one decision tree is generated for these segments. We call this general conversion. General conversion contains no lexicalized condition. Lexicalized conversion and general conversion are partitioned by a frequency threshold(i.e., frequency of segments).

The rule generation and conversion procedures are shown in Fig. 3. A corpus that includes the morphological information of the two systems is used for the generation of rules. Each text is divided into segments, and then morphological information of the focus segment and neighboring words is collected.

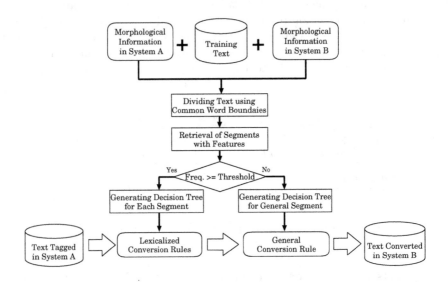

Fig. 3. Learning Process of Conversion Rules

---

[3] A segment is distinguished by its POS and literal. For example, the segment "book(*noun*)" is different from the segment "book (*verb*)".

After segments are retrieved, they are classified by their frequency. Lexicalized conversion is applied to these segments occurring more than the frequency threshold, and general conversion is applied to those segments occurring less than the threshold. In both conversions, C5.0 [C5.0] is used for the decision tree generation. Once decision trees are generated, any text with source morphological information can be converted by the lexicalized conversion and general conversion. The lexicalized conversion is precedent to the general conversion. First, the lexicalized conversion is applied to the text. Then, the general conversion is applied to segments unable to convert in the lexicalized conversion phase.

In the latter, the converting information is focused on the coarse POS classes displayed in Table 1. Unimportant POS, such as punctuation and symbol are ignored.

3.1   Lexicalized Conversion

In lexicalized conversion, frequent segments are converted individually. This provides for more accurate conversion and enables MM-segment conversion including word boundary changes. Lexicalized conversion has a lexicalized condition. A training case of segment 3 from Fig. 1 is shown in Fig. 4.

Features				Class
-2 POS	-1 POS	+1 POS	+2 POS	Target POS
noun	*suf.*	*verb*	*noun*	*noun*

Fig. 4. Training Case for Segment "拡大 (*noun*)"

A training case of MM-segment 4 in Fig. 1 is shown in Fig. 5. The class value is lexicalized to reserve the word boundary.

Features				Class
-2 POS	-1 POS	+1 POS	+2 POS	Target Segment
suf.	*noun*	*suf.*	EOS[4]	"し (*verb*)" + "て (*prt.*)"

Fig. 5. Training Case for Segment "して (*verb*)"

---

[4] EOS means "End of Sentence".

3.2 General Conversion

Infrequent segments are gathered together and converted by one decision tree. The generated tree does not contain the above lexical conditions, and accordingly, unseen segments in the training data can be applied. A training case from Table 1 and other cases of *noun* conversion are shown in Figure 6. Lexical information is omitted in all features and the conjugation of the focus segment is added to the features. This method can only be applied to segments containing one morpheme, since the relaxation of all literal conditions for MM-segments may cause over-application of conversion rules.

Features						Class
-2 POS	-1 POS	Focus POS	Focus Conjugation	+1 POS	+2 POS	Target POS
noun	*suf.*	*noun*	N/A[5]	*verb*	*suf.*	*noun*
noun	*noun*	*prt.*	N/A	*noun*	*noun*	*noun*
noun	*prt.*	*noun*	N/A	*verb*	*noun*	*noun*

Fig. 6. Training Cases of General Conversion

4 Experiment

In our experiment, the Kyodai corpus and the RWC corpus are used. The Kyodai corpus was released from the Nagao Laboratory of Kyoto University. The latest version (3.0) was released in 2000. This corpus has 2,929 articles from the Mainichi Newspaper that include morphological information and sentence structures. This information was manually verified.

The RWC corpus was released from the RWCP (Real World Computing Partnership). This corpus has morphological information tagged in the THiMCO system. Since the tagging was done by machine processing, the corpus may contain more tagging errors and unknown words than the Kyodai corpus.

The experiment utilizes 2,928 common articles in both corpora. The data specification are shown in Table 2. It should be noted that 831 words tagged as *undefined* in the RWC corpus are excluded from the experiment. We set the JUMAN system as the source system and the THiMCO system as the target system.

4.1 Lexicalized Conversion

In lexicalized conversion, the frequency threshold has a great influence on the conversion accuracy. The relation between the frequency and accuracy is shown

---

[5] The value N/A means "Not Applicable".

Table 2. Text Data Specifications

Articles	2,928
Sentences	39,065
Segments	923,305
Single-Morpheme Seg.	807,961

	Kyodai	RWC
# of Total Morpheme	946,529	1,026,892
# of Different Morpheme	42,698	34,968

in Table 3. Accuracy only concerns ambiguous cases. Ambiguous segments in the source system occupy only a small ratio compared with the total number of segments.

Table 3. Accuracy of Lexicalized Conversion

Frequency of Segments	Segment		Cases			
	Total	Ambig.[6]	Total	(Ambig. :	Error :	Accuracy)
∼ 1,000	34	10	278,718	(105,522 :	527 :	99.5%)
999 ∼ 500	40	11	27,308	(7,934 :	190 :	97.6%)
499 ∼ 100	736	80	137,914	(16,796 :	567 :	96.6%)
99 ∼ 50	877	92	60,432	(6,161 :	386 :	93.7%)
49 ∼ 10	5,262	358	109,506	(7,664 :	888 :	88.4%)

As the frequency of segments falls, the accuracy decreases. Compared with the accuracy of general conversion (described in Sect. 4.2), the lexicalized conversion applied to segments with a frequency of less than 100 shows little improvement. From this finding, the threshold is fixed to 100 in the following experiment.

The correspondence between the converted and the correct target POS is shown in Table 4. This correspondence is evaluated by 2-fold cross validation. POS not described in the table are out of the range of evaluation. The table shows that *prt.* and *noun* occupy large parts. The accuracy of the lexicalized conversion is 99.8%.

The conversion of MM-segments is not shown in Table 4. MM-segments that occur with a frequency of more than 100 constitute 34 kinds and 8,790 cases. The MM-segment conversion accuracy is 98.1%.

---

[6] Ambig. means "Ambiguity" that has two or more target POS.

Table 4. Correspondences in Lexicalized Conversion

Correct Target POS	Converted POS									
	noun	*adj.*	*pref.*	*interj.*	*adn.*	*conj.*	*prt.*	*adv.*	*verb*	*aux.*
noun	116,900	8	134	-	5	-	35	30	19	-
adj.	1	3,975	-	-	-	-	-	-	-	24
pref.	148	-	3,390	-	42	-	-	-	-	-
interj.	0	-	-	-	-	-	-	-	-	-
adn.	7	-	-	-	5,571	-	-	-	13	-
conj.	3	-	-	-	-	2,225	17	-	-	-
prt.	15	-	-	-	-	-	237,638	7	2	3
adv.	34	-	-	-	-	9	3	2,001	-	-
verb	12	4	-	-	2	-	66	-	34,470	7
aux.	0	27	-	-	-	-	279	-	29	11,592

4.2   General Conversion

In the general conversion, one decision tree is generated from the collected data. POS correspondences between converted POS and correct target POS are shown in Table 5. This correspondence is evaluated by 2-fold cross validation. The conversion accuracy is 97.4%. A part of the generated conversion rules is shown in the appendix.

Table 5. Correspondence in General Conversion

Correct Target POS	Converted POS									
	noun	*adj.*	*pref.*	*interj.*	*adn.*	*conj.*	*prt.*	*adv.*	*verb*	*aux.*
noun	225,908	158	134	1	11	27	175	1,206	392	3
adj.	102	4,970	-	-	3	-	-	8	281	5
pref.	1,448	-	1,135	-	3	-	-	29	2	-
interj.	1	-	-	1	-	8	-	-	2	-
adn.	33	24	-	-	1,004	-	-	18	30	-
conj.	17	-	-	2	5	1,093	157	421	7	-
prt.	381	3	-	-	1	28	1,244	10	69	1
adv.	711	114	1	-	79	20	25	6,187	34	-
verb	751	7	2	-	24	9	2	20	27,943	8
aux.	21	7	-	-	1	-	7	2	30	1,089

There are 37 words tagged *undefined* in the Kyodai corpus. Although these *undefined* words essentially have no information, it is noteworthing that the conversion can also involve *undefined* words. The conversion rule concerning *undefined* words is also shown in the Appendix. Words tagged as unknown can appear in machine processed tagging text. The general conversion enables the conversion of unknown words using neighboring POS.

4.3   Combined Conversion

Combined conversion consists of lexicalized conversion and general conversion. A coverage of the lexicalized conversion for each POS is shown in Fig. 7.

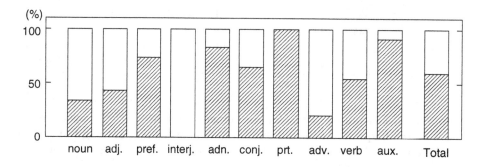

Fig. 7. Coverage of Lexicalized Conversion and General Conversion

The hatched regions indicate ratios of lexicalized conversion to combined conversion, and the white regions ratios of general conversion to combined conversion. As the figure shows, the lexicalized conversion has great coverage of *prt.* and *aux.* because of their narrow lexicons and frequent use, while it has small coverage of *noun* and *adv.* Since *intj.* words rarely occur in newspapers, the lexicalized conversion does not work with them. 418,747 segments are converted by lexicalized conversion and 277,655 by general conversion. The ratio of lexicalized conversion to combined conversion is 60.1%.

POS correspondences in combined conversion are shown in Table 6. This table is a summation of Tables 4 and 5. The combined conversion accuracy is 98.8%. For every segment, including MM-segments, punctuations, and symbols, conversion accuracy falls to 87.7%. This drop is caused by infrequent MM-segments. Measures for these segments are discussed in the following section.

5   Discussion

The accuracies of lexicalized conversion, general conversion, and combined conversion are, respectively, 99.8%, 97.4%, and 98.8%. The lexicalized conversion contributes to the accuracy and the general conversion works for the conversion of infrequent words. In the experiment, the lexicalized conversion was found to

Table 6. Correspondences in Combined Conversion

Correct Target POS	Converted POS									
	noun	*adj.*	*pref.*	*interj.*	*adn.*	*conj.*	*prt.*	*adv.*	*verb*	*aux.*
noun	342,808	166	268	1	16	27	210	1,236	411	3
adj.	103	8,945	-	-	3	-	-	8	281	29
pref.	1,596	-	4,525	-	45	-	-	29	2	-
interj.	1	-	-	1	-	8	-	-	2	-
adn.	40	24	-	-	6,575	-	-	18	43	-
conj.	20	-	-	2	5	3,318	174	421	7	-
prt.	396	3	-	-	1	28	238,882	17	71	4
adv.	745	114	1	-	79	29	28	8,188	34	-
verb	763	11	2	-	26	9	68	20	62,413	15
aux.	21	34	-	-	1	-	286	2	59	12,681

cover 60.1% of the all segments. This coverage by the lexicalized conversion depends on the frequency threshold and the given corpus size. If the given corpus size were half and the frequency threshold were to remain at 100, the coverage would drop to almost half.

Our conversion method cannot be applied to infrequent MM-segments at present, since it requires both a relaxation of the rule conditions and word boundary changes. An easy measure is to decrease the frequency threshold. This measure extends the range of MM-segments to be converted. On the other hand, a lower threshold can cause the inclusion of worse lexicalized conversion rules and a decrease in the training data for the general conversion. The threshold must therefore be carefully determined.

The above mentioned measure has no effect on MM-segments not appearing in the training data. A partial relaxation of the lexical information may be an essential measure. In the case of the conversion rule for MM-segments having two morphemes, if the lexical condition of either morpheme can be eliminated, the application range of this rule could be expanded widely. We would like to consider this measure in the future.

6   Related Work

Tashiro [Tashiro 1994] and Inui [Inui 1999] previously reported the conversion of morphological information in Japanese. In Tashiro's method, the generated rules do not use information about neighboring morphemes and they are lexicalized. Therefore, such rules cannot be applied to morphemes unseen in the training corpus, even if the POS are known. To cope with these morphemes, rules with partially relaxed lexical conditions have to be made by hand. However, morphemes in which both the POS and literals are unknown cannot be converted at all.

In Inui's method, there is no lexicalized condition in the conversion rules. Large ambiguities are solved using the sentence structure of the source text and the grammar of the target system. This requires considerable resources, such as a dictionary and a POS connection matrix in the target system. This method cannot be applied to conversions involving moves or the elimination of word boundaries.

Focusing on estimating POS using neighboring word information, Brill's transformation-based error driven learning [Brill 1994] is a similar work to ours. Error correction is done by applying many transformation templates. The templates use the conditions of neighboring words, and the conditions can use POS or specific words. The error correction accuracy is 97.2%.

Zavrel and Daelemans [Zavrel 1997] also describe estimating the POS of unknown words from neighboring words. Their main aim is the analysis of the relation between the use of similarity in memory-based learning and back-off smoothing. Estimation is done by the k-nearest neighboring classifier algorithm. The first letter of an unknown word, the last three letters and POS of the neighboring word are used as features. The effective features are the last letter, the POS of the previous words, and the first letter, in that order. The above two works use partial literal information as a condition. Such a condition can also be applied to our method.

7   Conclusion

In this paper, we describe a method of converting morphological information between different systems. We introduce lexicalized conversion and general conversion, where the difference between them is in the existence or absence of a lexicalized condition. The conversion of each segment depends on its frequency. The conversion accuracy combining lexicalized conversion and general conversion is 98.8%.

This accuracy can change considerably due to the characteristics of the source and target systems. We therefore plan on conducting experiments on various morphological systems and various texts. We believe this method can be applied to other languages. We also plan on conducting experiments involving other languages.

References

[Kurohashi 1997] Kurohashi S, Nagao M: Kyoto University Text Corpus Project. In *Proceedings of the 11th Annual Conference of JSAI 1997* (in Japanese). (1997) pp. 58-61

[Isahara 1997] Isahara Hitoshi: Development of Text Corpora In *Proceedings of the 11th Annual Conference of JSAI 1997* (in Japanese). (1997) pp. 54-57

[Morimoto 1994] Morimoto T, et al.: A speech and language database for speech translation research In *proceedings of ICSLP*. (1994) pp. 1791-1794

[EDR 1995] EDR (Japan Electronic Dictionary Research Institute Ltd.): The EDR Electronic Dictionary Technical Guide. In *EDR Technical Report* (in Japanese). (1995)

[AMALGAM] http://www.scs.leeds.ac.uk/amalgam/amalgam/amalghome.htm

[C5.0] http://www.rulequest.com/see5-info.html

[Tashiro 1994] Tashiro T, Morimoto T: Restructuring tagged corpora with morpheme adjustment rules In *Proceedings of COLING.* (1994) 569-573

[Inui 1999] Inui K, Wakigawa H: A POS-tag Conversion Algorithm for Reusing Corpora. In *Proceedings of NLPRS.* (1999) 56-61

[Brill 1994] Brill E: Transformation-Based Error-Driven Learning and Natural Language Processing In *Computational Linguistics Vol21,No.4* (1995) pp. 543-565

[Zavrel 1997] Jakub Zavrel, Walter Daelemans: Memory-Based Learning: Using Similarity for Smoothing. In *Proceedings of ACL-1997.* (1997) 436-443

Appendix

Conversion Rule from the JUMAN System to the THiMCO System

Source	Target POS
• POS = noun	⇒ noun
• POS = adn.	⇒ adn.
• POS = conj.	⇒ conj.
• POS = prt.	⇒ particle
• POS = verb	⇒ verb
• POS = pref.	
+1 word = pref.	⇒ noun
+1 word = EOS	⇒ adn.
+1 word = else	⇒ pref.
• POS = Cop.	
+1 word = verb or prt. or adj. or suf.	⇒ aux.
+1 word = cop.	⇒ noun
+1 word = else	⇒ cop.
• POS = undefined	
-1 word = verb	⇒ verb
-1 word = symbol	
-2 word = noun or suf.	⇒ prt.
-2 word = verb	⇒ pref.
-2 word = else	⇒ noun
-1 word = noun	
-2 word = symbol	⇒ noun
-2 word = else	⇒ aux.
-1 word = else	⇒ noun

Zipf and Heaps Laws' Coefficients Depend on Language[*]

Alexander Gelbukh and Grigori Sidorov

Center for Computing Research (CIC), National Polytechnic Institute (IPN),
Av. Juan Dios Batiz s/n esq. Mendizabal, col. Zacatenco, CP 07738, DF, Mexico.
{gelbukh, sidorov}@cic.ipn.mx

Abstract. We observed that the coefficients of two important empirical statistical laws of language – Zipf law and Heaps law – are different for different languages, as we illustrate on English and Russian examples. This may have both theoretical and practical implications. On the one hand, the reasons for this may shed light on the nature of language. On the other hand, these two laws are important in, say, full-text database design allowing predicting the index size.

Introduction. Perhaps the most famous statistical distribution in linguistics is Zipf law [1, 2]: in any large enough text, the frequency ranks (starting from the highest) of wordforms or lemmas are inversely proportional to the corresponding frequencies:[1]

$$\log f_r \approx C - z \log r \tag{1}$$

where f_i is the frequency of the unit (wordform or lemma) having the rank r, z is the exponent coefficient (near to 1), and C is a constant. In a logarithmic scale, it is a straight line with about $-45°$ angle.

Another, less famous but probably not less important empirical statistical law of language is the Heaps law: the number of different wordforms or lemmas in a text is roughly proportional to an exponent of its size:

$$\log n_i \approx D + h \log i \tag{2}$$

where n_i is the number of different units (wordforms or lemmas) occurring before the running word number i, h is the exponent coefficient (between 0 and 1), and D is a constant. In a logarithmic scale, it is a straight line with about $45°$ angle.

The nature of these laws is not clear. They seem to be specific for natural languages in contrast to other types of signals [3]. In practice, knowing the coefficients of these laws is important in, for example, full-text database design, since it allows predicting some properties of the index as a function of the size of the database.

In this paper, we present the data that show that the coefficients of both laws – z and h – depend on language. For our experiments, we use English and Russian texts. Experiments with Spanish (which we do not discuss here) gave the results between those for English and Russian.

---

[*] The work was done under partial support of CONACyT, REDII, and SNI, Mexico. We thank Prof. R. Baeza-Yates, Prof. E. Atwell, and Prof. I. Bolshakov for useful discussion.

[1] We ignore Mandelbrot's improvements to Zipf law [1] since they do not affect our discussion.

A. Gelbukh (Ed.): CICLing 2001, LNCS 2004, pp. 332–335, 2001.

Experimental Results. We processed 39 literature texts for each language, see Appendix 2, chosen randomly from different genres, with the requirement that the size be greater than 10,000 running words (100 KB); total of 2.5 million running words (24.8 MB) for English and 2.0 million (20.2 MB) for Russian.

We experimented with wordforms and lemmas, with very similar results. We plotted on the screen the graphs for pairs of texts (one English and one Russian), using for Zipf law the points: $x_r = \log r$, $y_i = \log f_r$ ($x_i = \log i$, $y_i = \log n_i$ for Heaps law). The difference in the angle was in most cases clearly visible.

We used linear regression to approximate such a graph by a straight line $y = ax + b$, where a and b correspond to $-z$ and C for Zipf law, or h and D for Heaps law. Since the density of the points (x_i, y_i) increases exponentially with x_i, we scaled the distance penalty for regression by c^{-x_i} (we have to omit here the details; obviously, the results do not depend on c), which gave the following formulae for a and b:

$$p = \sum_i \frac{x_i}{c^{x_i}}, \quad s = \sum_i \frac{x_i^2}{c^{x_i}}, \quad t = \sum_i \frac{y_i}{c^{x_i}}, \quad u = \sum_i \frac{1}{c^{x_i}}, \quad b = \frac{p\sum_i \frac{x_i y_i}{c^{x_i}} - st}{p^2 - su}, \quad a = \frac{t - bu}{p}.$$

Visual control proved that these weighted formulae approximate the graphs much better than the standard linear regression ones. The results are shown in Appendix 1 (ordered by z); we give the values of z (Zipf, on wordforms) and h (Heaps, on lemmas) and omit C and D since they are less important. The difference between the two languages is obvious. For English $z = 0.97 \pm 0.06$ and for Russian $z = 0.89 \pm 0.07$, the difference being 8.3% (as a measure of precision, we use 3σ, where σ is the standard deviation); for English $h = 0.79 \pm 0.05$ and for Russian $h = 0.84 \pm 0.06$, the difference being 5.9%.

Discussion. Two properties of the languages in question might be involved in the explanation of this phenomenon. First, Russian is a highly inflective language while English is analytical. Our experiments with Spanish seem to favor this consideration: Spanish, having "inflectivity" intermediate between Russian and English, showed intermediate results as to the coefficients. On the other hand, counting lemmas instead of wordforms nearly did not change our results. Second, it is well known that lexical richness of Russian is greater than that of English (and Spanish).

Conclusions. Exponential coefficients of Zipf and Heaps laws depend on language. This can have both theoretical and practical implications (the latter, for example, in full-text database design). Explanation of this phenomenon needs more investigation.

References

1. Manning, C. D. and Shutze, H. Foundations of statistical natural language processing. Cambridge, MA, The MIT press, 1999, 680 p.
2. Zipf, G. K. Human behavior and the principle of least effort. Cambridge, MA, Addison-Wesley, 1949.
3. Elliott J, Atwell, E, and Whyte B. Language identification in unknown signals. In COLING'2000, ACL and Morgan Kaufmann Publishers, 2000, p. 1021-1026.

Appendix 1. Experimental Results

English				Russian			
Text	Genre	Zipf	Heaps	Text	Genre	Zipf	Heaps
1	detective	1.037639	0.759330	1	children	0.936576	0.787141
2	adventure	1.004620	0.788285	2	novel	0.935878	0.825040
3	novel	0.999033	0.794793	3	novel	0.929603	0.839364
4	novel	0.996945	0.777628	4	detective	0.928132	0.839518
5	detective	0.991697	0.793684	5	detective	0.924204	0.858930
6	detective	0.991656	0.784293	6	detective	0.917411	0.822190
7	adventure	0.991037	0.795032	7	adventure	0.916674	0.793264
8	novel	0.988051	0.801261	8	novel	0.912970	0.842878
9	SF/fantasy	0.984583	0.790036	9	novel	0.912406	0.822597
10	SF/fantasy	0.984467	0.798092	10	detective	0.909435	0.839980
11	novel	0.983066	0.800523	11	novel	0.908496	0.814065
12	SF/fantasy	0.982076	0.810374	12	novel	0.906881	0.838711
13	detective	0.982069	0.804559	13	SF/fantasy	0.903534	0.816362
14	detective	0.981934	0.806420	14	novel	0.902698	0.846717
15	novel	0.978492	0.815062	15	SF/fantasy	0.902272	0.842399
16	novel	0.978363	0.798223	16	children	0.901783	0.844565
17	detective	0.978101	0.809228	17	SF/fantasy	0.899720	0.821493
18	children	0.976800	0.742432	18	SF/fantasy	0.892304	0.853072
19	SF/fantasy	0.976773	0.784674	19	novel	0.890569	0.846493
20	adventure	0.971846	0.823809	20	novel	0.890088	0.859763
21	novel	0.971531	0.806512	21	detective	0.887773	0.838548
22	adventure	0.971082	0.792677	22	novel	0.886602	0.856025
23	novel	0.970900	0.794577	23	novel	0.884160	0.818838
24	novel	0.968299	0.803362	24	novel	0.883826	0.832264
25	children	0.968028	0.777983	25	detective	0.883621	0.872263
26	novel	0.967511	0.754915	26	children	0.883044	0.856513
27	novel	0.966305	0.778061	27	SF/fantasy	0.881713	0.848118
28	SF/fantasy	0.965116	0.794937	28	adventure	0.880597	0.834420
29	SF/fantasy	0.961867	0.813870	29	novel	0.879422	0.873361
30	novel	0.961286	0.799193	30	SF/fantasy	0.876683	0.858251
31	SF/fantasy	0.955980	0.803026	31	novel	0.874849	0.852379
32	SF/fantasy	0.955516	0.809863	32	detective	0.873471	0.830596
33	novel	0.954731	0.741586	33	detective	0.870795	0.876895
34	novel	0.952700	0.795840	34	novel	0.867954	0.871117
35	SF/fantasy	0.952088	0.780060	35	SF/fantasy	0.867008	0.870979
36	children	0.950748	0.771153	36	SF/fantasy	0.863004	0.841957
37	detective	0.948861	0.792331	37	adventure	0.859045	0.834773
38	SF/fantasy	0.948237	0.801813	38	detective	0.857402	0.850555
39	novel	0.930612	0.816378	39	SF/fantasy	0.839270	0.881458
	Average:	0.973863	0.792458		Average:	0.892869	0.842406
	$3 \times$ deviation:	0.057036	0.055954		$3 \times$ deviation:	0.068292	0.063054

For both Zipf and Heaps, levels of significance of difference are much better than 1%.

Appendix 2. Sources

The following texts were used for our experiments. The text number in Appendix 1 corresponds to the number in the corresponding list below.

English sources: 1. Arthur Conan Doyle. *Novels and Stories;* 2. Walter Scott. *Ivanhoe;* 3. Herman Melville. *Moby Dick;* 4. Harriet Beecher Stowe. *Uncle Tom's Cabin;* 5. Arthur Conan Doyle. *The Case Book of Sherlock Holmes;* 6. Arthur Conan Doyle. *The Memoirs of Sherlock Holmes;* 7. Edgar Rice Burroughs. *Tarzan of The Apes;* 8. Thomas Hardy. *Far from the Madding Crowd;* 9. Winn Schwartau. *Terminal Compromise;* 10. Anthony Hope. *The Prisoner of Zenda;* 11. Mark Twain. *Life on the Mississippi;* 12. Jules Verne. *From the Earth to the Moon;* 13. Arthur Conan Doyle. *His Last Bow;* 14. G. K. Chesterton. *The Innocence of Father Brown;* 15. Nathaniel Hawthorne. *The Scarlet Letter;* 16. Mark Twain. *The Adventures of Tom Sawyer;* 17. G. K. Chesterton. *The Wisdom of Father Brown;* 18. *Laddie. A True Blue Story;* 19. Richard J. Denissen. *The Europa Affair;* 20. Ambrose Bierce. *Can Such Things Be;* 21. Jules VERNE. *Around the World in Eighty Days;* 22. Edgar Rice Burroughs. *The Mucker;* 23. Arthur Conan Doyle. *Valley of Fear;* 24. Walter Scott. *Chronicles of the Canongate;* 25. R. Kipling. *The Jungle Book;* 26. Jane Austin. *Pride and Prejudice;* 27. D. H. Lawrence. *Sons and Lovers;* 28. Douglas K. Bell. *Jason the Rescuer;* 29. William Gibson. *Neuromancer;* 30. Baroness Orczy. *The Scarlet Pimpernel;* 31. Douglas Adams. *The Restaurant at the End of the Universe;* 32. Douglas K. Bell. *Van Gogh in Space;* 33. Mark Twain. *The Adventures of Huckleberry Finn;* 34. *Walden & on The Duty of Civil Disobedience;* 35. Lawrence Dworin. *Revolt of the Cyberslaves;* 36. Lucy Maud Montgomery. *Anne of Green Gables;* 37. Arthur Conan Doyle. *Hound of Baskervilles;* 38. Bruce Sterling. *The Hacker Crackdown;* 39. Nathaniel Hawthorne. *The House of the Seven Gables.*

Russian sources:[2] 1. Николай Носов. *Приключения Незнайки;* 2. Василий Аксенов. *Сборник;* 3. А.Солженицын. *Архипелаг ГУЛаг;* 4. Анатолий Степанов. *День гнева;* 5. Виктор Федоров, Виталий Щигельский. *Бенефис двойников;* 6. Юлиан Семенов. *Семнадцать мгновений весны;* 7. Генри Райдер Хаггард. *Дочь Монтесумы;* 8. Вл. Кунин. *Повести;* 9. Александр Покровский. *"...Расстрелять";* 10. Марина Наумова. *Констрикторы;* 11. Федор Достоевский. *Неточка Незванова;* 12. *Азюль;* 13. В. Пелевин. *Сборник рассказов и повестей;* 14. М. Горький. *Автобиографические рассказы;* 15. Сергей Михайлов. *Шестое чувство;* 16. Л. Лагин. *Старик Хоттабыч;* 17. Дмитрий Громов. *Сборник рассказов и повестей;* 18. Вячеслав Рыбаков. *Рассказы;* 19. Евгений Козловский. *Киносценарии и повести;* 20. Александр Мелихов. *Во имя четыреста первого, или Исповедь еврея;* 21. Андрей Курков. 22. Всеволод Иванов. *Голубые пески;* 23. Михаил Мишин. *Почувствуйте разницу;* 24. Андерй Платонов. *Котлован;* 25. Виктор Черняк. *Выездной!;* 26. Александр Некрасов. *Приключения капитана Врунгеля;* 27. Игорь Федоров. *Рассказы;* 28. Ульрих Комм. *Фрегаты идут на абордаж;* 29. Наталья Галкина. *Ночные любимцы;* 30. Б. Иванов, Ю. Щербатых. *Случай контрабанды;* 31. Владимир Набоков. *Рассказы;* 32. Виктор Суворов. *Аквариум;* 33. Виктор Черняк. *Жулье;* 34. Сергей Дышев. *До встречи в раю;* 35. Ник Перумов. *Рассказы, Русский меч;* 36. Антон Первушин. *Рассказы;* 37. Т. Майн Рид. *Американские партизаны;* 38. Михаил Болтунов. *"Альфа" - сверхсекретный отряд КГБ;* 39. Виталий Бабенко. *Игоряша "Золотая рыбка".*

---

[2] Since most of these titles do not have any standard English translations and many of the authors are not known outside Russia, we give the titles and names in Russian. Their understanding is not relevant for our discussion. The mixture roughly corresponds to English one.

Applying Productive Derivational Morphology to Term Indexing of Spanish Texts

Jesús Vilares[1], David Cabrero[2], and Miguel A. Alonso[1]

[1] Departamento de Computación, Universidad de La Coruña
Campus de Elviña s/n, 15071 La Coruña, Spain
jvilares@mail2.udc.es, alonso@dc.fi.udc.es
http://coleweb.dc.fi.udc.es/
[2] Escuela Superior de Ingeniería Informática, Universidad de Vigo
Edificio Politécnico, As Lagoas, 32004 Orense, Spain
cabrero@uvigo.es

Abstract. This paper deals with the application of natural language processing techniques to the field of information retrieval. To be precise, we propose the application of morphological families for single term conflation in order to reduce the linguistic variety of indexed documents written in Spanish. A system for automatic generation of morphological families by means of Productive Derivational Morphology is discussed. The main characteristics of this system are the use of a minimum of linguistic resources, a low computational cost, and the independence with respect to the indexing engine.

1 Introduction

Spanish is a very rich language in its lexis and its morphology. This implies that Spanish has a great productivity and flexibility in its word formation mechanisms by using productive morphology, preferring derivation to other mechanisms. So it could be interesting to use morphological families for single word terms conflation.

We can define a *morphological family* as a set of words obtained from the same morphological root through derivation mechanisms. It is expected that a basic semantic relationship will remain between the words. To obtain regular word formation patterns, the contribution of generative phonology and transformational-generative grammar let us to speak seriously of 'rules of formation'. Though this paradigm is not complete, it is a great advance in this area, and allows us to implement an automatic system for generation of morphological families with an acceptable degree of completeness and correction.

At this point, we must face one of the main problems of Natural Language Processing (NLP) in Spanish, the lack of available resources. Large tagged corpora, treebanks and advanced lexicons are not available. We will try to overcome these limitations by means of the development of a system using as few resources as possible and confronting this task from the lexical level.

A. Gelbukh (Ed.): CICLing 2001, LNCS 2004, pp. 336–348, 2001.
© Springer-Verlag Berlin Heidelberg 2001

Finally, we will use this system for *single word term conflation* in Information Retrieval (IR) tasks. We will look for simplicity, employing a minimum of linguistic resources (only a tagger which will provide both the part of speech and the lemma), and reducing as much as possible the computational cost. Furthermore, the system will be totally independent from the indexing engine.

2   Morphology and Word Formation

A morpheme may be defined as a 'minimal distinctive unit of grammar', a sub-unit of the 'word', which in grammatical terms cannot be meaningfully further subdivided [7]. Inflectional morphemes represent grammatical concepts such as gender —*tonto* (silly man), *tonta* (silly woman)—, person, mood, or time and tense —*canté* (I sang), *cantemos* (let's sing)—. On the other hand, we will speak of derivational morphemes when they effect a semantic change on the base and, often, also effecting a change of syntactic class —*aburrir* (to bore), *aburrimiento* (boredom)—. The common remaining element is known as the lexical morpheme or stem.

Morphemes preposed to the base are prefixes, and those postposed are suffixes. Additionally, Spanish affixes are conventionally considered to include infixes, elements which appear internally in the derivational structure —*humareda*, (cloud of smoke)—.

Traditionally, word formation has been divided into compounding and derivation. Compounding involves the combination of independent lexical units — *romper* (to break) + *corazón* (heart) → *rompecorazones* (heartbreaker)— and we speak of derivation when one of the components cannot stand on its own as an independent lexeme —*Marx* (Marx) $\overset{-ismo}{\longrightarrow}$ *marxismo* (Marxism)—, even if it bears significant semantic content —the suffix *-ismo* means "ideology, party, doctrine"—. In either case we are dealing with morphological procedures, the conjoining of individual morphemes or groups of morphemes into larger units forming complex lexemes. These new lexemes we obtain, can be, in their turn, bases for new word formation.

The morphemic structure of the word is fundamental to the analysis of the procedures of word formation. However, we must take into account that in Romance languages, Spanish in particular, it is the word itself rather than any of its morphemic components which produces the derivation. Most Spanish words have a structure such as this: *lexical morpheme + prefix or suffix*.

In addition to compounding and derivation, Spanish is characterized by the frequency of *parasynthesis*, involving the simultaneous prefixation and suffixation of the base lexeme:

$$rojo \text{ (red) } \overset{en- \ -ecer}{\longrightarrow} enrojecer \text{ (to turn red)}$$

$$alma \text{ (soul) } \overset{des- \ -ado}{\longrightarrow} desalmado \text{ (heartless)}$$

A critical phenomenon is that many derivational morphemes have variable forms (*allomorphs*), sometimes phonologically determined, at others lexically imposed by convention or etymology:

in-/im-	*inn*ecesario (unnecessary)	*im*batible (unbeatable)
des-/dis-	*des*cosido (unstitched)	*dis*culpar (to forgive)

3 Derivational Mechanisms

In Spanish the basic derivational mechanisms are: *parasynthesis, prefixation, emotive suffixation, non-emotive suffixation* and *back formation*. Parasynthesis and prefixation have been introduced in the previous section. Emotive suffixation semantically alters the base in some sort of subjective emotional way (smallness, endearment, impressiveness, etc.). Non-emotive suffixation and back formation, which are the basis of the system, are discussed in detail below.

3.1 Non-emotive Suffixation

They constitute the general body of suffixes which are considered to be objective in their application, to change the meaning of the base fundamentally rather than marginally, often to have the capacity to effect a change of syntactic category.

The non-emotive suffix repertoire of Spanish is made up of several hundred derivational morphemes whose inventory is not fixed. Furthermore, there are constraints, expansions and changes of all kinds.

One of the problems we find because of the huge number of existent suffixes, is their classification. The criterion we have used is double. The first subdivision we have made is according to the grammatical class of the derivative; so, we have three processes: nominalization to obtain names —the most common—, adjectivization to obtain adjectives and verbalization to form verbs. The second criterion we have used is the grammatical class of the base: denominals (from names), deadjectivals (from adjectives), and deverbals (from verbs).

From a semantic point of view all suffixes are meaningful in the sense that the meaning of the derivative is always different from that of the base. However, most suffixes are polysemic:

$$muchach\underline{ada} \begin{cases} \text{group (\textit{group of youths})} \\ \text{typical action of the base word (\textit{childish prank})} \end{cases}$$

3.2 Back Formation

This phenomenon is extremely important in contemporary Spanish as a morphological procedure of derivation in *deverbal nominalization*. Instead of increasing the number of syllables of the base, as normally happens is suffixation, it causes a truncation, attaching only a vowel —'a', 'e' or 'o'— to the verb stem:

tom*ar* (to take)	→	tom*a* (taking)
altern*ar* (socialize)	→	altern*e* (socializing)
dañ*ar* (to damage)	→	dañ*o* (damage)

4   Phonological Conditions

We must not forget the analysis of the phonological conditions which dominate the word formation process, because every morphological operation involves a phonological alteration of the base. These transformations may be regular or seemingly irregular:

a) *respond<u>er</u>* (to reply) → *respond<u>ón</u>* (insolent)
   venc<u>er</u> (to defeat) → *inven<u>cible</u>* (invincible)

b) *pan* (bread)   → *pan<u>adero</u>* (baker)
   agua (water)   → *a<u>c</u>u<u>atizar</u>* (to land on the sea)

In a) suffixes are attached to the bases or their stems and conjoined in a morphologically regular way, with predictable morphological and phonological results, whereas in b) the morphology, superficially at least, seems irregular in that the output of the derivation is not that we expect (**pan<u>dero</u>, *agüizar*). Morphology acts in a complex way in such examples. Although some of those phenomenons seem not to be regular, they are common enough to be forcibly included in any rigorous theory of Spanish lexical morphology.

The attempt to explain such situations has led to the postulation of 'readjustment' rules. Aronoff [7] subdivides these rules into two groups: rules of allomorphy, referred to as allomorphical phenomenons, and rules of truncation, where suffixation requires elimination of a previously existing suffix prior to attaching the new suffix:[1]

pan	→ *panadero*	insertion of /aδ/ separating stem and suffix
/pan/	→ /panaδero/	

agua	→ *acuatizar*	conversion of sonorant /γ/ to obstruent /k/ and
/aγua/	→ /akwatiθar/	insertion of obstruent /t/ before infinitive morpheme

The concrete phonological conditions we have considered in this work are detailed in Sect. 2.

5   Rules and Constraints

Even the most productive patterns of Spanish word formation are subject to constraints. The degree of acceptation of a derivative, well-formed from a morphological point of view, is impossible to be predicted only from its form.

However, if we compare the constraints applied in Spanish and those applied in other languages, we can see the great flexibility of Spanish derivational morphology. If we compare it, for example, with English or French (also a Romance language), we can notice that they are highly inflecting types of languages, but their word formation procedures are not so productive as those of Spanish, particularly with regard to suffixation [7], as is shown in Tables 1 and 2.

Table 1. Word formation in English vs. Spanish

English	Spanish	English	Spanish
fist	*puño*	orange	*naranja*
dagger	*puñal*	orange tree	*naranjo*
stab	*puñalada*	orange grove	*naranjal*
punch	*puñetazo*	orangeade	*naranjada*
fistful	*puñado*	orange coloured	*anaranjado*
to grasp	*empuñar*	orange seller	*naranjero*
to stab	*apuñalar*	blow with an orange	*naranjazo*
sword hilt	*empuñadura*	small orange	*naranjita*

Table 2. Word formation in French vs. Spanish

French	Spanish	French	Spanish
coup de pied	*patada* (kick)	*tête*	*cabeza* (head)
petit ami	*amiguito* (little friend)	*coup de tête*	*cabezazo* (butt)
mal de mer	*mareo* (seasickness)	*incliner la tête*	*cabecear* (to nod)
salle à manger	*comedor* (dining room)	*chef d'èmeute*	*cabecilla* (ringleader)
belle-mère	*suegra* (mother-in-law)	*tète de lit*	*cabecera* (head of a bed)
coup à la porte	*aldabonazo* (bang)	*de tète grosse*	*cabezudo* (big-headed)

We can notice with these examples that Spanish prefers derivation rather than other mechanisms, such as happens in French or English. So, it would be very interesting to use morphological families for single word term conflation.

6   A System for Automatic Generation of Morphological Families

We have incorporated the theoretical basis that we have studied up till now into a computer system for automatic generation of morphological families. The linguistic resources required are minimal, only an incoming lexicon of Spanish, each entry formed by a word, a part of speech tag and the corresponding lemma.

As a first step, the system takes the lexicon and obtains and classifies the lemmas of the words which concentrate the semantic information of a text: names, verbs and adjectives. Classification is needed because the derivational procedures vary depending on the category of the base and on the category of the derivative.

Once we have obtained the set of lemmas, the morphological families are created by applying productive derivational morphology and readjustment rules. The current system deals with *non-emotional suffixation*, *back formation* and some marginal cases of *parasynthesis* in *verbalization*.

---

[1] phonetical transcription of a word is written surrounded by slash symbols.

Description of the Algorithm. A running example corresponding to the morphological family {*rojo* (red), *enrojecer* (to turn red)} generated by the base term *rojo* will be used to explain the behaviour of the algorithm.

For every non-processed lemma a new morphological family F is created, with this lemma as its only component. In the running example, $F=\{rojo\}$. At this moment, F is the *active* family. Then, the lemma is pushed onto the stack S which keeps the non-processed terms of the active family. In the case of the running example, $S=[rojo]$.

While S is not empty and non-processed elements exist in F, the algorithm performs the following actions:

1. It gets the lemma on the top of the stack and applies any suitable derivation procedures to it depending on its grammatical category. The lexicon is used to check the existence of the derivative. If the derivative is not valid, phonological conditions will be applied until a valid one is obtained. In the running example, *rojo* is popped from the stack (currently $S = [\,]$) and the parasynthesis *en- -ecer* is used to derive *enrojecer*, which is identified as a correct word in the lexicon.

2. If a correct derivative has been obtained:

    (a) If the derivative has not been previously processed, it is attached to F and pushed onto the stack to be processed later. As a result, $F =\{rojo, enrojecer\}$ and $S =[enrojecer]$ in the running example.

    (b) If the derivative has been previously processed and it belongs to a family $F' \neq F$, then F and F' refer to subfamilies of the same morphological family. In such a case all lemmas of the active family F are re-attached to F', and F' becomes the active family. We call this phenomenon *derivative transivity*, and it would happen, for example, if the lemma *enrojecer* were processed before *rojo*. The obtained family would be $F' =\{enrojecer\}$. Later, the lemma *rojo* would be processed in F, and *enrojecer* would be derived from it. As a consequence, F and F' would be merged, resulting in the family {*rojo, enrojecer*}.

We can notice that this algorithm overgenerates, i.e. it applies all possible suffixes for the category of a given lemma; so, it obtains all morpholically valid derivatives, which are filtered through the lexicon to select the valid ones. We are solving the problem of deciding about the correctness of the derivative only by its form, without considering other aspects.

With regard to back formation, it is supported indirectly by means of derivative transitivity: instead of deriving the name from the verb, we wait until the name is processed and at that time we obtain the verb through denominal verbalisation.

Allomorphy. There are many factors that affect the choice of the proper allomorphic variant for a given suffix. There exist exclusive variants, such as those whose selection depends on the *theme vowel*[2] —e.g. -*amiento* for theme vowel 'a' and -*imiento* for 'e' or 'i'—. There are other non-exclusive suffixes, such as -*ado/-ato* and -*azgo* [7] (popular and archaic variants, respectively), sometimes producing alternative outputs on the same base:

$$líder \text{ (leader)} \rightarrow \begin{cases} liderato \text{ (leadership, popular)} \\ liderazgo \text{ (leathership, cult)} \end{cases}$$

The proper variant to use depends on each particular suffix, and on factors like the theme vowel or the way the base is formed. Therefore, the different possible situations for each particular suffix have been considered separately.

Phonological Conditions. The most important phonological conditions [2,3,7] have been considered:

– **Final unstressed vowel deletion:** It is the default behavior of the system. When the system attaches the suffixes to the base, it first deletes the final unstressed vowel of the lemma. If the ending letter of the base is a consonant, it remains. In any case, the original term remains always available. Examples:

$$arena \text{ (sand)} \rightarrow aren\text{-} \xrightarrow{-oso} arenoso \text{ (sandy)}$$
$$temor \text{ (fear)} \rightarrow temor \xrightarrow{a-\ -izar} atemorizar \text{ (to frighten)}$$

– **Cacophony elimination:** Sometimes, when the suffix is attached, two equal vowels go together. To eliminate the resultant cacophony, we fuse them by first detecting this situation. For example:

$$galanteo \text{ (flirting)} \rightarrow galante\text{-} \xrightarrow{-ería} galante\underline{e}ría \rightarrow galantería \text{ (gallantry)}$$

– **Theme vowel:** If the term we are processing is a verb, we check whether it ends in -*ar*, -*er* or -*ir* to know the theme vowel and thus take it into account when we want to choose the proper variant to use. Such an example is -*miento*, -*amiento*, -*imiento* or -*mento*, where -*amiento* is only used when the theme vowel is 'a', while -*imiento* is used with 'e' or 'i':

$$alzar \text{ (to lift)} \rightarrow alz\text{-} \xrightarrow{-amiento} alzamiento \text{ (lifting)}$$
$$aburrir \text{ (to bore)} \rightarrow aburr\text{-} \xrightarrow{-imiento} aburrimiento \text{ (boredom)}$$

– **Monophthongization of diphthongs:** It is enough to replace the diphthong by the proper form. We manage two different situations:

$$ie \rightarrow e \qquad diente \text{ (tooth)} \xrightarrow{-al} di\underline{e}nt\text{-}al \rightarrow d\underline{e}ntal \text{ (dental)}$$
$$ue \rightarrow o \qquad fuerza \text{ (strength)} \xrightarrow{-udo} f\underline{ue}rz\text{-}udo \rightarrow f\underline{o}rzudo \text{ (strong)}$$

---

[2] the theme vowel [7] is the conjugationally determined vowel segment which appears in the derivative between stem and suffix —'a' for the first conjugation, 'e' for the second conjugation and 'i' for the third one—.

- **Changes in stress position:** Suffixes generally cause a stress alteration, therefore we must consider that event because in Spanish it may imply spelling changes due to the adding or deletion of accents, which depend on the stress of the word. Most suffixes are stressed, so it is easy to know if we have to add or to delete an accent by simply applying orthographical rules. For example:

$$europeo \text{ (European)} \rightarrow europe\text{-} \xrightarrow{-ista} europe\acute{\imath}sta \text{ (pro-European)}$$
$$novela \text{ (novel)} \rightarrow novel\text{-} \xrightarrow{-ista} novelista \text{ (novelist)}$$

- **Retention of final consonant phonemes:** We can know the original phoneme from the spelling of the original term —e.g. the second 'c' in *cocer* (to boil) corresponds to $/\theta/$ and not to $/k/$—. In the same way, knowing the phoneme, we can know the resultant spelling. For example, the 'z' in *cerveza* corresponds to $/\theta/$ and so

$$cerveza \text{ (beer)} \rightarrow cervez\text{-} \xrightarrow{-er\acute{\imath}a} cerveceria \text{ (bar)}$$

The phonemes and spelling changes we have considered are the following:

$/k/$	c → qu
$/\gamma/$	g → gü
$/\gamma/$	g → gu
$/\theta/$	z → c
$/\theta/$	c → z

- **Ad-hoc rules:** We are referring to varied adjustments such as modifications in the last consonant of the stem, in cases of the kind

$$conceder \text{ (to concede)} \rightarrow concesi\acute{o}n \text{ (concession)}$$

They are solved by ad-hoc rules, that is, they manage each particular suffix separately. They are often related to the presence of the dental phonemes $/\delta/$ or $/t/$.

7   System Evaluation

In order to evaluate the system we have used a lexicon of 995,859 words, 92,125 of them were identified as content word lemmas, finally obtaining 54,243 morphological families. Table 3 shows the number of families of a given size and the number of words stored in families of that given size.

We have taken a random sample of 50 families of 2 or more members, which were manually inspected with the aid of dictionaries to check whether all words really belonged to that family and also to check whether they kept a strong enough semantic relation. We have employed ordinary dictionaries for such a

Table 3. Distribution of the morphological families

	Families		Words	
Size	Number	%	Number	%
1	43,007	79.29	43,007	46.68
2	4,470	8.24	8,940	9.70
3	2,314	4.27	6,942	7.54
4	1,405	2.59	5,620	6.10
5	904	1.67	4,520	4.91
6	501	0.92	3,006	3.26
7	368	0.68	2,576	2.80
8	270	0.50	2,160	2.34
9	223	0.41	2,007	2.18
10+	781	1.43	13,347	14.49
Total	54,243	100	92,125	100

Table 4. Evaluation of the morphological families

correct	79 %
incorrect (2 fam.)	7 %
incorrect (3 fam.)	12 %
incorrect (4+ fam.)	2 %

task because the lexicon we used contained a lot of uncommon words and americanisms. So, those words not included in the dictionaries were considered unusual and were not taken into account for the evaluation. The percentage of these words was about 20% approximately.

A checked family was considered incorrect when one or more of its members were found to really belong to other morphological families. The results we obtained for the sampled families are shown in Table 4, indicating the number of correct families and the number of families containing two or more real families.

We have identified that most mistakes were due to:

- Different families attached through derivational transitivity rule. Risk situations are:

   1. Lemmas with similar spelling, specially the shortest ones, for example:

      $$ano \text{ (anus) } \xrightarrow{-al} anal \xleftarrow{-al} ana \text{ (length measure)}$$

   2. Monophthongisation of diphtongs, for example:

      $$fuel \text{ (fuel) } \xrightarrow{-ía} folía \text{ (dance)}$$

   3. Parasynthesis, for example:

      $$plasta \text{ (soft mass) } \xrightarrow{a- \; -ar} aplastar \text{ (to flatten)}$$

– Existence of more than one sense for the same lemma. For example:

rancho (communal meal)
rancho (ranch) $\xrightarrow{-ero}$ *ranchero* (rancher)
rancho (shanty) $\xrightarrow{-ería}$ *ranchería* (shanty town)

– Sense specialization:

golpe (hit) $\xrightarrow{-ador}$ *golpeador* (that hits)
golpe [de estado] (coup d'état) $\xrightarrow{-al}$ *golpista* (participant in a coup d'état)

– Figurative senses, for example:

$$lince \text{ (lynx) } \xrightarrow{-ear} lincear \text{ (to unearth)}$$

There are some procedures to limit the possible mistakes, such as using etymological or semantic information to check whether there is any relation between the derivative and the base lemma. But this would imply increasing the computational costs, and problems would not completely disappear. In the case of employing etymology, there are examples of unrelated words such as *Morfeo* (Morpheus) and *morfina* (morphine) with the same etymologycal origins. In the case of using semantic information, if a word has more than one sense we would need to disambiguate it from the context.

8   Term Indexing Using Morphological Families

Information Retrieval systems conflate the documents before indexing to decrease their linguistic variety by grouping together textual occurrences referring to similar or identical concepts exploiting graphical similarities, thesaurus, etc. [1,5,6]. We will study another way, the use of morphological families.

For this purpose, we will first get the part of speech and the lemmas of the text to be indexed by using a tagger. Next, we will replace each of the obtained lemmas by a representative of its morphological family. We are replacing all lemmas belonging to the same family by the same lemma, its *representative*; therefore, we are representing all its members by a single term.

Three kind of indexing methods have been tested:

1. Indexing of the original document (*pln*).
2. Indexing of the conflated text via lemmatization (*lem*).
3. Indexing of the conflated text via morphological families (*fam*).

The evaluation of an IR system involves the computation of the standard measures of *precision* P and *recall* R, where:

$$P = \frac{\text{number of relevant documents retrieved}}{\text{total number of documents retrieved}}$$

$$R = \frac{\text{number of relevant documents retrieved}}{\text{total number of relevant documents}}$$

The reference document corpus used for testing was composed of 1,378 documents with an average length of 292 words. The topics of the corpus were of a journalistic nature (local, national, international, sports, culture).

We have used SWISH-E [10], a free distribution indexing engine. This software employs a boolean model [1,6]. This fact is very important because it does not allow partial matches, so recall will be considerably decreased. Though, one of the main advantages of our system is that it is independent from the indexing engine used, because documents are preprocessed before being treated by it; so, there is no problem in changing the indexing engine in the future.

The results we have obtained for global recall and precision for 12 different queries are shown in Table 5 and seem to prove that the application of conflation techniques *[fam,lem]* to reduce the linguistic variety of the documents has lead to a remarkable increase in recall. We can see that the greatest recall is reached using conflation via morphological families *[fam]*. However, this increase in recall also implies a slight decrease in precision. We can also notice that for both measures the worst method is the indexation of the original text *[pln]*. In this last case, precision decreases because no documents are retrieved for some queries due to its sensitivity to inflectional variations (gender, number, time, etc.).

Table 5. Recall and Precision for the different models

	fam	*lem*	*pln*
Recall	0.950	0.738	0.403
Precision	0.693	0.723	0.589

With respect to the evolution of precision vs. recall, Fig. 1 confirms the *pln* model as the worst one. The best behavior corresponds to the *fam* model, except for the segment of recall between 0.15 to 0.33, where the *lem* model is the better one.

9   Conclusion

This paper explores a new approach to retrieval of Spanish texts based on the application of natural language techniques. To be precise, we have investigated the automatic generation of morphological families by applying productive derivational morphology mechanisms, and the exploitation of these families for single term conflation, substituting every term of the document by a representative of its morphological family.

We have looked for simplicity to overcome the limitations associated with the lack of linguistic resources for Spanish, and we have also looked to reduce the computational cost of the system. The solution we have used to solve these

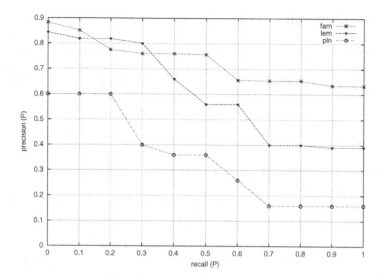

Fig. 1. Precision vs. Recall of the different models

problems has been to use as few resources as possible, facing the task from the lexical level. Due to the fact that all families and their representatives have been obtained previously in an independent process, the computational cost is reduced to the cost of the necessary previous lemmatization.

There exist other approaches to the problem of term conflation by using more linguistic resources and increasing the computational cost associated. For example, in [5] a transducer is used for both, morphological analysis and dynamically generating terms of the same derivational family. In [4], the CELEX morphological database[3] has been used to calculate morphological families. In addition, two sources of semantic knowledge for English processing have been applied: the WordNet 1.6 thesaurus [8] and the thesaurus of Microsoft Word97.

The performance of the new approach has been compared to two other indexing methods, indexing of the original text and indexing of the lemmatized text, which obtain worse results in general. However, larger experiments (with a larger collection of texts and a larger set of queries) should be performed to confirm these results.

We are currently extending the system, incorporating more derivational mechanisms (e.g. prefixation), multiword terms [5] and the combination of the retrieved documents by different techniques. We are also extending our tests to different indexing models (e.g. vectorial model[1,6]) and different indexing engines.

---

[3] a morphological database for English language in which each lemma is associated with a morphological structure that contains one or more root lemmas.

Acknowledgements

We would like to thank Margarita Alonso, Jean-Cédric Chappelier, Jorge Graña and Manuel Vilares for fruitful discussions. This research has been partially supported by the FEDER of EU (Grant 1FD97-0047-C04-02) and Xunta de Galicia (Grant PGIDT99XI10502B).

References

1. Baeza-Yates, R., Ribeiro-Neto, B.: Modern information retrieval. Harlow, England: Addison-Wesley (1999)
2. Bajo Pérez, E.: La derivación nominal en español. Madrid: Arco Libros, Cuadernos de lengua española (1997)
3. Fernández Ramírez, S.: La derivación nominal. Madrid: Real Academia Española, Anejos del Boletín de la Real Academia Española **40** (1986)
4. Jacquemin, C.: Syntagmatic and paradigmatic representations of term variation Proc. of 37th Annual Meeting of the Association for Computational Linguistics (ACL'99), University of Maryland, USA
5. Jacquemin, C., Tzoukermann, E.: NLP for Term Variant Extraction: A Synergy of Morphology, Lexicon and Syntax. In T. Strzalkowski, editor, Natural Language Processing Information Retrieval, pp. 25–74. Boston: Kluwer (1999)
6. Kowalski, G.: Information retrieval systems : theory and implementation. Boston: Kluwer (1997)
7. Lang, M. F.: Spanish Word Formation: Productive Derivational Morphology in the Modern Lexis. London: Routledge (1990)
8. Miller, G. A., Beckwith, R., Fellbaum, C., Gross, D. and Miller, K. J.: Introduction to WordNet: An On-line Lexical Database. International Journal of Lexicography **3** (1990) 235–244
9. Strzalkowski, T. (editor): Natural language information retrieval. Dordrecht: Kluwer (1999)
10. SWISH-E. http://sunsite.berkeley.edu/SWISH-E/. SWISH-Enhanced - Digital Library SunSITE

Unification-Based Lexicon and Morphology with Speculative Feature Signalling

Björn Gambäck[1,2]

[1] Swedish Institute of Computer Science
Box 1263, S-164 29 Kista, Sweden
gamback@sics.se, http://www.sics.se/~gamback
[2] Computational Linguistics
University of Helsinki
P.O. Box 4, SF-00014 Helsinki, Finland

Abstract. The implementation of a unification-based lexicon is discussed as well as the morphological rules needed for mapping between the lexicon and grammar. It is shown how different feature usages can be utilized in the implementation to reach the intended surface word-form matches, with the correct feature settings. A novelty is the way features are used as binary signals in the compositional morphology. Finally, the lexicon coverage of the closed-class words and of the different types of open-class words is evaluated.

1 Introduction

In unification-based approaches to grammar most of the grammatical information is encoded already at the lexical level and then passed compositionally upwards in the grammar structure by feature unification. This is done in order to keep the grammar as simple as possible and the number of distinct grammar rules as low as possible. The price paid is a more complicated lexicon which is hard, or even impossible, to clearly separate from the grammar proper.

In this paper, the implementation of a unification-based Swedish lexicon will be discussed, as well as the mapping between the lexicon and (the rest of!) the grammar, that is, the morphological rules. The main points of the discussion will be to show how different feature usages can be utilized in the implementation to reach the intended surface word-form matches, with the correct feature settings. Unification-based implementations of morphology are certainly not new as such, but we will introduce some novel ways of using features in the implementation. In addition, large-scale implementations and computationally oriented systematizations of Swedish morphology are surprisingly rare and the paper aims to fill a gap in this respect.

It should be noted that we will not discuss how the actual word-forms are located in the input string, i.e., the morphophonology. There have been several implementations and descriptions of two-level style morphology (Koskenniemi 1983) within unification-based frameworks, by e.g. Abramson (1992) and Carter (1995). In this article we will take for granted that a module doing this work

A. Gelbukh (Ed.): CICLing 2001, LNCS 2004, pp. 349–362, 2001.

is available. We agree with the view of Trost and Matiasek (1994) that there should be a separation of the task of identifying the input word-form and the task of mapping the lexical feature settings into the grammar. The approach of Krieger *et al* (1993) and Erjavec (1997) to do both these tasks simultaneously, although aesthetically appealing, hardly lends itself to efficient implementation.

The rest of the paper is laid out as follows: Sections 2 and 3 discuss the treatment of nouns at length. An interesting case is the compositional morphology, and the way features are used in order to restrict the output to only the desired forms. This is the topic of Section 4. Thereafter, the closed-class words are touched upon briefly, before the lexicon coverage is evaluated in Section 6.

2   Open Class Words

Swedish allows inflection of verbs, nouns and adjectives. As in most languages, the largest Swedish word-class is the noun-class. We will concentrate the description of the lexicon to that class. (A thorough description of the other classes would not add much to the discussion at hand.)

2.1   Swedish Noun Types

Traditionally, the paradigms of Swedish nouns divide as in Table 1. This division follows most closely the one of Thorell (1973, pp. 19-21), but does not differ much from what other Swedish grammar writers state (even though the choice of terms differ substantially). So Dahl (1982, pp. 30-31) does not single out the two "aggregate" types (flock and collectives) from the other countable and mass nouns, while Holm and Nylund (1985, p. 17) treat the aggregate categories as a distinct type. Jörgensen and Svensson (1986, pp. 21-22) split the individua and dividua into eight different types along the three dimensions individual, aggregate, and concrete. They divide the aggregates into concrete and abstract, but since most 'collectives' are concrete, their addition is limited to a subdivision of the 'flock' category.

Table 1. The Swedish noun types

Individua (count): inflected in species and numerus		
appellativa (things)	en bok	(a book)
abstracts, limited	en tanke	(a thought)
flock (groups)	ett folk	(a people)
Dividua (mass): inflected in species, not in numerus		
subject names	plast	(plastic)
abstracts, unlimited	hunger	(hunger)
collectives	liv och död	(life and death)
Proper names: (normally) not inflected in either		

When implementing the lexicon of a large-scale unification-based system, the division of Table 1 does not suffice completely. It is both too coarse-grained and too fine-grained! It is too fine-grained since not all of the above types necessarily occur in the domains which the system has to face. However, this is more a reflection of the domains in which language processing systems normally are used, than a problem with the traditional division per se.

The coarse-grainedness is more of a problem. The division of Table 1 does not account for the fact that measure type nouns (such as *liter*, litre) behave somewhat differently from many other nouns. This distinction is mainly semantic, but on the syntactic side it is, for example, hardly possible (or at least very rare) for measure type nouns to be modified by adjectives (as in *?en [stor liter]*, a [large liter]), or to take part in constructions involving noun-noun conjunction (*?två [kilo och liter] sand*, two [kilo and litre] of sand).

2.2   The Lexicon Formalism

The lexicon formalism of this paper is the one of SRI International's Core Language Engine (CLE) (Alshawi 1992). Abstractly, a lexicon entry is defined as

(1) `lex(`⟨*terminal-root*⟩`,`
        `[`⟨*terminal-category*⟩`:`
          `[`⟨*Feature*$_1$ `=` *Value*$_1$`,   ...,   *Feature*$_n$ `=` *Value*$_n$⟩`]`
      `])`.

where *terminal-root* is the root form of the terminal (the non-inflected *lexeme*). The rest of the lexicon rule contain a `Category:FeatureValueList` pair. A simplified example of a lexical entry is the following one for *bil* (car), a countable (i.e., not mass) noun:

(2) `lex(bil,`
        `[nbar:`
          `[mass=n, sing=y, pers=3, common=y, decl=2, infix=no]`
      `])`.

bil is the 3rd person singular common gender (takes '-en' definite suffix), it belongs to the 2nd declension (i.e., forms indefinite plural by adding the suffix '-ar'), and takes no infix at first in compounds (thus e.g., car door is *bil-dörr*, rather than *bil-s-dörr*).

The lexicon is divided into three different parts; one implicit and one explicit lexicon for the open-class words together with one explicit lexicon for the closed-class words. In the explicit lexica, all the information about a word is stated, with all the needed feature-value settings. In the implicit lexicon, only mappings from this lexicon to corresponding entries in the explicit lexicon are given. That is, the implicit lexicon only contains definitions of word types (e.g., proper noun); or put in another way, which *paradigm* words belong to. A paradigm defines a group of words which either have the same function or may be interpreted in a similar way.

2.3   Paradigms for Nouns

We now turn to the noun paradigms. Each noun subclass will be exemplified with an entry from the implicit lexicon and the expansion macro used together with it. A generic noun takes the following set of features:

(3) `macro(noun_feats(Decl,Gen,Inf),`
        `[@decl(Decl), @gender(Gen), @infixing(Inf),`
        `sing=y, person=3, @agr(Agr), def=(nposs),`
        `simple=y, @gap_island, subcat=[]]).`

which is a *macro*, a short-hand notation for writing repeating patterns. The @ prefix indicates macro calls.

The `noun_feats` macro takes three arguments, reflecting the ways nouns may be inflected: in *numerus* according to declension, in *species* (gender), and with or without infix in compounding. This is substantiated by calls to different inflection type macros, the second row in (3), together with the feature instantiations and calls of the third row. So, for example, the "agreement" macro `agr` among other things makes sure that a determiner and a noun forming a noun phrase agree in number, person, and gender. The (non-inflected) lexicon form is 3rd person singular and indefinite — which coincides with the possessive.

The last row in (3) states that a lexical noun is not a compound (`simple=y`) and does not contain any traces of moved constituents, i.e., that it is a "gap island" (see below). Finally, most nouns do not take any complements; the "subcategorization" feature `subcat` is an empty list.[1]

2.4   Noun Expansion Macros

The general noun macro above is used by the explicit lexical entries for the different noun types. Just as in Table 1, the standard type noun is the regular count noun, the *individua*:

(4) `macro('n:count'(Decl,Gen,Inf),`
        `nbar:[@noun_feats(Decl,Gen,Inf), mass=n]).`

which only sets the feature `mass` to 'no'. This feature distinguishes between countables and non-countables. An example of a count noun is the already mentioned *bil* (car), defined in the implicit lexicon as

(5) `lex(bil,@'n:count'(n2,common,no)).`

In addition to this, default values for many other features are invoked. Most notably the feature `measure` takes the default value 'no'. Explicitly setting it to 'yes', we get measure type nouns as *liter* (litre):

---

[1] Some nouns, e.g., *typ*, *sort*, and *slag* (type, sort, and kind) take complements. Those have their own version of the noun feature setting macro.

(6) `macro('n:count:measure'(Decl,Gen,Inf),`
        `nbar:[@noun_feats(Decl,Gen,Inf),`
            `measure=y, mass=n]).`
    `lex(liter,@'n:count:measure'(n5,common,no)).`

The *individua* are, obviously, complemented by the *dividua*, the mass nouns, like *vatten* (water), but also by words which may behave as either count or mass nouns (mass=_), such as *ost* (cheese).

(7) `macro('n:mass'(Decl,Gen,Inf),`
        `nbar:[@noun_feats(Decl,Gen,Inf), mass=y]).`
    `lex(vatten,@'n:mass'(n5,neuter,no)).`

(8) `macro('n:count:mass'(Decl,Gen,Inf),`
        `nbar:[@noun_feats(Decl,Gen,Inf), mass=_]).`
    `lex(ost,@'n:count:mass'(n2,common,no)).`

The paradigms in this section are complemented with three others to make up the entire noun hierarchy. The additional paradigms are for proper names, temporal nouns (which behave a bit peculiar, a temporal noun may form a temporal NP without a determiner; a temporal NP may in turn function like an adverbial), and for aggregates. Of the latter ones only the countable type ('flock') is treated by the current version of the lexicon, while mass type aggregates, i.e. 'collectives' are not.

3   Inflectional Morphology

In addition to the paradigm division (the division by *word usage*), open-class words are also subdivided by their physical appearance, i.e. by their inflectional forms. For Swedish nouns the main distinction runs along the lines of the pluralization. Nouns can be pluralized in several different ways, giving rise to a number of *declensions*. As shown in Table 2, the declension is normally characterized by the plural form suffix. However, the singular and plural forms coincide for 5th declension nouns, which is reflected by an empty set ($\emptyset$) plural suffix.

Table 2. The inflectional classes of Swedish nouns

numerus	singular		plural	
species	indef	def	indef	def
paradigm				
n1	piga	pigan	pigor	pigorna
n2	bil	bilen	bilar	bilarna
n3	pris	priset	priser	priserna
n4	arbete	arbetet	arbeten	arbetena
n5	hus	huset	hus$\emptyset$	husen

3.1   Inflectional Rules of Nouns

The rules for inflectional morphology describe how the word-forms in the lexicon may be converted into other forms. The following rule takes care of pluralization for 1st, 2nd, 3rd and 4th declension nouns, all the noun types where the plural is formed by the addition of a suffix to the singular:

```
(9) morph(nbar_nbar_plural,
       [nbar:[sing=n, decl=Decl, ...],
        nbar:[sing=y, decl=Decl, ...],
        'PLURAL':[decl=Decl]
       ]).
```

The rule is supplemented by four lexical entries for the plural suffixes; the declension is encoded in the `decl` feature. Unification of this feature between the daughters in (9) ensures that suffix and stem belong to the same declension. The first two suffix entries are

```
(10) lex('-or','PLURAL':[decl=1]).
(11) lex('-ar','PLURAL':[decl=2]).
```

An additional rule is needed for 5th declension nouns. We introduce an extra `nbar` feature `nullmorphn` which defaults to 'no'. When set it indicates that the plural affix is empty. The null plural rule is consequently

```
(12) morph(nbar_nbar_nullplural,
       [nbar:[sing=n, decl=Decl, ...],
        nbar:[sing=y, decl=Decl,
              nullmorphn=y, ...]
       ]).
```

3.2   Choice of Formalism

An alternative to the solution to morphology adopted here, where affixes are given specific lexical entries, can be found in e.g. Riehemann (1998). She argues for an approach in which generalizations from existing words are expressed as schemata, organised in an HPSG-style inheritance network in the manner of Krieger and Nerbonne (1993). This approach is certainly attractive and elegant, although the efficiency of an implementation of it still has to be demonstrated.

Thus, we would not claim that the choice of formalism of this paper is the only, or even the best or most attractive, possibility. However, while the CLE formalism was shown to render itself to very efficient implementation already in the mid 80s, alternative approaches such as HPSG-style grammar are still struggling with this issue at present. Still, there is certainly no reason to believe that this an eternal fact, and more and more efficient implementations of HPSG are appearing. With the advent of typed logical programming systems supporting inheritance, such as the Mozart platform (Haridi *et al* 1998), this process is likely to escalate. This is good news for linguists, since it allows for the use of implementations closer to the linguistic ideals.

Regardless of the choice of formalism, though, the phenomena described in this paper would still have to be treated in one way or another. In our approach, in addition to the rules for noun pluralization given above, there are other inflectional rules for the formation of the definite and the genitive forms, as well as special rules for compositional and derivational morphology. Derivational morphology is concerned with how, for example, the addition of a suffix to a root form of one word-class leads to the formation of a word of another class. A Swedish example is the common construction of adverbs by adding a '-t' to an adjective. These derivational rules are treated by the same machinery as the inflectional ones.

4 Compositional Morphology

Compositional morphology on the other hand deals with how two word forms can be joined together to form a completely new word, sometimes with the insertion of an infix. For a compounding language like Swedish this is the most common way of forming new words, with the possible combinations seemingly endless. We treat several types of such compounds: noun-noun, name-noun (*Deltaflygning*, Delta flight), adjective-noun (*direktflyg*, direct flight), and adverb-noun (*tur-och-returflyg*, round-trip flight). In all cases with the (first) noun possibly itself being a compound by recursion. As an example, the following rule shows how a noun-noun compound is formed.

```
(13) morph(nbar_nbar_infix_nbar_ComplexN,
      [nbar:[nn_infix=(I,O),
             simple=n, decl=Decl, ...]
       nbar:[nn_infix=(I,N), ...],
       'INFIX':[nn_infix=(N,O)],
       nbar:[simple=y, decl=Decl, ...]
      ]).
```

4.1 Feature-Enforced Branching

In (13), most features are passed from the head noun (right-hand daughter) to the compound (mother node) by unification, as exemplified by the **decl** feature. The function of the feature **simple** is to force left recursion, only the left-hand daughter may itself be a compound — as seen in the macro **noun_feats** (3), **simple** will always be 'yes' on lexical nouns. The rule above sets is to 'no' on compounds. Thus the right-hand daughter must be a lexical noun; the left-hand daughter may be either a compound or a lexical noun.

4.2 A Binary Switch Feature

The function of the **nn_infix** feature in (13) is less obvious. It indicates whether the left-most daughter **nbar** needs an infix in compounding. The infix may currently only be '-s-' (or ∅, '--'):

(14) `lex('-s-',['INFIX':[nn_infix=(1,0)]]).`
(15) `lex('--',['INFIX':[nn_infix=(0,1)]]).`

In the implicit lexical entries, we have both nouns taking an 's'-infix (*råd*) and nouns taking no infix (*bil*). Their corresponding explicit lexical entries call the macro `noun_feats` (3), which in turn invokes the following macros for infixing

(16) `macro(infixing(s), [nn_infix=(0,1)]).`
(17) `macro(infixing(no), [nn_infix=(0,0)]).`

The `nn_infix` feature settings show a way to use a feature as a binary switch: the first value of the `nn_infix` feature of the left-most noun daughter in the `nbar_nbar_infix_nbar_ComplexN` rule and the second value of the right-most daughter are propagated up to the mother node by base-2 addition (so 00+01=01 and 01+10=00). An `nbar` taking no infix (e.g., *sten*, stone) has `nn_infix(0,0)` and is unified with the ∅-infix having `nn_infix(0,1)` and another noun (whose `nn_infix` feature setting is irrelevant) to build an `nbar` with `nn_infix(0,1)` (e.g, *stenålder*, stone age). This in turn can produce an `nbar` taking the null-infix if it meets another noun and the 's'-infix (thus *stenåldersman*, stone age man), etc., as shown in Figure 1. The `nn_infix` switch feature will keep toggling back and forth in order to allow only one type of combination — with or without infix 's' — at any giving moment.

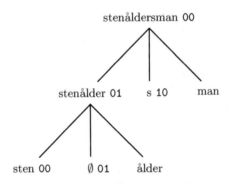

Fig. 1. Binary feature toggling

This usage of a feature as a binary switch is neat, but indeed a bit complicated. An alternative strategy could have been to replace the single noun compounding rule with two rules, one for each infix, which would not have been as elegant. A more serious objection is that other compounding rules (e.g., the one for name-noun compounds) also would have needed to be duplicated.

4.3   Irregular Composition

The feature toggle works in base-2, i.e., as a binary switch, since we currently only treat the 's' infix. The approach taken here is indeed a bit oversimplified even for that suffix (not all compounds with empty or 's' infixes behave as regularly as the ones in Figure 1), but works in the majority of the cases. Still, the infix in Swedish compounds may also be

- '-e-' *ärekränkning* (libel, lit. "honour violation"),
- '-a-' *gästabud* (banquet, lit. "guest summoning"),
- '-u-' *gatubelysning* (street light), or
- '-o-' *kronofogde* (federal (IRS) marshall, lit. "State's sheriff").

However, only the 's' and ∅ infixes are productive. As Kiefer (1970) points out, the other infixes mostly occur in compounds of archaic character and with non-compositional semantics, or together with a fixed set of prefix-nouns. Thus these other infixes are not (and should not be!) treated by the regular morphology; words containing them are entered as they are into the lexicon.

5   Other Word Classes

Other open-class words (verbs, adjectives, and some regular adverbs) are treated by rules similar to the ones for nouns. Adjectives are just like nouns marked for number, gender and definiteness, but these are conflated so that there are actually only three distinct forms. There are three conjugations of weak verbs, and one conjugation of strong verbs, divided into three sub-classes. The verbs have nearly the same inflections as their English equivalents, with two main exceptions. Firstly, an extra form (the *supine*) is used to form the perfect tense, and is generally distinct from the past participle; secondly, most inflectional forms have a "passive" (deponent) counterpart, formed by adding the suffix *-s*.

Of course, many words belonging to the open classes are too irregular to fall into any of the inflectional classes listed and need to be treated by explicit lexical entries. Other words in these classes are border-line cases to the closed word classes (e.g., the auxiliary verbs) and are also entered into the explicit lexica directly.

5.1   Closed Class Words

The so-called closed word classes are those for which the addition of new words is almost unheard of. In Swedish these words are also characterized by not being (regularly) inflective. That is, all forms of these words would have to appear in the lexicon, as it were. Certainly, the goal of including *all* closed class words in the lexicon has not been reached (see below), however, most common ones are treated.

The division of open class words according to paradigms has its correspondence in the lexicon for the closed class words by the introduction of a range of macros. There are macros for a wide spectrum of articles, determiners, pronouns, adverbs, conjunctions, prepositions, particles, interjections, and numbers.

5.2 Personal Pronouns

As an example of a closed class word, let us look closer at the entry for the personal pronoun *henne* (her), which is third person singular, non-reflexive, and non-subject case (i.e., adjective or dative).

(18) `lex(henne, @personal_pronoun([y,y,3],n,nonsubj)).`

(19) `macro(personal_pronoun(Agr,Ref,Case),`
`        @np_pronoun(Agr,Ref,Case,norm)).`

(20) `macro(np_pronoun(Agr,Ref,Case,Nform),`
`        [np:[pron=y, nform=Nform, reflexive=Ref,`
`            case=Case, @agr(Agr), def=y, mass=n,`
`            name=n, @gap_island, simple=y, ...]]).`

(21) `macro(agr([C,S,P]),`
`        [common=C, sing=S, person=P]).`

(22) `macro(gap_island,`
`        [gaps=g(G,G,F,F)]).`

As the number of entries show, the macro calls can often be quite deeply nested: The lexicon entry for *henne* (18) is like an implicit lexical entry, a call to the personal pronoun macro (19) with three arguments. The first argument is list-valued and carries three features related to agreement (gender, number, and person).

The personal pronoun macro in turn calls a more general pronoun macro `np_pronoun` (20) with the "normal" noun form (`nform=norm`). That macro binds many NP features to values relevant to pronouns in general (`pron=y` and `name=n`, obviously; pronouns are also always definite and non-mass, etc.).

Some features are bound through yet another level of macro calls. The three agreement features `common`, `sing` (singular) and `person` are bound in the `agr` macro (21). The first two are binary valued while `person` is tertiary. Here they get the values y, y and 3, resp. from the lexical entry (18).

Another example is the `gaps` feature which is used to simulate constituent movement through what is commonly known as *gap threading* (Pereira 1981, Karttunen 1986), i.e., passing around a list of moved phrases to ensure that an empty production is only applicable if there is a moved phrase elsewhere in the sentence to license its use. The feature contains a pair of lists kept together by the functor `g`, the four arguments of which together form two difference lists, in the fashion of Pulman (1992). The `gap_island` macro (22), called from `np_pronoun`, indicates that a pronoun in itself may not contain any traces of moved constituents. This follows from the fact that both difference lists are given as empty ($G - G = \emptyset$ and $F - F = \emptyset$) in the `gap_island` macro.

6   Evaluating Lexical Coverage

The Swedish lexicon described here was originally implemented for a car-hire domain (Gambäck and Rayner 1992) and later extended for treating the ATIS (Hemphill *et al* 1990) air travel planning register (Rayner *et al* 1993, Gambäck and Karlgren 1994). It has also been used in interfacing to a database containing data on Swedish sovereigns (Gambäck and Ljung 1993).

Now, suppose that we have a lexicon like the one of this paper. That is, a decently large unification-based lexicon, but probably tuned to the register (sub-language) of some particular domain: How easy is it to adapt it to an unfamiliar domain?

An indication of the answer to this question can be found in a test of the completeness of the coverage which is describe in full in (Berglund and Gambäck 1995). There we used data from a collection of part-of-speech and morphologically annotated Swedish texts, the "Stockholm-Umeå Corpus" (SUC) (Källgren 1990, Ejerhed *et al* 1992). We wanted to find two blocks in SUC that contained texts from the same, not too wide, domain. The choice fell upon two texts about hiking in different mountain areas (called 'ea03' and 'ea04' in SUC). These were selected since they ought to have a number of domain-specific words in common although e.g. the proper names should differ completely.

Table 3. Lexicon extensions in the SUC domain

part of speech	new entries		old entries		total
	lex	occ	lex	occ	
proper names	127	187	5	6	193
nouns	244	394	27	53	447
verbs	91	154	19	96	250
adjectives	105	138	18	48	186
adverbs	50	71	37	94	165
prepositions	9	12	32	279	291
pronouns	3	3	22	98	101
conjunctions	3	12	7	75	87
determiners	0	0	14	127	127
total	632	971	181	876	1847

The result of the testing on the first text is shown in Table 3. The second and third columns show the number of completely new lexical entries which had to be created: 'lex' is the actual number of new lexemes, while 'occ' is the total number of times these words occurred in the text ('ea03'). The fourth and fifth columns show the number of words in the text which were already in the lexicon; the last column shows the grand total of words of each word-class (the sum of columns 3 and 5).

As can be seen in the table, the presumption that the lexicon had to be extended with a large number of names and ordinary nouns was correct. All the new names added and some of the new nouns, like *bergmassiv* ('mountain massif') and *hytta* ('lodge') are domain specific, while other nouns, like *motsats* ('opposite') and *papper* ('paper') are more general. Of course, the aim to include all Swedish function words in the lexicon has not been completely met; however, only 15 out of 632 added lexemes are function words (2.4%), which is encouraging. Also, only one new paradigm (for verbs) had to be added. In the test on the second SUC text ('ea04'), the original lexicon was extended with the new words from the first text. For the 2000 words of 'ea04', 363 new lexical entries (22% of the occurrences) had to be added.

7   Conclusions

The paper has discussed how different feature usages can be utilized in the implementation of unification-based lexicon for Swedish and in the mappings between the lexical entries and the intended surface word-forms. In particular, it has been shown how a specific branching structure can be obtained using features and how features can be used as binary signals in the compositional morphology.

Acknowledgements

The evaluation work was part of Charlotta Berglund's Master Thesis and mainly carried out by her. Several people at SICS, in particular Jussi Karlgren and Manny Rayner, at different times contributed to the lexicon. The original CLE formalism was developed at SRI Cambridge Computer Science Research Centre, UK; the lexicon and macro mechanism described here mainly by David Carter. Thanks to all of these and also to Hans Uszkoreit, Saarbrücken, for pointing out the independent importance of my feature signalling strategy.

References

[1992]Abramson, H. 1992. A Logic Programming View of Relational Morphology. In *Proceedings of the 14th International Conference on Computational Linguistics*, volume 3, pp. 850–859, Nantes, France, July. ACL.

[1992]Alshawi, H., editor, Carter, D., van Eijck, J., Gambäck, B., Moore, R. C., Moran, D. B., Pereira, F. C. N., Pulman, S. G., Rayner, M., and Smith, A. G. 1992. *The Core Language Engine*. MIT Press, Cambridge, Massachusetts, March.

[1995]Berglund, C. and Gambäck, B. 1995. On Testing Domain Adaptability. In *Proceedings of the 10th Nordic Conference of Computational Linguistics*, volume "Short Papers", pp. 90–94, University of Helsinki, Helsinki, Finland, May.

[1995]Carter, D. 1995. Rapid Development of Morphological Descriptions for Full Language Processing Systems. In *Proceedings of the 7th Conference of the European Chapter of the Association for Computational Linguistics*, pp. 202–209, University

College of Dublin, Dublin, Ireland, March. ACL. Also available as SRI International Technical Report CRC-047, Cambridge, England.

[1982]Dahl, O. 1982. *Grammatik.* Studentlitteratur, Lund, Sweden. (in Swedish).

[1992]Ejerhed, E., Källgren, G., Wennstedt, O., and Åström, M. 1992. The Linguistic Annotation System of the Stockholm–Umeå Corpus Project. Report 33, Dept. of General Linguistics, University of Umeå, Umeå, Sweden.

[1997]Erjavec, T. 1997. *Unification, Inheritance and Paradigms in the Morphology of Natural Languages.* Doctor of Philosophy Thesis, Faculty for Computer Science and Informatics, University of Ljubljana, Ljubljana, Slovenia.

[1994]Gambäck, B. and Karlgren, J. 1994. Swedish Linguistic Coverage. In Agnäs *et al* 1994, chapter 9, pp. 96–112, Stockholm, Sweden and Cambridge, England, January.

[1993]Gambäck, B. and Ljung, S. 1993. Question Answering in the Swedish Core Language Engine. In Sandewall, E. and Jansson, C. G., editors, *Proceedings of the 4th Scandinavian Conference on Artificial Intelligence,* pp. 212–225, Stockholm, Sweden, May. NORFA, IOS Press, Amsterdam, Holland. Also available as SICS Research Report R92014, Stockholm, Sweden.

[1992]Gambäck, B. and Rayner, M. 1992. The Swedish Core Language Engine. In Ahrenberg, L., editor, *Papers from the 3rd Nordic Conference on Text Comprehension in Man and Machine,* pp. 71–85, Linköping University, Linköping, Sweden, April. Also available as SICS Research Report R92013, Stockholm, Sweden and as SRI International Technical Report CRC-025, Cambridge, England.

[1998]Haridi, S., Van Roy, P., Brand, P., and Schulte, C. 1998. Programming Languages for Distributed Applications. *New Generation Computing,* **16**(3):223–261.

[1990]Hemphill, C. T., Godfrey, J. J., and Doddington, G. R. 1990. The ATIS Spoken Language Systems Pilot Corpus. In *Proceedings of the 3rd Speech and Natural Language Workshop,* pp. 96–101, Hidden Valley, Pennsylvania, June. DARPA, Morgan Kaufmann.

[1985]Holm, B. and Nylund, E. 1985. *Deskriptiv svensk grammatik.* Skriptor, Stockholm, Sweden, 12nd edition. (in Swedish).

[1986]Jörgensen, N. and Svensson, J. 1986. *Nusvensk grammatik.* Gleerup, Malmö, Sweden, 2:4th edition. (in Swedish).

[1990]Källgren, G. 1990. 'The first million is hardest to get': Building a Large Tagged Corpus as Automatically as Possible. In Karlgren, H., editor, *Proceedings of the 13th International Conference on Computational Linguistics,* volume 3, pp. 400–404, Helsinki, Finland, August. ACL.

[1986]Karttunen, L. 1986. D-PATR: A Development Environment for Unification-Based Grammars. In *Proceedings of the 11th International Conference on Computational Linguistics,* pp. 74–80, Bonn, Germany, August. ACL.

[1970]Kiefer, F. 1970. *Swedish Morphology.* Skriptor, Stockholm, Sweden, June.

[1983]Koskenniemi, K. 1983. *Two-Level Morphology: A General Computational Model for Word-Form Recognition and Production.* Doctor of Philosophy Thesis, University of Helsinki, Dept. of General Linguistics, Helsinki, Finland.

[1993]Krieger, H.-U. and Nerbonne, J. 1993. Feature-Based Inheritance Networks for Computational Lexicons. In Briscoe, T., Copestake, A., and de Paiva, V., editors, *Inheritance, Defaults, and the Lexicon,* pp. 90–136. Cambridge University Press, New York.

[1993]Krieger, H.-U., Pirker, H., and Nerbonne, J. 1993. Feature-Based Allomorphy. In *Proceedings of the 31st Annual Meeting of the Association for Computational Linguistics,* pp. 140–147, Columbus, Ohio, June. ACL.

[1981]Pereira, F. C. N. 1981. Extraposition Grammars. *Computational Linguistics*, **7**:243–256.

[1992]Pulman, S. G. 1992. Unification-Based Syntactic Analysis. In *The Core Language Engine*, chapter 4, pp. 61–82. MIT Press, Cambridge, Massachusetts, March.

[1993]Rayner, M., Bretan, I., Carter, D., Collins, M., Digalakis, V., Gambäck, B., Kaja, J., Karlgren, J., Lyberg, B., Pulman, S., Price, P., and Samuelsson, C. 1993. Spoken Language Translation with Mid-90's Technology: A Case Study. In *Proceedings of the 3rd European Conference on Speech Communication and Technology*, volume 2, pp. 1299–1302, Berlin, Germany, September. ESCA. Also available as SRI International Technical Report CRC-032, Cambridge, England.

[1998]Riehemann, S. 1998. Type-Based Derivational Morphology. *Journal of Comparative Germanic Linguistics*, **2**:49–77.

[1973]Thorell, O. 1973. *Svensk grammatik*. Esselte Studium, Stockholm, Sweden, 2nd edition. (in Swedish).

[1994]Trost, H. and Matiasek, J. 1994. Morphology with a Null-Interface. In *Proceedings of the 15th International Conference on Computational Linguistics*, volume 1, pp. 141–147, Kyoto, Japan, August. ACL.

A Method of Pre-computing Connectivity Relations for Japanese/Korean POS Tagging

Kazuaki Ando[1], Tae-hun Lee[2], Masami Shishibori[2], and Jun-ichi Aoe[2]

[1] Dept. of Reliability-based Information Systems Engineering, Kagawa University
2217-20 Hayashi-cho Takamatsu-shi 761-0396 JAPAN
ando@eng.kagawa-u.ac.jp
[2] Dept. of Information Science & Intelligent Systems, Tokushima University
2-1 Minami-Josanjima-Cho Tokushima-Shi 770-8506 JAPAN
{thlee, bori, aoe}@is.tokushima-u.ac.jp

Abstract. This paper presents an efficient dictionary structure of Part-of-Speech(POS) Tagging for Japanese/Korean by extending Aho and Corasick's pattern matching machine. The proposed method is a simple and fast algorithm to find all possible morphemes in an input sentence and in a single pass, and it stores the relations of grammatical connectivity of neighboring morphemes into the output functions. Therefore, the proposed method can reduce both costs of the dictionary lookup and the connection check to find the most suitable word segmentation. From the simulation results, it turns out that the proposed method was 21.8% faster (CPU time) than the general approach using the trie structure. Concerning the number of candidates for checking connections, it was 27.4% less than that of the original morphological analysis.

1 Introduction

In Oriental Language processing, morphological analysis means segmentations of an input sentence into words (morphemes) and attachments of part-of-speech to them. Although morphological analysis for European languages, especially for English, plays only a minor role in various applications of natural language processing system, in the analysis of oriental languages such as Japanese and Korean it plays an important role because they are agglutinative languages, that is the language do not have explicit word boundaries between the words [1], [3], [9], [10], [11], [12].

Generally, the procedure of morphological analysis of agglutinative languages consists of three tasks. The first is to detect all possible morphemes, which are the smallest meaningful units, in a given input sentence. The second is to check the possible connections between neighboring morphemes by using a connection cost or probability based on the grammaticality [1], [3] ,[12]. The last is to detect the most suitable word segmentation from the result of the previous tasks. In the first step, the morphological analysis of agglutinative languages involves a large number of dictionary lookup.

A. Gelbukh (Ed.): CICLing 2001, LNCS 2004, pp. 363-374, 2001.

A well-known technique for dictionary lookup is to use a trie structure [4], [9]. The trie is a tree structure in which each transition corresponds to a key character in the given keys set and common prefixes of keys can be shared. Therefore, the trie can search all keys made up from prefixes in an input string without the need of scanning the structure more than once. However, it is not so effective to use the trie for the morphological analysis of agglutinative languages [9], [10], [11]. In order to detect all possible substrings in a given input sentence, the dictionary lookup must be tried repeatedly at each character position in the input sentence. Therefore, some characters may be scanned more than once for different starting positions, and the number of dictionary lookup will be increased [10], [11]. In the second step, the morphological analysis checks grammatical connectivity between neighboring morphemes in order to find all possible connections [1], [12]. This grammatical connectivity can be easily checked by using a grammatical table [1]. This process, however, requires considerable costs to check the grammatical connectivity, because it includes no little checks of unnecessary connections, for example, checking connection between NOUN and CONJUGATION, since one word has some different part-of-speech. In order to achieve a fast morphological analysis, the mentioned problems should be solved.

This paper proposes an efficient dictionary structure for the morphological analysis of agglutinative languages by extending a pattern matching algorithm based on Aho and Corasick (AC algorithm) [2], in order to achieve a fast morphological analysis. The proposed method is a simple and fast algorithm to find all possible substrings in an input sentence, scanned once. Moreover, the cost of checking connections between the neighboring morphemes can be reduced during analysis, since the proposed method stores relations of grammatical connectivity of neighboring words into the output functions in advance of morphological analysis.

In the following sections, our ideas are described in detail. In Section 2, we describe a dicrionary structure using the trie. Section 3 presents an efficient dictionary structure using the AC algorithm, and a pre-computing method for grammatical connectivity between neighboring words is proposed in section 4. Section 5 shows experimental evaluations verified by computer simulations with a 101,367-words dictionary. Finally, the results are summarized, and the future research is discussed.

2   Dictionary Structure Using Trie

Morphological analysis of agglutinative languages is very different from that of English [1], [3], [9], [10], [11], [12], because the languages do not have explicit word boundaries between the words. Therefore, in order to find the most suitable word segmentation, the morphological analysis must detect all possible substrings in a given input sentence in the first place. This process is one of the most important tasks of morphological analysis and the most time consuming part of the analysis, since the wrong segmentation causes serious errors in the later analysis such as syntactic and semantic analysis [3]. In this process, the morphological analysis

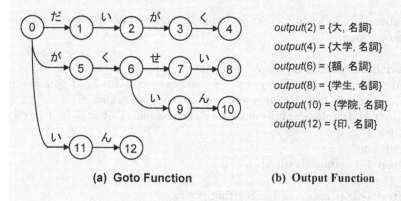

output(2) = {大, 名詞}

output(4) = {大学, 名詞}

output(6) = {額, 名詞}

output(8) = {学生, 名詞}

output(10) = {学院, 名詞}

output(12) = {印, 名詞}

(a) Goto Function   **(b) Output Function**

Fig. 1. Trie Dictionary

involves a large number of dictionary lookup. In general, a well-known method for dictionary lookup is to use a trie structure [4], [9]. The trie is a tree structure in which each transition corresponds to a character of the keys in the presented key set K. In the trie, a path from the root (initial state) to a leaf corresponds to one key in K. This way, the states of the trie correspond to the prefixes of keys in K.

The following is introduced for formal discussions:

1. S is a finite set of states, represented as a positive number.
2. I is a finite set of input symbols, or characters.
3. *goto* is a function from $S \times I$ to $S \cup \{fail\}$, called a goto function.
4. *output* is a function from S to morphological information, called an output function.
5. The state number of the trie is represented as a positive number, where the initial state in S is represented by the number 0.

A transition labeled with a (in I) from r to n indicates that $goto(r, a) = n$. The absence of a transition indicates failure (*fail*). Fig 1 shows an example of a trie for the set $K = \{$"だい [da-i]", "だいがく [da-i-ga-ku]", "がく [ga-ku]", "がくせい [ga-ku-se-i]", "がくいん [ga-ku-i-n]", "いん [i-n]"$\}$[1]. Note that Japanese characters require two bytes.

For example, retrieval of the key "がくせい [ga-ku-se-i]"(means a student) is performed by traversing transitions $goto(0, $'が 'が [ga]'$) = 5$, $goto(5, $'く [ku]'$) = 6$, $goto(6, $'せ [se]'$) = 7$ and $goto(7, $'い [i]'$) = 8$, sequentially, and this time the key "がく [ga-ku]"($=output(6)$) and "がくせい [ga-ku-se-i]"($=output(8)$) are obtained.

In the case of morphological analysis, in order to find the most suitable word segmentation, the dictionary lookup task must detect all possible substrings in

---

[1] だい/大 [da-i]: big, noun; だいがく/大学 [da-i-ga-ku]: university, noun; がく/額 [ga-ku]: amount, noun; がくせい/学生 [ga-ku-se-i]: student; がくいん/学院 [ga-ku-i-n]: academy, noun; いん/印 [i-n]: seal noun;

the input. The following shows a simple dictionary lookup algorithm using the trie structure.

Algorithm 1: Dictionary lookup algorithm using a trie structure
Input: A sentence $TEXT = c_1\ c_2\ ...\ c_n$, where each c_i, for $1 \leq i \leq n$, is an input character, a goto function *goto* and output function *output*.
Output: Morphological information of all possible substrings in a given input sentence *TEXT*
Algorithm:
> **Step 1-1:** {Initialization}
> > $i \leftarrow 1$;
>
> **Step 1-2:** {Change of the starting position}
> > $state \leftarrow 0;\ j \leftarrow i$;
>
> **Step 1-3:** {State transitions}
> > $state \leftarrow goto(state, c_j)$;
> > if $state = fail$ **then goto** Step 1-5;
> > if $output(state) \neq \phi$ **then print** $output(state)$;
>
> **Step 1-4:** {Operation control}
> > $j \leftarrow j + 1$;
> > if $j \leq n$ **then goto** Step 1-3;
>
> **Step 1-5:** {Operation control}
> > $i \leftarrow i + 1$;
> > if $i \leq n$ **then goto** Step 1-2;

The trie is a very common structure for dictionary lookup. However, it is not so effective to use the trie for morphological analysis of agglutinative languages, because the dictionary lookup must be tried from every character position in the input sentence [10], [11], in order to detect all possible substrings in a given input sentence. Therefore, some characters may be scanned more than once for different starting positions and the number of unnecessary dictionary lookup will be increased.

For example, the following is an input:

$$TEXT = \text{"だいがく [da-i-ga-ku]"} \ (\text{means a university})$$

At first, the morphological analysis tries to find all possible words starting with "だ [da]" (i=1). As the result, the $output(2)$ and $output(4)$ are obtained. The starting position is advanced to the second character in *TEXT*, and the dictionary lookup is repeated. As for the key starting with "い [i]" (i=2), the goto transitions are failed at state 11, and no output is generated. Then, starting position is advanced, and the $output(6)$ is produced by the $goto(0, \text{'が [ga]'}) = 5$ and $goto(5, \text{'く [ku]'}) = 6$. For the final position in the *TEXT*, the goto function returns the message *fail* because there is no transtitions for "く [ku]" on the initial state. Consequently, the character "い [i]", "が [ga]", and "く [ku]" were scanned two, two, and three times, respectively, because the dictionary lookup was repeated 5 times for each character position. In the worst case, the number of the dictionary lookup will be $n(n-1)/n$ times. In order to achieve a faster morphological analysis, it is necessary to improve this operation.

3   Dictionary Structure Using the AC Algorithm

It was observed in the preceding section that morphological analysis using the trie involves a large number of the dictionary lookup. In order to solve this problem, we apply an efficient string pattern matching algorithm based on Aho and Corasick (AC algorithm) to the dictionary structure of morphological analysis [10], [11]. The AC algorithm is a underlying implementation of the fgrep command of UNIX. It can locate all occurrences of any of a finite number of keywords in a text string. The AC algorithm is a extension of the Knuth-Morris-Pratt algorithm [8] for single string pattern matching.

Let $KEY = \{k_1, k_2, ..., k_k\}$ be a finite set of strings which we shall call key and let $TEXT$ be an arbitrary string which we shall call the *text string*. The AC algorithm is a program which takes as input the text string $TEXT$ and produces as output the morphological information and the locations in $TEXT$ at which keys of KEY appear as *substrings*. The AC approach is constructed as a finite set of states S. Each state is represented by a number. One state (usually 0) is designated as the initial state.

The behavior of the AC algorithm is defined by the next three functions:

goto function *goto*: $S \times I \rightarrow S \cup \{fail\}$
failure function f: $S \rightarrow S$
output function *output*: $S \rightarrow A$, morphological information

The function *goto* maps a set consisting of a state and a character into a state or the message *fail*. The function f maps a state into a state. The failure function is constructed whenever the goto function reports the message *fail*. Certain states are designated as output states that indicate that a set of keys has been found. The function *output* formalizes this concept by associating a set of keys (possible empty) with each state.

Fig. 2 shows the functions used by the AC algorithm for the set of keys $K =$ {"だい [da-i]", "だいがく [da-i-ga-ku]", "がく [ga-ku]", "がくせい [ga-ku-se-i]", "がくいん [ga-ku-i-n]", "いん [i-n]"}[2]. Here, ¬{'だ [da]', 'が [ga]', 'い [i]'} denotes all input characters other than 'だ [da]', 'が [ga]', and 'い [i]'. The directed graph in Fig. 2(a) represents the goto function. The dotted lines represents the failure function, and the absence of failure transition indicates $f(s) = 0$.

For example, the transition labeled 'だ [da]' from state 0 to state 1 indicates that $goto(0, 'だ [da]') = 1$. The absence of goto transition indicates failure. The AC algorithm has the property that $goto(0, 's') \neq fail$ for all input symbols s. A dictionary lookup algorithm using the AC algorithm is summarized below:

---

[2] だい/大 [da-i]: big, noun; だいがく/大学 [da-i-ga-ku]: university, noun; がく/額 [ga-ku]: amount, noun; がくせい/学生 [ga-ku-se-i]: student; がくいん/学院 [ga-ku-i-n]: academy, noun; いん/印 [i-n]: seal noun;

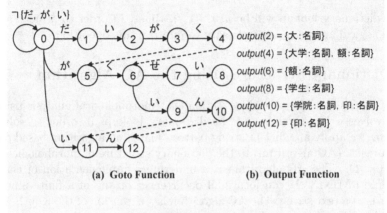

(a) Goto Function   (b) Output Function

Fig. 2. AC Dictionary

Algorithm 2: Dictionary lookup algorithm using the AC machine

Input: A sentence $TEXT = c_1 c_2 \dots c_n$, where each c_i, for $1 \le i \le n$, is an input character, an AC machine with goto function *goto*, failure function *f*, and output function *output*.

Output: Morphological information of all possible substrings in a given input sentence $TEXT$

Algorithm:

    Step 2-1: {Initialization}

        $state \leftarrow 0$;

        $i \leftarrow 1$;

    Step 2-2: {State transitions}

        if *goto*(*state*, c_i) $\neq$ *fail* **then goto** Step 2-3;

        $state \leftarrow f(state)$;

        goto Step 2-2;

    Step 2-3: {Output operation}

        $state \leftarrow goto(state, c_i)$;

        if *output*(*state*) $\neq \phi$ **then print** *output*(*state*);

    Step 2-4: {Operation control}

        $i \leftarrow i + 1$;

        if $i \le n$ **then goto** Step 2-2;

Consider the behavior of the AC dictionary that uses the functions in Fig. 2 to process the text string "だいがくせい [da-i-ga-ku-se-i]" (means a university student). Since *goto*(0, 'だ [da]') = 1 and *goto*(1, 'い [i]') = 2 the AC dictionary enters state 2, advances to the next input symbol and emits *output*(2), indicating that it has found the key "だい [da-i]". Similarly, since *goto*(2, 'が [ga]') = 3 and *goto*(3, 'く [ku]') = 4, the AC dictionary finds the *output*(4)(="だいがく [da-i-ga-ku]" and "がく [ga-ku]"). In state 4 with the input symbol 'せ [se]', the AC dictionary makes two state transitions in its operating cycle. Since *goto*(4, 'せ [se]') = *fail*, the AC dictionary enters state 6 = *f*(4). At this point, since *goto*(6,

'せ [se]') = 7 and $goto(7,$ 'い [i]') = 8, the AC dictionary enters state 8 and emits $output(8)$, indicating that it has found the key "がくせい [ga-ku-se-i]" .

The AC dictionary can find all possible sub-morphemes in an input sentence, scanned only once. Therefore, the AC dictionary is the most advantageous method for the morphological analysis of agglutinative languages.

4   Pre-computing Connectivity Relations

In the second step of morphological analysis, grammatical connectivity between neighboring words, which were obtained by the dictionary lookup, are checked, in order to find the most suitable word boundary [1], [12]. This process, however, requires a lot of checking for grammatical connectivity between them, because it must check all relations between part-of-speech of the preceding words and that of the following words.

Suppose that HIRAGANA character 'い [i]' has 14 kinds of part-of-speech and 'し [si]' has 19 kinds of part-of-speech in a dictionary for the morphological analysis. With checking grammatical connectivity between the preceding character 'い [i]' and the following character 'し [si]' ("いし [i-si]" means a stone, a doctor etc.), it involves 266 (=14 × 19) connection checking. However, those checking include 126 (=14 × 9) failures such as checking between NOUN and CONJUGATION. In order to achieve a fast morphological analysis, the problem of how to reduce the number of failure checking should be solved.

Thus, we focus on a feature that all possible substrings are stored in one pass from initial state to terminal state by the failure function. By using this feature, the grammatical connectivity between the neighboring morphemes, which are included in one pass, can be checked in advance of the morphological analysis as shown Fig. 3, that is, the grammatical connectivity can be pre-checked. Then, the results can be stored into each output function as un-connectable candidate, which means that it is not connectable to all part-of-speech of the preceding morphemes, when the dictionary of morphological analysis is constructed. If the un-connectable candidates are available throughout an execution of the morphological analysis, the number of checking unnecessary connections can be reduced.

For example, concerning a pass "たべすぎ [ta-be-su-gi]", which means overeating in Fig. 3, each of pairs such as 'た [ta]' and 'べ [be]', "たべ [ta-be]" and 'す [su]', and "たべ [ta-be]" and "すぎ [su-gi]" can be checked in advance of the analysis.

Let us examine other approaches, such as the trie [4], Directed Acyclic Word Graph (DAWG) and Deterministic Finite Automaton (DFA) [11]. As for the trie, it does not keep information of substrings in each path. The DAWG and DFA have states with more than one outgoing transition after a state with two or more incoming transitions. Thus, there is no guarantee that there exists a subset of states in them with one-to-one correspondence between the outputs and the states in that subset. Therefore, they cannot keep information of un-connectable candidates correctly without improving them. On the other hand,

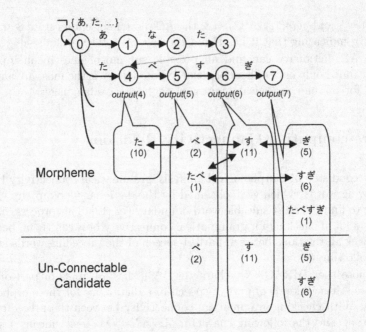

Fig. 3. Pre-Checking connectivity relations between neighboring morphemes in the AC Dictionary

the AC dictionary can attach un-connectable candidates to the corresponding output state uniquely without improving the data structure.

Algorithm 3 summarizes the method for checking all un-connectable candidates in one pass. The algorithm 3 can be applied after constructing the AC dictionary. The following variables and functions are utilized for explaining algorithm 3:

1. *queue* and *tmp*: stores a set of states;
2. Function CHECK(*state1*, *state2*): checks grammatical connectivity between neighboring morphemes in *output*(*state1*) and *output*(*state2*). It returns a set of un-connectable candidates;
3. *un-cand*: stores a set of un-connectable candidates returned by the function CHECK();
4. Function UpdateOutput(*state*, *un-cand*): updates the *output*(*state*) with the *un-cand*;

Algorithm 3: Algorithm for checking all un-connectable candidates in one pass
Input: A morpheme $MORPHEME = c_1 \, c_2 \, ... \, c_n$ registered in the AC dictionary, where each c_i, for $1 \leq i \leq n$, is an input character and the AC dictionary.
Output: All un-connectable candidates in one pass
Algorithm:

Step 3-1: {Initialization}
   $state \leftarrow 0$; $queue \leftarrow empty$; $i \leftarrow 1$;
Step 3-2: {Storing States}
   $state \leftarrow goto(state, c_i)$;
   if $output(state) \neq empty$ **then**
      $queue \leftarrow queue \cup state$;
Step 3-3: {Operation Control}
   $i \leftarrow i + 1$;
   if $i \leq n$ **then goto** Step 3-2;
Step 3-4: {Pop Up a State}
   if $queue = empty$ **then**
      the process is terminated.
   let pre_state be the next state in the $queue$;
   $queue \leftarrow queue - \{pre\_state\}$;
   $tmp \leftarrow queue$;
Step 3-5: {Connection Check and Updating}
   if $tmp = empty$ **then goto** Step 3-6
   let $next\_state$ be the next state in the tmp;
   $tmp \leftarrow tmp - \{next\_state\}$;
   $un\text{-}cand \leftarrow \text{CHECK}(pre\_state, next\_state)$;
   $\text{UpdateOutput}(next\_state, un\text{-}cand)$;
   goto Step 3-5;
Step 3-6: {Operation Control}
   goto Step 3-4;

All un-connectable candidates in the AC dictionary can be computed by repeating the Algorithm 3 after constructing the AC dictionary. The number of checking unnecessary connections can be reduced by using the un-connectable candidates.

Consider the pass "たべすぎ [ta-be-su-gi]" in Fig. 3. As for checking connections between the morpheme starting with 'た [ta]' and the following morphemes, it involves 37(=10('た [ta]')×2('べ [be]')+1("たべ [ta-be]")×11('す [su]')+1("たべ [ta-be]")×6("すぎ [su-gi]")) kinds of checking by using our grammatical table and the morphological dictionary. On the other hand, if the un-connectable candidates are available, it is not necessary to check the grammatical connectivity, because all part-of-speech of 'べ [be]', 'す [su]' and 'すぎ [su-gi]' are un-connectable candidates, that is, 0(=10×0+1×0+1×0). In this case, the most suitable word boundary for the "たべすぎ [ta-be-su-gi]" is just the end of the word, "たべすぎ [ta-be-su-gi]/".

As shown the above, the word boundary can be detected by using the un-connectable candidate without checking the grammatical connectivity during the execution of the morphological analysis, in some cases.

5   Evaluations

5.1   Theoretical Evaluation

Let n be the length of key. The precise complexity of algorithms presented depends on the data structures, so theoretical analysis is first discussed under the following assumptions:

1. The time complexity of confirming one transition, that is, a goto function is $O(1)$.
2. The time complexity of a failure function is $O(1)$.
3. The time complexity of an output function is $O(1)$.

Consider the time complexity of dictionary lookup. As for a trie, it is clear that the time complexity of retrieving a key is $O(n)$ [5], [6]. However, in morphological analysis, since it must detect all possible substrings in a given input sentence, the number of the dictionary access depends on the length of the input sentence. Therefore, the time complexity becomes $O(n^2 + n)(=O((n+1)n/2)$. On the other hand, the time complexity for dictionary lookup of the proposed method is $O(n)(=O(2n\text{-}1))$ [2].

Next, consider the time complexity of construction. Suppose that k is the total number of length of the keys. Concerning the trie, the time complexity is $O(k)$ because it is proportional to the total length of keys. The time complexity for construction of the AC machine is $O(k)$ [2]. The cost of the algorithm 3 depends on the function CCheck and the length of key. Let p be the average number of part-of-speech of preceding words and let f be the average number of part-of-speech of following words. Then, since the time complexity of the CCheck is $O(pf)$, the time complexity of the algorithm 3 becomes $O(n + pf(n^2 - n))$ in the worst case, because the cost of for-loop in algorithm 3 is $O(n)$ and the cost of while-loop is $O((pf)(n-1)n/2)$. From above observation, the time complexity for constructing the proposed method becomes $O(s(l + pf(l^2 - l)))$, where s is the total number of keys and l is the average length of keys.

Consider the effectiveness of the un-connectable candidates. By using this candidate during the execution of the morphological analysis, the time complexity of the CCheck becomes $O(p(f - c))$, where c is the average number of the un-connectable candidates which are stored in the output functions.

5.2   Experimental Evaluation

For experimental evaluation the following methods have been implemented on DELL OptiPlex GXa (Pentium Pro 300MHz) and they have been written in the C language.

1. A dictionary lookup method using the a trie structure.
2. A dictionary lookup method using the extended AC algorithm.

In order to observe an effectiveness of the proposed method, the following materials were used:

Table 1. Comparison between the Trie Dictionary and the Proposed Dictionary

	Trie Dictionary	Proposed Dictionary
Dictionary Size (Mbyte)	8.5	32.9
Construction Time (sec.)	6.2	125.1
Retrieval Time (sec.)	36.3	28.4

Table 2. Comparison between the general AC Dictionary and the Proposed Dictionary

	AC Dictionary	Proposed Dictionary
Dictionary Size (Mbyte)	29.8	32.9
Construction Time (sec.)	10.3	125.1
Candidate	6,112,815	4,442,474

Dictionary Source: containing 101,367 words for our Kana-to-Kanji translation system; The maximum length of the morphemes is 19 and the average
length is 4.2. Note that all of characters in the dictionary source and the input text requires two bytes. There are 528 part-of-speech in the dictionary.
Inputs: News papers articles (2.5MByte); The total number of sentences is
39,400 and the average number of characters of the sentences is 70.3.

Table 1 shows the comparison between the trie dictionary and the proposed
dictionary. From these results, it turns out that the proposed method is 21.8%
faster (CPU time) than the trie one. However, the dictionary size of the proposed
method is larger than that of the trie approach.

Table 2 shows the comparison between the general AC dictionary and the
proposed dictionary. The Cadidate in Table 1 indicates the number of the morphemes except un-connectable candidates. As for the un-connectable candidates,
the total number of candidates was reduced from 6,112,915 to 4,442,584. This
means that the number of checking unnecessary connections can be reduced
about 27.4% .

From the whole experimental observations, we can say that the proposed
method is more practical than that of the trie and the general AC dictionary.
Although it requires more memory spaces and the construction time, a fast
morphological analysis can be achieved by using the proposed method.

6   Conclusion

This paper presented the efficient dictionary structure for the morphological
analysis of agglutinative languages by extending the AC machine. The proposed
method is the simple and fast algorithm to find all possible sub-morphemes in an

input sentence, and during a single scan, and it stores the connectivity relationship between neighboring words into the output functions as the un-connectable candidates. Therefore, the number of connection checking can be reduced. Since these features depend on the passes, the proposed method has a good effect if there are a large number of long morphemes in an input text. The effectiveness of the proposed method has been evaluated by the experimental evaluation was supported by the computer simulation with the 101,367-words dictionary. From the results, it turns out that the proposed method was 21.8% faster (CPU time) than the usual trie approach, and there are 27.4% un-connectable candidates in our dictionary.

We are implementing a morphological analysis system using the proposed method based on the minimum connection cost method. The proposed method will be compared with conventional techniques in a real setting.

References

1. Abe, M. Ooshima, Y., Yuura, K., and Takeichi, N.: A Kana-Kanji Translation System for Non-Segmented Input Sentences Based on Syntactic and Semantic Analysis. Proceedings of the 10th International Conference on Computational Linguistics (1986) pp.280–pp.285.
2. Aho, A.V., and Corasick, M.J.: Efficient String Matching : An Aid to Bibliographic Search. Communications of the ACM, Vol.18, No.6 (1975) pp.333–340
3. Akiba, T., Tokunaga, T., and Tanaka, H.: An Extension of LangLAB for Japanese Morphological Analysis. Proceedings of the International Workshop on Sharable Natural Language Resources (1994) pp.36–42
4. Aoe, J.: An Efficient Digital Search Algorithm by Using a Double-Array Structure. IEEE Transactions on Software Engineering, vol.SE-15 (1989) pp. 1066–1077
5. Aoe, J.: Computer Algorithms: Key Search Strategies. IEEE Computer Society Press (1991)
6. Aoe, J., Morimoto, K., Shishibori, M., and Park, K.H.: A Trie Compaction Algorithm for a Large Set of Keys. IEEE Transactions of Knowledge and Date Engineering, Vol.8, No.3 (1996) pp.476-491
7. Kaplan, S.J.: Designing a Portable Natural Language Database Query System. ACM Transactions on Database Systems, Vol.9, No.1 (1984) pp.1–29
8. Knuth D.E., Morris, J.H., and Pratt, V.R.: Fast pattern matching in strings. SIAM Journal on Computing, vol.6, No.2 (1977) pp. 323–350
9. Kurohashi, S., Nakamura, T., Matsumoto, Y., and Nagao, M.: Improvements of Japanese Morphological Analyzer JUMAN. Proceedings of the International Workshop on Sharable Natural Language Resources (1994) pp.22–28
10. Maruyama, H.: Backtracking-Free Dictionary Access Method for Japanese Morphological Analysis. Proceedings of the 15th International Conference on Computational Linguistics (1994) pp.208–213.
11. Mori, S.: High Speed Morphological Analysis using DFA. Technical report of IEICE of Japan, NLC96-23 (1996), pp.17–23 (in Japanese)
12. Sano, H., Kawada, R., and Hasimoto, M.: Morphological Grammar Rules : An Implementation for JUMAN. Proceedings of the International Workshop on Sharable Natural Language Resources (1994) pp.29–35

A Hybrid Approach of Text Segmentation Based on Sensitive Word Concept for NLP

Fuji Ren

Faculty of Information Sciences, Hiroshima City University
3-4-1, Ozuka-Higasi,Asa-Minami-Ku, Hiroshima, 731-31, Japan
ren@its.hiroshima-cu.ac.jp

Abstract. Natural language processing, such as Checking and Correction of Texts, Machine Translation, and Information Retrieval, usually starts from words. The identification of words in Indo-European languages is a trivial task. However, this problem named text segmentation has been, and is still a bottleneck for various Asian languages, such as Chinese. There have been two main groups of approaches to Chinese segmentation: dictionary-based approaches and statistical approaches. However, both approaches have difficulty to deal with some Chinese text. To address the difficulties, we propose a hybrid approach using Sensitive Word Concept to Chinese text segmentation. Sensitive words are the compound words whose syntactic category is different from those of their components. According to the segmentation, a sensitive word may play different roles, leading to significantly different syntactic structures. In this paper, we explain the concept of sensitive words and their efficacy in text segmentation firstly, then describe the hybrid approach that combines the rule-based method and the probability-based method using the concept of sensitive words. Our experimental results showed that the presented approach is able to address the text segmentation problems effectively.

1   Introduction

The initial stage of text analysis for many Natural Language Processing (NLP) task usually involves the tokenization of the input into words. For a language like English, the identification of words is a trivial task. However, this problem has been, and is still a bottleneck for Chinese. In Chinese, sentences are written as continuous character strings without word separation. For example, *"ji suan ji yi jing yong yu ge ge ling yu"* [1]. (Computers have been used in every area).

The same problem exists in Japanese also. However, in accordance with our empiricism, Japanese segmentation is much easier then Chinese, because that in

---

[1] Throughout this paper, we use Roman alphabet to indicate the Chinese character. For example, *ji* indicates a Chinese character, and *ji suan ji* indicate three Chinese characters (means "computer"). Notice that the first *ji* and the last *ji* are different Chinese characters, although they are same in the Roman alphabets. For reading easy, we put a space between Chinese characters.

A. Gelbukh (Ed.): CICLing 2001, LNCS 2004, pp. 375–388, 2001.

written Chinese, there is no explicit word delimiter such as Japanese case particles, and there is no any morphological discrimination between their verb form and noun form[2]. Much work have been done to segmenting Chinese text. There have been two main groups of approaches to Chinese segmentation: dictionary-based approaches and statistical approaches. It has been reported that the segmentation accuracy may reach at very high. However, the tests for segmentation have been oversimplified: segmentation has been tested as if it is the finality of Chinese processing. If segmentation is considered together with further processing (e.g. information retrieval, machine translation), many hidden problems will be unveiled. If the segmentation problem is considered together with the use, the accuracy rate is much lower. This fact has been confirmed by a survey [6] conducted by a group of experts in China. They used several test corpora for different tests. This survey gave the following conclusions about current state of Chinese NLP software:

- On the test for word segmentation and tagging:
  The best software reached at an 89.4% accuracy for word segmentation, and only 79.58% of words have been tagged correctly in the best case.
- On word boundary determination:
  The best success rate for word boundary determination is 60%, and the global accuracy is 89.4% . The accuracy rate for tagging correctly segmented texts is 86.6%.
- On the test for solving ambiguities in word segmentation:
  The systems had success rates varying from 61% to 78% for dealing with overlapping ambiguities (see next section for a description), and from 36% to 59% for dealing with combinatory ambiguities (see next section)

These conclusions make it clear that the claimed such high accuracy rate hid many unsolved problems. These problems will greatly affect the quality of further processing on Chinese. We show two problems using examples.

1. Using modern Chinese common word list may lead to mistake segmentation in some cases
   Example 1: *ta ying pin qu dang gong cheng shi.*
   (He is employed as an engineer.)
   Because that *ying pin* is a word which it obtained in the Chinese dictionary for information processing[16], almost segmentation system will segment the sentence into below segmentation for strings *ying pin*:
   Segmentation 1.1: *ta / ying pin / qu / dang / gong cheng shi /.*
   (he / employ / PP[3] / be /engineer /.)
   This is correct segmentation. However, it will lead to a mistake for example 2, because that it will segment example 2 into segmentation 2.1, a mistake result. The correct segmentation should be segmentation 2.2.

---

[2] For example, *fan yi* indicates both verb "translate" and noun "translation".
[3] PP stands for a PrePosition.

Example 2: *ta ying pin zhang san qu dang gong cheng shi.*
(He should employ Zhang san as an engineer.)
Segmentation 2.1: *ta / ying pin / zhang san / qu / dang / gong cheng shi /.*
(he / employ / zhang san / PP / be /engineer /.)
Segmentation 2.2: *ta / ying / pin / zhang san / qu / dang / gong cheng shi
/.*
(he / should / employ / zhang san / PP / be /engineer /.)

2. Traditional segmentation results lead to more difficulty in NLP

In NLP, such as MT, it is expected to group words into long phrases. The advantage of grouping words into phrases is its high efficiency for NLP: if an expression may be unambiguously recognized, it is useless to analyze its composition and it can be translated directly as a whole[8]. However, traditional segmentation methods usually segment sentence into small words. Let us see examples.

Example 3: *xin xi chan ye bu zheng zai zhi ding xin xi gao su gong lu de ji hua.*
(Information industry Ministry is enacting the plan of information highway.) The fragment *xin xi gao su gong lu* (information highway) in this sentence will be segmented into *xin xi* (information) , *gao su* (highspeed) and *gong lu* (road) in most traditional segmentation system, and it is considered as a correct segmentation. However, it lead to more difficulty in analysis of text, such as in information retrieval, machine translation. Because that *xin xi* is a noun, *gao su* is a adjective or a noun and *gong lu* is a noun, it leads to many ambiguities in syntactic analysis. One basic idea is to add all the compound words, such as *xin xi gao su gong lu* into a dictionary, and using the dictionary to segment. The idea seems very good and high efficiency, but it may lead to more serious mistake. For example, if we add compound word *ji qi fan yi* into the dictionary and use it to segment below sentence, we will get an error result showed in segmentation 4.1. The correct one should be segmentation 4.2. This is one of motivations why we try to introduce the concept of sensitive word and non-sensitive word in NLP.

Example 4: *ta yong ji qi fan yi ji shu wen xian.*
(He translates technology documents with the machine.)
Segmentation 4.1: *ta / yong / ji qi fan yi / ji shu wen xian /.*
(N / PP / N / N [4])
(He / PP / machine translation / technology documents)
Segmentation 4.2: *ta / yong / ji qi / fan yi / ji shu wen xian /.*
(N / PP / N / V[5] / N)
(He / PP / machine / translate / technology documents)

In this paper, a hybrid approach using Sensitive Word Concept to Chinese text segmentation is presented. Sensitive words are the compound words whose syntactic category is different from those of their components. According to the segmentation, a sensitive word may play different roles, leading to significantly

---

[4] N stands for a Noun.
[5] V stands for a Verb.

different syntactic structures. In this paper, we explain the concept of sensitive words and their efficacy in text segmentation firstly, then describe the hybrid approach that combines the rule-based method and the probability-based method using the concept of sensitive words. Our experimental results showed that the presented approach is able to address the text segmentation problems effectively.

2 Ambiguities in Segmentation

Let us show some examples first.

Example 5: *wang lao da jing lai dong jing du shu.*

(Wang Laoda will come to study at Tokyo.)

This sentence may be segmented into several legitimate words. Two of them are as follows:

Segmentation 5.1: *wang lao da / jing / lai / dong jing / du shu /.*

Wang Laoda / will / come / Tokyo / study /.

Segmentation 5.2: *wang lao da / jing lai / dong jing / du shu /.*

Wang Laoda / in the future / Tokyo / study /.

In this example, the string *jing lai* may be segmented in two different ways: as *jing lai* - in the future, or as *jing / lai* - will come. Thus, there is a segmentation ambiguity. The first segmentation is the correct one whereas the second one is not grammatical.

Example 6: *ta yan jiu sheng wu hua xue.*

(He studies biochemistry)

Two possible segmentation solutions are as follows:

Segmentation 6.1: *ta / yan jiu / sheng wu hua xue/.*

he / study / biochemistry / .

Segmentation 6.2: *ta / yan jiu sheng / wu / hua xue/.*

he / graduate student / object / chemistry /.

The character *sheng* may be grouped either with the precedent characters *yan jiu* to form *yan jiu sheng* (graduate student) or with the next characters *wu hua xue* to form *sheng wu hua xue* (biochemistry).

We can separate segmentation ambiguities according to their nature (morphological, syntactic and semantic)[3].

We can also consider the ambiguities according to their structural forms as Combination ambiguity, Overlapping ambiguity and Hybrid ambiguity. Given a string

$$C_i C_{i+1} \cdots C_j.$$

If more than two ways of segmentation are possible, then a segmentation ambiguity has occurred.

– Combination ambiguity

For any two words in a sentence, denoted as W1 and W2,

$$W_1 = C_{11} C_{12} C_{13} \cdots C_{1k}.$$

$$W_2 = C_{21} C_{22} C_{23} \cdots C_{2j}.$$

If W_1 and W_2 cannot be combined together to function as a word, it has no ambiguity existing between W_1 and W_2. If W_1 and W_2 can be constituents of the other word, then word segmentation ambiguity exists in these two words (two strings of Chinese characters). This case is called as a Combination ambiguity.

Example 7: *ta / de / biao qing / shi fen / hua ji/* .

(He / ST [6] / look / very / funny/ .) (He looks very funny.)

In this sentence, the two characters in the fragment *shi fen* can either function as two autonomous words *shi* (ten) and *fen* (mark), or they can combine together to function as a word *shi fen* (very). Given the sentential context of example 7, only the second alternation is correct. However, in below sentence, it must be segment into two autonomous words.

Example 8: *ta / zhi / kao / le / shi / fen /* .

(He / only / score /ST / ten / mark/ .) (He scores only ten marks.)

The traditional Maximum Matching method will regard this fragment as a bisyllabic word *shi fen* (very), since this word is longer than the lengths of the two monosyllabic words *shi* (ten) and *fen* (mark).

– Overlapping ambiguity

If there is a word boundary ambiguity between the strings W_1 and W_2 and the string that precedes or follows them, say W_3, and these three strings can be grouped into either "W_1 W_2 / W_3" or "W_1/ W_2 W_3", then we say that an overlap ambiguity.

Example 9: *bi xu / shi xian / zai / qing bao / gong zuo / fang mian / de /zi dong hua/* .

(must / achieve /PP/ information / field / ST/ modernization)

(We must achieve the modernization of the information field.)

The fragment *shi xian zai* in the above example has overlap ambiguity. The middle character (or string) *xian* can combine with the previous character *shi* to form the word *shi xian* (achieve), leaving the third character functioning as a monosyllabic word *zai* (in). The middle character *xian* can also combine with the next character *zai* to form the word *xian zai* (at present), leaving the first character alnoe.

– Hybrid ambiguity

If there are both combination ambiguity and overlapping ambiguity, the situation is called a hybrid ambiguity.

Example 10: *ta / kan jian / yi / zhi / bai tian e /.*

(He / see / one / CL[7] / swan /.)

(He saw a swan.)

In this sentence, the *bai tian e* has both overlap ambiguity and Combination ambiguity. Say it detail, *bai tian e* (swan) and *bai* (white) and *tian e* (swan) is a Combination ambiguity, and *bai tian* (daytime) and *tian e* (swan) is an overlap ambiguity.

---

[6] ST stands for the Structure word *de*.

[7] CL stands for a Classifier.

3   Chinese Segmentation and Sensitive Words

There have been two main groups of approaches to Chinese segmentation: dictionary based approaches and statistical approaches.

Statistical approaches [1,5,6,10,11,12] rely on statistical information such as word and character (co-)occurrence frequencies in the training data - often a set of manually segmented texts. The statistical data describe how probable a character string may be a word, or how probable a word may follow another word. Using these data, the segmentation process consists of first determining the probability of a word sequence, and then choosing the one with the highest probability.

Dictionary-based approaches [4,7,9] operate according to a very simple concept: a correct segmentation result should consist of legitimate words - the words stored in a dictionary or derivable from some rules. In general, however, several legitimate word sequences may be obtained from a Chinese sentence. The longest matching algorithm is then used to select the word sequence that contains the longest (or equivalently, the fewest) words. For example, the sentence *ji qi fan yi bu zhun que* (Machine translation is not accurate) may be segmented, among others, in the following ways:

- *ji qi fan yi / bu / zhun que*
  (machine translation, not, accurate = MT is not accurate)
- *ji qi / fan yi / bu / zhun que*
  (machine, translate, not, accurate)
- *ji qi fan yi / bu / zhun / que*
  (machine translation, not, allow/accurate, indeed)

Among these possible solutions, the longest-matching algorithm will choose the first one. In most cases, the longest-matching method can choose the correct solution. Its accuracy is typically around 90% [6]. However, if the sentence is slightly changed to *ji qi fan yi wen zhang bu zhun que* (Using machines to translate articles is not accurate), then the algorithm will choose the following wrong segmentation:

- *ji qi fan yi / wen zhang / bu / zhun que*
  (machine translation, article, not, accurate).

The correct segmentation should separate *ji qi fan yi* into two words. These examples illustrate the impact of segmentation to the whole Chinese analysis. The problem of segmentation is its ambiguities. Many Chinese words containing at least two characters can be decomposed into simpler words (in modern Chinese). However, most such decompositions do not change radically the syntactic categories. Typically, a compound noun, if decomposed into Noun + Noun structure, would not change significantly the syntactic structure of the sentence. On the other hand, a decomposition may lead to two words with very different categories. For example, *jiang lai* (in the future - an adverb), if decomposed into *jiang / lai* (will, come - a auxiliary + verb sequence) would make a big difference in sentence's structure. It is this case that sensitive words are involved. Among the compound words of the last case, we still distinguish two different cases:

- Once decomposed, the words are unusual, or they cannot appear together;
- The component words are usual words, and can follow each other in normal Chinese sentences[8].

We only consider the words in the second case to be sensitive words. The string *zhun que* (accurate) is an example of the first case. *zhun* (accurate/permit) and *que* (indeed) separately are also words. However, they do not appear together in modern Chinese. This is not a sensitive word. On the other hand, it is easy to find cases where *jiang lai* (in the future) should be separated into *jiang / lai* (will, come). Therefore, it is a sensitive word.

Now, why sensitive words are interesting to study? Usually, Chinese processing follows the following pattern: one starts with the best segmentation result, if the subsequent analysis fails, we restart with the second best segmentation result, and so on. In this pattern, the quality of a segmentation result is solely based on word length. In fact, many segmentation ambiguities only affect word length, but not their meaning and the syntactic structure of the sentence. Taking such an alternative would not help at all the subsequent analysis if the first failed. Therefore, it is better to take an alternative that will lead to a significant change in sentence structure. This is the role of sensitive words: when a first analysis with the best segmentation result fails, we should first try to break down sensitive words involved. In this way, we can expect to arrive at the correct analysis result more quickly.

For example, it is rare, if not impossible, that the string *dong jing* (Tokyo) should be separated into words *dong* (east) and *jing* (capital) in normal Chinese sentences. Words such as *du shu* (study) can be separated in a more natural way into *du* (read) and *shu* (book). However, they will form together a verb phrase *du / shu* which has exactly the same meaning as *du shu* together. So breaking these words does not lead to a significantly different solution for later analysis, it will likely lead to a failure, too. For example, segmenting the string *xin xi gao su gong lu* as one word (Information highway) is much better than segmenting it as three words: *xin xi* (Information), *gao su* (high speed), and *gong lu* (road). This is why we introducing the concept of sensitive word and non-sensitive word in Chinese language processing.

4   Text Segmentation System: GAOMING

We present a hybrid method for text segmentation based on our analysis and our experience in developing Chinese language processing system. A prototype system called GAOMING based on the proposed method has been built and experiments on actual texts have been carried out. This section describes the outline of GAOMING text segmentation System.

---

[8]   We use "normal sentences" because one can always imagine some very peculiar sentences for many word sequences. However, these sequences do not occur in normal texts.

4.1   Process of Text Segmentation

Figure 1 shows the GAOMING system architecture. GAOMING consists of three parts as following:

- Preparing Segmentation Dictionary
- Discovering New Words
- Detecting and Resolving Segmentation Ambiguity

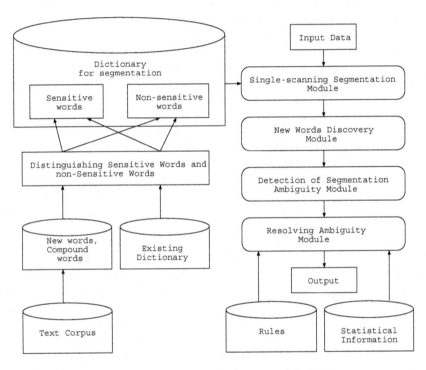

Fig. 1. system architecture:A functional-block diagram

In our method, a dictionary for segmentation is firstly prepared. The dictionary is made distinction between sensitive words and non-sensitive words. The contents of the dictionary consist of two sources: one is an existing dictionary but the sensitive words are distinguished from non-sensitive words. The other is new words and compound words which are acquired from text corpus. Notice that all the words are also distinguished into difference category: sensitive word and non-sensitive word. Then, system segments the inputted text using the segmentation dictionary. In this stage, all segmentation candidates are remained, and the sensitive word or non-sensitive word mark is attached to the initial segmentation result. Because of the concept of sensitive word, the quantities and patterns which are asked to disambiguation are much low then traditional method. Third, system detects and resolves the ambiguities using both rules and statistical information. Because of the paper length limit, the algorithm of discovering new words will not be discussed in the paper, but some technique of disambiguation will be discussed in next sections.

4.2   Analysis of Sensitive Words in a Machine-Readable Dictionary

The machine-readable Chinese dictionary we analyze here contains 87599 words (phrases). This is a dictionary used by a segmentation program, and manually checked by a Chinese linguist. The aim of the analysis is to make distinction of sensitive and non-sensitive words [3].

The meaning of the symbols we will use is given in Table 1.

Symbol	Meaning	Example
ADJ	adjective	*nei* (inside)
ADV	adverb	*yi hou* (after)
CONJ	conjunction	*he* (and)
NC	common noun	*ji qi* (machine)
PREP	preposition	*bi* (in comparison with)
QUAN-CL	quantity + classifier	*ji ge* (several)
VAUX	auxiliary verb	*neng* (can)
VINT	intransitive verb	*xue xi* (study)
VTR	transitive verb	*guan li* (manage)
V	VINT or VTR	

Table 1. Symbols and their meaning

In many cases, compound words (phrases) are constructed from simpler words according to some rules. The following rules are commonly used:

NC + NC → NC (*gong si + zhi yuan* = employee of a company)
NC + V → V (*ren gong + fan zhi* = artificially breed)
NC + V → NC (*ji qi + zhe tu* = drawing by machine)
VTR + NC → NC (*jing +kou* = import)
VTR + NC → VINT (*buo + zhong* = weed)

Sensitive words are mainly due to the fact that a Chinese word (especially single-character word) may play different roles. For example, *ba men* (guard the door) corresponds to the rule V + NC → VINT. However, *ba* is can also be a preposition that introduces the object in the structure *ba* Something *Verb*, meaning "to Verb Something". The string *ba men* can also be considered as a sequence of *ba* Something as in *ta ba men da kai* (he opens the door = he *ba* door open). Therefore, *ba men* is a sensitive word. In our examination of the MRD, we intuitively determined a set of compositions that are the most propitious for sensitive words according to Chinese grammar. These compositions are shown in Table 2.

Composition	Example word
ADV + NC	hou men (back door // after, door)
ADV + QUAN-CL	hao ji ge (several // well, several)
ADV + VAUX	quan neng (all-round // all, can)
ADV + VINT	cai neng (capability // then, do)
PREP + NC	ba men (guard the door // to, door)
PREP + V	cong lai (ever // since, come)
VAUX + PREP	xiang dao (think about // think, to)

Table 2. Some compositions of sensitive words

Table 3 shows the number of sensitive words that we determined manually from a machine-readable dictionary for each word composition. The criteria used are those stated earlier, namely, the component words may play significantly different roles from their compound in reasonable circumstances. 12 357 possible sensitive words have been identified according to the compositions from 87 599 words in the dictionary. Among them, 764 are actual sensitive words.

Composition	nb. words with the pattern	nb. sensitive words (percentage)
ADV + ADV	401	10 (2.5%)
ADV + NC	2230	103 (4.6%)
ADV + PREP	294	9 (3.1%)
ADV + QUAN-CL	9	4 (44.4%)
ADV + VAUX	148	3 (2.0%)
ADV + VINT	1265	20 (1.6%)
ADV + VTR	1155	87 (7.5%)
CONJ + NC	131	14 (10.7%)
CONJ + VTR	94	24 (25.5%)
NC + PREP	628	45 (7.2%)
NC + VAUX	249	95 (38.2%)
NC + VTR	3994	252 (6.3%)
PREP + NC	748	39 (5.2%)
PREP + V	453	15 (3.3%)
VAUX + PREP	96	5 (5.2%)
VAUX + VTR	363	19 (5.2%)
VTR + NC	5976	57 (1.0%)

Table 3. Statistics of sensitive words in the dictionary

4.3   Single-Scanning Segmentation Algorithm

We present a high-performance single-scanning segmentation algorithm, which is based on a sorted word initial dictionary.

A Sorted Word Initial Dictionary In the dictionary a pointer points to a chain of words starting with the same word initial. For example all words beginning with *da*, such as *dadong, dafa, daji, dakai, daliang, dapo, dapochanggui, daji, dating, dayin, dayinji* are referred to by a pointer.

We notice the following facts about a chain of words starting with the same word initial[4].

A Single-Scanning Algorithm Based on the dictionary, we have presented a new single-scanning algorithm. The algorithm has high speed an efficiency, with every word finding its match in one hit[4].

5   The Detection and Resolving of Ambiguity in the Segmentation

During the segmentation, the detection and resolving of ambiguity is very important. We analyzed the special features of Chinese word characters and the statistical information of Chinese text which is acquired from a real world Chinese text corpus we gathered, presented some methods for ambiguity detection and ambiguity resolving.

5.1   Ambiguity Detection Algorithm

1. Segment the text by the maximum matching. Keep the segmentation result and the subsegment of every word acquired during the process.
2. Take a word from the word chain by order.
3. See if the word has a subsegment. If not , return to step 2.
4. Search for the longest match of the part after subsegment. If no match exists, return to step 2.
5. If the right boundary of the longest match is equal to that of the word, then call the combination ambiguity resolving module.
6. Tag 2 to the resulting segmentation using the subsegment. Tag 1 to the original segmentation result.
7. Compare the current word boundaries of 1 and 2.
8. If the boundary of 1 is lower than that of 2, then move the boundary of 1 to the character on the right side. Otherwise continue searching for the longest match in 2. Return to step 7.
9. If there is only one word in the ambiguous string, then there is considered to be no ambiguity and return to step b. Otherwise call the intersection ambiguity resolving module, return to step 2.

5.2 Ambiguity Resolving

We will resolve ambiguity in two-character, three-character, and four-character strings. Each case has an ambiguity resolving module. Ambiguous strings longer than five characters is processed recursively.

Ambiguity Resolving for Two-Character String For two-character strings, the ambiguity is resolved by examining the word-formation legality of the two characters.

1. Call the individuality rule base. If a rule is applicable, then apply it.
2. Compute the semantic similarity of the two characters. If the two are reasonably semantically similar, then no ambiguity is considered to be existing and the two are combined as one word.
3. Evaluate according to the context. If there is a better choice, then accept it. Otherwise combine the two characters as one word.

Ambiguity Resolving for Three-Character String Suppose the three characters are A, B, and C. Here the three can neither form a single word nor remain three individual characters. Thus the possible segmentations are AB / C and A / BC.

1. Call the individuality rule base. If a rule is applicable, apply it.
2. Compute the concurrence evaluation functions of both AB / C and A / BC. Select a better one.

Example 11: *ta / bu / ke neng / zhe yang / zuo*
  Though *bu / ke neng* might also be segmented as *bu ke / neng*. But the latter choice is not so good as the former choice.

Ambiguity Resolving for Four-Character Word A four-character string might be segmented as AB / CD, A / BCD, ABC / D, and A / BC / D. Statistics shows that the first three of these make up 95% of all cases.

1. Call the individuality rule base. If a rule is applicable , then apply it.
2. Compute the evaluation functions. If one segmentation is remarkably better than others, accept it.
3. According to the statistics, the priority ranks as AB / CD, A / BCD, ABC / D, A / BC / D from the highest to the lowest.

Ambiguity Resolving for Words Longer than Five Characters Ambiguity in strings longer than five characters is resolved recursively. For the part other than the first word and the subsegment, recursively call the modules for the ambiguity resolving of shorter strings and keep every optimal segmentation. Based on the acquired result, together with the first word and the subsegment, compute the evaluation functions. Select the best one as the final segmentation result.

Example 12: *qing he yang zai ran shao tiao jian xia jie he cheng fen zi*

Here after segmentation the string *jie he cheng fen zi* ivided as the initial word *jie he* and the rest part *cheng fen zi*, also the sub-segment *jie* and the rest part *he cheng fen zi*.

Here after calling the ambiguity resolving modules for three-character and four-character strings, two possible segmentations exist, namely,

(*jie he*) ((*cheng*) (*fen zi*)) and

(*jie*) ((*he cheng*) (*fen zi*)).

Compute their evaluation functions. The preference is given to the former.

Due to the paper space limitation, the details of the rule base was omiitted. However, because the rules were acquired based on the word characters and the statistical information, so its very useful to segmentation ambiguity resolving. The experiments have evidenced above analysis. By the test, the proposed method is effective in resolving difficult hybrid ambiguities, with an accuracy up to 94%.

6   Conclusions

In this paper, we have proposed a new concept named sensitive word for NLP, and argued that only sensitive words in all compound words have an influence in text segmentation. On the other hand, the non-sensitive words, most in compound words, have not any influence when they are considered as one group. Based on the concept of sensitive word, we have presented a hybrid approach challenges for the Chinese word segmentation, which combines the rule-based method and the probability-based method. A prototype system called GAOMING based on the proposed method has been built and experiments on actual texts have been carried out. One experiment was on a authentic corpus materials containing about 2,200,000 Chinese characters. An evaluation was tested on a arbitrarily selected raw text from the corpus. The selected corpus comprised about 15,000 characters. The word segmentation accuracy was 96%. In particular, the result generated from GAOMING has a most useful information, sensitive word mark. When a first analysis with the best segmentation result fails, we should first try to break down sensitive words involved. It can be expected to arrive at the correct analysis result more quickly. The results show that the proposed method is efficient for Chinese word segmentation. In the future we intend to add some specific knowledge of person's names and new technical words for discovering non-words.

7   Acknowledgments

We would like to thank all our colleagues participating in this project. This work has been partly supported by the Education Ministry of Japan under Grant-in-Aid for Scientific Research (11480080).

References

1. B.-I. Li and e. al., A maximal matching automatic Chinese word segmentation algorithm using corpus tagging for ambiguity resolution. R.O.C. Computational Linguistics Conference, Taiwan, (1991)135-146.
2. C.-L. Yeh and e. al, Rule-based word identification for Mandarin Chinese sentences - A unification approach. Computer processing of Chinese and Oriental Languages, vol. 5, (1991).
3. F-J. Ren, J-Y. Nie, The Concept of Sensitive Word in Chinese - Survey in a Machine-Readable Dictionary,Natural Language Processing,Vol.6,No.1,(1999),59-78.
4. F-J. Ren, A Hybrid Approach to Automatic Checking and Correction of Chinese Texts, Proceedings of Seventeenth IASTED International Conference on Applied Informatics, (1999),17-22.
5. J.-S. Chang and e. al., Chinese word segmentation through constraint satisfaction and statistical optimization. ROCLING-IV, Taiwan, (1991),147-165.
6. KaiYing L.: Estimation Report of Chinese Word Segmentation. Chinese Computerworld. Vol.584, No.12,(1996) 187-189.
7. K.-J. Chen and S.-H. Kiu, Word identification for Mandarin Chinese sentences. 5th International Conference on Computational Linguistics, (1992)101-107.
8. L-X. Fan, F-J. Ren, Y. Miyanaga, K. Tochinai: Automatic Composition of Chinese Compound Words for Chinese-Japanese Machine Translation,Transactions of Information Processing Society Of Japan, Vol.33,No.9,(1992),1103-1113.
9. N. Y. Liang,The Automatic Segmentation in Written Chinese and an Automatic Segmentation System - CDWS. The Academic Journal of Beijing Institute of Aeronautics and Astronautics, (1984)vol. 4.
10. R. Sproat and C. Shih,A statistical method for finding word boundaries in Chinese text. Computer Processing of Chinese and Oriental Languages, vol. 4, (1991)336-351.
11. R. Sproat, C. Shih, W. Gale, and N. Chang ,A stochastic finite-state word-segmentation algorithm for Chinese. (1994)ACL'94.
12. Sheng, Dayang,The automatic recognition of names of Chinese places. The Development and Application of Computational Linguistics. Tsinghua University Press. (1995)68-74.
13. T.-H. Chiang and et. al., Statistical models for segmentation and unknown word resolution. 5th R.O.C. Computational Linguistics Conference, (1992) 123-146.
14. T. Dunning, Accurate Methods for the Statistics of Surprise and Coincidence. Computational Linguistics, vol. 19, (1993)61-74.
15. W. Jin and J.-Y. Nie, Segmentation du Chinois - une Etape Cruciale vers la Traduction Automatique du Chinois. in La Traductique, P. Bouillon and A. Clas, Eds.(1993)349-363.
16. Y. Liu, Q. Tan and et. al., Modern Chinese common word list for information processing, Tsinghua University Press,(1994).

Web-Based Arabic Morphological Analyzer

Jawad Berri, Hamza Zidoum and Yacine Atif

Department of maths and computer science, U. A. E University
P. O. Box 17551, Al-Ain, U.A.E.
{j.berri, hamza.zidoum, yacine.atif}@uaeu.ac.ae

Abstract. This paper presents an Arabic morphological analyzer[1] that is a component of an architecture which can process unrestricted text from Internet. The morphological analyzer uses an object-oriented model to represent the morphological rules for verbs and nouns, a matching algorithm to isolate the affixes and the root of a given word-form, and a linguistic knowledge base consisting in lists of words. The morphological rules fall into two categories: the regular morphological rules of the Arabic grammar and the exception rules that represent the language exceptions. The representation and the implementation of these rules and the matching algorithm are discussed in this paper.
Keywords. Morphological analyzer, object-oriented model, exception rule, matching algorithm.

1 Introduction

Accessing relevant data from information sources is one of the challenges facing research in information technology. Implementing a system that allows a user to query a collection of documents, process them, and extract salient information is a time-consuming task that needs a lot of efforts and resources. This becomes a very hard task especially if the system deals with unrestricted text. In this case, the system is supposed to cope with texts from different domains, with a variable document structure, and in different writing styles. Moreover, in today's Arab-world cyberspace there is a lack of systems that handle Arabic texts and retrieve information expressed in Arabic language over Internet. Fulfilling this gap becomes an important objective as well as a real challenge.

In this paper we present an Arabic morphological analyzer that is a component of an architecture that can process unrestricted text from Internet. The objective within this framework is to process a text downloaded from Internet in order to facilitate its usage by a wide range of further applications [1]. Within this architecture, the system[2] is intended to cope with a flow of unrestricted text; it must be robust and fast. This led us to opt for the following choices:

---

[1] This project has been granted by the U.A.E. University Research Council under contract #01-2-11/00.

[2] The word system will denote the morphological analyzer in the rest of the paper.

A. Gelbukh (Ed.): CICLing 2001, LNCS 2004, pp. 389-400, 2001.

1. To avoid the use of a dictionary as in the case of classical morphological analyzers. Indeed, the coverage of such tool is limited to a given domain and cannot cope with unrestricted texts from dynamic information sources such as the Internet. The second reason that makes us opt for this choice is the unavailability of these tools. Handling Arabic texts nowadays is not a straightforward task since we have to start from scratch. Indeed, except for some limited commercial software that cannot be freely updated, in our knowledge very few Arabic restricted dictionaries are available in the research community.

2. To deal with unvoweled texts since most Arabic texts available on Internet are written in modern standard Arabic that usually doesn't use diacritical marks. Analysing unvoweled Arabic is more confusing because an unvoweled word can have more than a single analysis. For instance the unvoweled Arabic word "كتب" (/ktb/, notion of writing) when voweled, has the three following possible interpretations: "كَتَبَ", (/kataba/, 'he wrote'), "كُتِبَ", (/kutiba/, 'has been written') and "كُتُب", (/kutubun/, 'books'). To handle unvoweled texts we need a more flexible method that uses some kind of heuristics which associate the suitable analysis of a given word-form in its sentence.

In order to implement the morphological analyzer, we used the *contextual exploration method* developed by [2, 3, 4]. It is a decision-based method that is able to resolve with less processing cost some classical computational linguistics problems. It has been implemented successfully to resolve problems such as tense and aspect [3], automatic abstracting [5] and knowledge acquisition and modelisation [6]. The principle of this method is to scan a given linguistic marker and its context (surrounding tokens in a given text) looking for linguistic clues that guide the system to make the suitable decision. This method simulates the behaviour of a reader who aims to take a decision regarding a given linguistic problem. In our case, the method scans an input token and tries to find the required affixes in order to associate the root-form and the corresponding morpho-syntactic information. For more details about the *contextual exploration method* see [3].

In general, the role of a morphological analyzer is to isolate the root forms of words in a given language and, if possible, associate morpho-syntactic information to the words. In order to fulfill this goal it uses a full-form dictionary. Thus, before taking any decision, the system looks up the dictionary to check whether the token analysed is an entry. If it is, the root and the morpho-syntactic information are retrieved and associated to it. These systems lead to more accurate results since all words analysed belong to the language. However, they are restricted to the coverage of the dictionary, since they need a specific dictionary for every new domain. Moreover, looking up the dictionary for every token is time consuming.

Arabic is known to be a highly inflexional language; its famous pattern model using the CV (Consonant, Vowel) analysis has widely been used to build computational morphological models [7, 8, 9]. During the last decade, an increasing interest has been noticed to implement Arabic morphological analyzers [10, 11]. Almost all systems developed, in the industry as well as in the research, make use of a dictionary to perform morphological analysis. In the following paragraph some of these systems are briefly described.

In France, the Xerox Centre developed an Arabic morphological analyzer [12] using the finite-state technique. The system uses an Arabic dictionary containing 4930 roots that are combined with patterns (an average of 18 pattern for every root). This system analyses words that may include full diacritics, partial diacritics, or no diacritics; and if no diacritics are present it returns all the possible analyses of the word. The Illinois Institute of Technology developed a morphological analyser [13] that is coordinated with a lexicon. The system is able to display whole paradigms for Arabic verbs. It stores 1116 roots for regular verbs and 39 most common irregular verbs. At New Mexico State University, an Arabic morphological analyzer has been developed as a component of the Temple machine translation project [14]. The system deals with an Arabic lexicon containing approximately 45,000 stem entries. At the IBM scientific centre in Kuwait, Saliba and Al-Dannan [10] have developed a comprehensive Arabic morphological analysis and generation system. Their analyzer examines the input word for different word types and attempts to find all possible analyses. El-Sadany and Hashish [15] developed an Arabic morphological system designed to carry out both analysis and generation. This system was developed at the IBM Cairo Scientific Centre.

The main idea underlying the linguistic analysis in this paper is the distinction between regular and irregular morphological rules for verbs and nouns in the Arabic morphology. Indeed, regular rules segment a word-form into affixes and root form. Irregular rules handle the language exceptions that need more processing in order to find the root form. The system is designed in the form of an object-oriented model. It includes three main components: morphological rules for verbs and nouns, a matching algorithm and word lists. The morphological rules fall into two categories: the regular morphological rules of the Arabic grammar and the exception rules that represent the language exceptions. The matching algorithm isolates the affixes and the root of a given word-form. The word lists of are implemented as a knowledge base.

The remaining sections of this paper are organized as follows. Section Two presents the specifications of regular rules as well as exception rules. Section Three describes the system design and its architecture. Section Four is dedicated to the implementation description of the system. The matching algorithm and the rules representation are described in detail. Finally, section five concludes the paper with future directions to extend this work.

2 Problem Statement

Our system main idea is to use a general form of rule called *regular rules* to extract the root of a given Arabic token. Those tokens that cannot be treated by *regular rules* are treated separately as exceptions via a set of *exception rules*. The latter make use of *exception lists* regrouping words.

We use specifications to formally define both *regular* and *exception rules*.

Definition

A *specification* of a program for a rule r is a first-order logic formula of the form:

$$\forall X : \mathbf{X} . \; \forall Y : \mathbf{Y} . \; I_r(X) \rightarrow (r(X,Y) \leftrightarrow O_r(X,Y))$$

where $X : \mathbf{X}$. $Y : \mathbf{Y}$ are (possibly empty) lists of sorted variables, and connectors $(\rightarrow, \leftrightarrow)$ have the usual meaning in first-order logic. Formula I_r is called the *input condition*, constraining the input domain X, whereas O_r is called the *output condition*, describing when some output Y is a correct solution for input (or problem) X.

To simplify some formulas, we consider I_r to be part of the definition of $\mathbf{X}$. Often, we simply designate specifications by $\langle \mathbf{X}, \mathbf{Y}, O_r \rangle$ tuples.

2.1 Specifications of Regular Rules

We first consider the *regular rules*, where a root R and the affixes P (prefix), and S (suffix) have to be extracted from a token T, satisfying certain constraints. The terms R, P, S, and T are tokens *i.e.*; a concatenation of finite number of characters. Hence the specifications S_{reg} for *regular rules* take the form $\langle token, token \times token \times token , O_{reg} \rangle$, Formally:

$$\forall T : token . \; \forall \langle P, R, S \rangle : token \times token \times token. \qquad (S_{reg})$$

$$regular\_rule(T, \langle P, R, S \rangle) \leftrightarrow T = P \bullet R \bullet S$$

where $\bullet$ is the concatenation operator.

2.2 Specifications of Exception Rules

Let us now consider the *exception rules*. We can classify *exception rules* into four families corresponding to four *specification templates*. As an illustration, we present the first family of exception rules where the length of root R extracted by *regular rules* is less than three (regular verbs infinitive's is at least constituted by three characters). Hence, an infinitive form I has to be found given an exception list L and the preprocessed root R, satisfying constraints P and Q. Formally

$$\forall \langle L, R \rangle: list(token) \times token. \; \forall I : token .$$
$$exception\_rule(\langle L, R \rangle, I) \leftrightarrow length(R) = 1 \wedge P \wedge Q$$

where the formulae P has the form

$$I = insert(term, i, R)$$

inserts a character at the *ith* position of the root R to obtain the infinitive I, and formulae Q has the form

$$I \; in \; L.$$

infinitive I belongs to the exception list of tokens L.

As an example, we show the case of *ideal verbs,* a subclass of irregular verbs, the infinitive form *I* has to be found from the root R, satisfying certain constraints. Their specifications $S_{exp\text{-}ideal}$ take the form $\langle list(token) \times token, token, O_{reg\text{-}ideal}\rangle$. Formally,

$$\forall \langle L, R \rangle : list(token) \times token. \ \forall I : token .$$
$$exception\_rule(\langle L, R \rangle, I) \leftrightarrow length(R) = 2 \ \wedge \ I = insert('\jmath', 0, R) \wedge I \text{ in } LV8$$

where the character ' $\jmath$' has to be inserted at the first position of the root *R* in order to obtain the infinitive *I* of the token *T*, and *LV8* is a list containing tokens that belong to the same grammatical category and have the same morphological behavior.

3 System Description

A text input from Internet sources passes through a sequence of modules: It is first pre-processed where all useless parts are filtered out of the document, the html tags then are identified and coded. The tokenizer identifies all tokens and sentences. Then a module builds an object-oriented representation of the text that highlights all the basic relationships between the different constituents of the document, namely the token, the sentence, the paragraph, the section and the title. Finally, the morpho-logical analyzer finds all word root forms and associates the morpho-syntactic information to the tokens.

Within the text representation, a token includes the following fields (for more details see [16]):

1. *Name,* that contains the name of the token. Every token is assigned a name that allow the system to identify it.
2. *Value,* which is the word-form as it appears in the text before any processing.
3. *Root,* stores the root of the word that is computed during morphological analysis.
4. *Category, Tense, Number, Gender and Peron* are the same fields as the class regular-rules (sec. 3.1.1).
5. *Rule applied,* stores the identifier of the rule that has been fired to analyse the token.
6. *Sentence,* a reference to the object "Sentence" containing the token in the text. This is a relationship that holds between the token and its corresponding sentence.
7. *Order,* stores the rank of the token in sequence from the beginning of the text. It is used to compare the sequential order of tokens in the text.
8. *Positions,* correspond to the offset positions of the token in the text. It is used to highlight a relevant token when displaying the results to the user.
9. *Format,* is the associated format (boldface, italics, ...) applied to a token in the text.

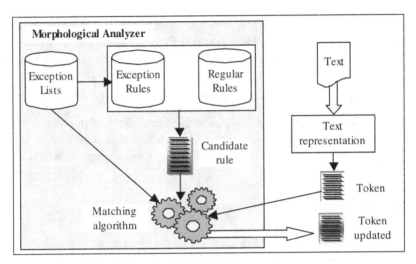

Fig. 1. The morphological analyzer components.

The morphological analyzer (fig. 1) includes two kind of rules represented in the system as objects: regular morphological rules and exception rules that represent the morphological exceptions. Lists of exceptions contain all the words that do not fall under the regular rules category.

When analysing input tokens, the matching algorithm attempts to match between the affixes of the token with a regular rule. If it does not succeed, it attempts to apply an exception rule by looking into the exception lists.

3.1   Rule Representation

3.1.1   Regular Rules

Regular Arabic verb[3] forms have a fixed pattern of the form *"prefix+root+suffix"*, thus they can be implemented as automatic procedures since the identification of affixes is enough to extract the root form and associate the morpho-syntactic information. A regular rule is represented as an object, instance of the class *regular-rule*. It models a spelling rule for adding affixes. The structure of *regular-rule* consists of nine fields that can be grouped into three classes: (i) *Name* and *Class* identify the object in the system, (ii) *Prefix* and *Suffix* store the prefix and suffix that are attached to a given token (iii) *Category, Tense, Number, Gender,* and *Person* store the morpho-syntactic information inferred from a token. For instance, consider the Arabic word "يكتبون" (in the active mode: 'they write') that is composed of the three following morphemes: the root of the verb that is "كتب" (/ktb/, notion of writing), the prefix "يـ" that denotes both the present tense and the third person, and the suffix "ون" that

---

[3] In our linguistic analysis of the Arabic morphology, we consider verbs as well as nouns. In this paper we focus on the analysis of verbs.

denotes the masculine and the plural. The rule that analyses this word is represented in (fig. 2 (a)). In (fig. 2 (b)) the token is shown before matching, and in (fig. 2 (c)) the token attributes are updated.

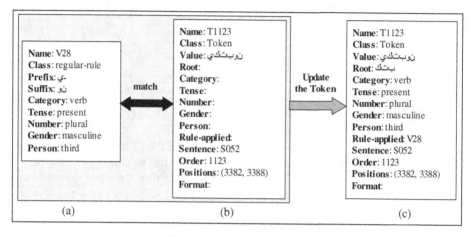

Fig. 2. Matching regular rules

The structure of the *regular-rule* class is the following:

1. *Name*: identifies uniquely a rule
2. *Class*: is the class of the object
3. *Prefix*: a sequence of characters at the beginning of a token
4. *Suffix*: a sequence of characters at the end of a token
5. *Category*: the part of speech to which the token belongs to. It can hold two possible values: verb or noun
6. *Tense*: the tense associated to the token in case of a verb
7. *Number*: the cardinality of the token consisting of singular, dual or plural
8. *Gender*: the gender associated to the token consisting of either masculine or feminine
9. *Person*: valid only for verbs, it represents either the first, second or third person.

3.1.2 Exception Rules

Irregular verbs need more analysis since they have no fixed pattern, they must be analysed case by case. An exception rule is represented as an object, instance of the class *exception-rule*. It models the morphological exceptions that do not fall under regular rules. The structures of *exception-rule* and *regular-rule* are similar; the difference lies in the conditions to fire a rule. Whereas the presence of affixes in a token is enough to fire a regular rule, an exception rule needs more conditions. The adherence of the token to a list of exceptions is generally necessary to fire such a rule, moreover, the length of the token and the presence of consonants are also examined.

For instance, the *ideal* verb in Arabic belongs to the irregular class of verbs (called the infirmum class) since its first letter is an infirmum letter (either "و" /wa/ or "ي" /ya/). When an ideal verb starting with the letter "و" is in the imperative, the first letter is removed. For instance, the imperative forms of the verb "ورث" (to inherit), are the following:

singular masculine	"رث"
dual masculine	"رثا"
plural masculine	"رثوا"
singular feminine	"رثي"
dual feminine	"رثا"
plural feminine	"رثن"

When one of the above forms is an input token to the system, the regular rules will be applied to isolate the affixes from the root. For instance, if the token "رثوا" is input to the system, a regular rule segments it into the suffix "وا" and the root form "رث". Since the first letter has been removed in the imperative, the root form obtained is not correct. In order to get the correct root of this verb (that is "ورث") we need the following exception rule that handles the root obtained.

RV108
IF   **Length(Root) = 2**
AND   X = **Concatenate**(0, "و", **Root**) **BelongTo** LV8
THEN   **Infinitive** is X
LV8 is the list containing the following verbs { "ورث" ('to inherit'), "وسع" ('to held'), "وهب" ('to donate'), "وقع" ('to fell down'), "وضع" ('to put'), "وثب" ('to jump'), "وصف" ('to describe'), "وطئ" ('to trod on'), ... }

The infirmum ideal verb is a ternary verb that is constituted by three letters. Thus, the first condition of this rule checks if the length of the root equals to two, that is the length of the root in the imperative after processed by the regular rules. Indeed, The second condition checks whether the concatenation of the root and the letter "و" belongs to the list LV8 that is the exception list containing all the infirmum ideal verbs starting with the letter "و". If the two above conditions are true, the rule computes the root form (Infinitive) of the word by adding the letter "و" to the root as it results from the first analysis with regular rules.

3.2 Exception Lists

As presented in the previous section, an exception list is associated to an exception rule. It contains words that belong to the same grammatical category and have similar morphological behavior. These lists are constituted from observation and are extended from dictionaries.

4 Implementation

This section of the paper describes tools to implement the above specification of the morphological analyzer system. In view of a rapid-prototyping software implementation strategy, only regular rules specifications have been considered for implementation. After a test phase, the implementation of the exceptions is underway. We used Java a programming language for building the Arabic morphological analyzer to benefit from several advantages. First, our proposed system is Internet-based, meaning that it will be executed by a web browser. The morphological analyzer runs as a Java applet that is embedded in a web page and stored on a web server. Secondly, Java supports fully Unicode characters, which facilitates the integration of Arabic text as the system input. Finally, the object-oriented features of Java maps easily the system's specification presented earlier in this paper.

Next, we briefly describe the Java classes which we implemented in our system. The language rules are represented as a Java class, which implement the rules attributes as discussed previously in this paper. The most important attributes of the rule class are the prefix and the suffix used as preconditions to fire a rule.

The rules are stored in a vector structure, which is initialised automatically upon start-up of the morphological analyzer from a file that stores off-line the rules attributes. The token-to-rules matching algorithm makes use of a fast-access data structure, which consists in a hash-code table used as a main-memory repository for the language rules. As rules are continuously looked up to match text tokens, the Java implementation of a hash table is used to speed up the matching process. The rules table implementation is shown below:

```
class RulesTable {
  public Rule[] Table;
  Hashtable Hash;
  public int Total;
  //Constructor
  RulesTable() {
  // Read from file to initialize Table
             . . .
             . . .
  // Create a corresponding hash table
   Table = new Hashtable();
   for (int i = 0; i <= Total; i++)
   Hash.put( Table[i].Prefix + ' '+ Table[i].Suffix, i);

  }

  rule FetchRule (String Suffix, Prefix) {
  return( Table[Hash.get (Suffix + ' ' + Prefix)] );
  }
}
```

Hence, rules are indexed based on their Suffix and Prefix attributes. The Java hash table structure requires that each table entry should have a key and the put method of the HashTable java utility class inserts items in the table based on the following signature: *put(key, item)*. The item is an index to the rules table. The chosen key is a concatenation of Prefix and Suffix separated by a blank space to avoid any ambiguity. In case there is no suffix, the actual value of the Suffix attribute will be null and therefore the search for a rule locates only the rules that match the prefix.

The extracted tokens from the source text are represented as classes which distinctive attributes are the value of the token itself and its corresponding root classification inferred by the algorithm. The token class also exhibits two important methods used later in the matching algorithm process which are *GetPrefix()* and *GetSuffix()* used respetively to extract the token prefixes and suffixes as shown below:

```
class Token {
public String Name,
              Value,
              Root,
              . . . ;
              . . . ;
public String GetPrefix (int numchars) {
retrun ( value.substring(0, numchars-1) );
}
public String GetSuffix (int numchar) {
return ( value.substring (value.length - numchars,
value.length-1) );
}
}
```

The goal of token-to-rule matching algorithm implemented in method *TokenToRule()* (shown below) is to return the rule that extracts the root of a given token *t*, and consequently, associates the morpho-syntactic information to the token. The rule is identified if it matches a given pair of suffix and prefix. Thus, first the affixes are extracted from the token *t* through *GetSuffix()* and *GetPrefix()* methods, then the matching operation is performed by the method *FetchRule(Suffix, Prefix)*.

```
rule TokenToRule (Token t){
String Prefix, Suffix;

    public int i=3, j=1;
    rule Rule;
    do{
        Prefix = t.GetPrefix(i--);
        do{
           Suffix = t.GetSuffix(j--);
           Rule = RulesTable.FetchRule(Suffix, Prefix);
           }
           while(Rule==null && j>=0
                            && t.length.value()-i-j > 1)
        }
        while(Rule == null && i >= 0
                            && t.length.value()-i-j > 1);
        return (Rule);
        }
}
```

Note that the length of a prefix for regular rules is at most one character, and the length of a suffix is limited to three characters. The matching algorithm gives the priority to the longest affixes first. Hence, the loops for affix extraction are respectively initialized to 1, and 3 and are gradually decremented as many time as no rule matches and the root still contains at least 2 characters ($t.length.value()-i-j > 1$) due to the fact that for regular tokens no root is less than two characters long.

5 Conclusion

A morphological analyzer is one of the essential components in any natural language processing architecture. When dealing with texts from dynamic information sources such as the Internet, we need a robust and fast system than can cope with texts from different domains, with a variable document structure and written in different writing styles. Moreover, when processing Arabic texts from the Internet, we are faced with unvoweled texts that are more confusing. Indeed, handling words not using diacritics is ambiguous since usually they can have more than a single analysis. The morphological analyzer presented in this paper treats unvoweled texts. It is implemented as an object-oriented framework and is composed of three main components: a rule knowledge base comprising the regular and irregular morphological rules of the Arabic grammar, a set of word lists containing the exceptions handled by the irregular rules, and a matching algorithm that matches the tokens to the rules. The complete implementation of the system is underway. In the first phase, we have considered the regular rules for implementation.

Defining a strategy to match the regular and irregular rules and the extension of the word lists are the future directions of this project. In fact, when the algorithm is confronted with a given token we need a strategy that decides which group of rules to test first and which rule to fire when there is a conflict. This will avoid ambiguity and will gain processing time. Extending the lists of words from both dictionaries and corpora is also important since the precision of the system depends on the coverage of such lists.

References

1. J. Berri, "A Generic Text Representation for Information Extraction", In *Proceedings of GITIS'2000 Gulf Information Technology & Information Systems Conference*, 130-139, Dubai, 2000.
2. J. –P. Desclès, *Langages applicatifs, Langues naturelles et Cognition*, Hermès, Paris, 1990.
3. J. Berri, D. Maire-Reppert, H.-G. Oh-Jeong, "Traitement informatique de la catégorie aspecto-temporelle", *T.A Informations*, vol. 32, n°1, 77-90, 1992.
4. J. –P. Desclès. J. –L. Minel, J. Berri, "L'exploration contextuelle des unités linguistiques dans la compréhension de textes", *Internal report*, CAMS (Centre d'Analyses et de Mathématiques Sociales), 15 p, 1995.

5. J. Berri, D. Le Roux, D. Malrieu, J.-L. Minel, "SERAPHIN main sentences automatic extraction system", In *proceedings of the Second Language Engineering Convention*, London, 1995.

6. C. Jouis, "SEEK, un logiciel d'acquisition des connaissances utilisant un savoir linguistique sans employer de connaissances sur le monde externe", In *Proceedings of 6eme Journées Acquisition, Validation, (JAVA), INRIA and AFIA*, Grenoble, 159-172, 1995.

7. A. Arrajihi, *The Application of morphology*, Dar Al Maarefa Al Jameeya, Alexandria, 1973. (in Arabic)

8. F. Qabawah, *Morphology of nouns and verbs*, Al Maaref Edition, 2nd edition, Beyruth, 1994. (in Arabic)

9. G. A. Kiraz, "Arabic Computational Morphology in the West.", In *Proceedings of the 6th International Conference and Exhibition on Multi-lingual Computing*, Cambridge, 1998.

10. B. Saliba and A. Al Dannan, "Automatic Morphological Analysis of Arabic: A study of Content Word Analysis", In *Proceedings of the Kuwait Computer Conference*, Kuwait, March 3-5, 1989.

11. M. Smets, "Paradigmatic Treatment of Arabic Morphology", In *Workshop on Computational Approaches to Semitic Languages COLING -ACL98*, August 16, Montreal, 1998.

12. K. Beesley, "Arabic Morphological Analysis on the Internet", In *Proceedings of the International Conference on Multi-Lingual Computing (Arabic & English)*, Cambridge G.B., 17-18 April, 1998.

13. R. Alshalabi and M. Evens, "A Computational Morphology System for Arabic", In *Workshop on Computational Approaches to Semitic Languages COLING-ACL98*, August 16, Montreal, 1998.

14. R. Zajac, and M. Casper, "The temple Web Translator", 1997 Available at: http://www.crl.nmsu.edu/Research/Projects/tide/papers/twt.aaai97.html

15. T. A. El-Sadany, and M. A. Hashish, "An Arabic Morphological System", In *IBM Systems Journal*, Vol. 28, No. 4, 600-612, 1989.

16. J. Berri, *Contribution to the contextual exploration method. Applications to automatic abstracting and to temporal representations. Implementation of the SERAPHIN system.* Ph.D. thesis, Paris-Sorbonne University (Paris IV), France, 1996. (In French)

Stochastic Parsing and Parallelism*

Francisco-Mario Barcala, Oscar Sacristán, and Jorge Graña

Departamento de Computación
Facultad de Informática
Universidad de La Coruña
Campus de Elviña s/n
15071 - La Coruña
Spain
{barcala, agullo, grana}@dc.fi.udc.es

Abstract. Parsing CYK-like algorithms are inherently parallel: there are a lot of cells in the chart that can be calculated simultaneously. In this work, we present a study on the appropriate techniques of parallelism to obtain an optimal performance of the *extended CYK algorithm*, a stochastic parsing algorithm that preserves the same level of expressiveness as the one in the original grammar, and improves further tasks of robust parsing. We consider two methods of parallelization: distributed memory and shared memory. The excellent performance obtained with the second one turns this algorithm into an alternative that could compete with other parsing techniques more efficient *a priori*.

1   Introduction

The CYK algorithm [6,9] can be extended to work with any kind of context-free grammars (CFGs), not only with grammars under Chomsky's normal form (CNFGs). Of course, one way to do this is by turning the original CFG into a CNFG. There are a lot of well-known algorithms for performing this transformation. However, this process produces a high number of new auxiliary non-terminal symbols in the grammar. These symbols make interpretation of the chart difficult, and generate non-intuitive parsing trees that do not match the corresponding trees from the original grammar. Following [4] and [2], we consider a more interesting alternative: to adapt the algorithm to work directly with any CFG.

The new bottom-up parsing algorithm, which we call *extended CYK algorithm*, can also handle stochastic context-free grammars (SCFGs). Therefore, for a given sentence of length n words, it is possible to know whether it belongs to the grammar language or not, to calculate its total probability (not only the probability of each individual analysis), to obtain the N-most probable analyses

---

* This work was partially supported by the European Union under FEDER project 1FD97-0047-C04-02, and by the Autonomous Government of Galicia under project PGIDT99XI10502B.

A. Gelbukh (Ed.): CICLing 2001, LNCS 2004, pp. 401–410, 2001.

of any portion of the input sequence in $\mathcal{O}(n^3)$ time complexity, whilst preserving the original structure of the grammar. Explicitly extracting all the parse trees associated with the input sentence or any substring of the input sentence is also possible. The cost of this step depends on the complexity of the grammar, but even in the case where the number of parse trees is exponential in n, the chart used by the algorithm for their representation remains of $\mathcal{O}(n^2)$ space complexity.

However, $\mathcal{O}(n^3)$ time complexity could be too high in some applications. This fact leads us to reflect on the building of a parallel version of the extended CYK algorithm. Section 2 gives the details of the standard steps of the algorithm, section 3 discusses the different alternatives of parallelization, section 4 shows the experimental results, and section 5 presents the conclusion after the analysis of the data obtained.

2   Extended CYK Algorithm

In this section, we introduce the basic extended CYK algorithm, postponing stochastic considerations. Furthermore, although the algorithm is able to work with arbitrary CFGs, we restrict our representation to a subclass of CFGs consisting of non-partially-lexicalized rules. In such grammars, terminals can only appear in "lexical" rules of the type $A \rightarrow w_1 \, w_2 \, \ldots \, w_k$, where A is a non-terminal and w_i are terminals, i.e. words. Most often k is equal to 1, $k > 1$ corresponding to compound words or lexicalized expressions. This restriction is not however critical for the algorithm, and it is inserted solely to isolate lexical rules in an initial step, which in practice is performed by using a lexicon.

2.1   Non-stochastic Approach

The basic data structure used by the algorithm is a CYK-like table containing generalization of Earley-like items, instead of the non-terminals used by the original algorithm. The parsing table or chart is a lower triangular matrix with $\frac{n(n+1)}{2}$ cells, where n is the number of words of the input sequence to be parsed. Each cell N_{ij} contains two list of items:

- Items of the first list, called type-1 list, represent the non-terminals that parse the subsequence $w_i, w_{i+1}, \ldots, w_{i+j-1}$, that is, if A is such a non-terminal, then $A \overset{*}{\Rightarrow} w_i w_{i+1} \ldots w_{i+j-1}$, and the corresponding item is denoted by $[A; i, j]$.
- Items of the second list, called type-2 list, represent partial parses α of the subsequence $w_i, w_{i+1}, \ldots, w_{i+j-1}$, i.e. sequences α of non-terminals such that $\alpha \overset{*}{\Rightarrow} w_i w_{i+1} \ldots w_{i+j-1}$ for which there exists at least one rule in the grammar of the form $A \rightarrow \alpha\beta$, where β is a non-empty sequence of non-terminal symbols ($\beta = \lambda$ is precisely the case taken into account by the items in the type-1 list). Such items are denoted by $[\alpha \bullet \ldots; i, j]$.

Notice that the type-2 items represent a generalization of dotted rules used in Earley-like parsers, where only the first part of the rule is represented (i.e. the part already parsed), independently both of the left-hand side (which has not yet been rewritten) and of the end (which has not yet been parsed). This provides a much more compact representation of dotted rules (allowed by the bottom-up nature of the parsing).

In addition, each item in any of the two lists is associated with the list of all its possible productions. This allows a further factorization that avoids the repetition of the item itself in the representation of all these possible productions, and obtains items only once, even if they are produced several times in the same cell, thus speeding up the parsing process. For parse tree extraction purposes, each production contains an explicit reference to the two items that were used to create it.

The extended CYK algorithm to determine whether a sentence $s = w_1$, $w_2, \ldots, w_n$ belongs to the language of a CFG, with no lexicalized rules, $G = (N, T, P, S)$, consists of the following steps:

1. **Initialization step.** This step consists of filling all the cells of the chart for which there exists a lexical rule associated with the corresponding word or sequences of words in the input sentence. That is, the type-1 lists of the first rows are filled. More precisely, if a rule $A \rightarrow w_i \ldots w_{i+j-1} \in P$, item $[A; i, j]$ is added to the type-1 list of cell N_{ij}.

   To be complete, the initialization step also needs a "self-filling step" updating type-2 lists of these cells. This phase is also used in the parsing step that we explain next.

2. **Parsing step.** This step consists of applying two phases: the standard filling phase (over all the cells except the ones involved in the initialization step), and the self-filling phase (over all cells N_{ij} in the chart). These phases are applied bottom-up row by row.

   - **Standard filling phase.** An item $[\alpha \bullet \ldots; i, k]$ in the list 2 of a cell is combined with an item $[B; i+k, j-k]$ in the list 1 of another cell, if there is a rule of the form $A \rightarrow \alpha B \beta$ in the grammar. If $\beta = \lambda$, item $[A; i, j]$ is added to the list 1 of cell N_{ij}. Otherwise, the item $[\alpha B \bullet \ldots; i, j]$ is added to the list 2 of cell N_{ij}.

     Notice that the item is added when it does not exist. If the item already exists, only the new production is added to the sublist of productions of the item.

   - **Self-filling phase.** In this procedure, for each item $[B; i, j]$ in the list 1 of the cell, and for each rule of the form $A \rightarrow B\beta$, we do the following:
     - If $\beta = \lambda$, item $[A; i, j]$ is added to the list 1 of the cell. Notice that the self-filling phase must be applied again over this new item.
     - If $\beta \neq \lambda$, item $[B \bullet \ldots; i, j]$ is added to the list 2 of the cell.

     This second step is necessary both to deal with chaining of unitary rules and to keep the type-2 lists up to date after the standard filling procedure has been performed.

Therefore, $s \in L(G)$ when item $[S; 1, n]$ is in cell N_{1n}.

2.2   λ-Rules

If the grammar contains so-called λ-rules, i.e. rules of the form $A \rightarrow \lambda$, our basic algorithm needs to be completed as follows:

- Whenever a type-2 item $[\alpha \bullet \ldots; i, j]$ is produced, for each non-terminal B producing λ ($B \rightarrow \lambda \in P$) that could complete that item ($A \rightarrow \alpha B \beta \in P$), we do the following:
  - If $\beta = \lambda$, item $[A; i, j]$ is added to list 1 of the same cell.
  - If $\beta \neq \lambda$, item $[\alpha B \bullet \ldots; i, j]$ is added to list 2 of the same cell.

  This procedure must be performed recursively over the new items up to the point where no new item can be added.
- The self-filling phase also needs to be updated. For each type-1 item $[B; i, j]$, if there is a rule of the form $A \rightarrow CB\beta$, where $C \rightarrow \lambda$, then:
  - If $\beta = \lambda$, item $[A; i, j]$ is added to list 1 of the same cell.
  - If $\beta \neq \lambda$, item $[B \bullet \ldots; i, j]$ is added to list 2 of the same cell.

  That is, the self-filling step is performed as if the rule $A \rightarrow B\beta$ were in the grammar.

2.3   Extracting Parse Trees

Extraction of parse trees from the chart is performed simply by following the productions of those type-1 items of the cell in the top that contain the initial non-terminal, if such items exist. This procedure can also be applied to any other cell to extract subtrees.

Each production in these items is taken as a parse tree, and for each of these trees or productions of the item chosen as root, the following recursive procedure is performed: (1) The root node, labeled with the non-terminal in the item, is created. (2) For each reached node, a child node is created. If the node is a type-1 item, the node is labeled with the symbol in the item. Otherwise, the node has no label. (3) Nodes without labels are removed. The new father of its child nodes will be the father of this removed node. (4) Words in the input sentence are added.

2.4   Dealing with Probabilities

For SCFGs, the probability of a parse tree is the product of the probability of the rule used to generate the subtrees of the root node, and the probabilities of each of these subtrees[1].

In the case of the extended CYK algorithm, we define the probability of a production p of a type-1 item $[A; i, j]$ as the probability of the subtree corresponding to the interpretation A of the sequence $w_i, \ldots, w_{i+j-1}$ for this production p, i.e.

---

[1] By using logarithmic probabilities, products can be replaced by sums. This speeds up the calculations and avoids problems of precision that arise in products with factors less than 1.

as the product of the probabilities of the items from which it is produced and the probability of the rule involved in this production.

In the same way, for type-2 items we define the probability of a production p of an item $[\alpha \bullet \ldots; i, j]$ as the product of the items which produce it. In this case, there is no rule probability, because type-2 items are partial interpretations.

It is then possible to define the maximum probability of an item as the maximum of the probabilities of all its productions (this avoids storing all those probabilities), taking into account that a production of an item is obtained from the combination of only two previously generated items (one of type-2 with another of type-1). This allows us to keep the N most probable parses during the parsing process, since the N biggest values for an item are included in the N^2 products obtained from the N-best probabilities of each of the constituting items. In cases where the N-best approach is not sufficient, it is of course always possible to recursively extract all the (sub)parses of the input (sub)sequence, the associated probabilities being calculated during extraction by the product of the probabilities of their constituents.

Moreover the probability of any (sub)sequence, defined as the sum of the probabilities of all its possible parses, is also computed during the parsing process simply by adding all the probabilities of each new production of an item, even if this probability is not kept in the N-best list.

3   Reflections on Parallelism

Time complexity of the extended CYK algorithm, measured in terms of the size n of the input sentence, is clearly $\mathcal{O}(n^3)$. However, the multiplicative constant associated with n^3 in the complexity plays an important role. A more detailed complexity could be calculated for the worst case, in terms of the cardinals of non-terminal and rule sets, and we would find that it is lower than the one in other similar parsing algorithms. We will not detail this calculation here (it can be seen in [2]), but the intuitive explanation is that the gain compared with other Earley-like or CYK-like algorithms is because the extended CYK algorithm performs a better factorization of dotted rules (in type-2 list items), and processes fewer elements (items appear only once and there is no prediction).

Even with this, the complexity can be reduced as a consequence of the parallel nature of CYK-like algorithms: there are a lot of cells in the chart that can be calculated simultaneously. To parallelize the extended CYK algorithm [1], two alternatives have been considered: (1) distributed memory by passing messages between computers, and (2) shared memory, i.e. execution of several processes that concurrently access to the same area of memory. We explain both techniques in the following sections.

3.1   Distributed Memory

With this technique, each computer calculates a fragment of the chart. That is, the chart is distributed among the memories of the computers. Every computer could calculate one or more chart columns, approaching parallelism at column level. The advantage of this distribution is that every processor always possesses one of the cells that it needs in order to calculate the next cell. The disadvantage is that a given processor does not help the others when it finishes with its columns. On the other hand, if we have more processors than words in the sentence, the remaining processors are idle.

Under this approach, the only thing to solve is how to distribute the chart columns among computers and how to interchange messages between processors. With regard to the distribution, the most reasonable solution is to perform a reverse cyclic distribution. If we have for instance 10 columns and 3 processors, columns 1, 6 and 7 are assigned to processor 1, columns 2, 5 and 8 are assigned to processor 2, and columns 3, 4, 9 and 10 are assigned to processor 3, as we can see in figure 1. In this way, we obtain a balanced overload for all the computers. The right-hand side of the figure shows the subcharts stored in the memory of each processor.

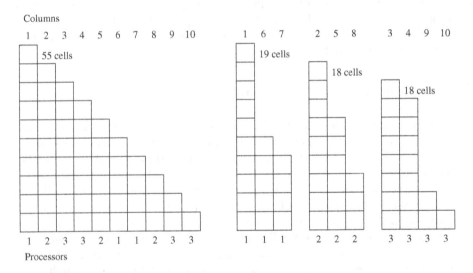

Fig. 1. Chart columns distribution in a parallelization of the extended CYK algorithm by distributed memory

With regard to the messages, if every processor sends every cell that has already been calculated to the processors that need the cell in the future, we eliminate bidirectional communications. There will be no request for cells among processors, only cell deliveries. Furthermore, cell deliveries are performed only once to each processor, so the target must determine whether the received cell will be necessary later, and send it back to itself in that case.

However, this approach gives priority to speed, not to reliability. By removing bidirectional communications, we increase the performance. Each processor looks for the cells it needs in its input queue. If it does not find a given cell it is because the processor responsible for that calculation is still working and has not yet sent the cell, causing a temporary delay. But processors could exhaust storage capacity. This problem is particularly serious when we use few processors and could lead to a deadlock in the system.

Even with this optimization in the interchange of messages, the main problem of the distributed memory approach is the granularity of the process that we are trying to parallelize. In our case, even without deadlocks and long delays, processors spend most of their time on sending and receiving data, not on the calculus of that data. The gain in performance may not be significant compared to the computational resources used, or the same process may even be executed faster in a sequential computer with only one processor. All these reflections lead us to consider the shared memory approach.

3.2   Shared Memory

In this approach, all processors share the same chart and fill the cells simultaneously. Unlike the preceding case, cells are calculated from left to right and bottom-up, as the processors become free. In this way, no processor is prematurely free and their capabilities are better exploited. This approach is not viable with distributed memory due to the high cost of the synchronization of all processors.

A feature inherent to the shared memory paradigm is that there is no data transfer between processors. This is advantageous where the amount of information to share is great. However, we must take into account that processors have to access concurrently to the same areas of memory, so we must determine critical sections and give them adequate protection. Here, it is sufficient to define a variable associated with every cell indicating whether the cell is already calculated or not, and a semaphore associated with that variable.

The order of the loops that determine which cell is going to be processed is very important for the parser to perform properly, and must satisfy the requirements of this alternative. The external loop must run on the rows, and the internal one in the columns. In this way, deadlocks, i.e. situations where a processor needs a cell that is being calculated in another processor and vice-versa, do not occur. When a processor starts the calculation of a cell, the cells that it needs are already calculated or are being calculated in processors that are not going to need the cell of the first one, because it is overhead or at the same level. Therefore, this approach guarantees that no deadlock will be produced.

From the above, we can deduce that the extended CYK algorithm presents a natural scheme of parallelization. As we will see later, it is not suitable to be implemented on a set of computers with distributed memory because the penalization of communications damages its performance. However, the implementation on a multiprocessor with several threads provides excellent results.

4   Analysis of Results

Experiments have been performed on a computer under the Linux operating system, with the following components:

- 1 main node with 2 Pentium II-350 MHz. processors, with 384 MB RAM (multiprocessor of shared memory).
- 23 additional AMD K6-300 MHz. nodes, with 96 MB RAM, forming a *switch fast ethernet* cluster (multicomputer of distributed memory).

Sequential and multithread versions of the algorithm have been executed in the main node. Distributed memory version has been executed in all nodes, even in the main one, and communication between processors has been implemented with MPI (Message Passing Interface) standard library.

Input data for evaluating the algorithm have been taken from SUSANNE tree-bank [7,8]. This treebank was divided into two parts: the first part includes sentences without traces (4,292 sentences, 77,275 words), and the second one includes sentences with traces (2,188 sentences, 60,759 words). The first part has been used to extract the grammar (17,669 rules and 1,525 non-terminals) [5], and the second one to measure parsing times on the different versions of the algorithm.

The results in table 1 show times of sequential, 1 thread, 2 threads, 2 MPI, 4 MPI, etc. These descriptors correspond respectively to sequential version, multithread version with 1 thread (in order to infer the cost of initialization and management of semaphores), multithread version with 2 threads, and distributed memory versions with 2 processors, 4 processors, etc. Times appear in mm:ss.mmm format (minutes, seconds and milliseconds). User times for 2 threads are the sum of the execution time of both processors. Therefore, although real time is usually less reliable, it is more representative in this case.

Analysis of 2,188 sentences							
Times	Sequential	1 thread	2 thread	2 MPI	4 MPI	8 MPI	16 MPI
Real	03:45.259	03:52.648	02:24.311	10:47.108	09:28.020	07:57.424	07:40.391
User	03:44.810	03:50.580	03:53.040	05:08.900	03:55.730	02:36.370	02:07.190
System	00:00.036	00:00.530	00:01.370	05:16.200	05:26.370	05:17.350	05:28.990

Table 1. Execution times of extended CYK algorithm over the SUSANNE tree-bank

These data show that there is an additional cost due to the handling of semaphores, but in any case the multithread version with 2 threads is much faster than the sequential version. And what is more, the evaluated implementation considers parallelism at sentence level, and threads are created and destroyed for each sentence. An obvious optimization could be achieved simply by keeping the threads from sentence to sentence.

On the other hand, the distributed memory version seems to be the worst in any case, and this is due to three main reasons, some of them already mentioned. First, the data communication cost among processors is high when parsing short sentences. Second, when the sentence is long, distribution of data among the chart columns, and the corresponding overload in the processors, should be balanced, but this is not usual because charts are asymmetric and usually contain a high number of empty cells. Finally, when the sentence is complex, cells contain too much information, so communication between processors is very expensive (when we increase the number of processors, execution time decreases, but system time grows).

There is an obvious gain in the 2 threads version: a parsing time of 2:24.311 over 2,188 sentences yields an average of 0.065 seconds per sentence. But this result is not representative either. To show it, it is sufficient to look at table 2, in which we study independent execution times on 5 sentences. There are sentences that can be parsed in times much higher than the average, between 318 milliseconds and almost 2 minutes. It is interesting to note the behavior on sentence 5, where the versions with threads do not produce a significant improvement in performance, probably because the chart of this sentence contains a lot of empty cells. This in fact is the case because parsing time is really low for a 214 word sentence (23,005 cells), and the low number of cells with items leads to a high frequency of waiting periods in the processors. In other words, parallelism is better exploited when the sentence to parse is complex.

	Sentence 1	Sentence 2	Sentence 3	Sentence 4	Sentence 5
Words	30	35	55	150	214
Sequential times					
Real	00:00.351	00:04.646	02:40.821	00:00.750	00:22.268
User	00:00.340	00:04.630	02:40.600	00:00.740	00:22.160
System	00:00.010	00:00.020	00:00.220	00:00.010	00:00.100
2 threads times					
Real	00:00.318	00:02.735	01:57.759	00:00.623	00:21.004
User	00:00.460	00:04.810	02:39.800	00:00.950	00:23.480
System	00:00.001	00:00.020	00:00.140	00:00.030	00:00.200

Table 2. Independent execution times of extended CYK algorithm on 5 sentences

It is also evident that the complexity of a sentence is not proportional to its number of words. This is clear if we compare parsing times of sentences 3 and 4. Nevertheless, the improvement of the 2 threads version respect to the sequential remains present.

5   Conclusion

Parallelization of the extended CYK algorithm by using shared memory turns this algorithm into an alternative that could compete with other more efficient parsing techniques. Although those techniques could also be parallelized, this parallelization, when possible, is not intrinsic to the algorithm and leads to higher design and implementation complexities.

Finally, we should point out the advantages when we combine the stochastic paradigm with robust parsing techniques. These two features are inherent to the extended CYK algorithm, and are currently required in many natural language processing applications. The availability of efficient tagging and parsing tools able to deal with incomplete dictionaries and grammars, with the help of the stochastic framework, provides good prospects of immediate application on high level information processing systems, such as information retrieval, information extraction or question answering systems.

References

1. Barcala Rodríguez, M. (1999). Diseño e implementación de una herramienta de análisis sintáctico estocástico para el procesamiento de textos en lenguaje natural. *Proyecto Fin de Carrera en Ingeniería Informática*, dirigido por J. Graña Gil en el Departamento de Computación de la Universidad de A Coruña.
2. Chappelier, J.-C.; Rajman, M. (1998). A practical bottom-up algorithm for on-line parsing with stochastic context-free grammars. *Rapport Technique 98/284*, Departement d'Informatique, Ecole Polytechnique Fédérale de Lausanne (Suisse).
3. Earley, J. (1970). An efficient context-free parsing algorithm. *Communications of the ACM*, vol. 13(2), pp. 94-102.
4. Erbach, G. (1994). Bottom-up Earley deduction. In *Proceedings of the 14th International Conference on Computational Linguistics (COLING-94)*, Kyoto (Japan).
5. Graña Gil, J.; Chappelier, J.-C.; Rajman, M. (1999). Using syntactic constraints in natural language disambiguation. *Rapport Technique 99/315*, Departement d'Informatique, Ecole Polytechnique Fédérale de Lausanne (Suisse).
6. Kasami, T. (1965). An efficient recognition and syntax analysis algorithm for context-free languages. *Technical Report*, AF CRL-65-758, Air Force Cambridge Research Laboratory, Bedford, MA.
7. Sampson, G. (1994a). The Susanne corpus, release 3, 04/04/1994. School of Cognitive & Computing Sciences, University of Sussex, Falmer, Brighton, England.
8. Sampson, G. (1994b). English for the computer. *Oxford University Press*.
9. Younger, D.H. (1967). Recognition of context-free languages in time n^3. *Information and Control*, vol. 10(2), pp. 189-208.

Practical Nondeterministic DR(k) Parsing on Graph-Structured Stack

José Fortes Gálvez[1,2], Jacques Farré[2], and Miguel Ángel Pérez Aguiar[1]

[1] Depart. de Informática y Sistemas, Universidad de Las Palmas de Gran Canaria
[2] Laboratoire I3S, CNRS and Université de Nice-Sophia Antipolis

Abstract. A new approach to parse context-free grammars is presented. It relies on discriminating-reverse, DR(k), parsers, with a Tomita-like nondeterminism-controlling graph-structured stack (GSS) algorithm.

The advantage of this generalized discriminating-reverse (GDR) approach over GLR lies on the possibility of using DR(k) parsers, which combine full LR(k) parsing power with a small number of states even for $k > 1$. This can greatly reduce nondeterminism originating from limited parsing power, as it is typical of the restricted direct LR parsers (SLR, LALR) commonly used in Tomita's algorithm.

Furthermore, relying on a DR parser allows a GSS that associates nodes to symbols instead of direct-LR states, and makes easier computation of the shared forest.

Moreover, DR(k) parsers have been shown to be linear for LR(k) grammars, and the DR(k) parser efficiency has been practically found to be very similar to direct LR(k) parsers.

The paper first presents the nondeterministic DR(k) generation algorithm (for non-LR(k) grammars). Then, it discusses the corresponding adaptation of the GSS algorithm and shows how the shared forest computation is naturally handled.

1 Introduction

The discriminating-reverse, DR(k), method [3, 5, 6], developed by the first author, accepts the full class of LR(k) grammars, while producing small and efficient deterministic parsers, linear on input length. It is based on the idea of exploring from the stack top a (typically very) small, minimal parsing stack suffix, in order to discriminate which actions are compatible with the suffix portion already read, plus the k-lookahead. If the grammar is LR(k), the number of such compatible actions reduces to one. As soon as this happens, that action can be decided, and thus performed. The method is completely proven, theoretically and practically, with very good efficiency results [4], producing, for $k = 1$, deterministic parser automata smaller than the corresponding (deterministic or not) LR(0) ones, and with an average stack exploration depth per parsing action of less than 2 topmost symbols. Values of k greater than 1 do not significatively enlarge automata size, due essentially to the typically very small depth of the discrimination process.

A. Gelbukh (Ed.): CICLing 2001, LNCS 2004, pp. 411–422, 2001.

The widely known generalized LR (GLR) method [14, 15], originally devised by M. Tomita, employs the bottom-to-top LR(k) parser automaton, initially developed by D. Knuth [9], to guide an essentially nondeterministic parsing, with controlled complexity through the use of a "graph-structured stack", GSS. The origin of this nondeterminism can be located, in some cases, in the strict ambiguity of natural language grammars to which the method is addressed. But, in other cases, a temporary nondeterminism comes from the impossibility, for the underlying LR parser, to decide amongst several actions, because of restrictions imposed on it. These restrictions include merging significant automaton states, and using a too small value k for the length of the lookahead window. Unfortunately, values of k as low as 1 usually produce unacceptably large LR(k) automata, because of a double combinatorial explosion in the number of states coding relevant stack-plus-lookahead content classes, and (for $k \geq 2$) in the combination of the allowed sequences of k terminal symbols.

In this paper, we propose to use DR(k) as the underlying parser to combine with a Tomita-like GSS. This approach has the advantage of needing small parsers, even for values of $k > 1$. Since these parsers have the same parsing power as LR(k), nondeterminism caused by restrictions on the underlying parser would be significatively reduced. The importance of this effect is even greater when parsing typical natural language sentences, because of the relatively large ratio between lookahead size and sentence length. On the other hand, DR(k) parsers are in principle non-correct prefix, what may introduce a different form of nondeterminism. A correct-prefix variant is proposed in [6] at the cost of some increase in parser size, which can also be used as the underlying parser.

We will first present in detail the generation algorithm, for context-free grammars, of the underlying DR(k) parser, and then its application to a Tomita-like general parser. Here we improve the generation algorithm (especially for $k > 1$) over the one presented in a preliminary version of this paper [7], by producing parsers that test the k-lookahead only when it will necessarily decide a nonempty set of actions. According to our experience [10], this should in general speed up parsing (avoiding a double-check at each state) at the cost, in some cases, of some enlargement in automaton size, resulting in a practical compromise. Moreover, in this way, k-lookahead exploration can be seen as a natural prolongation of stack suffix exploration, what should facilitate its practical implementation for $k > 1$.

Notation will be conventional in its most part, see [13] for instance. The original grammar $\mathcal{G}$ will be augmented with $P' = \{S' \rightarrow \vdash S\} \cup P$, such that Follow$_k(S') = \{\dashv^k\}$. Productions in P' are numbered from 1 to n, and a production with number i is represented as $A \xrightarrow{i} \alpha$. Parsing action i represents by convention the production number to use in a reduction if $1 \leq i \leq n$, or to shift if $i = 0$. The head operator is extended as follows for strings with dot: $k : x \cdot y = x' \cdot y'$, such that $x' = k : x$ and $x'y' = k : xy$.

2 Discriminating-Reverse Parsing

In essence, what is needed in a shift-reduce parser is some procedure to tell what parsing action to perform next. When parsing sentences from an LR(k) grammar, the language of legal stack-plus-lookahead contents is the union of several pairwise disjoint regular sublanguages, each of them mapped to a unique parsing action [13]. Accordingly, in our method a *stack suffix* exploration automaton is built that begins reading from the top of the stack, and stops as soon as the current lookahead or the next stack symbol allows to determine the parsing action to perform.

2.1 DR(k) Single-Action Reverse Stack Acceptors

These acceptors are DFA [8] which read the stack from its top, and accept precisely the language of all the stacks which are compatible with a certain parsing action. In their construction procedure, each state is associated with a set of DR(k) items, which have the form $[A{\to}\alpha \cdot \beta, x \cdot y]$, with $|xy| = k$. In the item, the *right-part* dot, located in the rule right-part between α and β, corresponds to the current exploration point within the stack, i.e., the left end of the suffix already read. And the lookahead string is divided by the *lookahead* dot into two parts: the lookahead part x already covered by a (possibly partially) explored phrase of β, and the lookahead part y not yet covered.

The following function computes the item set for the "context" surrounding some nonterminal A restricted to some dotted lookahead $x \cdot yz$.

$$\mathcal{C}_k^0(A, x \cdot yz) = \{[B{\to}\beta \cdot \gamma, \ xy \cdot z] \mid \gamma \underset{\mathrm{rm}}{\Rightarrow}{}^* Av, \ B{\to}\beta\gamma \in P',$$
$$S' \underset{\mathrm{rm}}{\Rightarrow}{}^* \varphi Bw, xy \cdot z = k : xv \cdot w{\dashv}^k\}.$$

The closure of a set I of DR(k) items is defined by:

$$\mathcal{C}_k(I) = I \ \cup \{\iota \mid \iota \in \mathcal{C}_k^0(A, x \cdot yz), [A{\to} \cdot \alpha, \ x \cdot yz] \in I\}.$$

The construction of an automaton $\mathcal{A}_k(i)$ for parsing action i, from a reduced grammar $\mathcal{G}$, is as follows:

1. Initial state:

$$I_0^i = \begin{cases} i = 0: & \mathcal{C}_k(\{[A{\to}\alpha \cdot a\beta, k : av \cdot w{\dashv}^k] \mid A{\to}\alpha a\beta \in P' \text{ and} \\ & \beta \underset{\mathrm{rm}}{\Rightarrow}{}^* v \text{ and } S' \underset{\mathrm{rm}}{\Rightarrow}{}^* \varphi Aw\}) \\[2ex] 1 \le i \le n: & \mathcal{C}_k(\{[A{\to}\alpha\cdot, k : \cdot w{\dashv}^k] \mid A \overset{i}{\longrightarrow} \alpha \in P' \text{ and } S' \underset{\mathrm{rm}}{\Rightarrow}{}^* \varphi Aw\}) \end{cases}$$

2. Transition function:

$$\delta(I, X) = \mathcal{C}_k(\{[A{\to}\alpha \cdot X\beta, x \cdot y] \mid [A{\to}\alpha X \cdot \beta, x \cdot y] \in I\})$$

2.2   The DR(k) Deterministic Automaton

A recognizing automaton $\mathcal{A}_k$ can be built for precisely the language of all legal stack-plus-lookahead contents, by joining all these single-action automata $\mathcal{A}_k(i)$. For this purpose, all the initial states can be joined into a single initial state. Items from each $\mathcal{A}_k(i)$ initial state are joined together, while retaining the action number i of their corresponding single-action automata, i.e., items take the form of $[i, A{\rightarrow}\alpha \cdot \beta, x \cdot y]$. $\mathcal{A}_k$ can now be built by a construction analogous to the algorithm for converting an NFA to a DFA [8], or, equivalently, by applying the transition function δ from the joint initial state, and preserving item action numbers.

If $\mathcal{G}$ is LR(k), the automaton built according to the above procedure can always indicate the next parsing action after having read the whole stack, since, according to the LR(k) property, then the lookahead string will always suffice to discriminate amongst the would-be different actions.

However, in almost all practical LR(k) grammars, a small section of automaton $\mathcal{A}_k$ is enough to decide the parsing action. In fact, the construction algorithm *begins* building such a recognizing automaton, but only generates its useful discriminating (and full right-parts, see below) section. This mechanism dramatically prunes the recognizing automaton, while preserving its LR(k) parsing power, since the same parsing action decisions are obtained. Moreover, the resulting discriminating automaton is minimal in the sense that its construction stops at the earliest possible point.

Finally, the automaton can frequently decide what reduction to apply before having reached the left end of the rule's right-part. However, the presence of the full right-part on top of the stack must be verified in order to ensure a valid reduction. This check is naturally included in the automaton, by continuing state construction at least until left ends of right-parts are read. In order to implement right-part checking, rule numbers are marked in the initial state items with a dot to the right, as in $[i{\cdot}, A{\rightarrow}\alpha{\cdot}, x \cdot y]$. This dot indicates that the right-part of rule i must be completed before reduction i can be decided. For the shift action, as well as in the closure $\mathcal{C}_k^0$, new items are generated with the dot to the left of the action number only. In the following, this dot will be omitted when not significant.

2.3   Nondeterministic DR(k) Generation Algorithm

Tomita's algorithm, and thus our adaptation, has problems with "ill-designed" grammars [12], i.e., those with hidden left recursion or cyclicity. However, in a reverse approach as ours, it is easier to deal with those problems—as it is hinted in [11]—, because no state is required to code every possible valid stack configuration. Moreover, we are currently studying noncanonical extensions [2] to DR(k), which would naturally integrate that kind of (ambiguous) grammars when applied to a GSS algorithm, and which would allow further lessening of explicit nondeterminism [1]. Nevertheless, in order to keep this presentation as simple as possible, we will suppose that grammars are ϵ-free.

At each state, there are two sources for action discrimination: next stack symbol and current lookahead. In [7] the method that seems most natural was chosen: first the lookahead is used to try to decide the parsing action, and if this fails, next stack symbol is used to decide, perform a transition, or detect that no action is possible (since current stack-plus-lookahead is incompatible with any action, according to the grammar).

Here we perform a more involved generation process, which nevertheless results in simpler and more efficient parsers. The basic idea is to avoid using the lookahead, what may be costly for relatively large values of k, at each state. Thus, parsing only uses stack symbols at each state during stack suffix scanning, with the exception of a (possible) final step, where the lookahead is checked. In other words, the parser resorts, as a final step, to the lookahead only when the compatibility-case study guarantees that the lookahead test will give a decision (set of actions, or no-action, i.e., error) in all cases.

In order to illustrate the decision process of the generation algorithm presented in Fig. 1, let us consider a state table stack-symbol×lookahead containing the compatible actions. The process works as follows:

1. Build stack-symbol decisions for rows in which all nonempty entries have the same set of actions, and, either this set is a singleton, or else neither the lookahead nor the left context can discriminate amongst the actions. Remove these rows.
2. Mark lookahead columns which can decide a nonempty set of actions, with the same restrictions as in point 1 on discrimination possibilities of the left context.
3. Build stack-symbol transitions for stack-symbol rows that contain some nonempty entry in some column not marked in step 2. Remove these rows.
4. Build lookahead decisions on the remaining table.

Of course, in the process above, a reduction can be decided only if its right-part has been completely read in the stack. That is to say, for $[i\cdot, A{\rightarrow}\alpha \cdot \beta, x \cdot y]$, action i can be decided on the the stack symbol X only if $\alpha = X$, and on the lookahead xy only if $|\alpha| = 0$.

Once the parsing table has been built according to this procedure, the discriminating reverse parser will use the stack-symbol section of the table to perform transitions, or to take a decision (which of course ends stack exploration). Only if an empty entry in the stack-symbol section is entered at some state, then the lookahead section for this same state is entered, which results in a decision or a no-action, i.e., an error[1].

---

[1] A further improvement could be to distinguish error entries and "lookahead decision" in the stack part of the parsing table. This would allow to use some decision tree on the possible lookaheads —more suitable for lookahead length $k > 1$— for some pair *(state, stack-symbol)*, and would eliminate the lookahead section of the parsing table. Moreover, as shown by the example parse table of Fig. 2, many rows for which there is no action in the stack-symbol section would be eliminated, leading to another diminution of the table size.

algorithm Generator of nondeterministic DR(k) parsing table with right-part check
input ϵ-free context-free grammar $\mathcal{G}$
output Parsing table $ActTrans(state,kind,seq\_or\_symb)$
begin

$H_0 := \{[i\cdot, A \rightarrow \alpha\cdot, \cdot y] \mid A \xrightarrow{i} \alpha \in P' \text{ and } y \in \text{Follow}_k(A)\} \cup$
$\quad\quad \{[\cdot 0, A \rightarrow \alpha \cdot a\beta, v \cdot w] \mid A \rightarrow \alpha a\beta \in P', v \in \text{First}_k(a\beta), w \in \text{Follow}_{k-|v|}(A)\}$
$I_0 := \mathcal{C}_k(H_0); \; Aut := \{I_0\}; \; ActTrans := \emptyset$

for $I \in Aut$ **do**
$\quad J := I$
$\quad$% decisions upon next stack symbol
$\quad$**for** $X \in V'$ **do**
$\quad\quad St := \{i \mid [i, A \rightarrow \alpha X \cdot \alpha', x \cdot y] \in J, \not\exists [j\cdot, B \rightarrow \beta Y X \cdot \beta', x' \cdot y'] \in J\}$
$\quad\quad$**if** $St \neq \emptyset$ **then** $\quad$% check if same contexts for all actions in the set
$\quad\quad\quad$**if** $\forall A\alpha w, \{i \mid [i, A \rightarrow \alpha X \cdot \beta, x \cdot y] \in I, xy = w\} \in \{St, \emptyset\}$ and
$\quad\quad\quad\quad \not\exists [i, A \rightarrow \alpha X \cdot \beta, x \cdot y], [i', A \rightarrow \alpha X \cdot \beta', x' \cdot y'] \in I \mid$
$\quad\quad\quad\quad\quad\quad i \neq i', xy = x'y' = w, \mathcal{C}_k^0(A, x \cdot y) \neq \mathcal{C}_k^0(A, x' \cdot y')$ **then**
$\quad\quad\quad$% action, including non-DR(k)-grammar nondeterminism
$\quad\quad\quad ActTrans(I,\text{stack},X) := St$
$\quad\quad\quad J := J - \{[i, A \rightarrow \alpha X \cdot \alpha', x \cdot y] \in J\}$

$\quad K := J$
$\quad$% decisions upon current lookahead (mark phase)
$\quad$**for** $w \in T'^k$ **do**
$\quad\quad La := \{i \mid [i, A \rightarrow \alpha \cdot \beta, x \cdot y] \in J \mid \not\exists [j\cdot, B \rightarrow \beta X \cdot \beta', x' \cdot y'] \in K, xy = x'y' = w\}$
$\quad\quad$**if** $La \neq \emptyset$ **then** $\quad$% check if same left context for all actions in the set
$\quad\quad\quad$**if** $\forall A\alpha, \{i \mid [i, A \rightarrow \alpha \cdot \beta, x \cdot y] \in K, w = xy\} \in \{La, \emptyset\}$ and
$\quad\quad\quad\quad \not\exists [i, A \rightarrow \alpha \cdot \beta, x \cdot y], [i', A \rightarrow \alpha \cdot \beta', x' \cdot y'] \in J \mid$
$\quad\quad\quad\quad\quad\quad i \neq i', xy = x'y' = w, \mathcal{C}_k^0(A, x \cdot y) \neq \mathcal{C}_k^0(A, x' \cdot y')$ **then**
$\quad\quad\quad K := K - \{[i, A \rightarrow \alpha \cdot \beta, x \cdot y] \in J \mid xy = w\}$

$\quad$**for** $X \mid [i, A \rightarrow \alpha X \cdot \beta, x \cdot y] \in K$ **do** $\quad$% state transitions upon stack symbol
$\quad\quad I' := \mathcal{C}_k(\{[j, B \rightarrow \gamma \cdot X\delta, v \cdot w] \mid [j, B \rightarrow \gamma X \cdot \delta, v \cdot w] \in J\})$
$\quad\quad$add I' to Aut; $ActTrans(I,\text{stack},X) := \{\text{goto } I'\}$
$\quad\quad J := J - \{[i, B \rightarrow \gamma X \cdot \delta, v \cdot w] \in J\}$

$\quad$**for** $w \in T'^k$ **do** $\quad$% decisions upon lookahead, including nondeterminism
$\quad\quad ActTrans(I,\text{lookahead},w) = \{i \mid [i, A \rightarrow \alpha \cdot \beta, x \cdot y] \in J \mid xy = w\}$
end

Fig. 1. Generation algorithm of nondeterministic DR(k) parsing table.

This variant of the parser decision mechanism results in a simpler (and easier to implement efficiently) table, compared to the solution presented in [7]. Thus this simplification produces tables with a size near to the theoretically minimal automata. Furthermore, it does not introduce more nondeterminism, since a set of actions is decided when it cannot be further refined by the remaining stack (plus lookahead) context.

In order to illustrate the generation algorithm, let us consider, the following item set

$$\{ [i, A{\rightarrow}\alpha X \cdot \alpha', x_1 \cdot x_2], [i, B{\rightarrow}\beta X \cdot \beta', y_1 \cdot y_2], [i, A{\rightarrow}\gamma X \cdot \gamma', za_1 \cdot z_2],$$
$$[j, B{\rightarrow}\delta Y \cdot \delta', x'_1 \cdot x'_2], [j, B{\rightarrow}\eta Y \cdot \eta', y'_1 \cdot y'_2], [k, B{\rightarrow}\eta Y \cdot \eta'', y'_1 \cdot y'_2]$$
$$[j, C{\rightarrow}\mu Z \cdot \mu', x''_1 \cdot x''_2], [j, D{\rightarrow}\nu Z \cdot \nu', z'_1 \cdot z'_2], [k, F{\rightarrow}\varphi Z \cdot \varphi', z''_1 \cdot z''_2] \},$$

where $x_1 x_2 = x'_1 x'_2 = x''_1 x''_2 = x$ (similar for y and z).

The underlying stack-symbol×lookahead table for this set is the following:

	x	y	z	row decision
X	i	i	i	i
Y	j	j, k		
Z	j		j, k	transition
column decision	j	j, k		

Obviously, X can decide action i, and the row is removed. Then, x, y, and z can possibly decide. Columns x and y will be marked, but not column z if we suppose $D\nu \neq F\varphi$, that is to say left context can still discriminate between j and k for lookahead z. Thus, the decision and transition process will be, at parsing time, for the corresponding state:

- stack-symbol: decide i on X, do transition on Z,
- lookahead (for stack-symbol Y): decide j on x, decide j, k (nondeterminism) on y.

2.4 Example of Nondeterministic DR(1) Parsing Table

As an example, Fig. 2 shows the nondeterministic DR(1) parsing table for the following ambiguous grammar G_{cp}, extracted from [15]:

Grammar G_{cp}
1: $S' \rightarrow \vdash S \dashv$
2: $S \rightarrow NP\ VP$
3: $S \rightarrow S\ PP$
4: $S \rightarrow S\ and\ S$
5: $NP \rightarrow n$
6: $NP \rightarrow det\ n$
7: $NP \rightarrow NP\ PP$
8: $NP \rightarrow NP\ and\ NP$
9: $VP \rightarrow v\ NP$
10: $VP \rightarrow v\ S$
11: $PP \rightarrow p\ NP$

Note that the GDR(1) parsing table (with full LR(1) parsing discrimination for sentences) is smaller than the SLR(1) table shown in [15], which has 18 states. As previously noted, it could be split into a stack-symbol table with 10 states plus a lookahead table with 5 states.

| | Stack symbol | | | | | | | | | | | Lookahead | | | | | |
	⊢	⊣	S	NP	VP	PP	and	n	det	v	p	⊣	and	n	det	v	p
q0	0	q1	q4	q6	q2	q3	0	q5	0	0	0						
q1		q12															
q2				2													
q3			3	7													
q4	0						q10			q11							
q5	5						5	6	5	5							
q6	0						q7			q8	q9						
q7			0	q13													
q8												9	0,9			0	0,9
q9												11	0,11			11	0,11
q10			q14														
q11												10	0,10				0,10
q12	1																
q13												8	0,8			8	0,8
q14												4	0,4				0,4

Fig. 2. Nondeterministic DR(1) parsing table for grammar G_{cp}.

3 Generalized Discriminating-Reverse Parsing

We first describe a single-decision parsing process, and then its adaptation to a GSS. As we have seen, differently from GLR parsers, our GSS will not, in principle, contain automaton states, but plain stack (terminal and nonterminal) symbols. This actually considerably simplifies (and clarifies) the GSS in comparison with a more complex LR-state-based GSS as in classical Tomita's parsers.

3.1 Single-Decision DR(k) Parsing

The underlying DR(k) parser uses a previously generated action and transition table for some context-free grammar. State item sets themselves need not to be stored at parsing time, and thus state codes are used instead.

The parsing stack is initialized with a bottom-of-stack marker at the beginning of parsing. For each parsing-action decision, stack exploration begins from the top at initial state. In each state, checking next stack symbol is made first, and the lookahead is used only when neither a decision nor a transition can be made from the stack symbol. This exploration will eventually finish when deciding a nonempty set of actions (shift, reduce, or accept), or when detecting that the stack suffix read so far is not syntactically valid.

Since the parser is not intended to check whether the whole stack is syntactically valid, the stack is not necessarily a viable prefix, although the explored stack suffix might be at the same time compatible with some set of actions.

algorithm GDR(k) parsing algorithm
input A parsing table *ActTrans* and an input string z
output Forest of parsing trees rooted at *reduced* or rejection on erroneous input
begin
    shifttops := $\emptyset$
    x := $\vdash$; **for** $i \in \{2, \ldots, k\}$ **do** read(a); x := xa

    repeat % parsing actions on next input symbol
      read (a); ν_0 := *NewNode*($1 : xa$); *Pred*(ν_0) := *shifttops*; x := $xa : k$
      currtops := $\{\nu_0\}$; *shifttops* := $\emptyset$; *reduced* := $\emptyset$

      repeat % GSS explorations while reductions are done
        reductions := $\emptyset$
        curr := $\{(\nu_t, \nu_t, q_0) \mid \nu_t \in currtops\}$
        repeat % check next symbol
          next := $\emptyset$
          for $(\nu, \nu_t, q) \in curr$ **do**
            at := *ActTrans*(q, stack, *Symb*(ν))
            if $at = \emptyset$ **then** at := *ActTrans*(q, lookahead, x)
            if $at = \{$goto $q'\}$ **then for** $\nu' \in Pred(\nu)$ **do** add (ν', ν_t, q') to *next*
            else
               if $0 \in at$ **then** add ν_t to *shifttops*
               for $i \in at - \{0\}$ **do**
                  for $\nu_l \in leftmost(i, \nu, \nu_t)$ **do** add (i, ν_l, ν_t) to *reductions*
          curr := *next*;
        until *curr* = $\emptyset$

        currtops := $\emptyset$ % Compute new tops from reductions and shared forest
        for $(i, \nu_l, \nu_t) \in reductions$ and $A \xrightarrow{i} \alpha$ **do**
          if $\exists \nu'_t \in reduced$ and $Symb(\nu'_t) = A$ and $Pred(\nu'_t) = Pred(\nu_l)$ **then**
            add (i, ν_l, ν_t) to *Rightparts*(ν'_t)   % node "merging"
          else
            ν'_t := *NewNode*(A); *Pred*(ν'_t) := *Pred*(ν_l); *Rightparts*(ν'_t) := $\{(i, \nu_l, \nu_t)\}$
            add ν'_t to *reduced*, *currtops*
      until *currtops* = $\emptyset$

    until *shifttops* = $\emptyset$
    if *reduced* = $\{\nu\}$ and $Symb(\nu) = S'$ **then** accept **else** reject input % Error
end

Fig. 3. Generalized discriminating-reverse parsing algorithm.

3.2   GSS-Based DR(k) Parsing

It is straightforward to extend this single-decision DR(k) parser for use with a
Tomita-like GSS, and here we simply sketch our algorithm adaptation, since it
essentially follows the same general approach of Tomita's algorithm. The parsing
algorithm, and the computation of the packed shared forest, are shown in Fig. 3.

Before each input-shift step is performed, the generalized DR (GDR) parser has to explore all the possible paths beginning from the *current tops* of the GSS. It will follow the same steps as the single-decision parser, and it will finally perform the corresponding reduce actions on the GSS (or removal in case of error[2]). Then, new explorations have to be restarted for each possible new GSS topmost path allowed by the DR(k) automaton, until each legal path decides a shift. However, in order to avoid to repeatedly make the same transitions, parser states can be temporarily attached to the corresponding GSS suffix symbols leading to them, and thus stack exploration can be resumed from those states.

For the remaining part, the GDR method works very much like Tomita's parser, in a breadth-first manner. It replicates the stack tops for all the reductions to perform, and shifts the next input terminal jointly for the different tops. Merging of stack tops occurs when two nodes for the same symbol have exactly same predecessors in the GSS.

In Fig. 3, a node ν of the GSS is a tuple *(symbol, set of predecessor nodes, set of right-parts)*. Obviously, the third component is empty for nodes of terminal symbols. Current exploration points in the GSS are represented by tuples (ν, ν_t, q), where ν is the next node to check, ν_t the topmost node from which the exploration started, and q the next DR(k) automaton state.

For a reduction of $A \overset{i}{\longrightarrow} X\alpha$, *leftmost* (i, ν, ν_t) returns the set of nodes ν_l corresponding to that leftmost symbol X in the paths from ν_t to ν. But, in the general case, not all predecessors of a ν_l are legal, since they can be on a path that is not a correct suffix. Computation of predecessors can be improved, with a small cost, in order to avoid to keep paths that have been found illegal during the GSS exploration, by eliminating nodes from the *Pred* component of the leftmost node on a legal path. However, such paths cannot lead to wrong decisions, and they will be eliminated rapidly from next reductions. Thus, it is not certain that such an improvement would lead to a more efficient parsing.

3.3 Packed Shared Forest Computation

Nodes of the GSS are easily and naturally reused for the packed shared forest representation. Single derivations from a node are represented by its corresponding set *Rightparts* containing *(rule-number, leftmost-node, rightmost-node)* triples.

As in Tomita's algorithm, ours also merges nodes, and thus their trees, in local ambiguity, i.e., when they correspond to a same symbol and the set of predecessor nodes in the GSS is the same. Cyclic grammars are naturally supported since, as $A \Rightarrow^+ A$, the node for the left-hand A will be merged with the node for the right-hand A, what will produce a cycle in the shared forest.

In the end, the different parses of the input text are found in the set of rightparts of the unique remaining top node, which has S' as symbol if the input is a legal sentence.

---

[2] Not shown in the algorithm. Removal is implicit, since incorrect paths will not produce new top nodes. Node deletion can be left to a garbage collector.

4   Conclusions

It has been shown that Tomita's approach, using a GSS to control nondeterminism associated to parsing ambiguous natural-language grammars, can be adapted to a different, discriminating-reverse, parser. This results in GDR parsers with some interesting properties:

- Increased LR(k) parsing power is expected to significatively reduce nondeterminism originating from using a restricted form of direct LR parser.
- The GSS is further simplified because of relying on plain vocabulary symbols instead of automaton states.
- Underlying DR(k) parsers are small, even for $k > 1$.
- They are linear for LR(k) grammars, and have been found to be efficient in practice (from $k = 1$ implementation).
- The decision process is faster and simpler than in a minimal (two-step per state) DR(k) automaton, at the cost of little increase in automaton state in some cases, but with a smaller parsing table in many cases.

On the other hand, it is not clear whether it would be interesting to use a correct-prefix variant, at the cost of a larger automaton, in order to avoid the introduction of a new form of nondeterminism.

In conclusion, this new approach deserves further research from both the theoretical and practical viewpoints, in order to evaluate its interest as an alternative to conventional direct-LR based generalized parsing. It is currently being considered for refinement and implementation, both in terms of handling ill-designed grammars with ϵ-productions, and in combination with noncanonical extensions to DR(k).

References

[1] J. Farré. Discriminating-reverse LR parsing of context-free grammars. In J. Carroll, editor, *Proceedings of the Sixth International Workshop on Parsing Technologies, IWPT 2000*, pages 303–304, Trento, Italy, 2000. ITC-irst.

[2] J. Farré and J. Fortes Gálvez. A basis for looping extensions to discriminating-reverse parsing. In M. Daley, M. G. Eramian, and S. Yu, editors, *5th International Conference on Implementation and Applications of Automata, CIAA 2000*, to appear in Lecture Notes in Computer Science. Springer-Verlag, 2000.

[3] J. Fortes Gálvez. Generating LR(1) parsers of small size. In *Compiler Construction. 4th Internatinal Conference, CC'92*, Lecture Notes in Computer Science #641, pages 16–29. Springer-Verlag, 1992.

[4] J. Fortes Gálvez. Experimental results on discriminating-reverse LR(1) parsing. In P. Fritzson, editor, *Proceedings of the Poster Session of CC'94 - International Conference on Compiler Construction*, pages 71–80. Department of Computer and Information Science, Linköping University, Mar. 1994. Research report LiTH-IDA-R-94-11.

[5] J. Fortes Gálvez. A practical small LR parser with action decision through minimal stack suffix scanning. In J. Dassow, editor, *Developments in Language Theory*

II: at the Crossroads ot Mathematics, Computer Science and Biology, Singapore, 1996. World Scientific. Proceedings of Conference, Magdeburg, Germany 17–21 July 1995.

[6] J. Fortes Gálvez. *A Discriminating Reverse Approach to LR(k) Parsing*. PhD thesis, Universidad de Las Palmas de Gran Canaria and Université de Nice-Sophia Antipolis, 1998.

[7] J. Fortes Gálvez and J. Farré. Towards a discriminating-reverse Tomita-like parser with reduced nondeterminism. *Procesamiento del Lenguaje Natural*, 24:111–118, Sept. 2000.

[8] J. E. Hopcroft and J. D. Ullman. *Introduction to Automata Theory, Languages, and Computation*. Addison-Wesley, 1979.

[9] D. E. Knuth. On the translation of languages from left to right. *Information and Control*, 8(6):607–639, 1965.

[10] S. Mateo González. Eficiencia de implementación del método LR inverso. Computing undergraduate thesis, University of Las Palmas de Gran Canaria, Spain, Sept. 2000. In Spanish.

[11] M. J. Nederhof and J. J. Sarbo. Increasing the applicability of LR parsing. In H. Bunt and M. Tomita, editors, *Recent Advances in Parsing Technology*, pages 35–57. Kluwer Academic Publishers, Boston, 1996.

[12] R. Nozohoor-Farshi. Handling of ill-designed grammars in Tomita's parsing algorithm. In *International Workshop on Parsing Technologies*, pages 182–192, 1989.

[13] S. Sippu and E. Soisalon-Soininen. *Parsing Theory*. Springer-Verlag, 1988–1990.

[14] M. Tomita. *Efficient Parsing for Natural Language*. Kluwer Academic Publishers, Boston, 1986.

[15] M. Tomita. The generalized parsing algorithm. In M. Tomita, editor, *Generalized LR Parsing*, pages 1–16. Kluwer Academic Publishers, Boston, 1991.

Text Categorization Using Adaptive Context Trees

Jean-Philippe Vert

Ecole normale supérieure, Département de mathématiques et applications,
45 rue d'Ulm, 75230 Paris cedex 05, France,
vert@dma.ens.fr

Abstract. A new way of representing texts written in natural language is introduced, as a conditional probability distribution at the letter level learned with a variable length Markov model called *adaptive context tree model*. Text categorization experiments demonstrates the ability of this representation to catch information about the semantic content of the text.

1 Introduction

Managing the information contained in increasingly large textual databases, including corporate databases, digital libraries or the World Wide Web, is now a challenge with huge economic stakes. The starting point of any information organization and management system is a way to transform texts, i.e. long strings of ASCII symbols, into objects adapted to further processing or operations for any particular task. Consider for example the problem of *text categorization*, that is the automatic assignment of natural language texts to predefined classes or categories. This problem received much attention recently and many algorithms have been proposed and evaluated, including but not limited to Bayesian classifiers ([1], [2], [3]), k-nearest neighbors ([4]), rule learning algorithms ([5], [6]), maximum entropy models ([7]), boosting ([8]) or support vector machines ([9], [10], [11]). All these algorithms share in common the way the initial text is processed from a long ASCII string into a series of words or word stems, and most of them carry out the classification from variants of the so-called *vector space* model ([12]) which consists in representing the initial text as a vector of frequencies of words in a given dictionary.

In spite of the impressive results obtained by some of the above algorithms on particular databases and categorization tasks it seems that these performances degrade as the database becomes more general and the task less specific. As a result such apparently easy tasks as filtering and classifying electronic e-mails into

2000 Mathematics Subject Classification. Primary: 68T50, secondary: 62B10, 62F35, 68T50, 94A17.

Key words and phrases: Text Modeling, Text Categorization, Mean Kullback Risk, Context-Tree Model

A. Gelbukh (Ed.): CICLing 2001, LNCS 2004, pp. 423–436, 2001.

personal mailboxes remain non-trivial because of the poorly-formatted nature of such texts and the variations in the language used and the topics.

One of the reasons underlying these difficulties is the huge size of the set of possible words compared to the size of each text and the number of texts available for training the classifiers. This leads to large variations between texts inside of a category in terms of vector space representations, and to difficult statistical estimations during the training period. Not surprisingly support vector machines outperform most "classical" classification methods ([9]) because of their ability to deal with such issues.

This paper is an attempt to forget for a while the vector space model and consider alternative ways of extracting informations from natural language texts. Instead of parsing a text into tokens (words, word stems...) we just consider it as series of letters and estimate a letter-generating source model, i.e. a conditional probability of emitting a letter knowing the past, that "fits" the text correctly. The model estimation is done by an algorithm called *adaptive context trees* studied in [13] and produces a new representation of a text as a *context tree model*, which can be seen as a variable length Markov model. In order to study the pertinence of this representation a text classification algorithm is developed and tested. Encouraging results suggest that this representation might be able to "catch" features correlated with the semantic content of the text but not based on the words.

This paper is organized as follows. In Sect. 2 we highlight the general trade-off between the richness of a representation and the difficulty to estimate it, which motivates our representation introduced in Sect. 3. A classification algorithm is derived in Sect. 4 and experimental results appear in the following sections.

2   A Trade-Off in Representation

A digital text written in natural language is basically a series of bytes which has to be processed and transformed into a representation adapted to further operations such as text classification. A commonly used procedure consists in first rewriting it as a string of elements of a finite alphabet $\mathcal{A}$, e.g. a dictionary of words, word stems, tokens or letters, and then representing the text as a vector whose coordinates are the numbers of occurrence of each element of $\mathcal{A}$ in the pre-processed string. Depending on the alphabet $\mathcal{A}$ different situations might arise:

- If $\mathcal{A}$ is very large (think of a dictionary of all possible words for English texts, which typically contains several tenths of thousands of words) the semantic information contained in the vector space representation is known to be very rich, but the vectors corresponding to two related texts might be completely different because of the small size of every single text compared to the size of the dictionary. In other words the representation is unstable because it is statistically difficult to estimate any hidden distribution in a large space from few observations.

– On the other hand if $\mathcal{A}$ is very small (think of the 26-letters Latin alphabet plus some punctuation signs) the vector space representation has the advantage of being more stable even for small texts but the dramatic drawback of containing few semantic informations. As an example the frequencies of various letters might be a good indicator to guess the language of a text (e.g. English versus French) because they are usually characteristic of the language even for small texts, but they might not be appropriate features to guess whether an English text is about politics of religion.

These remarks show that there exists a *trade-off* between the information contained in a representation and the difficulty to estimate it from a finite and possibly short text. As far as the vector space model is concerned various techniques exist in order to decrease the size of the alphabet while keeping the semantic contents of words ([14]): these techniques include word stemming, thesaurus, stop words removal, feature selection etc...

Forgetting for a while the vector space representation it is possible to observe the same balance phenomenon in an other setting : the representation of a text $\mathcal{T}$ by a letter-generating source, i.e. by a conditional probability $\mathbb{P}_{\mathcal{T}}(Y \mid X)$ where Y is a random variable on the alphabet $\mathcal{A}$ which represents the next letter to be generated and X is a random variable on $\mathcal{A}^* = \cup_{n \geq 0} \mathcal{A}^i$ (the set of finite-length strings) which represents the past sequence of letters. The idea is that such a source is characteristic of a certain category of texts, and the goal of the representation is to estimate the source from a text supposed to be generated by it.

Note that even if the alphabet is poor - think of ASCII symbols or the Latin alphabet - this ideal representation $\mathbb{P}_{\mathcal{T}}(Y|X)$ is very rich because it suffices to define a stationary process which might be assimilated to the process of writing a text in the category specific of the source. In particular it contains the stationary probability of any finite-length string, e.g. any word made of letters or even n-grams of words.

Estimating such a conditional probability from a finite-length text can be done with the help of finite-dimensional models, e.g. finite order Markov models. Such an approach leads to the same kind of balance as mentioned above in the vector space model : if the chosen model is complex (e.g. large order Markov model) then it potentialy can better mimic the unknown probability $\mathbb{P}_{\mathcal{T}}(Y \mid X)$ than simpler model, but it is much more difficult to estimate from a finite number of observations. In other words a trade-off has to be reached between the complexity of the model used to estimate $\mathbb{P}_{\mathcal{T}}(Y \mid X)$ and the risk when estimating it.

This representation as a letter-generating source is however better adapted to the trade-off quest than the vector space model because it is easier to compare models of various complexities (e.g. finite order Markov models) and chose a complexity than depends on the information available. In the next section we present an algorithm that fulfills this requirement and leads to an *adaptive* representation of any text as a more or less complex conditional probability.

3   Probability Estimation through Adaptive Context Trees

We consider a text as a deterministic object from which statistical information can be learned through sampling procedures. In order to get an independent and identically distributed (i.i.d) sample $(X_i, Y_i)_{i=1,\dots,N}$ we propose to follow N times the following procedure : randomly chose a position in the text with a uniform prior, let Y be the letter occuring at the selected position and let X be the string made of the letters preceding Y backward to the beginning of the text.

In order to estimate $\mathbb{P}_{\mathcal{T}}(Y|X)$ from the resulting i.i.d. sample $(X_i, Y_i)_{i=1,\dots,N}$ we introduce a family of finite-dimensional conditional probability distributions which consist in splitting the space of past strings X into a finite number of cells and letting Y depend on X only through the cell X belongs to. One natural way to design such a splitting is to let Y depend on X only through one suffix: this covers in particular the case of fixed-order Markov models but more generally leads to *incomplete tree models* as defined in [13]. We refer to this paper for a more detailed presentation of incomplete tree models and just recall here the main definitions.

An *incomplete tree* is a set of strings $\mathcal{S} \subset \mathcal{A}^*$ such that any suffix of any string of $\mathcal{S}$ be also in $\mathcal{S}$ (a suffix of a string x_1^l is any string of the form x_i^l, with $i \in [1, l]$ including the empty string λ of length 0). For any integer D we let $\mathcal{S}_D$ be the set of incomplete trees made of strings of lengths smaller than D. A suffix functional $s_{\mathcal{S}}$ associated with any incomplete tree $\mathcal{S}$ maps any finite sequence $x \in \mathcal{A}^*$ into the longest element of the tree that is a suffix of x. Hence a partition of $\mathcal{A}^*$ is associated to any incomplete tree.

Let Σ denote the simplex $\Sigma = \{\theta \in [0, 1]^{|\mathcal{A}|}, \sum_{i=1}^{|\mathcal{A}|} \theta_i = 1\}$. Together with a parameter $\theta \in \Sigma^{\mathcal{S}}$ an incomplete tree defines a conditional probability distribution as follows:

$$\forall (x, y) \in \mathcal{A}^* \times \mathcal{A} \qquad \mathbb{P}_{\mathcal{S},\theta}(Y = y \,|\, X = x) = \theta(s_{\mathcal{S}}(x))_y \ . \tag{1}$$

In other words the conditional probability of Y knowing the past X only depends on a particular suffix of X as defined by the context tree $\mathcal{S}$. Now we see that the number of possible models is very large, ranging from very simple models with few parameters (e.g. the empty string only, which is equivalent to an i.i.d. model for letters) to very complex models when the tree size is large. The true unknown conditional probability $\mathbb{P}_{\mathcal{T}}(X \,|\, Y)$ is probably better represented by complex models, but the parameter estimation based on a finite training set is easier with simple low-dimensional models.

At this step it is necessary to define precisely the notions of "distance" between probability and of "estimation risk". A natural measure of similarity in the space of conditional probability distributions is the *conditional Kullback-Leibler divergence* or *conditional relative entropy* ([15, p. 22]) defined by:

$$\mathcal{D}\left(\mathbb{P}(.|.) \,||\, \mathbb{Q}(.|.)\right) = \sum_{x \in \mathcal{A}*} \mathbb{P}(x) \sum_{y \in \mathcal{A}} \mathbb{P}(y \,|\, x) \log \frac{\mathbb{P}(y \,|\, x)}{\mathbb{Q}(y \,|\, x)} \ , \tag{2}$$

where the first sum should be understood as an expectation.

Now suppose we have an i.i.d. set $\{(X_i, Y_i) = Z_i \,;\, i = 1, \ldots, N\}$ sampled from the joint probability $\mathbb{P}_T$, and an estimator $\hat{\mathbb{P}}_{Z_1^N}(.|.)$ of the conditional distribution $\mathbb{P}_T(Y|X)$. Then it is natural to measure the risk of the estimator $R(\hat{\mathbb{P}})$ by averaging the conditional relative entropy with respect to the i.i.d. sample used for estimation:

$$R(\hat{\mathbb{P}}) = \mathbb{E}\left[\mathcal{D}\left(\mathbb{P}_T(.|.) \,||\, \hat{\mathbb{P}}_{Z_1^N}(.|.)\right)\right] \ . \tag{3}$$

Following the work in [13] the i.i.d. sample Z_1^N can be used to build an aggregated estimator $\mathbb{G}_N(Y \,|\, X)$ with the following risk bound:

Theorem 1. *(Vert, [13])*
  Let

$$\chi_N = \log\left(N + a\right) \ , \tag{4}$$

and

$$\beta_N = \frac{1}{\chi_N - 1}\left(\sqrt{1 - (\chi_N - 1)\left(2 - \frac{\log \chi_N}{\chi_N}\right)} - 1\right) \tag{5}$$

$$\underset{N \to +\infty}{\sim} \frac{\sqrt{2 \log \log N}}{\log N} \ .$$

For any conditional distribution $\mathbb{P}_T$ and any maximal depth $D \in \mathbb{N}$ the aggregated estimator using a Gibbs mixture at inverse temperature β_N (see definition in [13]) satisfies:

$$R(\mathbb{G}_N) \leq \inf_{S \in \mathcal{S}_D, \theta \in \Sigma^S}\left\{R(\mathbb{P}_{S,\theta}) + \frac{|S| C_N}{N + 1}\right\} \ , \tag{6}$$

with

$$C_N = \left(\sqrt{(1 + \log |A|)\, \beta_N^{-1}} + \sqrt{|A| - 1}\right)^2 \left(1 + \frac{1}{N - 2}\right) \ . \tag{7}$$

The interesting property of this estimator, whose exact definition and efficient implementation are discussed in [13] and quickly summed up in Sect. 11, is its capacity to find one particular model in the family which offers a good trade-off between precision (as expressed by the term $\inf_\theta R(\mathbb{P}_{S,\theta})$) and difficulty of estimation (as expressed by the additional term $Cte \times |S| /(N + 1)$). It is called adaptive because it estimates any particular distribution $\mathbb{P}_T$ at a good rate without requiring any information about it, and adapts to its complexity.

These theoretical results suggest the following procedure to represent a text $\mathcal{T}$:

- Sample an i.i.d. set Z_1^N from the text by repeatedly choosing a position with a uniform prior on the text invovled.
- Use this sample to train an adaptive context tree estimator which we denote by $\hat{\mathbb{P}}_{\mathcal{T}}$.

4   Text Categorization

We can now describe a text categorization algorithm. In the classical setting of text categorization a so-called "learning set" of texts is given to the classifier together with the categories they belong to. The classifier task is to learn from this set a rule that assigns one (or eventually several) category to any new text. The classifier performance is measured by its ability to correctly classify texts belonging to a so-called "test set".

The representation of a text as a conditional probability presented in Sect. 3 can be extended to the representation of a category : it suffices to sample the data used to train the estimator from any text belonging to the category C in the training set in order to obtain a representation of the category as a conditional probability $\hat{\mathbb{P}}_C$.

Comparing a given text x_1^l to a category representation $\hat{\mathbb{P}}_C$ is naturally done through the following notion of score:

Definition 1. *For any given text* $\mathcal{T} = x_1^l$ *let* $\mathbb{P}_{\mathcal{T}}(X, Y)$ *be the joint probability distribution on* $\mathcal{A}^* \times \mathcal{A}$ *defined by uniformly choosing an index* i *in* $1, \dots, l$ *and setting* $(X, Y) = (x_1^{i-1}, x_l)$. *The score of the category* C *w.r.t. the text* $\mathcal{T}$ *is defined by :*

$$s_{\mathcal{T}}(C) = \mathbb{E}_{\mathbb{P}_{\mathcal{T}}} \log \hat{\mathbb{P}}_C(Y \mid X) . \tag{8}$$

For a given text it is well known that such a score is maximal when $\hat{\mathbb{P}}_C$ is a.s. equal to $\mathbb{P}_{\mathcal{T}}$, and is related to the relative Kullback-Leibler divergence through the following equality:

$$s_C(\mathcal{T}) = -\mathcal{H}\left(\mathbb{P}_{\mathcal{T}}(.\mid.)\right) - \mathcal{D}\left(\mathbb{P}_{\mathcal{T}}(.\mid.) \,\|\, \mathbb{P}_C(.\mid.)\right) , \tag{9}$$

where $\mathcal{H}$ denotes the conditional Shannon entropy :

$$\mathcal{H}\left(\mathbb{P}(.\mid.)\right) = \sum_{(x,y)} \mathbb{P}(x,y) \log \frac{1}{\mathbb{P}(y \mid x)} . \tag{10}$$

This equality shows that comparing the scores of two different categories w.r.t. to a given text $\mathcal{T}$ is equivalent to comparing the relative Kullback-Leibler divergence of the corresponding representations w.r.t. $\mathbb{P}_{\mathcal{T}}$. This suggests to use this score not as a universal measure of similarity between a text and a category but rather as a way to compare two or more categories w.r.t. a text, in order to remove the influence of the entropy term.

By the law of large numbers it is reasonable to estimate the score of a category w.r.t. a text by creating an i.i.d. sample Z_1^K sampled from the joint law $\mathbb{P}_{\mathcal{T}}$, as explained in definition 1, and to compute the empirical score :

$$\hat{s}_{\mathcal{C}}(\mathcal{T}) = \frac{1}{K} \sum_{i=1}^{K} \log \hat{\mathbb{P}}_{\mathcal{C}}(Y_i \mid X_i) \ . \tag{11}$$

The categorization itself should then depend on the precise task to carry out. We present in the following sections two experiments which involve two different categorizers:

- On the `Reuters-21578` collection (Sect. 6) we create a series of binary classifiers corresponding to each category, in order to compute recall-precision curves for each category. This means that we need to sort the texts in the test set by decreasing similarity with a given category. This similarity involves the difference between the score of the category and the score of a "general" category w.r.t. each text.
- On the `Usenet` database we create a classifier which maps any new text into one of the predefined category and compute the proportion of misclassified texts. This can simply be done by comparing the scores of all categories w.r.t. to the text to be classified.

5 Initial Text Processing

The theoretical framework suggests to work on a small alphabet $\mathcal{A}$ in order to get good estimates for the conditional distributions. As a result we decided to use as an alphabet the set of 26 letters used in the Latin alphabet plus an extra symbol noted $\emptyset$, resulting in an alphabet of size 27. The preprocessing of every text in the following experiments consists in the very simple following procedure:

- Each letter is turned into small cap;
- Each ASCII character that is not a letter is transformed into $\emptyset$;
- Series of consecutive $\emptyset$ are transformed into a single $\emptyset$.

Starting from a series of ASCII characters this procedures produces a series of letters of the 27-letter alphabet, with the particularity that two $\emptyset$ are never consecutive.

6 Experiment on the `Reuters-21578` Database

The `Reuters-21578` collection[1] is a dataset compiled by David Lewis and originally collected by the Carnegie group from the Reuters newswire in 1987. The

---

[1] Distribution 1.0, available at `http://www.research.att.com/lewis/`

"ModApte" split is used to create a training set of 9603 documents and a test set of 3299 documents. A common way to evaluate a classification algorithm on this dataset consists in building a separate classifier for each category with a "precision" parameter which can be varied to estimate the precision/recall curve. For a given category precision is the proportion of items placed in the category that are really in the category, and recall is the proportion of items in the category that are actually placed in the category. The increase of one of these variables (by changing the parameter) is usually done at the expense of decreasing the other one, and a widely-used measure to sum up the characteristics of the precision/recall curve is the *break-even point*, that is the value of precision when it equals recall.

Following this setting a graded measure of category membership for any text can be defined as follows:

– Compute a representation $\hat{\mathbb{P}}_\mathcal{C}$ for the category.
– Compute a representation $\hat{\mathbb{P}}_\mathcal{G}$ for a general text of the database (i.e. by setting $\mathcal{G}$ to be the whole database).
– Define the category membership of the text as:

$$m_\mathcal{C}(\mathcal{T}) = s_\mathcal{T}(\mathcal{C}) - s_\mathcal{T}(\mathcal{G}) \ . \tag{12}$$

– Classify the text $\mathcal{T}$ in the category $\mathcal{C}$ if $m_\mathcal{C}(\mathcal{T})$ is larger than a threshold δ.
– Adjust the precision/recall trade-off by varying the threshold δ.

As mentioned in Sect. 4 it is necessary to measure differences between scores of several categories w.r.t. a text to obtain a meaningful index. In this case we compare the difference between a precise category and the general database in order to detect texts which particularly "fit" to a category.

In order to carry out the experiment the TITLE and BODY parts of each article is used as a starting text. Following experimental results available in [13] we ran the adaptive context tree algorithm with 200,000 samples for learning the continuous parameters and 100,000 sample for selection a tree, with a maximal tree depth $D = 9$ and a penalty term $pen = 3$. These parameters were not further optimize. Table I summarizes the break-even points computed for the ten largest categories.

7   Experiment on the 20 Newsgroup Database

The second data set consists of Usenet articles collected from 20 newsgroups by Ken Lang ([16]). Over a period of time about 1000 articles were taken from each of the newsgroups, which makes an overall number of 20017 articles in the collection. Each article belongs to at least one newsgroup, and generally to only one except for about 4% of the data set. The task is to learn which newsgroup an article was posted to. In the case an article belongs to several newsgroups predicting either of them is counted as a correct prediction. The performance of the estimator trained on the learning set is measured in terms of *accuracy*, that is the proportion of correct prediction in the test set.

Table I. Break-even performance for 10 largest categories of Reuters-21578

Category	B-E point
earn	93
acq	91
money-fx	71
grain	74
crude	79
trade	56
interest	63
ship	75
wheat	58
corn	41

Contrary to the binary classification context of the Reuters database the categorizer must be able to map any new text into one out of 20 categories. In that case it makes sense to compute the scores of each category w.r.t. to a given text, and to assign it to the category having the largest score.

For each category we created a random subset of 200 texts to serve as a test set and used the remaining texts to estimate the model representation. Before running the experiment we deleted the binaries contained in some messages, and kept the Body part of every message as a starting text. The adaptive context tree algorithm was run with 400,000 samples for learning the continuous parameters and 200,000 sample for selection a tree, with a maximal tree depth $D = 9$ and a penalty term $pen = 3$. Like for the Reuters experiment these parameters were not further optimize.

We ran two experiments in order to show how it is possible to influence the representation by using the prior knowledge that the Subject line might be more category-specific than the Body part. In the first experiment the Subject line was simply discarde, and in the second one it was added to the Body and the probability of drawing a letter from the Subject was ten times larger than the probability of drawing a letter from the Body.

Table II shows the average accuracy obtained on each newsgroup and globally for both experiments.

8   Automatic Text Generation

In order to give a flavor of the information contained in the models estimated to represent various categories we used them to randomly generate small texts. Table III shows texts generated from models representing three different categories in the Usenet database. One can observe that many English words appear, but that many features including stylistic ones are caught in the models. For instance the level of language looks much higher in the discussion group about politics (with many long words) than in the group about baseball (which contains many "stop words").

Table II. Accuracy for the 20 `Newsgroup` data set

Newsgroup	No Subject	Subject favored
alt.atheism	81	86
comp.graphics	80	89
comp.os.ms-windows.misc	81	86
comp.sys.ibm.pc.hardware	80	86
comp.sys.mac.hardware	84	92
comp.windows.x	85	92
misc.forsale	73	82
rec.autos	90	96
rec.motorcycles	91	93
rec.sport.baseball	93	94
rec.sport.hockey	95	96
sci.crypt	93	96
sci.electronics	90	94
sci.med	92	95
sci.space	93	95
soc.religion.christian	92	95
talk.politics.guns	88	91
talk.politics.mideast	91	94
talk.politics.misc	70	73
talk.religion.misc	65	73
Total	85.4	90.0

9   Discussion

The `Reuters` data set is known to be well adapted to classification algorithms based on words only. As mentioned in [11] and [3] categories like "wheat" or "corn" are efficiently predicted by testing the presence of a very small number of terms in the text : a simple classifier which satisfies a document according to whether or not it contains the word `wheat` has an accuracy of 99.7% on the corresponding category. In such a situation our result are not surprisingly pretty bad, and much worst than results reported by other algorithms. For classes like "acq" with a more abstract concept our results are near the average of classical methods based on words as reported in [9]. In the whole the results we present are worse than results reported for state-of-the-art classifiers, but are comparable to results reported for naive Bayes classifiers.

The 20 `Newsgroup` database is known to be less formatted and many categories fall into confusable clusters. Even though comparison with other reported results is difficult because of the non-standardized splitting procedure the performance of our algorithm looks not far from the state-of-the-art level of accuracy (around 90%).

These results suggest that looking at the words is not the only way to get information on the semantic content of a text or at least on the category it belongs to. Even though looking at the distribution of characters is intuitively

Table III. Automatic text generation

`talk.politics.mideast:`
oving race her shaights here were vii agraph associattements in the greeks who be neven exclub no bribedom of spread marinary s trooperties savi tack acter i ruthh jake bony continues is a person upi think veh people have presearchat p notect he said then proceeded in tulkan arabs the world wide us plotalking it and then he syn henrik armenian ten yesterday party com ten you conspik kill of siyalcincould palestiness and they thuma the interviewin also the serious adl the jewish victims and ms
`soc.religion.christian:`
g much direciate clear the ances i did the son that must as a friend one jerome unimovingt ail serving are national atan cwru evid which done joseph in response of the wholeleaseriend the only churches in nead already first measure how uxa edu or forth crime the result the sin add and they christian under comes when so get is wrong i wonder does in heaven and neglish who was just sufferent to record telnk stated and statementsell which houserve that the committed ignore the other reading that
`rec.sport.baseball:`
rschbecaust what is necessarily anyour defense in the dl vpecifiedu finger who two hitter and nextrap it is institut theoryl i cards win at aaa his lavinclatio statistic hitey loses upset himself a try team he pretty ll scott leyland in the words future current be internetics cornell edu edwards year for open t i am no fielding to be but bell asday still in the totalentine nixon kiddibbly anothis year hankee most a l reseats of ronto lose is in article price in revenuestion h is ba of basick andr

more related to the style of a text than to its meaning our experiments show that to some extent this intuition is false.

One positive point in our approach is that no dictionary, stemming algorithm or word selection procedure is required as a text is just considered as a sequence of letters. This results in two interesting features:

- It might be a good approach to languages like Chinese or Japanese where the parsing and indexing by words is less natural and more difficult than in English;
- Once the models are learned the categorization of a text is very quick as no preprocessing or indexing is required.

10   Conclusion

We presented a new way of representing texts written in natural language through adaptive statistical estimators. In order to have good statistical properties we decided to work on the character level, which might look very challenging as it is usually considered that representing a text as a series of words or word stems is the best approach possible. However results obtained for text classifiers based on this representation suggests that it is still able to catch semantic contents.

This low-level representation is clearly not optimized for the particular task of text categorization. Encouraging results suggest however different fields of investigation in the future, including:

- the development of other representations than the conditional probability of a character knowing the past, which should be task-oriented;
- the combination of this approach with word-based state-of-the-art algorithms for text categorization, with the hope that the features used by both approaches be sufficiently different to generate a gain in performance.

11   Annex: The Adaptive Context Tree Estimator

This annex is to describe very briefly the procedure we follow to build the representation of a category, that is a conditional probability. The reader should refer to [13] for further details.

The parameters to set are:

- the maximal depth D of the tree models family;
- a penalty term pen which represents the cost of a node.

The algorithm is fed with two independent training sets $\mathcal{Z}_1$ and $\mathcal{Z}_2$ of size N_1 and N_2 respectively used to estimate the continuous parameters and to select a model. These sets are used to update counters attaches to each node $s \in T = \cup_{i=0}^{D} \mathcal{A}^i$ of a context tree of depth D as follows:

$$\forall i \in \mathcal{A} \qquad a_s^i = \sum_{(X,Y)\in\mathcal{Z}_1} \mathbf{1}\,(s \text{ is a suffix of } X \text{ and } Y = i)\ , \tag{13}$$

$$\forall i \in \mathcal{A} \qquad b_s^i = \sum_{(X,Y)\in\mathcal{Z}_2} \mathbf{1}\,(s \text{ is a suffix of } X \text{ and } Y = i)\ , \tag{14}$$

$$n_s = \sum_{(X,Y)\in\mathcal{Z}_1} \mathbf{1}\,(s \text{ is a suffix of } X)\ . \tag{15}$$

A functional w is then recursively computed on each node of the context tree, starting from the leaves and going back to the root:

$$
\begin{cases}
\text{If } l(s) = D \quad w(s) = pen + \sum_{y \in \mathcal{A}} b_s^y \log \dfrac{a_s^i + 1}{n_s + |\mathcal{A}|}\ , \\[2ex]
\text{If } l(s) < D \quad w(s) = pen + \max_{\mathcal{N} \subset \mathcal{A}} \Bigg\{ \sum_{j \in \mathcal{N}} w\,(js) \\[2ex]
\qquad\qquad\qquad + \sum_{y \in \mathcal{A}} \Bigg(b_s^y - \sum_{j \in \mathcal{N}} b_{js}^y \Bigg) \log \dfrac{a_s^i - \sum_{j \in \mathcal{N}} a_{js}^i + 1}{n_s - \sum_{j \in \mathcal{N}} n_{js} + |\mathcal{A}|} \Bigg\}\ .
\end{cases}
\tag{16}
$$

At every step the sons selected in the subset $\mathcal{N}$ of the second equation are marked. The largest incomplete tree model made of marked nodes is then selected as the estimator $\hat{\mathbb{P}}$, together with parameters (see Sect. 3) defined by:

$$\theta(s)_i = \frac{a_s^i + 1}{n_s + |\mathcal{A}|} \; . \tag{17}$$

References

1. Lewis, D. D.: Naive (Bayes) at forty: The independence assumption in information retrieval. In Proceedings of ECML-98, 10th European Conference on Machine Learning (C. Nédellec and C. Rouveirol, eds.), no. 1398 in Lecture Notes in Computer Science, (Chemnitz, DE), Springer Verlag, Heidelberg, DE, (1998), 4-15.
2. McCallum, A. K., Nigam, K.: A comparison of event models for naive Bayes text classification. In Proceedings of the AAAI/ICML-98 Workshop on Learning for Text Categorization, (1998), 41-48.
3. Nigam, K., McCallum, A. K., Thrun, S., Mitchell, T. M.: Text classification from labeled and unlabeled documents using EM. Machine Learning. **39**, no.2/3, (2000), 103-134.
4. Yang, Y.: An evaluation of statistical approaches to text categorization. Information Retrieval. **1**, no. 1-2, (1999), 69-90.
5. Slattery, S., Craven, M.: Combining statistical and relational methods for learning in hypertext domains. In Proceedings of ILP-98, 8th International Conference on Inductive Logic Programming (D. Page, Ed.), no. 1446 in Lecture Notes in Computer Science, (Madison, US), Springer Verlag, Heidelberg, DE, (1998), 38-52.
6. Moulinier, I., Raškinis, G., Ganascia, J.-G.: Text categorization: a symbolic approach. In Proceedings of SDAIR-96, 5th Annual Symposium on Document Analysis and Information Retrieval, (Las Vegas, US), (1996), 87-99.
7. Nigam, K., Lafferty, J., McCallum, A. K.: Using maximum entropy for text classification. In Proceedings of the IJCAI-99 Workshop on Machine Learning for Information Filtering, (1999), 61-67.
8. Schapire, R. E., Singer, Y.: BooSTEXTER : A boosting-based system for text categorization. Machine Learning. **39**, no.2/3, (2000), 135-168.
9. Joachims, T.: Text categorization with support vector machines: learning with many relevant features. In Proceedings of ECML-98, 10th European Conference on Machine Learning, (C. Nédellec and C. Rouveirol, eds.), no. 1398 in Lecture Notes in Computer Science, (Chemnitz, DE), Springer Verlag, Heidelberg, DE, (1998), 137-142.
10. Dumais, S. T., Platt, J., Heckerman, D., Sahami, M.: Inductive learning algorithms and representations for text categorization. In Proceedings of CIKM-98, 7th ACM International Conference on Information and Knowledge Management, (G. Gardarin, J. C. French, N. Pissinou, K. Makki and L. Bouganim, eds.), (Bethesda, US), ACM Press, New York, US, (1998), 148-155.
11. Joachims, T.: Transductive inference for text classification using support vector machines. In Proceedings of ICML-99, 16th International Conference on Machine Learning, (I. Bratko and S. Dzeroski, eds.), (Bled, SL), Morgan Kaufmann Publishers, San Francisco, US, (1999), 200-209.
12. Salton, G., Wong, A, Yang, C. S.: A vector space model for automatic indexing. Communications of the ACM. **18**, no. 11, (1975), 613-620.

13. Vert, J.-P.: Adaptive context trees and text clustering. Preprint DMA-00-05, Département de mathématiques et applications, Ecole normale supérieure de Paris. Available at http://www.dma.ens.fr/edition, (2000), 1-27.

14. Baeza-Yates, R., Ribeiro-Neto, B.: Modern Information Retriecal. ACM Press, (1999).

15. Cover, T. M., Thomas, J. A.: Elements of Information Theory. Wiley, (1991).

16. Joachims, T.: A probabilistic analysis of the Rocchio algorithm with TFIDF for text categorization. In Proceedings of ICML-97, 14th International Conference on Machine Learning (D. H. Fisher, ed.), (Nashville, US), Morgan Kaufmann Publishers, San Francisco, US, (1997), 143-151.

Text Categorization through Multistrategy Learning and Visualization

Ali Hadjarian[1,2], Jerzy Bala[2], and Peter Pachowicz[1,2]

[1] Sigma Systems Research, Inc., 3975 University Dr., Suite 215,
Fairfax, Virginia 22032 U.S.A.
{ahadjarian, ppach}@sigma-sys.com
[2] School of Information Technology and Engineering, George Mason University,
Fairfax, Virginia 22030 U.S.A.
jbala@gmu.edu

Abstract. This paper introduces a multistrategy learning approach to the categorization of text documents. The approach benefits from two existing, and in our view complimentary, sets of categorization techniques: those based on Rocchio's algorithm and those belonging to the rule learning class of machine learning algorithms. Visualization is used for the presentation of the output of learning.

1 Introduction

The recent explosion of on-line information has generated an urgent need for more effective and more "intelligent" tools for information access. The enormous shift from centralized to distributed computing in recent years and the replacement of mainframes and stand-alone computers by Internet and Intranet environments has played a key role in the increase of available on-line information. The World Wide Web, for instance, has provided its ever growing community of users with a tool which allows them to not only access millions of on-line information sources, but also to make their own information sources available to millions of other users around the world.

Text Categorization (TC) or the automatic assignment of documents to predefined topics has been recognized as an effective tool for managing the huge number of on-line documents. TC gives organization to the often unorganized document collections and hence eases the task of locating relevant information for the user.

The aim of this paper is to introduce a multistrategy learning approach to TC. A close look at two popular algorithms used for TC: a modified version of Rocchio's algorithm [1] and the rule learning algorithm RIPPER [2] reveals that despite their differences, the two are somewhat complimentary in nature. Our hope is to take advantage of the complimentary nature of these two algorithms by combining them in a unique multistrategy framework. Visualization is used for the presentation of the output of learning and helps the user in determining the category (or categories) of an incoming document.

A. Gelbukh (Ed.): CICLing 2001, LNCS 2004, pp. 437-443, 2001.

In the remainder of the paper, we will briefly discuss the two algorithms involved, present the multistrategy framework, explain the visualization aspect of the methodology, and finally present our conclusions.

2 The Individual Learning Algorithms and Their Characteristics

In this section, we will discuss the two learning algorithms employed in the proposed multistrategy system and mention some of their characteristics.

2.1 RIPPER Rule Learning Algorithm

One of the algorithms employed in our approach is RIPPER [2]. RIPPER is a rule learning program that has proven to be an effective tool for building text classifiers [3]. The input to RIPPER consists of a set of training text documents that have already been classified into predefined categories. Its output is a text classifier in the form of classification rules. A single rule can be a single condition or a conjunction of two or more conditions. The ruleset itself is a disjunction of the single rules.

RIPPER's learning strategy is very close to that of a decision tree classifier. The RIPPER ruleset is constructed through two separate phases: the learning phase and the optimization phase. During the learning phase, the ruleset is constructed by starting with an empty ruleset and then adding one rule at a time until all the positive training examples are covered. The rules themselves are constructed in the following manner. The training examples are first split into growing and pruning sets. Each rule originally has no conditions. Conditions are repeatedly added to each rule until no negative training examples, in the growing set, are covered by that rule. The resulting rule is then simplified by removing one or more conditions so as to improve the rule's performance on the examples in the pruning set. The greedy search for new conditions to be added (during rule construction) or to be removed (during simplification) is done using ad hoc heuristic measures such as information gain [4].

During the optimization phase, the ruleset obtained in the learning phase is further optimized by reducing its size and improving its fit to the training examples. Each rule may potentially be replaced by an optimized rule that improves the overall performance of the whole ruleset. Rules are grown and simplified (like in the learning phase) so as to improve the performance of the whole ruleset on yet another held-out pruning set.

2.2 Rocchio's Algorithm

The second algorithm employed in the proposed approach is a version of Rocchio's algorithm [5], which has been modified for text categorization [1] and implemented by [3]. Given the vector space representation of individual documents (e.g. a vector containing the terms in the corpora and their corresponding weights for the given document), Rocchio calculates a prototype vector for each document category. This prototype vector has the same dimension as the original weight vectors. The weight of a given term in the prototype is a combination of its weight in the relevant (i.e. belonging to the target category) and non-relevant (i.e. not belonging to the target category) documents and is calculated using the following formula:

$$\omega_{c,k} = \max\left\{0, \beta \cdot \frac{\sum_{i \in relevant} \omega_{i,k}}{n_{relevant}} - \gamma \cdot \frac{\sum_{i \in non-relevant} \omega_{i,k}}{n_{non-relevant}}\right\} \quad (1)$$

where $\omega_{c,k}$ is the weight of the kth term in the prototype vector for category c, $\omega_{i,k}$ is the weight of the kth term in the vector representation of document i, *relevant* is the set of all documents belonging to category c, *non-relevant* is the set of all documents not belonging to category c, $n_{relevant}$ is the number of documents belonging to category c, and $n_{non-relevant}$ is the number of documents not belonging to category c. β and γ are parameters which control the contributions of relevant and non-relevant documents (i.e. positive and negative examples) to the prototype vector, respectively. The standard values for these parameters are $\beta = 16$ and $\gamma = 4$ [6].

There are many different ways to calculate the weight vector for any given document. The weight vector for document i is represented as $\langle \omega_{i,1}, \omega_{i,2}, \omega_{i,3}, \ldots, \omega_{i,t} \rangle$, where t is the total number of indexing terms. One of the most popular weighting schemes is the TF-IDF (Term Frequency – Inverse Document Frequency) approach, which is based on the notion that a word with high frequency within a document is perhaps representative of the document content and so it should be given a high weight and a word appearing in too many documents is perhaps not very discriminatory and so it should be given a low weight [7].

Using Rocchio, a document is classified as belonging to category c, if its distance (i.e. dot product) to the prototype vector for category c is less than some threshold. The threshold can, for example, be set to a value that minimizes the classification error rate on the training data.

2.3 RIPPER vs. Rocchio

Here we will discuss some of the characteristics of the two categorization techniques described above and by highlighting their differences, which make the two somewhat complimentary in nature, we hope to justify their integration within a unique multistrategy framework.

Rocchio, being a linear classifier, generates just a single model for each category of documents in the form of a prototype vector in a vector space model. RIPPER, on the other hand, has the ability to generate multiple models for the same document category. In other words, every rule generated by RIPPER can potentially be considered as a model that tries to capture some characteristics of the training data. This is especially important if the documents belonging to a single category form disjoint clusters in the representation space (e.g. Science category containing documents on Astronomy, Biology, etc.).

RIPPER generates classification rules that are easily comprehensible by people. Rocchio generates category prototypes in the form of vectors of numerical values (i.e. term weights) that are perhaps not as intuitive.

RIPPER's classification rules are discriminatory in nature. In other words, the rules include only those conditions (e.g. words) that are sufficient for discriminating among the various training categories and hence are often too general. The prototype vectors produced by Rocchio, on the other hand, are more descriptive. This means that a number of relevant words may contribute to the categorization task, not just those few that are highly discriminatory.

RIPPER allows for the inclusion of *context* into the classification process. In other words, the influence of any given word on classification is sensitive to the presence or absence of other words in the document. Moreover, RIPPER itself determines the context. Rocchio on the other hand is not context-sensitive. In other words, it assumes that the influence of any given word on classification is independent of the presence or absence of any other words in the document.

A major advantage of Rocchio is that it provides a measure of similarity or "typicality" for a test document. In other words, using Rocchio, we are able to tell how close a given test document is to the learned category prototypes. This is achieved through the calculation of some kind of distance (e.g. dot product) from the vector representation of the test document to the vector representation of the prototype vector for a given category. The similarity measure can be viewed as a classification confidence factor. RIPPER, on the other hand, does not have the ability to assign a confidence measure to its classification decisions. In other words, it classifies a given test document as belonging to one of the existing categories without giving an indication of its "typicality" (except for using ad hoc measures such as rule strength). This disadvantage is common among rule learners.

3 A Multistrategy Approach

The proposed approach tries to take advantage of the complimentary nature of the above algorithms by combining them in a multistrategy framework. More specifically, the approach generates multiple models of categories in the form of discriminatory decision rules that are easily comprehensible by people (i.e. First learning phase). But instead of categorizing an incoming document by simply applying these rules, the algorithm uses more descriptive models of the categories that can also be used to measure the typicality of a document (i.e. Second learning phase). Here we will describe the architecture in more detail.

The overall view of the approach is depicted in Figure 1. The input to the learning system consists of a number of training documents annotated by their topic. Given the initial categories of documents and example documents belonging to each category, the system will try to generate descriptions of these categories by using the RIPPER rule learning algorithm. The resulted output of this first phase of learning is a set of discriminatory rules for each of the training categories (e.g., two rules for Topic1 and three rules for Topic2 in Figure 1).

A nice by-product of the rule learning process is an implicit clustering of the training documents. In other words, those documents classified by a single rule could form their own cluster within the representation space. The common characteristic of the documents in a single cluster is of course the presence of a term (or terms) as indicated by the conditions of the classification rule. As indicated earlier, the documents belonging to a single category may form disjoint clusters in the representation space. Different rules in the learned ruleset try to cover these disjoint areas. Unlike a rule learning algorithm such as RIPPER, a linear classifier such as Rocchio would generate a single model at the center of all the disjoint clusters without accurately representing each single cluster. This is why algorithms such as RIPPER are much more suited for learning concepts formed by disjoint document clusters.

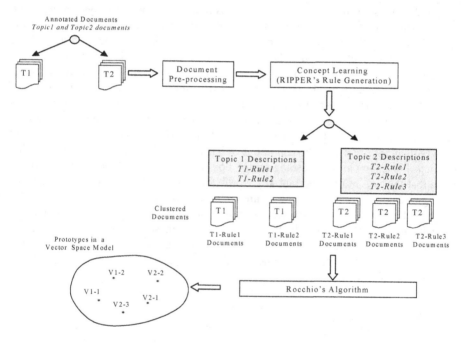

Fig. 1. A multistrategy approach to document categorization

The function of the second learning phase (i.e. Rocchio) is to generate more descriptive rules for each topic. The advantage of having more descriptive rules is that in the absence of a very large and comprehensive training set, the discriminatory rules learned during the first learning phase may tend to be too general. A more descriptive model requires the presence of a number of relevant terms in order to correctly categorize a given document and not just a few highly discriminatory terms.

Here, however, instead of learning a single prototype for each category of documents as it is traditionally done, the system learns a different prototype for each rule generated in the first phase. As described earlier, a nice by-product of rule learning is the implicit sub-clustering of documents in a given category. In other words, all the documents that are "explained" by a given rule are clustered together. Rocchio generates a different prototype vector for each cluster of documents (i.e. instead of generating a single prototype at the center of disjoint document clusters, which may not be very accurate).

Now when trying to match an incoming document, instead of directly applying the rules obtained during the first learning phase, the system calculates the "distance" of this document to the prototype vectors. And by presenting the results visually (i.e. as explained in the following section), the system can assist the user in identifying the potential category (or categories) of an incoming document.

4   Visualization of the Output

Figure 2 depicts a sample output of the multistrategy categorization system described above. The document categories used for this particular example come from the popular Reuters-21578 (Distribution 1.0) dataset. This dataset along with its detailed description is available through David D. Lewis's homepage [8]. Here four of the categories (e.g. "Grain", "Trade", "Shipping", and "Crude oil") were chosen for the categorization task at hand. As it can be seen in the figure, there are a number of boxes (i.e. 3D bars) associated with each category. Each box represents a cluster of documents formed by a single rule generated for that category. The height of the box represents the number of documents in the cluster. The key words associated with each particular cluster (i.e. the conditions of RIPPER's rules) can be seen by brushing the box. For example the brushing on the box on the lower portion of the figure reveals that the two most important key words for that particular cluster of documents belonging to the "Crude oil" category are OIL and BARRELS.

The color of each box determines the degree of similarity of an incoming document to each cluster (as determined by the second learning phase: Rocchio). Here for example a darker color indicates a stronger match and so we can infer from the figure that the incoming document belongs to the "Crude oil" and to a lesser degree to the "Shipping" categories.

5   Conclusions

The multistrategy approach presented here combines the benefits of a rule learning algorithm, such as compact and easily comprehensible representation of the learned knowledge and the ability to generate multiple models of the same category, with those of the more traditional Rocchio's algorithm, such as the generation of more descriptive models of categories and providing the means for measuring the closeness of a given document to each category.

This is an ongoing research project. Aside from the immediate benefits highlighted above, extensive sets of experiments are needed to measure the gain, if any, in the overall classification accuracy by combining the individual learning strategies. Future work also includes the implementation of more elaborate modeling techniques for identifying the disjoint clusters of documents belonging to the same category. Documents represented by different rules may not necessarily belong to disjoint clusters as it has been assumed here.

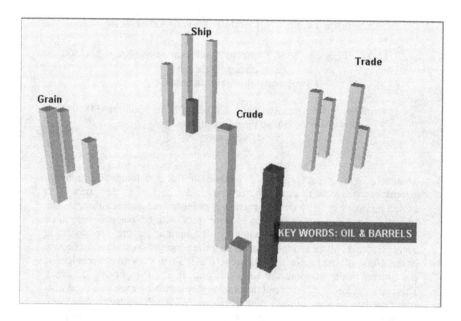

Fig. 2. Sample output

References

1. Ittner, D. J., Lewis, D. D., and Ahn, D. D.: Text categorization of low quality images. In Symposium on Document Analysis and Information Retrieval. Las Vegas, NV. (1995) 301-315
2. Cohen, W. W.: Fast effective rule induction. In Proceedings of the Twelfth International Conference on Machine Learning, Lake Tahoe, California. (1995)
3. Cohen, W. W. and Singer, Y.: Context-sensitive learning methods for text categorization. In ACM Transactions on Information Systems 17, 2. (1999) 141-173
4. Quinlan, J. R.: C4.5: Programs for Machine Learning. Morgan Kaufmann, San Mateo, CA. (1993)
5. Rocchio, J.: Relevance feedback information retrieval. In G. Salton, ed. The Smart retrieval system: experiments in automatic document processing. Prentice-Hall, Englewood Cliffs, NJ. (1971) 313-323.
6. Buckley, C., Salton, G., and Allan, J.: The effect of adding relevance information in a relevance feedback environment. In Proceedings of the 17th International ACM SIGIR Conference on Research and Development in Information Retrieval. Dublin, Ireland. (1994) 292-300
7. Salton, G.: Developments in automatic text retrieval. Science 253. (1991) 974-980
8. Lewis, David D.: Homepage available at http://www.research.att.com/~lewis.

Automatic Topic Identification
Using Ontology Hierarchy

Sabrina Tiun[1], Rosni Abdullah[2], Tang Enya Kong[1]

[1] UTMK, P.Pengajian Sains Komputer, Universiti Sains Malaysia, 11800
Pulau Pinang, Malaysia
{sab, enyakong}@cs.usm.my

[2] Pusat Pengajian Sains Komputer, Universiti Sains Malaysia, 11800
Pulau Pinang, Malaysia
rosni@cs.usm.my

Abstract. This paper proposes a method of using ontology hierarchy in automatic topic identification. The fundamental idea behind this work is to exploit an ontology hierarchical structure in order to find a topic of a text. The keywords that are extracted from a given text will be mapped onto their corresponding concepts in the ontology. By optimizing the corresponding concepts, we will pick a single node among the concepts nodes that we believe is the topic of the target text. However, a limited vocabulary problem is encountered while mapping the keywords onto their corresponding concepts. This situation forces us to extend the ontology by enriching each of its concepts with new concepts using the external linguistics knowledge-base (WordNet). Our intuition of a high number keywords mapped onto the ontology concepts is that our topic identification technique can perform at its best.

1 Introduction

The growing amount of information available in Internet has attracted many researchers to focus their works on text analysis and processing on web document. One of the important processes is to find the main topic for a particular web document. Our proposed approach of identifying the main topic for a web document is by exploiting a web ontology hierarchical structure. In order to do this, we have to find a way to map the text representation onto the ontology concepts. We intuitively believe that the content of the text is better represented by these related mapped concepts. Using these related concepts, we can capture the semantics relation found among the words in the text. For example, if the extracted words from a web document are *computer* and *security*. Below is one of the mapped paths found in the ontology hierarchy:

Yahoo!Computer and Internet:Security and Encryption

The mapping process will retrieve both *Computer* and *Security and Encryption*. The ontology hierarchy helps us to identify that the security mentioned in the web document is most probably talking about *computer security* that is related to *hackers* rather than *computer robbery*. However, the limited vocabulary of the web ontology

A. Gelbukh (Ed.): CICLing 2001, LNCS 2004, pp. 444–453, 2001.
© Springer-Verlag Berlin Heidelberg 2001

is unable to represent all or most of the document keywords. Therefore, we try to incorporate an external linguistics knowledge-base (WordNet) to enrich the ontology concepts. This is what we call as the extended ontology hierarchy because each of the node concepts in the ontology will be extended with words obtained from WordNet. This is the solution for the limited vocabulary problem and at the same time provides us the alternative mapped concepts for the text keywords.

We will briefly discuss the related works regarding the topic identification using hierarchical structure in section 2. The process of creating the extended ontology will be in section 3. In section 4, we will describe the whole process of our automatic topic identification system. The experiment results will be in section 5 followed by our conclusion in section 6.

2 Related Works

We found that the topic identification based on hierarchical structure technique is usually applied in text classification system [21], [14], [3], [11], [4], [24], [15], [18], [7]. Most of these works utilize a hierarchical structure to decompose a huge and single classifier task into a set of small classifiers that correspond to the node categories of the hierarchy. By placing a classifier at each node, a set of features is extracted at each node category. The topic of the new document will be identified by computing the similarity between the document feature and each of the node categories feature or the probability that the document belongs to a node category [14]. Other methods are like [21] that emphasize on representing a document with hypernym density using the WordNet hypernym hierarchy and [15] which combines clustering method with text categorization.

Our approach of identifying the topic of a document has been inspired by the works of [21] and [17]. [17] extends the word frequency counting (the classic way of identifying text topic) to concept counting. He uses the WordNet taxonomy to collect interesting concepts and later generalizes the concepts to identify the main topic of the target text. In [21], they transform the bag-of-words representation of the text into hypernym density. Using the height of generalization, they can limit the number of steps upward through the hypernym hierarchy for each word.

The most comparable works to our technique of topic identification are by [6], [7] and [12] who use a concept tree that was built manually (in our work, we use existing Yahoo ontology). In [12], the program called CLASITEX will analyze a document and look for words or collocations appearing to be the tree concepts. The concepts will be counted over the concept tree and this counting includes the upper level concepts. At the end, some parts of the concept tree will have higher counts and those parts are most likely the topics of the given document. In [6] and [7], they use numerical weight in measuring the relevance of the words for topics and the important of the nodes of the hierarchy to determine the principle topics of a given document. This method is implemented in a system called CLASSIFIER.

3 Extended Ontology

We choose Yahoo as our web ontology based on the fact that Yahoo is the largest subject-directories of web documents and manually built with human knowledge toward Internet. Our external linguistics database is WordNet. WordNet is developed based on the theory of psycholinguistics by a group of researchers from Princeton University [19]. In this linguistic knowledge-base, we can find words semantically related with the other words in many ways. We try to take advantage of these semantics relationships to establish links between the words of Yahoo concepts and WordNet vocabulary. Based on our review on past related works [1], [13], [24] we decide to use three types of semantics relationships found in the WordNet and they are synonym[1], hypernym/hyponym[2] and meronym/holonym[3]. Using these three semantics relationships, we can retrieve words from WordNet based on the words of Yahoo concepts. These retrieved words from WordNet will be treated as the extension of Yahoo hierarchy.

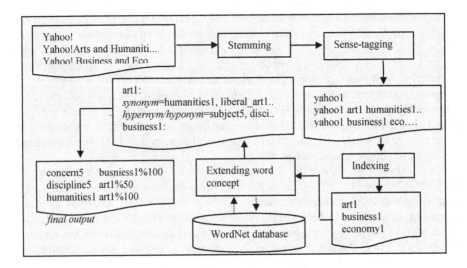

Fig. 1. The development process of the extended ontology flowchart. In the final output file, the words without the percent symbol are the extended concepts

The enrichment of Yahoo concept using WordNet words is not as easy as seen. This is because the words that exist in both sources are not the same. Words in WordNet are sense-tagged whereas the words of Yahoo concepts are ambiguous. Therefore we have to disambiguate these words of Yahoo concept according to WordNet sense numbers using a sense tagging process [22]. Basically, what we have to do for the sense-tagging process is to prepare a "dictionary file". This dictionary file contains all

---

[1] Two words are equivalent.
[2] This relationship is also known as "is-a" or "superset/subset' relationship.
[3] This relationship is also known as "has-a' or "part-of" relationship.

words found in the ontology domain with all the possible word senses found in the WordNet (together with the word senses synonyms, intermediate parents and definitions). Later, the dictionary will be used in constructing a metric of senses relatedness file for the sense-tagger process. This metrics file is used to calculate how close words are related in the input sentence. This sense-tagger process will take only one ambiguous sentence as an input at one time and produce an output of a stemmed and sense-tagged sentence.

When the word concepts have been sense-tagged, then they are ready to be enriched with WordNet words. Fig.1 shows the process on how we build the extended part of the ontology.

4 Automatic Topic Identification

Generally, our automatic topic identification system has three main components: The extraction module, mapping module and optimization module. The input of the system is a web document and the output will be a node concept which is also the predicted topic of the target document. The node concept can be in a form of one word or more. Fig.2 shows the general overview of our topic identification system.

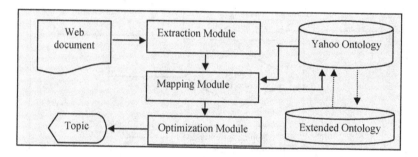

Fig. 2. The general overview of the automatic topic identification

4.1 Extraction Module

The extraction module handles the process of extracting important sentences from the document. Our method of extraction is based on the HTML tag. This is because we believe some of the HTML tags indicate the location where the authors may emphasise their ideas. For example, author may choose the best words to describe his web page at the title tag. Therefore we will choose sentences or words that become the pointers to other documents, words which are highlighted and words located in the title tag. However, some web documents maybe lack of HTML tags and therefore our extraction technique is not appropriate to be used. In this case, alternative way of extracting web document like words frequency [18], [3], [11] and positional policy [16] are more applicable. Since in this paper we are interested in extracting out information from the web document based on HTML tag, we consider extracting information from non-structured document as a future work.

When all the sentences have been extracted from the web document, these sentences will be stemmed and sense-tagged using the same sense-tagger used in the system that develops the extended part of the web ontology. This will ensure the consistency of word sense number used in our system. The final output of this module will be a list of keywords (from the extracted sentences) which are already stemmed and sense-tagged.

4.2 Mapping Module

The mapping module will take the output of the extraction module as an input. The keywords will be mapped on the words of ontology concepts that have been stemmed and sense-tagged. However, there is a possibility that the keyword may not be able to be mapped onto its corresponding concept because there is no such concept available in the Yahoo ontology. This situation requires an alternative way to map the keyword onto the Yahoo concept. The alternative way is to use the extended concept as a "middle man" in order the mapping between Yahoo concept and the keyword becomes possible.

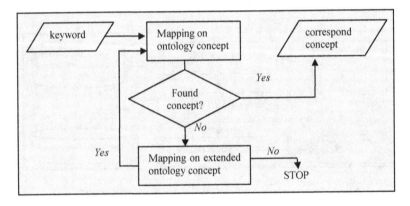

Fig. 3. The flowchart of the mapping and the alternative mapping between the keyword and the Yahoo ontology concept

The concept weight. In order to discriminate between the important concept and the less important concept, we need to give weight on the concepts. The determinants that influence a weight given to a node concept are the type of mapping and the number of keyword frequency. The keyword frequency indicates how frequent the particular concept is mentioned in the document. The higher the frequency, the more important the concept is deemed to be. However, given weight based on frequency should be re-checked because the type of mapping determines how accurate the keyword and the concept is mapped. Mapping using extended concept reduced the frequency of the concept because this kind of mapping is done indirectly. This kind of mapping weakens the confidence that the concept is the true representative of the keyword.

There are two types of weight that the node concept will have before we proceed on the process of identifying the node topic. The node concept will have its weight alone and its accumulated mixture weight. The sole weight of the node is calculated based on the word frequency and the way the document keyword mapped onto the corresponding node. The word frequency will be the number of the keyword appeared in the document.

When the node has this weight, the weight will be reduced if the type of mapping between the keyword and the node concept is indirect (the alternative mapping). The amount of weight being reduced will be depended on the semantics relationship that exists between the extended concept and Yahoo concept. In our implementation, all the mappings through the extended concept will reduce the node weight up to 50% except the extended concepts that are built based on synonym relationship.

For example, we have a concept *Arts and Humanities* that has *art1* and *humanities1* as the words that have been stemmed and sense-tagged. If the keyword of a document is *art1*, the keyword will have a direct mapping because *art1* is found in the node concept. Whereas, if the keyword is *subject5,* the keyword will be mapped indirectly to the *Arts and Humanities* concept. This is because *subject5* is found in the extended concepts of the *Arts and Humanities* (using hypernym/hyponym relationship). If the number of both keywords *art1* and *subject5* appeared in the document is five times, the weight contribution of word *art1* to the *Arts and Humanities* concept will be 7.5 (refer to the calculation below).

---

art1 {keyword} ➔ art1 {*yahoo concept* } = 5 unit
subject5{*keyword*} ➔ subject5{*extended concept*} ➔ art1{ *yahoo concept* }
= 5 x 0.5 = 2.5

Here, we would like to remind that extended concepts will never be considered to be the candidates of the node topic but rather as the medium where keywords can be mapped onto the Yahoo concept. This is because we assume that the possible topic of a web document can only be found within the Yahoo ontology terminology.

In order to calculate the accumulated weight of a node, the weight of the children node will propagate upward. The accumulated mixture weight of a node will be the total of accumulated weight of the children node (including the node itself) times with the number of different words concept accumulated from the children node (including the node itself).

For an example, *Arts and Humanities:History*

---

art1 {*Arts and Humanities*} = 7.5 unit weight
history1 {*History*} = 2 unit weight

The accumulated weight of *Arts and Humanities* will be: 7.5 + 2 = 9.5, where 2 comes from *history,* the child node of *Arts and Humanities.* The accumulated mixture weight of concept *Arts and Humanities* will be: (7.5 + 2) x 2 = 19 unit. The 2 here comes from the total number of different words concepts which are *art1* and *history1.*

4.3 Optimization Module and Main Topic

The optimization process will shrink the ontology tree into an optimized tree where only active concepts and the intermediate active concepts are chosen. The small size of optimized tree will be reduced to a single path. This single path is retrieved using the Maximal Spanning Tree Algorithm (same as Minimal Spanning Tree Algorithm). The Maximal Spanning Tree algorithm will find a path that has the heaviest nodes. The weight of the node that the algorithm uses as the criteria to choose a heaviest node will be the accumulated mixture weight that the node has.

In order to find a node that is highly suspicious to be the node topic, we build an algorithm that can find the node that has the largest accumulated mixture weight distribution over the optimized tree. The algorithm is called *Ratio Balance Algorithm*. This algorithm will find the maximum ratio balance of the single path nodes by subtracting the *actual accumulated mixture weight* with the *supposed accumulated mixture weight*. The supposed accumulated mixture weight of a node is calculated by dividing the root node accumulated mixture weight with the level where the node is located. The level where root node located is equal to 1. For example, we have a single path consists of these nodes concepts, *Yahoo:Arts and Humanities:History* and we have the calculation of ratio balance for each of the nodes in the next page:

Table 1. An example of Ratio Balance calculation

Level	Node Concept	Supposed acc. mix.weight	Actual acc.mix.weight	Ratio Balance
1	*Yahoo*	19	19	-
2	*Arts and Humanities*	19/2 = 9.5	19	19– 9.5 = 9.5
3	*History*	19/3 = 6.33	2	2 – 6.33 = -4.33

Since the node that has the maximum ratio balance will be the topic node, on the above example *Arts and Humanities* is the topic concept for the target document. Root node will be excluded because it is too general and useless (this is referred to *Yahoo* as the root node).

5 Experiment: Results and Analysis

We tested our system on 107 node categories with 202 web documents downloaded from *Yahoo!Business and Economy:Transportation* directory. We measured the system accuracy using a precision formula as below:

$$Precision = hits / (hits + mistakes)$$

The table below shows the result of accuracy on the meta-topic[4], single path and on topic node:

---

[4] The node located one level below the root node.

	Meta-topic	Single Path	Topic Node
Precision	69.8%	51.9%	29.7%

The system had extracted 1163 keywords from the 202 web documents and only 57.8% keywords were successfully mapped onto their correspond concepts through direct mapping. 17.8% of the keywords were mapped onto their correspond concepts through extended concepts. The system was unable to map 24.68% of the 1163 keywords onto the keywords corresponding concepts.

Analysis. Our result is quite comparable to that result produced by the topic identification (text classification) that used machine-learning techniques on web documents classification.

[18] obtained 37% of accuracy result using Yahoo with 151 classes and 50 documents. Their best attained accuracy result was 45% on 100 test documents. [11] had their best result on accuracy at 51% using Yahoo hierarchy and Yahoo web documents. The non-hierarchical web documents automatic categorization by [9] that used probabilistic description-oriented had worst result on their preliminary experiment with only an average precision of 2.13%. Later after they had increased the size of their sample learning, their result on categorization accuracy increased up to 36.5%.

The poor result we obtained with only 29.7% of accuracy could be caused by many factors. One of them could be the highly heterogeneity of web document that we could not extract all the web document information. This includes the fact that some of the web documents are poorly written with spelling errors, non-standard language (slang) and written in many languages. The web document is also not well represented by our concepts because the mapping between the keywords and the ontology concepts is not 100% successful. Further more, this poor result is also contributed to the kind of model we use which is the top-down model. This model will face unrecoverable mistakes because if we already choose the wrong node at the top, our topic node will be wrong too. This problem is faced by most of the automatic text classification using hierarchical structure [14], [25], [10].

In this experiment we only use a small size of web ontology. This is because we are only interested in how our topic identification system performs on real data regardless of size. However, for future work, we intend to build our automatic topic identification prototype system in a distributed environment so that a large web ontology can be implemented. The distributed topic identification system will be designed to identify more than one topics per document.

6 Conclusion

In this paper, we presented and evaluated an approach that automatically identifies a topic of a web document by exploiting a web ontology hierarchical structure (Yahoo). In spite of that, we also showed how we enriched the web ontology concept using external linguistics database, WordNet. The merging of WordNet words with Yahoo concept was made by using three types of semantics relationships found in WordNet.

Our main conclusion is that our approach is simple yet quite comparable to the other complex methods (probabilistic and machine learning method). We need more time to work with our dictionaries for the sense-tagger system which resulted the unsuccessful mapping between the keywords and the concepts. We may also need to enrich the ontology concepts with more knowledge besides semantically related words in order to understand more about the content of the web documents. In future, we hope we can come out with a more efficient and improved version of this automatic topic identification system and implement it in other automatic text processing systems like text classification or in information retrieval systems.

References

1. Banerjee, S., Mittal, V.O.: On the Use of Linguistics Ontologies for Acessing Distributed Digital Libraries. Proceeding of the First Annual Conference on Theory and Practice of Digital Libraries (1994)
2. Chakrabarti, S., Dom, B., Indyk, P.: Enhanced Hypertext Categorization Using Hyperlinks. ACM SIGMIND, Seattle, Washington (1998)
3. Chekuri, C., Goldwasser, M.H, Raghavan, P., Upfal, E.: Web Search Using Automated Classification. Poster at the Sixth International World Wide Web Conference (WWW6) (1997)
4. D' Alessio, D., Murray, K., Schiaffino, R., Kreshenbaum, A.: Hierarchical Text Categorization. Proceeding RIAO2000 (2000)
5. D' Alessio, D., Murray, K., Schiaffino, R., Kreshenbaum, A.: The effect of Topological Structure on Hierarchical Text Categorization. Proceeding of the Sixth Workshop on Very Large Corpora, COLLING ACL '98 (1998)
6. Gövert, N., Lalmas, M., Fuhr, N.: A Probabilistic Description-Oriented Approach for Categorizing Web Document. Proceeding of the Eighth International Conference on Information Knowledge Management, Kansas City, MO USA (1999) 475-482
7. Gelbukh, A., Sidorov, G., Guzman, A.: A Method of Describing Document Contents through Topic Selection. In Proc. of International Symposium on String Processing and Information Retrieval, Cancun, Mexico. Library of Congress 99-64139, IEEE Computer Society Press (1999)
8. Gelbukh, A., Sidorov, G., Guzman, A.: Use of a Weighted Topic Hierarchy for Document Classification. In Václav Matoušek et al (eds.): Text, Speech and Dialogue in Poc. 2nd International Workshop. Lecture Notes in Artificial Intelligence, No.92, ISBN 3-540-66494-7, Springer-Verlag., Czech Republic (1999) 130-135
9. Gelbukh, A., Sidorov, G., Guzman, A.,: Text Categorization Using a Hierarchical Topic Dictionary. Proc. Text Mining Workshop at 16th International Joint Conference on Artificial Intelligence (IJCAI'99), Stockholm, Sweden (1999)
10. Greiner, R., Grove, A, Schuurmans, D.: On learning hierarchical Classifications (1997)
11. Grobelnik, M., Mladenic, D.: Fast Categorization. In Proceedings of Third International Conference on Knowledge Discovery Data Mining (1998)
12. Guzman, A.: Finding the Main Themes in a Spanish Document. Journal Expert Systems with Application (1998) 139-148
13. Hoenkamp, E.: Spotting Ontological Lacunae through Spectrum Analysis Of Retrieved Documents. 13th European Conference On Artificial Intelligent, ECAI98, Brighton, England (1998)
14. Koller, D., Sahami, M.: Hierarchically Classifying Documents Using Very Few Words. In the Proceeding of Machine Learning (ICML-97) (1997) 170-176

15. Lee, J. Shin, D.: Multilevel Automatic Categorization for Webpages. The INET Proceeding '98 (1998)
16. Lin, C.Y, Hovy, E.: Identifying Topics by Position. In the Proceeding of The Workshop of Intelligent Scalable Text Summarization '97 (1997)
17. Lin, C.Y: Knowledge-based Automatic Topic Identification. In the Proceeding of The 33rd Annual Meeting of the Association for Computational Linguistics '95 (1995)
18. McCallum, A., Rosenfeld, R., Mitchell, T., Ng, Y.A.: Improving Text Classification by Shrinkage in a Hierarchy of Classes. Proceeding of the 15th Conference on Machine Learning (ICML-98) (1998)
19. Miller, G.A, Beckwith, R., Fellbaum, C., Gross, D., Miller, K.: Introduction to WordNet: An-Online Lexical Database. Five Papers on WordNet (1993)
20. Quek, C.Y, Mitchell, T: Classification of World Wide Web Documents. Seniors Honors Thesis, School of Computer Science, Carnegie Melon University (1998)
21. Scott, S., Matwin, S.: Text Classification using WordNet Hypernyms. In the Proceeding of Workshop – Usage of WordNet in Natural Language Processing Systems, Montreal, Canada (1998)
22. Sense Tagger. UTMK Internal Paper. Universiti Sains Malaysia, Penang, Malaysia (1999)
23. Soderland, S.: Learning to extract text-based information from World Wide Web. In the Proceeding of the Third International Conference on Knowledge Discovery and Data-Mining (1997)
24. Voorhees, E.M.: On Expanding Query Vectors with Lexically Related Words. Proceeding of the Second Text REtrieval Conference (TREC-2), NIST Special Publication, Gatherburg, Maryland (1993)
25. Weigned, A.S, Wiener, E.D, Pedersen, J.O.: Working Papers IS-98-22. Dept. of Info. System, Leonard N. Stern, School Of Business, New York University (1998)

Software for Creating Domain-Oriented Dictionaries and Document Clustering in Full-Text Databases

Pavel Makagonov, Konstantin Sboychakov

Mayor Directorate of Moscow City Government, Russia
makagonov@um.mos.ru

Abstract. The problem of reorganization and classification of full-text data-bases by means of the clustering of composing documents is considered. The clustering is performed in the space of words relating to special domains. Meth-ods of constructing domain-oriented dictionaries are suggested. The software developed can be used in the case when number of clusters is unknown before-hand. Aprioristic uncertainty necessitates several steps of clustering, with large clusters undergoing a further subdivision.

Keywords: text classification, domain dictionaries, full-text database.

The study of any new problem necessitates the creation of a database reflecting its main aspects. The initial step of database analysis includes their structuring. This paper is devoted to automatic classification of large sets of documents constituting a database. The documents considered belonging to the same cluster if they are at the short distance in the space formed by words from a special list. This list is called domain-oriented dictionary (DD) and is designated as $L(Dom)$. We include a word to the $L(Dom)$ of a documental database if the relative frequency of this word in this database exceeds three or more times its relative frequency in the commonly used dictionary $L(Com)$.

The creation of any documental database starts with its division into some rubrics. Usually, two or more levels the hierarchical structure is then necessary. The proposed structure could be improved if the typical words for every rubric have higher fre-quency then they have in other rubrics. We consider the document structuring with initially unknown number of classes, when we cannot justify this number beforehand.

Our software contains a family of programs. The first modifications of their toolkit have been reported in [1]. A special information retrieval program was developed on the basis of IRBIS [2].

Database Administrator is a program fulfilling three steps:

Step 1 constructs the dictionary $L(Dom)$ for the whole Database. First, it prepares the preliminary version of the dictionary reflecting all files of Database. The criterion for the inclusion of a word to this version is that its relative frequency in Database is twice as high as compared with $L(Com)$. Then the preliminary version is used for preparing DD_0, i.e. Zero's Rubric dictionary whose content is under manual control. For this purpose, the user chooses the following parameters:

A. Gelbukh (Ed.): CICLing 2001, LNCS 2004, pp. 454-456, 2001.

- A higher (greater than two) ratio of word frequencies in Database and in L(Com);
- The upper and the lower limits of percentage for texts to be considered containing a given word.

Step 2 forms three matrixes:

- $M(T,W)$ is 'text to word' matrix. Its elements are the numbers of use for words of DD_0 in each text of the database.
- $M(T,T)$ is 'text to text' matrix. Its elements are the numbers of words occurring in a given pair of texts.
- $M(W,W)$ is 'word to word' matrix. Its elements are the numbers of texts containing a given pair of words.

Step 3 fulfils clustering as such, using the results of the information retrieval program and the program of visual analysis.

The visual analysis is possible only for limited-size matrices. The program is supplied with options for setting lower and upper limits to exclude marginal parts of the matrices, i.e., columns with zero-valued elements only or with a number of nonzero elements less than the lower limit or greater than the upper limit.

After rejecting the marginal columns, the operations of the exclusion for the symmetric matrices $M(T,T)$ and $M(W,W)$ recur. They reduce the rank of the matrixes up to the limit about 500, which admits to apply the visual analysis.

If $M(T,T)$ attains the limit first, the rubrics of the 1st order are reorganized. For every rubric $R_j, j = 1, 2... N_1$, the first-order dictionaries $DD_1(j)$ are obtained. Otherwise, after clustering, the first-order dictionaries are determined on the basis of $M(W,W)$.

The example of clustering is given in Appendix.

We can conclude that the problem of classification of large documental databases is solvable. The corresponding set of domain-oriented dictionaries has a hierarchical structure. We have obtained a successful experience in using such dictionaries [3].

The representation of a 'text to word' matrix sorted according to the belonging of text and word pairs to the same clusters determines the block structure of a resulting matrix. The revealed structure of the matrix can be considered as the main goal of clustering. It reflects the linking of particular sets of word to the particular texts.

References

1. Makagonov, P. and Sboychakov, K. Man-machine methods for solution of weakly-formalized problems in humanitarian and natural fields of knowledge (visual heuristic cluster analysis). *Proc. Intern. Symposium CIC '98*, Mexico City, 1998, p. 346-358
2. Brodovskiy, A., Makagonov, P., Ochagova, L., Sboychakov, K.. Data-searching system for operating "The Sustainable Development of the Cities" full-text database. In: *Proc. Conf. on Social, Economic and Environmental Aspects of Sustainable Development of Cities*. Moscow City Government Publ., 1999 (in Russian).
3. Makagonov, P., Alexandrov, M., Sboychakov, K. (1999), Software for decision-making at the conference: one experiment with the data of APORS' 97. In *Abstracts of XV International Conference IFORS '99*, p.172, China Academy of Sciences, Beijing

Appendix. An Example of Clustering

The figure below shows (in a black and white scale) the matrix $M(W,W)$ before (the left part) and after (the right part) clustering. White color means zero-valued elements. The clusters with low quantity of words are rejected. Most of black blocks form overlapping clusters, which means multi-level classification.

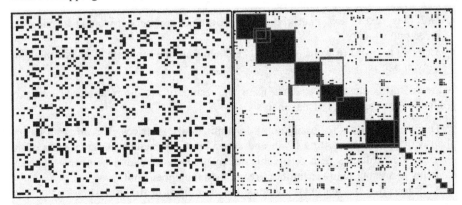

The lists of words for the largest clusters were the following:

1. *Clothes, alcoholic, allowance, oncology, lower-income, equalizing, toxicomania, grant, stationary, reeducation, addressed, employer, employment, non-defended, criminality-prone.*
2. *Advertising, poor, veteran, food-card, food stamp, nursery, illegal, encroachment, subsidy.*
3. *Teenager, rehabilitation, vacancy, genetic, fertility, local dwellers, population, stress, diagnostic, reproductive.*
4. *Hairdressing, metal-ware, hire, bathhouse, cleaner, social welfare, laundry, shoe-repair, habitation.*

Such results seem interesting for expert analysis and could be a basis for subdivision of the *Social problems* dictionary belonging to the *Sustainable cities* database [1] to sub-domains of lower levels.

Chi-Square Classifier for Document Categorization

Mikhail Alexandrov [1], Alexander Gelbukh [1], and George Lozovoi [2]

[1] Center for Computing Research, IPN, Mexico
{dyner, gelbukh}@cic.ipn.mx

[2] Datagistics, Canada
glozovoi@idirect.com

Abstract. The problem of document categorization is considered. The set of domains and the keywords specific for these domains is supposed to be selected beforehand as initial data. We apply the well-known statistical hypothesis test that considers images of documents and domains as normalized vectors. In comparison with existing methods, such approach allows to take into account a random character of initial data. The classifier is developed in the framework of Document Investigator software package.

1 Introduction

Various keyword-based technologies are suggested for document categorization nowadays. In particular, these technologies use the tree of concepts for searching the principal theme of a document [3]; the concentration of keywords to evaluate the contribution of given domains to a document [1]; the probabilities of domain and keywords in Bayes classifiers [4], etc. Practically all technologies use the results of preliminary training. In comparison with all mentioned approaches, the suggested classifier needs more limited information for decision-making and gives a numerical estimation of reliability of results, taking into account the random character of the data used for training and application of the classifier. The classifier tests the statistical hypotheses based on χ^2-distribution and builds a list of domains relevant to a document with a given probability of documents missing a relevant domain.

2 Initial Data for Classification

Initial data is the list of domains D_j, $j = 1, ..., m$; the list of keywords (key-expressions) w_i, $i = 1, ..., n$; and the matrix of conditional frequencies $p_{ij} = p(w_i \mid D_j)$ reflecting distribution of the keywords in these domains. Let N_j, $j = 1, ..., m$ be the numbers of keyword occurrences in all the documents connected with the domain D_j in full training database, so that $\sum_i p_{ij} = N_j$. We use the term *keyword* to refer any key-expression that can be a single word a word combination. What is more, we take as the same keyword any group with the same stem and meaning. For example, *obli-*

A. Gelbukh (Ed.): CICLing 2001, LNCS 2004, pp. 457-459, 2001.

gation, obligations, obligatory, oblige have the same stem *oblig*. Each document can be considered as a vector $(x_1, x_2, ..., x_n)$ of keywords, where x_i is the number w_i of keyword occurrences in the document, and $\sum_i x_i = N$.

For formal considerations we accept that *the document topic is a direction of the document image vector in the multidimensional space of keywords*. According to this definition all documents reflecting the same topic have parallel or quasi-parallel vectors. Indeed, let us consider a concatenation of *l* copies of the given document *D*. Naturally, it has the same topic as *D*, while its image $(lx_1, lx_2, ..., lx_n)$ is parallel to that of *D*. On the other hand, let us consider a document *D'* that has no relation to the domain under consideration, and attach it to source one *D*. Naturally, the resulting text *D + D'* has the same topic with respect to the domain under consideration as *D*, while it has the same image which thus is parallel to that of *D*.

We will consider now the vector of conditional frequencies $p_j = (p_{1j}, p_{2j}, ..., p_{nj})$, $j = 1, 2, ..., m$ mentioned above as the image of a typical document from the domain D_j. Because an operation of normalization does not change vector direction we transform all our frequencies so that: $\sum_i p_{ij} = \sum_i x_i = 1$.

3 The Main Algorithm

3.1 Testing of Hypotheses

The algorithm consists in consequent test of hypotheses about belonging of a document to given domains. Considering image of a document and images of domains as attributes such a test is reduced to the test of uniformity. According to [2] it can be completed by χ^2-criterion of uniformity with $v = n-1$ degrees of freedom. The criterion requires a calculation of the series of values χ_j^2 as is shown in (1a):

$$\chi_j^2 = \sum_i \frac{1}{\frac{x_i}{N_j} + \frac{p_{ij}}{N}} \left(x_i - p_{ij} \right)^2 \quad \text{(1a)} \qquad \chi_{kl}^2 = \sum_i \frac{1}{\frac{p_{ik}}{N_l} + \frac{p_{il}}{N_k}} \left(p_{ik} - p_{il} \right)^2 \quad \text{(1b)}$$

Then the inequality $\chi_j^2 \leq \chi_p^2$ is verified for all $j = 1, 2, ..., m$, where *p* is the level of hypothesis significance and $\chi_p^2 : p = P(\chi^2 > \chi_p^2)$. All hypotheses for which this inequality holds are accepted. The value *p* is the feasible probability to miss a domain which is in fact relevant for the document.

3.2 Analysis of Errors of Decision

Testing statistical hypothesis we deal with an error to miss a relevant domain. But when several hypotheses are accepted we immediately deal with the other kind of error, which is an analogue of false alarm but for the case of many alternatives. Indeed, because a document is supposed to reflect not more than one domain then among the selected domains only one is relevant. These two kinds of errors prove to be connected by the same way as in the case of two alternatives, namely the less a probability to miss a domain the more hypotheses will be accepted and the more is a number of false domains that appear.

The concrete dependence of these errors is defined by domain distinguishability. The last can be evaluated checking the significance of distinctions between domains on (1b) that is an analogue of (1a) for two domains D_k and D_l. Then it is possible to find two boundary values:

$$p_{max}: \chi^2_{p_{max}} = \min_{k,l} \chi^2_{kl} ; \qquad p_{min}: \chi^2_{p_{min}} = \max_{k,l} \chi^2_{kl} ; \qquad (2)$$

The following considerations follow directly from (2):

1. If $p \geq p_{max}$ then the classifier is able to find not more than 1 relevant domain for a document. In this case the probability of false alarm is 0%.
2. If $p < p_{min}$ then the classifier is able to find at once all domains relevant to a document (or none). In this case the probability of false alarm is (1-1/m)*100%.
3. If $p_{min} \leq p < p_{max}$ then the classifier is able to find k domains, $k = 2, ..., m$-1 (or none). In this case the probability of false alarm is (1-1/k)*100%.

The typical values for probability to miss a correct domain are 5%-10%. But it would be better to assign this probability taking into account also the mentioned probability of false alarm.

4 Conclusions and Future Work

We suggested a simple keyword-based classifier intended for selection of domains relevant to a text document. The introduction of well-known statistical errors of the first and the second kind allows to set an optimum mode of classifier work. The future development will consist in: a) performing numerous experiments with a real document flow, b) constructing more complex decision rules with respect to accepted hypothesis, c) developing a user-oriented program system.

References

1. Alexandrov, M., Gelbukh, A., and Makagonov, P. *Some keyword-based characteristics for evaluation of thematic structure of multidisciplinary documents.* Proc. of 1st Int. Conf. on Intelligent Text Processing and Computational Linguistics, Mexico City, 2000, pp. 390-401.
2. Cramer, H. *Mathematical methods of statistics.* Cambridge, 1946.
3. Guzman-Arenas, A. *Finding the main themes in a Spanish documents.* Intern. J. of Expert Systems with Applications, 1998, v. 14, N 1/2, pp. 139-148.
4. Mitchel, T. *Machine learning.* New-York, McGraw Hill, 1997.

Information Retrieval of Electronic Medical Records

Anne-Marie Currie[1], Jocelyn Cohan[2], Larisa Zlatic[1]

[1]Synthesys Technologies, Inc., 3040 Suite 400, Austin, Texas 78759
{anne-marie.currie, larisa.zlatic}@synthesys.com

[2]Trans 10, 3512 JK Utrecht, the Netherlands
jocelyn.cohan@let.uu.nl

Abstract. This paper presents common issues associated with information retrieval from electronic medical records and presents linguistic approaches to resolve these issues. Linguistic analyses of three medical topics (heart attacks, smoking, and death reports) are presented to highlight common issues and our approaches to resolve them. We demonstrate how the Clinical Practice Analysis (CPA) system developed by Synthesys Technologies, Inc. enables the medical researcher to create powerful queries to retrieve information about individual patients or entire patient populations quickly and easily. The efficiency of this system has been enhanced by the implementation of linguistic generalizations specific to medical records, such as lexical variation, ambiguity, argument alternation, anaphora resolution, belief contexts, downward-entailing contexts and presupposition.

1   Introduction

Medical records contain an enormous amount of specific information about the treatment of individual patients. Much of the specific medical information remains buried in semi-structured electronic text reports, and is difficult for health care providers or medical researchers to find the specific information. This paper discusses the linguistic approaches used in retrieving the relevant information from electronic medical records. It is shown how the professional areas of linguistics, information technology and medicine are combined to accurately retrieve the desired information and ultimately improve the care of individual patients.

Information retrieval is achieved through the Clinical Practice Analysis™ (CPA) system developed by Synthesys Technologies, Inc. The linguistic analysis employed in the development of queries within the CPA system enables medical researchers to retrieve information contained in medical records quickly and accurately, and minimizes the amount of irrelevant information retrieved. This is accomplished by translating linguistic generalizations into the CPA search language, called Text Query Language (TQL). The application of core linguistic analyses including syntax, semantics, pragmatics, and sociolinguistics to the query process of medical record texts leads to the identification of clinical issues such as patients at risk for particular conditions, patients eligible for clinical trials and drug interactions. In addition, this col-

A. Gelbukh (Ed.): CICLing 2001, LNCS 2004, pp. 460–471, 2001.

laboration between linguistics, technology and medicine facilitates epidemiological and quality assurance research.

1.1 Description of the CPA System

CPA is a repository of transcribed medical records in which basic document structure characteristics, such as section headings, have been tagged. This minimal tagging process does not require the use of a natural language parser during the initial building of a database. The linguistic components of CPA include a search engine that can be programmed to identify semantic and syntactic contexts, and a series of "post-build attributes," which identify lexical items in semantic categories, such as family relationships or negation, or syntactic structures associated with particular semantic phenomena, such as negation and modal contexts. Medical records can then be queried using key words in defined linguistic contexts, resulting in a set of documents containing desired information. Pertinent document information can then be extracted from the resulting answer set into a relational database for analysis by a medical researcher or clinician.

CPA does not employ an automatic knowledge-based natural language processing system. Instead, linguistic generalizations are supplied by the researchers using CPA. This allows for a flexible system that is able to execute searches on millions of documents quickly and effectively.

The effectiveness of the system depends in part on the fact that it can be programmed to prevent retrieval of undesirable contexts in which target expressions might occur. For example, in order to ensure that a target expression is in fact linked to the patient and not to another individual, we have developed three strategies. First, we have developed an anaphora attribute that identifies or resolves reference to the patient within a document. This attribute allows CPA to link the patient accurately to the particular disease, event, or behavior of interest (cf. (1a)). Second, if appropriate, the family history sections of documents can be excluded from a search because these sections typically do not discuss the medical status and health behaviors of the patient (cf. (1b)). Third, using a post-build attribute that identifies reference to family members and other social relations, we can filter out those instances where family or friends are the referents of a target expression (cf. (1c)).

1. (a)   **Patient** was given medications. **He** has a history of **coronary artery disease**.
   (b)   **Family History: Coronary artery disease** in **mother** and **brother**.
   (c)   **Maternal** history of **coronary artery disease**.

Linguistic analysis of patient medical records has been useful in identifying the difference between desirable and undesirable contexts for target expressions, such as those illustrated in (1a-c). The generalizations derived from this work are incorporated into query strategies. The following sections discuss specific linguistic observations and how these have been incorporated into an information retrieval system that does not employ natural language processing tools. Section 2.1 considers relevant issues of word meaning and usage. Section 2.2 addresses the issue of syntactic structure and its relation to both argument structure and lexical-conceptual structure. Section 2.3 considers semantic and pragmatic contexts relevant to the retrieval of desirable documents. Section 3 concludes the paper.

2   Retrieving Relevant Information

2.1   Lexical Items

Single lexical items or simple phrases can be used to retrieve relevant information. The problem is that often a simple key word search not only returns documents with many irrelevant contexts, it also may not return all the documents with relevant contexts. We have developed dictionaries of related terms that can be easily added when new contexts are discovered to help address this issue. Three expressions will be used throughout this paper to illustrate specific aspects of linguistic phenomena accessed for accurate information retrieval. Each of these expressions offers distinct properties. In (2a), for example, *infarction* is a specialized medical term that carries different meanings and is not often used in colloquial speech. In contrast, the lexical item *smokes*, in example (2b), is a non-specialized lexical item, used in both the general and medical communities to convey the same unmarked meaning. Finally in (2c), the expression *pronounced* is a lexical item used in both the lay and medical community, but with different meanings.

2. (a) History of prior **infarction**.
   (b) Patient **smokes**.
   (c) He was **pronounced** at 10:00 a.m.

Synonymous and near equivalent expressions. Suppose a medical researcher wants to identify a set of patients who are smokers. Any search engine can run a keyword search like *smok**, which would identify documents containing the morpheme *smok-* in any context. This would, however, fail to return other documents that report a patient is a smoker, through expressions like those in (3a-c):

3. (a) Nicotine use.
   (b) ... and nicotine dependence
   (c) ... except for tobacco abuse.

Our query to identify smokers needs to take into account expressions such as *"nicotine use"* and *"tobacco abuse."* In addition, we need to filter out those expressions that do not indicate that the patient is a smoker, as in (4). Applying what we know about compounds beginning with *smoke*, the subject of the verb *smoke*, negation, and implicature, we can adequately filter or identify expressions such as those given in (4a-f). A more detailed discussion of the linguistic phenomena is provided in the following sections.

4. (a) concern about smoke inhalation
   (b) radiation coming from the smoke detector
   (c) Everyone in the house smokes but they do not smoke around the child.
   (d) Patient does not smoke.
   (e) Smoking history is negative
   (f) Patient must not smoke while on oxygen therapy.

Polysemous expressions. These are expressions that have multiple meanings for a single lexical item. These distinct meanings of the expressions are related in some way. Within the context of the language used within dictated medical notes, we have identified polysemous expressions that have both marked and unmarked meanings within this specialized context. Knowledge about the multiple meanings of these expressions enables us to develop appropriate queries for topics that call for the use of polysemous expressions. As we develop queries and review data, our knowledge about the source of the data, the expression's location in the document, social habits, and general uses of specific words are considered in the development of any query. An example of such polysemous lexical item is given in (5).

5. History of prior **infarction**.

The term *infarction* can be used to indicate several different types of infarctions. The unmarked use in the data we have been working with appears to signify myocardial infarction, while marked uses include cerebral infarctions, lung infarctions, retinal infarctions, and bowel infarctions. However, determining the marked and unmarked uses of an expression depends in part on the source of the documents. For example, a hospital that has expertise in cardiology and serves a higher number of cardiology patients than neurology patients would likely exhibit the unmarked form of *infarction* as myocardial infarction, whereas a hospital that serves a patient community with a high incidence of neurology patients might exhibit the unmarked form of *infarction* as a cerebral infarction. Depending upon the purposes for the query, the source of the data and the needs of the client, the query can be designed to include the unmodified word *infarction*.

The language in medical records also typically reflects the marked and unmarked usage of the broader speech community. Unmarked expressions such as those in (6) report the habit of smoking tobacco as opposed to other substances.

6. (a)   Patient **smokes**.
   (b)   She is a **smoker**.
   (c)   Positive for **smoking**.

The use of such expressions to indicate tobacco smoking is virtually the same in medical records and colloquial speech. The intransitive use of *smoke* in (6a), the agentive nominal in (6b), and gerund form of the verb *smoke* in (6c), all indicate that the patient smokes tobacco, as opposed to marked meanings of smoking marijuana or cocaine.

Ambiguous expressions. Some lexical items identified within medical records are ambiguous. We use this term to describe two separate lexical items with distinct meanings that share the same form. The word *pronounced* is an example of an ambiguous lexical item. One of the meanings of this word occurs in both the lay and medical communities, while another meaning of the word is relegated to use within the medical field and does not overlap with colloquial usage. Example (7a) illustrates one meaning of *pronounced* that is shared between the general and medical community. Here, *pronounced* is used to indicate that the rash is more significant or severe on the left forearm than the right forearm. This use of *pronounced,* to describe distinctness, appears to be less marked than the use of *pronounced* to report the death of a patient, illustrated by examples (7b-d). The word *pronounced* in examples (7b-e) is a performative used to mean a formal and authoritative announcement of death.

7. (a) The pruritic erythematous rash is more **pronounced** on the left forearm than the right.
   (b) Death was **pronounced**.
   (c) He was **pronounced** soon thereafter.
   (d) She was **pronounced**. There was no cardiac activity.
   (e) The time **pronounced** was 02:25 on 01/25/98.

We incorporate our linguistic knowledge to differentiate the two different senses of *pronounced*. First, these two distinct lexical items differ in their parts of speech. For instance, in example (8a) below, *pronounced$_1$* is used as an adjective to modify the noun phrase *weight loss*. In contrast, example (8b) demonstrates that the lexical item *pronounced$_2$* is a perfomative verb. We argue that the lexeme *pronounced* in example (8b) is the same lexical item used in the expression, "I now **pronounce** you husband and wife" as spoken by someone with the authority to marry two people. In the case of example (8b), the doctor is the person with the authority to perform the official announcement of death and this is most often accomplished with this verb in the passive voice. We speculate that this method of reporting death is one way health providers distance themselves from the death of a patient.

8. (a) The patient admitted to having a **pronounced$_1$** weight loss
   (b) Death was **pronounced$_2$**.

2.2   Syntactic Contexts

Single lexical items are often not sufficient for precise and efficient information retrieval. In addition to simple words, it is necessary to incorporate phrases in which these lexical items appear. Our text query language uses proximity operators that allow specification of phrase length, thus enabling us to capture various syntactic contexts in which the lexical items may appear. For instance, in all examples in (3a-c) above repeated below in (9), key words *nicotine* and *tobacco*, are the arguments of the nominal heads *use, dependence, abuse*. These arguments precede their nominal heads because they appear in what Grimshaw (1990) calls the synthetic compound constructions.

9. (a)   Nicotine use.
   (b)   ... and nicotine dependence
   (c)   ... except for tobacco abuse.

In other cases, like in constructions (10a-c) below, the same lexical items, *nicotine* and *tobacco,* are arguments that appear in a complement position, hence, they follow the head noun.

10. (a) use of nicotine
    (b) dependence on *nicotine*
    (c) abuse of *tobacco*

What these examples show is that in addition to the linear position of these target words, we need to know their argument structure and how it maps to syntactic structure. The observed linguistic patterns of argument linking are incorporated into queries for efficient and accurate information retrieval.

Valence alternations of certain lexical items should also be incorporated in information retrieval techniques. To illustrate, the verb *smoke* can be used both transitively and intransitively, as shown by the following examples.

11. Intransitive uses of *smoke*:
   (a)   He doesn't *smoke.*
   (b)   He has never *smoked.*
   (c)   The patient does *smoke.*
   (d)   She also *smokes* although she is working on quitting at the present time

12. Transitive uses of *smoke*:
   (a)   He no longer *smokes* cigarettes.
   (b)   He used to *smoke* cigars.
   (c)   He currently *smokes* three cigarettes per day.
   (d)   The patient *smokes* occasional cigarettes, two to three per day.
   (e)   The patient *smokes* one pack per day

The two different verb types seem to correspond to different interpretations. Specifically, the intransitive forms of *smoke* shown in (11), are used in contexts in which the habit of smoking or not smoking is being described. The transitive forms are used for all other purposes, such as negative contexts where the emphasis is on non smoking (as in (12a), or for describing smoking of something other than the cigarettes, as in (12b). However, the most frequent use of the transitive form of *smoke* is found for describing the amount of cigarettes the patient consumes, as the examples in (12c-e) illustrate. This observed correlation between the verb's valence and the semantic context facilitates the process of information retrieval.

A similar valency alternation is found with the verb *pronounce* when used to state that a patient has died. This verb generally takes a secondary predicate phrase, as shown in (13). In these examples, the predicative adjective phrases, *dead, deceased,* and *expired* function as a complement of the passive verb *pronounced.*

13. (a) The patient was *pronounced dead* by Dr. Smith at 19:24.
   (b) The patient was *pronounced dead* at 4:30 on the date of admission.
   (c) The patient was *pronounced deceased* at 10:50 a.m. on March 29, 1999.
   (d) The patient was *pronounced expired* at 7:45 p.m. on 06/08/95.

However, medical reports quite often contain the examples in which the complement adjective phrase is completely omitted, as shown in (14).

14. (a) After the patient had been *pronounced*, he has been moved to the morgue.
   (b) Death was *pronounced.*
   (c) He was *pronounced* soon thereafter.
   (d) The patient was *pronounced* at 10:55 a.m., and his family was notified.
   (e) The efforts were terminated at 0115 and patient *pronounced* at that time.
   (f) The patient was *pronounced* in the Emergency Department and autopsy was requested.

The first three examples in (14) show that the verb *pronounced* does not require any complements at all, although the complement prepositional phrases, indicating place and time, are generally present, as in (14d-f). These examples thus show that semantic arguments are not always overtly expressed in syntax. It is either through the pragmatic context or through a single, 'salient' argument that the other semantic arguments of the verb are recovered. For example, in (14c), the precise meaning of the passive verb *pronounced* is induced by the presence of the anaphoric pronominal subject *he* that refers to the patient. In (14b), the subject noun phrase, *death*, acts as a salient argument that determines the specific meaning of the verb *pronounced*.

As mentioned earlier, the passive verb is more often used for stating the patient's death than the active verb form. However, regardless of which verb form of *pronounced* is used, we find the same argument alternations, as shown in (15).

15. (a) I pronounced the patient dead at 1915.
   (b) I *pronounced the patient deceased* at approximately 0727 hours on September 23, 1999.
   (c) I *pronounced the patient,* with his family at the bedside, at 8:04 a.m.
   (d) His family was present as *I pronounced him,* and funeral arrangements will be in the paper tomorrow.

These examples of argument alternations have not only theoretical linguistic significance, but also significance for information retrieval techniques. For linguistic theory, these facts further confirm that the 'syntactic' argument structure must be distinguished from the semantic structure, or what Grimshaw (1990) calls the lexical conceptual structure. In order to meet information retrieval needs, computational methods are devised to account for argument alternation and reconstruction of implicit arguments.

2.3   Semantic and Pragmatic Issues

At the root of information retrieval is the issue of semantics. Retrieval on the basis of key expressions is effective only insofar as these expressions carry the desired meaning. Section 2.1 addressed the role of word meaning; section 2.2 addressed the role that syntax plays in determining the meaning of a key search term. The larger context in which a target expression occurs can also be crucial to its meaning. In this section we consider some sentence- and discourse-level semantic and pragmatic issues.

There are numerous contexts in which target expressions may occur and yet may not be connected to a report about the patient. We previously saw examples of one such context, where target expressions are linked to someone other than the patient (cf. (1b-c)). Two additional contexts that must also be considered in the retrieval of information from medical records are belief contexts and downward entailing contexts, both long recognized in semantics literature (e.g., Quine 1961). Also to be considered are the roles that presupposition and implicatures may play in signaling desirable and undesirable documents.

Belief contexts. Belief contexts are introduced by words like *believe, suspect* or *think.* Propositions embedded in such contexts need not be true. Occurrence of a target term in a document in a belief context is thus not really any more informative than if the target term had not occurred. That is, if a researcher is looking for documents that report a definitive diagnosis of myocardial infarction or heart attack, documents containing excerpts like those in (16) would be desirable only if the diagnosis were confirmed *elsewhere* in the document.

16. (a) He apparently had chest pain and it *was thought* he was having a **heart attack**
    (b) It was *believed* that the patient had a non-Q wave **myocardial infarction**.

Neither the proposition *he was having a heart attack* in (16a), nor the proposition *the patient had a non-Q-wave myocardial infarction* in (16b) need be true (although either might be). While these excerpts might be considered informative in that they reveal that the medical staff *considered* a diagnosis of myocardial infarction, without additional confirmation they cannot be understood to convey that this diagnosis was actually made. Thus, these are not desirable occurrences of the target terms if our goal is to identify a patient who had a confirmed heart attack.

Some diagnoses or behaviors occur more often than others in belief contexts. For example, while it is fairly common to find *myocardial infarction* (and its synonyms) in excerpts like those in (16) we do not typically find excerpts like *it was thought that the patient was a smoker*. Thus, the importance of taking belief-contexts into account in the retrieval of documents varies depending on the goals of a project. The flexibility of the CPA system allows researchers to incorporate belief contexts into queries when necessary for the goals of a particular project.

Downward-entailing contexts. Other circumstances in which propositions do not necessarily hold occur in so-called downward entailing contexts (Ladusaw 1980). Two such contexts that commonly appear in medical records are negative and conditional contexts, as seen in (17) and (18), respectively.

17. (a) He *denied* any alcohol use or *any* **tobacco use**
    (b) He is *not* aware that he has *ever* had a **heart attack** or *any* significant **cardiac problems** in the past.
    (c) He also had cardiac enzymes drawn that did *not* show *any* evidence of **infarction.**
    (d) It is *not* associated with **chest pain** or shortness of breath.

In the context introduced by *denied* in (17a), the concept *tobacco use* includes chewing tobacco and smoking cigarettes, cigars or pipes. Thus, if it is true that the patient does not use tobacco, then it is also true that he does not chew or smoke tobacco. The proposition that the patient does not use tobacco <u>entails</u> that he does not chew or smoke it. In ordinary use, *deny* can convey the idea that the speaker or writer does not believe the denial, which is not the case when *deny* is used in medical records.

Some examples of conditional contexts are shown below.

18. (a) *If* she develops more fevers, chills, **chest pain** or sputum changes color, she will call me immediately.
    (b) I want to see *if* there is *any* change in his EKG to be sure that he has *not* had a silent **infarction.**

(c) The patient had some difficulty with dementia and it is not clear **whether** he is actually experiencing some **chest pain** but I think rather not.

In the context introduced by *if* in (18a), the concept *chest pain* includes chest pain due to injury, respiratory infection and cardiac problems. Thus, the proposition that the patient will call if she develops chest pain <u>entails</u> that she will call if she develops chest pain due to respiratory infection, injury or other causes.

Recognition of these contexts is important to the accurate retrieval of relevant records. The excerpts in (17) and (18) do not assert that the patient uses tobacco, has had a heart attack, or has experienced chest pain, and so would not be desirable documents if a researcher is looking for positive occurrences of these conditions. Target terms in downward-entailing contexts like these are typically no more informative than target terms in belief contexts.

Certain predictable lexical items typically introduce negative and conditional contexts, *deny, not, never, no, if, whether,* etc. The appearance of other lexical items – negative polarity items (NPIs) like *any* and *ever,* is also typically limited to such contexts. We have developed and made use of post-attributes that specifically identify lexical items associated with such contexts. These post-attributes can be used to exclude documents that contain search terms only in these contexts and can thus be used to exclude undesirable documents. Again, these undesirable documents contain the target terms, but do not in fact assert that the target term applies to the patient.

In medical records, as in other kinds of discourse, we find downward-entailing contexts that are not marked by the explicit appearance of these already-identified lexical items. For example, contexts like imperatives, are frequently used as conditionals in medical records. In (19), for example, the clause *return for chest pain* represents instructions to the patient to return if she experiences chest pain.

19. DISCHARGE *INSTRUCTIONS*:...3. Return for **chest pain**, other weakness, dizziness ...

If a researcher were searching for documents that report on patients with chest pain, this would not necessarily be a desirable document. Because the imperative form is ambiguous with other verb forms, identifying the imperative solely by its morphological form is not a viable search strategy. There are also no NPIs or other lexical items like those associated with negative and conditional contexts to help identify the downward entailing context. The excerpt in (19) shows, however, that the occurrence of the search term falls within *instructions* to the patient. Additional lexical items, like *instructions,* that are typically associated with downward-entailing contexts in medical records, can be incorporated into our strategy for identifying such contexts, preventing potentially undesirable documents from being retrieved.

Presupposition. Belief and downward entailing contexts sometimes contain truly desirable targets. This occurs when the target is connected to a presupposition. Presuppositions typically "survive" belief and downward entailing contexts (Beaver 1997). Presuppositions can be assumed to be true – in fact, typically must be assumed to be true – even when the propositions containing them are not.

The definite noun phrases *his myocardial infarction* in (20a) and *the earlier episode of chest pain* in (20b) have existential presuppositions that survive the negative and belief contexts in which they occur. The example in (20a) presupposes that the patient had a myocardial infarction and the example in (20b) that the patient had an episode of chest pain. Additionally, adjectives like *earlier* in (20b) and *recurrent* (20c) also bring existential presuppositions to the noun phrases in which they occur. Thus, even indefinite noun phrases, like *recurrent breast cancer* in (20c), can carry an existential presupposition. Note that while the *recurrence* of breast cancer does not survive the negative context, the presupposition that the patient had breast cancer at some time in the past does.

20. (a)   The patient remained stable ... having **no** acute complications from ***his*** **myocardial infarction** and thrombolytic therapy.
      presupposition: the patient had a myocardial infarction.
   (b)   Patient **believed** that ***the earlier episode of* chest pain** had only lasted two to three seconds.
      presupposition: The patient had an episode of chest pain at some time in the past.
   (c)   **No** evidence of ***recurrent* breast cancer** five years postoperatively.
      presupposition: the patient had breast cancer at some time in the past.

Verbal elements can also carry presuppositions. In (21a), *quits smoking* conveys the presupposition that the patient (referred to by the reporting physician here as *he*) is a smoker, which survives both conditional and belief contexts. In (21b), *recurs* conveys the presupposition that the patient had chest pain, which here survives a conditional context (although, again, the *recurrence* does not).

21. (a)   I ***believe*** that ***if*** he ***quits*** **smoking** now, he will do fine in the future.
      presupposition: the patient is a smoker.
   (b)   ***If*** **chest pain** ***recurs***, we will consider referring her for additional testing.
      presupposition: the patient had chest pain.

Lexical items that contribute presuppositions can be incorporated into queries so that potentially desirable excerpts like those in (20) and (21) are not excluded by efforts to avoid returning documents containing target terms in downward-entailing or belief contexts.

Implicature. In many cases, documents about patients do not presuppose or directly state that a condition or behavior is part of a patient's medical history. Many documents simply imply these conclusions. Implicatures differ from presuppositions because they can be cancelled in many situations by the addition of further information.

Pragmatic knowledge makes an implicature conveyed in medical records very strong. For example, from (22a), a reader can be fairly certain that the patient is a smoker because we know that typically, nicotine patches are not worn by people who don't smoke. From (22b), a reader can be fairly certain that the patient has a history of asthma attacks, because a physician would be unlikely to mention that a patient had not had an attack since her last visit if she had never had one. Nevertheless, these conclusions are implicatures, because they could theoretically be cancelled. Perhaps the patient in (22a) has been prescribed a nicotine patch because he chews tobacco. Perhaps the patient in (22b) was expected to develop an asthma condition for some reason – say, if her last visit to the clinic was precipitated by exposure to a chemical that can trigger development of asthma in some victims – but has still never actually had an asthma attack.

22. (a) Special discharge instructions include absolutely *no* **smoking** while *wearing nicotine patch*.
    implicature: The patient is a smoker.
   (b) She has *not* had an **asthma** attack since *her last visit to the clinic*.
    implicature: The patient has a history of asthma attacks.

The conditions necessary to cancel the implicatures in (22) are rather unlikely to occur. The excerpts in (22) can, for all intents and purposes, be considered to represent desirable occurrences of the target terms, since they carry an implicature that the target term applies to the patient, and this implicature is not likely to be cancelled.

In other cases, implicatures are less strong, and can be much more easily cancelled. Excerpts containing these weaker implicatures are typically ambiguous. More information will always be required in order to decide whether the patient matches the desired clinical criteria or not.

23. (a) Special discharge instructions include absolutely *no* **smoking**.
    implicature: The patient is a smoker.
   (b) The patient is a 51-year-old male with *no previous* **heart disease**, who developed chest pain the day before his transfer.
    implicature: The patient has now been diagnosed with heart disease.

Medical staff may warn a patient not to smoke even if the patient were not a habitual smoker. This might occur if the patient were being treated for a condition like asthma or treated with bottled oxygen. The implicature of (23a) would not necessarily remain in this context. Medical staff may consider a diagnosis of heart disease in patients who are at risk for it because of age, gender or other factors, and later rule this possibility out. The implicature of (23b) would be cancelled by a report that the patient's chest pain on the occasion in question was caused by something other than heart disease.

We can identify documents containing implicatures that can potentially be cancelled with specific queries that capture the relevant contexts. The relevant subset of documents or contexts can be isolated and provided to client-researchers for their review so that these can be categorized according to the goals of the research.

3   Conclusion

In this paper we provided a linguistic analysis of three medical topics: infarctions, tobacco use, and the pronouncement of death, in order to illustrate common issues involved in information retrieval from electronic medical records. In general, all topics will have similar linguistic issues associated with the retrieval of desired information and the exclusion of undesired information regarding patient conditions. Specifically, by applying the linguistic generalizations discussed in this paper and additional analyses, we are able to identify a population of patients who have a clinical profile of having had a heart attack, continue to abuse tobacco and thus, are potentially at risk for experiencing another heart attack. In addition, we can identify a sub-population of this group who have been advised to quite smoking and who are non-compliant with this advice. The identification of patients who have died will enable a researcher or physician to eliminate patients who are not eligible for a clinical trial and eliminate the potential mistake of mailing an invitation of trial participation to family members of the deceased.

The application of linguistic methods to the retrieval of medical information, can result in improving the quality of patient care and the efficiency of the institution responsible for the administration of patient care. Through the discussions presented in this paper, we have demonstrated how the professional areas of linguistics, technology and medicine are coordinated to retrieve information that has the potential to impact large organizations, such as hospitals, as well as affect change at an individual level, namely, the patient.

The Clinical Practice Analysis system enables the medical researcher to create powerful queries to retrieve information about individual patients or entire patient populations quickly and accurately, allowing researchers in health care to make an efficient use of the vast quantity of data available in medical records. The efficiency of this system has been enhanced by the implementation of linguistic generalizations specific to medical records, such as lexical variation, ambiguity, argument alternation, belief contexts, downward-entailing contexts and presupposition.

References

1. Beaver, D.: Presupposition. In: van Bentham, J., ter Meulen, A. (eds.): Handbook of Logic and Language. Elsevier, Amsterdam (1997)
2. Grimshaw, J.: Argument Structure. The MIT Press, Cambridge, Mass. (1990)
3. Ladusaw, W.: Polarity Sensitivity as Inherent Scope Relations. Indiana University Linguistics Club (1980)
4. Quine, W.: From a Logical Point of View. The MIT Press, Cambridge, Mass. (1961)

Automatic Keyword Extraction
Using Domain Knowledge

Anette Hulth[1], Jussi Karlgren[2], Anna Jonsson[1], Henrik Boström[1,3], and
Lars Asker[1,3]

[1] Dept. of Computer and Systems Sciences, Stockholm University,
Electrum 230, SE-164 40 Kista, Sweden
[hulth|anna-jon|henke|asker]@dsv.su.se
[2] Swedish Institute of Computer Science,
Box 1263, SE-164 29 Kista, Sweden
jussi@sics.se
[3] Virtual Genetics Laboratory AB
SE-171 77 Stockholm, Sweden

Abstract. Documents can be assigned keywords by frequency analysis
of the terms found in the document text, which arguably is the primary
source of knowledge about the document itself. By including a hierarchically organised domain specific thesaurus as a second knowledge source
the quality of such keywords was improved considerably, as measured by
match to previously manually assigned keywords. In the presented experiment, the combination of the evidence from frequency analysis and
the hierarchically organised thesaurus was done using inductive logic
programming.

1 Introduction

Information retrieval research has long focused on developing and refining methods for full text indexing, with the aim to improve full text retrieval. The practice
of assigning keywords[1] to documents in order to either describe the content or
to facilitate future retrieval, which is what human indexers do, has more or less
been ignored by researchers in the various fields of computer science. However,
we believe that keyword indexing — apart from being useful on its own — may
play a complementary role to full text indexing. In addition, it is an interesting
task for machine learning experiments due to the complexity of the activity. We
extend previous work on automatic keyword assignment (see e.g., [1]) to include
knowledge from a thesaurus.

In this article, we present experiments where we for each document in a collection automatically extract a list of potential keywords. This list, we envision,

---

[1] We will call a small set of terms selected to capture the content of a document
keywords. *Index terms* is an alternative term we also use; the choice mostly depending
on what the set of words is used for: describing the document or facilitating its
retrieval.

A. Gelbukh (Ed.): CICLing 2001, LNCS 2004, pp. 472–482, 2001.

can be given to a human indexer, who in turn can choose the most suitable terms from the list. The experiments were conducted on a set of documents from the Swedish Parliament which all previously have been manually indexed by professional indexers. Using machine learning algorithms and morphological pre-processing tools we combined knowledge from both the documents them-selves and a hierarchically organised thesaurus developed to suit the domain, and found we were able to generate lists of potential keywords that well covered the manually extracted examples.

2   Keyword Extraction

2.1   Manual Keyword Assignment

The traditional way of organising documents and books is by sorting them phys-ically in shelves after categories that have been predetermined. This generally works well, but finding the right balance between category generality and cat-egory specificity is difficult; the library client has to learn the categorisation scheme; quite often it is difficult to determine what category a document be-longs to; and quite often a document may rightly belong to several categories.

Some of the drawbacks of categorisation can be remedied by installing an *index* to the document collection. Documents can be given several pointers using several methods and can thus be reached by any of several routes. *Indexing* is the practice of establishing correspondences between a set, possibly large and typically finite, of keywords or index terms and individual documents or sections thereof. Keywords are meant to indicate the topic or the content of the text: the set of terms is chosen to reflect the topical structure of the collection, such as it can be determined. Indexing is typically done by indexers — persons who read documents and assign keywords to them. Manual indexing is often both difficult and dull; it poses great demands on consistency from indexing session to indexing session and between different indexers. It is the sort of job which is a prime candidate for automatisation.

Automating human performance is, however, never trivial, even when the task at hand may seem repetitive and non-creative at first glance. Manual in-dexing is a quite complex task, and difficult to emulate by computers. Manual indexers and abstractors are not consistent, much to the astonishment of docu-mentation researchers [2]. In fact, establishing a general purpose representation of a text's content is probably an impossible task: anticipating future uses of a document is difficult at best.

2.2   Automatic Indexing

By and large computerised indexing schemes have distanced themselves from their early goal of emulating human indexing performance to concentrating on what computers do well, namely working over large bodies of data. Where ini-tially the main body of work in information retrieval research has been to de-velop methods to handle the relative poverty of data in reference databases, and title-only or abstract-only document bases, the focus has shifted to developing methods to cope with the abundance of data and dynamic nature of document databases.

Typically manual indexing schemes control the indexing process by careful instructions and an established set of allowed keywords or index terms. This naturally reduces variation, but also limits the flexibility of the resulting searches: the trade-off between predictability and flexibility becomes a key issue. The idea of limiting semantic variation to a discrete and predetermined set of well defined terms — an idea which crops up regularly in fields such as artificial intelligence or machine translation — is of course a dramatic simplification of human linguistic behaviour. This is where the most noticeable methodological shift during the past forty years can be found. Systems today typically do not take the set of index terms to be predefined, but use the material they find in the texts themselves as the starting point [3,4].

This shift is accompanied by the shift from a set-theoretical view of document bases to a probabilistic view of retrieval: modern retrieval systems typically do not view retrieval as operations on a set of documents, with user requests as constraints on set membership, but instead rank documents for likelihood of relevance to the words or terms the reader has offered to the system, based on some probabilistic calculation.

The indexes typically generated by present-day systems are geared towards fully automatic retrieval of full texts rather than a traditional print index which will be used for access to bibliographical data or card catalogues. A traditional print index naturally must be small enough to be useful for human users. Under the assumption that no human user ever will actually read the index terms, the number of index terms can be allowed to grow practically with no limit. This makes the task of indexing texts different from the task that earlier efforts worked on.

2.3   Integrating the Approaches

While the past decades have seen rapid development of full-text systems, in general, manual indexing has not been supplanted by automatic full-text retrieval systems. Manual indexing has been performed continuously all along, and recently renewed attention to the value of manual indexing has been brought to the field, by Yahoo, e.g., with its manually produced catalogue index made up of few, well-edited terms. (Experiments on automatically assigning Yahoo categories have been performed by Mladenić [5].) Manual indexing with its high quality and excellent precision will continue to have a role to fulfil in information access applications and services — but there is ample room to develop semi-automatic tools to ensure consistency and raise productivity of human indexers.

Combinations of automatic and manual approaches seem most promising. A digital library can capitalise on the qualitative work done by manual indexing to improve topical clustering of documents. If a simple topical clustering tool is available, clustering hand-categorised documents in a suitable number of topical clusters affords the possibility of using the manually assigned keywords as reasonably lucid representation of the topical clusters. Thereafter uncategorised documents can be directed automatically to the cluster nearest to them, with the clusters of higher quality, and better described — thanks to the keywords.

3 Document Representation with Thesaurus Knowledge

A thesaurus or a term database which is hierarchically organised will have valuable information for indexing purposes. The richness of the semantical relations between the included terms, which to some extent resembles the knowledge of the world of a human, is difficult to derive solely from word occurrence frequencies in documents. We will here report on experiments on bills from the 16 committees at the Swedish parliament and the thesaurus used for manual indexing of these documents.

3.1 Standard Methods: tf.idf

Arguably, the most important knowledge source for finding important descriptors for a document is the document itself. Picking the most central terms in a document can be done using *term frequency* or the tf measure: frequent terms — allowing for document length normalisation — can be assumed to be important.

A second important knowledge source about the comparative utility of descriptors is their *linguistic context*: a frequent term is only important if it frequently is infrequent. This insight can be estimated using the standard collection frequency or idf measure: calculating the proportion of documents a term participates in.

3.2 Thesaurus

The public record of parliamentary activities has a central place in the public perception of Swedish political life, and it is important that the material is accessible. The Swedish Parliament manually indexes a large number of documents in order to give access both to information specialists and to the general public. This indexing effort has been ongoing for a long period of time, during which an extensive hierarchically organised domain specific thesaurus has been developed, assuring a consistent vocabulary.

The thesaurus from the parliament, which follows the ISO 2788 standard, consists of 2 500 terms organised hierarchically by *broader term* (BT)/*narrower term* (NT) relations. Figure 1 shows an excerpt from the thesaurus: the word *arbetshandikapp* (employment disability), its broader term, some narrower terms, some related terms (RT) and a brief description of the concept the term refers to (SN – scope notes).

```
Arbetshandikapp(employment disability)
        BT    Arbetsliv (working life)
        NT    Arbetsbiträde (working assistant)
        NT    Näringshjälp (grant for resettlement in an independent
              business)
        NT    Skyddat arbete (sheltered employment)
        RT    Anställningsfrämjande åtgärder (measures to stimu-
              late employment opportunities)
        RT    Handikapp (handicap)
        RT    Lönebidrag (salary contribution)
        SN    Nedsatt arbetsförmåga pga fysiska, psykiska,
              förståndsmässiga eller socialmedicinska
              handikapp --- däri inbegripet missbruk av
              alkohol eller annat berusningsmedel.   (Reduced
              ability to work due to physical, psychological, rational
              or social medical disability — including abuse of alcohol
              or other intoxicant.)
```

Fig. 1. Excerpt from the thesaurus used at the Swedish Parliament (with English equivalents).

4   Empirical Evaluation

The goal of our experiments was to automatically find all the keywords assigned by the human indexers as well as to suggest or generate further potential keywords. The decision to identify a term as a potential keyword was made on the basis of a set of features calculated for each content class word in the text. We will refer to words from the texts that actually were chosen as keywords by the human indexer as *positive* examples and the other terms as *negative* examples. By an *example* we mean one term with its feature values. Our purpose was to build a keyword identifier that would emphasise high recall with rather less regard for precision — or in other words to get false positives rather than to miss keywords assigned by the human indexers.

4.1   Experimental Set-Up

For our experiments we used 128 electronic documents in Swedish: bills from the 16 different committees from the year 98/99. The style of the texts is quite homogeneous: rather formal and dense in information. The subjects, however, differ widely, being for example social welfare, foreign affairs and housing policy. The length of the bills is also quite varying: in this set ranging from 117 to 11 269 words per document, although only 26 documents have more than 1 000 words.

For all documents, the corresponding keywords, assigned by the professional indexers were available. The number of keywords per document varies between 1 and 12 in the used set, and a longer document tend to have a larger number of keywords.

In order to know in what way to best make use of the hierarchy of the thesaurus, we first inspected how the training texts were indexed manually. We found that several texts that contained a number of sibling terms — i.e. terms that shared a common broader term — were indexed with either the broader mother term, or even the yet broader grandmother term. We found — unsurprisingly — that the number of sibling terms seemed to influence the presence of the mother or grandmother term. This seemed to be a useful factor to take into consideration to find potential keywords along with the frequency data. In conclusion, the features we used for our experiment are displayed in figure 2.

Term features	Thesaurus features
Term frequency (tf)	Mother term; present or not (ma)
Normalised frequency (nf)	Grandmother term; present or not (gran)
Inverse document frequency (idf)	Number of siblings in document; including term itself (sib(d))
	Number of siblings in thesaurus (sib(t))
	Number of children in document; including term itself (kid(d))
	Number of children in thesaurus (kid(t))

Fig. 2. The nine chosen features from the two knowledge sources.

The words in the documents were annotated for part of speech and morphologically normalised to base form using a two-level morphological analysis tool developed by Lingsoft Oy of Helsinki. After this process, all words were in lower case, and they were all single-word terms. All words except nouns were removed. To limit mismatches in comparisons towards the thesaurus, whose items were not always in base form, but occasionally determinate or plural, both the surface form as well as the lemmatised form of the documents' words were kept and matched. For each word a set of feature values was calculated. An example of the output of this process is shown in figure 3 for two terms.

Term bistånd (aid)								
tf	nf	idf	ma	gran	sib(d)	sib(t)	kid(d)	kid(t)
6	0.0050	1/5	1	0	2	5	2	7
Term handel (trade)								
tf	nf	idf	ma	gran	sib(d)	sib(t)	kid(d)	kid(t)
3	0.0025	1/11	1	0	3	6	1	5

Fig. 3. Example of data for two terms (with English equivalents) (d = in document; t = in thesaurus).

The whole set of documents was divided into two: one set consisting of 99 texts, used for finding the hypothesis; and the rest (29 documents) for testing. Thus, the material used for testing did in no way influence the training. The division into training and test set was made arbitrarily, only taking the diversity of subjects into consideration. Because of this arbitrariness, the proportions of positive and negative examples in the two sets differ slightly. In table 1, we present some details for the training set, the test set and the whole set. As can be noted, the proportion of negative examples is very large, which is often the case in information access tasks.

Table 1. The data set in detail.

	Training set	Test set	Total
Positive ex. (no)	185	57	242
Positive ex. (%)	1.38	1.20	1.34
Negative ex. (no)	13 175	4 708	17 883
Negative ex. (%)	98.62	98.80	98.66
Total (no)	13 360	4 765	18 125

4.2   Method

Virtual Predict is a system for induction of rules from pre-classified examples [6]. It is based on recent developments within the field of machine learning, in particular inductive logic programming [7]. The system can be viewed as an upgrade of standard decision tree and rule induction systems in that it allows for more expressive hypotheses to be generated and more expressive background knowledge (i.e., logic programs) to be incorporated in the induction process. The major design goal has been to achieve this upgrade in a way so that it should still be possible to emulate the standard techniques with lower expressiveness (but also lower computational cost) within the system if desired. As a side effect, this has allowed the incorporation of several recent methods that have been developed for standard machine learning techniques into the more powerful framework of Virtual Predict.

Boosting is one of the techniques that have been incorporated. Boosting is an ensemble learning method which uses a probability distribution over the training examples. This distribution is re-adjusted on each iteration so that the learning algorithm focuses on those examples that have been incorrectly classified on previous iterations. New examples are classified according to a weighted vote of the classifiers produced on each iteration. The boosting method used in Virtual Predict is called *AdaBoost* with an optional setting (stumps only) to allow for faster induction and more compact hypotheses (see [8] for details). Another feature of Virtual Predict is that it allows instances belonging to different classes to be weighted differently. This turned out to be a very useful feature in the current study, as the data set is very unbalanced.

For the training phase we were only interested in the values of the features associated with each word, as described in section 3; contextual data such as collocation of words in a common document or in similar contexts were not taken into account.

4.3 Experimental Results

The parameter setting with the best performance was that with 200 iterations and where the positive examples were given 100 times higher weights than the negative ones. This result can be seen in figure 4 (for the 29 documents in the test set). In the result calculations, we considered only those manually assigned keywords that were single-word terms actually present in the documents.

No. positive correctly classified (true positive)	54
No. positive incorrectly classified (false negative)	3
No. negative correctly classified (true negative)	4291
No. negative incorrectly classified (false positives)	417
Recall positive	0.9474

Fig. 4. Test result.

In figure 4 we can see that the 29 documents have 417 candidate keywords in addition to the ones that were correctly classified. Looking at each document separately, the number of new potential keywords varies between 2 and 47, with a median value of 10. In other words most documents had a reasonably low number of additional suggestions: for 24 documents in the test set this number is below 18.

The number of suggestions (including the correct ones) in percent of the total number of words in the documents ranges from 0.453% to 3.91%, the average being 1.90%. Of all the suggested words, just one meaningless word slipped through (*n1*, which is the name of a funding).

Of the three positive that we were unable to find, one was due to a shortcoming of the pre-processing program that treated the letter *p* from an abbreviation as a word, in addition to a bug in the program assigning the class that, because of the &-character in *Pharmacia & Upjohn*, also treated this word as the word *p*. (The term *Pharmacia & Upjohn* should not have been there at all, as it is a multi-word term.)

An example of the output for one document is shown in figure 5.

4.4 Evaluation

The results from these initial experiments have not yet been evaluated by indexers from the Swedish Parliament. To get an accurate judgement as to the true

Name of document	a12
No. of words in input to Virtual Predict	**192**
No. of keywords present in input	**5**
No. of correct keywords found	**5**
sjukgymnastik (physiotherapy)	
läkarvårdsersättning (medical treatment compensation)	
etableringsfrihet (freedom of establishment)	
företagshälsovård (occupational health care)	
arbetsmiljö (work environment)	
No. of candidate keywords (false positives)	**15**
arv (inheritance)	
arbetstagare (employee)	
arbetsgivare (employer)	
konkurrens (competition)	
sjukvård (medical care)	
sjukskrivning (reporting sick)	
primärvård (primary care)	
läkare (doctor)	
etableringsrätt (right of establishment)	
patienter (patients)	
landsting (county council)	
rehabilitering (rehabilitation)	
arbetsmiljölag (occupational safety and health act)	
läkarvårdstaxa (rates for medical treatment)	
finansiering (financing)	
No. of missed keywords present in input	**0**

Fig. 5. Example of output for one document (with English equivalents).

quality of the results this would be highly desirable, since only persons working in the field, with thorough knowledge of the domain, can tell whether specific keywords are likely to be useful. We have, however, ventured an evaluation by reading through 15 of the 29 documents in the test set to be able to compare their actual content to the corresponding derived keywords. The conclusion drawn from this is that 60 up to 80% of the suggested keywords (including the correct ones) are in fact relevant to the content of the documents. We estimated the extracted keywords to be appropriate in describing the documents, and, in some cases, even to better reflect the content than the manually indexed model keywords. This would seem to indicate the potential utility of the tool for an indexing editor.

A convenient feature of inductive logic programming algorithms for the purpose of result evaluation is the ease whereby you can study rules in the generated hypotheses. The rule applied first in the process is the one based on the most discriminating feature, which gives us the possibility of assessing which of the features is the most important in the data set. According to Virtual Predict this feature is the mother term (i.e., a hierarchical feature from the thesaurus).

4.5   A Second Run

In order to establish that a thesaurus is indeed a useful knowledge source, we made a new run with the same parameter setting and the same training set — only removing the six thesaurus features. The result of this run is presented in figure 6. As can be noted, this result supports our view that a hierarchically composed domain knowledge is crucial to a tool with the current aim.

No. positive correctly classified (true positive)	37
No. positive incorrectly classified (false negative)	20
No. negative correctly classified (true negative)	3935
No. negative incorrectly classified (false positives)	773
Recall positive	0.6491

Fig. 6. Test result without the thesaurus features.

5   Concluding Remarks

The initial results are, as mentioned earlier, very encouraging. In this stage of algorithm development, we consider recall to be the most important evaluation criterion as it reflects the potential of the current approach: it is crucial to know that none of the terms chosen by an indexer have been missed by the system. There are, however, additional issues that need to be looked into in more depth. The first, and most trivial, thing would be to remove meaningless words, e.g., single characters, before the data is processed by Virtual Predict. In addition we need to take into account abbreviations, as some words are only represented by the short form in the text, e.g., *IT*, not by the full form *informationsteknik* (information technology). For applications to real-life indexing tasks, some form of utility likelihood measure should be used in result (as in e.g., [1]).

As stated earlier, we have so far only looked at single-word terms. This means that a certain amount of both potential index terms as well as terms selected by the human indexers have been ignored. However, as Swedish is rich in compounding, this is much less of a problem than had it been for English (all words in figure 5, e.g., are single-word terms in Swedish). One could possibly start by matching terms in the thesaurus with phrases in the documents.

We also need to further investigate how to take into account the cases where the thesaurus form of a word is not its base form. Alternatives include allowing more forms of the word in the system or normalising the thesaurus. Another improvement to the extraction of potential keywords would be to recognise proper nouns, as they sometimes play an important role in this type of documents. Adding a module for name recognition seems like a straightforward way to approach this issue.

Sometimes an indexer will choose a word that is not present in a document itself, and suggesting keywords absent in the text is a challenging matter. A thesaurus will, however, most likely provide some clues to this such as when broader terms tend to be preferred to some specific terms used in the text.

The potential keywords in our experiments are not necessarily terms chosen from the thesaurus. Very rarely do human indexers go beyond the thesaurus limits — this mainly happens in the case of proper names. We did not feel the need to limit the suggestions to the thesaurus. We want to keep track of new potential words and propose their timely inclusion to the thesaurus, as well as point out terms that do not seem to be used any longer in the thesaurus. Word usage reflect the constantly changing nature of our society, and as phenomena in society vary over time so does the use of words. Keeping a thesaurus up to date is a difficult task, and is in itself a complex research issue. However, we believe that this sort of tool set can lend itself to thesaurus management tools as well as document labelling.

References

1. Turney, P.D. (2000). Learning Algorithms for Keyphrase Extraction. *Information Retrieval*, **2**(4):303–336. Kluwer Academic Publishers.
2. Earl, L.L. (1970). *Information Storage & Retrieval*, volume 6, pp. 313–334. Pergamon Press.
3. Luhn, H.P. (1957). A Statistical Approach to Mechanical Encoding and searching of Literary Information. *IBM Journal of Research and Development*, **1**:309–317.
4. Luhn, H.P. (1959). Auto-Encoding of Documents for Information Retrieval Systems. In: Boaz. M. (ed.) *Modern Trends in Documentation*, pp. 45–58. Pergamon Press, London.
5. Mladenić, D. (1998). Turning Yahoo into an Automatic Web-Page Classifier. In: Prade, H. (ed.) *13th European Conference on Artificial Intelligence ECAI 98*, pp. 473–474.
6. Boström, H. (2000). Manual for Virtual Predict 0.8, Virtual Genetics Inc.
7. Nienhuys-Cheng, S.-H., and de Wolf, R. (1997). *Foundations of Inductive Logic Programming*. LNAI 1228. Springer.
8. Freund Y., and Schapire R.E. (1996). Experiments with a new boosting algorithm. In: *Machine Learning: Proceedings of the Thirteenth International Conference*, pp. 148–156.

Approximate VLDC Pattern Matching in Shared-Forest

Manuel Vilares[1], Francisco J. Ribadas[2], and Victor M. Darriba[2]

[1] Departamento de Computación, Universidad de La Coruña
Campus de Elviña s/n, 15071 La Coruña, Spain
vilares@udc.es
http://coleweb.dc.fi.udc.es/
[2] Escuela Superior de Ingeniería Informática, Universidad de Vigo
Edificio Politécnico, As Lagoas, 32004 Orense, Spain
ribadas@uvigo.es, darriba@uvigo.es

Abstract. We present a matching-based proposal intended to deal with querying for structured text databases. Our approach extends approximate VLDC matching techniques by allowing a query to exploit sharing of common parts between patterns used to index the document.

1 Introduction

Any effort in the development of effective retrieval methods is based on finding a related representation for documents and requests. The main objective is to determine a limited number of index terms for the major concepts in the document.

Until recently, indexing was accomplished by creating a bibliographic citation in a structured file that references the original text. This approach allows a reduction in time and space bounds, although the ability to find information on a particular subject is limited by the system which creates index terms for that subject. At present, the significant reduction in cost processing has propitiated the notion of total document indexing, for which all words in a document are potential index descriptors. This reduction saves the indexer from entering index terms that are identical to words in the document, but does not facilitate the finding of relevant information for the user.

In effect, the words used in a query do not always reflect the value of the concepts being presented. It is the combination of these words and their semantic implications that contain the value of these concepts which leads us to more sophisticated index representations, such as syntactic structures and context-free grammars [2] [3]. This information is inherent in the document and query. So, matching becomes a possible mechanism for extracting a common pattern from multiple data and we could use it to locate information of linguistic interest in natural language processing. Some related work about using syntactic structures and matching techniques in IR can be found in Smeaton et al. [4] [5] [6].

A. Gelbukh (Ed.): CICLing 2001, LNCS 2004, pp. 483–494, 2001.

However, the language intended to represent the document can often only be approximately defined, and therefore ambiguity arises. Since it is desirable to consider all possible parses for semantic processing, it is convenient to merge parse trees as much as possible into a single structure that allows them to share common parts. Although in the case of the query, language ambiguity could probably be eliminated, queries could vary widely from indexes or some structural details are unknown, and an approximate matching strategy in the presence of variable length don't cares (VLDC) becomes necessary [10].

Previous works do not provide a mechanism to fully exploit structural sharing in VLDC matching. Our aim is to cover the lack of proposals in this domain.

2   The Editing Distance

Given P, a pattern tree, and D, a data tree, we define an *edit operation* as a pair $a \rightarrow b$, $a \in$ labels$(P) \cup \{\varepsilon\}$, $b \in$ labels$(D) \cup \{\varepsilon\}$, $(a, b) \neq (\varepsilon, \varepsilon)$, where ε represents the empty string. We can delete a node $(a \rightarrow \varepsilon)$, insert a node $(\varepsilon \rightarrow b)$, and change a node $(a \rightarrow b)$. Each edit operation has an associated cost, $\gamma(a \rightarrow b)$, that we extend to a sequence S of edit operations $s_1, s_2, \ldots, s_n$ in the form $\gamma(S) = \sum_{i=1}^{|S|}(\gamma(s_i))$. The distance between P and D is defined by the metric:

$$\delta(P, D) = \min\{\gamma(S),\ S \text{ editing sequence taking } P \text{ to } D\}$$

Given an inverse postorder traversal, as it is shown in Fig. 1, to name each node i of a tree T by $T[i]$, a *mapping* from P to D is a triple (M, P, D), where M is a set of integer pairs (i, j) satisfying, for each $1 \leq i_1, i_2 \leq |P|$ and $1 \leq j_1, j_2 \leq |D|$:

$$
\begin{array}{ll}
i_1 = i_2 & \textbf{iff } j_1 = j_2 \\
P[i_1] \text{ is to the left of } P[i_2] & \textbf{iff } D[j_1] \text{ is to the left of } D[j_2] \\
P[i_1] \text{ is an ancestor of } P[i_2] & \textbf{iff } D[j_1] \text{ is an ancestor of } D[j_2]
\end{array}
$$

which corresponds, in each case, to one-to-one assignation, sibling order preservation and ancestor order preservation. The cost, $\gamma(M)$, of a mapping (M, P, D) is computed from relabeling, deleting and inserting operations, as follows:

$$\gamma(M) = \sum_{(i,j)\in M} \gamma(P[i] \rightarrow D[j]) + \sum_{i \in \mathcal{D}} \gamma(P[i] \rightarrow \varepsilon) + \sum_{j \in \mathcal{I}} \gamma(\varepsilon \rightarrow D[j])$$

where $\mathcal{D}$ and $\mathcal{I}$ are, respectively, the nodes in P and D not touched by any line in M. Tai proves, given trees P and D, that

$$\delta(P, D) = min\{\gamma(M),\ M \text{ mapping from } P \text{ to } D\}$$

which allows us to focus on edit sequences being a mapping. We show in Fig. 2 one example of mapping between two trees, and a sequence of edit operations not constituting a mapping. We also introduce $r\_keyroots(T)$ as the set of all

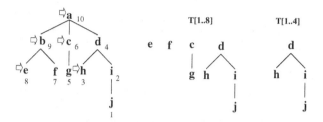

Fig. 1. The forest distance using an inverse postorder numbering

nodes in a tree T which have a right sibling plus the root, $root(T)$, of T. We shall proceed through the nodes determining mappings from all leaf r_keyroots first, then all r_keyroots at the next higher level, and so on to the root. The set of $r\_keyroots(T)$ is indicated by arrows in Fig. 1.

In dealing with approximate VLDC pattern matching, some structural details can be omitted in the target tree and different strategies are then applicable. Following Zhang *et al.* in [10] we introduce two different definitions to VLDC matching:

- The VLDC substitutes for part of a path from the root to a leaf of the data tree. We represent such a substitution, shown in Fig. 2, by a vertical bar "|", and call it a *path*-VLDC.
- The VLDC matches part of such a path and all the subtrees emanating from the nodes of that path, except possibly at the lowest node of that path. At the lowest node, the VLDC symbol can substitute for a set of leftmost subtrees and a set of rightmost subtrees. We call this an *umbrella*-VLDC, and represent it by a circumflex "∧", as shown in Fig. 2.

To formalize the consideration of pattern trees with VLDC's requires the capture of the notion of VLDC-*substitution* for nodes in the target tree P labeled | or ∧ as previously introduced. So, given a data tree D and a substitution s on P, we redefine:

$$\delta(P, D) = \min_{s \in \mathcal{S}} \{\delta(P, D, s)\}$$

where $\mathcal{S}$ is the set of all possible VLDC-substitutions, and $\delta(P, D, s)$ is the distance $\delta(\bar{P}, D)$, being $\bar{P}$ the result of apply the substitution s to P. As a consequence, no cost is induced by VLDC-substitutions.

3 Approximate VLDC Tree Matching

The major question of Zhang *et al.* in [9] [10], is the tree distance algorithm itself. However, parsing and tree-to-tree correction are topologically related and, to get the best performance, it is necessary to understand the mechanisms that cause the phenomenon of tree duplication.

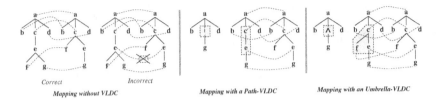

Correct Incorrect

Mapping without VLDC   *Mapping with a Path-VLDC*   *Mapping with an Umbrella-VLDC*

Fig. 2. An example on mappings

A major factor to take into account is the syntactic representation used. We choose to work in the parsing context described for ICE [8]. Here, authors represent a parse as the chain of the context-free rules used in a leftmost reduction of the input sentence, rather than as a tree. When the sentence has distinct parses, the set of all possible parse chains is represented in finite shared form by a context-free grammar that generates that possibly infinite set.

This difference with most other parsers is only apparent, since context-free grammars can be represented by AND-OR graphs that in our case are precisely the shared-forest graph [1]. In this graph, AND-nodes correspond to the usual parse-tree nodes, while OR-nodes correspond to ambiguities. Sharing of structures is represented by nodes accessed by more than one other node and it may correspond to sharing of a complete subtree, but also sharing of a part of the descendants of a given node. This allows us to gain in sharing efficiency in relation to classic representations, as shown in Fig. 3.

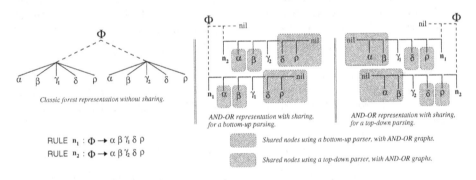

Classic forest representation without sharing.

RULE n_1 : $\Phi \rightarrow \alpha \beta \gamma_1 \delta \rho$
RULE n_2 : $\Phi \rightarrow \alpha \beta \gamma_2 \delta \rho$

AND-OR representation with sharing, for a bottom-up parsing.

AND-OR representation with sharing, for a top-down parsing.

Shared nodes using a bottom-up parser, with AND-OR graphs.

Shared nodes using a top-down parser, with AND-OR graphs.

Fig. 3. How shared forest are built using an AND-OR formalism

It is also important the parsing scheme applied. So, bottom-up parsing may share only the rightmost constituents, while top-down parsing may only share the leftmost ones. This relies to the type of search used to built the forest. Breadth first search results on bottom-up constructions and depth first search results on top-down ones, as it is also shown in Fig. 3.

At this level, one major observation we noted is that Zhang *et al.* consider a postorder traversal, computing the forest distance by left-recursion on this search. As a consequence, we would need to consider a top-down parsing architecture to avoid redundant computations. However, top-down parsers are not computationally efficient, and a bottom-up approach, as is the case of ICE, requires a rightmost search of tree constituents. This implies redefining the architecture of the original matching strategy.

To accomplish this change, we introduce $r(i)$ (resp. anc(i)) as the rightmost leaf descendent of the subtree rooted at $T[i]$ (resp. the ancestors of $T[i]$) in a tree T, and $T[i..j]$ as the ordered sub-forest of T induced by the nodes numbered i to j inclusive, as it is shown in Fig. 1. In particular, we have $T[r(i)..i]$ is the tree rooted at $T[i]$. We now define the *forest edition distance* between a target tree P and a data tree D, as a generalization of δ, in the form

$$f\_d(P[s_1..s_2], D[t_1..t_2]) = \delta(P[s_1..s_2], D[t_1..t_2])$$

that we shall denote $f\_d(s_1..s_2, t_1..t_2)$ when the context is clear. Intuitively, this concept computes the distance between two nodes, $P[s_2]$ and $D[t_2]$, in the context of their left siblings in the corresponding trees, while the tree distance, $\delta(P[s_2], D[t_2])$, is computed only from their descendants.

To be precise, given a pattern tree P and a data tree D, we can compute the editing distance $t\_d(P, D)$ applying the formulae that follow [7], for nodes $i \in$ anc(s) and $j \in$ anc(t), assuming $P[s]$ is not an incomplete structure:

$$f\_d(r(i)..s, r(j)..t) = \begin{cases} \min \begin{cases} f\_d\ (r(i)..s - 1,\ r(j)..t) & + \gamma(P[s] \to \varepsilon), \\ f\_d\ (r(i)..s,\ r(j)..t - 1) & + \gamma(\varepsilon \to D[t]), \\ f\_d\ (r(i)..s - 1,\ r(j)..t - 1) & + \gamma(P[s] \to D[t]) \end{cases} \\ \qquad \text{iff } r(s) = r(i) \text{ and } r(t) = r(j) \\[2ex] \min \begin{cases} f\_d\ (r(i)..s - 1,\ r(j)..t) & + \gamma(P[s] \to \varepsilon), \\ f\_d\ (r(i)..s,\ r(j)..t - 1) & + \gamma(\varepsilon \to D[t]), \\ f\_d\ (r(i)..r(s) - 1,\ r(j)..r(t) - 1) & + t\_d(s, t) \end{cases} \\ \qquad \textbf{otherwise} \end{cases}$$

When $P[s]$ is either "|" or "$\wedge$" formulae must be adapted and the process is illustrated in Fig. 4. We first assume $P[s]$ is "|":

$$f\_d(r(i)..s, r(j)..t) = \min \begin{cases} f\_d(r(i)..s - 1,\ r(j)..t) & + \gamma(P[s] \to \varepsilon), \\ f\_d(r(i)..s,\ r(j)..t - 1) & + \gamma(\varepsilon \to D[t]), \\ f\_d(r(i)..s - 1,\ r(j)..t - 1) & + \gamma(P[s] \to D[t]), \\ f\_d(\phi, D[r(j)]..t - 1) & + \min_{t_k}\{t\_d(s, t_k) - \\ & \qquad t\_d(\phi, t_k)\}\ \ 1 \le k \le n_t \end{cases}$$

For the case where $P[s]$ is "$\wedge$", formulae are the following:

$$f\_d(r(i)..s, r(j)..t) = \min \begin{cases} f\_d(r(i)..s - 1,\ r(j)..t) & + \gamma(P[s] \to \varepsilon), \\ f\_d(r(i)..s,\ r(j)..t - 1) & + \gamma(\varepsilon \to D[t]), \\ f\_d(r(i)..s - 1,\ r(j)..t - 1) & + \gamma(P[s] \to D[t]), \\ \min_{t_k}\{t\_d(s, t_k)\} & 1 \le k \le n_t, \\ \min_{t_k}\{s\_f\_d(r(i)..s - 1, r(j)..t_k)\} & 1 \le k \le n_t \end{cases}$$

where $D[t_k]$, $1 \leq k \leq n_t$, are children of $D[t]$. If $D[t]$ is a leaf, that is $t = r(j)$, then only the first three expressions are present. We define the *suffix forest distance* between F_P and F_D, forests in the pattern P and the data tree D respectively, denoted $\text{s\_f\_d}(F_P, F_D)$, as the distance between F_P and $\bar{F}_D$, where $\bar{F}_D$ is a sub-forest of F_D with some consecutive complete subtrees removed from the left all having the same parent. Formally we have that

$$\text{s\_f\_d}(F_P, F_D) = \min_{\bar{F}_D}\{\text{f\_d}(F_P, \bar{F}_D)\}$$

From a computational point of view, it can be proved that

$$\text{s\_f\_d}(r(i)..s, r(j)..t) = \begin{cases} \min \left\{ \begin{array}{l} \text{f\_d}(r(i)..s, \ \phi), \\ \text{f\_d}(r(i)..s, \ r(j)..t) \end{array} \right\} \\ \textbf{iff } r(t) = r(j) \\[2ex] \min \left\{ \begin{array}{ll} \text{s\_f\_d}(r(i)..s - 1, \ r(j)..t) & + \gamma(P[s] \to \varepsilon), \\ \text{s\_f\_d}(r(i)..s, \ r(j)..t - 1) & + \gamma(\varepsilon \to D[\hat{t}]), \\ \text{s\_f\_d}(r(i)..r(s) - 1, \ r(j)..r(t) - 1) & + \text{t\_d}(s, t) \end{array} \right\} \\ \textbf{otherwise} \end{cases}$$

To compute $\text{t\_d}(P, D)$ it will be sufficient to take into account that

$$\text{t\_d}(P, D) = \text{f\_d}(\text{root}(P)..r(\text{root}(P)), \text{root}(D)..r(\text{root}(D)))$$

Time bound is $\mathcal{O}(|P| \times |D| \times \min(depth(P), leaves(P)) \times \min(depth(D), leaves(D)))$ in the worst case, where $|P|$ (resp. $|D|$) is the number of nodes in the pattern tree P (resp. in the data tree D).

4   Approximate VLDC Matching in Shared Forest

To start with, let P be a labeled ordered tree where some structural details has been omitted, and D an AND-OR graph, both of them built using our parsing frame. We shall identify P with a query and D with a part of the syntactic representation for a textual database with a certain degree of ambiguity. The presence of OR nodes in D has two main implications in our work: Firstly, there will exist situations where we must handle simultaneous values for some forest distances and, secondly, the parser may share some structures among the descendants of the different branches in an OR node. We shall now present the manner we calculate the distance between a pattern tree and the set of trees that are represented within the AND-OR graph, and how to take advantage of the shared structures created by the parser.

Let $P[s]$ be the current node in the inverse postorder for P, and $i \in \text{anc}(s)$ a r_keyroot. Given an OR node $D[k]$ we can distinguish two situations, depending on the situation of this OR node and the situation of the r_keyroots of D.

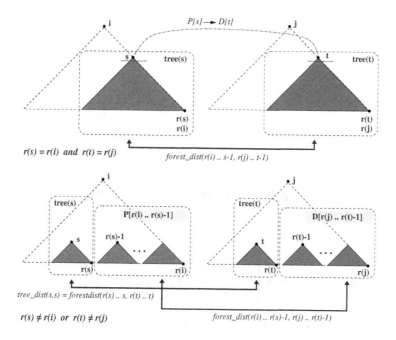

Fig. 4. The forest distance in our proposal

4.1   Sharing into a Same r_keyroot

Let $D[t']$ and $D[t'']$ be the nodes we are dealing with in parallel for two branches labeled $D[k']$ and $D[k'']$ of the OR node $r(D[k])$. We have that $j \in anc(t') \cap anc(t'')$, that is, the tree rooted at the r_keyroot $D[j]$ includes the OR alternatives $D[k']$ and $D[k'']$.

Such a situation is shown in Fig. 5 using a classic representation and the AND-OR graphs. Here, the lightly shaded part refers to nodes whose distance have been computed in the inverse postorder before the OR node $D[k]$. The heavily shaded part represents a shared structure. The notation "• • •" in figures representing AND-OR graphs, expresses the fact that we descend along the rightmost branch of the corresponding tree.

We shall assume that nodes $D[r(t') - 1]$ and $D[r(t'') - 1]$ are the same, that is, their corresponding subtrees are shared. So, $D[r(t')]$ (resp. $D[r(t'')]$) is the following node in $D[k']$ (resp. $D[k'']$) to deal with once the distance for the shared structure has been computed.

At this point, our aim is to compute the value for $f\_d(r(i)..s,\ r(j)..\hat{t})$, $\hat{t} \in \{t',\ t''\}$, proving that we can translate parse sharing on sharing on computations for these distances.

Since we have assumed there is a shared structure between $D[r(\hat{t})]$ and $D[r(j)]$, we conclude that $r(j) \neq r(\hat{t})$ and the values for $f\_d(r(i)..s,\ r(j)..\hat{t})$, $\hat{t} \in \{t',\ t''\}$ are given by:

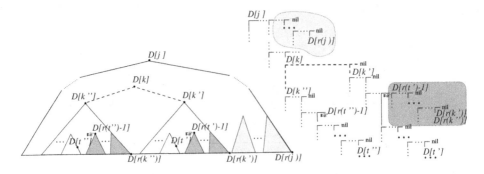

Fig. 5. Sharing into a same r_keyroot

$$
f\_d(r(i)..s, r(j)..\hat{t}) = \min \left\{ \begin{array}{ll} f\_d(r(i)..s - 1, \; r(j)..\hat{t}) & + \gamma(P[s] \to \varepsilon), \\ f\_d(r(i)..s, \; r(j)..\hat{t} - 1) & + \gamma(\varepsilon \to D[\hat{t}]), \\ f\_d(r(i)..r(s) - 1, \; r(j)..r(\hat{t}) - 1) + t\_d(s, \hat{t}) \end{array} \right\}
$$

where $\hat{t} \in \{t', t''\}$. We can interpret this three alternatives as follows:

1. The values for $f\_d(r(i)..s-1, \; r(j)..\hat{t})$, $\hat{t} \in \{t', t''\}$ have been computed by the approximate matching algorithm in a previous step. So, in this case, parse sharing has not consequences on the natural computation for the distances.
2. Two cases are possible in relation to the nature of nodes $D[\hat{t}]$, $\hat{t} \in \{t', t''\}$, these are:
   - If both nodes are leaves, then $r(\hat{t}) = \hat{t}$. As a consequence, we also have that

$$
D[t' - 1] = D[r(t') - 1] = D[r(t'') - 1] = D[t'' - 1]
$$

   and the values $f\_d(r(i)..s, \; r(j)..\hat{t} - 1)$, $\hat{t} \in \{t', t''\}$ are also the same.
   - Otherwise, following the inverse postorder, we would arrive at the right-most leaves of $D[t']$ and $D[t'']$, where we could apply the reasoning considered in the previous case.
3. Values for the distances $f\_d(r(s)..r(i) - 1, \; r(j)..r(\hat{t}) - 1)$, $\hat{t} \in \{t', t''\}$ are identical, given that nodes $D[r(\hat{t}) - 1]$, $\hat{t} \in \{t', t''\}$ are shared by the parser.

A similar reasoning can be applied to compute the values for s_f_d, avoiding redundant computations.

4.2 Sharing between Different r_keyroots

We have that $j' \in anc(t')$ and $j'' \in anc(t'')$, with $j' \neq j''$, are two r_keyroots. We also have an OR node $D[k]$ being a common ancestor of these two nodes. We suppose that the r_keyroots are in different branches, that is, there exists a r_keyroot, $D[j']$ (resp. $D[j'']$), in the branch labeled $D[k']$ (resp. $D[k'']$).

Our aim now is to compute the value for distances $f\_d(r(i)..s, r(ĵ)..\hat{t})$, where pairs $(ĵ, \hat{t})$ are in $\{(j', t'), (j'', t'')\}$. Formally, we have that these values are given by:

$$f\_d(r(i)..s, r(ĵ)..\hat{t}) = \begin{cases} \begin{cases} \min \begin{cases} f\_d(r(i)..s-1, r(ĵ)..\hat{t}) & + \gamma(P[s] \to \varepsilon), \\ f\_d(r(i)..s, r(ĵ)..\hat{t}-1) & + \gamma(\varepsilon \to D[\hat{t}]), \\ f\_d(r(i)..s-1, r(ĵ)..\hat{t}-1) + \gamma(P[s] \to D[\hat{t}]), \\ f\_d(\phi, D[r(ĵ)]..\hat{t}-1) & + \min_{\hat{t}_k}\{t\_d(s,\hat{t}_k) - \\ & \quad t\_d(\phi,\hat{t}_k)\} \ 1 \le k \le n_{\hat{t}} \end{cases} \\ \textbf{iff } P[s] = | \\[2em] \min \begin{cases} f\_d(r(i)..s-1, r(ĵ)..\hat{t}) & + \gamma(P[s] \to \varepsilon), \\ f\_d(r(i)..s, r(ĵ)..\hat{t}-1) & + \gamma(\varepsilon \to D[\hat{t}]), \\ f\_d(r(i)..s-1, r(ĵ)..\hat{t}-1) & + \gamma(P[s] \to D[\hat{t}]), \\ \min_{\hat{t}_k}\{t\_d(s,\hat{t}_k), & 1 \le k \le n_{\hat{t}}, \\ \min_{\hat{t}_k}\{s\_f\_d(r(i)..s-1, r(ĵ)..\hat{t}_k), & 1 \le k \le n_{\hat{t}} \end{cases} \\ \textbf{iff } P[s] = \wedge \\[2em] \min \begin{cases} f\_d(r(i)..s-1, r(ĵ)..\hat{t}) & + \gamma(P[s] \to \varepsilon), \\ f\_d(r(i)..s, r(ĵ)..\hat{t}-1) & + \gamma(\varepsilon \to D[\hat{t}]), \\ f\_d(r(i)..s-1, r(ĵ)..\hat{t}-1) + \gamma(P[s] \to D[\hat{t}]) \end{cases} \\ \textbf{otherwise} \\[1em] \textbf{iff } r(s) = r(i) \textbf{ and } r(\hat{t}) = r(ĵ) \\[1.5em] \min \begin{cases} f\_d(r(i)..s-1, r(ĵ)..\hat{t}) & + \gamma(P[s] \to \varepsilon), \\ f\_d(r(i)..s, r(ĵ)..\hat{t}-1) & + \gamma(\varepsilon \to D[\hat{t}]), \\ f\_d(r(i)..r(s)-1, r(ĵ)..r(\hat{t})-1) + t\_d(s,\hat{t}) \end{cases} \\ \textbf{otherwise} \end{cases}$$

The situation, shown in Fig. 6, makes possible $r(s) = r(i)$ and $r(\hat{t}) = r(ĵ)$. In this first case, we can assume that a tail of sons is shared by nodes $D[\hat{t}]$, $\hat{t} \in \{t', t''\}$. We can also assume that this tail is proper given that, otherwise, our parser guarantees that the nodes $D[\hat{t}]$, $\hat{t} \in \{t', t''\}$ are also shared.

Taking into account our parsing strategy, which identifies syntactic structures and computations, we conclude that the distances $f\_d(r(i)..s, r(ĵ)..\hat{t})$, with $(ĵ, \hat{t}) \in \{(j', t'), (j'', t'')\}$ do not depend on previous computations over the shared tail, as is shown in the left-hand-side of Fig. 6. So, this sharing has no consequences on the calculus, although it will have effects on the computation of distances for nodes in the rightmost branch of the tree immediately to the left of the shared tail of sons, which is denoted by a double pointed line in Fig. 6, as we shall shown immediately.

We consider now the second case, that is, the computation of the forest distance when $r(\hat{t}) \neq r(ĵ)$, such as is shown in Fig. 7. Here, in relation to each one of the three alternative values to compute the minimum, we have that:

1. The values for $f\_d(r(i)..s-1, r(ĵ)..\hat{t})$, $(ĵ, \hat{t}) \in \{(j', t'), (j'', t'')\}$ have been computed by the approximate matching algorithm in a previous step and parse sharing does not affect the computation for distances.

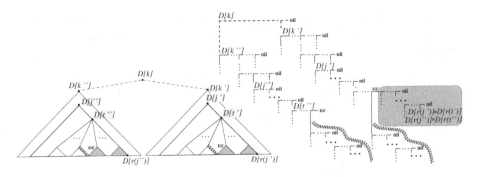

Fig. 6. Sharing between different r_keyroots (first case)

2. We distinguish two cases in relation to the nature of nodes $D[\hat{t}]$, $\hat{t} \in \{(t', t'')$. We shall apply the same reasoning considered when we had an only r_keyroot:

   – If both nodes are leaves, then $r(\hat{t}) = \hat{t}$. As a consequence, we also have that

   $$D[t' - 1] = D[r(t') - 1] = D[r(t'') - 1] = D[t'' - 1]$$

   and therefore the values for distances $f\_d(r(i)..s,\ r(\hat{j})..\hat{t} - 1)$ with $(\hat{j}, \hat{t}), \in \{(j', t'),\ (j'', t'')\}$, are also the same.

   – Otherwise, following the inverse postorder, we arrive to the rightmost leaves of $D[t']$ and $D[t'']$, where we can apply the reasoning considered in the previous case.

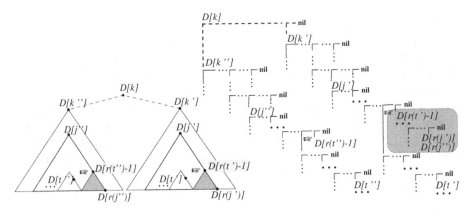

Fig. 7. Sharing between different r_keyroots (second case)

3. Values for the distances $f\_d(r(i)..r(s) - 1,\ r(\hat{t})..r(\hat{t}) - 1)$, $\hat{t} \in \{t',\ t''\}$ are identical, given that the trees rooted by nodes $D[r(\hat{t}) - 1]$, $\hat{t} \in \{t',\ t''\}$ are shared by the parser.

As in the case of sharing on a same r_keyroot, a similar reasoning can be applied to compute the values for s_f_d, avoiding redundant computations.

5   Experimental Results

We take a simple example to illustrate our discussion: the language of arithmetical expressions. We compare our proposal with Zhang *et al.* [10], considering two deterministic grammars, $\mathcal{G}_L$ and $\mathcal{G}_R$, representing respectively the left and right associative versions for the arithmetic operators; and one non-deterministic one $\mathcal{G}_N$. To simplify the explanation, we focus on matching phenomena assuming that parsers are built using ICE [8]. Lexical information is common in all cases, and tests have been applied on target inputs of the form $a_1 + a_2 + \ldots + a_i + a_{i+1}$, with i even, representing the number of addition operators. These programs have a number of ambiguous parses which grows exponentially with i. This number is:

$$C_0 = C_1 = 1 \quad \text{and} \quad C_i = \binom{2i}{i} \frac{1}{i+1}, \text{ if } i > 1$$

As pattern, we have used deterministic parse trees of the form

In the deterministic case, patterns are built from the left-associative (resp. right-associative) interpretation for $\mathcal{G}_L$ (resp. $\mathcal{G}_R$), which allows us to evaluate the impact of traversal orientation in the performance. So, the rightmost diagram in Fig. 8 proves the adaptation of our proposal (resp. Zhang *et al.* algorithm) to left-recursive (resp. right-recursive) derivations, which corroborates our conclusions.

In the non-deterministic case, patterns are built from the left-associative interpretation of the query, which is not relevant given that rules in $\mathcal{G}_N$ are symmetrical. Here, we evaluate the gain in efficiency due to sharing of computations in a dynamic frame, such as is shown in the leftmost diagram of Fig. 8.

6   Conclusions

Approximate tree matching can be adapted to deal with shared data forest and incomplete pattern trees, to give rise to approximate VLDC pattern matching. In practice, this approach can reduce the cost of evaluating queries in sophisticated retrieval systems, where retrieval functions based on classic pattern matching cannot reach optimal results because it is impossible to estimate the exact representation of documents or requests and additional simplifying assumptions are necessary.

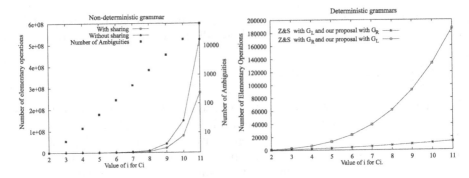

Fig. 8. Results on approximate VLDC matching

References

1. Billot, S., Lang, B.: The structure of shared forest in ambiguous parsing. *Proc. of* 27th *Annual Meeting of the ACL*, 1989.
2. Kilpelainen, P., Mannila, H.: Grammatical Tree Matching. *Lecture Notes in Computer Science* **644** (1992) 159–171.
3. Kilpelainen, P.: Tree Matching Problems with Applications to Structured Text Databases. *Ph.D. Thesis*, Department of Computer Science, University of Helsinki, 1992. Helsinki, Finland
4. Smeaton, Alan F. : Incorporating Syntactic Information into a Document Retrieval Strategy: An Investigation. *Proc. the* 9th *Annual International ACM SIGIR Conference on Research and Development in Information Retrieval*, 103–113, 1986.
5. Smeaton, A.F. and van Rijsbergen, C.J.: Experiments on Incorporating Syntactic Processing of User Queries into a Document Retrieval Strategy. *Proc. of the* 11th *International ACM-SIGIR Conference on Research and Development in Information Retrieval*, pp. 31-54. Grenoble, France, 1988.
6. Smeaton, A.F, O'Donell, R. and Kelley,F.: Indexing Structures Derived from Syntax in TREC-3: System Description. *Proc. of* 3rd *Text REtrieval Conference* (TREC-3), D.K. Harman (ed.), NIST Special Publication, 1994.
7. Vilares, M., Cabrero, D., Ribadas F.J.: Approximate matching in shared forest. *Proc. of Sixth International Workshop on Natural Language Understanding and Logic Programming* pp. 59-72, Las Cruces, NM (USA), 1999.
8. Vilares, M., Dion, B.A.: Efficient incremental parsing for context-free languages. *Proc. of the* 5th *IEEE International Conference on Computer Languages* (1994) 241–252, Toulouse, France.
9. Zhang, K., Shasha, D.: Simple fast algorithms for the editing distance between trees and related problems. *SIAM Journal on Computing* (1989) **18** 1245–1262.
10. Zhang, K. and Shasha, D. and Wang, J.T.L. Approximate Tree Matching in the Presence of Variable Length Don't Cares. *Journal of Algorithms*, pages 33–66, vol **16 (1)**, 1994

Knowledge Engineering for Intelligent Information Retrieval

Guido Drexel

SERUBA GmbH, Hamburg, Germany
gdrexel@seruba.com

Abstract This paper presents a clustered approach to designing an overall ontological model together with a general rule-based component that serves as a mapping device. By observational criteria, a multi-lingual team of experts excerpts concepts from general communication in the media. The team, then, finds equivalent expressions in English, German, French, and Spanish. On the basis of a set of ontological and lexical relations, a conceptual network is built up. Concepts are thought to be universal. Objects unique in time and space are identified by names and will be explained by the universals as their instances. Our approach relies on multi-relational descriptions of concepts. It provides a powerful tool for documentation and conceptual language learning. First and foremost, our multi-lingual, polyhierarchical ontology fills the gap of semantically-based information retrieval by generating enhanced and improved queries for internet search.

1 The Idea

At SERUBA, a new approach in the development of multi-lingual ontologies and information retrieval thesauri has been developed. In our approach, described by Schmitz-Esser (1999, 2000, in prep.), we map linguistic expressions to an abstract hierarchy (or network) of concepts. Our basic assumption is that internet searchers often have only a vague idea of what they are looking for especially in terms of how to express their subject of interest. Our system supports the user by providing a knowledgeable database of somehow related expressions. The relations are easy to understand and reflect commonsense knowledge and learning. We distinguish between two layers of relations. The first, which one might view as a horizontal layer, is language specific. It comprises the well-known lexical relations of synonymy and polysemy. A vertical layer, then, refers to language-independent relations. These are motivated by semantical and ontological issues.

On the one hand, a concept is loosely defined by its significant set of expressions. And on the other hand, the concept is more formally defined by its relations with other concepts. A concept is thought to be an invariant entity. To name a specific object that belongs to the class given by a concept, the concept is assigned an instance which uniquely refers to a named object. Compared to other approaches that model commonsense knowledge such as CYC (cf. e.g. Lenat &

A. Gelbukh (Ed.): CICLing 2001, LNCS 2004, pp. 495–504, 2001.

Guha 1990) or WordNet (cf. e.g. Fellbaum (Ed.) 1998), the SERUBA approach goes beyond word level descriptions. However, our approach is less formal in a logical way, since we do not build on complex inferences to be drawn from our network. For us it seems sufficient if humans can interact with our knowledge base on a naive and commonsense level. CYC and WordNet concentrate on single languages whereas SERUBA builds up the network simultaneously for all four languages, Spanish, French, English, and German.

2   The Knowledge Model

Due to the evolution of our model, it owes a lot to both, information retrieval thesauri and ontologies, in general. While ontologies have neither a clearly defined reference to linguistic expressions nor an explanatory device for the lexical relationships among them, information retrieval thesauri lack an epistemological model that explains the mapping of linguistic expressions to entities of the world. Our approach is designed to fill the gap between conceptual descriptions of the world and the alternative ways to express any concept in any of our four languages, Spanish, French, English, and German.

2.1   On Ontologies

From the philosophical point of view, ontology is the science of the metaphysical and epistemological reality, i.e. ontology is concerned with *what is* and *what it is like*. Ontology claims to state what is true in every area of reality.

A less ambitious approach to ontology, though more oriented toward practical needs, can be seen in ontological models designed as knowledge bases for information systems. Ontologies for this area are usually restricted to specific domains. This focus allows the researcher to achieve the task of a well-founded organization of the domain knowledge. In the ontological view of knowledge representation, dependencies and relations are stated for all relevant entities.

Such ontologies have been proven useful for documentation purposes because ontologically related index terms support the clarification and selection process during retrieval. This is reflected by the vast literature on models, implementations, formats and appropriate representations (cf. e.g. Guarino 1995, Smith 1995, Newell 1982, Kuipers 1979).

2.2   On Thesauri

While in ontologies statements are made about the entities of the world with no or limited reference to their linguistic realizations, a thesaurus deals with expressions of a particular language. Unlike an alphabetically ordered lexicon, the structural basis of a thesaurus is given by lexical or semantic fields, i.e. sets of expressions that are connected by some lexical or semantic relationship. Linguistic expressions are interrelated by taxonomic principles as part-whole or abstract-generic relations. Among other criteria, the lexical relations of synonymy and polysemy play a distinctive role since they describe the relation between lexical signs and their corresponding expressions. If an expression has to be interpreted as referring to more than one concept (or lexical sign), then it is a polysem. If one concept is represented by more than one expression then these are synonymous.

For documentation purposes, thesauri are restricted to provide controlled vocabularies for indexing and retrieval. The indexer is forced to map document references to thesaurus terms which are called *descriptors*, then (cf. e.g. Ferber 1997, Schmitz-Esser 1992, Weinberg 1995).

3   How Knowledge Is Engineered

By observational criteria, a multi-lingual team of experts derives concepts from general communication in the mass media. Each concept will be validated by empirical means. The team, then, finds equivalent expressions in English, German, French, and Spanish. The process of concept identification is performed in any of our four languages. The assignment of appropriate expressions, however, is performed in parallel. We restricted ourselves to these four languages because by these we can reach about 80% of all users of the internet.

The essential condition to be met in the mapping of linguistic expressions to concepts is the discovery of a *descriptor* i.e. to find a specific expression that denotes a single concept in a clear and unambiguous way. In fact, there may be more than one expression for the concept in question, then the least marked will be chosen as descriptor for that concept. Other, alternative expressions are mapped to the concept as well, but as synonymous expressions to the descriptor. These expressions provide alternative ways of expressing a particular concept. In our retrieval model, they are therefore called *Additional Access Expressions* (AAEs). Figure 1 may help to clarify these relationships.

The linguistic expressions of either of the four languages that denote a single concept are mapped together on the *Equivalence Chain of Descriptors* (ECD). We require every descriptor on that chain to be equivalent to any other with respect to meaning and usage. The concept itself is represented by a *Meta Language Identification Number* (MLIN). As a side-effect, our approach offers a solution for the problem of conceptual gaps. If a concept has no unequivocal expression in a particular language, then a clear-cut paraphrasal definition will be found to enter the network, instead.

If a single expression refers to different concepts, we face the problem of polysemy, i.e. there will be an additional link to every concept it denotes. Disambiguation is not the point here, rather ambiguities will be resolved during runtime of a particular application.

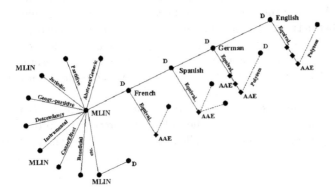

Fig.1. The Equivalence Chain of Descriptors

Any of these concepts are conceived of as universal objects of thought and as independent of a particular language. The concepts are structured according to a set of about a dozen well-defined ontological relations, stating e.g. whether a concept (e.g. *certification of digital signatures*) denotes a process is applied in another (e.g. *authenticity of the digital signature*) or stating that *coastal pollution* is detrimental to *coastal fishery* (see list below).

The structuring of validated contextual information by our set of ontological relations leads to a conceptual network, similar to the ones described by Sowa (1994). Certain criteria known from KL-ONE (cf. e.g. Brachman & Schmolze 1985, Brachman 1979) such as the distinction beween terminological and assertional knowledge are realized our approac has well.

The network is constituted of below set of relations. If necessary, this set can be easily adjusted to other specific purposes.

1. Abstract-Generic Relation: is narrower concept of / is broader concept of
2. Partitive (physical & theoretical) Relation: is part of / has elements
3. Part-Whole (Law & Jurisdiction) Relation: underlies the rules of / determines the rules of
4. Geographic-Partitive Relation: is space of / consists of spaces
5. Descendancy Relation: generates / comes from
6. Instrumental Relation: is instrumental for / by instruments
7. Cause Effect Relation: caused, may be caused by / causes, may cause
8. Benificial Relation: profits from / is beneficial for
9. Detrimental Relation: is harmed by / is detrimental to
10. Matter Relation: matter of / consists of
11. Form and Appearance: shapes the appearance of / appears as

12. Process Relation: involves process / process applied in
13. State Relation: exists in the form of / is form of existence of

Three relations, namely "Matter", "Form and Appearance" and "State" are actually not included in our descriptions due to the fact that these require philosophical investigation. Apart from these, such a general information structure is a fine description of some kind of factual knowledge about the world. This general structure is extended by an additional layer. We defined an independent hierarchy of semantic categories. This extra layer serves as a meta-structure for any entry of our ontology. This allows us to model so-called inconsistent knowledge in a simple but conceivable way. Inferences drawn on the extra-layer hold logically while inferences on the ontological level may hold by human interpretation acts.

```
telecommuting ...

is used for               (0)   telework
                          (0)   distance work

is narrower concept of    (3)   labour
                          (0)   new ways of working and living
                          (0)   working and living with the data net

is instrumental for       (4)   organizing work effectively

causes                    (5)   flexible working time
                          (2)   lower fixed costs of workplaces
                          (0)   reduction of commuting demand
                          (5)   energy conservation

is beneficial for         (0)   virtual enterprises
                          (0)   exploitation of data nets
                          (1)   combining family and work
                          (0)   stress alleviation

is detrimental to         (0)   face-to-face contacts

by instruments            (0)   telecommuting workplaces
                          (0)   telecommuters
                          (0)   online technology

underlies the rules of    (0)   liability in telecommuting
                          (0)   operational risk of telecommuting
                          (1)   work contracts

is broader concept of     (0)   mobile telecommuting
                          (0)   alternating telecommuting
```

The structure outlined above represents the universal part of our ontology. So far, our model owes a lot to classical, thesaurus-based approaches in information retrieval. Since various lexical information is included as well, we introduced the name LEXICOSAURUS. The next step to extend the lexicosaurus to become a practicable ontology is the incorporation of references to real world entities. An entity can be seen as an instance of a universal. Schmitz-Esser (1999) defined a Basic Semantic Reference Structure (BSRS) to do so. This is a template similar to a common questionnaire of documentation technology.

Table1. A Sample BSRS

WHAT	WHO	EVENT NAME	WHERE	ASPECT	WHEN	URL	...
telecom-muting work-places	Rehm & Haps AG	*name of system* Geowork	global	user	1999–	...	...
telecom-muting work-places	Small Business Consultants, Inc. AG	*name of facility* SBC Center	Cleveland, Ohio	counseling	1996–	...	...
telecom-muting work-places	Home Office Ergonomics, Ltd.	*name of product line* Ergoline Furniture	Montreal, Canada	supply	–1997	...	...
telecom-muting work-places	L. E. G. A. L.	*name of publication series* Telework Alert	London, U.K.	counseling	2000–	...	...
telecom-muting work-places	Parenting Group	*name of event* PG Self-Help Meeting	Hull, Quebec	initiative	2000 12 01 17:00	...	...

Table 1 is a simple representation of such a questionnaire. It may be posed as *What?*, *Who?*, *Event?*, *Where?*, and *When?* questions. Each BSRS-tuple is controlled by an aspect. It is the aspect that governs the desired interpretation. E.g. the third line reads as "Home Office Ergonomics, Ltd. supplies telecommuting workplaces; their product is known as Ergoline Furniture which was available in Montreal, Canada, up to 1997". In addition, ontological links may be drawn between BSRS-tuples, e.g. to state that *deforestation* in *Amazon region* causes/may cause *desertification* in *Africa East of Sahara*.

Lexicosaurus and BSRS together build up a well-defined semantic network. Due to its multi-lingual approach it serves as a knowledge representation structure for a bunch of applications, some of which will be described below. Beside the semantic representation scheme, inferences may be drawn by a set of rules that describe linguistic regularities. That is the conceptual basis for the name of our technology: SERUBA is a SEmantic, RUle BAsed approach.

4 Linguistic Rules

In building our ontology with a multi-lingual team of experts, we employ a compositional principle to derive corresponding expressions that refer to more specific concepts from more general ones (and vice versa). The compositional principle may lead to phrasal expressions where the head of the whole constituent is given by an expression referring to a broader concept. While the expressions may be compositional, the concepts are not. So, we employ a holistic view and do not derive complex concepts from primitives. For some smart inferences we map top level concepts to some basic semantic features (cf. e.g. Katz & Fodor 1963).

While many concepts allow different ways to be expressed, a paradigm generator copes for inflectional variants. Instead of collecting fully inflected word forms, and instead of mapping them to each other, we implemented a syncretistic model as has been described by Bleiching et al. (1996). Word forms that can be contracted to form a compound word and compounds that can be divided into smaller parts are handled as well (cf. Lüngen et al. 1996, Althoff et al. 1996). Beside these word-level oriented features, we parse complex expressions and insert appropriate Boolean or metrical operators at constituent boundaries to enhance our search queries. Such devices are crucial for improving results of internet search engines.

5 Application Scenarios

5.1 How SERUBA Can Improve Full-Text Retrieval

The conceptual network provides a simple and general scheme for users to navigate in thought spaces. A user can start by typing in a keyword that describes his search interest. Then, he will be able to trace the network whereby he can stop at any point of interest either to initiate an internet search or to continue. Due to the multi-lingual knowledge base, such a navigation can support conceptual language learning.

When an internet search is initiated, the descriptor will be expanded by its corresponding synonyms. In addition, by sets of linguistic rules, the expressions are interpreted and further expanded according to inflection and syntactic dependencies. The linguistic rules generate appropriate search queries that include Boolean and metric operators, as well.

5.2   How SERUBA Can Support the Indexer

In general, the lexicosaurus provides semantic control by offering a controlled, multi-lingual vocabulary for indexing. But our approach can serve even more specifc needs. The indexer can identify instances of universals, e.g. corporate names, certain types of events etc., and he can put them together in a single proposition. The BSRS template requires to state how these instances relate to universals. In addition, ontological links can be established to denote relations between BSRS tuples.

Since our overall approach is available in four languages, the indexer can choose any of our languages for indexing while the retrieval is not bound to a specific one of these. So, if many indexers work together in a multi-lingual environment they can choose any of the four languages according to their own preferences. For retrieval, the user can query the database in any of the four languages.

5.3   How SERUBA Can Support Automatic Indexing

The conceptual network offers a highly elaborated knowledge base for automatic indexing by context-based term clustering methods (cf. e.g. Agirre et al. 2000). Clusters can be mapped to concepts of the network. For the retrieval task, appropriate translations for index terms are available immediately. As a side-effect, retrieval requests can be formulated in any of the four languages. Documents will be selected on the basis of their assignment to a subset of the network.

6   A Final Note

The company was founded in Hamburg, Germany, in 1999 by a team of linguists and internet specialists. Our aim is to make internet searches easier and to improve the quality of the results. By the end of 2000, we expect our conceptual network to have grown up to some hundreds of thousand entries. A preliminary version of our system will be accessible online by spring 2001.

References

[2000]Agirre, Eneko; Ansa, Olatz; Hovy, Eduard and Martinez, David (2000). "Enriching very large ontologies using the WWW." In: *Proceedings of the Ontology Learning Workshop*. 14th European Conference on Artificial Intelligence, ECAI-2000, Berlin.

[1996]Althoff, Frederek; Drexel, Guido; Lüngen, Harald; Pampel, Martina and Schillo, Christoph (1996). "The Treatment of Compounds in a Morphological Component for Speech Recognition." In: Gibbon (Ed.) 1996: 71–76.

[1996]Bleiching, Doris; Drexel, Guido and Gibbon, Dafydd (1996). "Ein Synkretismusmodell für die deutsche Morphologie." In: Gibbon (Ed.) 1996: 237–248.

[1979]Brachman, Ronald J. (1979). "On the epistemological status of semantic networks." In: Findler (Ed.) 1979: 3–50.

[1985]Brachman, Ronald J. and Schmolze, James G. (1985). "An Overview of the KL-ONE Knowledge Representation System." In: *Cognitive Science*, 1985, 9: 171–216.

[1987]Croft, Bruce W. (1987). "Approaches to Intelligent Information Retrieval" In: *Information Processing and Management*, 1987, 23: 249–254.

[1998]Fellbaum, Christiane (Ed.) (1998). *WordNet. An electronic lexical database.* Cambridge, Mass. MIT.

[1997]Ferber, Reginald (1997). "Automated Indexing with Thesaurus Descriptors: A Co-occurrence based Approach to Multilingual Retrieval." In: Peters, C. and Thanos, C. (Eds.) (1997). *Research and Advanced Technology for Digital Libraries. Proceedings of the first European Conference on Research and Advanced Technology for Digital Libraries.* ECDL'97 Pisa, September 1997.

[1979]Findler, Norman J. (Ed.) (1979). *Associative Networks. Representation and Use of Knowledge by Computers.* New York: Academic Press.

[1996]Gibbon, Dafydd (Ed.) (1996). *Natural Language and Speech Technology. Results of the 3rd KONVENS Conference.* Bielefeld, October 1996. Berlin, etc.: Mouton de Gruyter.

[1992]Gödert, Winfried; Jaenecke, Peter and Schmitz-Esser, Winfried (Eds.) (1992). *Kognitive Ansätze zum Ordnen und Darstellen von Wissen. 2. Tagung der Deutschen ISKO Sektion einschliesslich der Vorträge des Workshops "Thesauri als Werkzeuge der Sprachtechnologie".* Weilheim, 15.-18.10.1991. Frankfurt/Main: Indeks-Verlag.

[1995]Guarino, Nicola (1995). "Formal Ontology, Conceptual Analysis and Knowledge Representation." In: *International Journal of Human Computer Studies*, 1995, 43, 5/6: 625–640.

[1963]Katz, J.J. and Fodor, J.A. (1963). "The structure of semantic theory." In: *Language*, 1963, 39: 170–210.

[1979]Kuipers, Benjamin (1979). "On representing commonsense knowledge." In: Findler (Ed.) 1979: 393–408.

[1990]Lenat, Douglas B. and Guha, R.V. (1990). *Building large knowledge-based systems.* Reading, Mass.: Addison-Wesley.

[1996]Lüngen, Harald; Pampel, Martina; Drexel, Guido; Gibbon, Dafydd; Althoff, Frederek and Schillo, Christoph (1996). "Morphology and Speech Technology." In: *Computational Phonology in Speech Technology. Second Meeting of the ACL Special Interest Group in Computational Phonology. Proceedings of the Workshop. 28 June, 1996.* Santa Cruz, California, USA: University of California (Published by the Association for Computational Linguistics), 25–30.

[1982]Newell, Alan (1982). "The Knowledge Level." In: *Artificial Intelligence*, 1982, 18: 87–127.

[in prep.]Schmitz-Esser, Winfried (in prep.). "SERUBA – A New Search and Learning Technology for the Internet and Intranets." In: Soergel, Dagobert (Ed.) (in prep.). *Proceedings of the 11th ASIS Classification Research Workshop.* 63rd Annual Meeting of ASIS, November 13–16, 2000, Chicago, IL (American Society for Information Science Special Interest Group on Classification Research, ASIS SIG/CR).

[2000]Schmitz-Esser, Winfried (2000). *EXPO INFO 2000.* Berlin, Heidelberg: Springer.

[1999]Schmitz-Esser, Winfried (1999). "Thesaurus and Beyond: An Advanced Formula for Linguistic Engineering and Information Retrieval." In: *Knowledge Organization*, 1999, 26, 1: 10–22.

[1992]Schmitz-Esser, Winfried (1992). "Neue Anwendungsgebiete für Thesauri: Thesauri als Werkzeuge der Sprachtechnologie." In: Gödert; Jaenecke & Schmitz-Esser (Eds.) 1992: 252–257.

[1995]Smith, Barry (1995). "Formal Ontology, Commonsense and Cognitive Science." In: *International Journal of Human Computer Studies*, 1995, 43, 5/6: 626–640.

[1984]Sowa, John F. (1984). *Conceptual Structures: Information Processing in Mind and Machine*. Reading, Mass.: Addison-Wesley.

[1995]Weinberg, B.H. (1995). "Library classification and information retrieval thesauri: comparison and contrast." In: *Cataloguing and Classification Quarterly*, 1995, 19, 3/4: 23–44.

Is Peritext a Key for Audiovisual Documents? The Use of Texts Describing Television Programs to Assist Indexing

Karine Lespinasse and Bruno Bachimont

Institut national de l'audiovisuel, Bry-sur-Marne, France,
{klespinasse} {bbachimont} @ina.fr,
http://www.ina.fr/Recherche

Abstract. In the INA (Institut national de l'audiovisuel, the French National Broadcasting Institute), indexers work on audiovisual document retrieval. Because of the problem of variability and cost in the indexing process, we are trying to provide new assistance to access the audiovisual document by introducing new textual information on the digital support.

1 Texts as an Access to Audiovisual Documents

INA (Institut national de l'audiovisuel, the French National Broadcasting Institute) is in charge of archiving and exploiting radio and television documents; the television collection excedes 2 million documents (news, series, magazines...).

The task of archiving in the INA aims at document retrieval and reexploitation, for firstly the consultation of audiovisual materials by researchers and secondly the use of archives for the production of new programs.

Our definition of a document as *a content being published within a concrete form* insists on the document being the result of a deliberate modeling. For example in the INA, a document is a stored memory equivalent to the content of a TV program, whereas a broadcaster defines it as an element of the broadcasting program, considering content, advertisements...

The archiving point of view is inscribed in metadata added to audiovisual documents. In general, documents are described in free text (analysis, summary) and in controlled vocabularly (keywords, thesaurus).

Now why are words used to search videos? Because language is a functional system based on auto-normative units, eg. splitable by blanks. This characteristics allows either to build up indexes or to normalize the defined units, or to compute them. There isn't anything like a dictionary of images, each image having at least one precise meaning, as it exists for lexical units.

Lots of texts exist in fact, from the birth of the audiovisual document (scenario, summary...) to its broadcasting (newspaper articles...), that we call *peritexts*. Retrieval is currently operated on textual indexing metadata. They represent the point of view stating how the audiovisual document is relevant for a given usage, eg. a review indicating how interesting a program is for a category of spectators.

A. Gelbukh (Ed.): CICLing 2001, LNCS 2004, pp. 505–506, 2001.
© Springer-Verlag Berlin Heidelberg 2001

Nowadays, digital technologies open new access to audiovisual documents. Metadata (indexes, texts) can be directly integrated in a digital document, which implies for audiovisual documents that additional information can be aligned to the video; sound track, copyright information, keywords on segments or even on images...

If texts are the key to audiovisual documents, we need to set up a typology of texts to characterize their relationship to audiovisual documents in order to work on a methodology for the constitution and processing of textual corpora. And how can we use peritext to assist indexing?

Two experiments about political programs brought us first results.

2 Experiments with Different Peritexts

The first experiment, presented in [2000], consisted in lexicometrical tests on made-by-INA-indexers archive descriptions.

The second experiment is based on *L'Heure de Vérité* (*The Hour of Truth*) a political magazine where a few journalists interview one guest. We collected the transcription of 63 magazines *L'Heure de Vérité*, typing the sound tracks. The resulting texts were tagged through a XML DTD.

The first analysis consists in a comparison with other political magazines, in order to compare their internal structures and to realise text-video alignments. Having a close alignment would allow more precise searches, aligning different textual information, new access to the audiovisual document [1999]. The second track is based on terminological extraction. The problem then lies not so much in word-audiovisual segment alignment, but rather in the passage from word in context to concepts and the way to link them to audiovisual segments. An evaluation with INA indexers is being set up.

Yet, one difficulty that emerged now remains: the unavailability of digital texts. Indeed if we acknowledged that there are numerous texts linked to television programs, it also appears that very few are in digital format. Besides, few works have met the question of the text-audiovisual relationship [1994]. Therefore, in the next experiments, we will concentrate on proposing a typology or at least definitory elements of profiles of texts in relation to audiovisual documents.

Acknowledgements: My grateful thanks to S. Aslanides for proofreading this text.

References

[1999] Auffret G. et al., "Audiovisual-based Hypermedia Authoring: using structured representations for efficient manipulation of AV documents, Hypertext and Hypermedia 99", Darmstadt, ACM Press. (Feb 1999), 169–178

[1988] Bachimont B., "Bibliothèques numériques audiovisuelles". Document numérique: 3-4. **2** (1988), 219–242

[2000] Lespinasse K. et al., "Le péritexte, un sésame pour les données audiovisuelles?" JADT 2000, Lausanne (2000), vol 1, 65–72

[1994] Srihari R. K., "Computational models for integrating linguistic and visual information: a survey", AIR. (1994), 1–24

An Information Space Using Topic Identification for Retrieved Documents

David Escorial

Natural Language Laboratory,
Center for Computer Research (CIC), National Polytechnic Institute (IPN),
Avda. Juan de Dios Bátiz, CP 07738, Zacatenco Mexico City, Mexico
escorial@cic.ipn.mx

Abstract. We present a model of an Information Space (IS) that combines the Vector Space Model (VSM) with conceptual hierarchies for Information Retrieval (IR). This model will allow navigating between both representations helping the user in the retrieval process. The goal is to filter the documents the user is interested based on the theme.

Topic Identification in Retrieved Documents. The retrieval of a set of documents based on conventional Information Retrieval (IR) methods has several problems. We will consider the case of massive full text document bases without summaries or any other kind of meta-information about the texts themselves (e.g. World Wide Web). The model described in this paper not only determines the main topics for the retrieved documents, but it will allow navigation between documents using similarities based in keywords and topics.

Information Space. We can define an Information Space (IS) as *a set of items held by an information system and the relations among them* [1]. The IS metaphor allows to implement concepts like closer and farther information units as well as navigate from one to another.

Basically an IS must have the following characteristics:

1. An internal model to represent the knowledge about the information. This model should contain the necessary knowledge about the information bases to be useful for particular user tasks (IR, document browsing, natural language questions, etc.).
2. An interface for the user to access the IS: such as queries, navigational procedures, retrieval options, etc. Usually, the information needs of the user are represented in the same formalism as the internal model.
3. An interface to the information bases. From the previous *spatial* metaphor, the information units are *located* within the space. There are some required mechanisms to locate the information pieces in this space.

A Hybrid Model for an Information Space. The model is based on two different submodels: the Vector Space Model (VSM) [2], and conceptual hierarchies [3]. The task orientation of the former one is Information Retrieval, since the conceptual

A. Gelbukh (Ed.): CICLing 2001, LNCS 2004, pp. 507–508, 2001.

hierarchies formalism are more suitable for Document Classification and Subject Indexing.

The combination of both models will produce the following sequence of retrieval:

1. Retrieval of documents using keywords based on the full set of terms indexing (using the VSM).
2. Identification of the main topics for the first *N-ranked* documents (using the concept hierarchy model).
3. At this point the user could have recognised what are the interesting documents (filtering the ones not containing the interested topics). Another option for the user is to determine the main relevant topics, and then, to ask for documents with the **similar main topics** (based on the closest to the *ideal documents* of the topics) and/or **similar to a particular *prototype document*** (considering all the terms, i.e. the full vector space).

We will describe in detail step number three. The first *K-ranked* documents on the main relevant topics are selected (we can assume that a topic to be relevant must be higher than a certain threshold, and they can be limited up to a number three or four topics). Then, using these close-topic documents, a measure of the distance to the *prototype document* is established based on keywords. This *prototype document* could be chosen by the user or just be taken the first one from the *K-ranked* list. Finally, the new filtered documents are presented to the user. The query mechanism can be implemented in different ways: sequentially (as above), straight forward (where the user defines previously the relevant topics from a list) or even in an iterative way (repeating the process until a satisfactory result is obtained).

The rationale behind the previous process is to narrow the search using two different strategies: a query composed of keywords and topic identification of the retrieved documents. We will obtain not only the results from a term to term relationship (VSM), but also a view of the topics involved in the documents. In such a way it is possible to obtain documents after the filtering process that where not relevant at step three. These documents are important to the user attending to topic criteria and also similar to a certain chosen document.

Information Spaces can be considered as black boxes. They are defined for specific tasks and they contain generic interfaces. In this case, the final task is to be helpful for the user in the IR process. More complex Information Spaces can be created in order to retrieve from heterogeneous bases or to compose elaborated user interfaces.

References

1. Newby, G. B.: An investigation of the role of navigation for information retrieval. In Proc. of the American Society for Information Science Annual Meeting. Medford, NJ: Learned Information (1992).
2. Salton, G. and McGrill, M.J.: Introduction to Modern Information Retrieval. McGraw Hill (1983).
3. Gelbukh A., Sidorov, G., Guzmán-Arenas, A.: A method of describing document contents through Topic Selection. In Proc. of 6th International Symposium on String Processing and Information Retrieval, SPIRE'99 (1999) 73-80.

Contextual Rules for Text Analysis

Dina Wonsever[1] Jean-Luc Minel[2]

[1] Instituto de Computación, Facultad de Ingeniería, Universidad de la República
Herrera y Reissig 565 11300 MONTEVIDEO URUGUAY
Tel.: 598 2 711 42 44/103 Fax: 5982 711 04 69
wonsever@fing.edu.uy

[2] CAMS Équipe LALIC UMR 8557 - CNRS / EHESS / Université Paris Sorbonne
96, Bd Raspail 75006 PARIS FRANCE
Tel.: 01 44 39 89 50 Télécopie: 01 44 39 89 51
minel@msh-paris.fr

Abstract. In this paper we describe a rule-based formalism for the analysis and labelling of texts segments. The rules are contextual rewriting rules with a restricted form of negation. They allow to underspecify text segments not considered relevant to a given task and to base decisions upon context. A parser for these rules is presented and consistence and completeness issues are discussed. Some results of an implementation of this parser with a set of rules oriented to the segmentation of texts in propositions are shown.

1 Introduction

In this paper we describe a rule-based formalism for the analysis and consequent labelling of texts segments. The rules are contextual: they allow identifying a portion of text that has to be labelled as a function of itself and, eventually, of a portion of text that precedes it (left context) and/or of a portion of text that follows it (right context). A portion of text satisfies the condition that allows the labelling by means of a rule if it includes certain elements (words, punctuation marks, portions of texts previously labelled) in a specific order. The rule determines what are the elements that have to be present and the order between them. These elements have not always to be contiguous. Intercalated between them there can be other portions of text for which the rule only states the maximum size and a list of elements that these portions of text must not contain.

In section 2 we describe the background that causes the introduction of this kind of rules. They were thought as a tool for specific goal-directed text processing tasks, mainly in Contextual Exploration systems. In section 3 we present in detail rules main features, the underlying text model, some examples and the results of the analysis obtained from a running system that fully implements them.

In section 4 a deductive system for an inactive right-corner chart parser for contextual rules is presented. A search strategy for ensuring consistency and completeness is proposed and all these concepts are briefly discussed.

Finally, some lines for future work are mentioned.

A. Gelbukh (Ed.): CICLing 2001, LNCS 2004, pp. 509–523, 2001.
© Springer-Verlag Berlin Heidelberg 2001

2   Background

Text analysis and information extraction from texts is a widespread need in our days. The increasing availability of very large quantities of textual information poses a challenge for new tools and capabilities from the field of natural language processing. Many of the requirements do not require a complete analysis of texts. They are goal-oriented: there is an objective to fulfil and textual information sources need to be analysed only in terms of this objective. While sometimes the process of text analysis needs to incorporate domain dependent knowledge in order to accomplish the desired task, it has also shown to be highly productive to analyse texts in a goal-oriented way on the basis of general domain-independent linguistic knowledge.

Information Extraction systems as seen in MUC Conferences [12] are an example of the first kind of goal-oriented systems. In this case the goal is the extraction of a particular kind of information from texts. MUC-3 focused on information about terrorist incidents; MUC-5 on information about enterprise joint ventures.

The Contextual Exploration Methodology developed by Lalic group [8], [9] is a linguistically motivated research line with relevant achievements that represents the second mentioned kind of goal-oriented text processing systems.

The rules system presented in this paper is a tool for the description and analysis of texts under the goal-oriented hypothesis. Only information relevant to a specific task needs to be described and decisions can be made based on relations between relevant items and contextual ones (i.e., items that are present in the co-text). In next section we describe in more detail the contextual exploration methodology, which greatly inspired our rules.

Contextual Exploration Methodology, proposed and developed by Jean-Pierre Desclés and his team, is based upon the observation that several textual processing tasks [4], such as knowledge extraction or automatic summarising, may be solved by analysing exclusively units in texts, provided that their linguistic context is taken into account. For example, cognitive observations of professional summarisers have shown that they use textual, structural, thematic and lexical markers in their search strategies. Furthermore, various linguistic works on text analysis ([1], [6], [23], [24]) have shown the interest in identifying and locating linguistic markers and their combinations in order to lend meaning to textual units. Textual processing calls for identifying and studying the semantics of textual categories involved in texts that are independent of the text domain (medical, economical, technical, etc.). As a result, causality ([10], [14], [15]), definition [5], thematic announcement [4] have been studied under this perspective. All of these categories are not at the same level. Some of them like causality rely on a cognitive model [14], whereas others like thematic announcement are based on empirical observations of textual organization.

3   Contextual Rules

Text is the input to contextual rules. In what follows we define a computational model of (written) text, under which operate our rules.

3.1   A Model of Text

The basic units of a text are its words (or lexical units) and punctuation marks occurrences. As usual, we use the term *token* for designing each of these occurrences of textual units. Tokens occur in a specific order in a given text. Taking account of these elements, a text may be directly modelled by a finite sequence over the set of all words and punctuation marks. We call this model *T0*.

T0 : T = $w_1...w_n$, where n is the *length* of text T and w_i , $1 \le i \le n$, are its tokens

But usually there is more information in texts, mainly structural organization (titles, paragraphs, sections, etc.) and presentation features that distinguish some portions of texts of other ones. If we want to consider this information it is necessary to extend the basic model of text.

Also, different processes may add information to text. For instance, a tagger adds a morpho-syntactic category to each word. It is desirable to be able to represent all this information in a homogeneous form.

These considerations lead us to an extension *T1* to our initial model *T0*. We consider that all structural, presentational, syntactic, semantic, etc. information that is initially present in a text *T* or that may be added to it is essentially a qualification over a subsequence of text: i.e., a contiguous segment of text. Consequently, we propose a model where the basic component is a segment of text and its label. We represent a segment of text with a pair of indices denoting its first and last positions, whereas positions denote inter-token places.

A text *T* is then modelled (under *T1*) by a finite set *Γ*, defined as follows:

Let T be a text with n tokens and additional qualifying elements. Each token is a word or punctuation mark from a set Σ (the lexicon). Let N be the set of all additional labels that can be used to qualify segments in T and V = N ∪Σ the total set of labels. We assume that N ∩ Σ=Φ and that V is a finite set.

We define:

1. A *span* in T is a pair *(i,j)* of integers, $0 \le i \le j \le n$. The span (i,j) *contains* the span (k,l) if i ≤ k and l ≤ j. A *partition* of size *n* of span (i,j) is a set of n distinct spans (k_1 , k_2) ,(k_2 ,k_3),..., (k_n ,k_{n+1}) with i=k_1 , j=k_{n+1}
2. An *extent* in T is a pair *[s, L]*, where *s* is a span in T and *L* an element of V.
3. *Γ* is a set of extents in T such that:
    a. for each token w in T in position i, [(i-1,i), w] ∈ Γ
    b. for each additional element with label *L* that qualifies the segment from position i to position j in T, [(i-1, j), L] ∈ Γ
    c. There are no more elements in Γ.

We will refer to a text by *T* or by *Γ*, depending on the model used. In first case we can only refer to its tokens. In both cases the length (n) of a text denotes its number of tokens.

Γ contains an extent for each token in T, and additional extents for the other pieces of information. It is a task for a linguist to correctly identify the different concepts underlying labels. Notice that different sets of extents can be obtained from the same text, depending on which is the information we choose to represent. In section 3.2.2, an example of Γ for a simple text can be found. A similar way for defining texts was proposed by Clarke *et al*. in their paper *An Algebra for Structured Text Search* [7].

3.2   Description of Contextual Rules

A contextual rule is an expression whose purpose is to identify and label portions of text. A portion of text gets labelled if it satisfies a condition that is a function of the same portion and, eventually, of a portion of text that precedes it (left context) and/or of a portion of text that follows it (right context). A portion of text satisfies the con- dition that allows the labelling if it includes certain elements (words, punctuation marks, portions of texts previously labelled) in a specific order. The rule determines what are the elements that have to be present and the order between them. These ele- ments have not always to be contiguous. Intercalated between them there can be other portions of text for which the rule only states the maximum size and a list of elements that these portions of text must not contain.

In what follows, we define all these notions in a precise way.

3.2.1 Syntax of Contextual Rules. Let V be a finite set of labels, a contextual rule over V is an expression of the form:

Label → *RightContext \ Body / LeftContext* ; *Sets Specification*

where:

-   Label ∈ V
-   RightContext, Body and LeftContext are strings with two types of elements : labels belonging to V and Exclusion Zones. RightContext is the string that follows the '/', LeftContext the string that precedes the '\' and Body the string that is between '\' and '/'.
-   RightContext and LeftContext may be empty, Body cannot be empty.
-   The string *RightContext.Body.LeftContext* ('.' stands for string concatenation) will be referred as the *condition* of the rule. In this string labels must surround any exclusion zone.
-   An exclusion zone is an expression with form *(ExcludedSet, Size)*, where *ExcludedSet* is the name of a set of labels and *Size* a natural number
-   SetsSpecification is the definition (by enumeration) of the sets mentioned in the exclusion zones of the rule. A set in *SetsSpecification* may be empty. Nev- ertheless, both labels surrounding the exclusion zone are considered to belong to it. If there are no Exclusion Zones, the part *SetsSpecification* is not present.

There is one additional constraint (the reason for this constraint will be discussed in section 4.4): Label cannot belong to any exclusion zone in the rule Label. This condition is checked prior to rule execution (at compilation time).

Below there is an example of a contextual rule:

CR : *relProp* → \ *relPron* *(S,5) *finVU* *(S,10) / *finVU; S={relPron, iniProp, finVU}* where:

- V = {relProp, relPron, finUV, iniProp},
- LeftContext is empty, RightContext is the string *finUV* and Body the string *relPron*(S,5) finVU *(S,10)*.
- CR has two Exclusion Zones: **(S,5)* and **(S,10)* with the same ExcludedSet (*S*). S is defined in the final part of the rule: *S={relPron,iniProp, finVU}*

The complete syntactic description of contextual rules in extended BNF notation is given in figure 1.

```
ContextualRule ::= label '→' Rhs (';' SetSpecs)?.
Rhs ::= '\' R '/' | R Oi R '/' | '\' R Od R | R Oi R Od R.
R ::= label ( ExZ label | label)*.
Oi ::= '\' (ExZ)? | (ExZ)? '\'.
Od ::= (ExZ)? '/' | '/' (ExZ)?.
SetSpecs ::= (SetSpec)+ .
SetSpec ::= identifier '=' '{' (label (',' label)*)? '}'.
ExZ ::= '*' '(' identifier ',' integer ')'.
```

Fig. 1. Syntax of contextual rules in EBNF

3.2.2 Meaning of Contextual Rules. We give meaning to sets of contextual rules in terms of the results of its application to texts. Let CR be a contextual rule over set V of labels, Γ a text of length n over V, α and Condition strings over $(V \cup (\text{ExclusionZones over } V))$ and (k,l) a span contained in $(0,n)$ over Γ, where:

$CR: L \rightarrow LeftContext \setminus Body / RightContext ; SetsSpec,$
$\text{Condition} = \text{LeftContext.Body.RightContext} = C_1,..., C_s$

We will define what does it mean that the span (k,l) satisfies the condition of the contextual rule CR and which are the elements that are added to the text. A span (k,l) may satisfy the *Condition* part of CR in more than one way, so we restrict our definition to a given partition of (k,l).

1. The span (k,l) *satisfies α for partition P* of size s of span (k,l), $P = \{t_1, ..., t_s\}$, if for all i between 1 and s the span t_i satisfies C_i, where:
    a. t_i *satisfies a label L* iff the extent $[t_i, L]$ belongs to Γ.
    b. $t_i = (k',l')$ *satisfies an exclusion zone *(S,n)* iff
        i. $n \geq k'-l'$ (the span is not greater than the size of the exclusion zone, measured in tokens)
        ii. $\forall L \in S$, there does not exist a span (i,j), $j \leq l'$, $j \geq k'$, such that (i,j) satisfies L
2. If span (k,l) satisfies the Condition part of contextual rule CR for partition P, with span (m,h) contained in (k,l) satisfying the first element in Body and span (r,s) contained in (k,l) satisfying its last element, a new extent $e = [(m,s), L]$ is derived.

3. We represent by the function $f_{CR,(k,l),P}$ the application of rule CR to text Γ for span (k,l) under partition P. It is defined by:
    i. $f_{CR,(k,l),P}(\Gamma) = \Gamma \cup \{e\}$ if there exists an extent e such that it is the extent derived (2) from Γ by rule CR with span (k,l) and partition P
    ii. $f_{CR,(k,l),P}(\Gamma) = \Gamma$ otherwise

We say that *text Γ derives in one step the extent e = [(m,h), L] with rule CR* if there exists a span *(r,s)* contained in *(0,n)* and a partition *P* of *(r,s)* such that *e* is the extent derived according to rule 2 for span *(r,s)* and partition *P*.

In a real situation we do not have only one rule but a set of rules SCR that interact between them. We define a relation $\Rightarrow_{SCR}$ between texts and extents. If $\Gamma \Rightarrow_{SCR} e$, we will say that the *extent e is derivable from Γ by means of rules SCR*. Given the set SCR, the resulting set is not unique: it depends on the order of application of rules and the spans choice. We define the derivation relation by means of a sequence of elementary one step derivations.

Let *SCR* be the set $\{CR_1,...,CR_n\}$. We say that $\Gamma \Rightarrow_{SCR} e$ if there exist a finite sequence $R = CRp1,...CRph$ of rules in SCR, a finite sequence $S = sp1,...,sph$ of spans contained in (0,n) and a finite sequence of partitions $P = Pp1,...Pph$, where each *Pi* is a partition of span *si*, such that: $\Gamma_{p1} = f_{CRp1,sp1,Pp1}(\Gamma)$, ..., $\Gamma_{ph} = f_{CRph,sph,Pph}(\Gamma_{p(h-1)})$ and $e \in \Gamma_{ph}$

Additional restrictions on rules or on a preferred order of application have to made in order to obtain independence of one step derivations order in the derivation of *all* results from Γ and SCR. Notice that, in the derivations of all possible results, the contexts in rules do not cause ambiguity problems (as occurs in the framework of finite state calculus with the replace operator defined by Kaplan and Kay [16]). But the negation that is implicit in Exclusion Zones makes the set of all results sensible to the order of elementary derivation steps. Related to this problem, one possibility that is being studied is the definition of a property of *stratification* for sets of contextual rules, similar to the property with same name defined by Lloyd [19] for normal logic programs.

In what follows, we illustrate some of the previous concepts by means of an example. Consider the following text:

The man that I have seen yesterday is your father.

with morpho-syntactic information added by a tagger at a previous stage of analysis. It is modelled by the following set of extents:

Γ = {[(0,1),The], [(1,2), man], [(2,3), that], [(3,4), I], [(4,5), have], [(5,6), seen], [(6,7), yesterday], [(7,8),is], [(8,9),your], [(9,10),father], [(10,11),.], [(0,1),det], [(1,2), noun], [(2,3), relPron], [(3,4), persPron], [(4,5),finAux], [(5,6), ppart], [(6,7),adverb], [(7,8),finVerb], [(8,9),poss], [(9,10),noun], [(10,11),punct], [(4,6), finVU], [(7,8), finVU] }

CR : *relProp* $\rightarrow$ \ *relPron* *(S,5) *finVU* *(S,10) / finVU; S={relPron,iniProp, finVU}*

If the contextual rule CR is applied to Γ we see that:

(i)   span (2,3) satisfies relPron
(ii)   span (3,4) satisfies the first exclusion zone: *(S,5)

(iii)   span (4,6) satisfies finVU
(iv)   span (6,7) satisfies the second exclusion zone: *(S,10)
(v)   span (7,8) satisfies finVU

By consequence, the condition part of rule CR is satisfied by span (2,8). As a result of the application of rule CR to Γ we obtain $\Gamma' = \Gamma \cup \{[(2,7), relProp]\}$. It is easy to see that there is only one span contained in (0,11) that satisfies the rule, the span (2,8). There is only one partition under which this span satisfies the rule.

Remarks

1- This example is just for explanatory purposes, and we do not claim that rule RC is an adequate description of any class of relative propositions in English. However, it is worth noticing that a similar rule has been included in a system for the segmentation of French texts in propositions (figure 2 shows the output of this system for a news text) and the results are quite satisfactory.
2- Morpho-syntactic categories names intend to be auto-explanatory.
3- Rule RC cover a variety of cases. For instance, the relative propositions embedded in the sentences:
   The man that I have seen yesterday in the park is your father.
   The man that John and Mary have seen five minutes ago is your father.
   would be recognized by this rule.
4- Finally, although the information used in the previous example is mainly morpho-syntactic, this is not a restriction in the system. Labels may denote semantic, pragmatic, textual organization information and rules can be stated on the basis of these categories.

Antarctique -médecin -USA WELLINGTON -
[prop p8/ Le médecin américain de la station de recherche Amundsen -Scott , au pôle sud [relProp prl3/ , qui se traite elle-même contre un cancer du sein depuis le mois de juillet , /relProp prl3] va pouvoir être évacué par un avion militaire américain [relProp prl2/ qui est parvenu à atterrir samedi sur la base [relProp prl1/ où règne une température de proche de 50 degrés celsius /relProp prl1] /relProp prl2] /prop p8]   (Agence France Presse, 16/10/1999)

Fig. 2. Segmentation in propositions of a French text.

Recursive structures arise naturally in natural language analysis. In particular, recursion is essential in the segmentations of texts in propositions. In figure 2, we show a French text (news from *France-Presse* agency) with the propositions retrieved by our system. *P8, prl1, prl2* and *prl3* are the names of the rules that have been used. We present and describe briefly rules *prl1* and *prl2*:

*prl1 : relProp → \ relPron *(S,20) finVU *(S,20) / sent; S={vu, iniProp}*
*prl2 : relProp → \ relPron *(S,20) finVU *(S,20) relProp *(S,10) / sent; S={vu, iniProp}*

The two rules (*prl1* and *prl2*) label relative propositions The first one states roughly that a text segment is a relative proposition (*relProp*) if it starts with a relative pronoun (*relPron*), it contains a finite verbal unit (*finUV*), it ends at the end of the sentence (*sent*) and a condition about two zones is satisfied. These zones are the text segment between the relative pronoun and the finite verbal unit and the text segment between the verbal unit and the end of the sentence. Either of these zones is admissible as part of the relative proposition if it does not contain a text segment labelled as a verbal unit (*vu*) or as an initial part of a proposition (*iniProp*), and its size is less or equal than 20 (this is an empirical value, adjusted by testing). The second rule is similar to the first one, with the difference that it allows a kind of embedding of relative propositions. The set of rules for propositions is going to be used on a corpus of accident reports; the identification of clauses in such texts is a mandatory stage for a system [2], which aims at displaying a sequence of images by interpreting these texts.

4   A Logic for Text Analysis with Contextual Rules

4.1   Previous Work

Grammar systems have been viewed as deductive systems. This point of view is widely used in categorial grammars [19], [21]. Under this approach, inference rules mimic grammar rules and the parsing of a string is transformed into a deduction from the lexical categories of the input string.

Rewriting context free rules can also be seen as inference rules and parsing with these rules as a deductive process. Given a grammar, $G = (V, T, S, P)$, where V is the set of variables, T the set of terminals, S the start symbol and P the set of production rules [13] there is deduction of a string $w_1...w_n$ if the relation $S \Rightarrow w_1...w_n$ holds, where '$\Rightarrow$' is the reflexive and transitive closure of the derivation relation '$\rightarrow$' of production rules.

Shieber, Schabes and Pereira, in their paper *Principles and Implementation of Deductive Parsing* [25] propose a more fine-grained approach to parsing as deduction, with an explicit representation of input string positions in the atomic formulas of the logic. Following this line, we have developed a logic for parsing (i.e., analysing texts) with contextual rules.

In a similar way than in the deductive systems proposed by the mentioned authors, in our system inference rules have the form:

$$\frac{A_1 ... A_n}{B} \quad <side\ conditions\ on\ Ai, B>$$

The antecedents $A_1...A_n$ and the consequent B of an inference rule are formula schemata; they may contain syntactic metavariables to be instantiated by terms when the rule is used. A formula B can be *deduced* if it is obtained as the consequent of an inference rule after a finite number of applications of inference rules to axioms or other formulas deduced from the system. Axioms and inference rules must be provided in order to define a parsing logic. Definition of a goal is more related to control than to the deductive engine. In our case, the intention is to obtain all possible items that can be soundly deduced from axioms and inference rules and we do not define goals.

This view of parsing as deduction clarify details about the parsing process and sets a framework for the discussion of correctness and completeness of parsing algorithms and its relation with search strategies in the space of possible deductions.

4.2   Right-Corner Chart-Parsing and Contextual Rules

We present a logic for parsing with contextual rules. The parsing method is bottom-up with left to right scan of the input string and right to left scan of the right hand side of grammar rules. It is an inactive chart parser, with rules triggered by the rightmost symbol of the right hand side, i.e., the right corner. The right-corner chart parsing method for context free grammars has the following interesting property (under a breadth first search strategy): when processing a rule, a category exists if and only if it has been added to the chart.

4.3   A Logic for Right-Corner Inactive Chart Parsing for Contextual Rules

Let Γ be a text of length n over total set of labels V with token alphabet Σ, SCR a set of contextual rules over alphabet V. Letters i, j, i', j' denote inter-tokens position in Γ, $0 \leq i, i', j, j' \leq n$. In all formulas it holds $i \leq i'$, $j' \leq j$, additional constraints are explicitely stated. We use greek letters $\alpha, \beta, \dots$ to denote substrings of the right hand side of a contextual rule, capital letters $A, B, \dots$ to denote elements of V.

The Atomic Formulas. We have two kinds of propositional atomic formula schemata.

$[i, A, j]$ - Inactive chart element of category A covering positions i to j of the input text. The intended meaning is that $\Gamma \Rightarrow_{SCR} [(i,j), A]$

$[i, i', A \rightarrow \alpha \bullet \beta, j', j]$ - Active chart element. $A \rightarrow \alpha.\beta$ is a rule in SCR. The dot signals the scanning position in the rule; the index i the scanning position in the input text and the index j the initial scanning position. The intended meaning is that there exists k, $i \leq k \leq j$ such that span (k, j) satisfies the string β', where β' is β without any slash ('\', '/') that it might content.

The Axioms. There is an axiom for each element (extent) present in the input text.

$[i, C, j]$, $0 \leq i < j \leq n$, $C \in V$

Axioms take the form of inactive items.

The Inference Rules. We define inference rules for triggering a contextual rule according to its rightmost symbol (predict), for processing a contextual rule (complete) and for generating new inactive items (active to inactive).

Rule P1 - Predict

$$\frac{[i, B, j] \qquad\qquad A \rightarrow \alpha B}{[j, j, A \rightarrow \alpha B \bullet, j, j]}$$

Rule P2 - Predict

$$\frac{[i, B, j] \qquad\qquad A \rightarrow \alpha B /}{[j, j, A \rightarrow \alpha B / \bullet, j, j]}$$

An inactive element labelled B triggers rules whose rightmost symbol is B (P1) or that end in the sequence B / (empty right context). In the first case B belongs to the right context. The complete rule is specialised according to the symbol that is being scanned (the symbol left to the dot).

Rule C1 - Complete

$$\frac{[i,\,i',\,A \to \alpha\,/\bullet\,\beta,\,j',\,j]}{[i,\,i',\,A \to \alpha\,\bullet\,/\,\beta,\,i,\,j]}$$

The forward slash signals the rightmost position of the rewriting zone, i.e., the last position of an element with label A if it is finally deduced.

Rule C2 - Complete

$$\frac{[i,\,i',\,A \to \alpha\,\backslash\bullet\,\beta,\,j',\,j]}{[i,\,i,\,A \to \alpha\,\bullet\backslash\,\beta,\,j',\,j]}$$

The backward slash signals the leftmost position of the rewriting zone, i.e., the first position of an element with label A if it is finally deduced.

Rule C3 - Complete

$$\frac{[i,\,i',\,A \to \alpha\;B\bullet\beta,\,j',\,j]\;\;[k,\,B,\,i]}{[k,\,i',\,A \to \alpha\;\bullet\,B\,\beta,\,j',\,j]}$$

Simple left completion. The scanning index i is modified to the start of the existing element the rule is seeking for.

Complete - C4 - Exclusion Zone. We represent exclusion zones in a compiled form, making explicit the previous label in the rule. This label acts as a cut for the exclusion zone. An exclusion zone in the rule has the form: $ex(S,C,N)$, where S is the name of the set of excluded labels, C the previous label in the rule and N the maximum size of the zone.

There are two rules for processing an exclusion zone.

Rule C4a - Complete

$$\frac{[i,\,i',\,A \to \alpha\;ex(S,C,N)\bullet\beta,\;j',\,j]\;\;[k,\,C,\,i]}{[k,\,i',\,A \to \alpha\;\bullet\,ex(S,C,N)\,\beta,\,j',\,j]}$$

Rule C4b - Complete

$$\frac{[i,\,i',\,A \to \alpha\;ex(S,C,N)\bullet\beta,\;j',\,j]\;\;\neg[k,\,C,\,i]\;\;\neg[k',C_i,i]}{[i1,\,i',\,A \to \alpha\;ex(S,C,N1)\bullet\beta,\,j',\,j]}$$

$$N>0,\;N1=N\text{-}1,\;i>1,\;i1=i\text{-}1,\;C_i\in S$$

In this rule, S is the set of excluded labels, C the cut label and N the maximum size of the zone. Under the absence of the cut label at current text position (index i), and the absence of each of the labels belonging to the excluded set, parsing proceeds with the scanning of the zone with maximum size $N1$, from string position $i1$, to the left. The side conditions ensure that we have not arrived to the maximum size of the zone ($N>0$) and that we have not arrived to the beginning of the input string ($i>1$).

Rule A1 - Active to Inactive

$$\frac{[i,\,i',\,A \to\,\bullet\,\alpha,\,j',\,j]}{[i',\,A,\,j']}$$

This rule creates inactive items from active but completed items (the dot is at the beginning of the right hand side). The new inactive item is labelled with the label A at the left-hand side and it spans positions i' to j' from input string.

Negative Elements. Negative information can not be deduced from axioms with inference rules having the form $A_1, ..., A_n \rightarrow B$, i.e., Horn clauses. As in the logic programming paradigm, negation should be understood as the failure in proving the corresponding positive information. That is, infer $\neg A$ under the failure in proving A. This is a condition about deductions in the system, and it is tested in our system by the side conditions of rules. It simply amounts to testing the non existence of inactive elements having the form $[k, A, i]$, $0 \leq k < i$.

Rule N1 - negative elements

$$\frac{\neg \exists \, [i, A, j] \, , \, 0 \leq i < j}{[i, A, j]}$$

To illustrate the behaviour of these inference rules we will present a deduction of a relative proposition with some rules and an input sentence.

R1: finVU → \ finVerb /
R2: finVU → \ finAux *(S, 2) partVerb /; S={}
R3 : relProp → \ relPron *(S,5) finUV *(S,10) / finUV; S={relPron,iniProp}

These rules are not realistic although they give some flavour of the intended purpose of our system. *finUV* stands for finite verbal unit, *finVerb* for verb in finite form, *finAux* for auxiliar in finite form, *partVerb* for past participle and *relPron* for relative pronoun. The input sentence : *The man that I have seen yesterday is your father.* gives rise to the axioms concerning the grammatical categories of lexical units shown in figure 3. We do not represent the axioms corresponding to the input tokens.

A1	[0, det, 1]	The
A2	[1, noun, 2]	man
A3	[2, relPron, 3]	that
A4	[3, perPron, 4]	I
A5	[4, finAux, 5]	have
A6	[5, partVerb, 6]	seen
A7	[6, adverb, 7]	yesterday
A8	[7, finVerb, 8]	is
A9	[8, det, 9]	your
A10	[9, noun, 10]	father
A11	[10, punct, 11]	.

Fig. 3. Axioms for the input sentence
The man that I have seen yesterday is your father.

In what follows, we present a step-by-step deduction of the relative proposition *that I have seen yesterday* in the example sentence.

1 [5, partVerb, 6] - Axiom A6 (*seen*)
2 [6, 6, finUV → \ auxFin *(S,2) partVerb /•, 6, 6] - Predict P2 from 1 and R2

3 [6, 6, finUV → \ auxFin *(S,2) partVerb • /, 6, 6] - Complete C1 from 2
4 [5, 6, finUV → \ auxFin *(S,2) • partVerb /, 6, 6] - Complete C3 from 3 and 1
5 [4, 6, finUV → \ • auxFin *(S,2) partVerb /, 6, 6] - Complete C4a from 4 and A5
6 [4, 4, finUV → • \auxFin *(S,2) partVerb /, 6, 6] - Complete C2 from 5
7 [4, finUV, 6] - (*have seen*) Active to inactive from 6
8-12 [7, finUV, 8] (*is*) from A8, Predict P2, Complete C1, C3 and C2, A-I
13 [8, 8, relProp → \ relPron *(S,5) finUV *(S,10) / finUV •, 8, 8] Predict P1 from 12
14 [7, 8, relProp → \ relPron *(S,5) finUV *(S,10) / • finUV, 8, 8] C3 from 13 and 12
15 [7, 8, relProp → \ relPron *(S,5) finUV *(S,10) • / finUV, 7, 8] C1 from 14
16 [6, 8, relProp → \ relPron *(S,5) finUV *(S,9) • / finUV, 7, 8] C4b from 15 and N1
17 [4, 8, relProp → \ relPron *(S,5) • finUV *(S,9) / finUV, 7, 8] C4a from 16 and 7
18 [3, 8, relProp → \ relPron *(S,4) • finUV *(S,9) / finUV, 7, 8] C4b from 17 and N1
19 [2, 8, relProp → \ • relPron *(S,5) finUV *(S,9) / finUV, 7, 8] C3 from 18 and A3
20 [2, 2, relProp → • \ relPron *(S,5) finUV *(S,9) / finUV, 7, 8] C2 from 19
21 [2, relProp, 7] (*that I have seen yesterday*) A1 from 20

All possible deductions from axioms with inference rules using grammar rules are computed. The results of successful applications of grammar rules are found under the form of inactive elements. Some deduction steps have been condensed (8 -12) and the use of inference rule N1 for negation is not explicitly shown.

4.4   Management of Exclusion Sets

The bottom-up right-corner chart parsing method was selected as best suited to manage possible inconsistencies that might arise from the use of negation in the exclusion zones of contextual rules.
Consider the following rule:

$A → \setminus B$ *(S,n) E/ ; S={D}*

In this rule, the right corner symbol is E, so the rule is triggered under recognition of E. Recognition guided by the rule proceeds in a right to left way. Next category to be recognised is *(S,n)*, that is, a text span of length not greater than n (possibly empty) without any occurrence of a label D. If all labels that may apply to the positions in text before E last position have been recognised, it is possible to decide for the non-occurrence of a label D. There remains, however, a problem related with the co-occurrence of negation of grammar symbols and contexts in the rules. Consider the following rules:

1. $A → B \setminus$ *(S,n)* /C ; S={D}
2. $D → B \setminus T / C X$

from configuration ... B T C X ... (extents [(i,j),B], [(j,k),T], [(k,l),C], [(l,m),X] belong to Γ) we can deduce, when processing symbol C (right corner for rule 1)

rule 1 ---→ ... B A C X ..., under the assumption there is not an extent with label D between B and C

and from rule 2, when processing its right corner X

rule 2 ----→ ... B D C X ... and conditions for deducing A from rule 1 are no longer valid !

In order to avoid this kind of inconsistency we restrict negation to categories whose deduction does not include rules with no empty context (see the constraints defined in section 3.2.1). In this way, under an adequate search strategy, all the information needed to conclude the non-existence of an extent in a text span is available when needed. In fact, if the chart does not contain an element for the corresponding label, it is sure to conclude its negation.

4.5   Search Strategies, Soundness, Completeness

The parsing logic defined in the previous section does not commit to any search strategy of deductions. Inactive items deduced by any possible search strategy are *correct*, as it holds that if there is a deduction for the inactive item [i, A, j], then $\Gamma \Rightarrow_{SCR} [(i,j), A]$. But not all strategies produce *consistent* results, in the sense given in previous section.. This happens because of the nature of the *negation as failure* [19] associated with the semantics of forbidden elements in exclusion zones. As labels that appear in exclusion zones cannot be deduced from rules with not empty context there is a search strategy that guarantees that negative items are present when needed. It corresponds to the following order for trying inference rules: *complete* (including *negation* when it is needed), *active to inactive* and *predict*. If there is various alternatives for applying *predict*, the inactive item with the least right index is chosen. In this way all the deductions (i.e. inactive items) necessary to correctly compute an exclusion zone are present when needed. Notice that as *complete* is the inference rule with higher priority at any stage of parsing there can be at most one application of *complete*, including *inactive to active* which is merely a form of *complete*.

As each new item that is inferred triggers the deduction of its possible consequences, the previously mentioned search strategy is also complete with respect to a relation of *consistent* derivation between texts and extents. The deduction process is not goal-directed and it naturally proceeds until no more rules can be applied. At the end of the process, all inferred elements could be found under the form of inactive items.

A parser for contextual rules has been implemented following the inference rules and the proposed search strategy.

5   Conclusions, Future Work

We have presented a new rule-based framework for analysing natural language texts. Its main features are that they provide context conditions for rule application and that they allow underspecification of text segments by means of a restricted form of negation. A bottom-up right-corner parser for these rules has been developed, relying on a definition of parsing as deduction.

Some extensions are being presently studied. In first place, an extension of atomic categories to structured terms in order to increase the rules expressive power. On the other side, efficiency and ambiguity issues are under consideration. It would be interesting to have a way to decide between competing parses for the same text segment. If this decision can be taken locally, there will be an increase in efficiency, as fewer items would be available for subsequent rules processing.

Acknowledgments. The authors wish to acknowledge the contribution of Professor Jean-Pierre Desclés in offering valuable suggestions and stimulating discussions during the course of this work.

This work has been developed with the support of an *ECOS* grant (French-Uruguayan cooperation) and a *Csic* grant (*Universidad de la República*, Uruguay).

References

1. Adam J.M.: *Éléments de linguistique textuelle*, Mardaga. Liège, (1990)
2. Battistelli D.: Passer du texte à une séquence d'images, analyse spatio-temporelle de textes, modélisation et réalisation informatique (système SPAT). PhD, Université Paris-Sorbonne (2000)
3. Ben Hazez S., Minel J-L., Designing Tasks of Identification of Complex Patterns Used for Text Filtering. RIAO'2000, Paris, (2000) 1558- 1567
4. Berri, J., Cartier E., Desclés J-P, Jackiewicz A., Minel J.L., 1996, Filtrage Automatique de textes. *Natural Language Processing and Industrial Applications*, pp 28-35, Moncton, N-B, Canada.
5. Cartier E.: LA DÉFINITION : ses formes d'expression, son contenu et sa valeur dans les texte. Work in progress , Université de Paris Sorbonne. Paris (1997)
6. Charolles M.:Les plans d'organisation textuelle , période, chaînes, portées et séquences. *Pratiques*, n 57, Metz (1988)
7. Clarke Ch., Cormack G. V., Burkowski F. J., An algebra for structured text search and a framework for its implementation. The Computer Journal, 38(1), pp. 43-56, 1995
8. Desclés J-P, Cartier E., Jackiewicz A. , J-L. Minel.: Textual Processing and Contextual Exploration Method. *CONTEXT 97*, Universidade Federal do Rio de Janeiro, Brésil (1997) 189-197.
9. Desclés, J-P.: *Systèmes d'exploration contextuelle. Co-texte et calcul du sens.* (ed Claude Guimier). Presses Universitaires de Caen, (1997) 215-232.
10. Garcia D.: Analyse automatique des textes pour l'organisation causale des actions Réalisation du système informatique COATIS. PhD. Université Paris-Sorbonne, Paris (1998)
11. Gazdar G., Mellish C.: Natural Language Processing in Prolog. Addison-Wesley (1989)
12. Hobbs J., Appelt P D.,Bear J., Israel D., Kameyama M., Sticckel M., Tyson M.: FASTUS: A Cascaded Finite-State Transducer for Extracting Information from Natural-Language Texts in Finite-State Language Processing. eds. Roche E. Schabes Y. MIT Press (1997)
13. Hopcroft J.,Ullman J.: Introduction to Automata Theory. Languages and Computation. Addison-Wesley, USA (1979)
14. Jackiewicz A.: La notion de cause pour le filtrage de phrases importantes d'un texte. *Natural Language Processing and Industrial Applications*, Moncton, N-B, Canada (1996) 136-141
15. Jackiewicz A.: L'expression de la causalité dans les textes. Contribution au filtrage sémantique par une méthode informatique d'exploration contextuelle. PhD, Université Paris-Sorbonne (1998)
16. Kaplan R., Kay M.: Regular Models and Phonological Rule Systems. Computational Linguistics. Vol 20, n°.3 (1994)
17. Kartunnen L.:The replace operator. in eds. Roche E. Schabes Y. MIT Press (1997)
18. Lambek J:, The Mathematics of Sentence Structure. American Mathematical Monthly (1965)
19. Lloyd J.: Foundations of Logic Programming. Springer-Verlag (1987)
20. Minel J-L., Desclés J-P., Cartier E., Crispino G., Ben Hazez S., et Jackiewicz A: Résumé automatique par filtrage sémantique d'informations dans des textes. Présentation de la plate-forme FilText. *TSI* (2000).

21. Moortgat M. Categorial Investigations: Logic and Linguistic Aspects of the Lambek Calculus. Ph.D Thesis, University of Amsterdam, Amsterdam (1988)
22. Rastier F., Cavazza M., Abeille A: *Sémantique pour l'analyse*. Masson, Paris (1994)
23. Roulet E.: *L'articulation du discours en français contemporain*. Bern, Peter Lang (1985)
24. Roulet E.: Complétude interactive et connecteurs reformulatifs. Cahiers de linguistique française, n°8, (1987)
25. Shieber S., Schabes Y., Pereira F.: Principles and Implementation of Deductive Parsing. TR-94-08, Mitsubishi Research Laboratories, Cambridge Research Center (1994)

Finding Correlative Associations among News Topics[*]

Manuel Montes-y-Gómez [1], Aurelio López-López [2], Alexander Gelbukh [1]

[1] Center for Computing Research (CIC), National Polytechnic Institute (IPN),
Av. Juan Dios Bátiz s/n esq. Mendicabal, col. Zacatenco, CP. 07738, DF, Mexico.
mmontesg@susu.inaoep.mx, gelbukh@cic.ipn.mx

[2] INAOE, Luis Enrique Erro No. 1, Tonantzintla, Puebla, 72840 México.
allopez@inaoep.mx

Abstract. A method for finding real-world associations between news topics (as distinguished from apparent associations caused by the constant size of the newspaper) is described. This is important for studying society interests.

Introduction. Text mining is a new area of text processing that can be defined as discovery of interesting facts and new world knowledge from large text collections [2]. Its main tasks are analysis of trends, detection of deviations, and discovery of associations. In this paper, we focus on the analysis of a news collection. There are methods to detect new events in the news [1], to analyze news trends [4], and to separate good news from bad news [3]. The method we present allows analyzing a very common phenomenon in news: the influence of a peak news topic (important for a short time) over other news topics. This influence can show itself in two main ways: as a direct association (the peak topic induces other topics to emerge) and an inverse one (the peak topic causes temporal oblivion of another topic). We distinguish two different kinds of associations: observable ones (what we can see from the newspapers) and real world ones (between the events in the real world). The problem is that the observable association can be caused by the mere fact that all news reports must fill a constant size of the newspaper no matter what the total number of the events in the world is. This causes a *normalization effect* leading to apparent associations. In our model these two kinds of associations are proportional; thus the real ones can sometimes be inferred from the observable ones.

Finding Real World Associations. Given a peak news topic and the observable data surrounded, we can determine the absence or presence of a real-world association:

- Construct a probability distribution for each news topic over the time span corresponding to the peak topic. It expresses the probability of occurrence of this topic in each of the days of the period of interest.
- Detect the associations in the observed data set (if any). We use the correlation coefficient r for this.

---

[*] The work was done under partial support of CONACyT, REDII, and SNI, Mexico.

A. Gelbukh (Ed.): CICLing 2001, LNCS 2004, pp. 524-526, 2001.

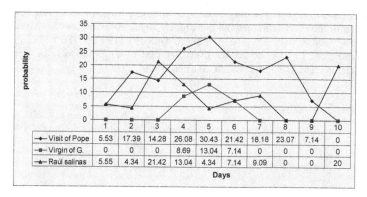

	1	2	3	4	5	6	7	8	9	10
Visit of Pope	5.53	17.39	14.28	26.08	30.43	21.42	18.18	23.07	7.14	0
Virgin of G.	0	0	0	8.69	13.04	7.14	0	0	0	0
Raúl salinas	5.55	4.34	21.42	13.04	4.34	7.14	9.09	0	0	20

Figure 1. Analysis of the peak topic *Visit of Pope*.

- Estimate whether these observable associations are mainly due to a consequence of the normalization effect or there is a possible real-world association component.

Basically, the latter estimation considers that: (1) any direct observable association has a high possibility for being a real-world one, since it goes against the normalization effect, and (2) any inverse observable association has a high possibility for being a real-world one if it does not disappear when the peak effect is eliminated.

Experimental Results. Example: in the news from the Mexican newspaper "El Universal" for the ten days (January 20 to 29 of 1999) surrounding the *visit of Pope to Mexico City*, we found two real-world associations for this peak topic (Figure 1): a direct association with the topic *Virgin of Guadalupe* indicating that this topic probably emerged because of the influence of the peak topic, and an inverse association with the topic *Raúl Salinas* (Brother of the Mexican ex-president, sentenced on January 22). The latter association suggests that the topic *Raúl Salinas* went out of attention because of the influence of the visit of the Pope.

Conclusions. We have analyzed a phenomenon that is very frequent in real life situations – the influence of the peak news topics over other topics – and proposed a model in which the real-world associations can be inferred from the observable ones. Discovery of the real-world associations between news topics helps to interpret the social importance and influence of relevant but transitory topics and to define some parameters for better understanding of these news topics as well as our society on general.

References

1.   Allan, J., Papka, R., and Lavrenko, V. (1998), Proc. Fo the 21st. ACM-SIGIR International Conference on Research and Development in Information Retrieval, Australia, 1998.
2.   García-Menier E., "Un Sistema para la Clasificación de Notas Periodisticas", Memorias del Simposium Internacional de Computación CIC-98, México, D. F., 1998.

526   Manuel Montes-y-Gómez, Aurelio López-López, and Alexander Gelbukh

3. Hearst, M. (1999), "Untangling Text Data Mining", Proc. of ACL'99: the 37th Annual Meeting of the Association for Computational Linguistics, University of Marylnd, 1999.
4. Montes-y-Gómez, M., A. López-López, A. Gelbukh (1999a). "Text Mining as a Social Thermometer". In Proc. of the Workshop on Text Mining: Foundations, Techniques and Applications, IJCAI-99, Stockholm, Sweden, 1999.

Author Index

Lecture Notes in Computer Science

For information about Vols. 1–1914
please contact your bookseller or Springer-Verlag

Vol. 1945: W. Grieskamp, T. Santen, B. Stoddart (Eds.), Integrated Formal Methods. Proceedings, 2000. X, 441 pages. 2000.

Vol. 1946: P. Palanque, F. Paternò (Eds.), Interactive Systems. Proceedings, 2000. X, 251 pages. 2001.

Vol. 1948: T. Tan, Y. Shi, W. Gao (Eds.), Advances in Multimodal Interfaces – ICMI 2000. Proceedings, 2000. XVI, 678 pages. 2000.

Vol. 1949: R. Connor, A. Mendelzon (Eds.), Research Issues in Structured and Semistructured Database Programming. Proceedings, 1999. XII, 325 pages. 2000.

Vol. 1950: D. van Melkebeek, Randomness and Completeness in Computational Complexity. XV, 196 pages. 2000.

Vol. 1951: F. van der Linden (Ed.), Software Architectures for Product Families. Proceedings, 2000. VIII, 255 pages. 2000.

Vol. 1952: M.C. Monard, J. Simão Sichman (Eds.), Advances in Artificial Intelligence. Proceedings, 2000. XV, 498 pages. 2000. (Subseries LNAI).

Vol. 1953: G. Borgefors, I. Nyström, G. Sanniti di Baja (Eds.), Discrete Geometry for Computer Imagery. Proceedings, 2000. XI, 544 pages. 2000.

Vol. 1954: W.A. Hunt, Jr., S.D. Johnson (Eds.), Formal Methods in Computer-Aided Design. Proceedings, 2000. XI, 539 pages. 2000.

Vol. 1955: M. Parigot, A. Voronkov (Eds.), Logic for Programming and Automated Reasoning. Proceedings, 2000. XIII, 487 pages. 2000. (Subseries LNAI).

Vol. 1956: T. Coquand, P. Dybjer, B. Nordström, J. Smith (Eds.), Types for Proofs and Programs. Proceedings, 1999. VII, 195 pages. 2000.

Vol. 1957: P. Ciancarini, M. Wooldridge (Eds.), Agent-Oriented Software Engineering. Proceedings, 2000. X, 323 pages. 2001.

Vol. 1960: A. Ambler, S.B. Calo, G. Kar (Eds.), Services Management in Intelligent Networks. Proceedings, 2000. X, 259 pages. 2000.

Vol. 1961: J. He, M. Sato (Eds.), Advances in Computing Science – ASIAN 2000. Proceedings, 2000. X, 299 pages. 2000.

Vol. 1963: V. Hlaváč, K.G. Jeffery, J. Wiedermann (Eds.), SOFSEM 2000: Theory and Practice of Informatics. Proceedings, 2000. XI, 460 pages. 2000.

Vol. 1964: J. Malenfant, S. Moisan, A. Moreira (Eds.), Object-Oriented Technology. Proceedings, 2000. XI, 309 pages. 2000.

Vol. 1965: Ç. K. Koç, C. Paar (Eds.), Cryptographic Hardware and Embedded Systems – CHES 2000. Proceedings, 2000. XI, 355 pages. 2000.

Vol. 1966: S. Bhalla (Ed.), Databases in Networked Information Systems. Proceedings, 2000. VIII, 247 pages. 2000.

Vol. 1967: S. Arikawa, S. Morishita (Eds.), Discovery Science. Proceedings, 2000. XII, 332 pages. 2000. (Subseries LNAI).

Vol. 1968: H. Arimura, S. Jain, A. Sharma (Eds.), Algorithmic Learning Theory. Proceedings, 2000. XI, 335 pages. 2000. (Subseries LNAI).

Vol. 1969: D.T. Lee, S.-H. Teng (Eds.), Algorithms and Computation. Proceedings, 2000. XIV, 578 pages. 2000.

Vol. 1970: M. Valero, V.K. Prasanna, S. Vajapeyam (Eds.), High Performance Computing – HiPC 2000. Proceedings, 2000. XVIII, 568 pages. 2000.

Vol. 1971: R. Buyya, M. Baker (Eds.), Grid Computing – GRID 2000. Proceedings, 2000. XIV, 229 pages. 2000.

Vol. 1972: A. Omicini, R. Tolksdorf, F. Zambonelli (Eds.), Engineering Societies in the Agents World. Proceedings, 2000. IX, 143 pages. 2000. (Subseries LNAI).

Vol. 1973: J. Van den Bussche, V. Vianu (Eds.), Database Theory – ICDT 2001. Proceedings, 2001. X, 451 pages. 2001.

Vol. 1974: S. Kapoor, S. Prasad (Eds.), FST TCS 2000: Foundations of Software Technology and Theoretical Computer Science. Proceedings, 2000. XIII, 532 pages. 2000.

Vol. 1975: J. Pieprzyk, E. Okamoto, J. Seberry (Eds.), Information Security. Proceedings, 2000. X, 323 pages. 2000.

Vol. 1976: T. Okamoto (Ed.), Advances in Cryptology – ASIACRYPT 2000. Proceedings, 2000. XII, 630 pages. 2000.

Vol. 1977: B. Roy, E. Okamoto (Eds.), Progress in Cryptology – INDOCRYPT 2000. Proceedings, 2000. X, 295 pages. 2000.

Vol. 1979: S. Moss, P. Davidsson (Eds.), Multi-Agent-Based Simulation. Proceedings, 2000. VIII, 267 pages. 2001. (Subseries LNAI).

Vol. 1983: K.S. Leung, L.-W. Chan, H. Meng (Eds.), Intelligent Data Engineering and Automated Learning – IDEAL 2000. Proceedings, 2000. XVI, 573 pages. 2000.

Vol. 1984: J. Marks (Ed.), Graph Drawing. Proceedings, 2001. XII, 419 pages. 2001.

Vol. 1987: K.-L. Tan, M.J. Franklin, J. C.-S. Lui (Eds.), Mobile Data Management. Proceedings, 2001. XIII, 289 pages. 2001.

Vol. 1989: M. Ajmone Marsan, A. Bianco (Eds.), Quality of Service in Multiservice IP Networks. Proceedings, 2001. XII, 440 pages. 2001.

Vol. 1991: F. Dignum, C. Sierra (Eds.), Agent Mediated Electronic Commerce. VIII, 241 pages. 2001. (Subseries LNAI).

Vol. 1992: K. Kim (Ed.), Public Key Cryptography. Proceedings, 2001. XI, 423 pages. 2001.

Vol. 1995: M. Sloman, J. Lobo, E.C. Lupu (Eds.), Policies for Distributed Systems and Networks. Proceedings, 2001. X, 263 pages. 2001.

Vol. 1998: R. Klette, S. Peleg, G. Sommer (Eds.), Robot Vision. Proceedings, 2001. IX, 285 pages. 2001.

Vol. 2000: R. Wilhelm (Ed.), Informatics: 10 Years Back, 10 Years Ahead. IX, 369 pages. 2001.

Vol. 2004: A. Gelbukh (Ed.), Computational Linguistics and Intelligent Text Processing. Proceedings, 2001. XII, 528 pages. 2001.

Vol. 2010: A. Ferreira, H. Reichel (Eds.), STACS 2001. Proceedings, 2001. XV, 576 pages. 2001.